An
Intellectual History of
Psychology

AN INTELLECTUAL HISTORY OF

PSYCHOLOGY

Daniel N. Robinson

GEORGETOWN UNIVERSITY

MACMILLAN PUBLISHING CO., INC.

NEW YORK

Collier Macmillan Publishers

LONDON

◻◻◻◻◻◻◻◻◻◻◻◻◻◻◻◻◻◻◻◻◻◻◻◻◻◻

*To my colleagues and students
in the College of Arts and Sciences,
Georgetown University*

/9233

Copyright © 1976, DANIEL N. ROBINSON

Printed in the United States of America

Macmillan Publishing Co., Inc.
866 Third Avenue, New York, New York 10022

Collier Macmillan Canada, Ltd.

Library of Congress Cataloging in Publication Data
Robinson, Daniel N
   An intellectual history of psychology.

   Includes index.
   1. Psychology—History. I. Title. [DNLM: 1. Psychology—History.   BF121 R659i]
BF81.R65   150'.9   75–12672
ISBN 0–02–402420–1
      Printing: 1 2 3 4 5 6 7 8   Year: 6 7 8 9 0 1 2

ACKNOWLEDGMENTS

The dedication page indicates my indebtedness to colleagues and students at Georgetown University. The ambiance of the College of Arts and Sciences transforms many informal relationships into constructive and genial tutorials. In this connection I should pay special thanks to several of my associates. Professor Fred S. Keller was ungrudgingly helpful on a number of occasions calling for first-hand accounts of behaviorism in its inchoate stages. He is not likely to agree with my own assessment of the movement but, were it not for his forbearing tuition, my judgments would be far less deserving of attention. Professor Tom L. Beauchamp displayed his usual penetration in discussing some of the more difficult philosophical passages and, while he too will not applaud all of my interpretations, he will recognize his counsel in those which might be particularly apt. I should also cite Professor Robert W. Ayers for introducing me to the writings of George Poulet and Frances Yates.

A number of chapters were typed and proofread by Margaret Heliotis and Debra Fain and I take this opportunity to acknowledge their kind assistance. Joseph Falzone, my production supervisor at Macmillan, also left nothing to be desired.

Finally, Francine Robinson, the best friend a husband ever had, has touched every page with the thoughtful attention she has always given to everything I hold dear.

PREFACE

Psychologists are justifiably proud of the most recent decades of research claimed by the discipline. On the strength of this record, the professional community is given more and more to describing psychology as a "behavioral science." Increasingly we discover a confident belief that the great variety of psychological issues will ultimately be embraced by the tenets of physiological psychology and behaviorism. In fact, the findings and methods of these two specialties have become the *lingua franca* of psychologists of every persuasion who now seem more committed than ever to the notion that most past controversy was largely semantic or merely innocent.

This contemporary outlook has much to recommend it but it has another side wherein enthusiasm stretches well beyond the achievements of the discipline. It is an enthusiasm that forges an unattractive and unproductive attitude—one that rejoices in psychology's liberation from "metaphysics" and greets warily any attempt to call attention to those dark periods when mere philosophers trifled with the mind. The history of psychology, by this light, has value only to the extent that it points to that heroic age when the world of letters was abandoned by the patrons of science. History, then, is the tool with which we date the birth of *real* psychology—*our* psychology.

Texts addressed to the history of psychology have, inadvertently one would hope, encouraged this attitude and have, in turn, been colored by it. When we assay these books we find disconcerting evidence of two of the most common and most sinister errors to which historians of ideas succumb. The first tends to reduce intellectual history to a form of bibliographic biography. Texts guided by this false and trackless light urge even the vigilant reader to believe that great minds appear without reason in every epoch and anticipate issues that will engage all later thinkers. These are the books that would have us revere Aristotle because he was wise enough to share our interests or "modern" enough to foresee our problems. The second error, which comes from the same shop, imposes upon historiography a charming form of "domino theory." Writers unable to resist this promote the view that a gentle idea presses against its neighbor and thereby unfurls a bolt of reasoning that conveniently stops at our own front door. Where the first error removes intelligence from its culture, the second would reduce intellectual history to a chain letter.

These errors and their effects participate in something of a *folie à deux*. Modern psychology proclaims its attachment to experimental modes of inquiry and histories of modern psychology proceed to describe how that was historically inevitable. Modern psychologists seek to establish the associationistic basis of learning and historians of psychology recall for us that Aristotle, too, found merit in the idea. Soon, the contemporary taste becomes the standard by which to assess the achievements of all earlier times. Since the Patristic philosophers appear to have missed the importance of physiology, there is no reason to burden the modern student with their unenlightened concerns. Indeed, why bother at all to recount those weary centuries between Epicurus and Galileo when the mind of man was trapped by faith and chained to rationalism?

If this perspective resulted in no more than porous scholarship, if it merely restricted the commerce psychologists might have with the larger realm of thought, there would be cause for embarrassment but not alarm. The fact is, however, that this perspective has had alarming consequences, promising to hold the discipline in that state of infancy so defensively portrayed by our historians. History is not simply a subject to be learned. It is a method by which we can attempt to explain ourselves and our world. Historical scholarship, properly conceived, is not an actuarial exercise leading to correct datings. It is misused when wielded in such a way as to populate a Hall of Fame. The historian who praises antiquity for anticipating the affairs of his own time is an apologist whose efforts can never rise above the level of self-congratulation. The historian who builds his own bridges and forces the ideas of the past to traverse them, or who presents his own age as the adult form toward which prior and childish epochs have been moving, is merely spinning tales.

Contemporary psychology has a past and it has a future. The future is under no compulsion to mimic our endeavors and the past had no way of knowing what we would select for study. Previous ages engaged the energies of thoughtful people who, for a variety of reasons, adopted certain strategies in an attempt to comprehend and improve the human condition. It is of importance to us to study their accomplishments and failures not because we will learn how far we have come but that we will be more acutely aware of how culture conditions the mind. The value, or at least a major value, of studying scholastic psychology is to learn how readily complex issues can be absorbed by a *Zeitgeist*, how completely a cultural perspective can dominate the process of thought. We study the Athens of Pericles to discern the climate within which speculative discourse is possible. In short, we review the history of ideas to remind ourselves of the powerful role of belief, symbol, metaphor, and custom in those affairs that we might otherwise consider to be separate, personal, and independent.

I noted previously how modern psychology has become affiliated with modern science and the strong tendency of contemporary psychologists to describe their interests and methods in the idiom of science. These are historical facts and as such they warrant critical examination by all who are interested not only in psychology but in human invention at large. The historian's responsibility does not end with the fact, it begins with it. What is responsible for the adoption of this scientific idiom? What were the intellectual and cultural factors that contributed to this turn? Why did previous ages not adopt this model? What was it about older formulations that resulted in their abandonment? What criteria or findings or arguments succeeded in producing this altered perspective? What does the new view have to recommend it and what buttresses are essential to its survival? These are *historical* questions and only indirectly *chronological* questions. They are the questions to which the present work is addressed.

D. N. R.

CONTENTS

□□□□□□□□□□□□□□□□□□□□□□□□□□□□

Philosophical Psychology

1

The Study of History and the Nature of Science

This book is addressed to the intellectual history of psychology. In our time, it is common to hear psychology referred to as a "behavioral science" or, in William James' terms, the "science of mental life." Not everyone who writes on the subject agrees that psychology is a science and there are some who have argued that, given its nature, it cannot be so called. While this point of view has not had much of an effect on those actually engaged in psychological research, it cannot be ignored by a historian. If psychology is to be judged as a science, no matter how young it might be in this regard, then its origins are to be sought in the history of science. If, on the contrary, our current ardor for the scientific has merely dressed up psychology in the garb of science and temporarily blinded us to its essentially nonscientific character, the historian must find the true roots of the discipline and the forces that conspired to create the illusion. In either case, the historian's role is not a passive one. He is not to sit back before the great chronological map of thought, pick out what seems to be "psychological," and pass it on as *the* history of psychology. Rather, he must interpret and analyze the history of ideas in an attempt to discern the conditions favoring the creation of any discipline and imparting a given character to it.

One would think it too obvious even to mention that the historian is obliged to define the subject of the history he is writing. Yet, it is not uncommon to find histories of psychology uncritically accepting the things contemporary psychologists happen to be engaged in and, from these ventures, work back in time to discover precedents. Such datings are not to be scorned, because they are often of use to subsequent analyses, but as historical contributions they are incomplete and potentially

3

misleading. Suppose, for example, that someone were to write a history of witchcraft, dividing the subject into twenty chapters, each covering a period of two centuries. Suppose, further, that each chapter presented accurate dates for the specific performances of witches—in 3150 B.C. a witch named Nefer flew over the Island of Cos on a ray of light; in A.D. 1585 a witch in Milan by the name of Francesca transformed the Prince's son into a toad. Suppose, finally, that our author, in the name of objectivity, never paused to ask whether such events really happened or why people believed they did or why they said they did. Suppose our author never gave the slightest hint of his own incredulity and never offered an alternative to the notion of witchcraft. Under such circumstances the informed reader could only judge that the author was an innocent; the innocent reader could only conclude that he was reading a chronicle of actual events. We would insist, at last, that the author was not a historian at all. To insist otherwise would be to fail to appreciate what historical analysis is all about.

This brings us to the purpose of this first chapter: the nature and use of historical studies and the character of science. What are we to expect from the historian? What are we to learn from the history of psychology? If modern psychology is judged to be scientific, what does it share with the rest of science? If it is not scientific, what in its subject or in its history is responsible? What in its history convinced many that it should be scientific? Briefly, what were the ideas that animated and guided its evolution?

We will return to these questions often in succeeding chapters and more pointedly in the last chapter. In order to establish the criteria that must be adopted if answers are to be plausible, it is necessary to examine two broad ideas: the idea of history and the idea of science. What do we have in mind when we look to history and what do we mean when we refer to science?

The Idea of History

"It is generally thought to be of importance to a man that he should know himself: where knowing himself means knowing not his merely personal peculiarities, the things that distinguish him from other men, but his nature as a man. . . . Knowing yourself means knowing what you can do; and since nobody knows what he can do until he tries, the only clue to what man can do is what man has done. The value of history, then, is that it teaches us what man has done and thus what man is."

So wrote R. G. Collingwood in the introduction to his treatise *The Idea of History*.[1] We come close to the purpose of the present book by substituting "psychology" at appropriate places in the passage above. Our best sense, indeed our only reasoned guesses about the future of psychology must proceed under the light of history. The same is to be said of any sound comprehension of contemporary psychology. It requires us to appreciate its roots in history and its branching dependence upon other disciplines.

We might profitably stay a while with *The Idea of History*, for in it Collingwood sets down important distinctions between history and the mere dating of events. History for Collingwood is science; it answers questions of a *causal* character. Knowing that William the Conqueror landed in England in 1066 is to possess a fact of history much as knowing that an orange weighs ten ounces is to possess a fact of science. But a collection of such facts is neither history nor science. It is not until these facts are understood according to principles, not until they are sought by a tested method, that they begin to comprise a science. As Collingwood put it:

> "Science in general . . . does not consist in collecting what we already know and arranging it in this or that kind of pattern. It consists in fastening upon something we do not know, and trying to discover it."[2]

If memory were perfect and impartial, if commentators were accurate and in agreement, there would be little need for historians. The interested student could open the record, review the sequence of events, and lay claim to knowledge of an older time. Our need of history is based on the fact that memories are imperfect and often lost; that only a camera records with complete neutrality, and even the camera is pointed toward one event and away from others; that contemporaries do not always agree upon either the nature or the order of events. Even if photographic records of historic events were available, we would still not have the essential product of historiography: *interpretation*. Facts occur in a context as well as in an order. Where intellectual history is involved, the relevant contexts are beyond the compass of one observer's memory, even a memory aided by the camera. Intellectual history, as a history of ideas, cannot even rely on the faded relics of an antique war or the ceremonial vessels of an old belief. It is tied to words that, unlike spears or cups, are used differently at different times and often intend more than they convey. Thus, intellectual histories are frustrated by all the obstacles facing other forms of historical inquiry, and then some. The thin lines of evidence diverge while the witnesses, out of ignorance, fear, or sloth, fail to reflect accurately the ideas of their period. Not only do words themselves obstruct a later reckoning, but the modern analyst further darkens the record with his own biases.

These biases were insightfully exposed by Giovanni Battista Vico[3] (1668–1744), one of the first great historians of the modern world. He reminds us of the constant temptation to revere antiquity beyond all sense of proportion. This prejudice not only colors our evaluations but may even lead to quantitative errors, errors in estimating wealth or population or longevity. We also fail to recognize the subtle chauvinist who writes about his own people in large-case. Most common of all historiographic blunders, Vico insists, is the tendency to identify the character of an age by studying the thoughts of its scholars. Vico is one of the first historians to recognize that scholars are not representative of the time in which they live. They differ from the rest of their contemporaries in interests, in schooling, even in basic values. For example, the importance of understanding Aristotle's theory of the soul cannot be to learn *the* Athenian conception of the soul. The average Athenian, more likely than not, seldom thought of the question and, had he been privileged to discuss the matter with Aristotle, would have probably found the philosopher's treatment bizarre. We are, then, called upon to search the myths and rites of antiquity, the poems and correspondences of the age, in order to unearth the popular view. Once located, it is nearly invariably different from the sage's.

Vico also warned against imputing too much credibility to those who have provided eyewitness accounts. The fact that Tacitus wrote about events in his own time does not mean that he was conceptually closer to them. He wore the distorting lenses of his epoch. His travels were limited. He spoke and read in but two languages. His resources were saddled to a primitive technology. Lacking the methods of modern scholarship (methods only recently developed by linguists, archeologists, physicists, etc.) a Tacitus or a Herodotus or a Livy could examine earlier eras only through the eyes and fables of those who came before.

Finally, Vico presents the pervasive error of *scholastica successionis civitatium*, the scholastic succession of states. This error moves us to believe that when an intellectual development occurs sequentially in two different countries, it occurred in the second through the direct influence of the first. Since, for example, Adelardus spoke in the twelfth century of the earth's motion and since Copernicus was generous in his reading habits, Copernicus must have got the idea from Adelardus (or Cicero or Aristarchus or Nicole Oresme, etc.). By this view, an idea is the pebble of a uniquely enlightened time dropped by philosophers on the calm lake of slumbering minds. The idea disturbs first one culture, then the next, *seriatim*. The historian's challenge is to work back from the ripples to the source and, thereby, to discover the first source of all our wisdom. Vico, as with Aristotle earlier, knew that such orderly succession was seldom the case. Ours is a questioning and a theorizing species which does not rest at length. There is hardly a notion prized by any age that was not entertained by many others at many different times and quite independently. Accordingly, a mere chronology of ideas would not only fail to be a history of ideas but would fail to be true. We can say, with measurable confidence, that an event of a certain kind occurred for the first time or, at least, that no earlier record has been found. But we cannot date the first appearance of a thought or a point of view.

The Greeks invented philosophy as a discipline, as a form of inquiry regulated by rules and organized around a set of questions. They were, in this narrow sense, the first philosophers. But it would be ridiculous to argue that Thales was the first human being to recognize that *"it is hard to be good."* We explore the history of ideas to learn how others have dealt with problems facing us, what others have considered important, and the factors that seemed to have caused events of consequence. One inescapable product of our study is a chronology, but it is surely not the goal. We expect the historian to tell us when things happened much as we expect the modern astronomer to tell us the position of the planets on the day Caesar was killed. But we expect much more. We believe the astronomer because his calculations are based on laws—laws fashioned in the light of criticism, objective measurement, and multiple observations. We expect as much from the historian. Not that his explanations will unfold inexorably from the fixed "laws" of history, but they will be framed according to the very best evidence available and will, therefore, yield the truest picture of what happened and why it happened.

In the epilogue to *The Idea of History*, Collingwood ventures, with characteristic decisiveness, to place psychology in perspective. He argues that psychology's chief mistake was to identify with the physical sciences and to adopt, by that act, methods wholly futile to its enterprise. Psychology, Collingwood insists, can answer its questions only by transforming its methods to those of history:

> "To regard [psychology] as rising above the sphere of history, and establishing the permanent and unchanging laws of human nature, is therefore possible only to a person who mistakes the transient conditions of a certain historical age for the permanent conditions of human life."[4]

It is not necessary to accept Collingwood's prescriptions for psychology in order to appreciate the subtler point he raises. A science concerned with the determinants of human conduct, with the character of human perception and emotion, will find in the annals of civilization a laboratory more varied and rich than any we could hope to re-create. This part of Collingwood's instruction is unimpeachable, and it is this part that urges us to study history if we are to study psychology.

In attempting what has been described as an intellectual history, an author commits himself to something different from chronology and, in attempting an intellectual history of psychology, one must be concerned with far more than academic psychology. This said, the following pages may seem to belie the premise for, in fact, a chronological succession does emerge. This, however, is a concession to custom and convenience and is not to be viewed as the fallacy of *scholastica successionis civitatium.* One age does not impart momentum to the next as would a pair of colliding billiard balls. Where ideas are concerned, we must not even think that an age has died. There is no question but that psychological scholarship, at any time since Socrates, has been influenced by Greek thought. Yet a study of the Socratics is not enough. Succeeding generations did not passively assimilate the *Dialogues* but interpreted them in altered contexts and for diverse purposes. Often enough the "Greek view" is advanced by a modern who discovers only later that someone else had said very much the same thing. Thus the following chapters could easily have been arranged not as a succession of epochs but as a collection of problems; for example, the problem of knowledge, the problem of conduct, the problem of values. Indeed, if there is anything that one age may be said to inherit directly from its predecessor, it is these problems. There are, however, at least two disadvantages courted by the "great questions" model. First, it leads to wearying redundancy, since nearly every age has come to advance the same varied set of answers to the same great questions. To choose one example, the range of informed opinions on the question of human goodness or wickedness is neither broader nor livelier in contemporary scholarship than it was in the days of Aristotle or even Plotinus. Still, although the richness of opinion may not have deepened over the ages, the chain of fact and the rules of evidence have advanced, even if sluggishly. Knowledge, after all, in some compartments is cumulative, and of these compartments a chronological accounting is essential. Knowledge is most cumulative in the sciences and, to the extent that modern psychology seeks membership in the family of science, we are advised to explore the pattern of its growth.

Perhaps the more compelling reason for adopting the chronological model—and here an author's laziness is stripped of all disguise—is simply that it is easier to compile evidence and interpret it within one era at a time. We can say—in one sentence—that questions of importance and daring answers to them have appeared repeatedly and often independently in every civilized epoch. We can say this, but we cannot show it until books are scored the way symphonies are and until readers can sight-read the simultaneous performances of strings, brass, woodwind, and tympany.

Having adopted—no matter how grudgingly—a sequentialist approach, and knowing that no caveat will be heeded by everyone, there is still the problem of identifying more or less discrete periods in intellectual history. Did the Athenian Age, for example, ever really end? The world still speaks of justice, still searches for truth, still houses democracies of a sort. Only the more literal-minded would require an Athenian Age to remain in Athens. And, since all forms of Roman Arts and Letters were utterly suffused by "Greek thought," on what conceptual basis do we defend such locutions as the Roman Empire, the Age of the Caesars, the Augustan Period? Is the American Constitution an American constitution, or is it John Locke's vision of government? Is it, then, an English constitution or a modified form of Roman Republicanism? Questions like these could be raised to challenge any suggestion of historical discontinuity, and they are valid. We may illustrate the problem with a popular example. When we date the Renaissance from 1350 to 1600 we are submitting at least four propositions: first, that there was, at some earlier time, a classical outlook; second, that this older age vanished or entered a period of prolonged hibernation; third, that at a definable time, the hibernation ended and a renascence of perspective and achievement took place; and fourth, that this rebirth itself ran a given course only to be replaced by something discriminably and even dramatically different. These propositions can be sustained or rejected depending on what we choose to make use of when we decide to define an "age." Religiously, the Renaissance mind was probably closer to the neo-Platonism of the Dark Ages than it was to the Thomistic Aristotelianism of the later Middle Age. If by *renaissance* we mean to imply a rebirth of that which made classical Athens famous, we must account for the startling fact that the Italian Renaissance did not produce a single philosopher of historic consequence.[5] And, as for the vaunted humanism of the period, few Greek philosophers would have found much to recommend it. But here we anticipate ourselves. The point to be made is that (and with due respect to Vico, Hegel, and Spengler) history is not cyclical and what sometimes makes it seem so is the mere recurrence of certain politico-philosophic dispositions. The conditions responsible for these are always different the second (third, fourth, etc.) time around. In no historically defensible way may we contend that the Renaissance was a re-creation of the Athenian *Zeitgeist* or that the eighteenth-century Virginia plantation was "medieval." Such descriptions can be no more than metaphorical and will often lead to ludicrous conclusions.

If we are clear in our recognition of the artificiality of abrupt historical transitions, we can gain the advantage that labels give to memory without suffering the burden they impose on judgment. Since history is neither constant nor cyclical, we must be prepared to perceive change without expecting duplication. We must seek orderliness but not historic necessity. Where the second billiard ball must move (if our laws in physics are to endure), the King may not. He may, for example, be sleeping. And, as we place people and events under sadly general categories, we must not forget that they are people more similar to ourselves than different—just as hopeful, confused, frustrated. We have no reason to assume that because they thought about different matters, they thought in different ways, or because they perceived their condition differently, they either had no perception at all or lacked one that could be defended. "They," after all, are "We"; otherwise our inquiry would be no more than comparative anatomy.

If the metaphor of the family is not too homespun, we might profitably view the several epochs as relatives, each with a set of distinguishing features but each nonetheless related to every other; related but not mechanically related. Some relatives leave diaries, portraits, photographs, and even handsome bequests. Others leave only a certain record of good will and tolerance. Still others remain ever a mystery. They said little, traveled less, and wrote nothing. Occasionally distant cousins show features more in common than brothers, and certain children seem to bear no resemblance at all to either parent.

When we treat historical inquiry as a kind of genealogy, we not only whet our intellectual appetite with a mixture of fancy and vanity but we also set certain traps. We invite the error of *scholastica successionis* like the fellow who first learns that his great-uncle was Turkish and now knows why he likes black coffee. There is no gene for liking black coffee and, if there were, it seems to have wandered out of Turkey with amazing speed and diffusiveness. Nor is there a gene for iambic pentameter, for twelve-tone harmony, or for painting madonnas. We do not understand the wealth of Uncle John and the poverty of his brother by exploring their pedigrees. To carry the metaphor to its limit, we do not explain the difference between ages by measuring their breeding practices. Therefore, the sense in which the following chapters are devoted to the various epochs of *Western* civilization is geographic only. Indeed, had it not been for Arab scholars, the chapter covering Aristotle might be less than a page.

The Idea of Science

The subject matter of psychology is as old as reflection. Its broad aims are as dated as human societies. Man, in any period, has not been indifferent to the validity of his knowledge, unconcerned with the causes of his behavior or that of his prey and predators. Our most distant ancestors, no less than we, wrestled with the problems of social organization, child rearing, competition, authority, individual differences, personal safety. Solving these problems required insights—no matter how untutored— into the *psychological* dimensions of life. Thus, if we are to follow the convention of treating psychology as a young discipline, we must have in mind something other than its subject matter. We must mean that it is young in the sense that physics was young at the time of Archimedes or in the sense that geometry was "founded" by Euclid and "fathered" by Thales. Sailing vessels were launched long before Archimedes discovered the laws of buoyancy, and pillars of identical circumference were constructed before anyone knew that $C = \Pi D$. We do not consider the ship builders and stone cutters of antiquity physicists and geometers, nor the ancient cave dweller a psychologist merely because he rewarded the good conduct of his children. The archives of folk wisdom contain a remarkable collection of achievements, but *craft*—no matter how perfected—is not *science*, nor is a litany of successful accidents a discipline. If psychology is young, it is young as a *scientific* discipline but it is far from clear that psychology has attained this status.

Distinctions between those ventures that are scientific and those that are not often blur under careful analysis. This is one reason why science and technology are often confused. Perhaps the most common distinction is drawn along the lines of method; that is, science is credited with a unique approach to a problem. While this is a useful means of drawing attention to one salient feature of scientific inquiry, it is limited by the fact that many types of inquiry—types that are not themselves scientific —share those methods common to science. All forms of serious scholarship strive for impartiality, attempt to uncover reliable facts, seek orderliness, and are based upon more or less well-defined procedures. The manner in which a physician conducts an examination, the steps followed by a detective attempting to solve a crime, and the weighing of evidence by a properly instructed jury, all conform to the canons of objectivity, and even may depend on careful measurements. These, however, are not instances of science, although they involve certain activities that are implicit in scientific inquiry. We may say, then, that although particular methodological considerations are a necessary feature of science, they are not sufficient to distinguish science from other endeavors.

At still another level of discourse, science is described as unique in terms of limiting its attention to the *material* world, insisting upon *sensible* phenomena as objects of investigation. This distinction is insufficient because it fails to exclude certain nonscientific activities (e.g., automotive repair) and fails to include important scientific theories whose terms, at present, do not correspond to known physical features of the universe.

To the foregoing we might add the behavioristic or "operationistic" definition of science according to which science is merely what scientists do. This sort of definition was strongly recommended by modern philosophical pragmatists. We find a version of it in Justice Holmes' definition of Law as that which allows him to predict what a judge and jury will do with a matter brought before them.[6] H. L. A. Hart aptly dismissed this definition in part because it failed to establish the basis on which judge and jury came into being in the first place, a basis that necessarily assumed Law.[7] A pragmatic definition of science fails for the same reason: it neglects the basis on which there might be "scientists" to do anything.

Notwithstanding the merits of these distinctions, we must note their inadequacy. The methodological criteria are too broad; the materialistic criteria are both too broad and too narrow; the operationistic criteria beg the question. To define science we must overcome these limitations and introduce a more discriminating criterion. This turns out to be *explanation*. We distinguish science from all that is not science in terms of the logical character of its explanations. For illustrative purposes, recall Newton's contribution to astronomy. Every high school student can recite Newton's explanation of why apples fall and why the moon, while "falling," never hits the earth. The explanation is the famous universal law of gravitation. According to it, all objects exert an attractive force upon all other objects. The magnitude of this force is directly proportional to the masses of the bodies and is inversely proportional to the square of the distances between them. But, did Newton *explain* why the moon remains in orbit? There is no simple answer. Philosophers of science have devoted volumes to the issue without settling it.

In everyday conversation, we say an explanation has been given when an answer has been offered to a question beginning with the word *why*. When we ask "Why is the sky blue?" we seek an explanation that will disclose those factors causing the sky to be blue. But a moment's reflection will reveal that the question calls for quite an elaborate explanation. In a certain respect a complete explanation is not even possible.

The color of the sky is imparted by the sun's radiation. This radiation is emitted as a continuous distribution of wavelengths and each distinct wavelength is uniquely affected by the various layers of atmosphere between the sun's and the earth's surfaces. Radiation within a certain range of wavelengths will pass through the atmospheric strata relatively easily. Other wavelengths will be distorted, others absorbed, others reflected away from the earth. There are instruments that will allow us to measure how much energy at each wavelength is reaching the earth, but this will not allow an answer to the question *"Why is the sky blue?"* because "blue" is *perceptual*, not merely or simply physical. In fact, "blue" is not physical at all! Thus, to explain the blueness of the sky, we must inquire into the determinants of human color vision, and this inquiry involves assumptions and procedures quite different from those involved in measuring the sun's radiation. We might underscore this difficulty of explanation by noting questions of the sort, "*Why did Jack die?*" or "*Why did Sparta war with Athens?*" The difficulty is not that explanations cannot be offered but that *exhaustive* explanations may be impossible or utterly impractical.

Before we examine how scientific explanations are framed in such a way as to evade this difficulty, we might consider explanations of the ordinary sort. These often take the form of exercises in naming or of mere tautologies while appearing to the unsuspecting as bona fide explanations. We find a useful example of the former in Molière's *The Physician in Spite of Himself*, in which the hero is called upon to explain why Lucinde is dumb. Sganarelle, the charlatan, assumes the posture of professional authority and announces that Lucinde is dumb "*from a loss of speech.*"[8] Sganarelle has, of course, explained nothing. He has merely substituted "loss of speech" for "dumb." Molière was intending to be sardonic, to draw attention to the emptiness of much of what passed for scholarship in the seventeenth century. But in our own time and with similar magisterial seriousness, "explanations" as specious as Sganarelle's are abundant. We learn, for example, that nations go to war because our species is aggressive; that children are hostile toward their parents because of an "Oedipal complex;" that marriages dissolve because modern couples find it difficult to live together; even that the principal cause of unemployment is that too many people are out of work! It is apparent that scientific explanations would not have to go very far to improve upon these.

The questions raised above—"*Why is the sky blue?*" "*Why did Jack die?*" "*Why did Sparta war with Athens?*" "*Why is Lucinde dumb?*"— are questions admitting of factual replies. We call them *empirical* questions because they can be settled by recourse to publicly observable data. Not only *can* answers to such questions be tested but they *must* be tested before we accept them as correct. Such questions, that is, empirical questions, are the only ones amenable to scientific explanation. There is, however, another type of question that calls for a different sort of answer. It is the type that refers not to evidence but to rules of argument. It is not an empirical question but a logical one or, to use the more discriminating term, an *analytical* one. Such questions as,

"Why are 3 + 5 equal to 8?"
"Why does a square contain 360 degrees?"
"Why is an orange a fruit?"

are illustrative. One notes readily that the answers we give to these questions are going to be different from those called for by *"Why did Jack die?"*, etc. A square is *defined* as a polygon containing four sides of equal length and consisting of four right angles. Thus, a square contains 360 degrees *by definition* and we explain the fact as a *logical necessity;* that is, calling any polygon that does not satisfy these criteria a "square" constitutes a logical contradiction. In contrast to empirical questions, which are answered by statements of fact, analytic propositions are evaluated according to the rules of logic. These rules preserve whatever truth there is in our assertions across cases. The most venerable, dating back to Aristotle, are the rules of the syllogism. If the syllogism is valid and if its premises are true, its conclusion *must* be true:

Major Premise: ALL MEN ARE MORTAL.
Minor Premise: SOCRATES IS A MAN.
Conclusion: SOCRATES IS MORTAL.

If ALL HUMAN BEINGS ARE AGGRESSIVE and if JOHN IS A HUMAN BEING, then it necessarily follows that JOHN IS AGGRESSIVE. But note that the syllogism does not tell us that, in fact, the premises are true; only that if they are, the conclusion must be true as well. Deductive logic provides us with rules of reason, not with evidence. And we must have something to reason *about* before the rules become useful. Deductive logic tells us to be wary of John only if, in fact, all men are aggressive and if, in fact, John is a man. It tells us that, indeed, adolescent boys will be fearful of their fathers if, in fact, they are driven by an "Oedipal complex" but not that there is such a complex or even what such a complex is. What it does tell us, however, is that if all we mean by "Oedipal Complex" is the fearfulness displayed by adolescent boys toward their fathers, then the statement ADOLESCENT BOYS ARE FEARFUL OF THEIR FATHERS BECAUSE OF THE OEDIPAL COMPLEX is a concealed tautology, that is, a statement in which the subject and predicate terms are synonyms. Tautologies are necessarily true and generally useless in the practical affairs of life.

We are now in a position to return to the question of scientific explanations. We begin by understanding that they are not merely logically consistent, nor are they only hypothetical. That is, unlike the syllogism, which is indifferent to the factual status of its premises, the scientific explanation must be concerned with that which is factually the case.

Scientific explanations must possess certain formal properties—properties that have been discussed since the time of Aristotle but were not formally articulated until the nineteenth century. Subsequent refinements in the model of scientific explanation have led to what is now called the "Hempelian" model, after the philosopher of science Carl Hempel.[9]

Hempel and his colleagues have introduced a number of nuances and complications to the model, but we need only review its principal features.

Every scientific explanation contains a statement of the event to be explained, the *explanandum*, and the statement that is the explanation, the *explanans*. The following criteria then apply:

1. The explanans must be a general or "covering" law, universally applicable to the class of events of which the explanandum is an instance.
2. The explanans must be true.
3. The explanandum must be logically deducible from the explanans.
4. The content of the explanandum must be empirical.
5. In summary, once the antecedent conditions have been stated, the explanandum (typically, an observed effect) becomes logically required by the covering law (explanans) of which it is an instance.

These conditions describe the "Covering Law" model or "hypothetico-deductive" model. Perhaps the most demanding feature of Hempel's version of the model is that the *explanans* be true. We will return to this point shortly. The first criterion, however, would appear to be the one which most modern philosophers of science would insist upon; any scientific explanation *must* refer to a universal law. What this does is remove scientific explanations from the larger domain of explanatory language. To answer the question "Why did Jack die?" with "Because his heart stopped beating" would not, in and of itself, constitute a scientific explanation, since no covering law is explicated although one may be implied. It is useful to list a variety of explanations that would fail the test imposed by the covering-law model. It is not necessary to state the questions since, given the explanations, the reader will recognize the sort of questions that would produce them:

"Because he felt like doing it."
"Because she is at that period in life."
"Because children like ice cream."
"Because dogs are loyal to their masters."
"Because he wants to do what is right."

Clearly, as "answers", these statements are neither universally true nor even lawlike. They are *ad hoc* inventions designed to account for a particular occurrence. In brief, they do not connect *causally* a specifiable set of antecedent conditions with a particular outcome. We would not accept as an answer to "Why do apples fall?" the reply "Because they feel like it." Nor would "The moon is loyal to its orbit" be a satisfying response to "Why does the moon remain in orbit?" If psychology is to take its place among the other sciences, its explanations must conform to those explanatory criteria that guide the other sciences. It is not enough that psychologists choose as *explananda* those psychological features that lend themselves to accurate measurement. No matter how precisely we describe an experimental outcome, no matter how painstaking we are in quantifying our descriptions of behavior or perception, such descriptions can never constitute scientific explanations until they are provided within the framework of *general laws*, if in fact they can be.

With respect to the second criterion, it would seem that the Hempelian demands may be somewhat overdrawn. This criterion insists that an explanation is not scientific unless the *explanans* is true and the event to be explained is logically deduced from it. In other words, a statement cannot pretend to be a scientific explanation unless the laws involved are true laws. According to this view, Newton's explanation of time-dependent and mass-dependent events was unscientific because Newton was not aware of Relativity and, therefore, was not able to make the necessary corrections for objects moving at velocities approaching the speed of light. Note that what is asserted here is not that Newton's explanation was wrong but that *it was not scientific.** This feature of the Hempelian model is unsettling for several reasons. First, it reserves scientific status to the sorts of statements which science, at any given time in its progress, cannot be sure of; that is, at what point can we assert that Law-X is true, unequivocally and eternally? As of now, we are confident that Einsteinian modifications of Newtonian physics are true and necessary. Tomorrow, something radically different and more compelling may surface. Are we then to say that Einstein's explanations were *unscientific?* Second, the insistence that the *explanans* be true assumes that the laws of nature are invariant; that from the beginning to the end of time, the causal links joining natural occurrences will change neither in shape, nor number, nor complexion. Thus the second criterion leaves no room for the possibility of two different explanations of the same event being not only equally scientific but equally true. Third, statements of the antecedent conditions are always modifiable, and the modifications can be so extreme as to allow any number of equally "true" general laws. The formal expression of this possibility is sometimes called the Duhem-Quine thesis:

"Any statement can be held true, come what may, if we make drastic enough adjustments elsewhere in the system . . . no statement is immune to revision."[10]

---

* Hempel, of course, accepts empirical laws or reliable empirical generalizations as provisional scientific explanations.

If we accept Quine's dictum, then any explanation can be revised to any degree and still remain consistent with the facts so long as we are willing to make drastic enough "adjustments" in the remainder of the system and, as Lakatos[11] has observed, the "system" may be the entirety of science.

The third criterion is the one that makes the Hempelian model *hypothetico-deductive*. It ties explanation in science to the strictures of formal logic. In practice, it takes the form:

If angular momentum is conserved and if X is angular momentum, then X is conserved.

In this respect, the general laws of science may be viewed as the major premises of a syllogism and the *explananda* its conclusion. Accordingly, the antecedent conditions would serve as minor premises. Of course, the explanations usually offered by behavioral and social scientists have this characteristic; a general law is either invoked or implied and the particular event of interest is attributed to the workings of this law. However, while the form of such explanations is Hempelian in the broadest sense, the substance rarely is. This is so because the conditions required by the first and the fourth criteria are not satisfied. That is, the "laws" in the behavioral and social sciences typically are either not true or are not universal, and the *explananda* are often devoid of empirical content. Again, it profits the discussion to cite illustrative questions from psychology:

"Why are people prejudiced?"
"What is it that motivates George?"
"Why is there such moral lassitude among our leaders?"
"Why is Thomas so much more intelligent than Earl?"
"Why is society so tasteless aesthetically?"
"Why is the South conservative?"
"Why does Jane repress her true feelings?"

The *explananda* in these interrogatives are mainstays of modern conversation: prejudice, motives, morality, intelligence, taste, conservatism, repression. One cannot read the learned journals long nor speak at length to a neighbor without hearing these nouns or their equivalents. The fact is, however, they are devoid of empirical content, at least in the form offered above. Indeed, those who endorse *behavioristic* psychology invariably point to the fourth criterion: a scientific explanation must refer to *empirically* knowable events, processes, and phenomena. We will evaluate this claim and its role in modern schools of psychology in subsequent chapters. For now, it is only necessary to appreciate that an uncritical adoption of the Hempelian model would require the simultaneous adoption of some form of behaviorism or physiological psychology as the only possible scientific psychology. This will be explored in the final chapter.

The citizen of the modern world—a decidedly "scientific" world—reading about the nature of scientific explanations may be struck by the obviousness of it all. He may well say to himself, "Well, certainly, such explanations should include universal laws, and should refer to the real (empirical) world." However, although it is true that a scholar here and there had suggested such prescriptions since the time of the Ancients, it has only been in the past century that this view of explanation has been anything but radical. Powerful obstacles have opposed its acceptance—obstacles never completely absent, not always irrational, not without merit. Salient among these is, of course, *authority:* the authority of religion, of custom, of taste, of competing scientific perspectives and, perhaps especially, the authority of success. It is difficult to convince anyone to abandon a way of doing things or a way of looking at things when, by his lights, his own method has been successful. The sixteenth-century intellectual, asked to choose between the universe of Ptolemy and that of Copernicus quite understandably found the Copernican alternative less compelling. Ptolemy had located the earth in the center of the universe—a sphere within a larger sphere. The sun and the rest of the heavens revolved around us and we remained fixed. Had this geocentric theory been ludicrous, had it violated good sense and normal perception, had it conflicted with basic values and the general temper of reflective minds, it would have occupied only the briefest interval in the history of ideas. Instead, it stood in the closest accord with reason, observation, and belief. Everyone *saw* the movement of the sun across the sky. No one experienced the motion of the earth. Indeed, if the earth were moving, would not a constant breeze always exist and pass in the same direction? Would we not fall off a spinning ball?

Modern man, who has witnessed lunar exploration and who has seen photographs of Venus, still speaks of the sun as rising in the east and setting in the west. In all respects but the intellectual, he remains a Ptolemaicist or, at best, a reluctant Copernican. His ancestors, committed to the view that God was so ensnared by metaphor that He had to locate the center of His concern in the center of His heavens, found the Copernican alternative not only unconvincing perceptually but theologically repugnant. And, in the court of last recourse, the court of commerce, nothing was to be gained by abandoning Ptolemy. Sailors, since the fleets of Phoenicia, navigated successfully, and farmers of the Nile anticipated the tides unerringly without the benefit of Copernican revisionism.

By the sixteenth century, astronomy, politics, and commerce in the

West had been conditioned by Roman Catholic orthodoxy. It was the official religion in the same sense that the Church of England now is except that the moderating influences of parliamentary government were absent. This distinction, of course, is a major one. Moreover, the Church had been engaged in nearly three centuries of struggles culminating in the Lutheran reform movement. Luther and Copernicus were contemporaries, and in times of strife there is the strongest temptation to consider all departures from convention as springing from the same source. With orthodoxy under attack, its defenders treated inquiry as sedition and neutrality as heresy. Unlike Luther's criticisms, Copernican theory suffered the special burden of appearing foolish to the lazy mind. The Duke of Saxony could support Luther in the interest of freeing Germany from Roman control. The peasants of Northern Europe could find in Luther one who would protect their marginal resources from the voracious appetite of the Basilica of St. Peter, that grand architectural conception of Julius II which nearly bankrupted the papacy. But no one had much to gain from vain speculation on the orbits of the planets and, given the implications of the Copernican theory, many thought there was much to lose. In the letters exchanged between Kepler and Galileo, the reluctance to publish their views is based less upon fear of censure by the Church than ridicule by the authorities of science. Kepler writes:

"You advise us by your personal example and in discreetly veiled fashion to retreat before the general ignorance and not to expose ourselves or heedlessly to oppose the violent attacks of the mob of scholars. . . . It is not only your Italians who cannot believe that they move if they do not feel it, but we in Germany also do not endear ourselves with this idea."[12]

Authority, when it succeeds in retarding the progress of science or of knowledge in any form, does not do so in spite of the "people" but, more typically, in their behalf. We are not to view the Renaissance Church as forcing the average citizen to abandon a collection of scientific truths —truths that appealed immediately to the reason and senses of the layman, truths more compelling than any alternative in the arsenal of faith. With few exceptions, authority never works this way. It is a product as much as a cause of its epoch. It is, in a word, the reflection of a *Zeitgeist*. The hypothesis of a moving earth had been advanced by Arisarchus in Ancient Greece, by Cicero, by Nicole Oresme, the French bishop in the court of Charles V, and, no doubt, by many others. Surely Christianity was not moving the sun in the Athens and Rome of antiquity. Nor was the earth kept in place by the Roman Church of the Renaissance. It was kept still by that great, hulking, mass of citizens who had other things to do and who were certainly not going to go to war over the idle visions of a Polish astronomer. The revolutions attributed to Copernicus, Newton, Darwin, and Einstein were *scientific* revolutions, and it is only the generous historian who will treat these intellectual advances as popular or cultural revolutions. Nonetheless, great scientific ideas do find climates that are uniquely receptive, climates in which revolutions of a very different sort are in progress. It is only when the most visible institutional authorities come under general suspicion, when the popular forces are prepared to labor against the very traditions that spawned them, that renegade perspectives from every quarter become tolerated and even solicited. And, in the great cycle of things, the revolutionary perspective soon becomes the new authority against which succeeding visionaries must do battle.

It has been argued by some, and most notably by Thomas Kuhn,[13] that the appearance of revolutionary ideas in science is not simply correlated with generally nurturing intellectual climates but that the scientific achievement itself is but one consequence of altered sociocultural perspectives. According to this view, science is an essentially cultural creation to be understood in psychological and motivational terms. The essential elements of this thesis, often called the *Kuhnian* thesis, include the following: (1) science is to be interpreted in psychosocial terms; (2) it is *not* to be understood as a set of sudden "earthquakes" but as a somewhat staid, "puzzle-oriented" process; (3) little of its research is extraordinary; rather, nearly all of it is, to use Kuhn's term, *normal* research intended to reveal how cleverly the scientist can prove what is well established; (4) it is a conservative rather than a revolutionary enterprise whose executors are judged more in terms of their ability to fit in than stand out.

Kuhn's influential work, *The Structure of Scientific Revolutions* (1962), has become one pole in a lively controversy known as the Kuhn-Popper debate. Where Kuhn would interpret science *psychologically*, Sir Karl Popper has insisted[14] that it can only be understood *logically*. Popperian science is "subjectless" in the sense that its nature is independent not only of the psychological dispositions of scientists but also of the particular problems to which science is addressed. Science, for Popper, is problem-oriented, not puzzle-oriented. That is, it is concerned with the validity of significant theories. What Kuhn considers to be "normal" science, the Popperian does not consider to be science at all. To the extent that a scientist is engaged in work that can only be appreciated within a given cultural or sociological context, to the extent that he is attempting merely to reconcile his research to that which is generally accepted by the scientific community, to the extent that the research is devoid of revolutionary potential—to these extents, Popperian science is not involved.

In a conciliatory spirit, we might suggest that the major disagreement between Kuhn and Popper vanishes when we picture Kuhn as describing what science has been historically, and Popper asserting what it ought to be. The tension, however, will not relax so easily. Kuhn's proposition is stronger than what a mere historical account would entail. It is that science is *scientists* and the latter are *psychological* entities, not just *logical* ones. As a result, science must be, at base, a psychological venture. The successful scientific revolution, accordingly, can take place only after the theory to be replaced has failed to satisfy needs of an extra-logical nature—needs that are economic, political, spiritual. The scientific theory that accommodates these needs will not be replaced by one that does not. Few scientists will search for such a theory; fewer will embrace it if it is unearthed. At a particular point in the evolution of science, the vast majority of scientists are "practitioners," performing the socially significant work of reproving, reasserting, and otherwise honoring those great scientific achievements of the past which define what science is for the practitioners. These achievements, which Kuhn calls *paradigms,* are the intellectual boundaries within which scientific inquiry can proceed. Without the paradigms there is, quite simply, no work for the practitioners!

On the Kuhnian account, science can and does form its own cult, its own priests, its own commandments. Membership entails ceremony and rites, not to speak of loyalty and vows. Rather than an invention of the human understanding designed to spare civilization the heavy encumbrances of superstition and unreasoning authority, science becomes yet another form of authority. And, as with different types of superstition and belief, those of science are not eliminated by the positive intrusions of logic but collapse from within. The myths and shibboleths of science dissolve only when they fail to do the work that society expects of its science.

The Popperian account accepts little of this. Popper contends that the validity of scientific propositions is and always could be assessed in terms utterly foreign to "sociologistic" analysis. In his well-known "falsification" hypothesis, Popper offers a litmus test for those who wish to weigh the scientific substance of a claim: is the claim stated in such a way as to apprise the listener of those procedures that would unequivocally establish the claim as false if it is, indeed, false? And by "procedures" Popper means more than the mechanical or methodological steps involved in research. He means the logical, *syntactical* procedures employed in phrasing the claim and in tying it to the observational domain to which it refers. The rules of the syllogism are not to be affirmed or suspended as society wishes, and the logic of science does not rest on taste. A scientific theory either explains what we can observe and explains with accuracy and reliability or it does not. It is either testable or it is not. When properly tested, it either passes or fails. When we advance our theory and conduct our tests, we know more than we did before. We know about the enduring features of the real world and we can predict how it will behave. Our predictions must be confirmed or the theory must be abandoned. That which deviates from these prescriptions is not science, "normal" or otherwise. Lest we abandon too quickly what is true, Popper leaves room for some dogma—not the dogma of conventional authority but the kind of "dogma" that permits dialogue of an essentially Socratic nature to take place, the dogma we have in mind when we begin a sentence with *"For argument's sake, let us assume that . . ."* In contrast to Kuhn's powerful *paradigms*, these Popperian dogmas are mere aids to debate and reflection. The scientist is prepared to forfeit them at any time they threaten to obstruct the search for truth. Of the Kuhnian paradigms, Popper collects them under what he calls The Myth of Framework.[15] He insists that no scientist, properly called, fashions theories or tests them according to these assumed dictates. Of course, all inquiry proceeds within a framework, but this framework itself is the very entity that true science challenges and tests. The paradigms which Kuhn would have exerting control over science are those which Popper has science modifying or replacing.

It would be difficult to challenge Kuhn's contention that most of what presents itself as science now or in any previous time is "normal" rather than extraordinary. The scientific literature is filled with studies of a replicative nature in which some little nuance has been added to an otherwise well-worn field of inquiry. Brazen challenges to the authority of extant theories are rare to the point of near invisibility. At first glance the professional journals would, indeed, seem to be the setting for puzzle-solving rather than problem-solving, and the contributors do appear to be guided by a desire to prove that orthodoxy is enlightened rather than by the compulsion to refute what is taken as fundamental truth. In other words, at a superficial level of analysis, science is Kuhnian, and our comprehension of its character requires sociological technique. But on further reflection, this description can be modified. The scientist must balance two otherwise conflicting duties: the duty to preserve truth when it is discovered and the duty to expose error. Any scientifically useful theory will be pregnant with implications. A theory such as Darwin's or Einstein's contains enough predictions to keep scientists productively occupied for generations. What may look like mere "busy work" is often an essential, albeit small, step in the long march from hypothesis to relative certainty. Grand theories, cosmic in their scope, often rise and fall on the smallest discrepancies. Science has learned that the slightest fact cannot be ignored, that a good study is worth repeating often, that every potentially significant variable must be examined, that in science, error is usually oversight rather than ignorance.

Properly understood, every experiment is potentially "revolutionary." That most studies fail to inaugurate a revolution is only to say that our major theories appear to be correct in their major respects and that, consequently, our tests of their validity generally do not reveal basic flaws. In time, of course, experiments of a more imaginative nature will be conducted and our perspectives on the universe, on life, on our own nature, will be revised. These revolutionary studies depend on scientists of genius equipped with the steadily evolved findings of prior generations. Not everyone entering a laboratory can be expected to be a Galileo, but this fact surely does not reduce science to a game of socially accepted puzzles. It has always been the case and probably will continue to be the case that popular acceptance of a scientific theory rests on what can be imprecisely called sociological considerations. To the extent that the man in the street believed that Darwin had made him a monkey, he was not about to adopt a Darwinian perspective. Many scientists shared this attitude, and Kuhn must be applauded for exposing this weakness in the scientific community. But the Darwinian revolution occurred nonetheless and it occurred because it was a *scientific* revolution, the kind—the only kind—whose fate is ultimately indifferent to the will or hopes of the man in the street.

Darwin's theory was stated in a form amenable to experimental tests and, in modified form, it passed these tests. It was confronted by fact and it survived the confrontation. Scientists might have been unwilling to accept the theory, but all of them knew the point at which they would have to; and this, after all, is what is meant by the *logical* structure of science. The Darwinian *explanans* was a universal law; the *explananda* were empirical and were logically deducible from the *explanans;* the resulting explanations were, in Popper's sense, *syntactically* necessarily connected to the theory. The facts on which the theory depended were available and the facts predicted by the theory were discovered. No alternative explanation assimilated or predicted the same facts as efficiently, completely, and accurately. When the shouting subsided and the misunderstandings were swept away, anyone educated in the standards of scientific explanation was required, by the force of logic, to accept the Darwinian account as possibly true and in no way necessarily false. And this, finally, is the nature of scientific discovery: When it takes place, *we know that we know.*

Psychology and History

From the foregoing, the reader should be in fuller possession of the objectives of the present work. There is simply too impressive a list of skeptics to permit the easy conclusion that psychology is a science. Accordingly, subsequent chapters will be addressed to the ideas that defined the psychological perspectives of a given era. Throughout, we will confront arguments for and against a *science of the mind*. More important, we will examine the general, intellectual, and cultural conditions favoring either the scientific or the nonscientific perspective. To this extent the following chapters are "Kuhnian" in orientation, but this is not to suggest that science itself is. The author's bias is decidely Popperian. At the same time, the historian must take note of what people actually do and of the principal determinants of their actions and ideas. At the end of the nineteenth century, psychology emerged as a scientific discipline, but it did not achieve this through Popperian processes. It was presented to the world of ideas as a science *before* the fact. In short, it had the pretension but not the evidence. However, from the historian's point of view it is less important that people consider something to be so or good or necessary than it is to discover why they are committed to such views. The remainder of this book, then, is an extended answer to the questions, "How did contemporary psychology come about and take the form it now displays?" and "In the light of history, what judgments of this contemporary form seem warranted?" This second question is a sensitive one and requires a comment here.

One of the most widely accepted rules of etiquette in modern historical scholarship is that the historian never argues that the past is prologue: that what has occurred u..der such and such conditions will ever occur again even in roughly the same way. With equivalent orthodoxy, and in keeping with the quest for that elusive raiment, objectivity, historians also insist that their interpretations are not intended to tell contemporaries what they *ought* to do. Yet, if historians never overcame their reluctance to predict or to wag a finger, their books would be far thinner and would appear in essentially tabular form. Try as we may, our histories will always contain a prophetic element and will rarely be devoid of a scolding. When the historian of science recounts the strenuous efforts and odd reasonings of those eighteenth- and nineteenth-century futurists, struggling to create perpetual motion machines, and when he reviews Helmholtz's part in putting a stop to these affairs, he is surely urging us not to renew the program. In the plainest terms, he is both prophesying that the program will fail and recommending that his contemporaries invest their energies in more promising ventures. Similarly the political historian who traces the rise of the National Socialists in the Germany of the 1930s to the paralyzing terms of the Versailles Treaty is telling posterity something about the consequences of treaties of a certain type, not just the one signed at Versailles. History cannot be a lesson unless it is at least loosely prophetic. And, if it is even loosely prophetic, it is at least loosely prescriptive.

The present work also includes prophesy and prescription. There is little question but that Psychology's decades of foundering are attributable to a constellation of causes that history can disclose. Some of the present difficulties, while of a more sophisticated and technical shade, appear to be residuals of earlier error. Were a historical analysis to ignore these residuals, it would gain "objectivity" only at the price of usefulness. The history of Psychology points at least generally to those paths the discipline is likely to take. It even anticipates those that might well be dead-ends.

References

1. R. G. Collingwood, *The Idea of History*, Oxford University Press, New York, 1972. This quotation is taken from page 10 of the Introduction. We owe the availability of this work to Professor T. M. Knox who edited these essays after Collingwood's death in 1943, at the age of 52. Knox was a close associate of Collingwood's. His Preface to the edition is important to an understanding of Collingwood's program of which *The Idea of History* is but illustrative.

2. Collingwood, op. cit., p. 9.

3. The most accessible source for the works of Giovanni Battista (or Giambattista) Vico is the translated edition, *The New Science of Giambattista Vico* by T. G. Bergen and M. H. Fisch, Cornell University, New York, 1970. This is an abridgement of the 1948 translation by the same translators. Vico's historiographic method is well illustrated in Book Three, the *Discovery of the True Homer*. On his complaint about earlier historians, a delineation of their flaws, and his own approach, see *Elements*, Book One, Sec. II. On the error of *scholastica successionis*, see XIII–146 of the *Elements*.

4. Collingwood, op. cit., p. 224.

5. This observation will be amplified and explained in Chapter 6, with apologies to Erasmus, Luther, Pico, et al.

6. Oliver W. Holmes, *The Path of the Law*, Collected papers (1920), p. 173.

7. H. L. A. Hart, *The Concept of Law*, Oxford University Press, London, New York, 1961.

8. *Plays by Molière*, Modern Library edition, New York, 1924.

9. See especially the collection in C. Hempel's *Aspects of Scientific Explanation and Other Essays in the Philosophy of Science*, New York, Free Press, 1965.

10. For the original see Quine, *From a Logical Point of View*, Harvard University Press, Cambridge, Mass., 1953; also the discussion by Imre Lakatos in *Criticism and the Growth of Knowledge*, edited by Lakatos and Musgrave, Cambridge University Press, 1970, pp. 184–189.

11. Lakatos, op. cit.

12. In *The Portable Renaissance Reader*, edited by J. B. Ross and M. M. McLaughlin, Viking, New York, 1973.

13. Thomas Kuhn, *The Structure of Scientific Revolutions*, University of Chicago Press, 1962.

14. Karl Popper, *The Logic of Scientific Discovery*, 1959. Also see the article in Lakatos and Musgrave, op. cit., titled "Normal Science and Its Dangers." On science as "subjectless," see his, "Epistemology Without a Knowing Subject" in Rootselaar and Staal (eds.), *Proceedings of the Third International Congress for Logic, Methodology and Philosophy of Science*, Amsterdam, 1968, pp. 333–73.

15. Popper, "Normal Science and Its Dangers," op. cit.

2

□□□□□□□□□□□□□□□□□□□□□□□□□□□□□

Psychology in the Hellenic Age

FROM THE PRE-SOCRATICS TO THE DIALOGUES

The Site

Using a map of the modern world, a crude rectangle can be constructed by connecting Messina, in Sicily, to Taranto some 200 miles to the north and east and, as the base of the rectangle, connecting Messina with Söke on the Aegean coast of Turkey about 75 miles south of Izmir. The resulting figure will yield an area approximately the size of Montana. Within this limited region and in a period of less than 150 years, the following births occurred: Anaxagoras, Parmenides, Zeno, Pericles, Empedocles, Sophocles, Euripedes, Aeschylus, Socrates, Herodotus, Thucydides, Xenophon, Protagoras, Plato, and Aristotle. By extending the time back another century, we can include Thales, Anaximander, and Pythagoras. The resulting two centuries—the time covering, roughly, the rise of the Pythagoreans to the flowering of Aristotle's scholarship—comprise the Hellenic epoch of Classical Greece—an epoch not anticipated by any prior age and, in the most significant respects, unmatched thereafter.

It would be reassuring to us and our posterity if we could explain the appearance of the classical world in a set of swift, declarative sentences. Indeed, popular histories are rather given to reducing the entire achievement to (1) a slave economy which permitted scholars the freedom to think and argue; (2) long periods of sunshine and clear skies which lessened the daily concern for shelter; (3) the cultivation of perspective by foreign influences imported by a peninsular Greek commerce; (4) the invasion of the Dorians from northern Europe; and (5) the mere refinement of older Minoan and Mycenaean accomplishments.

27

None of these factors is able to explain Classical Greece and, in certain respects, each of them is contrary to fact. Slave economies are virtually coeval with the history of civilization. Egypt, Assyria, Phoenicia, Babylonia, Lydia, Persia, Crete—for as far back as the evidence will take us—were bloated with slave labor. Greece depended on slaves to no greater extent, and certainly enjoys a far better record of caring for them. Indeed, when periods of peace prevailed such that the number of slaves decreased, the cost of slave labor may well have been prohibitive.[1] Moreover, the fraction of the Greek citizenry in a position to benefit from such labor was vanishingly small. A sudden increase in the number of slaves often resulted in a commensurate increase in unemployment, overpopulation, and the resulting pressure on a fragile economy. No one had more leisure than the pharaohs of Egypt, but the long line of them yielded not one philosopher.

The clear skies of Greece, for whatever aesthetic benefits they showered, allowed the sun to scorch the earth further. Only 20 percent of Greek soil could be cultivated. By the sixth century, the country was not able to feed itself without extensive foreign trade. This fact did bring the Greeks into contact with the non-Greek world, but it hardly supports the contention that Greece borrowed its civilization. To argue otherwise is to invite the question, *"Borrowed from whom?"* More to the point, the regions that contributed most to Greek commerce were the very ones the Greeks themselves had settled and had settled for that purpose. Ionia and her offshore islands (Samos, Lesbos, Chios) on the western edge of Asia Minor were Greek colonies, as were the regions in southern Italy and Sicily. This is not to ignore trade between Greece and such non-Greek cultures as those of Egypt, Persia, Lydia, and Assyria, but when we examine these cultures we find little to identify with the dominant features of Greek civilization.

As for the Dorian invasion, it is not at all clear where the Dorians came from, nor is it clear what they brought with them. By the sixth century, when historical accounts become available and credible, we find the Doric "race" occupying areas in the southwest of Asia Minor, principally the cities of Cnidus and Halicarnassus and the islands of Rhodes and Cos. These regions do not figure centrally in the Classical attainment. In the wars with Persia, the Dorians seem to have quit early and, given their excessive concern with "racial purity," it is not likely that they sought to influence the course of non-Doric culture. The later architecture of Dorian holdings in Sicily is, in major respects, quite in line with styles cultivated in the Hellenic (Greek) period.[2] The Dorians are mentioned only once in the *Odyssey* but later appear in numerous areas of the Greek world. Thus they did invade and they did push out the people and the cultures standing in their way. We need not doubt, therefore, their excellence in war, but we have no reason to believe that the elements of civilization borne by them even approximated those of their victims. That they may have been, as they were wont to assert, the original Hellenes is a possibility which, if true, has little bearing on the origins of the Classical period some seven centuries later.

The world inherited by the Dorians or, better, confiscated by them is the older world of Mycenae and Crete. Again, the Dorians' role here is not one of passing an older culture on to the Hellenes but, rather, destroying or neglecting it. The differences between the Hellenic epoch and those of Crete and Mycenae are certainly more significant than the similarities. Hellenic art cannot be derived from Mycenaean; the Hellenes cremated the dead, whereas the Mycenaeans buried theirs; the gods of Homer bear no resemblance to those of Mycenae.[3] Thin strands connect the architecture of the two civilizations and there are other points of convergence as well, but to focus on these is to invite an instance of *scholastica successionis civitates*.

The Classical Age did not, of course, spring forth from the brow of Zeus, nor was it a mere accident. It was caused by historical circumstances too numerous to exhaust. We must examine several that seem to play a salient part while recognizing that those discussed above did not.

Our principal sources of knowledge about the rise of Greece from 1200 B.C. are the epic poems of Homer and Hesiod, who wrote in the eighth century before the Christian era. The surviving contributions of Hesiod are *Works and Days* and the *Theogony*. The former describes his life as a modest farmer, and the latter attempts to recount the genealogy of the gods. The social and ethical character of agrarian life can be traced in *Works and Days*, while our understanding of the roles and responsibilities of the deities is informed by his *Theogony*. The Homeric epics are the *Odyssey* and the *Iliad*. It used to be something of a commonplace to insist that the two poems were not authored by the same hand. Iron, for example is occasionally mentioned in the *Odyssey* but not in the *Iliad*, suggesting that the latter was written prior to the Iron Age. What must be kept in mind, however, is that epic poems were created to be sung, to be recited by lonely shepherds huddled around an evening fire, or to be taught to children as lessons in history and as rules for life. Each generation, each tribe and village, added something to the original. The *Odyssey* and *Iliad* received by the Greece of Herodotus were surely different from the original compositions. It is in this sense that there were many Homeric poets, although some single Homer may well have been the spirit behind both works. By the sixth century there were "official" copies of both poems, and a number of Greeks, especially Ionians, earned a modest living teaching and interpreting the stories. There is no question but that the intellectual flavor of Greek life from the sixth to the fourth centuries was dominated by the sagas, idiosyncrasies, and fortunes of Homer's heroic figures. The poems trace the major battles, cite the important buildings, sing praises to the major tyrants, and expose the weaknesses of the greatest gods. We learn of migrations, military strategies, taxation, customs, ethics, superstition, cuisine, clothing, and population in a historic period that is otherwise silent.

In addition to the epic poets, our sources include the art and architecture of the period which tell so much about religion, standards of living, and technology. Later came coins stamped with the images of kings and generals, and tax rolls documenting the major demographic features of the period. Thus, history was being written long before Herodotus (484–425) recorded the chronicle of the Persian Wars or Thucydides (460?–400?) described the Age of Pericles and Athens' fate at the hands of Sparta. Finally, we have the hearsay evidence of the major Greek and Roman writers from Plato and Aristotle in the fifth and fourth centuries B.C. to Plutarch in the second century of the Christian era.

The Eve of Greatness

The Greek world of the seventh century received a moral and cultural legacy from the epic poets, chiefly Homer and Hesiod. Politically, it enjoyed relative serenity. Trade was limited, although emigration had already become common. The country was little more than a collection of independent principalities scratching a modest agrarian existence from the soil. Coinage had yet to disturb the simple commerce of the farmer. The potentates of Egypt, Assyria, Lydia, and Media were too busy with one another to threaten the Hellenes into solidarity. Athens was yet to be reckoned with, although she was the mother city of many who had recently settled the Ionian coast and its islands. It was the Ionians who were to initiate the coming cultural epoch—Ionians undisturbed by the greater Lydian nation to the east whose borders were under constant pressure from the Assyrians.

Seventh-century Greece was a collection of innocent and still relaxed polarities: economically, the polarity between farmer and aristocrat; culturally, between urban and rustic life; religiously, between the rational, Olympian sons of Homer and the mystery-laden Orphics with eastern (Thracean?) roots. This last polarity emerges most visibly in the sixth century with Ionian philosophy leading the cause of urbane reasonableness and with the Orphic cults rising to prominence in the south of Italy. These settlements aside, mainland Greece on the eve of sixth-century greatness was little more than the pages of *Works and Days*. Cities, whose populations and even limited commerce created the need for at least the rudiments of government, were controlled either by a party of "first families," the Aristocrats, or were ruled by hereditary monarchs or were controlled by the so-called Tyrants. This last term, which over the centuries has become pejorative, was used to describe any political-military leader whose position of authority was not constitutionally granted. As often as not, the reigning Tyrant was popular, respected, even revered. Certain regions had long and valued traditions of a given form of rule. Athens, since its earliest life, was governed by the Aristocrats; Sparta, by monarchs.

Except in the most densely populated areas, Greek territory was controlled by clans or phratries. Originally, these were probably groups that had settled a region at about the same time, emigrating from a common locale. The clan held its territory in communal fashion and, on the death of a member, his holdings would revert to the clan as a whole rather than to his family. Since possessions were thus controlled, the pressures to remain within the clan were undoubtedly great. The Dorian insistence on racial exclusiveness is but one sign of what must have been a very general and very fierce tribal identity. Blood feuds were common. It was believed that the spirit of a murdered clansman would work revenge upon his own clan until his murderer was executed and that his blood would spoil the earth for harvest, and his soul would appeal to the Olympians to deny good fortune to those who ignored the wrong that had been done him.

There is no question but that these people, reared on Homer and, to a lesser extent, Hesiod, had a strong sense of justice, an unyielding moral code, a devotion to independence. In Athens, discretionary matters were decided by the *Archon*, an appointed (later, elected) arbiter through whom the landed families were usually able to protect their interests. We understand the functions of the *Archon* more fully when we observe that the periods in which the office was vacant were referred to as *anarchia*.

The spiritual climate of the sixth-century Greek world was unique and remained unique as the empire formed. The Greeks were as superstitious as their eastern neighbors and were as eager to please their gods as were the citizens of earlier and later civilizations; but they were not *religious*. The distinction between superstition and religion is a broad one. Its major feature is the presence or absence of a prophet who speaks with the authority of the divine. The ancient Greek world, for whatever reason, was conspicuously devoid of prophets. Her prominent oracles, including that vaunted figure at Delphi, were notoriously uneven in their judgments and almost comically ambiguous in their prescriptions. One would guess that nearly everybody knew that oracles were for sale, that they strived harder not to offend monarchs and generals than to remain on the good side of Zeus, and that they were often best understood in terms of petty grievance and venality.

Although the Greeks honored the Olympians, they simply ignored or rejected anyone who might have posed as a prophet.* The epic poetry was rich enough in metaphor to serve as a daily guide to a life of justice, courage, and hope. It did not associate particular forms of misconduct with punishment in an afterlife. The wages of sin were essentially economic; for example, the soil would refuse to yield a harvest. But unlike their Jewish contemporaries or their Christian successors, the Greeks of the ancient world did not enjoy a received body of truths or a code of transcendent principles. The effects of this were at once positive and negative. On the positive side, the absence of such received principles permitted a freedom of interpretation and a creative approach to the spiritual dimensions of life. This, we must assume, had a subtle but very pervasive part in the evolution of Philosophy. There is an undeniable correlation between the quality of philosophical scholarship generated by a people and the relative paucity of "received truths" or, at least, the general inclination against accepting such truths. On the negative side, the absence of a rational and codified body of religious principles induced, necessarily it would seem, the average Greek to adopt the strangest assortment of superstitious beliefs and conduct. It also reduced his laws, at least until the time of Solon, to a collection of *ad hoc* ordinances, rewritten as the demands of the moment required. In the pre-Solonic period, justice was little more than a combination of trade agreements and spirited revenge.

The epic poetry made much of the genealogy of the gods and this was incorporated into daily affairs in the form of hereditary monarchies, family feuds, and a general nativistic outlook on human nature and the human condition. Nativism, separated from its roots in genetic science, is little more than fatalism. Without a formal and rational religious doctrine, a fatalistic people will be engulfed by a kind of situation-ethics; that is, if I take advantage of my neighbor, it is only because it was "in the

---

* I use the term "prophet" here in the sense of one proclaiming himself to be appointed by the gods for the purpose of explaining the divine will to the human community. The ancient Greek world was, of course, steeped in superstition and displayed the all-too-common reverence for witchcraft, prognostication, omens, and curses. Epigraphical studies have yielded ample evidence of the Greek citizen's eagerness to visit evil upon his enemies by invoking the powers of the deep. While the orthodox followers of Olympianism probably were less guilty of this, there were competing and less Homeric cults much given to superstitious excess. Even in Homer, of course, ghosts figure centrally. That the better minds of the period had only contempt for such occult practices and devotions is evident from the stern rebukes offered in Plato's *Republic* (Book II, [364]) and *Laws*, (X, [909b]; XI, [933a]).

cards," so to speak, and therefore utterly consonant with the whims of Fate.

Even as we admire the staggering achievements of the Hellenic epoch, we must remain mindful of the cruelty and barbarity of the age. The achievements of the few and the failings of the many were both dependent, to a significant degree, upon the looseness and inconstancy of the Hellenic religious commitment. Indeed, it was not until the critical minds of the pre-Socratics were trained on Olympus itself that the first signs of religious orthodoxy appeared. In brief, the Ancient Greek appears to have been rather oblivious to his religious convictions until the early philosophers presented a challenge to them. Thus challenged, the Greek of antiquity tended to respond with the same bigotry and nervousness that have been abiding partners in the history of persecutions and war.

In its most general expression, the religious tone of sixth-century Greek life was neither speculative nor psychological.[4] The gods were immortal, man was not, and therefore man was best advised not to pretend to any understanding of the divine. In rigid hierarchic fashion, the Greeks accepted the supremacy of divine will, followed by the temporal supremacy of the will of the king. Morality or ethics ($\epsilon\theta\eta\kappa\omega s$) translated quite literally into habit or custom: what was right was what the gods, and the kings in whom right was vested, did and decided. It was right *because* they did it. Only later, when economic forces created rigid economic classes, when poverty captured large numbers of farmers, when coins and banks and commerce were used to establish or wipe out fortunes overnight, did speculative morality appear. As power flowed from kings first to the aristocrats and next to the people, a new rationale was required. But even at this later date the distance between gods and men was still accepted as unbreachable, and as a result speculative morality took a philosophical rather than a theological turn.

The gods of Homer did not always get along with one another. Occasions would find them carrying on at cross purposes. This fact allowed the Greeks considerable room in choosing a course of conduct. That is, for almost any form of conduct, a divine example could be found with relative ease. Perhaps the most vivid expression of those moral antagonisms that are implicit in polytheistic societies is to be found in a comparison of the followers of Dionysos with those of Apollo. The central elements of Dionysiac belief and practice are portrayed in the *Bacchae* of Euripedes. Unlike the Olympians, Dionysos is mortal and, therefore, can plead and comprehend the case for man. Borrowed from the East (Lydia?), his gift is the gift of sensual life—one that frees the otherwise dominated Greek woman to revel in the pleasures of the flesh, one in which wine and night and passion conspire to elevate human emotion to the near-godliness of transcendent joy. Over and against this Dionysian vision is set the deliberative and ordered life of the Apollonian—a life of proportion and control, of inquiry and restraint, of law and justice. More than one philosopher, from antiquity to the present, would attempt to understand the unsteady march of civilization in terms of a conflict between the Dionysiac and Apollonian dimensions of man.

In subsequent pages, when we review Socratic ethics and its emphasis upon *harmony* and the Aristotelian conception of happiness as the soul's accord with virtue, we must keep in mind this already ancient conflict, or perceived conflict, between passion and reason. In fact, a defensible method of categorizing both pre-Socratic and Socratic approaches is through the use of this conflict: the Pythagoreans so devoted to Apollonian rationalism as to insist upon the utter abandonment of a life of the senses; Anaxagoras conceiving of Mind as the ultimate reality; Aristotle attempting to reconcile the spiritual and the material; finally, the post-Aristotelians taking his materialism so far as to reduce the meaning of life to Dionysiac ecstasy. The Homeric legacy, never missing from any expression of Greek belief, was sufficiently flexible and sufficiently removed from the daily affairs of the people to keep the spiritual climate chaotic and to encourage philosophers to impose or suggest their varied solutions. How their speculation was received depended, as has been true ever since, upon the economic, political, and military realities of the day.

On a scale modest by modern proportions, the Greek world had achieved a balance of power among her leading city-states. The Athenian navy was still more commercial than military and posed no threat to Sparta. The latter, soon to become the architect and center of the Peloponnesian League, could not interfere with Athens except on land and, with a hostile Argos and neutral Thebes in Sparta's path, such a venture was not undertaken. Maintaining the balance of power was important to all the states, so that a change in the leadership of any one of them or the signing of treaties among a few of them aroused suspicion and encouraged defensive countermoves. A look at the map of the period discloses the possibilities for manoeuvring. Excessive friendliness between Athens and Argos would place hostile forces behind any Spartan expeditions toward Corinth. The Spartan occupation of Salamis or Aegina would pose a threat to Athenian commerce in the west. Spartan accords with Thebes or Thessaly could only expose Athens to attack from the north. Control of both Aegina and the southern port of Sunium might prevent an Athenian vessel from ever getting through the Saronic Gulf to the Mediterranean.

As trade beyond the mainland became more important, the privileged position of Athens drew attention to her every move. Sparta, essentially

GREECE and the PERSIAN EMPIRE ca. 500 B.C.

1. Corcyra (Corfu)	10. Samos	19. Megara
2. Corinth	11. Miletus	20. Plataea
3. Salamis	12. Rhodes	21. Artemesium
4. Sparta	13. Crete	22. Clazomenae
5. Chalcidice	14. Athens	23. Ephesus
6. Propontis	15. Euboea	24. Colophon
7. Lemnos	16. Chalcis	25. Smyrna
8. Lesbos	17. Argos	
9. Chios	18. Gulf of Corinth	

foreclosing the possibility of ever controlling the Aegean, drove west to capture the Messenians and thereby create a path to the Ionian Sea and Italy beyond. Thus, had there been no departure from the tradition at all, a tension among the principal city-states would still have been unavoidable. Once the non-Greek world became essential to the economic survival of all Greek states, the aloof and ostensibly unassimilable independent units were bound to violate the status quo. That the greatest tension would be between Athens and Sparta was due to many factors: the commercial and strategic which have already been cited; the ideological, with Sparta retaining many features of the Homeric age; the spiritual, with Athens enjoying a liberalization through the influence of Ionian teaching and with Sparta still clinging to a very literal reading of scripture. Indeed, it is only in Sparta and, to a much lesser extent in Megara, that the Homeric king (*Basileus*) survives, a king whose genealogy traces back to the Olympians themselves. When we take note of the differences between these two cities, when we recognize the extent to which the fortunes of each depended on the containment of the other, we can only ask why war between them occurred so late. Given, that is, that the traditional ingredients of war were abundant by the dawn of the sixth century, why did it take until 460 for the rupture to occur?

Part of the reason for the rupture was the expedient of internal and regional stabilization. Sparta throughout most of the seventh century was striving for hegemony in the Peloponnesus and her most immediate concern was Argos. Argos was just north and thus occupied a strategic place along the northern trade route from the Corinthian isthmus. Megara, just east of the isthmus, was ruled by Tyrants and, from the Spartan perspective, this was sufficient to cause alarm. In Athens, matters were even more diverting. A young member of the aristocratic oligarchy, Cylon, conspired to install himself as Tyrant (shortly after marrying the daughter of the Tyrant of Megara* [c. 604][5]). Miscalculating the temperament of the commoners, Cylon made his move only to see his faction decimated. He escaped, but those who had sympathized with or supported his attempted *coup* were slaughtered. The aftermath of this event tells us much about the moral sensibilities of the period. The citizens were overcome by the brutal treatment they had inflicted upon the conspirators. They viewed their actions as courting the enmity of the gods. They feared that the stains upon their soil would blight their crops as much as their character. Accordingly, they appointed Draco as *Archon* and demanded that laws be ordained putting an end to butchery.

Little is known of the resulting "Draconian" measures, which, it is said, were extremely severe, but since many of them were subsequently incorporated in the laws framed by Solon, we are not to assume that Draco's code was especially "Draconian."[6] We know that Solon was appointed Archon in 594 and that his revised constitution was the turning point in Athens' march toward democracy. Solon succeeded, we must recall, not merely by genius but by the will of a citizenry at the end of its tether. The massacre of Cylon's followers was but the most vivid manifestation of hates and frustrations that had been accruing for at least a decade. Earlier in the seventh century money had been introduced

---

* Tyranny was rare. The Megarians were held in general contempt for tolerating tyrants. Indeed, the Ionian Greeks had difficulty even comprehending the reverence paid by Lydians and Persians to their kings.

and before long the once proud agricultural communities of the Athenian state were nearly in bondage. They received few coins for their labors, and the costs of supplies and conveniences rapidly grew to inflationary proportions. Archons, whose oath of office included a commitment to the protection of all aristocratic holdings, made a nagging situation desperate. Many farmers, judged guilty of not honoring their debts, had their property confiscated and were even sold, with their families, to slave merchants. Others were forced to abandon their land and become migrant laborers on foreign shores. The aristocrats, who had long been respected both by the seafarers and the farmers, were now objects of fear and contempt. The State was evolving into an essentially feudal system but there were neighbors across the Aegean who were on the threshold of empire.

By the time of Solon's appointment it was obvious even to the oligarchs that the trends of the past two decades could not continue. They were not, however, prepared for Solon's reforms. Ignoring those terms of office that had created the problems he now faced, Solon began his Archonate by eliminating all debts of land and by proclaiming free all citizens whose debts had placed them in bondage. As he defied the rich, he defied the clans by permitting each person to bequeath his holdings as he saw fit, although the inheritance rights of legitimate sons remained in force. He ordered the minting of new coins, a procedure that corresponds today to the devaluation of a currency. Athenian goods became more accessible to the Athenian. Blood feuds were condemned, violence proscribed, personal liberties expanded. The latent devotion to law, a devotion nurtured by the supreme orderliness of the Olympian vision, found expression in the Solonic code. Solon's graduated tax structure, his injunctions against the abuse of slaves, his formal recognition of the perquisites of outstanding contributors, his invariant loyalty to the canons of fairness, made his name synonymous with law itself.

As these developments were occupying and changing the character of Athens, Sparta too was immersed in her own "identity crisis." Having been the principal settlement since the 1100s of the joyless Dorians, Sparta had evolved into the infantry of the Ancient world. In the ninth (?) century, her laws had been laid down by Lycurgus—laws better suited to the breeding of circus animals than the governance of human beings. The terms of the Spartan Code are so faithfully incorporated into George Orwell's *1984* that they warrant little attention here. The Doric racial obsession found expression in ordinances pertaining to mating. "Errors" were corrected by infanticide. Meals, dress, music, athletics—in short, the full spectrum of daily life—came under Lycurgean review. At the time of Cylon's abortive ploy, Sparta was facing the same domestic problems that attach to any prolonged period of fascist rule. Her isolationism led her to reject the new monetary systems that were enriching the non-Laconian Greek world. Distrust toward her countrymen forced her to direct her economic interests toward Egypt and toward the lesser developed colonies of Italy. With every Spartan farmer required to return a fixed percentage of his yield to the kings (Sparta had two at a time) and the nobility, the yields were predictably modest and increasingly noncompetitive. Through awesome discipline and a less than enlightened sense of the value of human life, she terrorized her enemies and, with the exception of Argos, brought the entire Peloponnesian territory to heel. But saddled by a code that most of the Greek world found unintelligible, and ever on the verge of domestic strife, Sparta was simply not prepared to invite a confrontation with Athens as the sixth century began. There is no telling how long this counterproductive, uneasy state would have lasted had not a threat from the outside intervened to bring all the Hellenes together. This feat would be accomplished a century after Solon by the expansionistic zeal of Persia. Until then, however, Athens continued to grow in culture, prestige, commerce, and tolerance while Sparta remained, as always, vigilant.

Philosophy—The Ionian Invention

The situation of the seventh-century Ionians was unique in the Greek world. Their settlement of the Aegean islands and coastal cities of Asia Minor was prompted initially, we would expect, by scarcity on the mainland and by attractive trading prospects. Their homeland was for the most part Attica, meaning that Athens was their mother city. We have noted that the Lydian kings were preoccupied with problems to the east with the result that the Ionians enjoyed uncommon independence in the light of their status as foreigners.

If the history of immigrant experiences in modern times is applicable, we can conjecture that the Ionians displayed that same "pride of race" witnessed among displaced citizens the world over. Fear of assimilation seems to be an abiding condition of wandering people. That the earliest Homeric scholars should appear in Ionia is, therefore, quite in keeping with tradition. The further one removes himself from the culture of his childhood, the more strenuously he asserts its virtues and protects its uniqueness. The Ionian of the seventh century was quite possibly more Greek than his Athenian cousins. As a military force, the Ionians had a well-deserved reputation. Indeed, the success of Psammetichus I, who expelled the Assyrians from Egypt and restored the throne of Pharaoh (reigned as Ptsamik I from 663 to 609 B.C.), was due in large measure to the aid he received from Ionian mercenaries.

During Ptsamik I's reign of fifty-four years, Ionia was not only the brightest jewel of the Greek world but Miletus, the major Ionian city, was the cultural capitol of Western civilization.[7] Even after the fall of Miletus to Persia (494), Ionia remained a source of intellectual achievement and a model of political resistance for the rest of the Hellenic world. Her prosperity was secured by the fact that she made the finest fabrics in the world as well as the most beautiful pottery and had a navy that allowed both products to move freely from the Bosphorus in the north to Sybaris on the southeastern coast of Italy. For more than a century her only economic rival was the nearby island of Samos, a rival whose main effect was one of prompting the Ionian achievements to even greater heights.

Ionia's cultural rival, at least during the century beginning at about 650, was Sybaris, the Italian colony north of Croton. The Sybarites were the cosmopolitans of the Italian world, the middlemen between Greek and Etruscan traders. That the cultural rivalry would include, sooner or later, rival philosophical camps appears, in retrospect, inevitable. Here were Ionian cities—Miletus, Samos, Colophon, Ephesus, Clazomenae, Mytilene—preserving and asserting their Homeric character, outdoing one another in representing and reflecting their traditions. Deriving their inspiration, perhaps from Athens, their independence from the unique problems of their Lydian neighbors, and their wealth from hegemony of the Aegean, the Ionians rapidly forged a distinctive culture which sailed with goods as far as the western towns of Sicily. At the same time, Croton, Sybaris, Elea, Reggio, and Tarentum, the leading trading centers in *Magna Graecia*, were entering a period of prosperity and growing urbanity. These Italian Greeks were a "new breed," so to speak, viewing the Ionians as more or less tradition-bound. The parallel with, say, Americans at the beginning of the present century and their English forebears would not be strained. Coincident with these developments was the Ionians' daily commerce, in Egypt, in Lydia, in Sicily, with diverse religious, political, and cultural forms.

These were the ingredients that created the philosophical spirit. They may be present and philosophy may not prosper, but when they are lacking, philosophers do not appear. We may even argue that the absence of any one of them will retard the philosophical mind. Ionian wealth would surely not have been enough; nor would political independence from the mainland; nor military self-sufficiency; nor mere travel; nor even the nurturing elements of the Homeric legacy, with its reassuring contention that every Greek was protected from Olympian heights. We are to praise the Ionians less for founding Philosophy than we would condemn them had they not.

Before examining the contribution, we might quickly review the roster:

MAGNA GRAECIA ca. 500 B.C.

Thales, Anaximander, and Anaximenes were from Miletus; Heraclitus from Ephesus; Anaxagoras from Clazomenae; Pythagoras from Samos; Xenophanes from Colophon. In the Italian reaches of the Ionian influence, we record Philolaus from Tarentum; Empedocles from Acragas; Zeno and Parmenides from Elea. North of the Ionian cities, in Thrace and the centers along the Black Sea, the names of Protagoras, Democritus, and Leucippus are added. These are the figures who outlined the issues with which Plato and Aristotle would contend and which have caught the imagination and frustrated the minds of scholars for two millennia. The movement would culminate, of course, in Athens.

In 585 the Lydians reached temporary accords with the Medes such that Ionian autonomy was threatened. In 546 Croesus, the legendary King of Lydia, was dethroned by Cyrus and the Persian Empire took form. Samos, unlike Miletus, was congenial to the new rule seeing in it an opportunity finally to eclipse the Milesian influence. With the help of Samos, Croton destroyed Sybaris (525), and the youth of Miletus went into mourning.[8]

While the Ionian civilization was reaching its peak, mainland Greece was still in the throes of political organization and strategics. Solon's reforms, although inspired, were far from perfect in that they made no provision for those who had lost farms and homes during the pre-Solonic turmoil. The dissatisfaction of the poor residents and the returning exiles provided the archon, Peisistratus, with the cooperation Cylon had expected but never received a century earlier.* Peisistratus became Tyrant in 546 and for twenty years orchestrated the economic and cultural affairs of Athens. During his reign the "official" Homeric epics were recorded and widely disseminated in a uniform manner. The Panathenaic games became the most important cultural instrument on the mainland, permitting scholars and artists from the entire Greek world to meet and infect one another with new ideas.

The growing prestige of Athens led predictably to countermoves by Sparta, now the center of a Peloponnesian League, whose character was more military than cultural or commercial. In 510, under Cleomenes, Spartan forces defeated those led by the sons of Peisistratus. Cleomenes appointed Isagoras, an Athenian aristocrat, as archon but his reprisals directed at the former supporters of the Peisistratians proved self-defeating and even with the help of Spartan militia Isagoras was unable to retain power. As the fifth century drew near, Athens was under the rule of Cleisthenes, whose reforms established Athens as the center of the Greek world. The two reforms of greatest significance were (1) the "first families" were replaced with representative government based upon geographic (rather than hereditary) tribes, and (2) aliens with skills were permitted to enjoy the full privileges of citizenship. The effect of the latter was to encourage large numbers of skilled and even prosperous foreigners to settle in the Athenian realm. Many of the immigrants were the cultivated and resourceful Ionians escaping the Persian menace. In 494 this menace materialized in the complete subjugation of the Milesians, an event that even distracted the Spartans from their obsessive hostility toward Athens. Then, in 490, under the leadership of Xerxes, the Persians invaded mainland Greece, an act which, as no other could have done, united the Hellenic peoples from Thrace to Sunium. We need not inquire into the details of this war nor the wars that followed between Sparta and Athens and led ultimately to the Macedonian takeover of the Greek

---

* A startled Herodotus goes far to explain the popular support of Peisistratus by describing the manner in which this twice exiled ruler was reintroduced to the Athenians. There was, in one of the provinces, a six-foot beauty named Phya. Megacles and Peisistratus had her dressed in full armor and had heralds announce to the Athenians that Athena herself would deliver Peisistratus to the city. Herodotus tells us that the arrival of the chariot, driven by this "goddess," was greeted by an adoring mob, completely taken in by the ruse (*Persian Wars*, Book I, Ch. 60). Again we are reminded not to identify the character of an age too much with the wisdom of its intellectuals.

world. It is only necessary to recognize the factors at work in the rise of Ionian civilization and those that reduced the Ionian fortunes but with benefits to Athens.

The Pre-Socratic Philosophers

It is especially important when assaying the outlook and contribution of the pre-Socratics to keep two considerations in mind. First, we have very few of their writings[9] and, second, many of the later commentators on whom we must rely are far from unimpeachable. If Thales or Pythagoras ever set a thought to paper, all evidence is lacking. What survives of Anaximander's scholarship is some five sentences and only one by Anaximenes. We have nearly 140 fragments of Heraclitus of which perhaps several dozen require serious attention; that is, we can, at little peril, ignore items of the sort, *"Don't revel in mud."* We are more fortunate where Empedocles and Democritus are concerned, less fortunate in the case of Protagoras. All told, the major figures of the pre-Socratic achievement can be investigated directly through rather fewer than one hundred pages of modern text. Indirect evidence suggests that the group was responsible for perhaps as many entire books. Liberally, then, we may lay claim to 1 percent of their original contributions.

The credibility of post-Socratic commentators is questionable on several grounds. Plato and Aristotle, as well as their immediate disciples and later enthusiasts, were consciously engaged in the creation of new systems of philosophy. History teaches us that such climates tend to nurture both a disrespect for and a lack of comprehension of the older ideas. Many leading spokesmen of the Renaissance, for example, ignored the massive contributions of the twelfth century and thereby mistakenly credited their own age with discoveries that were already well worn a century earlier. Imagine, to cite a parallel example, if Darwin had not published his views; if all we had in our attempt to recreate his position were the writings of his critics or of those with competing theories. We must also recall the bitterness that prevailed between, on one coast, Samos and Miletus and, on the other, Croton and Sybaris. Pythagoras, born at Samos, became important in the political affairs of Croton, where he had taken up residence. It was the same Croton that overwhelmed the Sybarites and thus struck a blow directly at Miletus. As noted above, young Milesians dressed in mourning when, in 525, the news of the collapse of Sybaris was received. We can only wonder, in the light of this history, how fair a hearing the philosophy of a Samian living in Croton would get in a Milesian court.

We are also to recall that the peak of the Socratic development was reached in an Athens whose character had been shaped by Pericles (490–429). The *Academy* was founded by Plato only thirty-eight years after Pericles' death. Socrates and Pericles were contemporaries. The second and decisive Peloponnesian War (431–404) was won by Sparta and, predictably, the Athenian intellectual searched for the point at which things took a wrong turn. In attempting to express anew the (glorified?) humanism of the Age of Pericles, the Socratics insisted that all previous Philosophy was heaven-oriented (i.e., *cosmological*), whereas theirs was man-oriented (i.e., *anthropological*). Historians to the present day are tempted to honor this distinction which, on closer examination, is hardly defensible.[10]

Not only did the pre-Socratics concern themselves with matters lower than the heavens, but we must also analyze more closely why the Socratics did not study the heavens. The reasons are not purely intellectual. Both Protagoras and Anaxagoras suffered the wrath of the Athenian orthodoxy by investigating the secrets of the heavens. The Athenian man in the street was willing to tolerate philosophical speculation as long as things were going well, but once the political or financial or military fortunes of the city were in jeopardy, he was quick to find scapegoats. That the *Fragments* of the pre-Socratics are often ambiguous, that the Pythagoreans were committed to keeping their wisdom private, and that the Age of Pericles itself was rife with censorship—all prove that the Hellenic epoch was never really tolerant, or, if tolerant, was never completely nurturing of speculation. A passage from Plutarch's *Lives* drawn from the biography of Nicias is suggestive:

"People would not then tolerate natural philosophers, and theorists, as they called them, about [the laws of the heavens]; as lessening the divine powers by explaining away its agency. . . . Hence it was that Protagoras was banished and Anaxagoras cast in prison . . . and Socrates, though he had no concern whatever with this sort of learning, yet was put to death. . . . It was only afterwards that the reputation of Plato . . . because he subjected natural necessity to divine and more excellent principles . . . obtained these studies currency among all people." (See[15].)

Notwithstanding this sort of social pressure on their scholarship, we still must attribute these interests of the pre-Socratics principally to bona fide intellectual motives.

The concerns of pre-Socratic philosophers appear to be four in number—the same four that have guided speculation ever since. These were Theology, Physics, Ethics, and Psychology. Their mission—and here too modern analogies abound—was to discover those unifying principles that would explain the various problems associated with these four areas of concern.

In theological speculation the central issue was that of origins. The earth was populous and the heavens more so. Could these entities have come from nothingness? Was there a time before all creation? Is there a time beyond all life and substance? Was there some fundamental substance, some irreducibly common agent, from which all present complexities evolved?

These questions formed the basis on which speculation in Physics rested. Now, Physics in any age tends to be dominated by one or another of its special departments. Our own period focuses on atomic phenomena. Previous periods were devoted to electrical, optical, and mechanical phenomena respectively. These interests are often prodded by economic and practical exigencies as well as by technological advances that anticipate scientific comprehension; for example, it is only *after* an unlikely object floats that one is pressed to explain how it happens. That the pre-Socratic Physics is water-oriented should be of little surprise. All living things required water, a fact of common perception. Civilization was carried on the seas. Egypt ascended to power through irrigation. Water dominated Greece the way electronics dominates our contemporary Western life. Since nothing known could live without it, many believed that life was created within it. To ridicule Thales,* then, for insisting (if he did) that everything, fundamentally, is water is criticism lacking a mirror.

Theological and scientific speculation raised questions in *Ethics* then as it does now. The Homeric tradition had given each person, each city, each crop, its own special role and niche, ordained by Olympian laws. Without Homer, the office of Archon, the Greek loyalty to law and commitment to reason become incomprehensible. But once the philosophers begin to travel, begin to learn of other gods and other systems, begin to suffer at the hands of those who never heard of Zeus, this picture of an exclusively Homeric universe begins to fade. If all, man included, is water, can water be said to have an *obligation?* Can mere matter have an *ethical* claim on matter? Are not the gods as well constrained to obey *natural* law? Finally, are we the result or the cause of our gods, our laws, our convictions?

These questions, broadly comprehended, are questions in *Psychology.* The answers handed down by the pre-Socratics cover quite the same

---

* Even if Thales did not single-handedly, as it were, bring geometry from Egypt to Hellas, he still enjoyed the reputation of being one of the Seven Sages. His influence on the Pythagoreans (he may even have been a teacher of Pythagoras) appears to be great. We may also observe the interest of contemporary astrophysicists in water and moisture as they search the heavens for life-bearing planets.

range as that existing since. When Democritus tells us that *"more men become good through practice than by nature,"* when Protagoras insists that *"of all things, the measure is man,"* and when Anaxagoras argues that *"through the weakness of the senses we cannot judge the truth,"* we unearth the roots of that historic battle between empiricists and idealists. Xenophanes observed that the gods of the Aethiopians had snub noses and black hair; those of Thrace, grey eyes and red hair; and Heraclitus knew that every animal *"is driven to pasture with a blow."* Thus the relativity of styles of belief and the power of punishment were well-established notions without the aid of modern Sociology and Behaviorism.

Even the scanty fragments in our possession prove that the pre-Socratic philosophers had widened their compass to embrace law, science, morality, and art. Their particular interest in the elements—in water, air, earth, and fire—was not at the forfeiture of psychology or even biology. Recall that these men lived in a world new to currency, that the silver mines of Laurium were just beginning to yield their fortunes, that gold was clearly and threateningly on the horizon. For all we know, the pre-Socratic emphasis on the elements may have been instigated by practical forces. We would not seriously transgress the laws of historical interpretation by viewing this emphasis as a youthful Alchemy.

Whatever the practical interests of the pre-Socratics, there is no gainsaying their grasp of what we now recognize as the great imponderables. Ancient sources credit the Pythagoreans with a *numerological* theory of truth according to which the ultimate realities of the Universe are reducible to orderly, mathematical, relationships. In response to this (Crotonian!) vision, Heraclitus the Ephesian posed his theory of fluxes—a theory insisting that the laws of the Universe were statistical, that the salient events in nature were ever shifting in quality and magnitude, that our knowledge would always and necessarily be true for a short time only. We would be overly charitable to the pre-Socratics to credit them with any more than an inkling of the "uncertainty principle." But in broad, philosophical terms, the Pythagorean-Heraclitean controversy is very much a version of such modern tensions as those between "free will" and "determinism," absolutism and relativism, even positivism and the humbler forms of skepticism. The Olympians were reasonable but not perfect. Fate (*Moira*) guided their fortunes as well as our own. For Heraclitus, a physics devoid of this element of chance or luck or fortune was naive, and supporters of such a physics could only be guided by a kind of spiritual geometry. For the Pythagoreans, as best as we can tell, the laws of geometry were at once unfailing and, at the same time, part of the same natural world as everything else. Ultimately, on this account, the Universe itself must be reducible to such laws. Lest we underestimate the subtlety of the issue, we must note that it is only in our own century that we have been able to untangle the "lawfulness" of mathematics (which is merely a kind of verbal lawfulness) from the statistical regularities of the physical world.

Our debt unquestionably is to Plato and Aristotle. We are not directly beholden to the pre-Socratics, for indeed we know so little about them. But the debt of Plato and Aristotle to these now nearly forgotten philosophers is enormous. Plato's *Gorgias* and *Protagoras* are obvious illustrations of the pre-Socratic bequest. Less obvious are the *Physics* and *De Anima* of Aristotle, which might not have been written had not the pre-Socratic challenge been made.

Imperial Athens

The combined might of Sparta with her Lacedaemonian followers and Athens with her Attic and Ionian allies ultimately routed the forces of Persia. From the earliest battle, that legendary confrontation at Marathon (490), to the complete decimation of the Persian fleets at Salamis (479) and Mycale (476), Athens grew steadily in military power. Spartan strength and prestige at the start of the Persian Wars were unequaled. Her generals commanded the infantry in the major battles and even were nominally in charge of naval operations despite the meagerness of the Spartan fleet. But in 483 Themistocles rose to power in Athens and within three years had brought her to naval supremacy. One by one, major Persian holdings—Samos, Miletus, Sestos—were liberated. Athens became the center of the *Delian League* and could count on nearly every city-state in Attica for allegiance and for tribute. Xanthippus, the father of Pericles, was the influential Athenian general who persuaded the Delian states to assimilate the Greek colonies of Asia Minor. Sparta, at the time, always suspicious, always isolationistic, preferred not to get involved. The result, of course, was that Athens not only enjoyed unchallenged control of the Aegean but also the security of an axis of loyalties extending from the walls of her city to Thessaly.[11]

While Athens secured free access to the sea, tribute from a score of allies, and power abroad, Sparta retreated into her endless squabbles with Argos, her attacks upon her own heroes, and her "Spartan" form of diplomacy. While the wars with Persia lasted, the accords between Athens and Sparta were maintained. But, with the Persian menace under control and with the spread of Athenian influence everywhere, the old enmities resurfaced. Sparta had once warred with Athens over the issue of tyranny within Athens. Now she confronted the mounting tyranny of Athens throughout the Hellenic world. Athens controlled commerce, and no city in Greece could survive without it, not even Sparta. The Athenian navy was the principal obstacle to renewed Persian adventurousness. Ionian forces, from Sunium to the Bosphorus, were at Athens' disposal. Even Cyprus, on two occasions, nearly became an extension of Athenian influence.

The rise of Athens intensified the ageless competition for political control within the city itself. With the growth of naval power and the resulting increases in wealth and commerce, Athens experienced an emerging "middle class" and the attendant rise in expectations. The historic ruling families were now a vanishingly small fraction of the city's population and their traditional source of power—their agricultural holdings—were of diminished significance. Athens was the center of an empire, and the simple divisions of Solon were hopelessly dated. As the conservative voices shouted to preserve the old distinctions, an overwhelming chorus masked them in the din of *Réal Politik*.

The spokesman for this new vision, its leader and the most conspicuous political figure in Athenian history, was Pericles (490–429). His appeal to the commoner was irresistible. A wealthy man, the son of a successful commander and of one of the first families, he disposed of much of his money through public works. His closest friends were Anaxagoras the philosopher, Pheidias the sculptor who gave us the Parthenon, and Aspasia, that remarkable woman from Miletus whose genius became a legend in a man's world. As the philosophy of Anaxagoras argued that the human intellect gave form to the physical world, Pericles set out to prove that reason was invincible. He undertook massive public works in art, architecture, and education. Employment in Athens was full and proud. He extended the right to hold office to the previously disenfranchised. He sung the virtues of the intellect where, before, only courage in battle was praised. He insisted that rights impose responsibilities, that power must recognize obligation, that good birth demands good works. His was the gospel of hopefulness—a faith in the human potential freed from the chains of superstition, fear, and avarice. On the eve of the Peloponnesian War, this man of means, this spiritual architect of the Acropolis, pleads with his countrymen: *"Go out yourselves, destroy your possessions and prove to the Peloponnesians that you will not submit simply to save them."*[12] Later, as the wars raged on, Pericles would deliver (or so Thucydides would aver) one of the most moving speeches in the history of rhetoric. As the Athenians convened to honor their fallen brothers, Pericles searched, as every leader has since, for words that might make tragedy redemptive. Perhaps he succeeded most when he said of the dead that

"they were worthy of Athens."

Historians are agreed that the Peloponnesian Wars were inevitable but are divided in explaining the causes. For Thucydides, the simple envy of the non-Athenian was responsible, but this is hardly likely. Contemporaries of Pericles were wont to blame him for the start of war. He had, after all, written a decree preventing Megara from trading within the Athenian economic community. He had also orchestrated a telling defeat of the Corinthians, who by 459 were growing intolerant of the uses Athens made of contributions to the Delian treasury.* He attempted, moreover, to establish Athenian power in Egypt—an attempt that failed, and encouraged dissent at home and confidence among the Spartan states. Soon, such otherwise tame protectorates as Euboea were in sporadic revolt. By 446 Athenian claims in the Peloponnesus were withdrawn and Athens was forced to establish a thirty-year truce with Sparta. Inexorably, tensions mounted. Finally, in 433, a naval battle between Corcyra (today's Corfu) and Corinth took place in which part of the Athenian fleet aided the Corcyrians. Now powerful Corinth was in a position to demand Spartan support—to insist that, unchecked, Athens was a threat to every city in Greece. The time was right. Athens was torn by political dissension. Freedom creates a thirst for itself, and Pericles never did spread it as liberally as his supporters wished. The aristocracy, always bitter toward him, were now openly defiant. Sparta analyzed the situation: Athens was militarily overextended, her colonies were restless, her treasury was becoming depleted, her leader was under a domestic attack, her mercenaries were accessible to bribery, her citizens were softened by the good life. Pericles, eager to establish an Athenian empire once and for all—and no doubt aware of the unifying force of war—was not reluctant to see the inevitable become actual.

As the Spartans weighed the Corinthian arguments, Thebes, ever hostile to Athens, invaded Plataea, which was under Athenian protection. She captured nearly 200 Thebans and murdered them, an act the Athenians were too late to prevent. Outraged, the Spartan armies marched on Plataea. In the spring of 431 the Peloponnesian Wars were under way.

To make matters worse, Athens in 430 was visited by a devastating "plague," which over a period of several years may have cost her a quarter of the population. Pericles' enemies insisted that in walling Athens against attack he had created conditions ideal for the spread of disease.†

---

* The Delian League was intended to serve as an organization for mutual defense. Thus the funds received by Athens should in principle have been reserved exclusively for military use. In applying these funds to projects that were purely Athenian, Pericles violated at least the spirit of the agreement, if not the letter.

† It is not clear what this "plague" was. From the symptoms described by Thucydides, it may not have been bubonic plague. Indeed, it seems to have been more like a form of influenza or malaria, the latter being rather common at the time. Given the population of Athens, the spread of such a disease was obviously not the result

Others, we can be sure, believed the gods had punished Athens for submitting to the will of a man whose closest friend, Anaxagoras, was a heretic and whose consort was a *hetaira*. Pericles was discharged from his post as *strategos* (commander) in 430 and when recalled several months later was so ravaged by illness that he died in office (429).

Our purposes are not served by examining these wars nor by reviewing the causes of the ultimate defeat of Athens (404). We need only note that during the twenty-eight years of struggle nearly every vestige of the Periclean vision was wiped away. The enemies of democracy saw in the success of Sparta the powerlessness of freedom in the face of discipline. The commoners, now called upon to sacrifice all for an ideal, turned on those very intellectual forces that had made Athenian life a privilege. Pheidias, Anaxagoras, and Aspasia were all brought up on charges. A revival of the old-time religion of revenge replaced the cultivated and confident spirit of Athenian justice. The life of Athens, no matter how historic in proportion, had been forged from the toil of other States which now saw Sparta and her allies as liberators. As the war pressed toward the final Spartan triumph, Athenians sought guilt in one another. Supporters of Pericles were *ostracized,** democrats were imprisoned, and reactionary zeal filled the void created by departing pride. The pendulum swung again and a peculiar revolutionary fury made even the restored democracy a vice.

---

of walls surrounding the city. (*The Peloponnesian Wars*, translated by Benjamin Jowett, #47–53, Washington Square Press, New York, 1963.)

On the general contempt the Athenians developed toward Pericles, consult *Plutarch's Lives*. Plutarch informs us that Pericles was born with a somewhat elongated head and that, when his reign fell on hard times, the comic poets made much of the deformity. Teleclides, for example, was to have written,

"Fainting underneath the load
Of his own head: and now abroad
From his huge gallery of a pate
Sends forth trouble to the state."

Plutarch also relates the influence of Parmenides and Zeno on the intellectual development of young Pericles but reserves to Anaxagoras the central role of teacher. Of this philosopher, Plutarch notes that Athenians called him *Nous*, a nickname for his universal genius. In the same passage, Plutarch summarizes the philosophy of Anaxagoras thus:

". . . he was the first of the philosophers who did not refer the first ordering of the world to fortune or chance . . . but to a pure, unadulterated intelligence."

Plutarch's attributions where Anaxagoras is concerned were, no doubt, popular but only because of a general ignorance of the full sweep of pre-Socratic thought. Anaxagoras opposed the "statistical" theory of *fluxes* defended by Heraclitus but surely was not the first philosopher to impute a rational design to the Universe. (See *Plutarch, The Lives of the Noble Grecians and Romans*, John Dryden, translator. The authoritative modern edition is that revised by Arthur Hugh Clough (1864) and republished by The Modern Library, Random House, New York.)

* *Ostracism* is used here as the technical term for a ten-year period of exile.

During the turmoil, one family enlists our interest, the family of Ariston and Perictone, the latter marrying her uncle, Pyrilampe, after Ariston's death. This was the aristocratic family that numbered Socrates and Pericles as friends and Plato as a son.

Plato

As with the Evening Star and Morning Star, the identities of Socrates and Plato dissolve into one another when either is observed long enough. Socrates (469?–399) was the master, and by his own admission a "gadfly" flitting through the markets and assemblies of Athens and pricking the conscience of the complacent. It is likely that Plato not only knew him in childhood but that he was introduced to many members of the Socratic circle. Except for superficial comments offered a generation later by Xenophon,[13] our only record of Socrates' life and ideas is that recorded by Plato in the monumental *Dialogues*. Historians have labored to resolve the "Platonic" and the "historic" Socrates, and the "Socratic" and the "historic" Plato. Some scholars have applauded the genius of Plato by imputing to him full credit for all the ideas in the *Dialogues*. Others have reduced Plato to little more than a stenographer with a commendable memory. If we are to believe Plato's account, offered in his *Second Epistle*, then we must conclude that

> "there is not and never will be a work of Plato; the works which now go by that name belong to Socrates, embellished and rejuvenated."[14]

Socrates, in many ways, was a creation of the Age of Pericles. He was in his early twenties when Pericles was at his peak and, consequently, when proper Athenian society found Anaxagoras fashionable. His friends included Charmides and Alcibiades, both aristocrats, as well as Plato's prestigious stepfather. That his fate should follow the same course as Pericles' is no surprise. He questioned every assumption, ridiculed cant, doubted the obvious, rejected fees for his instruction, lived a simple and virtuous life, and attracted the love and loyalty of the finest young minds of his city. In short, he could not have been more offensive! Accused and convicted of heresy and the corruption of youth, he stood resolutely behind the laws of Athens and drank the poison while protesting his innocence. As the political giant, Pericles, had died in office thirty years earlier, Socrates died in office as well. He died debating the meaning of justice, the need for law, the rule of reason over greed. No one can read his last encounters in the *Crito* and the *Phaedo* without sensing not only the end of a great life but the end of a great age.

In the last decade of Socrates' life, while Plato was in his twenties, the Athenian empire had been reduced to a shambles. Spartan victories revived Persian intervention throughout Ionia and even on Attic soil. Athenian assaults on such friends and weaklings as Melos and hopeless attempts in Sicily produced both shame at home and contemptuousness abroad. The democratic system of Pericles was overthrown by the Athenian oligarchs in 411, restored (excessively) in 410, and gradually became transformed into a slovenly bureaucracy begging to be ignored by a serious Mediterranean world. Political hacks rose to power on "I-told-you-so" platforms and quickly diverted attention from their ineptitude by launching inquisitions into the affairs of their predecessors. Witch-hunts were common and double agents abundant. Men such as Alcibiades would lead a fleet one year and be exiled as friends of the Persian king the next. Socrates was the most famous and the most tragic sacrifice to the frustrations of decline, but he was only one of very many. The salient lessons of the *Dialogues* are to be understood against this background. Indeed, in the *Seventh Epistle*, Plato, a child of wealth, groomed for leadership, relates his decision to retire from the chaos:

". . . (O)ur city was no longer governed according to the customs and institutions of our fathers . . . the letter of the laws, and our customs were giving way to an even greater corruption and disrespect . . . when I considered these things, seeing everything being driven helter-skelter, my head was in a whirl. . . . I realized that all existing states without exception had irremediably bad constitutions. . . . So, in praise of true philosophy, I was obliged to say that through it alone can we recognize what is right for states as well as individuals."[15]

The intellectual range of the *Dialogues* is universal. They analyze all the problems introduced by the pre-Socratics and in the process advance others that only the Socratics seem to have conceived. We, of course, shall investigate but a narrow set of these topics—the set that still survives in contemporary psychological scholarship. Broadly defined, the set contains four major elements: (1) *The Problem of Knowledge*, (2) *The Origins of Reason*, (3) *The Problem of Conduct*, and (4) *The Problem of Governance*. The first of these contains the Platonic position on sensation, perception, and memory. The second is addressed to psychological and psychosocial development. The third is devoted to the determinants of behavior and to the tension between the rational and emotional dispositions. The fourth is the foundation of modern social studies and the psychology of interpersonal influence. An analysis of these four issues follows.

The Problem of Knowledge

Few of the *Dialogues* are confined narrowly to a single problem. Those that are—for example, *Charmides* (temperance), *Lysis* (friendship), and *Laches* (courage)—tend to be brief and even casual. The major works are intense and far-ranging. Very nearly all of them at least touch on the problem of knowledge; in several it is the central issue. Of the former, *Republic* is the most illustrious and illustrative; of the latter, *Parmenides*, *Theaetetus*, and *Meno*. In addition to these, we obtain perhaps an exhaustive comprehension of this part of Socratic psychology through the *Seventh Epistle, the Laws, Phaedo, Euthydemus, Timaeus*, and the *Protagoras*. Plato does not give himself a part in any of these, and in the earliest (e.g., *Parmenides*), we have conversations occurring during his infancy. The *Dialogues*, then, are not to be read as literal transcriptions but as textual materials put into a dialectical format for purposes of instruction at the Academy.

It is also worth noting that Socrates is not the source of all "Socratic" wisdom, nor does the Socratic view pass without challenge. The teachers in the *Parmenides* are Zeno and Parmenides, and it is young Socrates who is caught up in contradictions and *lacunae*. Even later and in no less a work than the *Republic*, Socrates has all he can do to keep up with the contrary perspectives advanced by Glaucon and Adeimantus. He is by no means the victor in the *Protagoras*, nor will the impartial reader be easily convinced by the principal conclusion of the *Meno*. Thus the problem of knowledge confronted by the Socratics and the theory invented to solve it do not describe for us *the* Athenian view or *the* Ancient perspective. They do, however, establish the boundaries within which the problem can be addressed. They expose the frailties of overly confident "solutions."

In its most innocent and most vexing form, the problem of knowledge is this: *How can we ever be sure that we know something?* For a philosophy such as that of the Socratics—a philosophy concerned with virtue, with government, and with society—it is obvious that the problem of knowledge itself must be comprehended before any specific branch of it can be dealt with. It makes no sense, for example, to inquire into the question of justice or courage or love until we have established that inquiry itself is valid and that its results are true. Thus, the *sine qua non* of the Socratic method is the initial development of a workable epistemology. It is this epistemology that will distinguish the knowable from the unknowable, truth from mere opinion, reality from mere appearance.

The final position taken by the Socratics on the question of knowledge was part invention and part reaction. The reaction was to the teachings of the major Sophists. We observe this most vividly in the opening scene of the *Meno*. Meno is a young aristocrat recently returned to Athens from Thessaly, where the sophist Gorgias is influential. He is accompanied by a servant who proves to be the pivotal figure in the dialogue.

In something of a teasing manner, Meno tells Socrates that he would like to be able to return to Thessaly equipped to instruct his Thessalian friends in the virtuous life and, accordingly, would hope that Socrates might share the truth with him. Socrates, ever on guard, explains that until he knows what Meno construes virtue to be, he surely could not prescribe a virtuous life. Meno, we might guess, has learned a trick or two from Gorgias and now poses a typical Sophist paradox:

"And how will you enquire, Socrates, into that which you do not know? What will you put forth as the subject of enquiry? And if you find what you want, how will you ever know that this is the thing which you did not know?"[16] [80]*

Meno's challenge is based on the contention that all inquiry is impossible, since (1) if we are ignorant, we have no starting point for an inquiry and (2) if we are informed, no inquiry is needed. Socrates' reply takes advantage of the fact that Meno's servant is a young, uneducated "barbarian." Socrates begins to question the boy about geometric forms which Socrates draws in the sand. The boy answers a number of questions by "yes" or "no" as Socrates leads him on to a version of the Pythagorean theorem. Little by little, and not before hosting several conceptual errors, the boy approaches and finally attains the understanding of the relationship between the diagonal of a square and its area. On no occasion does Socrates actually *tell* the servant. He merely paces him through a series of logico-mathematical steps until the insight appears. The exercise is meant to prove the first principle of Socrates' theory of knowledge: *knowledge is a reminiscence;* that is, the knower *has* the truth. He doesn't learn it; he merely recalls it with the aid of instruction.

The centrality of this position to the entire Socratic psychology (and epistemology) cannot be overdrawn, for if we believe that knowledge is memory we will accept the dialectical method of uncovering it. Moreover, we will give to *experience* a place of no special importance; to *reflection*, a place of unparalleled importance. The dialectical method, after all, is not simply a kind of conversation. Rather, it is a careful delineation and criticism of premises, an analysis of meanings, an assessment of implications. Through it the student is expected to learn not

---

* Numbers in brackets refer to manuscript pages from Stephens. See note[16] for explanation.

only what is true but why he has failed to discern this truth previously. The "learning" is, of course, but recollection.

With respect to experience, the *Dialogues* could not be more consistent. Under the indirect influence of Pythagoras and the direct influence of Parmenides and Zeno, Socrates rejects the senses as agents of truth. We discover in the *Theaetetus* [161], as well as in the *Timaeus* [43], and again in the "Cave Allegory" of the *Republic* that Socrates defines the dominant mission of philosophy as the rejection of the world of appearance. Anaxagoras, thriving in the reasonableness of Pericles' Athenian state, had elevated *nous*, or mind, to the summit of the real world. Protagoras had contended that *"Man is the measure of all things,"* a contention that would have extended the modest *idealism* of Anaxagoras to a wanton *subjectivism*. It is in the *Theaetetus* that Socrates directly challenges Protagoras' maxim:

"I am charmed with his doctrine, that what appears is to each one, but I wonder that he did not begin his book on *Truth* with a declaration that a pig or a dog-faced baboon, or some yet stranger monster which has sensation, is the measure of all things; then he might have shown a magnificent contempt for our opinion of him by informing us at the outset that while we were reverencing him like a God for his wisdom he was no better than a tadpole. . . . For if truth is only sensation, and no man can discern another's feelings better than he, or has any superior right to determine whether his opinion is true or false, but each, as we have several times repeated, is to himself the sole judge, and everything that he judges is true and right, why, my friend, should Protagoras be preferred to the place of wisdom and instruction, and deserve to be well paid, and we poor ignoramuses have to go to him, if each one is the measure of his own wisdom?"[17] [161]

As the *Theaetetus* proceeds, Socrates offers examples of the weaknesses of the sensationist position. Not only do brute animals have keen senses but so, as well, does the infant. Still, these beings cannot be said to know merely because they can see. Or, examined in another way, we continue to know that which is no longer visible. If knowledge were only and always perception, knowledge would cease when the objects of perception were removed. Not only this, but our knowledge would be in constant flux because of the ever-changing world of sense. Thus the sick Socrates, the standing Socrates, the reclining Socrates would all be different Socrates. But those who *know* Socrates are, in fact, not confused by these changing appearances. Rather, the soul and not the senses is able to read through these changing features and discover the real, unchanging, essential Socrates; that is, the *true form* of Socrates that survives all change:

> "Then knowledge does not consist in impressions of sense, but in reasoning about them."[18] [186]

To the extent that the method of dialectical analysis can succeed or fail, the *Theaetetus* fails. Indeed, at the end, Socrates is still frustrated by his inability to establish what knowledge is as opposed to what it is not. He succeeds in distinguishing between the specific factual knowledge acquired through the senses and the more significant general principles known to the mind [185] and he also notes the difference between opinion—which may be and often is false—and knowledge which, by definition, cannot be false [188]. Socrates also uses the *Theaetetus* to present his theory of memory according to which experiences are recorded as something like wax impressions. The durability of the impression depends on the frequency of the experience and the purity of the wax [191–195]. The former point is, of course, traditional *associationism*, while the latter is but another expression of the Socratic emphasis on the hereditary differences among men with respect to character and quality of mind. Notwithstanding the originality of these ideas, we still must judge the *Theaetetus*, *in toto*, as an incomplete and rather tortuously argued cognitive psychology. However, where it fails, the *Republic* succeeds: in clarity, consistency, scope, and completeness.

The *Republic*, historically understood as the Socratic theory of government and, therefore, as that Dialogue comprising Socratic *Political Science* is, on another account, really Socratic *Psychology*. Recall that in Book II, when the group (Glaucon, Thrasymachus, and Adeimantus) implores Socrates to analyze the principal features of justice and to establish how the just man is always happier than the unjust, Socrates warns them that such a task requires *"very good eyes"* [368]. He explains his remark by invoking the metaphor of a nearsighted person who can read distant letters only when they are greatly enlarged. Thus, to examine the nature and functions of the individual, the philosopher who does not have very good eyes must enlarge his object. Accordingly, Socrates chooses the State as the enlargement of man's personal nature. By constructing the perfect State, the philosopher will necessarily comprehend those characteristics that would produce the perfected human being (Book II [368–369]).

There is a temptation, in attempting to summarize the psychology of the *Republic*, to cull a group of handy quotations and with them argue that Plato anticipated all modern schools of psychological science or that he subscribed zealously to some narrow view of man and society. We might, for example, offer those sections of Book III in which the citizens are categorized as men of gold, men of silver, and men of brass and iron, framed so differently by the gods that some necessarily shall rule and others serve [415]. This passage—which, by the way, Socrates introduces as one of the convenient *fictions* a leader may have to foist on the people—stands in close accord with Book V (459–460) in which pre-arranged marriages and controlled breeding will be used to create the class of Guardians, following the practice of breeders of hunting dogs. There is no question but that Socratic Psychology is *nativistic;* that is, it assumes hereditary biases in the formation of human character and human intelligence. With equal consistency, Socratic Psychology is nativistic in locating our ideas within the soul prior to experience—indeed, prior to our very birth (*Phaedo*, 73–76).[19] But quite as many passages can be cited in which the emphasis is on education, experience, and commerce with contemplative friends. Meno's servant, surely no man of gold by Socratic standards, still reveals (recalls) his knowledge of the "true form" of the right triangle. Much as Socrates himself requires an enlargement of man to deal with man we—farsighted where he was nearsighted—must step back from the lines of the *Republic* in order to comprehend its meaning.

The *Republic* can be understood only by recognizing the conditions surrounding its authorship. The Athens of Pericles has disintegrated, and the enduring fact is that Sparta was victorious and Athens was not. In the *Laws*, Plato will insist that Greece survived the assaults of Persia not because Athens was victorious at Salamis and Artemisium but because the Spartans prevailed at Marathon and Plataea (IV–707). In the same *Laws*, Plato worries that maritime wars (those on which Athens rested her security) foster a form of cowardice. The Spartans—strong, self-denying, regimented, orderly, traditional—have become, by the time of the *Republic*, the model. We need not search the annals of Orphism or the mystery cults of Sicily to find the roots of Platonic asceticism and puritanism. In his *Seventh Epistle* and *Laws*, Plato is unequivocal in his respect for the political order and military achievements of fifth-century Sparta. What the *Republic* struggles to achieve is a reconciliation of the opposing elements of the Athens of Pericles and the Sparta of Pausanias. In this glorious but fated attempt to reconcile the irreconcilable, the *Republic* lays bare the fundamental tensions between law and freedom, pragmatism and moral absolutism, fact and value, passion and reason, power and justice. As the various institutions and actions of the perfect Republic are argued into being, we can watch quietly a coterie of valiant scholars striving to find a place in the great buzz of a declining age—a hopeful and reasonable order in their fallen house of cards. These are men no longer sure of their loyalties, their obligations, their basic values.

They, unlike the confident Ionians of the previous century, have been abandoned by the gods of Homer. The proverbs of Thales, and the optimism of Anaxagoras, to which in his last hours Socrates looks with longing and disappointment (*Phaedo* 97), are seen to be too simple. In a phrase, the *Republic* is an invention of the discontented and disaffected who will give up on this world:

> "Until philosophers are kings, or the kings and princes of this world have the spirit and power of philosophy, and political greatness and wisdom meet in one, and those commoner natures who pursue either to the exclusion of the other are compelled to stand aside."
>
> (*Republic*, V, 473)

They will not succumb to a Heraclitean theory of fluxes according to which the chaos around them is to be accepted as a fact of nature. Instead, they will make chaos unnatural.

To describe the Socratics as discontented and disaffected is not to say they were sullen or even pessimistic. Good humor obtains even in the saddest of the *Dialogues*, the *Phaedo*. Rather, we are to recognize Socrates and his pupils as the enlightened and reflective critics of an age and to realize that such philosophers, in any period, will perceive themselves as unheard by, even inaudible to "those commoner natures." As critics they observed power falling into the hands of polemicists whose only talent was the ability to tell the masses what they wanted to hear. Seeing an entire population deluded by the trappings rather than the essence of greatness, they rejected perception as a means by which knowledge might be apprehended. Watching a world tossed in seas of change, they searched for that which never changed and called it truth. Noting the sad fate of a people moved by passion, they devoted themselves to impersonal reason and argued well enough for what came to be known as *Rationalism* to make it the "official" philosophy until the seventeenth century.

The *Republic*, like every Utopia offered since, holds out many things but bears the most disenchanting portents of boredom. The *Republic* is a model of virtue, temperance, courage, justice, proportion—all the qualities that attach to the Platonically perfect individual. Character is guaranteed by heredity and instruction. Law is blind in the received sense, and justice swift. Population is carefully regulated with each city limited to 5040 citizens, a number defended because it can be divided evenly by every integer from 1 to 10, and then some. Plato does not mention the plague of 430, but it is likely that the recommendations against crowding derived in part from public health concerns. We also detect in this emphasis upon orderly division a retrospective appreciation of Pericles' land reforms.

Education in the Republic was to be carefully orchestrated. Those epic poems disclosing a lack of virtue among the gods were proscribed as were works of fiction and "panharmonic" music. No wonder that Lord Russell, reflecting on this State in the 1940s, would dismiss the entire enterprise as unblushing totalitarianism.[20]

We are concerned here not with the Utopianism of the *Republic* but with its theory of knowledge and this is illustrated most clearly in the "Cave Allegory" of Book VII. Socrates speaks of prisoners chained in the bowels of a deep cavern, facing a wall on which, unbeknown to them, shadowy forms are projected. From the prisoners' perspective, the shadows are real, their movements self-controlled. By good fortune, one of the prisoners escapes and makes his way up to the light of day. Now, for the first time, he sees reality and recognizes that all his former understandings were but illusion. Returing to share his discovery, this "philosopher" is chided for having been blinded on his journey and no longer able to enjoy the truths of the cave.

We can now sketch the essential features of the Socratic theory of knowledge by combining the cave allegory with the attack on Protagoras in the *Theaetetus* and with the servant's lessons in the *Meno*. First, true knowledge is a knowledge of the permanent principles of the world, not the changing appearances. Thus, it is not a knowledge conveyed by the senses but by reason analyzing experience. For the sake of convenience, we shall refer to this doctrine as *Rationalism* and construe it to mean that knowledge of the world is of a cognitive rather than a perceptual nature.

Second, and consequently, all true knowledge is *recollection*. If it can be possessed but cannot be received through perception, then it is not acquired but unearthed. In other words, and as demonstrated by Meno's slave, we possess the eternal truths prior to experience. They are locked within the soul and become available to our consciousness only through philosophical (dialectical) training. This doctrine is *Nativism* and it asserts the existence of innate ideas. A corollary of Nativism recognizes innate differences among human beings such that certain minds will not be as quick or as successful as others in releasing their truths nor as complete as others in their possession of truths. Accordingly, some will be ineradicably superior to others in intelligence and virtue and they will, properly and inevitably, lead and protect the less fortunate. We shall refer to this corollary of Nativism as *Elitism*.

Finally, since the eternal truths do not depend on the (material) senses, since they are within the soul before birth and survive within the soul after death, they are truths of a nonphysical nature. They are, that is, *ideas* and they are the only ultimate reality of the universe. This, of course, is the doctrine of *Idealism* which has arrested the attention of every major philosopher of the past twenty-three centuries.

With this summary before us, we may proceed to the Socratic position on the origins of reason, an integral feature of Idealism.

The Origins of Reason

Of all the facets of Plato's writings, probably none has enjoyed more scrutiny than the so-called *theory of ideas;* this, despite the warning of the renowned translator of the *Dialogues,* Jowett, that Plato's "theory" is not clearly set forth, changes over the years, and is treated by Plato himself as a sort of guess[21] (p. 874). On the deserved authority of Jowett, we will not attempt to force a unified theory out of Plato. But this much is clear from the *Dialogues* and is nowhere contradicted in them: the *ideas* do not refer to facts, are not about things, and do not either arise within the body proper or die with it. In analyzing the sources of language, Socrates insists that we could not invent and agree on names for things unless we shared an idea of them (*Cratylus,** 389).[22] Because of their permanence, they must originate in God's mind (*Timaeus,* 28),[23] which the cleansed soul shall join after abandoning the dead body (*Phaedo,* 81).[24] Unlike the attributes (e.g., the good*ness,* just*ice*) of things, the ideas behold the things, themselves (e.g., the good, the just), which is simply another way of removing them from the arena of perception. The Socrates of the *Parmenides* shrinks back from treating all reality as nothing but idea because to do so would cause him

"to fall into a bottomless pit of nonsense," [130]

although in less nervous moments he

"sometimes begin(s) to think that there is nothing without an idea."
[Ibid.]

The Socrates of the *Phaedo* has learned, as Parmenides had predicted years earlier, not to fear such bottomless pits and now seems quite willing to reject all that is not idea.

From a psychological as opposed to a metaphysical point of view, we need not try to achieve coherence in the theories about ideas. We need

* The *Cratylus* offers the reader an example of Socratic philology. Not only did the Socratics invent dialectical philosophy but they were the first to recognize the importance of establishing the meaning of recurring terms.

recognize only that with respect to origins, the ideas, on any of the several Platonic accounts, are innate. Since they determine reality, they necessarily control perception, or else the perceptions are illusory. We might say that whereas the "commoner natures" know only what they see, the philosopher sees that which he knew *a priori*.

While the theory of knowledge is nativistic, it is not static. We have already noted the attention given to education and when we look into the specific program of education recommended for the Guardians we see that the Socratics explicitly subscribed to a stage-theory of cognitive development. The Athenian stranger who is the teacher in the *Laws* notes that virtue and vice in childhood are known to the young only as pleasure and pain (II, 653). Since children instinctively love what is pleasurable and hate what is painful, the principal task of the educator is to make sure that true virtue becomes the object of love, vice the object of hatred. Moreover, there are *critical periods* of development when the lessons of virtue are most effectively conveyed by music, since virtue fundamentally is a harmonious relationship between body and mind (*Laws*, II, 653–654; VII, 790–791). The aim is furthered by close contact between parent and infant, by the rhythmic rocking of the young:

". . . nursing and moving about by day and night is good for them all and . . . the younger they are the more they will need it; infants should live, if that were possible, as if they always were rocking at sea." (*Laws*, VII, 790)

The same theme is sounded in the *Republic* (III, 377; IV, 441–442). The young are out of harmony, so to speak. Reason and passion have yet to establish that unique accord that constitutes virtue. Music, dance, and other gymnastics must be employed because the very young mind is not yet able to assimilate rational principles directly. Thus, early education uses metaphor, not literal lesson. The success of education depends, of course, on the "quality of the wax" and, only under rare circumstances will the children of a lower class qualify for the life of a Guardian (*Republic*, II, 375–376). Instruction notwithstanding, heritable differences prevail and foreordain one's receptivity to education and the life created by it.

That the Socratic theory of the origins of reason focuses on heredity is entirely consistent with Socratic epistemology in general. Having established to his satisfaction that knowledge of principles cannot result from perception, Socrates must look beyond experience to find the source of virtue. All that is left, once experience is dismissed, is heredity. Any subsequent education must assume a genetic endowment or the education will fail. However, given the "right" genes, the individual will pass through stages of receptivity culminating in that adult stage in which philosophy can make its appeals to the latent knowledge of the soul.

If there is still some ambiguity surrounding these nativistic notions, it might be reduced by considering the Socratic approach to a specific and essential element of knowledge, our knowledge of *space*. In the *Timaeus*, the spokesman of the same name has been given the task of lecturing on the origin of the universe and the creation of living things, including human beings. Timaeus raises the question of the reality of ideas [51] and proceeds to distinguish between the true *opinions* formed by perception and *ideas* which are beheld by the mind but neither received through nor confirmed by the senses. Having treated that which appeals to sense and that which is contemplated only by the intelligence, he moves to a third "nature,"

"which is space . . . and is apprehended without the help of sense, by a kind of spurious reason, and is hardly real; which we, beholding as in a dream, say of all existence that it must of necessity be in some place and occupy a space." (*Timaeus*, 52)

We will confront a more extensive discussion of this theory of space perception in Kant for whom the nonsensory nature of space was also significant. Timaeus notes that space is not an object "out there," nor is it a mere concept in the sense of an opinion or belief. It is certainly not learned, nor is there any feature of the objects we locate in it that permits inferences about it. Quite simply, it is not an "it" but a disposition or, in Timaeus' terms, *"a kind of spurious reason."* Now, the instructed child will surely become more accurate in his space perceptions. His performance as an archer will improve, for example. But we cannot say that instruction has provided space perception itself. It existed *a priori* as a native endowment. Exposure to a world of objects triggers this *a priori* latent capacity of the mind. When we say that the Socratic theory of the origins of reason is nativistic but that it also gives education a major role, we are saying that reason is, in this respect, like space perception.

The Problem of Conduct

". . . you fancy that the shepherd or neatherd fattens or tends the sheep or oxen with a view to their own good and not to the good of himself or his master . . . that the rulers of states . . . are not studying their own advantages day and night . . . and so entirely astray are you in your ideas about the just and unjust as not even to know

that . . . the just is always a loser in comparison with the unjust."
(*Republic*, I, 343)

Here, then, is the challenge of Thrasymachus to Socrates' theory of
the good. In nearly modern terms, Thrasymachus points out that the
rich avoid taxation through wile, whereas the poor and just man sinks
further into debt. The tyrant, who were he a mere citizen would be
imprisoned for his conduct, is praised for the power, wealth, leisure, and
loyalty he commands. The unjust partner too gains advantage over the
just. In every sphere,

"injustice, when on a sufficient scale, has more strength and freedom
and mastery than justice." (*Republic*, I, 344)

Later, in Book II, Glaucon resumes the attack with the legend of
Gyges' Ring. The story is borrowed from Lydian lore and involves
Gyges (reputed to be an ancestor of Croesus), who has discovered a
ring in a crack in the earth created by an earthquake. Subsequently, while
assembled with fellow shepherds, Gyges mindlessly twists the ring and
immediately becomes invisible. After several trials, he realizes that he
can appear or disappear depending on how he twists this ring. Thus
armed with magical powers, he goes off to the royal court, seduces the
queen, murders the king, and assumes the throne [360]. The story told,
Glaucon now asks what we would do if we possessed Gyges' ring. If
there were two such rings and one were given to the just man and one
to the unjust man, how would each conduct his life if he knew that no
one could ever see what he did, that he could never be punished, cen-
sured, or found out? Between them, Thrasymachus and Glaucon have
advanced the problem of conduct in a form that has been recurrent in
the history of ethics and moral philosophy. The manner in which modern
Psychology addresses itself to human behavior is determined in large
measure by the arguments of Thrasymachus and Glaucon on the one
hand and Socrates on the other. The Glaucon-Thrasymachus theory may
be summarized this way:

1. Man, fundamentally, is a pleasure-seeking, pain-avoiding animal.
2. His behavior is controlled by fear, by the wish for honor and
   security, by the customs of the day.
3. His *verbal* endorsement of the canons of justice and fairness is
   merely a disguise for what, at root, is fear of reprisal.
4. When the risks are minimized and/or the gains are maximized, the
   citizen will abandon his (verbal) vows and rush to improve the
   material and social conditions of his life.

5. The order enjoyed by any state and the justice meted out by its rulers are a compromise between the interests of the people and the rulers' need for loyalty. Where the military power of the rulers is beyond challenge, their concern for the well-being of the citizens vanishes.

The apparent validity of the Glaucon-Thrasymachus theory was confirmed by the affairs of the Athenian state in which they lived. Their government, their fellow citizens, and the known world seemed blanketed by the most rueful forms of pragmatism, situation-ethics, and privatism. In the context, Socrates' devotion to some higher principle seemed childlike. In fact, Thrasymachus goes so far as to ask him if he is protected by a nurse (I, 343). To the compelling charges of Glaucon and Thrasymachus, a further assault on the sense of justice is added by Adeimantus. He insists that even when fear of reprisal by a neighbor or desire for personal gain is not clearly responsible for seemingly moral conduct, the individual is guided by hopes and fears of the afterlife. Furthermore, lest this concern for the soul's eternal fate interfere too much with material pleasure in this life, the citizens have developed ready tools for the easy expiation of sins (Book II, 363–365).

Socrates' task, we can see, is not an easy one. He must prove first that the way things are is not the way they have to be; second, that there is a way they *ought* to be; third, that the breach between *is* and *ought* is created by a failure of reason. He begins by likening the soul to the State. As the state contains three classes (merchants, auxiliaries, and counsellors), the soul is occupied by three principles: the rational, the appetitive, and the passionate (Book IV, 441). The just man is he who has harmonized these three principles such that reason controls appetite and, as an auxiliary to reason, passion strengthens the resolve (Book IV, 443).

This view of reason and appetite as opposing forces is as old as the Homeric epics and as current as psychoanalytic theories. *Harmony* is an abiding theme in Socratic philosophy, and the *Republic* makes frequent use of musical metaphors. Ancient Greek medicine employed music therapeutically, and the Spartan *ephors* were very careful in regulating the kind of music heard by the citizens. We can, with some confidence, attribute this interest to Pythagorean influences. The goal of the Pythagoreans, grandly conceived, was the purification of the soul. But, more modestly, they searched for those eternal truths of the universe which lay behind mere perception. The Pythagorean theorem in Geometry was one such truth, the geometric properties of the musical scale another. When we learn of the Socratic near-obsession with harmony and music, therefore, we must not consider it either the overworking of mere metaphor or the sign of premodern innocence. Instead, it is an integral feature of a general *cosmological* theory. The world of appearance, accordingly, is metaphor, whereas the world of truth is relationship. Just as the true form of the right-angle triangle is given not by some graphic display but by the equation $a^2 + b^2 = c^2$, so the true form of man is given by a mathematical (i.e., harmonic) relationship among the three principles: reason, appetite, passion. This conception entails belief in some supraworldly rational principle, the author of all eternal truths, the framer of all proportion, the agent of cosmic harmony. This cosmology, as we shall see in subsequent chapters, led directly to *Stoicism* and, less directly, to that genre of metaphysics normally identified with Leibniz. To subscribe to it is to recognize that the petty successes and failures of daily life are utterly irrelevant to the question of true human life. Once we agree that the soul whose elements are in discord is sick and dying and that the person so diseased is less than human, the question of his "happiness" carries no more import than an inquiry into the "happiness" of a toad. A man will not drink a potion, no matter how cool and sweet, if he knows it is lethal. The pleasure of the moment will not serve as a rational excuse for suicide, and we would judge the alternative view as one that only a madman could find compelling. Thus, one who drinks this potion is either mad or is ignorant of the consequences. This, in brief, is the Socratic position on injustice: it is perpetrated only by the mad or the ignorant and, from the *Timaeus* [86], it has already been established that madness and ignorance are both diseases of the soul. To inquire, then, whether the unjust are happier than the just is as ridiculous (IV, 445) as asking whether the diseased are happier than the healthy. If they are, they are mad or fools or ignorant or children.

At root, the problem of conduct is no more than another side of the problem of knowledge. The unjust man is one whose appetites rule his reason. Just as the person limited to perception will fail to know what he should, the person driven by internal sensuousness will fail to do what he should. Moral relativism could be true only if the epistemology of Protagoras were correct, for, if man *were* the measure of all things, then it would follow that each man's conduct would be based on the private truths of individual perception. Meno's slave would have as much of a right to judge of triangles before instruction as after, even though his judgments would differ, even conflict. The same Socrates who must reject the epistemological relativism of Protagoras must reject the moral relativism of Thrasymachus, Glaucon, and Adeimantus and for the same reason. The Pythagorean theorem does not rest its truth on public opinion. The laws of harmony are not eradicable by human cupidity. Both become accessible by philosophical examination which will lead also and inexorably to a life of temperance, justice, and spiritual health.

As Meno's slave needed instruction, so too do the citizens of the State. And this fact provides the framework for the Socratic theory of governance.

The Problem of Governance

In the section dealing with Plato in his *History of Western Philosophy*, Bertrand Russell seeks to demythologize our rapture with the wisdom of antiquity:

> "It has always been correct to praise Plato but not to understand him. This is the common fate of great men. My object is the opposite. I wish to understand him, but to treat him with as little reverence as if he were a contemporary English or American advocate of totalitarianism."[25] (p. 105)

It is rarely wise to contradict the insights of Lord Russell, though usually tempting. However, although Russell is quite correct in following the traditional description of Plato's *Republic* as totalitarian, he courts the same difficulties as those facing all unwavering opponents of totalitarianism. Plato was not ignorant of the virtues of democracy. He grew up in one rather more enobling, we may submit, than any that Russell directly experienced.[26] He was also well aware of how similarly the citizen's life proceeds under forms of government with merely different names. Plato's respect for Sparta and his high hopes for the tyrants of Syracuse are not plausibly reduced to an autocracy-loving disposition. In vesting full authority in the State, Plato only followed the logic of Socratic epistemology as confirmed by the tragic chaos of Athenian politics. The argument for totalitarianism, in the light of the *corpus* of Platonic philosophy, proceeds unhindered. As the soul is driven by rational, appetitive, and passionate faculties, so too is the State. The just man and the just State are those living under the light of reason: those able to control the appetites and harmonize them with the wisdom of the intellect. While men and States are born with the capacity for such harmony, the capacity is actualized only under the leadership and guidance of the philosophically enlightened. Without this guidance the pleasures and pains of the flesh, which are the only source of virtue for the child, continue to dominate the life of the adult. Mere sensuous experience in this world of appearance will only strengthen the body's hold on the soul.

As the soul will be governed either by a harmony of the faculties or by the tyranny of one of them, the State too *will* be led. The question, then, is how and by whom and to what end. To answer "democratically," "by the people," and "for their happiness" is to miss the entire thrust of Plato's social and philosophical analyses. There is, first of all, no conceivable state in which the will of every single citizen can be honored. Infants cannot be consulted, nor can the dumb, the mad, and the criminal. Even if all were queried, we would find few decisions recommended unanimously. The possibility, therefore, of tyranny by the majority is inescapable. What good is there for the minority to have a voice which, though heard, is never followed? This can sew only the seeds of rebellion. Moreover, history offers little to support any claim of majority-wisdom. That same majority on whom Pericles conferred power was quick to turn on him, to accuse him of vile and venal things. With equal dispatch, it sentenced to death Socrates,

> "concerning whom I may truly say, that of all the men of his time whom I have known, he was the wisest and justest and best." (*Phaedo*, 118)

In his counsel to kings, Plato represented the interests of the multitude, and his advice, he insists, would have been the same no matter what the form of government. But he was convinced of the difference between the best interests of the people and their knowledge of it. The outcome of the Peloponnesian Wars was but one sign of the costs of "self-determination."

On the question of happiness as the end of human life, enough has been said. The people can be "happy" in their vice, their madness, their ignorance, and even their servility. Contentment can, on the Platonic account, be no criterion of virtue in the State or the citizen. If true happiness, the harmony of the soul's faculties leading to a life of justice and temperance, is to be enjoyed by the citizens, they must be led to it. It will not be found accidentally. Since this fundamental end of all just Republics can be achieved only under conditions of peace at home and with adequate defenses against quarrelsome neighbors, the rule of law and the might of armies must be unchallengeable. Only education can enlighten and only the law can compel the citizen to receive instruction. If the young are to reap the benefits of philosophical tuition (*phronesis*), their homes and games, their adult models and leaders, must be exemplars. The child who is taught the idea of justice cannot be turned loose in a town whose adults are driven by lust, whose poets traduce the character of virtue, whose leaders live by deceit and craft. If harmony is the goal, the sources of dissonance must be removed. Some of these are accidents of nature (i.e., those born with infirmities) and these must be "exposed" (i.e., exposed to the elements). Regulated breeding can reduce these accidents to a minimum.

By the standards of contemporary states, including those that advertise a commitment to liberty under democracy, Plato's *Republic* may seem repugnant. Yet, even in America, there are laws proscribing consanguinous marriages, marriages of the mentally defective, even marriages by those with certain hereditary "defects." Public education is compulsory, curricula are established by State regents, religious rites are disallowed, abortion of the defective fetus is permitted—the list could be expanded. These are the traditional practices of a twentieth-century republican democracy. They embrace ordinances against pornography, libel, treason, indecent exposure, discrimination on a racial, sexual, or religious basis, and so forth. Each of these proscriptions entails the constriction of personal freedom. Plato would be the first to argue that totalitarianism is not an approach to governance restricted to any particular *form* of government. It is, instead, that approach which vests in any person or corporate entity the power to control the religious, aesthetic, intellectual, and moral expressions of the rest of the citizenry. Since, on this analysis, only anarchy can free the citizen of these constraints, *any* form of governmental control is dictatorial within the regions in which that control is exercised. That the powers are granted by the people and that (although it doesn't follow) they can be withdrawn by the people is not a principle of government but a fact of political reality. Under any form of government there is an explicit or implicit covenant formed between citizens and their officials:

"A State . . . arises . . . out of the needs of mankind; no one is self-sufficing, but all of us have many wants." (*Republic*, II, 369)

Plato, we see, advances a *Social Contract* theory of sorts and certainly recognizes the factors that initially bring people into communal affiliations. If this motivation is ignored or frustrated by any subsequent government, either the government will be replaced or the social organization will fall to pieces. His "totalitarian" regime does not ignore this implicit covenant; it seeks to expand it, to extend the range of contributions the State can make to the life of every citizen *while still remaining a State*. Since we have no record of any nation in the history of civilization contending that any popular right is absolute and beyond appeal, we must place the Platonic theory of social organization on the same continuum that includes democracy. The problem of governance is rooted in the inescapable tension between law and freedom. That man is basically good, which is a hypothesis to which the Plato of the *Republic* is not hostile, is of too little comfort in a State that suppresses this goodness or does nothing to nurture it. Once we grant to the State or demand from it the steps required for the actualization of the moral potential of its citizens, we are moved irresistibly to the Platonic region of the continuum. That Plato never envisaged a State controlling every detail of daily life is clear:

> "When they have made a good beginning in a play, and by the help of music have gained the habit of good order, then this . . . will accompany them in all their actions and be a principle of growth to them. . . . Thus educated, they will invent for themselves any lesser rules which their predecessors have altogether neglected." (*Republic*, IV, 425)

That he did not recommend an unbending discriminatory code based on class is even clearer:

> ". . . we never meant when we construed the State that the opposition of natures should extend to every difference but only to those differences which affected the pursuit in which the individual was engaged."* (*Republic*, V, 454)

And so, and with no intention to tarnish the memory of Russell, we must avoid such convenient epithets as "totalitarian" and not wave the banners of our liberalism in such a way as to confirm Glaucon's rule that

> "the highest reach of injustice is to be deemed just when you are not." (*Republic*, II, 361)

It is the problem of governance that finally requires a theory of knowledge based on eternal memories. The confrontation in the *Protagoras* makes this clear, and it is only in the *Republic* that Socrates finally extricates his argument from a web of irksome contradictions. In the earliest stages of his debate with Protagoras, Socrates succeeds in chastening the great Sophist. Representing the interests of his young friend Hippocrates, Socrates reviews the bases on which one studies with a master. If, for example, Hippocrates wished to be a sculptor, he would want to study with Pheidias. Or, if medicine were his goal, Asclepius would be the proper tutor. What is it, then, that Hippocrates would want to be were he to submit his mind to the influence of Protagoras? When Protagoras replies that Hippocrates would wish to excel in virtue, Socrates has his opening: *Yes, but can virtue be taught?*

---

* This form of discrimination is the basis of the so-called *meritocracy*. It would be fair to say that under any rational form of government it is exercised either *de facto* or *de jure*.

Socrates' failure in the *Protagoras* is the result of a skepticism that is absent in the *Republic*. In the former work, he is hoisted by his own petard, as it were, the moment he questions a pedagogical approach to virtue for, if it is not teachable, the entire philosophic movement loses its *raison d'être*. In the *Republic* we discover the seasoned approach to this problem. Virtue, defined as always as a harmony, is not taught any more than one is taught to hear harmony. The capacity to recognize harmony and distinguish it from dissonance is an integral feature of the undiseased senses. However, experience with music is necessary if this native capacity is to be realized and is to become useful to the listener. Virtue is the same. Except for those "accidents of nature," every man enters the world with a soul capable of comprehending the good. Under the guidance of an enlightened community, the child's moral development must pass successively through stages of enlightenment culminating in a love for and recognition of virtue. This notion, only touched upon in connection with space perception in the *Timaeus* and geometry in the *Meno*, finds fullest expression in the *Republic* and the *Laws*. The philosopher is not so much a tutor or instructor as he is an *educator*—one who leads the pupil to a confrontation with the otherwise camouflaged truths of the eternal universe. This pilgrimage can begin only after a renunciation of the world of sense, only after the dialectical method has revealed the contradictions and sophistries that hitherto had passed for wisdom. Thus, in the most basic respects, the solution to the problem of governance is education. And, since the character of the State and all its citizens is completely determined by the nature of this education, it cannot be optional, nor can it be administered by just anyone who happens to come along.

Hippocrates

Socrates and his disciples loom so large historically that we often neglect to note many other creative enterprises of the Hellenic era. Of these, Greek medicine may rank as high as Greek drama for, in significant respects, the Hippocratic method was as deliberately original as were the literary methods of Sophocles, Aeschylus, and Euripedes. In fact, when we come to examine the biological turn taken by Aristotle's natural philosophy, we must keep in mind the quiet influence of the Hippocratic school. While quiet—Hippocratics are mentioned only fleetingly in the *Dialogues* and, to my knowledge, not at all in Aristotle's major works— the medical scholarship of ancient Greece invades Aristotelian naturalism at nearly every point.

We noted in our discussion of the pre-Socratics that no rigid boundary existed to separate philosophical and scientific exposition. Philosophy and physics, morals and cosmology, were but altered aspects of the same truth. The Pythagoreans accepted this notion, so much so that their ethics and theology were thoroughly intermingled with their geometry. And physicians as well accepted this idea. Until the dialectical and speculative elements of philosophy were made dominant by the members of the *Academy* and until the *true forms* replaced observable nature as the subject matter of philosophical importance, medicine and philosophy were handmaidens to each other. Platonic *idealism*, whose central message was that of skeptical disregard for the evidence of experience, was not compatible either with the practice of medicine or with those findings uncovered in the medical clinics every day by a host of practical men.

Hippocrates, himself, is hard to date. The *Dialogues* make reference to *Hippocratics*, suggesting that Hippocrates was older than the *Dialogues*, and it is customary to assign his *floruit* to about 400. What we have of his medical treatises we owe principally to Galen (c. A.D. 130–200), but the oldest manuscripts available which purport to be translations of Galen's works are by authors living eight centuries after Galen.[27] While this renders more difficult the task of authenticating the various treatises attributed to Hippocrates, there is sufficient presumptive evidence from many different sources, including ancient ones, for us to reconstruct the essential character of the Hippocratic approach to and theory of disease.

With respect to the approach, it is uncompromisingly *empirical*. As philosophy became more speculative, the Hellenic physician became commensurately less interested in the philosopher's notions about health and disease. What survived of philosophy in Greek medicine were remnants of Pythagoreanism, which treated disease of any sort as a lack of harmony. As practical biologists, the followers of Hippocrates reasoned that the body itself, and especially the *humours* of the body, required harmoniousness. It was not uncommon for delerium and fits to be treated through the combination of specific foods and music. Diet was especially integral to therapy. In the Hippocratic works on *Epidemics* we find frequent reference to fever and cold, to "fluxes" or storms of the humours. Similarly remedies focus on sleep and rest, quietude and temperance. In the next chapter, we will see that Aristotle's theories of memory and perception also take recourse to the notion of restlessness or quietude of the mind and the perceiving faculties.

More important than the specific observations made by the Hippocratics was their commitment to observation. Greek medicine was enormously advanced and it served as a constant reminder that the world of sense and the empirical method of fact-gathering were suspended only at the peril of those who wished to learn and understand. When, in the next chapter, we applaud Aristotle's ability to incorporate a biological perspective into his discourses on the soul, on animals, on the faculties, and so forth, we may find ourselves surprised that in the light of the advances made by the Hippocratics, he was not *more* biological in his orientation. For in remaining committed to rationalism in his larger works, he failed to avail himself of findings that were already common in the treatment centers of Athens. Thus while Aristotle, with brave logic, assigned to the heart those functions that we now know have their seat in the brain, Hippocrates had already recorded the fact that injuries to either side of the head resulted in spasms on the contralateral side.[28] And, instead of employing the same logic to prove that the brain is devoid of blood vessels, he might have consulted any number of Hippocratic treatises on the venous supply to the brain.

It would be improper to attribute more modernity to Hippocrates than the record demands. His humoural theory of psychological dispositions accorded an unchangeably *phlegmatic* nature to some (and therefore to their children!), a *bilious* one to another, and the justification for such attributions was hardly rigorously empirical. Indirectly, this type-theory of personality and its correlated hereditarian proviso supported the eugenic excesses of the *Academy*. Still, in the main, Hippocrates and his followers come closer to the modern spirit of experimental science than perhaps any figure in antiquity. The Hippocratics specifically rejected that Platonic version of "hypothesis" according to which all discourse must begin with self-evident truths, regarding such hypotheses as antithetical to the good care of patients and an understanding of their diseases. In the place of these "postulates," the Hippocratics compiled a veritable handbook of symptoms, therapies, and results. In the process, and through the translations and influence of Galen, they came to dominate the practice and theory of medicine for over two thousand years. More subtly but just as surely, they required of any psychological philosophy that it address itself to the biological facts of man and to the relationship between those facts and any theory that might be advanced to explain a psychological process. The first to show this influence was Aristotle.

Résumé

The Socratic philosophers, whose achievements were immortalized and "rejuvenated" by Plato, advanced many of the core problems with which all subsequent psychological scholarship would have to contend. They insisted on a distinction between the factual knowledge gleaned by error-prone perception and that knowledge of general principles made possible by reason alone. Combined with this was the assertion that knowledge, properly understood, is a recollection of that which is implanted within the mind as a condition of its being mind. These theories survive to the present day in the form of theories of cognition and, in modified form, as genetic theories of intellectual capacity. At the same time, although independently of the Hippocratics, they advanced a "type" theory of human personality and proposed a eugenic approach to deal with it. In focusing on the *a priori* determinants of perception and cognition, they anticipated that modern school of psychology called *Gestalt* and, in the process, posed a set of problems for the more empirically oriented psychologists of later centuries.

Coeval with this birth of idealism was the development of Greek medicine along rigorously observational lines. Thus by the end of the Socratic era, there were competing methods recommended for the study of man: the purely rationalistic leading to the spiritual dimension and the purely empirical which could only end in materialism. It was to Aristotle that the task of reconciliation fell and one he completed with mixed results.

References

1. For a general discussion of the slave question, see A. E. Zimmern, *The Greek Commonwealth*, Oxford University Press, 1924; and, more recently, Gustave Glotz, *Ancient Greece at Work*, Norton, New York, 1967, especially Part III; Ch. 5. Note too that the truly massive works of the period (aqueducts, temples, municipal buildings) were usually built by free men. (*The Cambridge Ancient History*, Vol. IV, p. 121, edited by J. S. Bury et al., Macmillan, Inc., New York, 1926.

2. *The Cambridge Ancient History*, op. cit., p. 393.

3. E. M. Walker's excellent brief review in the 1947 ("vintage") edition of *Encyclopaedia Britannica* might profitably be consulted.

4. In my discussion of the Greek religious attitude, I have relied upon W. K. C. Guthrie's fine study, *The Greeks and Their Gods*, Beacon Press, Boston, 1950. My interpretation is not, however, identical to Prof. Guthrie's.

5. *The Cambridge Ancient History*, op. cit., p. 27–28.

6. *The Cambridge Ancient History*, op. cit. pp. 29–30.

7. On the influence of Miletus, consult *Herodotus*, Book I, 17–22; Book V, 23–25; also, *The Cambridge Ancient History*, op. cit., pp. 87–97; and Breasted, *A History of Egypt*.

8. *The Cambridge Ancient History*, op. cit., pp. 87–97.

9. Kathleen Freeman, *Ancilla to the Pre-Socratic Philosophers*, Basil Blackwell, Oxford, 1952.

10. Analyses of the major pre-Socratics may be found in the following: G. S. Kirk, *Heraclitus: The Cosmic Fragments*, Cambridge, 1962; Leonardo

Tarán, *Parmenides*, Princeton, N.J., 1965; J. A. Philip, *Pythagoras and Early Pythagoreanism*, University of Toronto Press, 1966.

11. Herodotus is, of course, our primary source. Consult also Chapter 5 of Hermann Bengtson's *The Greeks and the Persians from the Sixth to the Fourth Centuries*, Delacourte Press, New York, 1968.

12. Thucydides, *The Peloponnesian Wars, translated* by Benjamin Jowett, #143, Washington Square Press, New York, 1963. The quotation is taken from the funeral oration of Pericles. The words, of course, are provided by Thucydides and, while the speech is undeniably moving, it bears the stamp of political rhetoric.

13. Xenophon's *Memorabilia* includes a sketch of Socrates that is important for corroborative purposes. It was written at least thirty years after the death of Socrates.

14. For the collection of Plato's *Epistles* consult Glenn R. Morrow, *Plato's Epistles*, Bobbs-Merrill, Indianapolis, 1962. *The Second Epistle* from which the quotation is taken is of questionable authenticity. But the very same modesty is expressed in the *Seventh Epistle* (Section 341) whose authenticity is very well established. In translating the *Second Epistle*, we may substitute "idealized" for "embellished." On this reading, Plato may be admitting that he did more than merely adorn the teachings of Socrates.

15. Ibid.

16. The edition of the *Dialogues* used in the present work is *The Dialogues of Plato*, 2 vols., translated by Benjamin Jowett, Random House, New York, 1937. The bracketed numbers refer to the standard Greek manuscript of Stephens. All modern English translations retain these numbers in their margins. Thus, no matter which translation the reader consults, the bracketed numbers will refer to the same lines of the Greek text.

17. Ibid.

18. Ibid.

19. Ibid.

20. Bertrand Russell, *A History of Western Philosophy*, 14th ed., Simon and Schuster, New York (first printing, 1945). See especially pp. 104–105.

21. *The Dialogues of Plato*, translated by Benjamin Jowett, op. cit. The reader will gain useful insights into Platonic philosophy by reading Professor Jowett's *Index*. The *Index* is not merely an alphabetical list of terms but is, in addition, an analysis of the meaning of the terms in the context.

22. Ibid.

23. Ibid.

24. Ibid.

25. Bertrand Russell, *A History of Western Philosophy, loc. cit.*

26. See, for example, *America: 1938–1944* in Volume II, *The Autobiography of Bertrand Russell*, Atlantic Monthly Press, Little, Brown, Boston, 1968. Lord Russell confronted an intellectual intolerance far more severe, we might suspect, than any likely to be found in the Athens of Pericles.

27. The authoritative edition of the Hippocratic system is the translation by W. H. S. Jones, *Hippocrates*, 3 vols., Putnam, New York, 1923. Prof. Jones' introduction is most useful.

28. Ibid., Vol. III, *On Wounds in the Head*.

3

□□□□□□□□□□□□□□□□□□□□□□□□□□□□□□□□□□

The Hellenistic Age

ARISTOTLE, THE EPICUREANS, AND THE STOICS

Aristotle (385–322): His Philosophical Development*

Vico's warning against the glorification of antiquity tends to fall on
deaf ears when the full sweep of Aristotle's achievement presents itself.
Aristotle has had a more direct and enduring effect on more departments
of scholarship than any other single figure. More than one reverent
historian has described him as the last man to have known everything
that was known in his own time.

What we know of his life is spotty, mostly superficial. He was a
devoted student of Plato's from the founding of the Academy (367)
until the master's death (347), although he only figures significantly in
one of the *Dialogues*, the *Parmenides*. He was born in Stageirus, on the
eastern edge of the Chalcidice (see the map, p. 35) and was of Ionian
heritage. His father was personal physician to the Macedonian king,
Amyntas II, father of Philip II and grandfather of Alexander the Great.
Thus, a measure of the prestige enjoyed by the *Academy* can be gleaned
from the fact that a family of means and connections would send their
seventeen-year-old son to it for instruction.

It is customary to separate Aristotle's philosophical development into

---

* Except where indicated otherwise, all references to Aristotle's works refer to
The Basic Works of Aristotle, translated by Richard McKeon, Random House, New
York (1941). However, with respect to *De Anima*, which is central to Aristotle's
psychological theories, I have gone to the Greek text, by W. D. Ross, Clarendon
edition, Oxford, 1956. Quoted material is taken directly from Prof. McKeon's translation. In discussing these passages, I have introduced synonyms in order to render
Aristotle's arguments more meaningful to an audience of psychologists.

three stages.[1] In the first, he is a Platonist to the core—the author of now lost dialogues, the student of the *ideas*. Direction of the *Academy* fell to Plato's cousin, Speusippus, in 347, and this was either the cause or the mere coincidence attending Aristotle's departure from Athens. During the following twelve years (347–335) his busy life included his marriage to Pythias, his teaching of Alexander (342–336), his direction of the group of Platonists at Assos, and what must have been a reassessment of his own position on basic philosophical questions. Opportunity knocked with the death of Philip II and the accession to power of Alexander (335). Aristotle returned to Athens, established his own school, the *Lyceum*, and devoted the remaining thirteen years of his life to that body of thought posterity would call Aristotelianism. On the news of Alexander's death (323), he retired to Chalcis in the Euboea, recognizing that the Athenians, now free to express their wanton nationalism, would attack any and all Macedonian sympathizers. We are told that he left Athens so that that city *"would not sin against Philosophy a second time."*

Indirect evidence suggests that Aristotle arrived at the *Academy* after the Platonic circle had completed the *Theaetetus* and while it was engaged in the *Parmenides*. Professor Jaeger has argued convincingly that the challenges offered by the Aristoteles of the *Parmenides* would not likely have come from the teenager from Stageirus.[2] Indeed, though we do not have the early dialogues of Aristotle, we have overwhelming circumstantial evidence that they were consonant with the prevailing theories of the *Academy*. Several of them were, we may believe, merely updatings of older Platonic works, for example, the *Eudemus* vis-à-vis Plato's *Phaedo* and the *Gryllus* vis-à-vis Plato's *Gorgias*.[3] Among these earliest works, we do have the fragments of the *Protrepticus*,[4] which, although not a dialogue, is nearly orthodox Platonism. It is in this work that we find a defense of Anaxagoras' commitment to "contemplate the heavens" and recourse to the authority of Pythagoras. The world of *sense* is respected, but the world of *idea* is proclaimed:

> "Hence we should do all things for the sake of the goods that reside in man himself, and of these, that which is good in the body we should do for the sake of that which is good in the soul . . . wisdom is the supreme end."[5]

> "(W)e ought either to pursue philosophy or bid farewell to life . . . because all other things seem to be but utter nonsense and folly."[6]

Mingled subtly with this devotion to the soul and its ideas, however, are the soft intimations of a coming revolution:

". . . if life is preferred and valued on account of sense-perception, and if sense-perception is a sort of knowledge . . ."[7]

On the whole, Aristotle's earliest period of intellectual evolution is best viewed as a Platonic one. The "revolution" he initiated in his final years might be seen not so much as an attack on Platonism as it was the unique invention of Aristotelianism. The important differences between the Aristotle of the missing dialogues and the Aristotle of 335–322 may be noted.

First, the earliest Aristotle is a pupil, the latest a teacher. In the *Academy*, he received the problems of antiquity but through a medium and format not readily applicable to the *Hellenistic* Age. It is conventional to divide the *Hellenic* and *Hellenistic* epochs with the accession of Alexander (335).* Alexander sought to "Hellenize" first the Persians who fell before his armies and the then entire world. This attitude, although formalized by Alexander, was not foreign to his father. After all, it was Philip II who sent for Aristotle. Macedonian respect for Hellenic culture is not the way to put it. Rather, that which is called "Macedonian" is indistinguishable from "Hellenic." The courts of Amyntas II and his successors were *Greek* courts, which is to say, *Hellenic* courts. There was no competing Macedonian culture or perspective. For Philip and his son the enemy was Persia, never Athens. Aristotle, a visionary, must have recognized that the dialectical method was simply inapplicable to any ambitious program of Hellenization. Accordingly, the materials prepared for instruction at his *Lyceum* were lectures and were in book form. It appears certain that Aristotle had rejected the cultist view of philosophy-as-a-religion and had adopted the pedagogical view of philosophy-as-a-subject. The Platonic lesson, a debt to the Pythagoreans, was that philosophic wisdom purified the soul in which it resided—albeit latently —for all time. By the time of Alexander, a time in which Macedonian forces toppled city after city and nation after nation, the need was for constitutions, laws, and trade agreements. Alexander defeated his enemies so that he could save them and, for this, a useful philosophy was in order. It would be absurd to suggest that Aristotle sat in the *Lyceum* filling political prescriptions. Rather, he saw more clearly than his student the need for knowledge in an expanding empire. The program of study, the format, and the resulting works all point to this recognition. If Socrates was a gadfly, Aristotle was a university professor.

Second, Aristotle departed from the Platonic tradition in the depths

---

* The *Hellenistic* period is generally taken as that occurring from the time of Alexander's death (323 B.C.) to the beginning of the Roman emperorship of Augustus (30 B.C.); i.e., until the Augustan age.

of his inquiries. There can be no wider scope than the *Dialogues*, but they are clearly lacking in substantive content. This gap between general principles and factual information is one that Aristotle's teaching strived to remove. Where the Platonists of the *Republic* politely argued a constitution into being, Aristotle examined some 158 different and actual constitutions and analyzed their premises and the factual evidence standing in their support.* Where Timaeus would content himself with an explanation of space perception based only on "a spurious kind of reason," Aristotle would devote entire books to the subjects of vision, touch, taste, and so forth. Here the "revolution" is more of an evolution. Plato died before completing his program and this, sooner or later, would have had to embrace the special problems of science, politics, ethics, logic, psychology. To ignore these would have meant the transforming of philosophy into religion. Aristotle, in taking the baton, almost transformed it into science.

Finally, the Platonists were too willing to dismiss all but "ideas" as irrelevant. Neither Aristotle nor his contemporaries could share this luxury. Those rare passages in Aristotle that address Platonism in a contemptuous tone are invariably directed at the exclusionary elements of the Platonic program. Perhaps this is most easily noted in the two versions of the *Metaphysics:* an earlier one in which the first-person plural is used in the discussion of ideas, and the later version in which the third-person plural is used.[8] This grammatical shift is of significance. In this later version, those who subscribe to a separate sphere of reality, the sphere of *ideas*, and who regard the sphere of *appearance* to be but a distortion of the truth, have become "they" where once they were "we."

There is yet another analytical route to appreciating the evolutionary rather than revolutionary turn taken by Aristotle and his *Peripatetic* school. We noted in the last chapter the hostility of the Athenians toward "natural Philosophers" resulting in the exile of Protagoras and the temporary imprisonment of Anaxagoras. A half-century later, Socrates suffered an even worse fate, even though his teachings were essentially noncosmological, let alone theological. The charges brought against these philosophers were of the sort normally associated with lynch law, and the evidence marshaled by the prosecution was as rich in rhetoric and innuendo as it was shallow in fact. These conditions have a far more chilling effect on scholarship than those in which particular freedoms are curtailed or in which specific topics are proscribed. A law narrowly confining free speech, say, to apolitical themes is offensive and oppres-

---

* Later sources attribute to Aristotle the analysis of 158 constitutions. We do have his *Constitution of Athens*, but the vast bulk of the constitutionalist's effort has yet to be discovered.

sive, but even under such a law a good deal of inquiry can proceed. Indeed, had there been a law expressly forbidding public discussion of religion or the gods, the only *Dialogues* that would have been clearly in violation were the *Timaeus*, portions of the *Parmenides* and the *Republic* and, on the narrowest construction, a few passages of the *Phaedo* and the *Cratylus*.

But charges against "natural philosophy" or those imputing slander against religion and the corruption of youth are so general and ambiguous that, for the timid spirit, they will reduce speculation to platitude and proverb. The students of the *Academy* were not so timid, but we cannot help but notice the relative absence of daring in their approach to cosmological and theological matters. That so many pages would be addressed to goodness, to virtue, to the soul, and even to an afterlife and so few to the gods themselves must tell us something about the effect of Socrates' execution on his philosophical progeny. The bandwagon effect leading to the condemnation of men like Socrates was deftly aided by such gifted playwrights as Aristophanes, whose *Clouds* reduced philosophical inquiry to semantic banality. It is revealing that what poor old Strepsiades has learned from the philosophers in *Clouds* is that thunder is not produced by Zeus but by the "aerial whirlwind." Since we know that the Socratics had little if any interest in thunder and clouds, we must assume that Aristophanes selected themes that would reinforce the public suspicion of heresy even if these themes were completely foreign to Socratic discourse.

The conditions by Aristotle's *floruit* were, of course, very different. Philip II and Alexander settled the Persian problem once and for all and, in the process, removed the Theban threat as well. Athens had peace and security but at the price of fealty. However, Alexander could not have been more respectful and protective of Athenian culture had he been a native of Athens. In all signifiant respects, he was a *Hellene* first, a Macedonian second. His "appointment" as *autocrator* (commander-in-chief) was rather a formality, since his armies could not possibly be opposed by any single force in the Greek world. To the last, these armies served Greece and worked toward Hellenization with a zeal and discipline unrivaled in military history. Alexander's perception of the non-Hellenic world was, we may guess, similar to the early Victorian view of the non-British world—a mass of barbarians patiently awaiting the enlightenment of a higher culture, ready to adopt it as soon as its obvious superiority was revealed. That Alexander's ultimate goal was essentially cultural is clear. Indeed, if the authority of Plutarch is to be trusted, the following letter—or, at least, its message—gives us an unambiguous portrayal of this attitude:

"Alexander to Aristotle, greeting. You have not done well to publish your books of oral doctrine; for what is there now that we excel others in, if those things which we have been particularly instructed in be laid open to all? For my part, I assure you, I had rather excel others in the knowledge of what is excellent, than in the extent of my power and dominion. Farewell."[9] (p. 805)

With this position taken by the most powerful man in the world, it was not likely that an Athenian assembly would publicly attack scholarly inquiry. The view of knowledge as power was surely treasonous to the Socratic tradition, and there is no reason to believe that Aristotle shared it. But that is not important. What is important is that Alexander believed it and that this belief was enough to allow the *Peripatetics* to restore natural philosophy to the curriculum of the *Lyceum*. Those who may wonder why, then, Aristotle should have been so interested in natural science coming as he did from an *Academy* that ignored it, fail to distinguish between indifference and suppression.

The Problem of Knowledge

Aristotle's opening lines of the *Metaphysics* provide a clue to the extent to which his epistemology departed from the theories of the Academy:

"All men by nature desire to know. An indication of this is the delight we take in our senses . . . and above all others the sense of sight. . . . (T)his, most of all senses, makes us know and brings to light many differences between things."[10]

No self-respecting, orthodox Platonist could have authored this passage. Here, in *Metaphysics*, which Aristotle considered to be the "first philosophy," the break with Platonism was announced at the very outset. We shall see that the break was more of a fracture and that even the latter showed signs of mending at several points. Nevertheless the position taken in the beginning sentences was never abandoned: knowledge gained by experience, by the actions of the senses, is real and since it is real, the world of sense is also and necessarily real. If only in this limited context, Aristotle must be regarded as an *empiricist*—as the father of that variety of empiricism which succeeding philosophers in the empiricistic tradition adopted. It is in the same work, as we have noted, that

Aristotle removed himself from the *Idealism* of the Academy and, after weighing the arguments, rejected the theory of the *Forms*. To appreciate Aristotelian empiricism, we need to revisit the Platonic-Socratic perspective on the *Ideas*, the *Forms*, and the *Universals*. This time, we will examine these theories through Aristotle's criticisms of them. Some targets of his criticism cannot be located in the *Dialogues* but, since Aristotle did devote twenty years to a study of Plato's thought, we may safely conclude that he had access to a more detailed account of this thought than what has survived in the *Dialogues*. As discussed earlier, the *Academy* of the *Dialogues* existed in a politically charged and reactionary environment that undoubtedly induced nervous caution in the Socratics. The shifting and ambiguous character of the theory of Ideas, as it has come down through the *Dialogues*, may be attributed to self-imposed censorship of the written works. As a member of the *Academy*, Aristotle was able to receive the uncensored doctrines orally. This is not to say that Aristotle's review of these theories is at great variance with the *Dialogues*—only that what appears tentative and hypothetical in the *Dialogues* is presented as Plato's official position in the *Metaphysics*.

In the *Metaphysics*, Aristotle praised Socrates for developing inductive reasoning and for advancing the theory and the problem of universals [1078^{b}]*.[11] In the *Theaetetus* and the *Meno*, Socrates distinguished between perception of particular instances and general ideas, which themselves cannot be received through perception. The world "cat" is illustrative. We can see a particular cat but we only know (perceptually) that it is *a* cat because it answers to the description given by our general idea of *the* cat. In the simplest terms, the problem of universals is this: Since no single cat can be so identified unless there is some supra-individual class (i.e., a *universal*) of which it is an instance, is the *universal cat* real? Now, Socrates did not suggest that somewhere in the world a perfected, four-legged, mewing ideal cat sits sipping ideal milk. What he did suggest, however, was that true knowledge of what *a* cat is depends on a true idea of *the* cat as a universal. Since any particular cat can be no more than an approximation to the ideal, our perceptual knowledge of cats can only be an approximation to true knowledge of *cat*. That is, particular cats display good-*ness*. But perception will only be of the attribute and, unaided, will not penetrate through to the ideal. The ideal, of course, is the *idea:* that in which each instance shares but only shares imperfectly and incompletely.

On Aristotle's account, Socrates was credited with retaining the connection between a universal class and its perceptible instances, but the Platonists were rebuked for dissolving this connection:

---

* See note 11 for explanation of bracketed numbers.

"Socrates did not make the universals or the definitions exist apart; *they*, however, gave them separate existence, and this was the kind of thing they called Ideas." (*Metaphysics*, XIII, 4, 30–33) [12]

Aristotle was never more aggressive in his refutations of the teaching of the *Academy* than in Book XIII, Chapters 4–6, of the *Metaphysics*. The impression on reading these attacks is that Aristotle was committed to the study of the real world and that he recognized such a study could not be philosophically valid if the *Forms* were. His inquiries in anatomy, reproductive biology, and astronomy, on the Platonistic account, would have been no more than illusion. Only mathematical abstractions could be held in esteem by the Platonists, since only these dealt with the relationship between things and ideas. Moreover, only when things and the Idea of things were rendered identical could one say he had unearthed the *Form*. Since Aristotle's own program of study was brazenly nonmathematical, his defense of his own efforts necessarily involved a stern dismissal of the *Forms*. With these set aside, the study of perception, learning, memory, even dreams, could be pursued with philosophical impunity.

We will confront the problem of the Universals again below and in subsequent chapters. It not only was a subject of great importance to medieval scholars but also, in modified fashion, it continues to participate in contemporary theories of cognition and perception. Aristotle did not settle the issue, nor were the Platonistic versions of the problem exhaustive. He did treat the problem, however, as a logical and semantic one and thereby set the stage for the great *Nominalist-Realist* debates of the twelfth and thirteenth centuries. It is in those debates that we observe the fuller implications of the theory of Universals, and we reserve further discussion until our review of the Middle Ages. We need to note here only that in rejecting the theory, Aristotle freed himself to use the data of experience and the facts of sensible nature to study man and society from a point of view that was both rationalistic and empiricistic. This point of view was responsible for Aristotle's major psychological work, the *De Anima*.

The *De Anima* is translated as "on the soul," although περί ψυχη in the original Greek* does not introduce a religious subject. Rather, ψυχη

---

* Aristotle, *De Anima*. Greek text by W. D. Ross, Clarendon Press, Oxford. In describing ψυχη as the αρχη ζωων Aristotle is employing the language of the biologist. In his own Doric dialect, αρχη ζωων translates comfortably as the principal determinant of life or the first (chief) causal factor. Thus, it is not an extraphysical determinant but an essentially biological one or, at least, the text allows such a rendering.

διαλεκτικος, while generally translated as dialectical, may not refer here to the specific method of the Socratics but, more generally, to a disputatious rather than empirical method of discovery.

("psyche") is a life-giving or animating agent and, in the context of
Aristotle's essay, it is best understood as a term designating the motive
force underlying life itself. If the modern Christian conception of soul
were or could be stripped of all religious and theological colorations,
then the ψυχη of Aristotle's inquiry would translate as *soul*. Thus, when
he established the priority of the topic in his opening sentences, he treated
ψυχη as integral to our understanding of nature because it is the *first cause*
or prime principle (αρχη) of all life (ζωων). [402a]. The account he proposes to give is to be

"compatible with experience" [402b]

rather than merely argumentative (διαλεκτικως), another reference to his
divorce from the purely dialectical methods of the *Academy*. Again in
the first chapter [402b–403a] he identifies the emotions (anger, courage,
appetite) and the sensations as conditions of the soul and insists that they
can only exist through the medium of a body. Therefore, the "affections"
of the soul are to be conceived as *"materialized formulable essences."**
Behind this tortured locution is a simply stated and profound implica-
tion: an understanding of human psychology depends upon and is informed by our knowledge of the material (biological) conditions of life.
For the Aristotle of *de Anima*, the possibility of a *physiological* psychology was very real indeed.†

The essentially physiological character of his psychology appears frequently throughout his works including those that are not particularly
concerned with psychological matters. In his *Physics*, for example, he
opposes the Platonic notion of intellectual processes as turbulent and
offers, instead, the theory of quiescence: perception and intellect, if
they are to be precise and organized, require that the soul approach a
condition of rest. He attributes the inferiority of perception on the part
of children and the aged to the result of the "great amount of restlessness," and all such deficits are to be understood finally in terms of some
kind of alteration "of something in the body."[13] In his treatise on dreams
(*De Somnis*) he again accounts for the phenomenon in terms of sensory-
biological processes and offers the surprisingly modern hypothesis that

* This is an awkward construction. The Greek reads, ει δ ουτως εχει, δηλον οτι τα
παθη λογοι ενυλοι εισιν. It comes after Aristotle's discussion of our ability to feel, em-
pathically, the terror experienced by another person although there is no external
source of terror impinging on us. Then comes the above sentence which I translate
as: "Clearly it follows from this that the soul's empathic feelings are to be understood as properties deriving from the material body." (*De Anima*, Book I, Ch. I,
[403a; lines 24, 25]).

† See, for example, his *Physics* (248a) where he argues that the affairs of the soul
are brought about "*by alterations of something in the body*."

dreams are the result of our conscious experiences and our emotions.[14] Even that most complex of psychological features, memory, is treated in purely biological terms. In his *de Memoria et Reminiscentia* (*On Memory and Reminiscence*), which we will note again shortly, he discusses recollection as the "searching for an image in a corporeal substrate" (Ch. 2, 453a) and again explains the memory deficiencies of children, the aged, the diseased in terms of biological anomalies.

When we study the philosophers before Aristotle, we can uncover, here and there, a psychological orientation that is materialist in tone. This is certainly true of several of the pre-Socratics and it is also true of particular passages in the *Timaeus*. However, no predecessor could possibly or plausibly lay claim to the title of an early physiological psychologist, and this is precisely the title we may assign to Aristotle. He was the first authority to delineate a domain specifically embracing the subject matter of psychology and, within that domain, to confine his explanations to principles of a biological sort. That the entire body of Aristotelian philosophy does not fit into a materialist mold is clear; the philosopher himself goes to some lengths to make it clear. But on the narrower issues of learning, memory, sleep and dreams, routine perceptions, animal behavior, emotion, and motivation, Aristotle's approach is naturalistic, physiological, and empirical.

At the same time, he rejected the extreme materialism of Democritus, who judged soul and mind ($\nu o \upsilon \varsigma$) to be the same and insisted that both were reducible to atoms (*De Anima*, [405a]). In [407b] he dismissed the Platonic theory of soul-as-harmony or as proportion, since such hypothesized harmonies are not evident in biological systems. And in [408b], he specifically distinguishes soul from mind, the latter dwelling somehow within the soul but, unlike the soul, being imperishable. That *mind* itself is not merely certain mental faculties is clear from his treatment of the process of senility:

> ". . . in old age the activity of mind or intellectual apprehension declines only through the decay of some other inward part; mind itself is impassible." [4086]

Aristotle was not satisfied with any of the traditional theories of the soul and he devoted Book I to a critique of them. He concluded by attributing their deficiencies to the error of believing that there is only one function of the soul. He, on the contrary, noted that biological systems exist in varying degrees of complexity and, for each essential function, there must be a corresponding *psychic* (i.e., motive) principle. The functions advanced by Aristotle were the nutritive, the perceptive, the locomotor, and, in man alone, the rational. Any animal possessing an advanced function (e.g., reason) will also have the less advanced functions (perception, locomotion, nutrition). Each of these functions, moreover, may express itself in one *faculty* or in a variety of faculties. Perception may, for example, be limited to touch, or all five senses may be well developed (Book II, Ch. 3). Even in the case of the rational function, there may be only mere imagination or calculation as well.

After reviewing the special character of the five senses (Book II), Aristotle concerns himself with the mind and with the problem of how thought ever occurs in the first place if, indeed, it is not native, as the theory of *Ideas* supposed. His solution was to distinguish the actual from the potential: mind has the potential for thought, but for this to be actualized, it must be acted upon by the world. In a sentence that anticipated the seventeenth-century empiricism of John Locke, he described the mind in these terms:

"What it thinks must be in it just as characters may be said to be on a writing tablet on which as yet nothing actually stands written: this is exactly what happens with mind." [429b–430a]

The actual mechanics associated with learning are not treated in *De Anima* but are reviewed quickly in one of Aristotle's "little works" (*Parva Naturalia*) entitled *On Memory and Reminiscence*, to which we have referred. It is in this essay that he established repetition as the source of the strength of memories and argued for an *associational* mechanism. According to the theory, sensations set up a certain movement within the soul. This will subside in time, but if it has been produced often enough, it can be re-created or, at least, a likeness of it can be re-created. Through repetition (by custom or habit), certain movements reliably follow or precede others. Our attempts to recall are only attempts to initiate the right internal events. We must find the beginning of the appropriate series and, when we do, the entire train of associations is set in motion.

Notions similar to these were given in the *Physics* in which he went so far as to bring the moral sentiments under the control of biological processes:

". . . all moral excellence is concerned with bodily pleasures and pains," [247a]

and in which these sentiments are finally traceable to sensory experience. Thus, to the associationism of *de Memoria et Reminiscentia* he added a "pleasure principle" as well and thereby removed himself still further from the *Academy*.

If all we possessed of Aristotle's works were the *de Anima* and the *de Memoria et Reminiscentia,* we would be correct in concluding that his theory of knowledge was *empiricistic,* his theory of learning *associationistic,* and his psychology essentially *behavioristic.* His position would not differ greatly from that of, say, B. F. Skinner. That this is not the case is established beyond doubt by his other works, especially his *Posterior Analytics.* It is in these works that we find a narrowing of the differences between his epistemology and Plato's. Whereas the senses were accorded special honor in *de Anima* and *Metaphysics,* their limitations are examined more critically in the *Posterior Analytics.* We should not read inconsistencies into these several works. The mission of each essay is different. In *de Anima,* Aristotle was examining questions of an essentially psychological and psychobiological nature. In *Posterior Analytics,* the subject is methodology and, particularly, scientific methodology. The former work was devoted to the processes of learning and perception, the latter to rules of evidence that must be applied to reason and experience. In *de Anima,* we discover our relation to the sensible world. In *Posterior Analytics,*[15] we discover how a world of changes can still be knowable.

Aristotle was well aware of the theory of fluxes advanced by Heraclitus. He knew also that the *Academy* had turned away from the senses in part because of this theory. Heraclitus drew attention to the ever-changing nature of the sensible world and argued accordingly for a relativistic attitude toward knowledge. The Socratics, however, found little merit in a life of study that could yield only temporary truths. They looked, therefore, behind the shifting world of Heraclitus and found the *Ideas.* In the *Posterior Analytics,* Aristotle attempted to salvage truth, permanent truth from relativism but without subscribing to the received theories of the *Academy.* The position he took appears toward the end of Book I:

> "Scientific knowledge is not possible through the act of perception . . . one must perceive (things) and at a definite present place and time: but that which is commensurately universal and true in all cases one cannot perceive." [87b].[16]

Now to know "that which is commensurately universal and true" we must have certain standards of an essentially cognitive nature which allow us to organize the teeming and shifting facts of the physical world. That is, the physical object or event, to be knowable, must impinge upon some disposition or capacity of the mind which will give to the object or event features of a cognitively meaningful sort. Aristotle was not suggesting that the objects or events did not possess such features; that is, the mind invented them. Rather, he argued that to be knowable and known, these objects or events had to have features that were compatible with our very methods of knowing. These features were presented in his ten *Categories*[17] and are as follows: (1) *substance* (according to which a thing *is*), (2) *quailty* (e.g., the thing is *white*), (3) *quantity* (e.g., the white thing is *three feet* tall), (4) *relation* (e.g., the white things is *taller* than the red thing), (5) *place* (e.g., the thing is *there*), (6) *time* (e.g., it was there *yesterday*), (7) *position* (e.g., it is *standing* in the corner), (8) *state* (e.g., that horse is *shod*), (9) *action* (e.g., he *lanced* the blister), and (10) *affection* (e.g., *he was lanced*, i.e., *affected by* the lance).

These ten *Categories* are applied to objects and events in order that we might classify, judge, compare, and locate them in space and time. They are the categories that must be available if any object or event is to be known. To be sure, our perceptions are *of* these categories but are not the categories themselves. Indeed, were the categories not available prior to the act of perceiving, the objects of perception could not be classified according, for example, to time, place, quality, and so forth.

Aristotle's *Categories* was intended as an essay on logic. No part of it purports to be "cognitive" or, for that matter, even psychological. Much later, in the hands of Kant, these categories, in modified form, would serve as the foundation for an unmistakably cognitive theory. But even in the nonpsychological context in which Aristotle introduced them, the categories are offered as mental dispositions, as principles according to which the world of matter and the world of knowledge merge or at least enjoy the possibility of becoming acquainted.

The categories alone are just that: categories of knowledge—not the *scientific* knowledge of that "which is commensurately universal and true." It is only through what Aristotle called *demonstration* that such scientific knowledge is possible. As such terms are employed in modern times, one might be tempted to think that Aristotle was advancing a purely empiricistic method for obtaining true knowledge. This is decidedly not the case, and we must examine the Aristotelian meaning of *scientific* to see why.

Scientific knowledge is, according to Aristotle, demonstrative knowledge, not in the modern sense of experimental demonstration, but rather in the sense of rational or logical demonstration. At first blush, his position seems naive and characteristically ancient. Indeed, if we ignore the fact that he invented embryology by breaking open chick eggs at different stages of development[18] or that he established the shape of the earth by observing its shadow on the moon during eclipses[19] or if we neglect his feats of observational skill in *de Partibus Animalium*, we might attribute his theory of science to an utter ignorance of the powers of observation.* But we know better. We know that Aristotle was a gifted scientist. But he was a philosopher first and hence he could not accept mere *facts* as demonstrative *proofs*. The demonstrations he sought were to be of the syllogistic sort in which the major premise was the law of nature, the minor premise, a fact of nature, and the conclusion, a necessary and demonstrated *reasoned* fact. Socrates is not said to be mortal merely because he died. He was known to be mortal while he lived. *All* men are mortal and Socrates is a man. His death, on this account, is not a mere fact but a reasoned fact. Scientific knowledge, then, differs from perception by possessing the general (universal) principles which cover each and every particular instance. As we recall from Chapter 1, Aristotle's position was, in important respects, an anticipation of the modern canons of scientific explanation.

It is not easy to summarize the Aristotelian solution to the problem of knowledge. Where the Platonic theory of *Ideas* is exclusive, Aristotle's theory is inclusive. Definition, dialectic, sense perception, syllogistic reasoning, inference, and certain native capacities of the mind are all included. Experience conveys factual knowledge and, from this and through the steps of inductive inference, true initial premises are grasped. These are laws and from them can be deduced the particulars. How the mind grasps the "universal" when the senses can perceive only the particular brings us to Aristotle's account of the origins of reason.

The Origins of Reason

The problem of the universals has been "solved for all time" by every major period of philosophical speculation. Aristotle was the first to recognize that, in one form, the problem is a semantic one. From the thirteenth century on, there have been philosophers contending that it is only a semantic one. Still, there are perceptual and cognitive dimensions of this problem, and a good many psychologists have staked their research and theories on the premise that the problem is more than mere semantics. We can catch a glimmer of these cognitive and perceptual elements by recalling the "universal cat" and determining how to go about teaching a three-year-old what a cat is; that is, which animals should be

---

* In addition to classifying animals on the basis of external appearance, Aristotle either performed surgical dissections or made himself aware of the results of these. In his *Historia Animalium*, for example, he notes the striking similarity between the internal organs of man and those of the monkey, going so far as to say that the sets of organs resemble one another in all respects: τα εντος διαιρεθεντα ομοια εχουσιν ανθρωπω παντα τα τοιαυτα. (*Historia Animalium* [II, 502b]).

called "cat," "dog," "wolf," "lion," etc. The first step, and the simplest, is to bring in the family pet (a cat in this case), show it to the child and say "cat." If this is done often, we have it on the very best authority that most children will learn to say "cat" when this pet is displayed. But suppose this pet, a large gray tabby, is replaced by a Siamese. Will the child say "cat"? If so, what did the child learn from the original training? In just a few years the same child will correctly identify all species of things despite great intraspecies differences in size, weight, color, temperament, and condition of health. Now the temptation, to be sure, is to attribute this successful performance to generalization (or induction, as Aristotle would say). But to generalize, the child must be in mental possession of some class or genus over which particular instances can be generalized. In other words, we run the risk of accounting for the performance by assuming the very "universal" we set out to eliminate.

The *Posterior Analytics* begins with the declaration that *"All instruction given or received by way of argument proceeds from pre-existent knowledge,"* and it ends by addressing the sense in which knowledge is *pre-existent* [99b–100a]. It is in this last chapter that Aristotle embraced the nativistic theory of knowledge while seeming to reject it. He first scorns the nativistic account and then notes its compelling element:

"Now it is strange if we possess them [States of knowledge] from birth for it means that we possess apprehensions more accurate than demonstration and fail to notice them. If on the other hand we acquire them and do not previously possess them, how could we apprehend and learn without a basis of pre-existent knowledge?" [99b]

His only answer is that we do not have the knowledge at birth (thereby rejecting the nativistic theory of the *Ideas*), but we do have the *capacity* which is subsequently actualized through sense perception. And, while the senses themselves only detect the particular, their *"content is universal"* [100b], meaning that the mind is able to construct the universal from the data of experience. This is not orthodox Platonism by any means but, as a solution to the universal-particular element of the problem of knowledge, it is a compromise of the sort found in the *Theaetetus;*[20] that is, the senses do not convey knowledge, only that from which the reasoning can extract knowledge.

It is clear from both his *Nicomachean Ethics*[21] and from his *Rhetoric*[22] that Aristotle envisaged human psychology as an evolving process. The Platonists were two-stage theorists in their treatment of the mind. This followed naturally from the theory of *Ideas*. Since the *Ideas* are eternal and are present in the soul before birth, there are only two possible psychological states: one in which the individual is ignorant or mad, and one in which he is enlightened. The senses contribute nothing to true knowledge, and so the mere experiences of a lifetime may find the old man as deeply in the cave as a child. Aristotle, forfeiting this binary conception and willing to accept the facts of everyday experience, advanced a dynamic theory of psychological development. As an associationist, he recognized the role of practice and rewards and punishments in learning and memory. As a social observer, he noted the differences among the young, the mature, and the aged as regards emotion, reason, courage, loyalty, motivation. He knew that senility brought a decline to the faculties of perception and, consistent with his larger theory, this necessarily produced changes in all spheres of intellectual endeavor. For Aristotle, growth and decay were the abiding correlates of the natural world, including man. While some rational principle may survive the grave, the soul and its more prosaic faculties would not. The origins of reason were to be found in our biological character, in the progression of our development, in the commerce between mind and sense. Things that exist, exist for a purpose, and our purpose is to be, to become, to reason, and to die. That there is a Prime Mover responsible for setting the machinery in motion, a Cosmic Reason that has the goal of life in its Cosmic Mind, was taken by Aristotle as truths with all the persuasion of the syllogism. Not even Anaxagoras argued as compellingly for destiny as a rational principle. But with all this, Aristotle never conveyed the optimism of the Socrates of the *Phaedo*. For Aristotle, the affairs of man and of the Prime Mover are separated by an unrelenting breach. There is a plan but one not likely to disclose itself. Reason evolves, experience teaches, and societies, like each of us, come and go. Stoicism is on the horizon.

The Problem of Conduct

It is in Book VII of his *Politics*[23] that Aristotle made the principles of statecraft and those of individual excellence indistinguishable. If Plato chose his *Republic* to serve as an enlarged model of the individual, Aristotle's attention to the individual was almost invariably a preliminary stage leading to a discussion of the State. For him, man is first *"a political creature whose nature is to live with others"* (*Nicomachean Ethics* [1169b]). Every action of the individual (*Nicomachean Ethics*, 1094a) and the State (*Politics* [1252a]) aims at some good; otherwise, the action is involuntary and therefore to be judged either as accidental or performed in ignorance (*Nicomachean Ethics* [1110b]). This position, that all voluntary actions have some good as their goal, is but an instance of Aristotle's general teleological theory of nature. Over the centuries this theory has fallen on bad times, often because of a failure to appreciate either Aristotle's statement of it or the facts of nature it was designed to explain. Since it is an integral feature of his social, political, and psychological speculations, this is a convenient place to pause and analyze it.

It is principally in the first Book of the *Posterior Analytics* (especially [73a–75b]), Book II of the *Physics* [196a–197b], and Book I of the *Metaphysics* (all) that Aristotle states his position on causation and on the theory of *necessity*. His position is maintained consistently, so for convenience we can examine the version of it offered in the *Physics*. In the second chapter of Book II there appears an almost perfunctory acknowledgement that things can be said to be understood only when the causes are known. Aristotle offers the distinction between knowing *that* and knowing *why* [194b] and then goes on to discuss the different senses in which we say we know the "why" of an event. There are four:

1. If we examine a statue, there is a sense in which we attribute the cause of it to the substance of which it is made, for example, stone. Here, we have what Aristotle referred to as the *material* cause.

2. The difference between a lump of stone and a statue is that the latter has a certain essence or form—not any single one, but one that is not random. If we refer to this as the cause of the statue, we are invoking the Aristotelian notion of a *formal* cause. The same is true when we answer questions like "Why is the sum of the angles of a triangle equal to 180 degrees?" The answer is, of course, that a triangle is *defined* as a figure containing 180 degrees; that is, it is the *essence* of triangle or its *formal* cause.

3. Returning to the statue, one might attribute the cause of it to the changes produced by the hammer and chisel. Blow by blow, these changes lead to the finished work. A causal explanation based upon these actions expresses what Aristotle called the *efficient* cause.

4. If we stand in the Piazza Navona and ask someone the cause of the *Fountain of the Rivers*, it is not likely that the reply will include references to stone, definitions, or hammers. More likely a one-word answer will be given: *Bernini*. The cause of these statues is the sculptor's vision or genius: that which he intended even before selecting the stone, the site, or the cutting tools. In this sense, the cause of *Fountain of the Rivers* is the goal or end of the artist. This is what Aristotle meant by the *final* cause.

The concept of *final* cause is the teleological element in Aristotle's theory of causation and the element that Medieval theologians and philosophers exploited in giving Christian belief a scientific cast. Science, at least since the influence of David Hume (Chapters 7, 10), has restricted itself to the study of *efficient* causes and has viewed any form of teleological explanation with whimsy, contempt, or indifference. Putting aside such matters of taste, we must contend with *final causes* here as, indeed, we must in nearly every walk of life except experimental science. A jury presented with a first-degree murder case must decide whether the cause of Jane Doe's murder was John Smith's *intention*. That is, did Jane die because John went to the drawer, removed a revolver, drove to Jane's house, knocked on the door, entered, picked her out in a crowd and shot her; or did she die merely because the bullet penetrated her aorta? If the judgment is that the cause of Jane's death was aortic destruction, then the bullet is guilty and John goes free. Briefly put, as long as we hold people responsible for their actions, we are accepting the Aristotelian notion of final causes; that is, the cause of the action was an ulterior goal of the actor.

The inference made by Aristotle was that since final causes are common in the affairs of men and since men are part of nature, nature too must possess final causes. On this account, birds build nests in order to care for the young, and elephants kneel in the presence of kings as a sign of respect! From a modern perspective, Aristotle may (again) appear naive. We are tempted to excuse him, in a patronizing way, for failing to realize that motives and intentions are themselves (efficiently) caused by immediately preceding agents. Bernini's vision, after all, can be traced back to his training, his religion, the price of stone, and so forth. But the Aristotle of *De Anima* and *Politics* was quite aware of "conditioning" and "behavior modification" and surely would have argued that these are irrelevant to the issue. The issue is not *how* a given goal or intention was established. Rather, the issue or proposition is that outcomes are never completely understood until the final cause is apprehended, no matter what "caused" the final cause. That we may be "conditioned" to prefer Bach to Berlioz does not eliminate the fact of the preference.

We observed above that final causes appear regularly in daily life except for that part of daily life which some people spend doing experiments. We mean to include theoretical science in those enterprises that make appeals to final causes. When we account for the "red shift," for example, in terms of an "expanding universe" we are saying that event-A occurs because of a condition of nature that is lawful, immutable, and "written," as it were. Now Aristotle may have it that nature *intends* to expand, but this can be set aside either as an unknown or as a semantic problem attaching to the word *intention*. Without laboring over the virtues and vices of teleological explanations, we might merely examine a modern discussion of embryological development or evolutionary theory or cosmology to ascertain whether science has rid itself of final causes.

Aristotle committed himself to final causes, but had a nearly modern position on the *necessitarian* theory of causation. We will see in Chapter

7 that an essential feature of science since Hume is the rejection of necessitarian explanations. Since the question is treated in that chapter, only a sketch of it is given here.

To say that A occurs for an end or toward some purpose is to say that A does not occur accidentally. But in saying that it occurs for an end, must we conclude that it occurs necessarily? Aristotle tells us that most of the pre-Socratic philosophers explained natural events as *necessary* outcomes (*Physics*, II, 8 [198b]), by which they meant that natural laws govern natural events. He cites Empedocles' theory of natural selection (a loose approximation to Darwin's), which explains the growth and shape of teeth in terms of functions that promote survival. Animals not possessing the proper teeth perish (ibid). Empedocles is arguing for natural *necessity* in the sense of a law or principle of nature but would argue against final causes; for example, it does not rain *so that* the corn will grow, but because moisture, drawn up from the earth's surface and cooled necessarily produces rain. Empedocles' account is in complete accord with the contemporary aversion to final causes, but it conflicts with the contemporary rejection of necessity and, on this latter point, Aristotle proves to be the futurist. By modern (post-Humean) lights, he correctly abandons the necessitarian account, contending that

"what is necessary . . . is necessary on a hypothesis; it is not a result necessarily determined by antecedents." (*Physics* [200a]).

The paradox is that one so able to adopt a skeptical position on necessity is so unable to abandon teleology. Perhaps the explanation is to be found in Aristotle the political theorist—the man who proves that many different forms of government (i.e., *efficient causes*) can have and can produce the same end (i.e., final causes). Since men and States are not constrained (necessarily) to achieve their ends by one mode only, why assume that the balance of nature is? Perhaps we get the clearest picture of pragmatism joined to teleology in this passage:

"It is absurd to suppose that purpose is not present because we do not observe the agent deliberating. Art does not deliberate. If the ship-building art were in the wood, it would produce the same results *by nature*." (*Physics* [199b])

Aristotle here discerns the ultimate failure of the necessitarian position: it cannot account either for error or for genius. All events will seem necessary until exceptions are noted. And, by denying purpose, the necessitarian will have to find the ship in the wood, that is, without the ship builder.

Eventually the necessitarian and the teleological propositions must merge. Whether things are as they are by necessity or by design, the ultimate outcome is never in doubt. We may not know what it is, but we can be sure, on either account, *that* it is. Thus, even in his *Physics,* with a lusty attack on necessity, Aristotle laid the foundations for the coming ages of Stoic resignation. This, of course, was not his design.

We are now able to return to the Aristotelian approach to conduct and governance, an approach stripped of many of the Platonic ingredients. In abandoning the necessitarian theory, Aristotle was able to disclaim the nativistic theory of virtue: *"None of the moral virtues arises in us by nature"* (*Nicomachean Ethics, II,* 1 [19–20]). In its place, he introduced the empiricistic alternative: *"We are made perfect by habit"* (ibid). The perfection in question was the good defined as *"activity of the soul in accordance with virtue"* (ibid., I, 7 [1098a]).

Virtue in the Aristotelian system consists of intellectual and moral dispositions. The former is divided into philosophical wisdom and intelligence. The moral dispositions are those that conduce to liberalism and tolerance (ibid., [1103a]). Both classes of virtue result from "study and care" [1099b] and from teaching, growth, and habit. Aristotle even refers to the roots of the *Ethics* in the word *ethos* (εθως), which means habit or an exercised skill [1103a].

Opposing the central role given to the passions by members of the *Academy*, Aristotle insisted that all virtue is based on intention and choice, and since acts impelled by passion are involuntary the passions do not figure in an account of virtue [1106a]. Nor was he patient with idle speculation as a putative form of virtue. The virtuous man is one who *acts* virtuously because he intends to; that is, virtue is his goal and is, therefore, the final cause of his behavior [1105b]. Consistent with this behavioristic criterion was Aristotle's conviction that actions aim at pleasure and avoid pain [1104b]. This pattern is established in infancy and is therefore very difficult to alter [1105a]. Only rigorous education can succeed in transforming pleasure-seeking into virtue-seeking conduct [1179b–1180a].

Traces of Platonism can be found not only in the definition of the good as an accord between the soul and virtue (i.e., a kind of harmony) but also in Aristotle's emphasis on moderation. Virtue, he asserts, is *"a mean between two vices"* [1107a]: excess and deficiency. The virtuous life is one guided by Aristotle's golden mean. Vice in the person and the State is invariably an expression of excess or deficiency and an extreme expression of that, which in moderate degree, is an absolute good. The good monarchy, transformed by excess, becomes tyranny; aristocracy becomes oligarchy; timocracy, in which political power is based on property, becomes democracy [1160b].

The *Politics* was written as an adjunct to the *Nicomachean Ethics*. The former was supposed to be the practical expression of the latter's theoretical foundations. Yet when the two are read at one sitting, there are important contradictions. In the *Ethics*, Aristotle has founded the moral dispositions on the empirical base of experience and instruction. They do not exist "by nature," nor are they half-real *Ideas* or *Forms*. They are habits and they are instilled by education and steady application. When we transport this theoretical position to the pragmatic concerns of the *Politics*, the mismatch is astonishing, for now we are faced with shallow defenses of slavery, hereditary superiority, and the fecklessness of women [1253b–1255b]. Aristotle notes that virtuous men do not always have virtuous sons [1255b], but apart from these brief intervals of lucid consistency with the *Ethics*, he is drawn into the hopeless task of defending a hereditarian politics with an empiricistic ethics. For whatever value the *Politics* has had for political science, it is useless as a social psychology. There are brilliant analyses of the strengths and weaknesses of various forms of government, but even these are so infected with Platonistic stereotypes of human beings as to be of historical consequence only. One is forced to look beyond the scholarship for the cause, but this is always perilous. A few unanswered questions will suffice. Was the *Politics* a defense of Alexander against the Athenian democratic movement? Was the hopeful empirical outlook of the *Ethics* at variance with Hellenization? Is the *Politics* an elaborate, if unconscious, argument against ever having to grant the franchise to the endless line of slaves manufactured by the Macedonian triumphs?

If there is a place for "psycho-historical" analysis, this is not it. No one can embrace the whole of the human condition and remain unerringly consistent throughout. Aristotle's divorce from the Platonists was never resolute and never final. The *Politics* assailed the numbing features of the communalism of the *Republic* but argued for a curriculum nearly identical with Plato's. It insisted that the public welfare was the State's first obligation while contending that the individual exists for the State. Deformed children were to be killed, and abortions performed to limit population, while the dark Dorian rhythms would instill courage and fortitude in the survivors. On every page, the ghost of Plato casts gloomy shadows: grudging praise of Spartan might, the weakness engendered by a maritime fighting force, virtue as its own reward, speculation as the ultimate pleasure. Pedantry has submerged genius but has stopped short of polemic. One almost gets the impression of the *Lyceum* competing with the *Academy* for funds and for students by displaying how useful it is as a "think-tank": *tell us the government you want or want to overthrow and we will take it under advisement.* This impression is the more vivid because of the uncommon clarity of the *Politics*. Except for a few very minor works, there is nothing in the corpus of Aristotelian scholarship more fit for general consumption. It would not be surprising if *this* were the work that Alexander preferred not to be published. It should have been written by a Roman and, in fact, it was rewritten some years later by Cicero, the Stoic lawyer who helped Rome administer the world.

The Aristotelian Legacy

No figure prior to René Descartes was as important to the history of Psychology as Aristotle. His most general contribution was to locate the intellectual and motive features of mind in the natural sciences. He did this by advancing a psychobiological theory of the perceptual and rational faculties. While his own version of Empiricism did not go so far as to submit scientific truths merely to confirmation by the senses, it did establish the validity and importance of the world of sense. In the process, Aristotle presented the senses themselves as objects of study.

In this same empiricistic vein, Aristotle invented the first laws of learning, loosely drawn around the principle of association and animated by a pleasure principle. Except for his retreat in the *Politics*, he consistently emphasized the part played by early experience, education, practice, and habit in the formation of the psychological dispositions. In this way, he presented human psychology as a *developmental* subject, not one (Platonically) reducible to a few great truths.

His effect on science in general has aroused much speculation, and it was certainly a mixed effect. Subsequent scholars invested his works with unchallengeable authority for which, of course, Aristotle is not to blame. He promoted a rationalistic attitude in those who would seek the "first principles" of things—and on this the history of Science must vindicate him—but this attitude soon was extended to matters that Aristotle himself treated empirically. He recognized that necessity exists in nature only as the major premise of a syllogism, a view not fully appreciated again until the nineteenth century (see Chapter 10). Although his doctrine of final causes became a central theme in religious controversy, his fourfold theory of causation was of indisputable value to generations of scientists. And, on a loose reading, even the final causes are not alien to theoretical science as long as they are theologically neutral.

Aristotle lived at the end of Greece's Classical epoch and his works are a fitting tribute to the names that made this age what it was. And what it was, in fact, was nothing short of the birth of Western civilization. He labored to assemble and dissect all that was known and knowable. Had his effect upon us been less, we would not be so proud to discover his errors. It may be true, as one critic has insisted, that

> "practically every advance in science, in logic, or in philosophy has had to be made in the teeth of the opposition from Aristotle's disciples."[24]

But neither science nor logic nor philosophy is easily conceivable without him.

We have criticized his *Politics* as departing not only from a healthy empiricistic outlook but as sanctioning the cruelest forms of subjugation and elitism. What we have been less careful to note, however, is the place of the *Politics* in the development of that attitude upon which any system purporting to be civilized must rest: *constitutionalism*. It may indeed be the case that the *Politics* was but a justification for all that Alexander had done and was likely to do. There is, for example, evidence of a lost book of Aristotle's entitled *de Monarchia*. While careful to avoid direct attacks on the democratic zeal of Demosthenes and his followers, Aristotle saw all too clearly the consequences of substituting individual rights for social responsibility. In both the *Politics* and the *Nicomachean Ethics* he struggled to balance the rights of the citizen and the needs of the State. The particular balance he achieved depended of course upon the view he held of man's essential nature and the State's essential function. In considering man to be innately rational, inquisitive, and social, he was given to believe that discipline, self-sacrifice, and principled authoritarianism would find universal endorsement. Only those lacking reason (e.g., the "Natural Slave") would rebel. The ghastly circularity of this view would naturally lead to the assertion of nautral rights based upon birth—rights, which if challenged, could be challenged only by those who lacked the wit to recognize the inherent justice of it all. Notwithstanding the foregoing, however, Aristotle was undeviating in his support of a society ruled by law, a law ruled by ethics, and an ethics whose first principle was the welfare of the citizen. It is this interconnection among society, law, ethics, and the public good that comprises constitutionalism.

Alexander and the Prelude to Rome

Seeking to Hellenize the world, Alexander succeeded in diluting the power, influence, and identity of the Greek city-states. Their ultimate retreat to insignificance took the better part of two centuries, but by the year of his death (323) the outcome was clear.

Alexander is one of the most complex of historical personalities. Plutarch and other commentators described his mother, the beautiful Olympias, as a woman of schizophrenic suspiciousness and ambition. She has been implicated in her husband's death both directly and as a conspirator. For years, she maintained a separate residence in her native Epirus (modern Albania), consorting with divines and snakes as Philip II assembled his armies. Her influence on Alexander must have been considerable. If, as we are told, he came to consider himself a descendant of the gods, it could not have been an attitude inspired either by Philip II or Aristotle. We might even explain his comfort in otherwise strange Eastern settings in terms of childhood exposure to the cultism and mystical rites to which Olympias was drawn.

That Alexander may have hated his father for leaving him too few worlds to conquer is not entirely farfetched, for Philip II was a great and successful commander whose forces had withstood and nearly routed those of Persia. But Philip was merely a general. Alexander was a general, a missionary, and a prophet. His plan was to organize the known world around a set of philosophical propositions and to ensure its evolution under the guiding light of Hellenic virtue. Nothing was to obstruct his program. He overcame the greatest forces of the world: Persia, Lydia, Egypt, Syria, Thebes, all of Greece. Each conquest was followed by the appointment of administrative officers—usually natives—and the establishment of economic and cultural policies. His captains were betrothed to Eastern princesses, and the soldiers were commanded to marry the natives. He himself returned from his greatest triumph married to the daughter of Darius.

More than any prior figure in Western history, Alexander etched in the minds of his contemporaries that idea which is embodied in the term *individualism*. Cities were raised at his bidding. The Hellenic world received from his victories a profusion of gold and silver enormous even by contemporary standards. From the palaces at Babylon, Persepolis, and Susa alone he extracted the equivalent of some half-billion current dollars. In less than a decade, he transformed the Mediterranean economy from a collection of relatively independent bartering communities into a colossus of international finance. Trade routes were opened and widened; joint citizenship was established by law; merchants, bankers, lenders, and actuaries now competed with and soon overshadowed farmers, and even the Aristocrats. The Empire extended from Sicily to northern India; from the southern reaches of the Nile valley to the foothills of the Caucasus. A period of wealth and opportunity was launched for which there had been no precedent. The casualty, ironically, was the Greek way of life. As the Macedonian empire expanded almost beyond imagination, the once proudly independent city-state retreated to insignificance. None of the city-states possessed a natural resource to compete significantly with the trading nations. None of them, not even Athens or Sparta, could field an independent army of consequence. Moreover each of them, and Athens especially, hastened the waning of its stature by absorbing itself in intramural political bickering and intrigues. These cities, which had throughout their histories struggled so intensely to preserve their separate characters, were now abruptly exposed to a torrent of foreign influences. Against this blossoming international outlook, the provincialism of the city-state descended from the quaint to the ludicrous.

For a time, in cultural and intellectual matters, Athens retained a privileged position. Both the weight of history and the loyalty of Alexander guaranteed it. But soon, even Athens was more of a museum, an aesthetic resort, than a city still evolving. Money was to be made in the East, not in Athens, and her population diminished proportionately. The year before he died, Alexander paused briefly one afternoon in the little Egyptian fishing town of Rhacotis and announced to an incredulous entourage that he had decided this village would be the capital of the world. He lived long enough to lay the general plan and his successor, Ptolemy I, materialized it: *Alexandria.* By 200 this city contained the greatest library, the most respected scholars, the finest craftsmen, and many of the most wealthy families in the known world. It was now to Alexandria that one sailed to read Aristotle or to attend the plays of Sophocles. And as these Athenian creations were displayed and savored at the head of the Nile, wild flowers began to cover the steps of the Acropolis.[25]

We have no way of knowing how Alexander conceived of Hellenization. If he intended to fashion a Greek world with Athens at its geographic center, he clearly failed. If he hoped to bring Greek thought to the "barbarians" and to convert them thereby to the spirit of democratic individualism, he failed resoundingly. The same may be said if his scheme was to ensure the future of the Athenian way by casting its seeds broadly and entrusting their nurturance to an invincible army. The world immediately after his death absorbed and transformed the Hellenic spirit. Its geographic center was one with its economic center—first Egypt and then Rome. Moreover, if a conversion occurred, it was not in the intended direction. The Persian satrap did not renounce his loyalty to the Great King and embrace Athenian statism. More typically, he availed himself of joint citizenship (*isopolitaea*), marched to Athens with a case of gold coins, and assumed instant membership in the Aristocratic class. And, with regard to preserving the Athenian way, Alexander's generalship could not oppose the drift of history. Athen's energy was no longer sufficient to protect her position in the world. Whereas Alexander may have seen in Aristotle the flowering of Athenian culture, it was in fact ending with Aristotle.

What Alexander did achieve was the establishment of a rational approach to the problems of the world. In this he outstripped Pericles, which may be no more than to say that Aristotle was a better political scientist than Anaxagoras. He and his successors recognized cities as moral agents founded on law, preserving order, and erecting institutions able to enrich life through culture and commerce. This, of course, is the essence of Hellenism and, to the extent that contemporary Western life strives for or enjoys these conditions, Alexander must receive a share of the credit. He died much too soon to be recognized as an architect of these ultimate developments. In terms of direct, personal influence, he can only be accorded second honors: the honors reserved for one who keeps certain options available until other and more successful figures come along. The options kept alive by Alexander were Hellenic options and, had he failed in this, Western evolution would have suffered a potentially fatal setback. He did not convert the East, but he did neutralize it and thereby safeguarded those precious creations of the Athenian genius which would prove to be irresistible to the next great empire, that of Rome.

The Stoic and Epicurean Systems

In the previous chapter we noted the pre-Socratic interest in the physical properties of the world and contrasted this interest with the value-oriented philosophy of Socrates and his disciples. The pre-Socratics of Ionia developed their philosophical systems in a climate of commerce and growing prosperity. Socrates and the Academy of Plato flourished in the aftermath of the humiliating Athenian defeat at the hands of Sparta. While we must resist the allure of mechanical laws of causation in history, we must also acknowledge the regularity with which materialistic philosophies prosper in periods of empire and with which spiritualistic-idealistic philosophies emerge in the wake of destruction. With notable exceptions, intellectuals are apologists as well as critics, and so-called systems of thought are very often little more than rationalizations of the prevailing facts of life. The influence operates in both directions: political and economic forces affect the character of philosophy, and the latter works to maintain or modify those outlooks and institutions that define a period.

Democritus (c. 460–370), an influential contemporary of Plato's, had tried to promote a radical, materialist philosophy in the years following the Peloponnesian ordeal. He was the father of *Atomism*, teaching that Nature and her subjects were no more than aggregations of particles of matter distributed in infinite space. At the time, Democritus was held to be a skeptic. Today he would, no doubt, be judged guilty of a cliché. His failure to be taken seriously by the Socratics was not due to his being provably wrong but to his being provably irrelevant. The fundamental challenge to the Athenian philosopher from 404 B.C. to 350 B.C. was to explain the demise of Athenian power and to lay the groundwork for Athens' rebirth. *Atomism*, in this setting, was useless. Similarly, by 300 the world had neither a use for nor ready exemplars of the Platonic *Ideas* or *Forms*. Alexander was the first bona fide potentate of the West and was followed by men of even greater organizational talent. From 300 B.C. to the first century of the Christian era the Western world was Imperial. Its defining ethic was expansionism. Its language, accordingly, was the language of law, administration, and finance. The voices of philosophy that speak for this period are those of the Stoics and the Epicureans.

The founders of the Stoic and Epicurean movements were, respectively, Zeno of Citium (340–265) and Epicurus of Samos (342?–270), who established their schools in Athens. Each was influenced by the teachings of Diogenes the *Cynic* (412?–323)—Diogenes, who broke his only bowl when he saw a child drinking with cupped hands—Diogenes the enemy of pomp and privilege, as hostile to the Platonic *Ideas* as he was to Platonic elitism. From Diogenes, we may surmise that Zeno borrowed the naturalistic character of Stoic philosophy: the life of man is a life in and with nature, loyal to the laws of nature, passed in simple harmony with the seasons. This bridge from the Cynics to the Stoics is to be noted but quickly crossed, for the Cynics never approached the development of a coherent philosophical system, whereas Zeno and his successors did.

The philosophies taught by Zeno and Epicurus in Athens came to have their greatest impact not on the Greek but on the Roman mind. Indeed, although these two compatible philosophies evolved in Athens, they were not Athenian in their principal philosophical features. To be sure, each carried traces of Platonic and Aristotelian influence, particularly the Plato of the *Laws* and the Aristotle of the *Nicomachean Ethics*. Zeno and Epicurus were ethicists even more than they were philosophers. But unlike Aristotle, who succeeded in keeping his *Physics* and his *Ethics* apart, Zeno, Epicurus, and their disciples embraced a philosophical *monism* that had not been seen since the pre-Socratics. Their philosophies drew inspiration from nature (φυσης) such that government, reason, perception, the entirety of the human enterprise were to be comprehended in physical terms.

While not Athenian, the Stoic and Epicurean philosophies do reflect the evolution of Greek theological attitudes which, as we have noted, were only gently touched by the *Academy* and the *Lyceum*. As Greek economy and philosophy evolved, so too did the Greek religious outlook.

In his classic essay, *From Religion to Philosophy*,[26] F. M. Cornford has traced this evolution from that early Homeric period which found the gods obedient to destiny (*Moira*) and at the mercy of chance (*Lachesis*) to the era of Pericles, by which time reason had replaced destiny, and Zeus had arrogated to himself absolute power over the affairs of men and gods. In this same development, the earliest concept of law (*nomos*) as a dispenser (*nomeus*) of one's fair share or just proportion became transformed into the belief that the *will* of Zeus was the *law* of nature.

Even from this all too superficial sketch of the changes that took place in the popular religious outlook from the sixth to the fourth centuries, we can discern the fundamentalist or revivalist tone of Stoicism. The Stoic philosopher saw his contemporaries as having wandered too far from the older and purer respect for *Moira, Lachesis, Nomos*. While retaining the current emphasis upon the will, they insisted that its freedom was of a limited sort: we are free only as long as our will is reconciled to destiny and harmonized with the immutable *nomos*. Thus, in the *Vatican Fragments*[27] Epicurus urges that nature is not to be violated but obeyed (F. XXI); that we must not complain about what we lack but realize that all we have is the gift of fortune (F. XXXV); that death is our common bond and shared future (F. XXX). In this same tradition but four hundred years later, Epictetus (A.D. 60–120) summarized the central idea with that moving simplicity that defines the Stoic mind:

"Never say about anything, 'I have lost it,' but only, 'I have given it back.' "[28]

From its origins in the fourth century to its last and most eloquent spokesman, the Emperor Marcus Aurelius (A.D. 121–180), the Stoic philosophy struggled to foster a moral commitment while adhering to physicalism. The brilliant Lucretius (died 54 B.C.)—who anticipated Darwin, who proposed conservationist laws of matter and momentum, who rested his evidence on the veracity of common sense and tutored perception, and who scoffed at unavoidable death—this Lucretius, whose book[29] attempts nothing less than an explanation of all that exists and occurs, can offer not a sentence of advice to Caesar and Pompey. He cannot tell us how to distinguish the just act from the unjust, nor can he discover any final cause of life other than the grave. Even Marcus Aurelius, whose *Meditations*[30] were to teach us those principles of conduct and good taste that might bring some order to our lives, finally offers little more than a paean to quiet resignation.

It is often averred that Stoicism was in some way natural to the Roman mind, to the spiritual and political character of the Empire. But Stoicism was a varied system whose major architects focused on different problems and wrote in different periods. Moreover, there are points of conflict not only among the Stoics but within the writings of a given spokesman. Still, each one does reveal a side of Roman psychology, and we will benefit from a review of the connection between Stoic thought and the facts of Roman life.

The popularity of the early Stoics in Rome is explicable in terms of two abiding features of the Roman epoch: law and materialism. These are not easily reconciled. Law, if it is to rise above the mere threat of reprisal, must be principled. It must make logical and cognitive contact with what the citizen believes to be right and wrong. As a form of constraint, it must justify itself in terms of a higher good. Materialism, in its commoner forms, conduces to a practical frame of mind. Actions are evaluated in cost-benefit terms where the highest good can be assigned a price. The dilemma facing the Roman of the third and second centuries was no less than the conflict between historic moral restraint and sudden opportunities for colossal wealth. Rome, in its religion and society, had asserted the virtue of a quiet and conservative republican life. Rome, as a limitless empire, made the goods and resources of the entire world accessible to a crafty and acquisitive citizen. We can set against this tension the possibilities held out by Stoic and Epicurean maxims:

1. Nothing happens without a cause.
2. What we possess and what we lack are, equally, expressions of fortune.
3. Our brief lives are spent in search of little pleasures and the avoidance of great pain.
4. The ultimate reality of the universe, our souls included, is *atomic*. Matter, neither created nor destroyed, distributes itself according to Nature's laws.
5. The world is pretty much as we see it, since both it and our senses are merely matter in commerce.

These propositions and their easily multiplied corollaries permitted the Roman, in his public defense of national policy and his private justification of personal conduct, to bring traditional morality and current fancies into easy accord. The Stoics all agreed that prophecy was impossible and this, coupled with a necessitarian position on natural events, could only engender *situationism*. That is, if we can't predict the future, but at the same time the future is determined, we can neither praise nor blame ourselves for the manner in which conditions come to be. The right or wrong of an event is a product of the situation, and each person judges it by his best lights. No prophet can do it for him. As for these lights, they are the lights of reason that illuminate the knowable laws of nature and save us from fear and frustration.

Stoic materialism could not accept a transcendent soul. To believe that the soul can affect the body requires that the soul be destructible. Personal immortality, therefore, is out of the question, as is fear of punishment in the afterlife. Accordingly, man's only concern must be with life as it is lived from day to day. The goal is happiness which, in the last analysis, is freedom from pain. Since the quest for fame and power and riches usually leads to frustration and grief, the Stoic recommendation is for moderation. As with Socrates, Plato, and Aristotle, the Stoic emphasizes contemplation as the means by which true happiness is secured. Unlike Plato, the Stoics endorsed contemplation not for the good of an immortal soul but for comfort in a troubled life. The Roman aristocracy proceeded to study philosophy with all the enthusiasm one brings to other pastimes. In their thirst for culture, they imported hundreds of Greek scholars and thereby furthered the cause of Hellenization. Cicero stamped Roman law with Stoic reasonableness, and Nero traduced the lessons of Epicurus into a grotesque caricature. Situationism, ethical relativism, and materialism lent righteous complacency to periods of prosperity but left the Roman morally defenseless when more powerful forces began to dismantle the Empire. As Rome approached the peak of her achievement, Lucretius could observe that

"nearly everything men need for life lies right within their grasp and . . . existence is safe and sound."[31]

But two centuries later, when Augustan greatness had receded and the barbarians' steps grew louder, Marcus Aurelius would look back over the entire epoch and explain:

"Thou hast endured infinite troubles through not being contented with thy ruling faculty."[32]

The Stoics had insisted on a *monism*, which not only reduced human psychology to physical matter but united all the faculties—perceptive, locomotor, appetitive—into a rational whole. As long as Rome made men happy and kept them safe, the Stoic outlook remained the national faith. By the second century of the modern era, Rome was failing. Her government was steeped in petty corruption and endless intrigues. Her crops were failing and her gold reserves depleted. Reason could not deter the barbarian, nor could materialism provide salvation. The Age of Faith was at hand.

Roman Law

The last king of Rome in the ancient world was Tarquinius, deposed in 510. Just as sixth-century Greece formed its democracy from the conflicts between aristocrat and farmer, the Roman *Republic* was never more than a tense peace between the Patrician and the Plebeian. Rome had gained her safety and independence in Italia from the tough resolve of the common people, who demanded political power as their fee for saving the nation.

The king's place was taken by two magistrates, the *Consuls*, who served one-year terms. Initially, the Assembly (of Plebeians) and the Senate (of Patricians) were bodies of substantially unequal influence, the latter having legislative responsibilities and the former having little more than a forum for opinion. However, by 367 the law required that one of the Consuls be a Plebeian, and by 267, the decisions of the Assembly had the force of law.

When we credit Rome with giving Law to the Western world, we acknowledge a debt not to the ancient framers of the Roman Republic but to the Roman emperors and legal scholars of the third to the sixth centuries of the Christian era, that is, from Gaius in the second century to the Emperor Justinian in the sixth. Except for England's Common Law, which resisted Romanization with incomplete success, the body of European civil law has drawn its character nearly entirely from the Justinian Codes.[33] It was only after the Republic became an *Empire*— that is, with the accession of Octavian (Caesar Augustus) in 27 B.C.— that a carefully worded and efficiently interpretable body of laws became essential. Codification proceeded at the same rate as imperial expansion, beginning in the second century B.C. and culminating some five hundred years later. The most frenzied period of law writing was that set off roughly from the conquering of Carthage (201 B.C.) to Constantine's displacement of the capitol from Rome to Byzantium (A.D. 330).

Law limits, and what it limits is the access one party can have to the property or life or opportunity of another. The *Codes* of Justinian were but summaries of the limits articulated by a thousand years of thought and compromise. The famous *Twelve Tables* were ordered into existence in 451 B.C. by Romans who refused any longer to be taxed or punished through *ex post facto* judgments of the magistrates. Here in the market, stamped in bronze, were the limits on private conduct and the penalties for exceeding them. Even in this first publication of the Roman sense of law a distinction was made between those acts that threatened the State itself and those that damaged only another citizen. Thus, with the *Twelve Tables*, the separation of criminal law and civil law (i.e., the law of torts) was effected. Murder, which the Greeks had treated as a crime committed by one clan against another and which, accordingly, called for revenge against an entire family (or even town), was, in the Roman *Tables*, a crime against the State. Guilt was restricted to the perpetrator. It did not extend either to his relatives or to his descendants.

This difference between Greek custom and Roman law betokens a more fundamental difference in psychological perspective than might appear at first glance. In eliminating group liability, the Romans, if only unconsciously, were asserting *individual* responsibility. A man acts thus and so not because he is a member of this or that *phratry*, not because his father did, not because his entire lineage is stained by *Moira*. He acts as a rational agent and is as guilty for what he violates as he is honored for what he achieves. Under the later Stoic influence, Rome would more consciously expect the sudden appearance of exceptional personalities: those created by Nature to serve for the moment and then pass eternally into the impersonal stuff of the universe. But long before this philosophical rationale was put forth formally, the Romans seem to have been too practical to adopt the rigid hereditarian excesses of Hellas. Far more impressed with national differences, the Greek city-states were overcome by them. Able to recognize similarities, the Roman Republic assimilated and tolerated—even enjoyed—diversity. As a result Rome, at least for a while, seemed to be an Eternal City. The so-called Social War (91–88 B.C.), which gave full Roman citizenship to all Italians, was a brief and relatively bloodless encounter by the standards of civil wars. It serves as still another sign of Rome's pragmatic, utilitarian outlook.

In addition to rejecting group-liability, Roman law contained the concept of "thing-liability," which required that the damaging agent (a slave, a cow, a sword) be turned over to the injured party. This, of course, is individualism of then cosmic and now comic proportion. The idea was Stoic, by way of the Aristotelian *Final Cause*. Each thing has its natural purpose and, in deviating from that end for which it was intended, it is culpable and therefore punishable. (The Medieval court at Bâle, which ordered an egg-laying cock to be executed for conduct unnatural to its intended purpose,[34] displayed a lighter side of the Roman legacy.) In both "thing-liability" and the rejection of group-liability, the Romans showed not so much a respect for individuals as a belief that they were individuals.

Even as the Empire was overrun by the strangest tribes, the world's debt to Rome was acknowledged. Perhaps more than any single item, a published *Code* of the fifth century A.D. best signals both that of Rome which perished and that which has survived. It was titled *Lex Romana Visigothorum*, "The Roman Law of the Visigoths."

By the second century A.D., Roman law fully accommodated the several spheres of influence—interpersonal, international, domestic—through the distinct bodies of law, the *jus civile*, the *jus naturale*, and the *jus gentium*. The first contained those laws specific to individual states. The Roman traveler was expected to abide by Alexandrian codes, the Macedonian by Roman codes, and so forth. Through the Stoic influence, *jus naturale*, or "natural law," had a nearly biological significance. It was a body of law designed to respect the instinctive features of life, that which any given *species* of animal knows by nature. Here, the Aristotelian differentiation between higher law and human law was adopted as was Aristotle's insistence that this higher law was attainable through reason alone. The *jus naturale*, which, to the Roman Stoic, bore the stamp of inevitability, that is, that which *must* be followed, was translated by later Christian thinkers into normative ethics, that which *ought* to be followed. Finally, the *jus gentium* was the law that appeared to be accepted by all civilized nations. Whereas *jus civile* had a local and ethnic character, *jus gentium* seemed universal; for example, injunctions against homicide. The foreigner might plead ignorance of the *jus civile* of an alien city, but not of the *jus gentium* and never of the *jus naturale*. The distinction between *jus gentium* and *jus naturale* was that between custom (Lat. *mos;* Gk. εθως) and imperative (*lex;* νωμως). Again, the Roman sense of *Naturalis* was shaped by the Stoic adoption of Hellenic *Moira; fated* is the close reading.

By the end of the pre-Christian epoch, these careful classifications and eloquently argued legalisms were of little avail. Roman citizenship, now available to nearly anyone who had the good fortune to be defeated by the Roman legions, attracted an awesome diversity of groups to the city. Many were from Egypt and Asia Minor and had a long history of confusing power with divinity. Augustus, who inaugurated the Empire, began that train of emperorships known as the *Principate*, by which is meant, emperor-as-first-citizen. With Diocletian's reign (A.D. 284–305), the *Principate* became the *Dominate*: the emperor as lord, master, judge, jury. Just as Alexander entered Persia as an Athenian and came out a potentate, so the Roman emperor began as a Republican and ended as a god. Stoicism, Platonism, Final Causes, and *jus naturale* performed the rational groundwork for this transition. Masses of superstitious instant-citizens from the Nile Valley, from Thrace and Byzantium, from Persia, conspired with high taxes, civil discord, unemployment, and rebelling slaves to provide the political excuse for fascism disguised as godliness. Long before Alaric's Visigoths sacked Rome, long before Constantine abandoned it, long before a Roman emperor finally was deposed, a small but cohesive group assembled to create a new order based on a very different conception of human destiny. These were the Latin fathers of Christianity whose scholarly writings and moral and ethical prescriptions define the Patristic Age—an age of great faith in God but little in man—

an age seeking to find something of value in a terrible and terrifying world.

References

1. The definitive biography of Aristotle's intellectual development remains Werner Jaeger, *Aristotle: Fundamentals of the History of His Development*, Clarendon Press, Oxford, 1934.

2. Ibid., Ch. 1.

3. Ibid., Ch. 2.

4. Aristotle, *The Protrepticus*, translated by Anton-Hermann Chroust, University of Notre Dame Press, Indiana, 1964.

5. Ibid., p. 9.

6. Ibid., p. 44.

7. Ibid., p. 31.

8. Jaeger, op. cit., Ch. VII, Sec. II.

9. Plutarch's *Lives*, The Modern Library edition, translated by John Dryden and revised by Arthur Hugh Clough, New York, Random House.

10. Aristotle, *Metaphysics*, Book A (I).

11. Ibid. (Bracketed numbers refer to the line of text in the Greek. These numbers are conventionally employed in all translations.)

12. Ibid. Book XIII, 4, 30–33.

13. Ibid.

14. Aristotle, *De Somnis*, Ch. I, 459b; Ch. 3, 462b.

15. Aristotle, *Posterior Analytics*, especially Book II, Ch. 19.

16. Ibid.

17. Aristotle, *Categories*.

18. Aristotle, *History of the Animals*, Book VI, Ch. 3, English translation by A. L. Peck, Harvard, 1970.

19. Aristotle, *On the Heavens*, Book II, Ch. 14.

20. Plato, *Theaetetus* [186]. In *The Dialogues of Plato*, translated by Benjamin Jowett, Random House, New York.

21. Aristotle, *Nichomachean Ethics*, 1153b.

22. Aristotle, *Rhetoric*, 1389a and b.

23. Aristotle, *Politics*, 1252a.

24. Bertrand Russell, *History of Western Philosophy* (p. 202), Simon & Schuster, Clarion Books.

25. An excellent analysis of the economic conditions of the ancient Greek world and the effect on these conditions, and on Athens specifically, produced by the conquests of Alexander is Gustave Glotz's *Ancient Greece at Work*, Norton, New York, 1967.

26. F. M. Cornford, *From Religion to Philosophy: A Study in the Origins of Western Speculation*, Harper & Row, Harper Torchbooks, New York, 1957.

27. A collection of Epictetus' *Fragments*, reprinted from the *Vatican Fragments* appears in *The Stoic and Epicurean Philosophers*, edited by Whitney Oates, Random House, The Modern Library, New York.

28. Ibid., *Epictetus*.

29. Lucretius, *De Rerum Natura*. English translation by Palmer Bovie, New American Library, Mentor Book, New York, 1974.

30. Marcus Aurelius, *Meditations* in *The Stoic and Epicurean Philosophers*, op. cit.

31. Lucretius, *De Rerum Natura*, op. cit., Book VI.

32. Marcus Aurelius, *Meditations*, op. cit.

33. For an excellent review of Roman law and its principled basis, consult *Roman Law* by Barry Nicholas. Clarendon Press, Oxford, 1962.

34. G. G. Coulton, *Life in the Middle Ages*, Vol. III, Macmillan, Inc. New York, 1935.

4

□□□□□□□□□□□□□□□□□□□□□□□□□□□□□□

Patristic Psychology

THE AUTHORITY OF FAITH

Formative Conditions

The Ostragoths, the Visigoths, and the Vandals attacked Rome in waves and occupied various sections of the shrinking Empire. By A.D. 476, when the governance of Rome fell to Odoacer, the German "king," the seat of Empire had already been in the East for more than a century. However, under the *Dominate* of Justinian and the generalship of the Macedonian Belisarius, western expansion of the Empire proceeded swiftly, reclaiming Carthage, the south of Spain, southern Italy, all of Sicily and Sardinia. Thus it is not possible to give a date to the "fall" of the Empire. Gibbon thought it began to fall in the sixth century B.C., and popular histories more or less agree in treating A.D. 476 with uncommon reverence. The fact, of course, is that the city of Rome underwent a cultural and economic decline at least as early as the Social War (92–88 B.C.), and its unique Patrician republicanism was displaced by the democratic reforms of 267 B.C. Rome as the intellectual and spiritual center of the Empire had always been something of a translation, though not a literal one, of Hellenism. Thus, when Constantine set up court on the Bosphorus, he surely was not bringing something solely "Roman" to a people uniquely "non-Roman." He was merely continuing that policy launched six hundred years earlier of securing economic and military gains with the durable protections of Hellenism. It is not inconsequential that Christianity was included in the move, but it is also not the case that this added feature produced any rupture with tradition. A Christian emperor could demand respect and tolerance for the new faith; but this faith, at the time of Constantine, was neither sufficiently organized, nor was it carefully enough argued to affect the salient aspects of urban life. Law was still Roman, economy remained polyglot, and culture ever Greek.

The invading "barbarians" often included statesmen of high quality (Theodoric being a prime example) and were, after all, the rebelling forces of a *Roman* world. Infantries in every period burn more than they build and generally carry on in a way that the term "barbarian" seeks to describe. Soldiers in the Gothic and Vandal armies were no different from those in the later Crusades or, for that matter, those who fought under Pericles or Alexander. But the *Lex Romana Visigothorum* is enough to remind us that conquering forces are also captured, and especially so by cultural and political features more compelling than their own. As the Romans of the third century B.C. worked hard to master Greek, the Gothic leaders of the third and fourth centuries A.D. struggled with Latin, studied law, drafted treaties, and engaged in those varied labors that civilization imposes on rational man. Byzantium and Rome had strong commercial ties, exchanges of diplomats, and written agreements. Rome never was "Vandalized" in the sense in which it had been Hellenized— vandalized, yes, but not Vandalized.

As we discussed in Chapter 1, epochs do not appear and vanish, nor does one lead mechanically to the next, for there is neither "one" nor "the next." Historical processes are organic. The assorted elements of a preceding time are transformed before digestion. The entity so nourished gains strength and life through this assimilation. Just as the grazing animal never appropriates the character of grass, the assimilating culture is never a copy of that upon which it feeds. Rome was Hellenized only in a very general way. Doric, Ionian, and Corinthian architecture, for example, was obviously seminal in the creation of the Roman school, but even the untutored eye quickly notes the differences, just as no one could mistake the Supreme Court building in Washington, D.C., for a work of Pheidias' nor perceive that building as evidence that America had been Hellenized. The Roman Patrician and his sons learned Greek because they aspired to a life of civility and cultivation and believed that Philosophy was a subject conducive to such a life. Roman dramatists also looked to Athens for their models as Cicero did when theorizing on Law and Rhetoric. But we search in vain for a Greek who could file suit for plagiarism against Plautus, Ovid, Terence, Virgil, Cicero, Catullus. Lucretius expressed his debt to Epicurus and Epicurus to Democritus. But in Lucretius, the form is neither proverbial nor didactic; it is poetical. Moreover, it is argued in an entirely different way. Its scope is broader and deeper. *De Rerum Natura* speaks to a different world in a different tongue about eternal problems which are, paradoxically, eternal in a different way. Lucretius did not mimic Epicurus for the simple reason that he knew things that Epicurus did not. To argue otherwise would be to suggest that Einstein's modern contribution was no more than an updating of the ancient Theory of Fluxes.

As the Hellenic epoch survives, so too the Roman period is with us, and the ancient Hellenes and Romans, after recovering from our striking technology, would be quick to discern as much. They would read our essays on political leaders and note that we were still wrestling with the problem of virtue. They would explore our nontechnical articles on an expanding universe, on the divisibility of the atom, on the causes of mental illness and on East-West tensions and be reminded of the *Dialogues*, the Peripatetics, Xerxes, Darius, Alexander, Caesar. Everything would at once seem so different and so very much the same.

The foregoing is not to be construed as a restatement of the bromide *"Nothing is new under the sun."* A great many things are new not only in epochal measures but even daily. The task set for a historical analysis is one of separating the small number of *fundamental* innovations from the staggering multiplicity of trivial ones. Every day, in every nation, legislative bodies write new laws and ordinances that confine or liberate the conduct of citizens. Few of these proscriptions are of historic consequence. Not even every war is historically noteworthy. A historical analysis of psychology must uncover and examine prevailing psychological attitudes, both those explicitly recommended and those silently shared. It must lead to a judgment of the causes and major consequences of these attitudes, the form of their defense, the goals they furthered, and the actions they sought to justify or illuminate. For such an analysis, the emergence of Christianity must be counted as an occurrence whose importance to Psychology is matched, if at all, only by the Hellenic epoch.

Conditions in the first century of Christianity were generally peaceful and prosperous. Roman politics was still enjoying the calm created by Augustus (died A.D. 14). Nonetheless, it was already clear that the Emperors were not going to be able to keep the Empire together indefinitely. Increasingly, their power at home depended upon the good will of the generals. The *Principate*, inaugurated by Augustus, preserved at least the trappings of Republican government in that, as Emperor, Augustus respected the authority of the Constitution. He presented himself and was accepted as *primus inter pares:* first among equals. The expansion of the Empire, however, drew many citizens great distances from Rome and for extended periods. Roman generals, commanding with absolute authority, soon began to affect imperial pretensions and to use the strength and loyalty of their troops for political ends. Emperors expanded the reach of their own authority commensurately and, as noted in the preceding chapter, the *Principate* evolved into the *Dominate*. Increasingly, Emperors adopted the trappings and the substance of kingly office. To keep themselves steeped in riches that ornament such arrogance and to remain on the best terms with their generals and armies, these new Roman Lords imposed unbearable taxes on the Roman citizens. Taxation not only kept the spirit of sedition high but prompted emigration by many of the city's first families.

Corruption grew, as we have come to expect, from climates gripped by moral lassitude at the top. The once vaunted *Lex Romana* degenerated from overuse and self-seeking manipulation. The power of the Assembly was the first to wane, but soon even the Patricians could not rescue the Senate from imperial avarice. Even as early as the *Principate* of Nero (ruled A.D. 54–68) the Senate's authority to ratify legislation had been reduced to utter ritual. Some in the imperial succession even found the step from monarchy to *Divinity* invitingly small.* Constant and inept tampering with the constitution did not simply transform the Republic to a monarchial form of government. (There are, after all, constitutional monarchies.) Rather, it transformed the Roman citizen from one who revered law to one who learned how to evade or exploit its maxims. Philosophers, and especially those Stoic spokesmen whose commitment to natural law was sacred, were quick to perceive the hypocrisies and rationalizations of the leadership. Twice in the second century A.D. they were expelled from Rome, but the effects of four hundred years of Hellenization were ineradicable. There were too many literate, educated, and traditional Romans. They could be controlled but not converted by the will of the Emperor or the might of his guards. Dissension was widespread and public. Its suppression further weakened the resources of the government, not to say the loyalty of the Roman. Moreover, the claims of the Emperor which may have struck the tradition-bound Patrician as outrageous, soon appeared ludicrous in the light of his failure to defend the Empire against barbarian rebellions.

As long as the fortunes of Empire found a direct route back to the first citizens of Rome, there was a willingness to ignore moral and judicial perversions. However, when taxation increased to oppressive heights, when generals in the field openly defied the Emperor's command, when once tame Gothic settlements dismissed imperial edicts, refused to offer tribute, and even scattered the Emperor's Legions, the Roman citizen either abandoned his city or conspired against its ruler. We must emphasize, then, that Constantine's establishment of Byzantium as the capitol did not sacrifice Rome. It merely acknowledged formally what any perceptive person recognized: Rome was an economic shambles lacking the will and the resources to defend herself.

There are many casualties when a culture fails. The citizen who gave

---

* Nero, as is well known, claimed the status of a divinity and, even though he was ultimately scorned by the Romans, the latter were still willing to extend a similar status to his son Galba (Roman emperor A.D. 68–69).

up on Rome was surrendering more than a territory. He was, if only unconsciously, resigning from her philosophy and theology, her art and
letters, her laws, and her customs. Citizenship is a frame of mind, a for-
mula or rule for perceiving the world and one's connection with it. To be
a Frenchman or a German or a Dane is not merely to be born at a certain
latitude or to speak a certain language. It is to live and evolve in a psychological climate whose appeals to one's senses are of a national and historic
sort. It is to spend one's life quietly integrating rhythms, tastes, dances,
folklore, and habits that have parallels but no copies. To be a citizen is
not to be a certain "type" of person (whatever that may mean) but, instead, to have a frame of reference within which one can place and evaluate the diverse possibilities offered by an alien culture. It is not so much
a reluctance to be changed as it is an awareness that X or Y will constitute
a change and to be able, therefore, to decide whether or not to adopt it.
The sense of citizenship is what permits a family to anticipate the conditions of existence that will surround their later years, and their children's years; to be secure, even if constrained, in the knowledge of what
one's peers expect, what one's country will allow, and what one's efforts
will yield. In brief, citizenship confers a fundamental predictableness upon
our lives, so limiting the realm of choice as to make life manageable. If
the fall of Rome is to be dated, it occurred in that indeterminate span
when the man in the street could no longer articulate the protections and
obligations of citizenship, when to be a Roman implied little more than a
geographic accident of birth. Under these circumstances a new spiritual
possibility, a revised way of seeing the world, can claim the interest and
then the loyalty of many. Christianity in its early period had a political
adversary but not a moral one.

   In assaying the early Christian epoch, we must also be wary of adopting
that convention introduced by Renaissance writers of describing the
periods between themselves and Classical antiquity as "Dark" and "Middle." It is worth numbing the senses for a moment by listing the scholars
who filled this putative intellectual void: Epictetus (?60–120?), Origen
(?185–254?), Plotinus (205–270), Porphyry (?232–304), St. Jerome
(?340–420), St. Augustine (354–430), Boethius (480–525), John the Scot
(800/815–877?), St. Anselm (1033–1109), Peter Lombard (1100–1160/
64), Peter Abailard (1079–1142), Robert Grosseteste (1175–1253), Albertus Magnus (?1193–1280), St. Bonaventura (1221–1274), Roger Bacon
(?1215–1294), St. Thomas Aquinas (1225–1274), Duns Scotus (?1266–
1308), William of Ockham (1300–1349). If by a "dark" age we mean one
for which we have no record of lively philosophical speculation, only the
period between Boethius (*floruit* 520) and John the Scot (*floruit* 850)
could possibly qualify. This span of some 330 years is certainly not
longer than the period separating William of Ockham from Hobbes

(1588–1679) or Descartes (1596–1650), and it is this latter span of relative, philosophical inactivity that we revere with the name *Renaissance*.

It can be argued, to be sure, that the list of scholars offered above contains few philosophers of clear superiority; that only St. Augustine and
St. Thomas Aquinas ever came to figure significantly in subsequent philosophical developments. But by the same token, it may be argued that, since
Hobbes, only a handful of philosophers have produced works of unchallengeable durability. Athens at the peak of her intellectual energy and
Rome at hers never could claim general, popular enlightenment. Even in
our own century of compulsory education and high literacy there are
few scholars of truly historic proportion, and relatively few citizens able
to comprehend the essential teachings even of these few.

Philosophy is not the only standard available in gauging the darkness or
brightness of epochs. There is no doubt but that in art and architecture,
the years between (roughly) 500 and 1000 were frighteningly unproductive. Liturgical music and primitive crafts struggled to ornament a growing faith with pale copies of those poems and temples the ancients had
dedicated to their gods. It was not until the twelfth century that the
Christian world could claim near parity with its classical ancestry. The
twelfth-century Gothic cathedral ended five hundred years of architectural quietude as the thirteenth and early fourteenth, through Dante
(1265–1321) and Giotto (1266–1337), ended an interlude of literary and
artistic restraint. But even this disappointing record cannot be explained
simply in terms of intellectual or aesthetic impoverishment and less in
terms of religious orthodoxy or authoritarianism. In regard to the latter,
while the Church grew in wealth and membership under Constantine,
Christian hegemony in the Western world must be dated toward the end
of the so-called Dark Ages and, therefore, the authority of the Church
can hardly be used to account for that which it followed. As late as the
fourteenth century, the king of France was able to arrest an insolent pope
and confine the successors of Peter to the province of Avignon—the
"Babylonian Captivity" of 1309–1377.

All this is to say that whatever may have "darkened" the Western mind
from 500 to 800 was certainly not the mere political power of the Church
of Rome. The influence of Christian teachings was inextricably tied to the
failure of alternative schools and to the inability of political authorities to
protect the people from themselves and from alien forces. The cities of
the early Christian era were economically reckless, morally weak, politically corrupt, and generally destitute of that ineffable tone and energy
that urban life presents to the active mind. Cities afforded neither safety
nor affluence, little law, less order, even less hope. They were abandoned
not merely by many but by most of those who made the cities attractive
in the first place. Emperors, now deified, required coteries of flatterers in

philosophy and the arts. Their official biographers, whose lamentable fore-bearance reaches us through the *Scriptores Historiae Augustae*,[1] have contributed a lasting testimony to those special inanities bred by absolute power.

We are able to review these conditions in several paragraphs, but they required many decades to come about. The Greek language, which, in the Principate of Marcus Aurelius, was still the preferred mode of philosophical and high-cultural expression, was barely heard in Rome by the reign of Justinian. This fact does not support the theory that philosophy and culture failed because of a dearth of Greek scholars; rather, the latter deficiency was only one more sign of a flagging culture. The more telling sign, however, was the spirit of nostalgia that overcame many of the leading scholars and artists, and none more than Epictetus.

Epictetus and the Stoic Bridge to Christianity

It is always tempting to read a good deal into a bygone time by interpreting its incomplete remains. In the present instance, interpretation is aided by very much more than chipped statues and faded urns. By the second century, philosophers were quite self-consciously striving to re-kindle the old values, the old style of life, the Classical perspective. Where art and philosophy both point in the same direction, we can be confident in looking the same way.

Epictetus (c. 70–c. 120) was the last philosopher of that era which might safely be called Classical. He was a Stoic but, more important, one who sought to revive the purest form of Stoicism, the form that prevailed before the movement became bookish and pretentious. His *Discourses* were faithfully transcribed by his constant companion, Arrian, and have reached us almost completely intact.[2] We also have several dozen *Fragments* and his abbreviated *Manual*, the latter being a guide to proper living.

It is the *Discourses* that provide the fullest measure of his system. Revealingly, the philosopher most frequently cited is neither Epicurus nor Cleanthes, that is, the textbook Stoics, but Socrates. Only Socrates, who put his life on the line rather than forfeit his principles, is worthy of the name "philosopher," for the philosopher is not one who says or studies certain things but one who lives a certain kind of life. Plato and Aristotle led active lives. They sought recognition and a role in the affairs of State. Socrates, however, loved the quiet life—the life of contemplation in which passion served reason and the resolute will was his only master.

Epicurus had adopted Atomism in his Stoic (materialistic) belief. The universe as "atoms and a void" was a nearly senseless din orchestrated by gods in conflict and by indifferent Destiny. Man's only hope was for a life reconciled to knowable Natural Law and one passed among friends. While preaching the indestructibility of matter, Epicurus still denied the material soul the ability to retain a meaningful existence once the body "is broken up."

Epictetus, reflecting on Epicurean Materialism, had this to say:

"Epicurus understands as well as we do that we are by nature social beings, but having once placed our good not in the spirit but in the husk which contains it, he cannot say anything different.[3]

This is a fundamental break, a return to *dualism*. Epictetus was committed to a useful philosophy. He scorned those whose lessons were contrary to common sense or private experience. Just as he insisted upon philosophers living the philosophical life and not merely talking about it, he also insisted upon a philosophy that formally acknowledged what every sentient being knew to be true. One such fact, of course, was the reality of the will and its essentially *spiritual* nature. Unlike Epicurus, who reduced prophecy to charlatanism, Epictetus was willing to accept spiritual commerce with the future but condemned those who sought it as weak and fearful (Book II, VII).[4] The Epicurean injunctions against marriage and children were ridiculed by Epictetus as removing the very foundation of social life (Book III, VII).[5] The Platonist suspicion regarding the evidence of the senses was viewed with equal contempt, since Epictetus had little to say to one who

"has sensation and pretends that he has not; he is worse than dead."[6]
(Book I, VI)

In all, Epictetus reasserted the central position of reason in the affairs of life; the indispensability and accuracy of perception when guided by reason; the power of the individual will to withstand the commands of princes and kings; the true happiness of a life devoted to harmony with nature and to rational principles; the transitoriness of wealth, popularity, and worldly power; goodness as the end of human life. To these he added monotheism, convinced, like Aristotle, that heaven must have one ruler as every flock has one shepherd and every family one father.

Marcus Aurelius was greatly influenced by the *Discourses* and, if only for this reason, Rome's "official" philosophy was stoical until well into the third century. However, the Romans themselves had moved some distance from the reserved and resourceful lives advocated by Zeno, Cleanthes, and Epicurus. We are on surer footing to read Epictetus as an example of what philosophy was fighting, not what it was observing. The *literati* among Epictetus' contemporaries were moved more by Horace, Martial, and Juvenal. By a deft corruption of Epicurean teaching, the upper-class Roman of the second century traduced philosophical materialism into a rationale for sexual promiscuity, moral laxity, situationism, and general debauchery. Nero's reign (54–68) had set the tone and, within a half century, Romans forgot that he had been judged an enemy of State and they recalled only that degeneracy was a sign of power.

The Christian Alternative

As the Empire proceeded along the course to its destruction, two radically different remedies were available: Stoic resignation, virtue, and independence, and skeptical indifference and ridicule. The former, for obvious reasons, was unacceptable to the free-living aristocrats whose station in life depended upon the good will of the Emperor. Skepticism, unless reduced to comedy, is always too subtle and too removed to be adopted by the ordinary run of citizens. In declaring man to be basically a *rational* animal (Plato) and a *social* animal (Aristotle), and a *moral* animal (Epictetus), the philosophers of antiquity recognized only generally that he is a *psychological* animal. Thus, to tell him either that his perceptions are always illusory or that they are always correct is to tell him what he knows or firmly believes to be false. To tell him that he is *merely* matter is, in terms of the day-to-day realities of his life, to tell him what is useless. To assure him that Nature's laws will see him through life when Caesar's caprice ever threatens to end his life, when Vandals threaten to detroy his culture, when plague succeeds in killing his children is to remove the philosopher from serious consideration. At a time when life violated Stoic orderliness in every conceivable way, one could subscribe to Stoic doctrine only by denying that reality was real, or, following the Skeptic, by suspending all judgment entirely. Neither alternative was any more compelling in the second and third Centuries than it is now.

The conspiracy of circumstances that led to the rise of Christianity can only be fathomed in the loosest respects. Of the political and military conditions enough has been said. With these there came a mounting and ever more public cynicism.[7] The scorn of Tertullian's *de Spectaculis*,[7] which threatened carnal Rome with a Day of Judgment, is illustrative. Persecution of Christians under Nero, Trajan, and (even) Marcus Aurelius provided the poor and hopeless non-Christians with a daring and romantic model. The eloquence of such early religious philosophers as Plotinus and Origen merged with the Stoic mandate that the true philosopher live an exemplary life. Origen's devotion to an existence devoid of lust is documented by his self-inflicted emasculation. Then too Christianity went

beyond the Stoic resignation in the face of death to the celebration of
death which would free the soul to reunite with its Creator. To a worn
and weary peasantry, the Gospels offered eternal life hereafter and rewards that would beggar the vaults of Croesus.

From Stoicism the Christian fathers borrowed the conception of Nature as Law. From the Platonists, they received and embellished the ultimate reality of *idea* over sense. From Aristotelian teaching, by way of
Epicurus, Lucretius, and Epictetus, they assimilated the concept of *Logos:*
the underlying rational principle of the Universe. Against the Classical
philosophies, they rejected materialism and its gloomy pointless implications. As Plotinus put it,

> "Matter is not Soul; it is not Intellect, is not Life, is no Ideal-Principle,
> No Reason-Principle; it is no limit or bound, for it is mere indetermina-
> tion; it is not a power for what does it produce?"[8] (*Enneads*, III, 6.7)

The teachings of the early Christian fathers were simple and undog-
matic, at least with respect to details. Plain folk from all over the Empire
had to find resonant elements in the new faith and, from Paul of Tarsus
to the mystic Porphyry, the missionaries of Christianity were willing to
bend and accommodate. On fundamental principles, however, there was
no compromise. These principles have remained central to Christian belief
ever since: that every man is the child of God; that there is only one
God; that man was made to serve God in this world and, through good
works, to live eternally in His light; that the soul is the essential fact of
human life; that neglect of the soul is a sin to be punished; that no force
on earth can affect God's plan nor can earthly wisdom fully reveal it;
that God's goodness is the cause of all things; that in His goodness, He
sacrificed His only Son to take on the human coil and then die for man's
redemption; that in that sacred death, the soul's hope was reborn, and
man once more could aspire to God's good grace.

With these brief, uncomplicated declarations, the founders of the
Church of Rome offered an alternative. To an empire torn by fickle tyrants and ignorant chieftains, they offered brotherhood. To a mass facing
hunger, plague, and the violent death of warfare, they offered eternal life.
To the oppressed, the slave, the exile, they offered the reassuring genealogy of God as the Father of all. To the pagan and criminal, the wan-
derer and the corrupt, they offered redemption. The poor were con-
soled by the meaninglessness of earthly riches; the aristocrats, by the good
works the prosperous could do for their brothers. The army inherited by
young Constantine was already mostly Christian—as, indeed, was his
mother—and his most impressive victories were won under Christ's flag.
Thus, as the Stoics retreated to the serenity of philosophic speculation, as

the fools at court submerged themselves in the lusty favors of the Emperor, and as the Visigoths planned their assault on Rome itself, Christianity was laying claim to the hearts and minds of the Empire.

Christianity did not begin with a firm foundation in philosophy. Its earliest members were drawn from the poorly educated classes of Egypt, Greece, Asia Minor, Syria, Spain. Its spokesmen were no match for the urbane rhetors of Rome and Alexandria. Indeed, Tertullian had contributed a sneering anti-intellectualism to the movement that remained with it for almost five hundred years. Philosophy, after all, had failed. Those who converted to Christianity had, we may assume, tried the way of the philosophers and found it wanting. Moreover, a philosophical foundation required argument, public discourse, and that openness to interpretation which comes only after the religion is itself secure. Constantine, desiring unification more than scholarly debate, was less than congenial to bishops and priests with a flare for theological discourse. Thus, while we can examine the psychological factors that guided the evolution of Christianity, we cannot unearth a Christian psychology before the fifth century. Only then, with the confidence that comes from success, did the Fathers begin to create that studiously rational framework by which the Christian view of man can be taught in psychologically meaningful terms.

The Problem of Knowledge

It has become a tradition in discussions of the Patristic period to describe Christian belief as *neo-Platonism* and to defend this description with quotations from, on the one hand, Plotinus, Augustine, and Boethius, and on the other, the *Dialogues* of Plato. This tradition is at once apt and misleading. It is misleading on several counts. Despite the breadth and penetration of the *Dialogues*, no amount of shuffling of those pages containing the Platonic cosmology will yield theology, and Christian belief, whatever else may be said of it, is theological. Second, the spirit of Platonism is fatalistic;* that of Christianity, optimistic. The soul that abandons the dead body of the Platonist wanders through the universe in search of True Forms. The Christian soul confronts God face to face. The *Dialogues*, taken as a whole, recommend a contemplative, introspective life of quiet virtue. The Christian life is one of action and reform. Platonism is Rationalism *par excellence:* through dialectical reasoning, the mind can be led to the latent knowledge of the soul. However, the Chris-

---

* I do not mean fatalistic in the Stoic sense; rather, the Platonic system, which denies truth to the living and is otherworldly in its orientation, leaves the citizen adrift in his daily affairs.

tian belief is that all knowledge begins first with *faith* which leads to a *transcendental* awareness of God who is the creator of all and is, therefore, in all things. For the Platonist, reason is the light. For the early Christian, faith is the light and the path. In short, the Platonist would not know what one meant by "taking a truth *on faith*," while the early Christian could not imagine knowing any significant truth without it.

There is no doubt but that the early Christian theorists, when exploring the available scholarship, found many natural bonds between their beliefs and the Socratic system. Predictably, they turned to the *Dialogues* when it became necessary to place Christianity in a context that could invite the attention of the more intellectually inclined. This reading of early Christianity as neo-Platonist is correct. That which would have Christian thought *evolving* from Platonism is decidedly incorrect. This is movingly documented in St. Augustine's *Confessions*[9] in which he credits the *Hortensius* of Cicero with first whetting his philosophical appetite,[10] insists that Aristotle's *Categories* did him more harm than good,[11] and, while praising the Platonists for their appreciation of truth-as-incorporeal,[12] lauds Paul still more for identifying this truth with the grace of God.[13]

St. Augustine was, by far, the most influential philosopher in the history of Christianity, at least until St. Thomas Aquinas. He set the tone of Christian intellectual life for the better part of eight centuries. In limiting our analysis of the problem of knowledge, then, to Augustine, we court little risk of rendering an incomplete account.

Our understanding of the problem of knowledge in Augustinian terms begins with the realization that God is the ultimate truth and that to know God is the ultimate goal of the human will. Thus, inquiry of any sort must come to rest on this. Otherwise, it is mere vanity and doomed to error and corruption. We examine, for example, the nature of man only because in the process we will reaffirm the existence of God.[14] The inquiry must avoid the pitfalls of the senses and must reject, *a priori*, the gaudy materialism of the Stoics. In brief, the formal properties of the inquiry must be patterned after the Platonists. When Augustine visited the venerable Simplicianus, he reported his devotion to the Platonists, and Simplicianus praised him

> "for not having fallen upon the writings of other philosophers full of fallacies and deceits, after the rudiments of this world, whereas in the Platonists God and His Word are everywhere implied."[15]

However, the Platonists merely implicated God, whereas the Christian with reason led by grace, is able to *explicate* God's reality and command.[16] Now, what is this reason led by grace? It is, in Augustine's phrase, an *interior sense*. It is that nonsensory inner awareness of truth, of error, of the moral right, of personal obligation, and of personal identity. This interior sense is the judge of perception and, therefore, is not reducible to perception. It, unlike the five senses, perceives itself perceiving as it perceives each of the separate senses perceiving.[17] In modern parlance, this interior sense is no less than consciousness itself, but indeed it is something more than consciousness. It is a moral consciousness whose character is outlined, in a startlingly Freudian way, in the *Confessions:*

> "You commanded me to abstain from sleeping with a mistress. . . . But there still live in that memory of mine . . . images of the things which my habit has fixed there. These images come into my thoughts and though, when I am awake, they are strengthless, in sleep they not only cause pleasure but go so far as to obtain assent and something very like reality. . . . (H)ow does it happen that even in our sleep we do often resist and, remembering our purpose and most chastely abiding by it, give no assent to enticements of this kind?"[18]

For Augustine, it is not through the deliberations of the mind alone that one comes to know the truth of God. Rather, it is that there *is* mind which informs us of the divine agent. That the mind furnishes itself with number, with time, with memory—facts not discernible through perception alone—proved to Augustine the wisdom of the Platonists. They did not go far enough only because the Son of God had not seen fit to present Himself to the Hellenes. The life of Jesus, however, changed all that and thereby revealed those truths that mere philosophy could never discover.

What makes this early Christian philosophy a transcendental psychology is its insistence that man, as a child of God, shares in the divine wisdom and that through this fact and man's faith in it he can elevate his comprehension of the universe to a truly cosmic level. Put quite directly, the Christian pledge is that the faith conferred by grace and spiritual labor will equip the believer with the answer to man's most vexing question: " Where did we and the universe come from and what is our destiny?" The Platonists, whose Rationalism provided the broad philosophical guidelines of Christian theological discourse, had carefully segregated the true *forms* and the *Republic*. That is, Plato at his idealistic extremes, never complicated the affairs of State with those ultimate verities that only death could illuminate. He yearned for a Philosopher-King, but only because he sought a government organized around defensible, rational principles rather than one immersed in petty squabbles and situationism. Philosophy, after all, was a way of life recommended because it would make man happy. It would conduce to civility, justice, fairness, and virtue. In a word, it would allow aristocratic personages such as Plato and his circle to live out their years untrammeled by the bellicose strivings of "men of brass." To be sure, the *Phaedo* and the *Crito* are rich in their intimations of immortality, in their promise of an ultimate enlightenment. To this extent, the *Dialogues* qualify unambiguously as transcendental *philosophy;* that is, they assert the existence of extrasensory, immaterial truths of a finer quality and graver meaning than any accessible to earthbound man.

Christianity, however, went further. It required not a philosophical life but a religious one which, if neglected, led not to ignorance and its attendant unhappiness but to sin and the ultimate retribution. It replaced the true forms with the all-seeing vision of the timeless architect of all truth, an architect whose infinite love was carefully balanced against infinite justice. Where the *Republic* was the enlargement allowing a clearer view of human nature, Christian Man was the miniature in whom God's reality could be established. This shift in emphasis provided early Christian scholarship with a decidedly psychological caste. God was believed to be infinitely good, yet there was evil in the world. If this was not God's doing then there must be matters beyond God's control or else, and in contradiction, God must be the author of both good and evil. To reconcile this seeming paradox, Augustine addressed the apparent tension between free will and determinism, a tension that has been discussed vigorously ever since. If all human beings are God's children and all, therefore, are potentially able to see the light, those who do not must be converted; their souls must be saved even at the peril of their bodies. In this issue was to be rooted theories of the "just war," theories of justifiable homicide, psychological principles of conversion. Unlike the Platonist who had to die before spiritually confronting Beauty, Justice, and Truth, the Christian, through faith, received these in this life by revelation and was specifically charged with the task of sharing them with all mankind. This mission, as history soon illustrated, demanded more than a polite, philosophical debate among friends.

The early Christian's problem of knowledge was not one of uncovering the truth but one of transmitting it, one of readying the pagan for the light of faith. The problem thus conceived, Christian scholars inquired more deeply into the psychological, as opposed to the purely rational, factors governing human judgment and conduct. The *Confessions* are particularly indicative of the shift in orientation. Augustine, in this work, commenced the practice of public disclosure, admissions of guilt, expressions of piety and resolution. The point here is not that he discovered the "cathartic" method in psychotherapy—which, in a weak sense, he did— but rather that his attention was given over to that side of self and others that the Socratic dialectic had ignored, even condemned. Where Socrates merely counseled against the rule of passion over reason, Augustine laid bare the genuinely personal and psychological dimensions of the conflict. The *Dialogues*, then, were transcendental without ever attaining the character of Psychology. Aristotle's works were studiously psychological, assiduously nontranscendental. Augustine observed human nature in an unblushing, otherworldly idiom. Subsequent centuries would strip the Augustinian approach of its theological content, but the transcendental elements have never vanished.

Central to the Augustinian epistemology is his distinction between knowledge and wisdom, the former being

"a rational cognizance of temporal things,"[19]

while the latter is

"an intellectual cognizance of eternal things."[20]

For Augustine, intellect and reason were different faculties. Reason was, indeed, a guiding light by which we might navigate through a confusing world, but reason alone could not equip us with that sublime knowledge of the eternal. And, of course,

"it is not difficult to judge which is to be preferred or postponed to which."[21]

In Book X of the *de Trinitate* Augustine reviewed the essential character of mind and emphatically declared it to be incorporeal.[22] He argued, dualistically, that the mind, while not a substance, was able to direct the material senses to "find out" what was of interest to it. However, the mere fact that it was so able to have commerce with the world of things did not indicate to Augustine that it was a thing itself. He rebuked former philosophers, and especially the Stoics, for confusing the objects of the mind's interest with mind itself. He rebuked the great run of men similarly for allowing their minds to become confused between the opposite poles of sense impression and eternal wisdom. Set free of sensory deceit, the mind can know itself, reflect on itself, love itself. Only this way can it find God.

The Problem of Conduct

If there was one element in Patristic philosophy that set it apart from virtually all preceding systems, even that of the Platonists, it was its explicit *equalitarianism*. The Platonists subscribed unwaveringly to psychological nativism in accounting for the differences among men. The "convenient fiction" of *Men of Gold, Men of Silver, Men of Brass* served as the constant rationale for eugenics and as the occasional explanation for human corruption. Aristotle and his Peripatetics never abandoned the notion of the *natural slave* who, by constitution, could only follow reasoning but lacked reason itself. The rupture in this otherwise unbroken tradition is announced in The *City of God*.

> "For, 'let them', He says, 'have dominion over the fish of the sea, and over the fowl of the air, and over every creeping thing which creepeth on the earth.' He did not intend that His rational creature, who was made in His image, should have dominion over anything but the irrational creation—not man over man, but man over the beasts. . . . And this is why we do not find the word 'slave' in any part of *Scripture* until righteous Noah branded the sin of his son with this name."[23]

For the historian who wishes to draw a straight line from the *Academy* to St. Peter's, the Patristic insistence on the fundamental equality of man stands as a persistent barrier. Moreover, given this insistence, scholars of the early Church subscribed to political philosophies, theories of justice, and principles of education which, it is fair to say, would have astonished the orthodox Platonist. The presumption of natural equality is a powerful one—one that perforce will color nearly every other aspect of a moral and social philosophy. Thus, whatever superficial resemblances exist between the Platonists and Patristics—and there are many—this difference between their views is of overriding consequence. Augustine, Plotinus, Porphyry, Simplicianus, all acknowledged a variety of debts to Plato. They all admired the honorable life of Socrates. They all saw, in the theory of Forms, the kernel of Christian transcendentalism. Hardly a line concerned with the immortality of the soul was written in the first four centuries of Christianity which did not refer to the authority of the Platonists for intellectual support. Still, when the time came for Augustine to share his vision of God's eternal city, it was not the *Republic* from which he sought inspiration, nor was it Plato's *Laws* that provided the maxims by which the Christian ordered his conduct. The Platonists, for all their genius and fully in command of that subtlety of mind which raises philosophy above the level of mere opinion, never did escape the pervasive sociology of Hellenic tradition. When read in the light of this tradition, the *Dialogues* are lessons offered by an aristocracy to an aristocracy and with the express purpose of establishing that most enduring of class structures, one based on genetic differences amplified by regulated opportunity. While sophisticated and reasoned, the *Dialogues* incorporated those brooding notions of clan, phratry, and race, timeless in the Hellenic mind. Over and against these characteristics, Patristic psychology, at least as set forth by Augustine, rested upon a most poignant expression of universal brotherhood.

It is to be noted that the task of explaining human error and limitation becomes far more difficult when egalitarianism is presupposed. For Augustine and his later disciples especially, the burden was increased by the transcendental character of their egalitarianism. Not only were all human beings presupposed equal in the significant respects but were so by virtue of divine intervention. Because of this wedding of egalitarianism and transcendentalism, the problem of evil—of unchristian conduct—was the most vexing of all. The entity adopted to solve this problem was that of the *free will*. Without it, early Christianity would have been little more than Manichaeanism: the belief in a god of goodness battling eternally with a god of evil and with the fate of every soul hanging, stoically, in the balance. Without free will, evil had to be attributed to divine authorship, which was a notion not only heretical but one utterly incompatible with the very concept of sin and personal responsibility. Only by asserting freedom of the will were the Patristic philosophers able to reduce evil in the world to man's invention and simultaneously, to elevate man to the status of a morally responsible agent. However, although free will was able to achieve these desired results, it created still another and potentially more telling problem: if the human will is free, how can God be said to have knowledge of things to come? And, if God does not have such foreknowledge, how can He be said to be omniscient? This dilemma had been settled once by Cicero who, in his attacks on those Stoics who believed the future could be foretold, granted free will to man only at the expense of denying omniscience to God.[24] Augustine's attempted solution began with an analysis of Cicero's conclusion. Praising Cicero for his reason but reproaching him for a lack of that wisdom which faith bestows, Augustine argued that the proposition need not be and, in fact, is not of the "either-or" variety:

> "(T)he religious mind chooses both, confesses both and maintains both by the faith of piety. . . . God knows all things before they come to pass and that we do by our free will whatsoever we know and feel to be done by us only because we will it."[25]

An example may clarify Augustine's position, although the issue itself is neither settled nor, perhaps, is able to be settled. We may know as a matter of fact that freezing rains are drifting eastward from Chicago and will pass over New York tomorrow afternoon. We also know that John Smith must be in Washington, D.C., tomorrow night and, further, that

John Smith is not aware of the impending showers. Moreover, we know that the only way Smith can arrive in Washington on time, should his scheduled flight be canceled, is by railroad. This information allows us, though with less than divine prescience, to predict the following: Smith will arrive at the airport, will learn of the freezing rain, will discover, to his disappointment, that his flight will not depart, will consider his alternatives and will proceed to reserve a seat on the late afternoon coach to Washington. Smith, indeed, does precisely this and, later that night, we assure him that we knew he would *before* he knew he would. Nothing about our foreknowledge may properly be said to have denied Smith the right or ability to choose as he did.

This example is intended to clarify but not to validate the Augustinian argument. If, for example, we not only know of the freezing rains but can cause them and can also cause the cancellation of Smith's flight and, indeed, can also produce his need to be in Washington, then it is less than clear that Smith's actions are freely expressed. Still, even under these conditions, Smith may *believe* he is acting freely and, accordingly, we may judge him not merely in terms of what he does but in terms of what he *intends*. Conditions may conspire to limit our range of possible actions, but we can always strive to *want* to do what is right:

> "Wherefore our wills also have just so much power as God willed and foreknew that they should have; and therefore whatever power they have, they have it within most certain limits."[26]

The problem of conduct, on this analysis, is the problem of will: getting man to recognize his obligations to himself, as a child of God, to God as his creator, to his fellow men as brothers. Failure of the will is sin and is unnatural.[27] Nature does not counsel a man to seek evil. When he does, when he *intends* evil, he is making ill use of a good nature.[28]

Augustine's careful distinction between the content of an action and the intention behind—or, in modern psychological language, between behavior and motivation—departed from the ancient approach to law. Plato looked for men of good will as did Aristotle, Cicero, and many other pre-Christian thinkers. But the actual laws of Greece and Rome were concerned principally with civil damage suits and with actual crimes against the State or provable conspiracies. The ancient laws did not and could not reach into the private longings of a citizen and hold him accountable for his hopes. God, however, omniscient and omnipotent, was able to penetrate the most secret recesses of cupidity and hold punishment in store for the culprit. The term "God-fearing" aptly conveys the Patristic plan for the salvation of the soul. To achieve this salvation, the missionary allowed himself great privileges in dealing with the non-believer. Transgressions punished severely in this brief life would not become so habitual as to doom the perpetrator to eternal fires. Sacrifice in this brief life, no matter how degrading and frustrating, was well worth the moment of pain in return for everlasting joy.

Conversion to Christianity solved the problem of conduct as it solved the problem of knowledge. The Roman citizen could evade Caesar's notice, but all was visible to the all-seeing God. Caesar's guard could reward the brave act and punish the coward, but only God could know the true motive behind each and every act, and His rewards and punishments were of a very different sort:

"If a man does not pay his debt by doing what he ought, he pays it by suffering what he ought."[29]

The Patristic Legacy

Augustine was not the Church's only voice but was surely her most authoritative. His *Confessions*, taken as a whole, attacked intellectualism so broadly as to number too many casualties. *The City of God* inspired hope in an afterlife but necessarily reduced that great interest in daily life that is the mark of every truly "classical" period. His *de Trinitate* and *de Libero Arbitrio*, which made "the goodness of God the cause of all things," relentlessly drew attention and energy away from Stoic science, Aristotelian logic, and Platonic rationalism. To the extent that we consider an unornamented and disinterested search for truth to be a noble one and a positive enterprise, Augustine's influence must be judged harshly. His teachings and the eagerness and talents of his followers induced fear and humility of a sort antithetical to creativity and culture.

Viewed against the background of fourth- and fifth-century alternatives, however, the growth of Christianity seems by far the better course. Despite the fear and trembling, man was first introduced to a psychological-theological theory of natural equality which has been a guiding force in the Western world ever since. Despite what may appear to be spiritual excess, this Patristic psychology, through its transcendental elements, rescued the mind from the blind alley of skepticism and the nihilistic prophesies of unbridled materialism. In focusing on the will and intention, the Patristics must be credited with inventing the psychology of motivation. Then, too, if only to rebuke the philosophers of antiquity, Patristic scholars preserved the older tradition, held it safe in monasteries from the western shores of Ireland to the flatlands of Syria. For very many years, a darkness settled over the mind of Europe—a darkness sustained by hunger and fear, by the failure of men and of law. We must be mindful of Christianity's contribution to this long silence, but we must also recognize how long it might have lasted had Christianity failed, for it was during this same five hundred years that new empires formed, new barbarian kings rose to power, and new cults emerged. Had these kings and cults no adversary, what would Europe's fate have been? Without these Christians, who would have labored to retain the Hellenic record or Roman Law? What would have stood between the king's caprice and the dignity of every human being?

For five hundred years the secular and the clerical powers grew. Conflict and competition raged with predictable ferocity. The citizen was torn for centuries between the king's command and God's. The modern world waited until a great king sought lasting peace with a good pope, when in 800 Charlemagne was crowned by Leo III. During this long pause, thought did not cease. It was less public, less assertive, even less relevant than it had been for any time since the Classical period. It was not until the reawakening of the philosophical mind in the tenth and eleventh centuries that these public and assertive elements returned. Whatever ill effects the authority of Augustine may have produced, and there were ill effects, this same authority formed the foundation on which was constructed a veritable monument to reason. We are, perhaps, so ready to note the Augustinian emphasis upon faith and upon forces of an utterly transcendental nature that we forget his central philosophical maxim: *Reason should be master in human life.*[30] Indeed, rather than reinforcing the superstitions and innocent fears of his fellow Christians, he sought to dispel these very fears by relegating emotion of any sort to a rank lower than reason's. He railed not merely against lust but against terror as well. Far from attempting to foist belief upon the unsuspecting or controlling the conduct of the brethren through reckless propaganda, Augustine labored to know the truth and to free men through its power. This power was reason itself: that which separates not only man from beast but the fool from the wise.[31]

How, then, may we fairly summarize the Patristic contribution to evolving Psychology? In an all too general way, we can cite certain propositions of a distinctly early Christian shade which, over succeeding centuries, became an integral feature of psychological speculation but with more and more of the theological aspects stripped away:

1. Over and against the Stoic "nature philosophies," the Patristics accorded to man a position unique in the world. This bias not only prevented the establishment of an ethological or evolutionary perspective but also discouraged the application of scientific principles of any sort to questions about human knowledge, conduct, or will. This contribution was, on the whole, negative.

2. Because of the unique position of man vis-à-vis the balance of nature,

the Patristic scholars insisted that each person was individually responsible for his actions. The sense of personal responsibility, a responsibility each person has to every other, was nearly *invented* by the first fathers of the Church. In all the pages of Plato, Aristotle, and their disciples, we hardly find a line devoted to this humanistic mandate. Earlier philosophers had discussed law, obligation, punishment, and justice, but their principles seldom included simple, unadorned *love*, the love spawned by a sense of brotherhood and nurtured by that ineffable condition we call compassion. This contribution, we may conclude, was positive.

3. In their antimaterialist convictions, the philosophers of the early Church insisted upon *psycho-physical dualism* according to which the psychological characteristics of human beings were forever beyond physical analysis. In orthodox religious terms, the dualism was between "soul" and "matter"; later, between "mind" and "matter." In our own time, the issue survives as the so-called Mind-Body problem. The Greeks invented the problem, and Augustine solved it in a way that was satisfying for over one thousand years. This contribution, it would seem, was mixed. It retarded science but saved the world from a form of materialism that would have been nearly lethal at the time.

4. In carrying religiosity into every sphere of human concern, the Patristics reduced the daily experiences of men to triviality. They continued that Platonic tradition which held all perception suspect and sanctified this tradition with some powerful scripture. This led inescapably first to a modest and then a virulent anti-intellectualism. It combined the worst features of Stoic fatalism with the worst features of Platonic idealism and thereby created a scientific vacuum. This was its most negative effect, made worse when the political authority of the Church was finally able to render the position official.

5. Rationalism, when colored with mysticism, produced a psychology of what we might call *intuitionism*, the belief in the power of the mind to achieve transcendental awareness *in this life*. The Patristics called this by several names: the *interior sense*, the *light of faith*, *grace*. It was the agent that gives intention to our actions and thereby holds us accountable. This contribution survives in the form of theories of the unconscious, notions of unconscious motivation, and theories that assert the innate origins of our moral sensibilities. In considering the failure of this intuition to be evidence of a defect, the Patristics were—inadvertently, we might suspect—presenting a theory of psychological deviancy as disease. More significantly, they were advancing the otherwise subtle notion that mere conduct (behavior) is not enough in an attempt to understand individual psychology; only when an action is judged in light of the intention behind it can that action be said to be known. The Patristics were not behaviorists.

Galen (c. 130–200) : The Empirical Alternative

We noted in Chapter 2 that while philosophers concerned themselves with the eternal imponderables, the Hippocratics continued to assemble a collection of clinical observations and therapeutic outcomes. That is, they continued to develop Greek medicine as an essentially empirical science, indifferent or even hostile to the speculative excesses of the Socratics.

A similar division of labor occurred in the Patristic period. As the fathers of the Church struggled to integrate pagan philosophy, barbarian ritual, and Christian teaching, Galen and his followers contented themselves with the more immediate problem of curing the sick, relieving pain, and understanding the causes of death and disease. Galen not only kept the Hippocratic system alive for subsequent historians but kept the idea of empiricism alive for subsequent scientists. His most important psychological work was *On the Natural Faculties*,[32] in which he attacked not only the untested hypotheses advanced by philosophers concerned with biology but, more particularly, the very notion that an untested hypothesis has any place in biology.

We are not to treat Galen as a radical empiricist, however. He was a practical man, devoted to unearthing the facts of clinical medicine and was willing to employ any method promising success. With respect to rational deduction versus empirical induction, he had this to say:

". . . it is not our habit to employ this kind of demonstration alone, but to add thereto cogent and compelling proofs drawn from obvious facts . . . [which] can actually be recognized by the *senses*."[33]

We must also respect the *nativistic* elements in Galen's theories if we are to avoid the error of assuming that because he was methodologically empirical, he was (therefore) epistemologically empirical. A fair portion of *On the Natural Faculties* is directed against the extreme Epicureans and Stoics who contended that man is to be understood only in terms of matter and only in terms of experiential determinants. By natural faculties, Galen meant those that exist by nature and, therefore, do not come into being in the empirical sense. Included among these natural faculties are those of the soul and especially those that ultimately reveal themselves in the form of reason and intellect. His theory, then, is not far removed from that of the Platonic school:

"Some of these people have even expressly declared that the soul possesses no reasoning faculty, but that we are led like cattle by the impressions of our senses, and are unable to refuse or dissent from anything."[34]

Nature, however, knows better than these radical empiricists, for

"she skilfully moulds everything during the stage of genesis and she also provides for the creatures after birth, employing here other faculties again, namely, one of affection and forethought for offspring, and one of sociability and friendship for kindred."[35]

Thus, with respect to the emotions, the social "instinct," the maternal drive, and the affective dimension of life in general, Galen's position is uncompromisingly nativistic. He rejected specifically that brand of empirical materialism according to which organisms enter the world as *tabula rasa*, whose knowledge and behavior must await the mechanical instructions given in experience. To the extreme Epicureans who wished to believe that man begins his life as amorphous clay, and gains wisdom and virtue only through experience, man whose essential character is but the consequence of certain *channels* having been etched into his form from without, Galen offers this:

"Thus, every hypothesis of *channels* as an explanation of natural functioning is perfect nonsense. For, if there were not *an inborn faculty* given by Nature to each one of the organs at the very beginning, then animals could not continue to live . . . let us suppose they were steered only by material forces, and not by any special *faculties* . . . if we suppose this, I am sure it would be ridiculous for us to discuss natural, or, still more, psychical activities—or, in fact, life as a whole."[36]

Galen is not to be viewed as a philosophical rarity in the Patristic period since, on the fundamental question of human nature, his system makes ample provision for native (God-given) forces. It is even less a psychological rarity since, in its principal tenets, Galenism is neo-Platonist. However, as a scientist, he is rare on at least two counts: he insisted on accepting the data of experience *over* the force of logic when the two were in apparent disagreement, and he dismissed scientific hypotheses that were devoid of empirical content. In accepting the "psychical" aspects of man and animal as the consequence of genetic processes and, as a result, in remaining skeptical toward the possibility of environmental factors having much of an effect upon the human condition, he locates himself quite confortably in an age soon to become Dark. Nonetheless centuries later, when medieval philosophers would introduce once more the virtues of observation and experiment as methods by which the truths of nature might be uncovered, the debt to Galen would be recognized, and noted as a major one.

Galen did not present himself as a philosopher—quite the contrary— but his system of medicine was rife with philosophical implications. In opposing radical materialism (i.e., atomism), he found himself constrained to propose a life principle by which the organic world was to be distinguished from mere matter. He termed this principle, *spiritus anima*, a principle that would reappear repeatedly in subsequent centuries and notably in the "animal spirits" of Descartes. From Galen on, there would be a theoretical and philosophic tension between materialists and vitalists—the former insisting that the laws governing the physical world were sufficient to embrace not only living things but man and his faculties as well; the latter urging that life and its *psychic* attributes could not be explained without recourse to an extraphysical, "life-giving" principle. A fair share of the controversies waged throughout the history of psychology is based either directly or derivatively on this tension.

References

1. *The Scriptores Historiae Augustae*, 3 vols., David Magie, translator. Putnam, New York, 1922. These volumes contain the surviving biographies of the Caesars from Hadrian to Carinus. It seems that the works were commissioned principally by Diocletian and Constantine because a good many of them are dedicated to these emperors. The biographies were written by different authors, apparently six or seven, and are predictably uneven in style and accuracy. While following the format employed by Suetonius in his *Lives*, the biographers of the *Scriptores* seem far more given to falsification and deceit than their model.

2. *The Discourses of Epictetus*, translated by P. E. Matheson, in *The Stoic and Epicurean Philosophers*, edited by Whitney Oates, The Modern Library, New York, 1957; Random House edition, 1940.

3. Epictetus, *op. cit.*, Book I, XXIII.

4. Ibid., Book II, VII.

5. Ibid., Book III, VII.

6. Ibid., Book I, VI.

7. Tertullian, *de Spectaculis*. In *Corpus Scriptorum Ecclesiasticorum Latinorum*, H. Hoppe, Vienna, 1939. The most accessible, unabridged essays of Tertullian's in English appear in *The Fathers of the Church: Tertullian* (Apologetical Works) *and Minucius Felix* (Octavius). Fathers of the Church, Inc., New York, 1950. Rudolph Arbesmann, O.S.A., translator. It is in his letter to Scapula, the governor of Africa, that Tertullian insists on the right of every man to worship as he sees fit (op. cit., *Ad Scapulam*). In the *Apology*, he chastens the Romans for infanticide, proclaiming that the followers of Jesus will not even take the life of a fetus. Tertullian was one of those rare critics able to combine wit and judgment. He ridiculed the pagan excesses

of the Romans and, in the same breath, judged Origen's self-emasculation with the question: *"If God wanted eunuchs, could He not have made them?"*

8. Plotinus, *The Enneads*, III, 6.7. An English translation has been published by Pantheon Books, Random House, New York.

9. St. Augustine, *The Confessions*, translated by Rex Warner, Mentor, New American Library, New York, 1963.

10. Ibid., Book III, Ch. 4.

11. Ibid., Book IV, Ch. 16.

12. Ibid., Book VII, Ch. 20.

13. Ibid., Book VII, Ch. 21.

14. Ibid., Book V, Ch. 5; Book VII, Ch. 12.

15. Ibid., Book VIII, Ch. 2.

16. Ibid., Book VII, Ch. 21; and in, *On Free Will*, Book II, Ch. 15.

17. Ibid., Book X, Ch. 12, 13, 14; and in *On Free Will*, Book II, Ch. 4.

18. Ibid., Book X, Ch. 30.

19. St. Augustine, *De Trinitate*, Book XII, Ch. 15, in *Basic Writings of St. Augustine*, 2 vols., edited by Whitney Oates, Random House, New York, 1948.

20. Ibid.

21. Ibid.

22. Ibid., Book X, Ch. 6 and 7.

23. St. Augustine, *The City of God*, Book XIX, Ch. 15, *Basic Writings of St. Augustine*, op. cit.

24. This argument appears in Cicero's *De Divinatione*.

25. *The City of God*, Book V, Ch. 9, op. cit.

26. Ibid.

27. Ibid., Book X, Ch. 17.

28. Ibid.

29. St. Augustine, *On Free Choice of the Will*, Book III, Ch. 15, *Basic Writings of St. Augustine*, op. cit.

30. Ibid., Book I, Ch. 8.

31. Ibid., Book I, Ch. 9.

32. Galen, *On the Natural Faculties*, translated by Arthur John Brock. Putnam, New York, 1916. I call this his most important psychological work notwithstanding his authorship of an essay titled, *On the Affections of the Mind*. This latter work is finally no more than an attempt to understand delirium, fits, drunkenness, etc., in terms of the Hippocratic theory of the humours and the effects of an imbalance in the humours. It is not really a "psychological" treatise at all.

33. Galen, *On the Natural Faculties*, Book III, Ch. 2.

34. Ibid., Book I, Ch. 12.

35. Ibid.

36. Ibid., Book II, Ch. 3.

5

□□□□□□□□□□□□□□□□□□□□□□□□□□□□□□

Scholastic Psychology

THE AUTHORITY OF ARISTOTLE

The Historian's Problem

Portraits of imperial epochs such as those of the Pharaohs, of Alexander, and of the Caesars can be painted with relatively broad strokes. Empires are regulated by a set of laws. They are governed by a visible coterie of powerful men. They possess that unmistakably *imperial* tone of life. Their economies are based on a specific currency and depend on a few basic goods. They have rather transparent policies toward neighbors and rather well-articulated strategies for defense and conquest. They speak in one tongue that must be mastered by all who would share in the bounty and protections of citizenship. Portraits of Empire, then, are geometric. No matter how great the Empire, one always knows how much canvas is required to contain it. On the few occasions when an Empire succeeds, it becomes the focus of an Age. That is, its entire culture becomes its principal export, and this culture is of such a nature as to transform and dominate alternative cultures. The Empire that succeeds best and thereby creates a historically identifiable Age is one that places a durable mark on every feature of social life. Accordingly, when the Empire fails, nothing that defined it remains unchanged. Art, law, letters, economy, homelife, religion, politics, all display the signs of change as that which once animated all of them begins its decline. The historian's problem, in studying that almost fantastic period laboring under the deceiving title *Medieval,** is that it is a post-Imperial period—one occurring at the end

* There is no hard-and-fast rule for the dating of the Middle Ages (Medieval) or the Renaissance. The Frankish kingdom of Charlemagne and the Holy Roman Empire emerging from the Middle Ages created conditions in the ninth century

of an Empire, great even by the inflated standards of that genre. The problem, then, is not that the Medieval epoch lacks distinguishing features but that each of its features is a *feature-in-transition.*

As it is post-Imperial, the Medieval epoch is also pre-National. Indeed, the nations of Europe as received by modern times were Medieval inventions. Empires have an imperial character and nations a national character. But what is the "character of a transition" if not a contradiction? It is only after we appreciate the complexity of this question that we can be protected against those misleading commonplaces employed in describing and dismissing the "Middle" Age. According to these commonplaces, the period from Rome's capture (?) to the Renaissance (?) was filled with a tame and dull homogenization of thought and belief, with a feudal system that reduced the faithful to servility, with political, moral, and intellectual hegemony exercised by a clerical elite in league with dukes and princes.

With respect to the putative homogenization of thought and belief, it is only necessary to point to the difficulty of writing Medieval history to expose the error. It is far easier to describe that which was Hellenic or Roman than to summarize that which was distinctively Medieval. Indeed, it is precisely because the Medieval epoch was neither imperial nor national that the search for its character must be so laborious. Thought and belief—always ambiguous terms when applied to more than one person— were probably more heterogeneous from the sixth to the eleventh centuries than during any equivalent span before or since. That superstition was rampant is beyond question, but this superstition, as a pararational phenomenon, is a veritable symbol of heterogeneity of outlooks. That is, in order to render belief uniform, it is necessary to reduce it to a set of teachable principles, to put it on a rational and even quasi-philosophical level, to argue it into an apparently unimpeachable form. Formal religions take hold only *after* dislodging the superstitious mind. They replace superstition. In this respect, we cannot even discuss Catholicism as the "official belief" until well into the eleventh century and we must date its "hegemony" in the thirteenth.

The so-called feudal system was, of course, a variety of systems that evolved continuously over a period of centuries. It was never merely an

---

quite different from those existing in Europe before Charlemagne. Certainly the rise of the universities in the eleventh and twelfth centuries saw a general improvement in education. Distinctions between the Low Middle Ages and the High Middle Ages are not any easier. Many historians who refer to the High Middle Ages find themselves discussing the fifteenth century. Prof. Holmes, for example, has given us an excellent review of what he calls *The Later Middle Ages* (Norton, New York, 1962) and he brackets this period [1272–1485]. By 1485, Dante and Giotto have been dead for over a century and Pico Della Mirandola has already begun to make a name for himself.

alternative to anarchy and the daily threat of a violent death; it was the *only* alternative. As an essentially economic system, feudalism had much in common with Roman life in the second to fifth centuries; that is, the feudal lord or baron was the economic equivalent of the Roman governor or provincial. As a system of classes, feudalism gave the lord or baron a position quite that of chieftan in prefeudal tribal communities. Scarcity requires economy, and economy requires binding agreements which, in turn, demand authority. Whether this authority is vested in archons, consuls, chieftans, barons, or kings depends principally upon the size of the social-economic community and its historic sources. The contemporary American must be willing to sacrifice his life in the defense of his country, an obligation quite in line with the serf's. The same American has a servile relationship to laws, including those that tax his possessions, proscribe treason, and otherwise regulate his public conduct. Of course, he shares in the authorship of these laws and their amendment. But feudal life was also based on agreements by both parties, and these agreements had the force of law.[1]* The transformation of serfdom to slavery occurred late in the feudal period and, when it occurred, it was based on the same factors that Aristotle had articulated and that no ancient Solon found lacking in merit.†

Thus, it is only in the "High Middle Ages" (from, say, 1100 to 1350) that we can find written justifications for policies and socioeconomic arrangements that applied to a substantial fraction of the Western world. Only at these late dates does the term *Medieval* enjoy those documented and reflective elements that are necessary to a historical analysis. From A.D. 500 to 1000, we can examine certain people, even certain groups. But we are not able to add these varied settlements and arrive at the character of an age, let alone its psychological attitudes. We can only

* We would be guilty of romantic excess to contend that the serf's lot was either carefully recognized in law or wholesomely protected by it. Still, it was common for once free men to enlist themselves and their descendants into serfdom for essentially religious reasons or even for personal gain! R. W. Southern, in *The Making of the Middle Ages* (Yale University Press, 1959), recounts submission by one freeman for the purpose of gaining another vineyard. As Prof. Southern notes in his analysis of the documents of the period, servitude was considered the lot of every man, if only servitude to God. Thus, some men were "serfs to the serfs of God," finding in their servility only the proper conduct of a Christian, since "all men labour and serve, and the serf is a freeman of the Lord, and the freeman is a serf of Christ" (p. 104).

† Note that the same Greeks who reviled tyranny benefited from slavery. Plato's men of gold, brass, silver, and iron are models for those hierarchic classifications of citizens that until modern times, suffused every political organization in the Western world. The slave in Greece was one whose side lost the battle, whose birth was non-Hellenic, and whose debts could not be paid in any other way. The advent of the *Dominate* in the Roman Empire introduced to the Western community the precedent of man-as-god and, therefore, citizen-as-servant.

try to capture, in a series of snapshots, how the mind of the Middle Ages grappled with itself and with the awesomely unpredictable world around it.

Fear and Magic

The changes that overtook the West between the fifth and tenth centuries were colossal by standards both ancient and modern. There is so little in common between the Frankish kingdom of Charlemagne and the late empire of Justinian that even comparisons are difficult to establish. Of all the prevailing forces working to change the world, none was more significant than Islam. The transformations imposed by the disciples of Mahomet (571–632) were progressive, cumulative, and overwhelming. Successively, Mohammedanism overcame Persia (651), Syria (636), Egypt (642), north Africa (698), Spain (711), and even blockaded Constantinople (717). The resulting economic and cultural consequences derived most immediately from the fact that the Mediterranean itself no longer served Western interests. The searching thesis that the Middle Ages are to be understood principally in terms of Islamic control of the Mediterranean Sea was advanced by Prof. Henri Pirenne.[2] His own description of what had occurred cannot be improved:

> "The familiar and almost 'family' sea which once united all the parts of this commonwealth was to become a barrier between them. On all its shores, for centuries, social life, in its fundamental characteristics, had been the same; religion the same; customs and ideas, the same or very nearly so. . . . But now, all of a sudden, the very lands where civilization had been born were torn away; the Cult of the Prophet was substituted for the Christian Faith, Moslem law for Roman law, the Arab tongue for the Greek and the Latin tongue.
>
> The Mediterranean had been a Roman lake; it now became, for the most part, a Moslem lake. From this time on it separated, instead of uniting, the East and the West of Europe. The tie . . . was broken."[3] (p. 25).

The part of the world which we now identify as Europe had become enclosed. To the north, the Danes and Saxons presented a constant threat to the vestiges of Roman civilization. From Spain in the south, the invasion and piracy of the Saracens were irresistible. In the East, of course, Islam was supreme. That life, which once had been Mediterranean, now collapsed toward a safe European center, but it could not be moved northward intact. Instead, it degenerated into that form of tribalism which would evolve into feudalism. Even the secondary effects of the Mohammedan conquest were telling. Syria, for example, had been the major source of papyrus, and from 650 until the eleventh century the supply was virtually eliminated. The Arabic number system, which would animate European science and mathematics only after the fourteenth century, remained isolated from the Western mind. One can easily gauge the consequence of this isolation by attempting a problem in multiplication or division using Roman numerals.

Technology is the achievement of a settled people. It arises when an abiding problem, an abiding conflict with nature, insists on a solution; for example, the Egyptian farmer's need for water and the need to protect his crops from an overflowing Nile; the Athenian's desire to erect a temple with massive columns. Technological undertakings on a grand scale are pointless to those living a nomadic life. By the time the problem is solved, conditions have forced the nomad to a new but ever temporary home. Thus the threat and the reality of invasion, of piracy, of crop failures not only robbed the European of his culture but denied him the very geographic permanence that might make a new culture possible.

The mind that will invent science is one located in the realm of the predictable. We discover what is predictable in nature only through a process that must be called *historical*—either the personally historical process of one's own life or the culturally historical processes received from the writings of our predecessors. Both the scientific and the philosophical mind grapples, finally, with the problem of causation. The very concept of a cause is one nurtured by experiences that are distributed in an orderly way in time. Time, however, for the Medieval mind was far less metrical than it is to the modern mind. Indeed, the Medieval sense of time was as varied and mystical as those childish superstitions we have come to identify with the entire epoch. For the Medieval Christian, time had at least these two divisions: the brief and insignificant one in which his sinful life proceeded, and the cosmically enduring one in which the suffering or the joys of his soul would occur.

"Every day, every hour, thus without ceasing
I must finish my life, and recommence
In this death uselessly alive."[4]

Christian belief and its essential elements—baptism, death, and resurrection—fostered a perception of time devoid of scientific meaning and one not seen in philosophy since the age of the pre-Socratics: with each day, a rebirth. Neither the past nor the future could be connected by that cognitive thread we know as history. Medieval life passed in a series of otherwise disconnected moments. Its events were sudden, as sudden as the imminent apocalypse that would end all life, all time, all fear. Marc Bloch put it aptly:

> "These men, subjected both externally and internally to so many ungovernable forces, lived in a world in which the passage of time escaped their grasp all the more because they were so ill-equipped to measure it. . . . The truth is that the regard for accuracy . . . remained profoundly alien to the minds even of the leading men of that age."[5]

Without a sense of time, a sense reinforced and validated by empirical regularities, the concept of natural cause fails to overtake the unharnessed imagination. The Medieval mind, this mind without a clock, was scientifically and philosophically backward. As with children living in any age, the Medievalist's comprehension was superstition. A search for causes unguided by the light of former efforts, denied the merest tools of investigation, and upset by the intrusions of plague, starvation, and assault, must finally ascend only to the level of magic. Greek science never escaped rationalism far enough to become experimental. It failed, therefore, to establish the validity of its propositions. Medieval science never reached the stage of rationalism and it failed, therefore, even to produce a proposition. God had made the world, and man was forced to live in it. Neither man nor the world was to survive very long. The end would come "in the twinkling of an eye." What sign would there be? Who would be so bold as to reckon the moment God's will would assert itself? "What is man?", wrote Alcuin, the resident scholar in the court of Charlemagne. And he answers, "The slave of death, a passing wayfarer." And then, "How is man placed?—Like a lantern in the wind."[6] These are lines provided by a man who described himself thus: "Alcuin was my name: Learning I loved. Oh thou that readest this pray for my soul."[7]

The men and women who lived in this period endured circumstances more harsh than human beings had confronted since prehistoric times. The power of the Church was political, but neither its moral nor its religious lessons could penetrate that large and shifting body of tribes that remained trapped by the timeless rites and visions of the pagan. With gruesome weariness these men and women struggled to rationalize the effects of their woeful lives. Not only was death a release, but the decaying body of the dead parent was praised for its sweet smell. The soul of this body now enjoying the presence of God Himself may still come back to sanctify its former shell. Thus a lock of hair, a rotting bone, the bristle of a beard, may have the power to heal or to protect its possessor against the devil and his demons. In one immense though bounded universe, man and his planet, the stars, the moon, each blade of grass, all shared in God's all-seeing vision. As late as the thirteenth century, St. Francis would repeat this spirit of medieval life in words whose beauty has survived the tragedy of it all:

> "Praised be my Lord for brother wind
> And for the air and clouds and fair and every
>   kind of weather . . .
> Praised by my Lord for sister water
> Praised be my Lord for our sister, mother earth,
> The which sustains and keeps us
> And brings forth diverse fruits with grass and
>   flowers bright . . .
> Praised be my Lord for our sister, the bodily
>   death . . .
> For the second death shall do them no ill."[8]

It would be misleading to reserve to the Middle Ages the mind's domination by fear and magic. Every period of the human experience finds good sense in short supply. In our own century there are still tribes whose starving children must be deprived of milk so that rats may drink to satiety. Even among otherwise advanced nations of the modern world, it is not unheard of for governments to insist upon unswerving orthodoxy of political belief, and this insistence is reinforced by threats no less severe than those promised to the Medieval heretic.

There can be no doubt but that the pervasive fear of death had a paralyzing effect upon the few who might have made lasting contributions of an artistic or intellectual nature. Scripture was interpreted as predicting the world's end in A.D. 1000 or thereabouts, and to those who believed this—and we may suspect that a good many did—the notion of launching a major project of any sort would have seemed chimerical. Even for those who were unaware of the exact date of the apocalypse or who entertained a different date, the crucial fact was that there was *some* date and a not too distant one. That a fear of the end, both a personal and a worldly end, was generally held seems confirmed by the incessant rationalizations invented to control it. Death as freedom, as liberation, as rebirth, as escape—*death as a good*—abound in the literary evidence of the period.

The run of competent and occasionally great philosophers begins with St. Anselm (1033–1109). We are tempted to connect this resumption of intellectual pursuits with a fact that must have surprised a good many Christians—the fact that they were still alive after A.D. 1000! There were, of course, less airy considerations responsible for the reawakening, and we shall examine several of them. Nevertheless we are advised not to dismiss too eagerly what, to the modern mind, seems utterly incomprehensible: that scholarship, art, enduring institutions, and culture itself suffered neglect by a people generally persuaded that the world would not endure. Excepting this, however, we must be careful not to judge these people and their other characteristics in terms foreign to the rest of the story of civilization.

If we are to segregate the Middle Ages on any basis that might satisfy the demand for rigor we must avoid variables such as poverty, plague, fear, superstition, zealousness, faith, and the like. We find these generously represented throughout the course of history. What is different, however, is the ease with which the literate and even intellectually gifted Medieval citizen abandoned so completely those critical faculties that are the stamp of a tutored mind. That the citizens of a Medieval town would burn a pig at the stake for entering a house and "murdering" a baby is a saddening fact but is of the same cloth as Roman "thing-liability" or the Athenian belief that Pericles' wall was responsible for the plague of 430 B.C. Indeed, it is not far removed from the modern citizen's romance with "flying saucers" or the songs he sings to his plants. Contemporary man, notwithstanding the miracles of television, space travel, and air conditioning, is still willing and able to support a good many fortune-tellers and may even make decisions of great personal consequence on the position of Neptune in relation to Orion. But these practices, even were they exercised by the vast majority of educated men and women, would not tempt us to describe the twentieth century as primitive or superstitious. Rather, we would examine the writings of the finest thinkers and scholars of the period and attempt to discern what the critics of an age had to say about their civilization. That is, we would not stop once we had established that most people were foolish or witless. We would press on to learn if there were exceptions; if, somewhere in the boundless tedium of the epoch, there were pockets of enlightenment. Those who do what John Morley described as *the work of the world* are, after all, the conspicuous minority in any span but are sometimes able to elevate the entire world of their time to a place of historic significance.

What was unique about the Middle Ages, then, was not the record compiled by the struggling masses—a record that is essentially undeviating across time—but the record attained by those very figures who presumed to lead and by those who might pass for the best minds. In this respect, the achievements by scholars between Boethius (d. 525) and John the Scot (d. 877?) were dismal. This interval, coinciding with the expansion of Islam and the correlated scattering of the Western community, may be described legitimately as the Dark Age. It may, however, also be viewed as a period of regrouping and assimilation—the period when monks in the West of Ireland preserved the language of the Hellenes, when kings and popes sought economic and even cultural foundations for peaceful coexistence, when the threat of Islam forced the philosophically inclined believer to articulate arguments for Christianity to counter the challenge and the promise of the followers of Mahomet. It was also the period in which Arab and Jewish scholars could reflect upon the ancient wisdom of Greece and Rome and thereby begin to invigorate the growing empire intellectually. The principal effect upon the Islamic world was felt in medicine, science, and mathematics; that is, in the practical spheres of life that always dominate the concerns of an expanding kingdom. Avicenna (980–1037), whose Islamic rendition of Aristotelian thought came to pose an enormous set of questions for the thirteenth-century Western philosopher, was a physician concerned, we might suspect, more with the wisdom of Aristotle-the-Materialist than with that of Aristotle-the-Philosopher. Still, had it not been for Avicenna and his colleagues in the Islamic world of the eleventh century, the philosophical achievements of twelfth- and thirteenth-century Europe— achievements based so sturdily upon Aristotelianism—are nearly unimaginable.

When Charlemagne allowed himself to be crowned by the pope, he displayed that rare talent of the political genius who knows what the future will demand. More than any religious connotation that might have attached to the event, the coronation symbolized the rebirth of the Western world, a world now organized around a set of religious principles shared by both the temporal and the spiritual monarchs of that world. The result was at least the possibility of European unification against an enemy who, now, was a heretic as well. The Western king could now claim to defend a competing truth and one as great in its implications as that which impelled the soldiers of Islam.

We would overestimate Charlemagne's personal contribution to credit him with the creation of a European community of nations. This, of course, required centuries of turmoil and disaster. But his alliance with the Church of Rome did establish at least a sense of community in a part of the world which, for several hundred years, had succumbed to tribal indifference and innocent provincialism. He served as king of the Franks for thirty-two years (768–800) and, until his death (814) as Charles I, emperor of the Holy Roman Empire. His name has become so romanticized that we often are most willing to forget essential facts of his life and his time. For example: his army probably never numbered more than 5000; he could neither read nor write; with the exception of two full-sized skirmishes with the Saxons, his reign was nearly devoid of major battles, let alone wars; although an admirer of St. Augustine's *City of God*, neither he nor any one of his five wives could be considered especially devout; his kingdom and, later, his Holy Roman Empire was still nearly comically disorganized by modern standards, and the Church he served was hardly better organized.[9] But over and against these facts, the following are every bit as true and, finally, far more important: He was devoted to learning and committed to the education of his people. He imported Alcuin from England to establish a Palace School and strongly encouraged the bishops of the Empire to incorporate schools within the churches and abbeys. These schools and even the curriculum introduced by Alcuin[10] were the wellsprings of the Medieval university, an invention of the twelfth century. He was no Pericles, nor was Alcuin an Anaxagoras, but Charlemagne did restore respectability to learning and thus cut a seam in the heavy curtain that had darkened European scholarship for four hundred years. He restored some stability to the economy, provided at least the hint of safety for those who might otherwise have wandered, and planted the banner of Jesus in every major center of Europe from the Ebro River in Spain to the southern edge of Denmark.

To the extent that the modern Western world retains institutions, ideas, and a general perspective that are Greco-Roman in their broadest features, then, to that extent, Charlemagne can be said to have been a maker of the modern Western world. He did not eliminate fear or magic—though he legislated against both—but he created a climate congenial to their antagonist, reason.

The Revival of Rationalism

There was a twelfth-century Renaissance which, in purely intellectual respects, compared favorably with its more vaunted successor in the fourteenth and fifteenth centuries.[11] The most vivid signs of this general rekindling of energy and hope are, of course, the majestic Gothic cathedrals. Even today, in an age that has made bigness a virtue, these churches seem to be and are of gigantic proportion. Still more impressive is the fact that nearly all of them—at Paris, Chartres, Amiens, Laon, Beauvais, Rheims, LeMans, Tour, Orléans, Mt. St. Michel, at Canterbury and Oxford, at Prague and Cologne, throughout Europe and the British Isles—appeared in less than two hundred years. Coincident with their appearance were the revival of classical Latin, the resumption of serious philosophical inquiry and, most significantly of all to intellectual history, the passage from Saracen Spain to Christian Europe of the Arabic translations of Aristotle's works.

First slowly and haltingly but soon quickly and continuously, the authority of Aristotle challenges and overtakes the traditional authority of neo-Platonism. St. Anselm (d. 1109), who may be said to have initiated the philosophic revival, entitles his major work *Faith Seeking Understanding*, and argues patiently for the role of perception and reason in Christian life. His principal authority, however, is St. Augustine. Next, we confront the *Four Books of Sentences* of Peter Lombard (1100–c.1164), the influential religio-philosophical work of the time and one that proclaims even more forcefully the position of reason in the affairs of faith. Still, his authority is also Augustine, who directs us to find God with that quality of ours,

> "than which our nature has no better,
> which is the mind."[12]

But with Peter Abailard (1079–1142), the emphasis shifts to Aristotle, whom he calls "our prince" and who, for the next two centuries will be *The Philosopher*.

The revival of rationalism cannot be reduced to a single or even small set of causative agents. Nor is this the setting for an analysis of the variables involved. Charlemagne's contribution has been noted, a contribution sustained and reinforced by King Otto whose German kingdom enjoyed a mini-renaissance in the tenth century. St. Peter's, which had been assaulted by the Saracens as recently as 846, now commanded the brave loyalty of all of Christian Europe, and the Roman Church was able to administer more effectively the efforts of her monks and missionaries. Rome itself was now secure enough to serve as a center for grammar and law as the Empire sought to restore its classical character. Not only was the Empire secure against Islam but was now able to reclaim territories previously lost. By 1085 the recovery of Spain had proceeded as far as Toledo, and by 1118 it included Saragossa. The notorious *First Crusade* (1096) was, we must note, a mere expression of the revival and not an antecedent.[13] Thus, by the end of the twelfth century we find Europe in a state somewhat similar to that of Athens under Alexander—war, plague, and discord giving way to order, security, and growing prosperity; political instability submitting to the will of the great man; a visible but now conquerable foe providing the stimulus to cohesion. The nightmare had ended, man and his world were still existing, and the future—if only because there *was* a future—seemed far brighter.

Scholastic Psychology

Among those who write general histories of Western thought, there is a custom of reducing the works of Augustine to "neo-Platonism" and dismissing Thomas Aquinas as an "Aristotelian." The respect in which reductions of this sort are defensible is that which allows us to reduce all philosophy either to Platonism or Aristotelianism. It is true that Thomas Aquinas (1225–1274) has been *the* intellectual voice of the Roman Church since the fifteenth century and it is also true that his two major works, the *Summa Theologica* and the *Summa Contra Gentiles*, derive their inspiration from Aristotle. But derivation is not duplication. One could not reconstruct Thomistic thought merely from a knowledge of Aristotelian thought. The two philosophers undertook their works in vastly different intellectual climates, with vastly different orientations and with vastly different objectives. If we are to comprehend the Medieval view of psychological man, we must focus on Thomism not because Thomas Aquinas was the only or even most influential figure to raise the important questions but because his were the only works that included all the perspectives prevailing in his age. And if we are to comprehend the portion of Thomism that is distinctly psychological, we must first appreciate the problems facing Thomas and his Church in the thirteenth century. It will not do to establish certain identities between Aristotle and Aquinas on the soul, on the senses, on justice, and so forth. The caveman, the Roman, the Vandal, and the modern resident of London, all may be described as seeking "the good life," but they surely would define that life differently. To know only that all of them seek the good life is to know nearly nothing at all about them. Let us review briefly the problems confronting Aquinas in regard to human psychology and then proceed to his essentially Aristotelian solutions.

1. *Can man know God?* This is the central epistemological problem of the High Middle Ages. Peter Abailard, in his *Sic et Non* (*Yes and No*), had advanced some 158 theological questions answered in a contradictory way by Scripture and by the early Christian fathers. He was also one of several influential twelfth-century spokesmen to reject the real existence of Universals and to adopt *nominalism;* that is, to assert that only individual entities are real and that so-called Universals are merely names (*nomines*) invented to create a general class. By the time of Aquinas' *floruit*, there was a creeping skepticism toward doctrine and a growing demand for rational as opposed to spiritual proof. Can man know God, then, was just the most relevant member of the larger question, *Can man know anything?*

2. *What is man's duty to God?* This question assumes that the general epistemological question has been answered; that is, we know what man can know of God and God's will. Now what remains to be determined is man's obligation to self, to State, to his fellow man.

3. *What is sin?* In the ninth century, the Church was so disorganized that the pope was unable to provide Charlemagne with an official liturgy

for the celebration of the Mass.[14] By the thirteenth century, intense efforts were directed at rendering Christian practices uniform. The Holy Roman Empire was indeed an empire, requiring laws, agreements, and an understandable set of first principles. The historic *ius civile, ius gentium,* and *ius naturale* were reactivated but had to be reconciled with a body of belief far more detailed than the belief existing at the time of Justinian. Secular and clerical powers were now so intermingled that the citizen-believer desperately needed guidance for a lawful and Christian life. The concept of sin had to be refined in such a way that all—kings, bishops, and farmers alike—were aware of the specific obligations man had to his Creator.

4. *How is the will free?* Scripture had granted freedom of the will while insisting that God caused all things. In the previous chapter we reviewed the Augustinian resolution of this apparent conflict, a resolution not complete enough for the more enlightened and critical citizens of the thirteenth century.

5. *What is the end of man?* Budding Materialism had created the impression in many quarters that the soul might die with the body. Aquinas must fashion an explanation of the soul's mission and one which, at the same time, will not be caught in the logical traps set by Averroës and his Western disciples (e.g., Siger of Brabant). The Averroist position was pure Aristotelianism: the soul perishes with the body, since it is the soul that grants individual (personal) identity and since that which is individual is, necessarily, destructible. Only mind (*nous*) survives and this is the same in all people. Thus, personal survival is impossible.

Many other questions were taken up by Aquinas including some as fundamental to theology as these. However, we need explore only his treatment of these to establish his psychological perspective.

The Problem of Knowledge

Maurice deWulf summarizes Scholastic Psychology aptly:

"According to the medieval classification of the sciences, psychology is merely a chapter of special physics, although the most important chapter; for man is a *microcosm;* he is the central figure of the universe."[15]

Until the thirteenth century, the Medieval view of human nature was essentially Augustinian, which is to say Platonistic in its most defined features. The Holy Trinity served as a metaphor of human consciousness viewed, accordingly, as the trinity of *sense, reason,* and *intellect.* Each of these faculties was able to provide knowledge of a certain sort, but only the last (*nous: intellectus*) could discern truth itself.

John Scotus Eriugena, as early as the ninth century, could offer a more or less complete system of psychological philosophy by combining Platonic idealism with the tenets of Christian faith. In the *De Divisione Naturae*[16] (a work that is astonishing, given the sorry intellectual climate surrounding its authorship), he reaffirms the Platonic distinction between attribute (*accidens*) and essence (*substantia,* or less formally, *essentia*) and argues that the senses can apprehend only the former. That is, the senses as material agencies can be affected only by the material aspects of the world. These, being of an ephemeral and crude sort, have little direct connection with the ultimate and sublime reality of God. However, the gift of reason (*logos: ratio*) allows the perceiver to assimilate these crude physical facts in such a way as to appreciate the *supra*factual order and design of the universe. Even this higher sensibility, however, is limited because the order so disclosed is only an order among things; it is an ordering of effects but not an awareness of their true, nonphysical causes. It is only when the passive senses and the active reason deposit their contents into that spiritual realm of intellect that the fundamental truth of nature can be discerned. Since these truths are above and before *things,* since they are, alas, ideas, then that which discovers them must, itself, be immaterial. Man himself

"is a kind of intellectual idea held eternally in the mind of God."[17]

A distinguishing feature of the philosophical revival that took place in the twelfth and thirteenth centuries is the rejection of such extreme idealism. John Scotus Eriugena rejected the facts of sensation as truths and thereby spoke in defense of an idealism that could never advance beyond the point at which Plato left it. The Scholastic philosophers, though never abandoning the spirit of idealism, were willing to deal with the perceptible realities of nature as facts and as facts that expressed truths. We discover this willingness in St. Anselm's *Dialogus de Veritate,* which credits the senses with an accurate reflection of facts of nature while condemning the "interior sense" for deceiving itself by creating false opinions about sensation.[18] Truth for Anselm is finally the right perceived by the mind alone but, in this act of creative perception, the mind makes use of the accurate neutrality of the senses. It is this line of reasoning that led Anselm to his famous *Ontological Argument*[19] for the existence of God. While we need not analyze this argument—a complex and vexing one—we must note its psychological orientation.

Anslem advanced the theory that what the mind is capable of entertaining is, by that fact, real. In order for the mind to be impressed with an idea, it must enjoy a faculty that is compatible with that which might impress it. For example, if we are able to see color, it is not only because there is color but because nature has equipped the human faculties to be responsive to this feature of the world. A faculty does not exist for which there is no natural agency. Now, the mind, as an enlarged faculty, is able to comprehend

"that than which there can be nothing greater"

and this, finally, is God. Since we are able to comprehend the possibility of that *than which there can be nothing greater,*" the possibility is a reality.*

Anselm was not proposing to replace faith with reason, nor was he suggesting that God's existence in any way depended on the idea man has of it. He was not advancing a Platonic idealism either. Instead, and with the influence of a great and revered teacher, he was permitting faith to rest upon a rational foundation such that "mind" and "spirit" need not battle any longer. It remained only for Peter Lombard's best-selling *Four Books of Sentences* to persuade the Medieval faithful that God is known in his works, known through an intellect informed by perception. With this final spadework accomplished, the thirteenth century was able to host that grand synthesis—a synthesis of thought stretching back to Plato and Aristotle and, along the way, including Augustine, Boethius, John Scotus, Anselm, Peter Lombard—a synthesis that is *Scholasticism.* Although the ideas and theories comprising Scholastic thought are varied in both tone and origin, the synthesis itself can be attributed to two men, Albertus Magnus and his pupil, Thomas Aquinas. It is the latter's writings that present the Scholastic approach, indeed the Scholastic "solution," to the problem of knowledge. We may summarize this solution as follows:

1. Consistent with Aristotle, Scholastic psychology distinguishes between the factual knowledge of the senses, a knowledge that even the sensitive faculty of animals can possess, and the knowledge of principles

---

* Anselm's argument is neither trivial nor "subjective" as the latter term is currently employed. God's existence is not based simply on the fact that someone might conceive of it. Nor does the argument require, as some have suspected, that an island "than which none can be greater" exists because we conceive of one. First, there cannot be an island than which none can be greater because such an island would be the universe or would be infinite and, therefore, would not be an island. We can, according to the argument, have the conception only if the capacity for the conception were imposed upon our understanding and to be imposed, an agency commensurate with the conception itself must exist. This, at least, is the first step in approaching the subtle complexity of Anselm's argument.

that only reason can embrace. Thus, although experience can inform about things, it cannot provide us with a knowledge of laws. Put in another and more classical way, experience is and must be of particulars only, whereas reason comprehends the universals. It is from the particulars of sense that reason abstracts the universals. Reason is a faculty of the soul. In fact, the soul is an intellectual principle.[20] Over and against Aristotle, the Scholastics reject the corruptability of the soul.[21]

2. Animals, which lack the intellectual principle, survive by instinctual patterns of responding. Man, through reason, apprehends universals, and this allows him to fashion an infinite variety of solutions to his problems. He is neither limited in his judgments nor driven to accept nature instinctively.[22] Against Plato, the Scholastic system requires not only the true and factual status of sensations but also the need for a physiological (material) mechanism by which the senses inform the intellect.[23] On the occasion of physical death, the nutritive and sensitive faculties of the soul cease—for these required a body for their expression—but the will and the intellect survive.[24]

3. There is an agent-intellect (*agens intellectus*) that abstracts the form of a thing from its appearance. The senses can embrace only the attributes, but the intellect can discern the form.[25] Now this is not a Platonic process; that is, the form is surely not the idea by which the thing comes about. Rather, the form is in the matter as a principle, but the senses can respond only to the matter and not to the principle. Thus we do not "know" to what the senses respond. Knowledge is an abstraction based on principles of matter, but the principles themselves are of course immaterial. The psychology of knowledge, then, is a *cognitive* psychology, not an empirical psychology. For Aristotle, the *agens intellectus* was a kind of light, an interior light, that illuminated particulars in such a way as to allow reason to discover their principle. For Aquinas, this interior light is God.[26] The abstractions made possible by this light are not (Platonically) removed from the world of matter (though they themselves are not material) but reveal a nonsensory aspect of matter. We can be sure these features or principles are inherent in things or else we could not derive the abstractions from the evidence of sense: *Abstrahentium non est mendacium—The abstraction is no lie!* The connection between matter and principle or object and form is discovered, not invented, by the mind. As deWulf noted in his analysis of the Thomistic theory of knowledge:

"We perceive directly reality itself, and not our subjective modification of it. We perceive it thanks to a close collaboration between sense and intellect . . . truth is the correspondence between reality and mind."[27]

4. Human knowledge, in man's earthly life, is imperfect and this is because his reason is imperfectly equipped to grasp the divine essence. Faith has been made available to man so that the imperfections of reason will not cause him to stray from God. However, faith and reason do not conflict and cannot conflict, since both seek the same truths:

> "Science and faith cannot be in the same subject and about the same object; but what is an object of science for one can be an object of faith for another."[28]

Note, then, that Scholastic rationalism is of a limited sort. Reason can bring man only so far in his search for truth. Indeed, even with the aid of faith, the rational mind cannot know all in this life. Not only are all men limited as a *genus*, but not every individual enjoys the same rational faculty as every other individual. All men possess the agent-intellect but not necessarily in the same degree.[29] There will, therefore, be differences in achievement and comprehension. Moreover, since reason's operations are performed on the data of experience, those whose experiences are limited (such as children) or distorted (as in the case of the sick) will have an impoverished intellect.[30] During earthly life, which finds the soul united with the body,

> "it is impossible for our intellect to understand anything actually, except by turning to phantasms."[*][31]

These "phantasms" are the images that perception makes of objects. The child, the delerious, the enfeebled, all fail to record reality aptly and thus fail to understand. But even for them, there is an afterlife in which the soul no longer requires the senses, and truth no longer must be abstracted from sensible things.

5. Because of the foregoing, differences among men as regards their capacity for knowledge lead inescapably to governance by some and servility by others. Before the sin of Adam, man lived in a state of innocence. Even in this state, some would lead and others follow but *only* by common consent; in the state of innocence, slavery is repugnant.[32] However, ours is no longer a state of innocence. Through original sin and weakness of the will, man fails in his duty either by failing to perceive his duty or by failing to act once he has perceived it. In either case, the sin is a departure from the rule of reason.[33] It is the rule of reason that establishes the *eternal law* in man's mind. As one may know of the sun through its rays, so, with respect to eternal law,

---

* It is in this article that St. Thomas notes that "man is impelled in the consideration of intelligible things by being preoccupied with sensible things."

"every rational creature knows it according to some reflection, greater or less."[34]

Those privileged to know it clearly must lead those who are less fortunate. The will of the Prince is indeed the law of the land, but only insofar as the Prince discharges the responsibilities for which his office was created.

Particular Principles

In addition to advancing a general epistemological system that combined empirical and rational elements, the Scholastics also examined more specific psychological functions such as learning, memory, habit, emotion, and language. Throughout the thirteenth and fourteenth centuries the guiding maxim, *nothing is in the intellect which was not first in the senses*, remained, and to this extent Scholastic *applied* psychology was empirical. There should be no need to note, any more than there was in our review of the Aristotelian or Platonist psychologies, the Medieval recognition of reward and punishment as agents of change. Nor need we dally to record each instance of that ordinary insight by which "practice makes perfect" or "as the twig is bent, so grows the tree." It is only in the modern context of behavioral science that these prehistoric verities have been accorded the status of principles, and it is only in the same context that their precise measurement seems to be a worthy undertaking. For the record, we may note in passing that, yes, the Medieval student relied on similarity and vividness to help his memory for facts[35] and, most assuredly, domestic pets were trained by the disciplined dispensing of sweets and cuffings. There was, also, more than a casual interest in dreams, at least as much as every other epoch has displayed, from the Second Empire of Egypt to the contemporary clinics of New York. But more important than any of these to the future of a scientific psychology was the Medieval discovery, although a limited one, of the *experimental* approach to nature, initiated by Grosseteste and developed by Duns Scotus and William of Ockham.

Experimental Science

"[Robert] Grosseteste appears to have been the first medieval writer to recognize and deal with the two fundamental methodological problems of induction and experimental verification and falsification which arose when the Greek conception of geometrical demonstration was applied to the world of experience. He appears to have been the first to set out a systematic and coherent theory of experimental investigation and rational explanation by which the Greek geometrical method was turned into modern experimental science." (A. C. CROMBIE)[36]

When we list the achievements of the twelfth century, we must place, perhaps first on the list, the effective integration of rationalism and empiricism, of Aristotle's logic and Aristotle's experimentalism. In this connection, we must recall that Aristotle's principal failing as a scientist was rooted in an attachment to idealism inherited from Plato and never fully rejected. Having insisted that perception can never penetrate the unchanging truth of matter, Aristotle adopted the geometric, syllogistic method of analysis, the method of logical demonstration as opposed to empirical demonstration. His biological treatises (e.g., *De Partibus Animalium, De Generatione et Corruptione*) and his psychological works (e.g., *De Anima, De Somniis*) were, respectively, either factual at the expense of theory or theoretical at the expense of fact. Convinced that truth was entailed by propositions and not observations, he provided a science rich in logico-mathematical elegance but one largely devoid of practical significance. Only as a naturalist, carefully observing the habits and appearances of the animal kingdom, urging Alexander to order his troops to bring back specimens, reflecting on lunar eclipses, did he capture the spirit of modern science, but he did not impose upon this spirit the formal, theoretical terms required by any major scientific conceptualization.

Grosseteste and his colleagues at Oxford and, a little later, Albertus Magnus and others at Paris succeeded in joining these historically dissociated elements of the Aristotelian legacy. Aided by recent translations of Greek studies in optics and of Euclid's mathematical essays, they set out deliberately to establish scientific proofs through experimental procedures; that is, to bring logical analysis to bear upon nature only after recording natural events with precision.

In an important sense, the religious orthodoxy of the twelfth and thirteenth centuries had a salutary effect upon these scientific enterprises. Peter Lombard had offered convincing arguments for finding God in His works, and this notion was a veritable theological directive. Even before Aquinas formally distinguished between the truths of science and those of faith and showed how one did not conflict with the other, Peter Abailard had posited a dualistic psychology that placed perception and its objects exclusively in the material realm. Even more significantly, the orthodox believer—and Grosseteste was certainly one—had no doubt about the Final Cause, which is God, and therefore could examine *efficient* causes without fear of heresy. His credentials as an unrelenting enemy of Stoic and Epicurean Materialism were commendable. He never entertained the notion that nature was *only* material and so he felt and perhaps was freer to explore those respects in which it was *also* material.

It was in the twelfth and thirteenth centuries also that translations of Greek medical works became available. The Hippocratic school and its descendants down to Galen were uniformly practical in their approach to disease. Diocles, the nutritionist, never paused to assess the logical structure according to which cucumbers from Antioch soothed the bowels. Nor was it necessary to analyze the syllogistic terms applicable to muscle, nerve, and artery. Greek medicine was observational, cor-relational, practical—in short, clinical, as medical practice is to this day. It remained for the Medieval scientists to recognize that the methods that advanced medicine were useful in any branch of inquiry: optics, physics, astronomy. Of course, the resulting factual knowledge could not be of scientific consequence unless (rationally) tied to a general theory. What was necessary, then, was to enter the observational domain with a hypothesis, to record events predicted by that hypothesis, and then to deduce the chain of effects that must take place if observation and hypothesis are properly compatible. As examined in Chapter 1, this *hypothetico-deductive* process is *the* method of science.

Neither Aristotle nor subsequent generations of Aristotelians failed to recognize the value of observation. The Aristotelian refusal to incorporate experimental or even empirical procedures into the philosophical search for truth was based on the ancient, pre-Socratic distinction between the universal and the particular. Since perception could not record the uni-versal, and since only it is ultimately true, no observational science can possibly disclose the truth. We can assess the revolutionary break with this tradition in the following passages from Roger Bacon and from Duns Scotus:

"I now wish to unfold the principles of experimental science, since without experience nothing can be sufficiently known. For there are two modes of acquiring knowledge, namely by reasoning and ex-perience. Reasoning draws a conclusion and makes us grant the con-clusion, but does not make the conclusion certain, nor does it remove doubt so that the mind may rest on the intuition of truth, unless the mind discovers it by the path of experience. . . . Aristotle's statement then that proof is reasoning that causes us to know is to be understood with the proviso that the proof is accompanied by its appropriate experience, and is not to be understood of the bare proof. . . . He therefore who wishes to rejoice without doubt in regard to the truths underlying phenomena must know how to devote himself to experi-ment." (*Opus Majus*, Pt. VI, Ch. 1)[37]

We need not review the many actual experiments conducted by Roger Bacon in his attempt to confirm the value of this new science—one of them involved the use of a stone-prism to separate sunlight into the spectrum—in order to appreciate the modernity of his position. While not rejecting Aristotle's rationalistic approach to proof, Bacon tempers it with the undeniable, immediate proofs of controlled observation. Reason, the *interior* sense, works with perception (the *external* sense) and forges *certain* knowledge. Note that this is not the certain knowledge of the syllogism; that is, a purely logical certainty of the kind entailed by the Aristotelian notion of demonstration. Rather, it is empirically certain knowledge, something that neither Plato nor Aristotle was willing to endorse. The same idea is advanced by Duns Scotus:

> "As for what is known by experience, I have this to say. Even though a person does not experience every single individual, but only a great many, nor does he experience them at all times, but only frequently, still he knows infallibly that it is always this way and holds for all instances. He knows this in virtue of this proposition reposing in his soul: 'Whatever occurs in a great many instances by a cause that is not free, is the natural effect of that cause.' This proposition is known to the intellect even if derived from erring senses."[38]

Robert Grosseteste, Roger Bacon, and Duns Scotus, the "Oxford school," had successfully begun to delimit a new approach to epistemology that would be made official by William of Ockham (1300–1349) and would secure for Ockham one of the more celebrated positions in the history of science. Scotus pleaded for the validity of empirical knowledge. Ockham went even further by reserving to observation the very basis on which any universal concept might be formed. In strict nominalist fashion, he argued that the universal is the name invented by the perceiver to represent that class of particulars learned by experience. In the absence of sensory commerce with the particulars, no universal could be conceived. Logic will take man just so far in his quest for knowledge. At some point, he must temper or even abandon the formalisms of logic in favor of *evident* truths.

Ockham's razor, the maxim that has guided scientific explanation for six hundred years, was an instrument honed by many hands. Grosseteste, Thomas Aquinas, and Duns Scotus were as disinclined to "multiply causes unnecessarily" as was Ockham. Where he exceeded his predecessors was in examining more carefully the nature of the mind itself in attempting to assess the reality of universals and, for that matter, particulars. It is not surprising that Renaissance scholars would be able to identify more readily with the writings of Ockham, not because Ockhamism was liberally heretical, but because it was fundamentally *psychological*.

Ockham's Psychological Synthesis

Ockham was more deliberately psychological in his approach than any of his Scholastic predecessors or contemporaries. Both Thomas Aquinas and Duns Scotus, as well as Albertus Magnus, had addressed the issue of human reason and had even loosely posited psychological principles of perception, memory, and the will. Their efforts, however, were never more than *pre*theoretical and were never removed from the larger religiophilosophical context which was their central concern. Ockham, on the contrary, proposed specific psychological principles, proposed them in a rigorously theoretical manner, and brought these principles to bear upon religiophilosophic questions. Where others had taken the truths of theology as the starting point in their exploration of human nature, Ockham chose to employ the psychological dispositions of man in an attempt to discern the way in which theological conceptions came into being. His approach is not revealed in any single treatise on psychology proper but suffuses the entire range of his scholarship. We are indebted to Oswald Fuchs for his careful compilation of Ockham's *Psychology*, drawn from his major works.[39]

At the core of Ockham's psychological theory is the concept of *habit* (*habitus*) which, in the Latin of Ockham (and in the technical, philosophical Latin of the Romans as well), is understood as an acquired disposition, perfected state, or condition. It represents a qualitative change in the individual such that he is now able to do easily, or perceive readily, or behave effortlessly where, initially, these acts and experiences were difficult or incomplete.

Since the habit disposes the individual to conduct of a certain sort, it must either be present as a condition of his birth or it must be acquired. As dissatisfied with the Platonic solution in the *Meno* as was Aristotle, Ockham argues that habits must be acquired, since fundamentally they are dispositions toward specific objects. We cannot be born with the habit of dressing neatly, since nothing in our conception or gestation is able to anticipate fashion. Now, if our commonest habits require experience and practice, is there any reason to assume that any habit results from something different? Ockham's answer is *No:* all our habits are the result of experience; none is innate, including our moral habits or "virtues."

While Aristotle's associationistic theory of learning was similarly empirical, as is shown most clearly in his description of the newborn soul as a *tabula nuda* (*Nic. Eth.*, Bk. III, 430a) and in his *Posterior Analytics* in which he argues that we know principles through experience and practice (Bk. II, 100a), the Philosopher is not entirely consistent on the point. For, in the *Categories*, habit is rendered as essentially changeless (Sec. 8, 8b) and in the *Metaphysics* he is willing to consider habits of a certain sort as inherent (Bk. V, 1022b). Thus, Ockham is not to be judged merely as an Aristotelian. His theory is far less compromising in its empiricism. It is also far more specific in distinguishing between instincts and similar *physiological* dispositions and habits that are intellectual, gradual in their appearance, and changeable through disuse or conflict.

Consistent with his nominalist position on the question of universals, Ockham insisted that the habit conduces to a given act, is disposed to particular objects, is strengthened by the specific exercise of the act of which it is the habit. However, the mind—*not nature*—can (and does) come to create general categories in which are included acts and objects of a perceptibly similar nature. By a process of abstraction—in modern parlance, we would say *stimulus generalization*—the mind will relate habitually to a number of objects that resemble each other. Cautiously, Ockham avoids speculating on how this is done, describing the process only as *natura occulta*, a process of a hidden or secret nature. There is no universal outside the mind (*extra animam*) but one produced by the mind after frequent experience.

Ockham also discoursed on the passions and appetites that, by association with habits, motivated behavior of an appetitive variety. While insisting that some acts of the will are moral, they are *subjectively* moral in that they *are* acts of the will; that is, moral acts, like other habits, are acquired and therefore cannot be by necessity. Any absoluteness possessed by them must derive from God, not from the experiences of man.

William of Ockham is a fitting conclusion to the Scholastic period. His emphasis on human psychology serves as an introduction to the Renaissance, as does his focus on experience, experiment, and natural causation. Dante died in 1321, Ockham in 1349. Dante was, in all symbolic respects, the last spokesman for the distinctively romantic tone of Medieval life, a life in which allegory was real, fact suspect, nature threatening. Ockham, more than symbolically, is one of the first spokesman of the coming age, an age of confidence, individualism, and grandness coexisting with "natural magic," superstition, and nationalism.

Chivalry, Honor, and the Ideal Life

Of the various institutions, beliefs, and practices that serve to separate the Medieval epoch from other historic periods, none is as unique as chivalry. It is the embodiment of the popular psychology of the Middle Ages in the way that Scholasticism is the embodiment of the academic psychology of the period. And, like Scholasticism, chivalry resists easy classification. We begin to understand it as an idea only by recognizing how readily the Medieval mind blended fact and metaphor so completely as to create a cognitive reality that was nearly otherworldly. In his classical treatise, *"The Waning of the Middle Ages,"* Prof. Huizinga has described this feature of Medieval psychology thus:

"The conception of chivalry as a sublime form of secular life might be defined as an aesthetic ideal assuming the appearance of an ethical ideal. Heroic fancy and romantic sentiment form its basis. But medieval thought did not permit ideal forms of noble life, independent of religion. For this reason, piety and virtue have to be the essence of a knight's life. . . . The . . . revival of the splendor of chivalry that we find everywhere in European courts after 1300 is already connected with the Renaissance by a real link. It is a naive prelude to it."[40] (pp. 69–71)

Committed with as much earnestness as the Scholastics to the idea of natural order, but with far less criticality, the Medieval citizen perceived the world to be a set of established and immutable arrangements—arrangements of an hierarchic order with the Church supreme, her safety and prosperity in the hands of the nobility and, last in the chain of significance, the commoner. It made no difference whether this commoner was a plain farmer, a simple merchant, or a rich and cultivated Burgher. Unless one served God directly as a Cleric or a Knight, his position was of tragic or even comic irrelevance. Even as the lowest economic classes loomed in real importance, the members of these classes refused to acknowledge the growth of their own power. Riveted in the mind was the notion of eternal order, social level, and God's will animating both. We need not pause to criticize here. We can have sympathy or scorn, for example, for the hopeless attempts to reclaim Jerusalem, the "Holy Sepulchre," at a time when the Balkans were on the verge of falling to the Turks or for the oddly macabre tournaments in which life and limb were sacrificed in the name of honor. These are merely symptoms or correlates of a deeper set of values and a more fundamental perceptual bias:

"All realism, in the medieval sense, leads to anthropomorphism. Having attributed a real existence to an idea, the mind wants to see this idea alive, and can only effect this by personifying it. In this way, allegory is born. It is not the same thing as symbolism. Symbolism expresses a mysterious connection between two ideas, allegory gives a visible form to the conception of such a connection. . . . Embracing all nature and all history, symbolism gave a conception of the world, of a still more rigorous unity than that which modern science can offer. Symbolism's image of the world is distinguished by impeccable order, architectonic structure, hierarchic subordination."[41] (*Huizinga*, p. 205)

In parallel fashion, the Scholastic philosophers and the public at large interpreted and created nature according to a great scheme, each piece fitting its intended slot, each act serving an ultimate purpose, each event fulfilling the prophesy of the symbol. The two abiding conditions of the human coil, Love and Death, were dressed in rituals of unimaginable complexity, formality, and design. Pure sensuality, which has never vanished in any epoch, was disguised by the heavy curtain of Courtly Love that required honor before pleasure; that is, it required suffering and sacrifice as conditions for pleasure. In literature, the allegory reigned, particularly in the influential *Roman de la Rose* in which the union of lovers is preceded and attended by a veritable legion of virtues, saints, demons, and coordinators right up to and including the moment at which the "rose" is finally plucked.

The chivalric ideal represented and preserved the Medieval belief in man as created by God and, indeed, as created by God to serve specific and different functions. Classes, since they existed, were *intended* to exist for the same reason that the number "7," chosen by God for the planets, was sacred. The world, itself, is worth noting only as a symbol or metaphor of God's work and, when noting it correctly, one *must* find order, symbol, and the divine. Faith is the light, reason the guide, and suffering, honor, and humility the way. With the Pope as Plato's Philosopher-King, with the Knights as his Guardians, and with a world in which symbols enjoy the ultimate reality of the Ideas, the Medieval mind created a *Republic* where, in fact, a civilization was crumbling.

In observing the parallel development of a Scholastic theory of conduct and the chivalric ideal, we do not mean to suggest that the latter was a conscious product of the former. Whatever praise might be heaped on the knight-errant, it surely would not include an award for scholarship. Rather, we describe the development as *parallel* in that Scholasticism and chivalry reflect the same features of the High Middle Ages but in different ways. The citizen recognized distinct classes, each with distinct responsibilities. Thomas Aquinas set forth these distinctions more formally:

"For everything is for the sake of its operation, since operation is the ultimate perfection of a thing."[42]

However, not only do species differ in their inclinations, owing to a different plan God has for them, but individuals also differ from other members of the same species,

"and a sign of this is that that they are not the same in all, but differ in different subjects."[43]

It was not necessary for the noble of the thirteenth century to read the *Summa Contra Gentiles* in order to learn of his own special obligations, nor was it necessary for Thomas Aquinas to study the social arrangements of Court in order to discern that God has intended each man, uniquely, to participate in the divine adventure. We may ask, however, in the light of this encompassing perspective, how the High Middle Ages were saved from the doleful form of Stoicism that engulfed Rome in the late stages of the Empire?

In some respects, of course, the Medieval perspective must be judged as stoical. Every major Christian spokesman agreed that the universe and all its contents were under the influence of God's gaze and owed their existence and their destiny to His will. Except for the introduction of a personal and knowable Creator, the Medieval scholar in this respect is indistinguishable from the followers of Epicurus or Zeno or Epictetus. For that matter, he is not far removed from the Rationalist astronomers of the seventeenth century or any radical determinist of our own time. But the inclusion of a personal and a knowable God makes a great difference here, a difference great enough to call for restraint in assessing the stoic elements in Medieval thought. For the Medieval Christian, God has endowed man, and only man, with free will and thereby has permitted indeterminacy in human affairs. The price we pay for the freedom is, of course, *responsibility*. We can be said to sin only because we can be said to choose. Our actions are worthy of praise or blame only to the extent that they are voluntary. Scholasticism grants to animals only an instinctive disposition to move toward or away from objects depending on which of the animal's appetites are excited by the stimulus; that is, animals, on the Scholastic account, are *reflexive* but not *reflective*. Man, as a rational creature, can control his appetites and thereby resist actions—or, more properly, *reactions*—that the intellect knows to be in conflict with man's ultimate purpose. Both man and the animal act as they do according to a principle that exists within them; but, whereas the animal has only the appetitive principle, man has, in addition, the intellectual principle.[44] Accordingly, when man sins, it is not because the will has taken control of reason but because the latter has failed to note the evil that attaches to an otherwise pleasurable sensation.[45] This, we note, is entirely consistent with Aristotle's insistence that actions committed in ignorance are involuntary. Thus, to the extent that a man is rational, his will seeks the good, unless misled by sensation. To the extent that man rejects reason, he may free himself from blame but only at the forfeiture of all that attaches to being a man.

Scholastic Psychology and Its Implications

The two and a half centuries beginning in 1100 were among the most inventive in Western history. Not only did scholars such as Robert Grosseteste, Duns Scotus, and William of Ockham define and promote the experimental approach to knowledge, but even heads of state shared in the new learning. Prominent in the latter category was Frederick II, Holy Roman Emperor and king of Sicily (1194–1250). It was this "Renaissance man" who addressed philosophical and scientific questions to scholars throughout the realm and to the Arabs as well. It was he who, putting philosophy and religion aside, experimented with falcons, proving their ability to locate prey by smell by blindfolding them; who reared children in stark silence to determine whether Hebrew was the innate language of man; who tagged fish and returned them to the lake to determine their longevity.[46] Frederick II was not common in these respects among the political leaders of his time—in what age would such a king be common?—but he does appear in the earliest chapter of a new learning, *scientific* learning. He did not reject the Scholastic system, nor did the Renaissance that followed in any but the most carping respects. Rather, he was a product of Scholasticism as were Grosseteste, Scotus, and Ockham. Scholasticism was not a single body of truths or a rigid set of methods. It was not a cult or a version of Christianity. It was a *movement* and, as such, was as diverse as the other *isms* which fill the canvas of intellectual history.

In according man a central position in the Creation, Scholasticism defended this priority on grounds as psychological as they were theological: man, the animal with free will; man, with reason and intellect; man, made in the divine image; man, born in sin and ever on the edge of error; man, like God, to be known by his works.

These themes would be expanded and secularized over the next two hundred years and would take the form of Renaissance *humanism.* The chivalric ideal would be translated into the dignity of man. Experimentalism, under heavy pressures in a very practical world but one still spiritual in tone, would appear as a "natural magic." Man, a child of the Divine, would come to challenge the authority of pope and king alike.

It was not for the Middle Ages to achieve these. Instead, it set the stage. As a period discovering simultaneously experimental science and the special place of human reason in the great scheme, it brought psychology closer to its modern expression by removing it further from its transcendental heritage. That the Scholastics did not invent modern psychology is to be understood in terms of their unwillingness to take the decisive step of viewing man as an *object*. The Renaissance fared no better in this respect. In addition, the Scholastics were concerned more with systematizing than with manipulating nature. As a result, they succeeded in recognizing the systematic character of experimental science but not in initiating actual experimental programs. They were, in this regard, as aloof as the Greeks and they paid the same price—an impoverished technology. They were, their fleeting tilts with empiricism aside, rationalists to the core; that is, a generally impractical sort. But the age they forged, unlike so many in history, commands more respect the more we learn about it.

References

1. An excellent analysis of the legal and moral obligations existing between vassal and lord is provided by Marc Bloch in Ch. XIV, *Feudal Society*, University of Chicago Press, 1961. Translations of several original documents of interest appear in *The Records of Medieval Europe*, edited by Carolly Erickson, Doubleday, Garden City, N.Y., 1971, pp. 161–163. See also R. W. Southern, *The Making of the Middle Ages*, Yale University Press, New Haven, 1959.

2. H. Pirenne, *Medieval Cities: Their Origins and the Revival of Trade*, translated from the French by Frank D. Halsey. Princeton University Press, New Jersey, 1952.

3. Ibid., p. 25.

4. Cited in *Studies in Human Time* by Georges Poulet, Johns Hopkins Press, 1956, p. 10. Prof. Poulet has provided a most valuable study of the manner in which different epochs conceived of time and how these varied conceptions are revealed in the literary works of the periods.

5. Bloch, *Feudal Society*, op. cit., pp. 73, 75.

6. Cited in *Life in the Age of Charlemagne* by Peter Munz, Capricorn Books, New York, 1971 (p. 119).

7. Ibid., p. 122.

8. *The Canticle of the Sun* by St. Francis of Assisi, in *The Writings of St. Francis of Assisi*, translated by Fr. P. Robinson, Dolphin Press, Philadelphia, 1906.

9. Munz, op. cit. Prof. Munz has, in a remarkably organized and brief fashion, presented a clear and thorough picture of Charlemagne's world.

10. The *trivium*, which comprised half of the Medieval curriculum, was Alcuin's invention.

11. The most authoritative and seminal study of the renascent features of the period remains Charles Homer Haskins' *The Renaissance of the Twelfth Century*, Harvard University Press, Cambridge, Mass., 1927.

12. St. Augustine, *De Trinitate*, Book XI, translated by Whitney Oates, Random House, New York, 1948.

13. Haskins, op. cit., p. 14.

14. Munz, op. cit., p. 90.

15. Maurice de Wulf, *An Introduction to Scholastic Philosophy*, Dover edition, 1956 (p. 125).

16. John Scotus Eriugena, *De Divisione Naturae*, Book 4, Ch. 7–9. A good translation can be found in Vol. I, *Selections from Medieval Philosophers*, edited and translated by Richard McKeon, Scribner, New York, 1929.

17. Ibid., Ch. 7.

18. St. Anselm, *Dialogues de Veritate*, in McKeon, op. cit.

19. St. Anselm's *Ontological Argument* is presented and discussed in an excellent little volume, *The Ontological Argument*, introduction by Alvin Plantinga and edited by Richard Taylor. Doubleday, Anchor Books, Garden City, N.Y., 1965.

20. Thomas Aquinas, *Summa Theologica*, Question 75, Part I. All references to the work of Thomas Aquinas are based on the translations of Anton Pegis in the Random House edition of the *Basic Writings of Thomas Aquinas*.

21. Ibid., Question 75, Article 6.

22. Ibid., Question 76, Article 5.

23. Ibid., Question 77, Article 5.

24. Ibid., Question 77, Article 8.

25. Ibid., Question 79, Article 3.

26. Ibid., Question 79, Article 4.

27. de Wulf, op. cit., p. 45.

28. *Summa Theologica*, op. cit., Question 2, Article 4.

29. Ibid., Question 79, Article 6.

30. Ibid., Question 101, Article 2.

31. Ibid., Question 84, Article 7; Question 94, Article 1.

32. Ibid., Question 96, Article 4.

33. Ibid., Question 73, Article 7.

34. Ibid., Question 93, Article 2.

35. For an excellent and intriguing review of the techniques employed, over the ages, to improve memory, see Frances A. Yates' *The Art of Memory*, University of Chicago Press, 1966.

36. A. C. Crombie, *Grosseteste and Experimental Science*, Clarendon Press, Oxford, 1953, pp. 10–11.

37. Roger Bacon, *Opus Majus*, Vol. II, translated by Robert Belle Burke, University of Pennsylvania Press, 1928.

38. John Duns Scotus, *Concerning Human Understanding*. In *Philosophical Writings*, translated by Allan Wolter, Thomas Nelson & Sons, Ltd, London, 1962.

39. *The Psychology of Habit According to William of Ockham* by Oswald Fuchs, The Franciscan Institute, St. Bonaventure, New York, 1952.

40. Johan Huizinga, *The Waning of the Middle Ages*, Doubleday, Garden City, N.Y., pp. 69–71.

41. Ibid., p. 205.

42. Thomas Aquinas, *Summa Contra Gentiles*, translated by Anton Pegis, op. cit., Ch. CXIII (p. 223 in the Random House edition).

43. Ibid.

44. Thomas Aquinas, *Summa Theologica*, Question 6, Article 2, op. cit.

45. Ibid., Question 6, Article 4.

46. An excellent discussion of science in the Court of Frederick II is presented by Charles Homer Haskins in *Studies in the History of Medieval Science*, Frederick Ungar, New York, 1924, Ch. 12–15.

6

□□□□□□□□□□□□□□□□□□□□□□□□□□□□□□□□

Nature and Spirit in the Renaissance

Was There a Renaissance?

Often previously we have noted that abrupt historical transitions exist far more frequently in the historian's mind than in the world of events. At the same time, we have observed that dramatic alterations in perspective have occurred and that these have occasionally taken place on a relatively large scale. Two ready illustrations are found between the Augustan period of Rome and, say, the seventh century, and between the Homeric period of Greek history and the Age of Pericles. An equally vivid change in perspective occurred in far less time: that between the early empire of Charlemagne and the philosophical revival of the twelfth century. In comparing the members of any one of these apposed pairs, one is struck by the degree and number of differences in institutions, social organizations, political processes, aesthetic productions, and philosophical and psychological inclinations. This makes it all the more surprising that most general histories focus on the Renaissance and accord to it a status rare in the annals of historical analysis. It is a focus or emphasis that tempts the more critical reader or writer to overcompensate by denying anything original to the period. But this is a compensation well worth avoiding. Undoubtedly the Renaissance that flowered in *Quattrocento* Florence and spread throughout Europe by the sixteenth century is a period of change, and the changes either touched or completely altered the full range of psychosocial and political institutions. The Medieval Town gave way to the Renaissance City. Chivalry disappeared and Patronage took its place. The scholarship of devotion gradually relinquished first place to the art of analysis. The full partnership of Church and State increasingly became competitive, even combative. Secular authority grew, and economics came to challenge theology as the State's first science.

None of these events serves to establish the claim that a *renascence* occurred. They merely prove the obvious: society and civilization evolve, man is given to change, and new pressures call for new measures. But when scholars of the nineteenth century invented the term, they did not intend *Renaissance* to imply a mere evolution. Writers such as Walter Pater, T. A. Trollope, and John Ruskin sought explicitly to convey the notion of a *rebirth* and, specifically, a rebirth of the classical Greco-Roman approach to life. We need not cavil with this Victorian usage, for, although the nineteenth century created the term, it was the Renaissance scholars themselves who insisted that they were re-creating the classical outlook. Before attempting to assess whether, in fact, they succeeded, we are advised to reflect on the claim itself. In asserting their role as new classicists and by insisting that they were out to restore a particular set of values and institutions, the spokesmen of the Renaissance proved this at least: they viewed themselves in a historical context, they rejected what they considered to be the perspective of their immediate predecessors, and they recognized the evolutionary nature of social man. These very claims served notice on the Medieval view of man and society, the view of eternal order, of each man in his place.

Was there a Renaissance? If the term is to signify a renewed commitment to a contemplative and philosophical life, there surely was no Renaissance in Europe between 1350 and 1600. If it is meant to convey a renewed appreciation of the classical works, and especially the classical philosophical treatises, we need only recall that Lorenzo Valla (1405–1457), perhaps the period's most celebrated *philosophe*, was passionately contemptuous of very nearly every Greek and Roman thinker, with the possible exception of Epicurus.[1] Ficino's neo-Platonist "Academy" in Florence, (established through the support of Cosimo de' Medici) as well as Pietro Pomponazzi's Aristotelianism are sufficient in themselves to confirm the interest of Renaissance scholars in ancient philosophy. But, in the light of the feverish philosophizing that took place from the eleventh to the thirteenth centuries, this interest can hardly be called a *revival!*

The growth of trade, the establishment of banking agencies, the undertaking of massive public and religious works, all are features of the Renaissance but are by no means sudden in their appearance. Each can be traced, uninterruptedly, to Charlemagne, to the Ottonian monarchy of Germany, to the Lombards in Italy and the Norman kings in France. By the time of the Renaissance, each had attained a certain stability and centrality, but none was new.

In adopting the term—and it is one so grafted to the historian's lexicon that no argument will succeed in removing it—we not only impute a characteristic that was not unique to the period but we fail to acknowledge an attitude that was *born*, not reborn, in that period. There is a theme in Renaissance literature that for all intents and purposes is new to the world of letters—a theme that could hardly have found approval in Plato's *Academy* or the *Lyceum* or the court of Marcus Aurelius or the universities of the Schoolmen. It is the theme of the dignity of man, the theme insisting that the world was made for man. It is a theme not easily embraced by any term, though usually labeled as Renaissance *Humanism*.

Humanistic Psychology

"Universal providence belongs to God who is the universal cause. Hence, man, who provides generally for all things, both living and lifeless, is a *kind* of god. . . . Man alone abounds in such a perfection that he first rules himself, something that no animals do, and thereafter rules the family, administers the state, governs nations, and rules the whole world. As if he were born to rule, he is unable to endure any kind of slavery. Moreover, he undergoes death for the common weal, a thing which no animal does . . . (O)ur soul will sometime be able to become in a sense all things; and even to become a god."[2] (MARSILIO FICINO, 1474)

Living at a time when, more than ever before, the public commitment to improve the lot of the less fortunate ranks so high on the list of the affairs of state, we are often lulled into thinking that *humanism* has always referred to *humaneness*. Also, living as we do in an intellectual and cultural period in which religious orthodoxy and religious power are in scarce supply, there is a tendency to think of humanism as something of an antireligionism and to assume, thereby, that the humanism of the Renaissance was a movement away from the Church. Both of these constructions are false, and fundamentally so. The humanism of the Renaissance is quite simply inconceivable without Christianity and in no instance is it to be confused with altruism, charity, or a national dedication to the welfare of the unfortunate. It was first and foremost an *individualism* and an individualism of the rugged sort.

The so-called Hundred Years' War (1338–1453), for all the destruction it heaped upon the English and French contestants, had reestablished the image of the *Great Man* and had succeeded in firing a spirit of nationalism throughout a Europe that previously had been only a loose federation of Christian centers. From 1309 to 1377 the popes had been exiled in Avignon under a succession of French kings beginning with Philip IV (the Fair). This Babylonian Captivity would end only after the Hundred Years' War had reduced French influence in Italy. While it lasted, it made ever more clear the dependence of spiritual authority upon secular (i.e., military, economic, political) patronage. Florence of the fifteenth century was, above all other considerations, the creation of the Medicis whose genius for finance was undiminished from the time of Cosimo the Elder (1389–1464) to Cosimo the Great (1519–1574). Not content with remaking the economic and architectural face of Italy, this family covered all its bets by siring both Leo X and Clement VII.

Even more than great kings and merchants, the Renaissance city itself supported the growing sense of individualism. The medieval town had room for but a handful of leading figures. The Holy Roman Empire, like all empires, was of a scale to embarrass all but regal initiative or papal intervention. The city, however, was perfectly suited to the variety of economic and cultural competition that yields visible and, often, sudden heroes. This capacity of urban life to nurture individual excellence was recognized as clearly by the luminaries of the Renaissance as it is by those of us enjoying the light of history. Early in the fifteenth century, Leonardo Bruni, the chancellor of Florence, wrote his *History of the Florentines* in which he attributed much of the success of the city to the fact that it did not labor under the stultifying and regulatory influences of a Roman empire, or an empire of any sort. Charmed by Aristotle's *Politics* and thoroughly captivated by Plato's *Republic*, Bruni led his contemporaries to a reverence for their cities, a commitment to attain the confined greatness that only urban life allows.[3] It would take nearly another hundred years for the introduction of the first graduated tax, intended to provide relief for the poor, and when this tax was instituted the affluent Florentines were stubborn in their opposition. In other words, Bruni's praise of the city—the Renaissance idea of the city—was rooted in the conviction that man was born for a life of civility and cultivation, and the best men were born to a life bordering on the divine. The city was the place in which such men "made their mark." We will return to this at the end of this chapter.

The spirit of humanism was individualism but, literally, the term was intended to describe the intellectual pursuits held proper for the enlightened members of the urban centers of Italy. These pursuits revolved around the venerable *humane letters* or "humanities," as they are now called. The subjects comprising this domain were none other than the Greek and Latin classics and especially the dramatic and political works of antiquity. We have remarked several times that the Renaissance scholar was not much for careful, philosophical analysis, let alone philosophical originality. Petrarch himself, called by more than one historian the father of the Renaissance, goes to some length in an essay *On His Own*

Ignorance and That of Many Others[4] to prove the weaknesses and contradictions of those vaunted Greeks and Romans. Commenting on
Aristotle's treatment of happiness in the *Ethics*, he offers this, which is
enough to convey the flavor of his rebuke:

> "He knew so absolutely nothing of true happiness that any pious old
> woman, any faithful fisherman, shepherd or peasant is—I will not say
> more subtle, but happier in recognizing it . . . he saw happiness as
> much as the night owl does the sun."[5]

Renaissance humanism, then, was neither self-consciously humane nor,
in any modern sense, especially humanitarian. As a social and psychological agency, it was what might be called the final stage of chivalry:
an agency whereby the privileged class might work toward a noble and
honorable end. As an intellectual movement, it was devoted to a broader
range and a different type of classical scholarship than that which had
arrested the attention of the Scholastics. As a moral instrument, it was
intended (or at least used) to protect the cultural, artistic, and intellectual
prerogatives of aristocrats and the circles that formed around them.

On the question of the relationship between humanism and orthodox
Christian teaching, we should observe that the humanists came close to
heresy only in questioning the authority of Aristotle or Plato or Averroës; that is, they were not heretical at all. They merely recognized, as
Albertus Magnus had two hundred years earlier, that Aristotle was not
Jesus, was not a pope, and was not even a Christian and, therefore, was
capable of error; that the same could be said of any philosopher; that the
essential message of Christianity was not philosophical in the first place.
It is for these reasons that Renaissance humanism is better studied as
humanistic *psychology* than humanistic philosophy. The latter, a philosophy that seeks God through a study of man, had been nearly exhausted by the Schoolmen. But the Renaissance scholar, less concerned
with finding God than with understanding the complexities of his own
evolving society, was driven to a more immediate topic: human nature
and the human spirit. We can examine the conclusions and the methods
of the period by reviewing the theories of its principal spokesmen.

Petrarch (1304–1374)

No single work of Petrarch's stands as a psychological treatise nor, for
that matter, does the bulk of his scholarship qualify as philosophy. Like
Voltaire after him and Diogenes before, his position within the most
important intellectual movement of his age was earned more by the daily

effect of his letters, his immediate effect on his friends, his influence among political and financial luminaries, and his winning rebukes of those who might stand in the way of progress.

In his "book" on his own ignorance—a book that was really a long letter to his friend Donato—he attacks the aloof rationality of Aristotle with a poet's passion, insisting that man can be happy only when in possession of faith and immortality.[6] His own authorities are the Bible, St. Augustine, and Cicero. He rejects Aristotle not because the philosopher was wrong (which, by Petrarch's lights, he was) but because philosophy itself, and especially Aristotle's, failed to make men good, failed to make them happy.

> "It is one thing to know, another to love; one thing to understand, another to will."[7]

We find in Petrarch one of the principal elements of Renaissance thought, the element of skepticism toward intellectualism. Note that this is not a religious skepticism. Quite the contrary. Petrarch was concerned to re-create a healthier and purer climate of faith, one not torn and twisted by Scholastic analysis. He saw his opponents in the camp of the Aristotelians whose contempt for Plato caused them either to ridicule Christian belief or to insist that such belief be reconciled with the tenets of logic. The opposition, then, was none other than Medieval philosophy. By the fourteenth century, Scholasticism had invited many quasi-heretical factions who found the Aristotelian system congenial to the coy badinage the skeptic so readily heaps on those of simple faith and little learning. We should be less surprised, then, to learn that Petrarch, this father of Renaissance humanism, comes down emphatically against, of all things, freedom of speech:

> "So sweet does the word Freedom sound to everyone that Temerity and Audacity please the vulgar crowd, because they look so much like Freedom. Thus the night owls insult the eagle with impunity."[8]

We find in Petrarch four characteristics that will be present in every lasting achievement of the Renaissance mind: (1) suspicious and even hostile attitudes toward formal, philosophical speculation; (2) a restrained position on intellectual expression; (3) a dedication to spirit and the will within the traditional context of Christian belief; and (4) a practical disposition according to which the worth of a man is judged by his works more than his words. The first of these characteristics is principally responsible for the failure of the period to produce a philosophical system of the highest order; the second led finally to the Spanish Inquisition;

the third and fourth animated the monumental achievements in art and architecture. Collectively, these characteristics imparted to the entire epoch a tone often missed by those who discuss the Renaissance: it was an extraordinarily *conservative* era. If, as we may believe, architecture speaks as directly for the spirit of an age as do the words of that period, we need only compare the disciplined, line-and-angle proportions of the Renaissance palace with the free, "barbaric," imperfections of the Gothic cathedral. Without denying the beauty of either, without suggesting that one is superior to the other, we still must recognize a vanity, a pretense, and even a showmanship in the Renaissance structures when examined against the herculean innocence of Chartres or Mt. St. Michel. This distinction was first drawn by the Victorian art historian John Ruskin and it has been drawn no better since. We can develop a more complete understanding of the departure the Renaissance represents and of the variety of conservatism for which Petrarch spoke by examining Ruskin's analysis:

> "Of servile ornament, the principal schools are the Greek, Ninevite, and Egyptian; but their servility is of different kinds. The Greek master-workman was far advanced in knowledge and power above the Assyrian or Egyptian. Neither he nor those for whom he worked could endure the appearance of imperfection in anything; and, therefore, what ornament he appointed to be done by those beneath him was composed of mere geometrical forms . . . which could be executed with absolute precision by line and rule. . . . The Assyrian and Egyptian, on the contrary, less cognizant of accurate form in anything, were content to allow their figure sculpture to be executed by inferior workmen, but lowered the method of its treatment to a standard which every workman could reach, and then trained him by discipline so rigid, that there was no chance of his falling beneath the standard appointed. . . . The workman was, in both systems, a slave. . . . The third kind of ornament, the Renaissance, is that in which the inferior detail becomes principal, the executor of every minor portion being required to exhibit skill and possess knowledge as great as that which is possessed by the master of the design; and in the endeavor to endow him with this skill and knowledge, his own original power is overwhelmed, and the whole building becomes a wearisome exhibition of well-educated imbecility. . . . But in the medieval, or especially Christian, system of ornament, this slavery is done away with altogether; Christianity having recognized, in small things as well as great, the individual value of every soul. . . . It seems a fantastic paradox, but it is nevertheless a most important truth, that no architecture can be truly noble which is *not* imperfect. And this is easily demonstrable. For since

the architect, whom we will suppose capable of doing all in perfection, cannot execute the whole with his own hands, he must either make slaves of his workmen in the old Greek . . . fashion, and level his work to a slave's capacities, which is to degrade it; or else he must take his workmen as he finds them, and let them show their weaknesses together with their strength, which will involve the Gothic imperfection, but render the whole work as noble as the intellect of the age can make it."[9]

Petrarch pleaded the case for man as a child of God, man freed from the prescriptions and dissections of ancient wisdom, man perfectable, man noble. He spoke as well for pragmatism and for disciplined individualism, for a Christian type of freedom. If the Gothic cathedral has that ambiguous and ethereal character of a Platonic *idea*, the Renaissance city displays the orderly reasonableness of Aristotle's categories. But there is no contradiction in identifying Petrarch with both. He sought to remove belief from the context of philosophical debate but, at the same time, to restore the citizen to a life of participation and achievement of the sort proclaimed by the ancients. In separating, or seeking to separate, philosophy from religion and in striving to give the former a practical function, he was instrumental in furthering the late Medieval development that ultimately became the experimental science of Galileo. His attacks on Aristotle were not of philosophical consequence—most anti-Aristotelians of the Renaissance had a less than commanding comprehension of Aristotle—but were of general intellectual consequence. The authority of the Aristotelians, by the fourteenth century, had begun to retard and even repress philosophy and science. There is a general impression, and one not without severe limitations, that the modern world did not begin until the authority of Aristotle was overcome. To the very limited extent that this is true, Petrarch figures centrally.

Marsilio Ficino (1433–1499)

Ficino is of interest because he was selected by Cosimo de' Medici to lead the newly established Platonic "Academy" in Florence (1462). Renaissance Platonism, which was never a re-creation of pure, Platonic philosophy, was yet one more movement or attitude that served to challenge the authority of Aristotelianism. It is important to continue to refer to the contrary perspective or "the enemy" as Aristotelianism and not Aristotle, for much of the criticism and scorn displayed toward Aristotle was based on a failure to comprehend the philosopher's system. Moreover, the attempt to prove God's existence and nature rationally was a Scholastic attempt and one fashioned from Aristotle's methods and arguments; it was not Aristotle's chief aim.

Ficino was devoted to a synthesis of religious opinions and not to a furthering of the explicit rejection either of Aristotle or the Scholastic Aristotelians. He considered Platonist thought to be ideally suited to this synthesis and, accordingly, his psychology is primarily idealistic and nativistic. As with many philosophers before him and since, he viewed man as that special creation torn between the sensual world of appetite and the intellectual world of reason. In this struggle, the soul—as the repository of the appetites, the will, and the intellect—holds the middle ground. It can either be pulled by the call of the senses or elevated by the claims of reason.[10] Its intellective faculty strives to know the eternal truths, while its appetitive faculty can rest only after its pleasures have been won.

Ficino's challenge, and the task facing the new Academy in general, was no less than the historic challenge skepticism presents to the religious mind. It was not essentially different from Protagoras' rebuke of Socrates nor from Hume's quiet assault on belief of any kind. Although it is true that the Renaissance has not left an especially notable record of philosophical originality, it is also true that the period was one of intense debate and assimilation. The rationalism of the scholastics had proceeded to the point of converting virtually every religious claim into a hypothesis and one whose ultimate status would rest upon logic and evidence rather than on faith and revelation. The Thomistic proofs of God's very existence were fetchingly empirical where they were not coldly syllogistic, and it was not long before limitations of both the evidence and the logic were combined to forge seductive heresies. Where Thomas had offered reason as faith's complement, Lorenzo Valla (1405–1457) forcefully contended that the two were in entirely disparate realms of discourse. On the question of free will, for example, Valla had noted that while God's foreknowledge did not make our conduct proceed by necessity (just as our knowledge that the sun will rise tomorrow is not what causes it to rise), that character which predisposes us to act in certain ways was stamped on us by the will of God. Valla, then, in arguing from an hereditarian and preformistic base, anticipated the central themes of Calvinism and also weakened the belief in individual responsibility that Scholasticism had labored so long to instill.[11] His position was of the deterministic sort and even of that mechanical quality that defines so much of the Renaissance achievement.

Ficino and the Platonist revival are to be judged as agents of moderation more than reform. He and his colleagues were devoted to the restoration of a spiritual tone to the affairs of faith. Coupled with their classical outlook this commitment led unavoidably to a special attachment to Plato and the Patristic philosophers, an attachment that was less hostile toward Aristotle and the Scholastics than it was concerned with a side of life that rationalism seemed to neglect.

Giovanni Pico della Mirandola (1463–1494)

One of the more durable characteristics of that form of humanism advanced by the Florentines of the Renaissance was *optimism*. The leading spokesmen of the period were all infected with the idea of progress. They saw themselves as agents of change and this, after all, is the dominant element in the idea of freedom. Perhaps no one was more coherent in his assertion of this idea or more persuasive in bringing it to the foreground of Renaissance discourse than Giovanni Pico.

His *Oration on the Dignity of Man*[12] establishes the human community as unique—even by heavenly standards! It is in this essay that Pico thanks God for granting to man the freedom to change that even the angels do not possess. He notes that animals are tied to their instincts, mindlessly fulfilling the prescriptions of their species. The angels, enjoying a state of spiritual perfection, dedicate themselves eternally and immutably to the praise of God. Man, however, being neither instinctive nor perfected, is free to move in either direction: to degenerate to purely instinctual and sensual levels of existence, or to rise, through reason, to a nearly angelic station:

"If sensitive, he will become brutish. If rational, he will grow into a heavenly being. If intellectual, he will be an angel and the son of God. . . . Who would not admire this, our chameleon?"[13]

Here, then, is one reply to Ficino's conservative neo-Platonism and hereditarianism. Indeed, man is "stamped" by God in such a way as to be predisposed, but it is *freedom* to which he is predisposed. God has not limited man in that dire, constitutional way suffered by animals:

"On man when he came into life the Father conferred the seeds of all kinds and the germs of every way of life."[14]

The notion expressed here has a modern equivalent in the scientific maxim, *ontogeny recapitulates phylogeny:* each advanced species progresses through the developmental stages of the less advanced on its way to maturity. Pico was not, of course, advancing an embryological theory but a psychological one: as the individual confronts the challenge of life, he can use reason and intellect, thereby improving and developing these, or he can confine himself to the more primitive apparatus of survival shared with lower forms of life. Pico, persuaded that all philosophical systems finally agree on certain principles, insists that the only really *human* life for human beings is one in which devotion, experience, action, and contemplation are combined by the powers of reason. He does not reject Ficino; he assimilates his arguments. He does not shun the skeptic; he engages him in debate. He does not deny the stoic immutability of natural law; he merely excludes man from its reach. To the cynic who points accusingly at philosophers' inability to agree, Pico insists that Plato and Aristotle, Scotus and Thomas, Avicenna and Averroës, when properly understood, were in substantial agreement and never contradicted each other on fundamental matters.[15]

While we cannot agree with Pico, we must recognize in his conciliatory plan the desire of a practical and hopeful man to "get on with it." The *pax philosophica* he sought never came about, nor could it have. Had his contemporaries been more given to the creation even of an unsteady peace, had the disputatious voices found skepticism and cynicism less inviting, such excesses as the *Inquisition* might have been averted. This was not to happen. Instead, the new sense of personal freedom combined with growing literacy to create a direct threat to orthodoxy. Mere philosophical reactionism was soon to be replaced by zeal and the force it comes to command. Giovanni Pico, who praised the dignity of man, who observed the unique, human potentiality for change and growth, and who devoted himself to the creation of a *pax philosophica*, died a young man, kindly spared the experience of seeing books burned in the town square.

In addition to his direct influence, Giovanni Pico indirectly influenced Renaissance scholarship through his nephew and biographer, Gianfrancesco Pico della Mirandola (1469–1533). While perceiving his uncle as hero and genius, Gianfrancesco clearly was not attracted by the *pax philosophica* so earnestly desired by Giovanni. In his *Examen Vanitas Doctrinae Gentium* (1520), he unleashed an attack on Aristotle which, in its tone and interpretive deficiencies, served as a model for the subsequent two centuries of anti-Aristotelianism from which we have yet to recover fully.[16]

It is constructive to treat the two Picos together because they disclose the special, intellectual contradictions of the Renaissance and because these contradictions anticipated many of the psychological and social characteristics of the Reformation.

The history of discourse on the human character may be summarized under two great headings: "Nature" and "Spirit." Beneath the former we find naturalism, Stoicism, materialism, and, ultimately, scientific determinism and logical positivism. Below the latter are the near opposites of these: spiritualism, idealism, transcendentalism, psychological indeterminism, and romanticism. Every century or so the terms change but the essential positions remain stubbornly constant. In the Hellenistic period, the controversy was over the reality of the Platonic *Ideas*. Among the Scholastics, this controversy surfaced in the form of the *Nominalist-Realist* antagonism. In the individualistic climate of the Renaissance, it becomes a battle between neo-Platonists and Aristotelians. In the twentieth century, the labels are "Behaviorism" and "Mentalism"; in the eighteenth and nineteenth, "Empiricism" and "Idealism."

For the better part of five hundred years the method of analysis introduced to settle these disputes was logic and, more particiularly, Aristotle's brand of logic. Nature was to be described according to the *Categories*, and the truths of nature were to be unearthed and thence preserved through the infallibility of the syllogism. The Aristotle of the *Historia Animalium*, of *De Caelo*, and *De Partibus Animalium* was either ignored or never found. Thus, Aristotle the Rationalist dominated scholarship, while Aristotle the Empiricist enjoyed only the fleeting recognition of a Grosseteste, a Roger Bacon, a Duns Scotus.

From the earliest part of the Patristic period, theologians expressed concern for the intellectual hegemony Aristotle was coming to exercise over the new faith. Tertullian, with his Jovian impatience, dismissed the Philosopher as a pagan. Plotinus read him as if he were something of an Epicurean. The culmination of this early movement was, of course, Augustine's *Meditations* in which Plato received first honors and in which philosophy itself was relegated to a secondary position on matters of belief. The rediscovery of Aristotle in the twelfth and thirteenth centuries not only redressed the disproportionate status accorded to Platonism but led to such a veneration of Aristotle that his works soon served to arbitrate even questions of Scripture. By the fifteenth century the faith that Thomas Aquinas had sought to defend with reason had become, in many learned quarters, a mere branch of logic and rhetoric. Thus, within the fifteenth-century Florentine circles, we discover three scholarly movements: (1) the revival of Platonism as a system promising to overcome Aristotelianism; (2) a renewed Aristotelianism equipped to meet these neo-Platonist attacks; (3) Giovanni Pico's *syncretism*, by which all philosophical perspectives are searched for their truth-content and are assimilated, peacefully, into a grand Christian scheme.

To these we must add a fourth movement which, while it employed the scholar's traditional tools, was not scholarly in conception or in its mission. This was the anti-intellectual movement away from books, away from argument, away from analysis, away from proof. In its sincerest expression, it was led by Girolamo Savonarola's ceremonial burning of the books. In its meanest form, it was led by the mob who burned Savonarola himself. Between the extremes of piety and hate stand the efforts of such sober commentators as Lorenzo Valla and Gianfrancesco Pico—the former finding enough contradictions among the pagan philosophers to dismiss all of them in favor of simple Christian faith; the latter, reading Aristotle with such distorting lenses as to convert Aristotelianism into a Lockean form of Empiricism and then setting out to dismiss the Philosopher because the senses are less than perfect!

It was in the fifteenth century that the Church was able to cement its position politically. Concurrently, it found it necessary to cement its doctrines as well. Scholasticism had never been more than the gospel of an intellectual elite. Within its fraternity, only Ockham toyed with heresy. By the Renaissance, however, the secular branch not only was more educated and powerful than it had been since the second century but was increasingly at odds with the Church over economic and military issues. Philosophical disputes were no longer mere academic exercises. In a word, philosophy had become *relevant*. One moved through crowded Florence, confronting a wave of street-corner philosophers peddling a variety of interpretations, all documented with quips and quotes, and few bearing any connection to the ancient wisdom. Ideas had become politicized and intellectuals had become warriors. The authorities, both secular and clerical, agreed to determine truth in their own special manner and in 1478 the *Spanish Inquisition* was launched. For two hundred years Nature and Spirit would do battle: Nature, according to which man's dignity is a matter of record, his reason and power nearly limitless, his body and his artifices beautiful, his life and his city reasonable, his mind inquiring; Spirit, with its extraterrestrial vision, its sense of wonder and fear, its murky and ascetic renunciations.

The Renaissance has left unambiguous records of this useless but ageless conflict. Nature and natural*ism*, in their historic marriage to empiricism and materialism, are expressed equally in the art, architecture, and political organization of the Renaissance city and in the ruthless and terrifyingly reasonable exploitation of the weak, the dull, and the poor. Renaissance naturalism simultaneously elevated geometry to the level of aesthetics and developed corruption and deceit to the level of a science. The Aristotle of the *Metaphysics* could be used to justify my success and your failure on the basis of that unavoidable Final Cause toward which all our actions proceed. The Aristotle of the *Politics* and Plato's philosopher-king now made Machiavelli's *Prince* almost syllogistically necessary.

The poor and the ignorant, important to any age because of their numbers and their labors, were now compressed into bustling and prospering cities; they now had firsthand knowledge of what they were missing. Not since the Augustan period had the lowest classes been so close and in such constant commerce with the educated and affluent elite. Serving at the

Banquet of Reason, these plain people could not help but pick up many small but fascinating crumbs: the dignity of man, freedom of the will, Final Causes, necessary truths—heady notions, indeed. Unfortunately these leftovers mixed poorly with Spirit and spiritual*ism*. Final causes and necessary truths, when digested by those used to simpler fare, create the sense of predestination and inevitability. Thus the doctrines of Spirit, which helped to mold some of the most sainted, pious, and loving people in all the world, also bred terrified souls, looking for a witch to burn, a prophesy to fulfill, an astrological sign that would disclose their fate. Renaissance spiritualism reached the summit of the Christian ideal and sank to the depth of fanaticism.

The contradictions within and between those movements we have identified as *Nature* and *Spirit* would come to determine the diverging paths taken by philosophers in the seventeenth and eighteenth centuries and by psychologists in the nineteenth. We prepare ourselves for these developments by reviewing the Renaissance version.

The Hermetic Revival

In addition to installing Ficino as director of his new *Academy*, Cosimo de' Medici kept him busy by providing a steady infusion of Greek manuscripts to be translated. He was no more insistent regarding any of these than he was in the case of the *Corpus Hermeticum*, a collection of books thought to contain the preclassical religiomystical secrets of the disciples of Hermes. Tradition had it that Hermes descended directly from Zoroaster and that his genealogical successors included Orpheus, Aglaophemus, and Pythagoras himself. Thus, the "divine" Plato's philosophical inspiration derived initially from Egyptian mystery religions and only these possessed the purest theology. Ficino titled his translation of the *Corpus*, *Pimander*, and it became one of the most widely read and influential manuscripts of the period. Among its most devout patrons was Giovanni Pico. It was even greeted tolerantly by Pope Alexander VI.[17]

The Renaissance love of antiquity was based in part upon the general belief that the purest and most philosophical eras had been those of Greece and Rome and that, from that time, civilization had undergone steady deterioration. Added to this linear perspective on virtue was the suspicion that if one could penetrate history even further back, before Athens and Rome, to the very fountains of Greek wisdom, one would find the absolute essence of spiritual energy. Egypt always held a deep fascination for the Renaissance faithful, and the *Pimander* unleashed a wave of Egyptomania.

The *Hermes* legend, which the seventeenth-century scholar Isaac Casauban proved to be authored by various hands between A.D. 100 and 300, came to dominate the spiritual dimension of Renaissance life. By deftness of interpretation and through agile translation, Ficino was able to establish a nearly perfect compatibility between its central themes and those of the New Testament. More encouraging even than this surprising agreement was the possibility held out by the *Corpus Hermeticum* that man, in *this* life, could command supernatural powers and share in the cosmic spirit. The Egyptian priests had unearthed all the necessary chants, had discovered all the secret number combinations and alphabetical series, had divined all the essential astrological configurations, and had documented the most reliable talismans, foods, and ceremonies. Those experienced in their ancient art could summon the forces of heaven and partake in the Oneness of it all.

It was Hermetism that placed the sun at the center of cosmic concern, allowing the earth to move, a principle duly acknowledged by Copernicus in defense of his odd speculation. It was this same mystical wisdom that accorded the *Magus* (a kind of magician) the status of a priest. Finally, it was a fundamental tenet of the Hermetic gospel that man is an agent of change, a rational-spiritual force capable of altering Nature's course. That human dignity of which Pico wrote so movingly we now recognize as a product of the Hermetic revival. It proved to be a boon as well for alchemy, for the new (Copernican) astronomy, and for a good share of what passed for science from the sixteenth to the seventeenth century. Giordano Bruno's vaunted defense of Copernicanism was, in the last analysis, no more than Hermetism, bearing no relation to the scientific merits of the case. In addition, many of the most ardent assertions about the human will and man's dignity were made by those firmly rooted in the new Hermetism. Indeed, the Renaissance focus upon the will itself is, in considerable measure, attributable to the lessons of the *Pimander*.

As with so many facets of Renaissance life and thought, Hermetism preserved the worst of what was old and promoted the best of what was to be the new. Its emphasis upon the great cosmic reason which oversees all and upon the will of the "One" kept rationalism alive at a time when postscholastic fatigue might have produced pure cynicism. Still, its brooding cants, its nonsensical astrological and dietary hocus pocus, and its ritual fever conspired to keep many of the best minds of the period and most of the plain folks under the heaviest cowls of superstition and fear. The witchcraft of the sixteenth and seventeenth centuries is a direct legacy as were the rites and tortures invented to solve the problem. Great artists were inspired by Hermetic tenets; others were driven to depravity by the same tenets.

The competing alternatives, Nature and Spirit, were implicit in the

Hermetic system. Part of this system, through the development of *"natural magic,"* led ultimately to an interest in experimental science, the manipulation of nature. The other part, through "spiritual magic," produced the macabre banalities of exorcism, witch-hunting, and self-mutilation.

Piety Reaffirmed: Luther and Savonarola

We are not concerned directly with theological matters and, if we were, Martin Luther and Girolamo Savonarola surely could not be treated under the same heading. Nor, to be sure, is it warranted to accuse either of them for those pietistic reactions to the new learning that led ultimately to the most scandalous forms of oppression and censorship.

At one level, the two had several things in common. Both came from working-class families, both were priests, both were gifted students and avid readers of the classics early in life. Both were passionately opposed to luxury, pomp, and privilege. Both were defiant and belligerent. Neither gained materially from the fame he won. Both were God-fearing Christians without a skeptical bone in their bodies. But there was, at still a higher level and the one required by our present purpose, an additional similarity: Luther and Savonarola were overcome by and devoted their lives to promoting a mystical sense of life's meaning and each, in his own way, instilled in the masses an intense hostility for all the trappings of what history recognizes as civilization.

Savonarola's contempt for the Medicis was without limit or embarrassment. His skill at rhetoric and his exemplary life escalated him to the position of *de facto* dictator of Florence, where in 1497 he led the citizens in the "burning of the vanities." The "vanities" were paintings, books, precious stones, and related symbols of overly dignified man. He imposed upon his once comfortable brothers a life of severe denial and insisted that this was the model for every Christian, popes and princes included. He justified his actions on the basis of Scripture and direct, divine revelation, the latter permitting him to predict the fate of men and nations. His most vivid inspiration was the apparition of a burning sword commanding him to serve as God's gladiator, a vision amplified by dark voices, clouded skies, and by many other persuasive signs.

Luther too was directed to the clerical life by extrapersonal influences; in his case, a terrifying vision. Poor origins and mystical experiences combined with an agile mind to locate him as a professor of Theology at Wittenberg whose Castle Church was to receive his *Ninety-five Theses*. Like Savonarola before him, he reviled the practice of taxing the poor to enrich the Church. The *Theses*, in fact, were written in direct response to John Tetzel's sale of indulgences, the proceeds of which were to help defray the costs of Julius II's plans for St. Peter's, now being carried out under Leo X. But these disputes were only the most superficial aspects of a far more basic rift between Luther and those responsible for the affairs of the Church. At the core of the disagreement—a disagreement that produced no less than the *Reformation* itself—were competing conceptualizations of Christian man.

We can begin a summary of these conceptualizations only after apologizing for the very attempt to encapsulate in a few paragraphs an issue that has arrested the attention of hundreds of theologians and philosophers for four centuries. If it is hazardous to reduce Platonic philosophy to a dozen pages, it is reckless to treat Luther in less than one hundred. However, it is not his theology that concerns us here but his *psychology* and, where his theology is rife with complex and subtle elements, his psychology is daringly straightforward.

Luther's conception of man is completely derivative, where this adjective is intended to contrast with inventive. All he seeks to know about man can be found in the New Testament; indeed, most of what he believes can be known is given by Paul. In his written debate with Erasmus on the question of free will, he summarizes the efforts of Greek, Roman, and Scholastic contributions to the issue as instances of the "plagues [Satan] has bred from philosophy." Scripture tells Luther that God's will is the cause of all things and, therefore, man's will can count for naught. The fatalistic and predestinational refrains dominate his jeering reply to Erasmus[18] and, in case anyone may be deceived into believing that Luther is just playing the scholar's game, he adds this:

"Let me tell you therefore—and I beg you to let this sink deep into your mind—that what I am after in this dispute is to me something serious, necessary, and indeed eternal, something of such a kind and such importance that it ought to be asserted and defended to the death, even if the whole world had not only to be thrown into strife and confusion, but actually to return to total chaos and be reduced to nothingness. . . . Stop your complaining, stop your doctoring; this tumult has arisen and is directed from above, and it will not cease till it makes all the adversaries of the World like mud on the streets."[19]

His attack on reason[20] is the semantic version of the "burning of the vanities":

"What are the Universities, as at present ordered, but as the Book of Maccabees says: 'Schools of 'Greek fashion' and 'heathenish manners' full of dissolute living, where very little is taught of the Holy Scriptures and of the Christian faith, and the blind heathen teacher, Aristotle, rules even further than Christ. Now, my advice would be that the books of Aristotle, the 'Physics', the 'Metaphysics', 'Of the Soul', 'Ethics', which have hitherto been considered the best, be altogether abolished. . . . My heart is grieved to see how many of the best Christians this accursed, proud, knavish, heathen has fooled and led astray with his false words. God sent him as a plague for our sins."[21]

Luther's psychology, for which there are generous Patristic precedents, begins with the conviction that man is born in sin. Where the Medieval rites of chivalry and the Renaissance opportunities for patronage left room for good works to count in heaven, Luther leaves none: good works cannot be performed by an evil soul and a good one can be responsible for no evil. In short, until the spirit is clean it is in peril, and there is no public gesture of altruism or grandiosity able to remove this peril. (The so-called Protestant ethic traces back to Luther only in a very circuitous way.) Purification of the soul requires a renunciation of the flesh, and at this point the distinctions to be made between Luther and Plato are less than striking.

What is central to Luther's psychology is the *will*, since the spiritual status of man can only be assessed in terms of his intentions, and his intentions will either be inspired by God or by Satan. God's inspiration is, alas, *grace*. Without it, there is no hope; with it, no fear or danger. It will come to those who yearn for it and who, through the mystical effects of Scripture, prepare themselves to receive it. Those in the state of grace are doing God's work: the rest are sinners, and this latter category is sufficiently wide to embrace popes, bishops, priests, and kings!

His essay *On Christian Liberty*[22] was an inadvertent call to arms. It was in this work that Luther insisted on the essential political freedom of each and every Christian, answerable to God alone, working for God's glory only, a slave to none but the willing servant of all. His message reached a large and eager audience, but when the Peasants' War (1524–1525) erupted, an angry and amazed Luther quickly issued a polemic, *Against the Thievish, Murderous Hordes of Peasants*. If the Renaissance as a whole is an era of contradictions, Luther's life is an apt analogy. His works bristle simultaneously with Dante's conservative awe toward the legitimate Monarch and with Locke's dedication to liberal reform; with Pico's elevating recognition of the worth of every single human life and with that Augustinian sense of the triviality of temporal affairs; with Valla's contemptuous rejection of the Greeks and with his Thomistic penchant for phrasing his case along essentially Aristotelian lines.

Luther did not create the Reformation; he spoke its message. It was the message of an emerging class, one whose power was already hundreds of years old but only recently sensed. For all his intensity, we must conclude that he never realized how far his own spirit of rebellion and reform would take the world when matched by tens of thousands. In opposing exploitation or fear-mongering, he, as had Savonarola, succeeded only because he induced even greater fear. He threatened the Church through the masses, and the Church, predictably, threatened the masses. Where his own guide had been reason, he disdained its powers publicly. As it receded from the arenas of debate, the rack, the stake, and the ax took over. If there was one man in all of Europe who anticipated this grim outcome, it was Desiderius Erasmus, the Petrarch of the North.

Reason in Waiting

Thomas Macaulay may well have had Erasmus in mind when he wrote in his *History of England:*

"Every where there is a class of men who cling with fondness to whatever is ancient and who, even when convinced by overpowering reasons that innovation would be beneficial, consent to it with many misgivings and forebodings. We find also everywhere another class of men sanguine in hope, bold in speculation, always pressing forward, quick to discern the imperfections of whatever exists, disposed to think lightly of the risks and inconveniences which attend improvements, and disposed to give every change credit for being an improvement. In the sentiments of both classes there is something to approve but, of both, the best specimens will be found not far from a common frontier."[23]

In terms of his mission, Erasmus can be grouped with Savonarola and Luther: he was a reformer, an enemy of clerical abuse. Moreover, like the older Savonarola and the younger Luther, he was a scholar whose inspiration derived from Scripture. Here, however, the similarities end abruptly. Erasmus was a man of universal genius, one whose rare capacities would have surfaced in any age and under any circumstances. Those affairs of life and of state to which he directed his genius are neither national nor seasonal. They have been with us always, and Erasmus saw them with a clarity never surpassed. Luther himself noted as early as 1517, in a letter to John Lang, that Erasmus could not be counted on to further Luther's objectives because

"for him human considerations have an absolute preponderance over divine."[24]

The Renaissance was more of a "middle" age than its predecessor. It was the interim separating two millennia, one ancient and one modern, with our own age falling halfway into the latter. The burning question put to the best minds of the sixteenth century was whether one period could gently give way to the next or whether the new could arrive only upon the death of its parent. Erasmus, more than any other figure of the period, hoped and worked for the first of these possibilities—and failed.

Failure was inevitable. His time was one of desperation, foment, intrigue, unrelenting enmity. His temper was one of conciliation, wit, urbanity, graciousness. We can appreciate his merits more adequately only by realizing that as he wrote, witches were being burned, astrologers were being revered, and elixers were being concocted to rid the body of daemonic possession. Among the scholars of the day, invective and solemnity had all but replaced the search for truth. Europe was dividing itself between king and pope, between reason and passion, between obedience and revolution. Erasmus tried to hold these together, knowing all the while that it simply couldn't be done.

If Luther may be said to have had a "scriptural" conception of man, Erasmus must be said to have had an *Erasmian* view. To avoid this tautology is to court inaccuracy, for the Erasmian view is *sui generis*. That his conception was Christian can be admitted only if we recall his devotion to "St. Socrates." That his position on fundamental questions of faith was orthodox may be granted as long as we note his sympathy for the Skeptics,[25] his charming reproach of theologians in *The Praise of Folly*.[26] There was none more learned in Greek or Latin nor any more eager to promote classical letters but, unlike the Florentine *Graecophiles* who had gone past respect to adoration, Erasmus was wholesomely critical even of the most celebrated of ancient writers. His admiration of Lorenzo Valla[27] was based in large measure on Valla's willingness to scorn the ancients when they earned it.

Erasmian "psychology" is best summarized as practical and eclectic. It flies off every page of his *Colloquies*, the little works rewarded doubly by being condemned both by the Faculty of the Sorbonne *and* the Council of Trent.[28] Of special interest are those dealing with *Exorcism* and *Alchemy*. Not only are these twins of gloomy nonsense held up to ridicule but they are presented in such a way that to hold out any validity for either is to proclaim one's self an innocent. Perhaps the best of the lot is the one titled *Charon*, from the Greek mythological ferryman who brought the souls of the deceased across the river Styx. The colloquy is between Charon and Alastor, the latter querying Charon on the nature of his cargo, and on the varied problems confronted by one with a job such as his. Erasmus stages the colloquy in order to display the banality of war—especially the "just war"—and to depict the shabby rationalizations invented by zealots to justify what is finally homicide. Charon complains that the forests have gone bare feeding wood to witch-burners, and Alastor asks if it is true that the souls of Frenchmen and Spaniards are rather light! He then observes that many a bishop, whose life would not have amounted to much at all, grows rich and famous in time of war: "*They make more profit from the dying than from the living.*"[29] In *The Alchemist*, the master of the "art"—"*who knows no more about it than an ass*"—is no more than a swindler who wins his way into the greedy heart of a great University scholar. In *A Pilgrimage for Religion's Sake*, another simpleton is presented, this one believing that the Virgin Mary has sent him a note complaining of the requests she receives from gamblers, loose women, and so forth. He knows the letter is authentic because the handwriting matches that which wrote "venerabilis" on Venerable Bede's epitaph. And so, one by one, Erasmus pricks vanity, exorcises exorcism, gleefully laments superstition, and otherwise reminds man of his duty to the simple lessons of Christ's life and of the extent to which all the trappings invented to decorate that life serve only to obscure it.

Erasmus was not a scientist. Neither was he a philosopher, a dramatist, or a statesman as these ranks are customarily claimed and awarded. He was a judicious observer and, by this very fact, he pleaded the case for Nature. His letters, colloquies, essays, and adages spoke directly of the observable world—of its problems, its charlatans, its warmongers, its vanities, its follies. His works reflected not only the labors of a polished mind and sympathetic heart but the precision and objectivity earned by judgments when good sense, opened eyes, and freedom from cant address the universe. He was the noblest side of Renaissance humanism.

Leonardo da Vinci (1452–1519)

Of all the records left by the Renaissance, perhaps it is the paintings that offer the clearest evidence of the beliefs and attitudes of the era. The texts of the age are helpful but, owing to the censorship exercised over the written word, they are often of uncertain credibility. Even Savonarola, in his *De Divisione et Utilitate Scientiarum* (*On the Division and Utility of the Sciences*), accorded first place to philosophy and, revealingly, the lowest rung to Ethics, Economics, and Politics. But can we believe that this was his genuine position? Can we believe, that is, that one of the most potent political forces in Renaissance Florence, a man who made a mockery of the classical writings, actually held philosophy in the highest regard and politics in the lowest? In the same work, we are reassured to discover that it is *theology* that is the ultimate science and all the others that are subsidiary. Thus, when we read Savonarola's little treatise carefully, we note that philosophy is first among the servants of theology and that the latter, notwithstanding the rigors of Scholastic analysis, is fundamentally *spiritual.*

Contrast this confusing classification with Raphael's fresco, *The School of Athens,* painted about 1509. Center-stage is given to Plato and Aristotle around whom are arranged the seven liberal arts. This work captures the distinctively *Scholastic* flavor of Renaissance scholarship at least as effectively as any tract written by Valla, Pico, or Ficino. Raphael leaves no doubt in the viewer's mind: the creations of man fit neatly into categories; the categories complement each other but do not overlap; human invention appears in different degrees and one degree is more valued and true than a lower one; philosophy (Metaphysics), as Aristotle said, is the Queen.

Art historians have properly found significance in Raphael's inclusion of Painting among the notables in this fresco. The inclusion is *prima facie* evidence of the status achieved by the artists of the Renaissance and of their clear awareness of this status. But what is all the more apparent in this work, and there are literally hundreds of others that make the same point, is that the Renaissance mind, when it searched for the eternal truths, produced *Scholastic* solutions. It is precisely because of this that the only alternative for many of the Renaissance anti-Aristotelians was to reject all philosophy. Metaphorically we may say that the Renaissance scholar could examine the world and his fellow man through one of only two spectacles: either of philosophy, and this meant *Scholasticism;* or of theology, and this meant *Spiritualism.* To escape the categories meant to leave nature altogether, for what was "nature" other than quantity, quality, substance, state, position. If we are to contrast the truly exceptional philosophical minds of the Renaissance with the large Scholastic background, we begin by noting that Erasmus and Leonardo, through superficially different media of expression, escaped the categories *and did not abandon nature.*

It is always hazardous to rest a case on a single work, let alone a single paragraph. Nonetheless, if one were called upon to locate a brief statement within the *corpus* of Renaissance thought, a statement that completely anticipated the modern era, the following from Leonardo's *Book on Painting* could hardly be equaled:

"Many will think they may reasonably blame me by alleging that my proofs are opposed to the authority of certain men held in the highest reverence by their inexperienced judgements; not considering that my works are the issue of pure and simple experience, who is the one true mistress. These rules are sufficient to enable you to know the true from the false—and this aids men to look only for things that are possible and with due moderation—and not to wrap yourself in ignorance; if this has no good result, you would have, in despair, to give yourself up to melancholy."[30]

And, again, in his essay on *Physiology:*

"Though human ingenuity may make various inventions which, by the help of various machines, answer the same end, it will never devise any invention more beautiful, nor more simple, nor more to the purpose than Nature does."[31]

With respect to the soul, he retains this same, modest naturalism, leaving "to the imagination of friars, those fathers of the people who know all secrets by inspiration," the question of the soul's spiritual composition.

Leonardo wrote on the full range of scientific and engineering topics which would be the focus of attention for centuries. Many of his ideas and inventions would not be improved upon until our own time. His anatomical sketches can still be used for instruction in biology, just as his drawings of various devices can still inform the mechanical engineer. His genius as inventor and painter is so widely recognized and discussed that we need not tarry to revere it. In matters that came to be of importance to modern psychology, his greatest contributions were, of course, in the field of visual perception. He virtually discovered the geometric principles of perspective and, in the process, defined the conditions necessary for depth perception. He studied as well the factors conducive to illusions, to distortions of apparent size, to color contrast, to brightness-enhancement at boundaries, to the perception of motion.

His outlook was one of undaunted empiricism and his methods of inquiry followed accordingly. He shared with Aristotle the conviction that all knowledge begins with perception. To use his words, "wisdom is the daughter of experience."[32] He was duly respectful of reason, a capacity he enjoyed bountifully, but was unalterably opposed to the form of rationalism that required a rejection of the facts of experience. Reason and sense, for Leonardo, were conversant with different features of the knowable world, the former providing the certain truths of mathematics, the latter yielding the probable causes of natural events. He distrusted any science devoid of mathematical substance and he argued that any science, in its final stages of development, would be mathematical in form. This smacks of Cartesian science and also allows us to locate Leonardo, as a *theorist,* in the Rationalist tradition. However, in requiring that the scientist work with the clear and immediate evidence of sense *before* attempting to "mathematize" nature, he was unequivocally a methodological empiricist.

On the question of man's moral dispositions, Leonardo was less than modern, subscribing to an essentially Platonic position. Although willing to attribute failure and vice to bad experience and a lazy attitude, he also believed that people differed in their constitutional makeup; nature made some men golden, some brass, and so forth. However, *"The greatest deception men suffer is from their own opinions,"* and this seemed to be a sufficient injunction against excessive theorizing about human psychology. To know man, one must study him the same way one would go about studying anatomy, geography, and mechanics. The method is observational, the perspective naturalistic, and the descriptions quantitative. Long before Newton would immortalize experimentalism with the maxim *"Hypothesis non fingo!"* (*I frame no hypothesis!*), Leonardo had set the cornerstone.

Was There a Renaissance?

We end this brief analysis of Renaissance philosophical psychology with the question that began it. It is true that the period bracketed by 1350 and 1600 yielded no new philosophical system; that the dominant theme in intellectual circles was the one set by the Scholastics; that witchcraft, alchemy, necromancy, persecution, fear, and mysticism were abundant; that the chief concerns and controversies still centered around theological matters; and that the variable governing political life was the ageless quest for power. But it is also true that a strong and growing middle class began to assert itself; that skepticism was diffused more widely; that literacy and education extended to greater and greater numbers; that art and architecture of unprecedented appeal were created; that science and engineering attained a status not enjoyed since antiquity; that man and his planet were, in increasing fashion, assimilated to that system of thought we have called Naturalism. Intellectual epochs, as we have said so often, do not begin and end abruptly. While Leonardo preached the value of empiricism and experimentalism, Calvin contributed predestinationism—and Calvin's following was a good deal larger than Leonardo's.

To the extent that there is an irreconcilable antagonism between Naturalism and Spiritualism, the Renaissance is important as a period in which the options and obligations held out by each were made clear and pressing. Reading Calvin and Erasmus transports one back to Athens, to the spare and righteous life recommended by the Pythagoreans and the reasonable, cheery gospel of Anaxagoras. As the Catholic Church began to suffer from divisive pressures, various sects splintered away and, ironically, strived for a condition of spiritual life much like the one founded by the early fathers of Catholicism, itself. We do not underestimate the sincerity or intelligence of either the reformers or the orthodox in the fifteenth and sixteenth centuries to note the similarity between their convictions and those that once divided Plato and Aristotle, or Augustine and Aquinas, or Pythagoras and Anaxagoras. Nor do we trivialize their concern by observing the frequency with which it has been expressed and defended historically. In every age there are those who find excesses in the material conditions of life and who seek to rescue us from these by recommending—or imposing—blind obedience, discipline, denial, and humility. If they succeed, it is not long before still others perceive that human life must amount to more than these; that man must do what man can do; that happiness, a sense of dignity, a means of personal growth and individual achievement are as essential as food and shelter; that nature *is* what it appears to be; that what does not appear, alas, is not.

Naturalism and Spiritualism are not the property of any particular religion, nation, or time. There is no religion utterly devoid of one, nor was there ever an age in which both could not be found. Indeed, in any age, both usually have quite a following which is only to say that, in any age, the prospects and realities of war and inhumanity are considerable. It is also why our greatest peacemakers in the intellectual tradition tend to be of the *hypothesis-non-fingo* variety. It is surely not accidental that the greatest treatises authored in behalf of pacifism and humanitarianism have come from the likes of Plato, Aristotle, Epicurus, Thomas Aquinas, Pico, Erasmus, Leonardo, Hobbes, Locke, Hume, Kant; that is, from scholars who, whether "naturalists" or "spiritualists," were disinclined to offer eternal verities. Sentences beginning with "Man is basically . . ." or "Man is merely . . ." are generally offered by those whose minds are made up and it is not long before they add the actions we should take, given this truth they have uncovered. There was a Renaissance, then, and there are many recurring renaissances: to the extent that the best minds of a period write on their own ignorance, or a praise of folly or a paean to human dignity; to the extent that, with Aristotle and Plato, there is a recognition of the limits of intelligence and the complexity of social life; to the extent that individual differences are allowed, encouraged, and assimilated without destruction.

More specifically, there was a rebirth of independence which allowed secular knowledge to develop and be promulgated. The birth of public universities—as early as the twelfth century in Italy—not only extended higher learning beyond the walls of the abbey but also established practical subjects as appropriate topics for study and debate. The University at Padua was central to this movement. It was here that Pomponazzi rekindled Aristotelianism not as the foundation of theology but as the essential ingredient of naturalism. As Prof. Wade has observed:

"In analyzing his [Pomponazzi's] works,—*De Deo, De immortalite animae, De actione reale, De incantationibus, De fato et de libero arbitrio*—the modern historian is struck to see that the five problems with which the Paduan of the Renaissance was preoccupied (existence of God, immortality of the soul, nature of matter, free will, and good and evil, i.e., providence) are the same with which Voltaire struggled at Cirey . . . and strikingly similar to those which engaged the attention of Sartre, Camus, and the other existentialists in the twentieth century."[33]

The secular universities, the invention of the printing press, the migration of classicists from fallen Byzantium, the growth of nation-states and their kings as a check on papal authority, the mystical naturalism of the *Hermetic* truths, and the preceding two centuries of Scholastic intellectualism blended to form a truly original concoction. It would not be an exaggeration to call this novel mix the first *psychological* age, since no prior one was so completely introspective as the Renaissance. Where the quest for personal power had once been confined to an aristocratic few, the Renaissance citizen openly sought to make nature work for him: if orthodox, to make it work religiously; if Hermetic, to make it work magically; if humanistic, to make it work in his behalf politically and intellectually. Pragmatism had never been seen on so great a scale, not even in Augustan Rome. Even the fear of the period, its superstitions and mysticism, were pragmatic at the roots. Medicine, which was essentially Arab medicine, reacquainted the Western mind with Averroës in contexts largely devoid of theological (Scholastic) content. The latent message of Averroist medicine was the message of materialism, and those who absorbed it added to the ranks of naturalism. In the hands of a Pomponazzi, the Averroist form of Aristotelianism led unswervingly to a universe of "two truths": the truths of reason nurtured by perception, and the truths of faith confined to intuition. The latter are beyond proof, and, therefore, need not play a significant role in the affairs of the former. The leading humanists of the period—Erasmus, Thomas More, Montaigne—did not need Averroist science to adopt the same position.

The Renaissance did not succeed in separating Nature and Spirit in a way that might have dignified each. In requiring the two to coexist, the Renaissance scholar too often laced each with tenets of the other or talked himself into believing that each was only a different form of the other. It remained for seventeenth-century philosophers to divorce the two and to promote a notion of irreconcilability which survives to the present day.

The City

Of the several depressing spectacles allowing the twentieth century to call attention to itself, perhaps that of the modern city is the grayest. Millions of bodies are hurled about daily as they seek shelter and success in the faceless blocks of glass which pass for architecture. It is hardly surprising, then, that each year the historic cities of the Renaissance become more appealing to the pilgrim. Moreover, the appeal is based on something in addition to the exquisite beauty of any given building or any collection of art. It is based as well upon the unmistakable sense of order and proportion conveyed by the city *as city*. In an important way, it was the Renaissance that invented the idea of a city, at least as that idea survives, though weakly, in our own time. It is true that Plato's *Republic* and Augustine's *City of God* were addressed in a broad philosophical manner to the moral ingredients of urban life, but neither of these works actually set out to plan a city around definite aesthetic, practical, and political considerations. Not until the fourteenth century did an essentially philosophical vision materialize into conscious urban planning.[34] The vision was Leon Battista Alberti's (1404–1472) and its materialization the result of Nicholas V's genius. The latter (1397–1455), as pope, remade Rome. Prof. C. W. Westfall reviews the relation between Alberti and Nicholas V this way:

> ". . . Alberti's theory of architecture and Nicholas's program for papal government flow together. In his testament the pope outlined a purpose for buildings, and in his treatise the architect described the principles of design for such buildings. Buildings that were perpetual monuments to doctrine would also be architectonic structures conjoined into a city that would facilitate the activity of citizens whose love for God moves them to strive for the good through *virtu*. The pope, while governing the Church, would be a stinging *exemplum* of *virtu*, moving the lower members of the hierarchy to seek God actively. Rome and its buildings would be proper settings for Nicholas's exemplary actions."[35]

The leading architects of *Quattrocento* Rome and Florence were not mere designers. They were, in a manner of speaking, *manual philosophers* conditioned by Augustinianism to appreciate the city as teacher; the city as a moral agent and moral engine. Here, in the beauty and order of a structurally planned space, men and women and children would be constantly reminded of the obligation to impose beauty and order upon their lives and their wills. In this regard, the Renaissance city is not a sudden invention but the logical extension of the chivalric animus. When communities were scattered and fragile, it was the knight who kept lonely vigil over the human potential for sacrifices and honor. The military and economic security of the Church of Quattrocento Italy transformed the idea of city as fortress to that of city as agent.

Even with this enlarged set of responsibilities, the city retained an essentially chivalric character. That is to say, even under the more modern press of finance and political machination, the city retained the quality of a *symbol*—a largely medieval symbol. Where the silhouette of the knight, painted against a drear and portentous sky, once chilled the designs of a luckless felon, once fired the moral passions of children, once served to imbue peasant and priest alike with the spirit of God's justice and mercy, there now stood the outline of the city. Within this city, churches and houses, meeting halls and municipal offices, gardens and markets would be placed according to a plan. Streets would be laid in order to join related functions. Size would be employed as the symbol of significance. Each frieze and *filarete* not only ornaments a building but tells a story, teaches a lesson, recalls a value, intones an obligation, evokes a noble sentiment. True enough, these features of the Renaissance city can be found in the Athens of Pericles, in the Rome of Augustus, even the Paris of Albertus Magnus. But even at the peak of their cultivation, ancient Athens and Rome were not cities in the modern sense and medieval Paris was scarcely more than a university town. Florence and Rome in the Renaissance were cities on a grand scale even by modern standards. They were places in which one could find anything known or done by the civilized world. They possessed most of the wealth, nearly all of the art, the sum of the talent of the age.

There is a dark side to all of this too. Ancient Greece hosted a symbiotic arrangement between aristocrat and farmer. At the height of Athenian influence, the agricultural class still played a salient role in the affairs of state. The medieval township or fortress-community preserved this tradition. Even the Roman patrician revered the land and sought the pastoral reaches of the exurban territory for peace and reflection. The Renaissance city, however, as a valid city, began to change this and the change has progressed almost without a pause. By the fifteenth century, the needs of major cities have already begun to be insatiable. The countrysides become mere suppliers; their inhabitants, near-barbarians. Now, urbanism, urbanity, and the like are *the* culture, and the city is at once a symbol of some higher mission and a reality in its own right. That is, the possibilities it once announced are now obscured by the realities it presents to its citizens. Living becomes coping, and the quest for perfection gives way to the struggle for success. The chivalric ideal becomes perverted into the gaudy ritual of self-conscious heroism as the knight is displaced by the banker. The city takes on its own life and begins to use and abuse the citizen in return for which it offers mere services. Values give way to fashion, valor to competition, restraint and sacrifice to unimaginable poverty. As sociologically understood, the "modern world" begins with the Renaissance city which, ironically, was to reawaken the classical idea of life.

References

1. *The Renaissance Philosophy of Man*, edited by E. Cassirer, P. O. Kristeller, and J. H. Randall, University of Chicago Press, 1948, p. 147.

2. J. L. Burroughs, translator. "Platonic Theology," *Journal of the History of Ideas*, April 1944.

3. Eugenio Garin, *Science and the Civic Life in the Italian Renaissance*, translated by Peter Munz. Doubleday, Garden City, N.Y., 1969, pp. 21–48.

4. *Renaissance Philosophy of Man*, op. cit., *Petrarch*, translated by Hans Nachod, *On His Own Ignorance*.

5. Ibid., p. 74.

6. Ibid., p. 75.

7. Ibid., p. 103.

8. Ibid., p. 121.

9. Ruskin, *The Stones of Venice*, Vol. II, pp. 159–171, Reuwee, Wattley & Walsh, Philadelphia.

10. Marsilio Ficino, in *Renaissance Philosophy of Man*, op. cit.

11. Lorenzo Valla, in *Renaissance Philosophy of Man*, op. cit.

12. Giovanni Pico della Mirandola, in *Renaissance Philosophy of Man*, op. cit.

13. Ibid., p. 225.

14. Ibid.

15. Ibid., p. 245.

16. Charles B. Schmitt, *Gianfrancesco Pico della Mirandola and His Critique of Aristotle*, Martinus Nijhoff, The Hague, 1967.

17. Frances A. Yates, *Giordano Bruno and the Hermetic Tradition*. University of Chicago Press, 1964. This is a brilliant reinterpretation of the "phenomenon" who was Bruno. Prof. Yates notes that, far from a spokesman for the new science or a harbinger of seventeenth-century empiricism, or even a defender of Copernican theory, Bruno was a mystic, a Hermetist.

18. Yates, op. cit., p. 121.

19. Ibid., pp. 128–130.

20. Ibid., pp. 185–186.

21. Martin Luther, *Twenty-seven Articles Respecting the Reformation of the Christian State*. In Vol. I., *Introduction to Contemporary Civilization in the West*, edited by J. Buchler et al. Columbia University Press, New York, 1946 (p. 630).

22. Ibid., pp. 634–647.

23. Thomas B. Macaulay's *History of England*, Vol. I., Harper & Row, New York, 1849.

24. Heinrich Boehmer, *Martin Luther: Road to Reformation*, New York, 1957, p. 160.

25. *Luther and Erasmus: Free Will and Salvation*. Library of Christian

Classics, *Vol. XVII*, Westminster Press, Philadelphia, 1969. (P. 37, Erasmus' *De Libero Arbitrio*, translated by E. Gordon Rupp.)

26. Erasmus, *The Praise of Folly*, translated by Hoyt Hopewell Hudson, Princeton University Press, 1941.

27. *The Epistles of Erasmus*, translated by Francis Morgan Nichols, Vol. I., #26, Longmans, Green, London, 1901.

28. Erasmus: *Ten Colloquies*, translated by Craig R. Thompson, Bobbs-Merrill, Indianapolis, 1957.

29. Ibid., p. 116.

30. *The Literary Works of Leonardo Da Vinci*, edited by Jean Paul Richter, Vol. I. #12, pp. 116–117, Phaidon Press, Ltd, 1970.

31. Ibid., Vol. II., pp. 100–101 (#837).

32. Ibid., p. 240 (#1150).

33. Ira O. Wade: *The Intellectual Origins of the French Enlightenment*, Princeton University Press, 1971, p. 63.

34. A brilliant study of the origins of city planning in fifteenth-century Rome and Florence is Carroll William Westfall's, *In This Most Perfect Paradise: Alberti, Nicholas V, and the Invention of Conscious Urban Planning in Rome, 1447–55*, Pennsylvania State University Press, 1974.

35. C. W. Westfall, op. cit., p. 62.

From Philosophy to Psychology

7

☐☐☐☐☐☐☐☐☐☐☐☐☐☐☐☐☐☐☐☐☐☐☐☐☐☐☐☐☐

Empiricism

THE AUTHORITY OF EXPERIENCE

The Terms

We must not corrupt our hope, To prostitute our past-cure malladie
to Empiricks.
—SHAKESPEARE, *All's Well That Ends Well*, 1602

An empirical law, then, is an observed uniformity, presumed to be
resolved into simpler laws, but not yet resolved into them.
—J. S. MILL, *System of Logic*, 1846

A mere Rationalist (that is to say, in plain English, an Atheist of the
late Edition).
—SANDERSON, *Preface to Ussher's Power Princes*, 1670

According to rationalism, reason furnishes certain elements, without
which, experience is not possible.
—FLEMING, *Philosophical Vocabulary*, 1857

The empirical philosophers are like to pismires (ants). . . . The
rationalists are like the spiders.
—BACON, *Apoph.*, 1626

The earliest differentiation between rationalistic and empiricistic approaches to knowledge occurred among the ancient Greek physicians.
The Hippocratic school, devoted to observation and correlation, referred
to its members as *empirici* (Gk.: εμπειρικος = experience; πειρια = experi-

195

ment). Their competitors, drawn from Pythagorean and mystic quarters as well as from "rationalistic" schools, based their therapeutic procedures on theory, divination, occult signs, various formulae; that is, on principles or beliefs deduced from some more fundamental proposition. The Hippocratics were naturalistic and pragmatic; the non-Hippocratics, metaphysical or even mystical.

Over the centuries these two labels have been applied with such generous diversity that it becomes necessary, each time we use one of them, to qualify the usage in terms of a given period's prevailing sentiment. J. S. Mill, the "Saint of *Rationalism*," can hardly be considered a mystic!

The problem of definition and, therefore, comprehension, is made still more difficult by the ambiguous position of another *ism*, *idealism*, in relation to empirical and rationalistic epistemologies. Philosophical history is so divergent and subtle on the issues to which these labels refer that we are advised to pause at this point to indicate precisely what each of these terms and their derivative terms are intended to mean when used in this and succeeding chapters. It is always distracting to insert a glossary into a text but, in the present instance, the advantages outweigh the liability.

Rationalism and empiricism, as we know them today, have the inevitable Platonic and Aristotelian ancestry claimed by all philosophical persuasions but have more immediate origins in Renaissance humanism, hermetism, and skepticism. When historians tell us that the modern era of science did not begin until the authority of Aristotle was overcome, they are generally referring to the emergence of an experimental attitude and the suspension of purely logical approaches to discovery. However, this very experimental attitude, one that Aristotle possessed in abundance, is to be found most vividly in the "natural magic" of the sixteenth century and is, therefore, rooted in traditions of an essentially *theological* character. Unlike Aristotle's own empirical attitude, which was that of the detached, disinterested observer of nature—an attitude reinforced by the simple desire to discover the makeup of the physical and animal world—Renaissance empiricism and experimentalism derived from the motive to control and manipulate nature, to make nature conform and obey, to *change* the world. It is this difference that accounts, in large part, for the inextricable connection between science and technology in the Renaissance and for the otherwise surprising indifference of Greek science toward technology. In this we have one more instance of the failure of the Renaissance to achieve that which it proclaimed to be its central mission: the re-creation of the classical outlook.

Renaissance rationalism too was given more to the "spiritual magic" of the Hermetic legacy than it was to that classical version of rationalism best represented by Anaxagoras and Aristotle. In their contempt for the Scholastics and, therefore, for the Aristotelian foundations of Scholasticism, Renaissance rationalists such as Giordano Bruno looked beyond the tidy veracity of the syllogism for still grander truths. These were to be found first in the eternal Platonic *Ideas* and, on closer inspection, in the preclassical visions documented in the *Corpus Hermeticum*.

The modern era, then, did not begin either with the science of the Renaissance or with its suspicion of Aristotle. It didn't begin in the Renaissance at all except to the extent that the quiet skepticism of Erasmus and the insolent skepticism of Gianfrancesco Pico are precursors to the *Novum Organum* of Francis Bacon (1561–1626). We will direct our attention to this work and its author presently, but first we must underscore these facts: (1) Renaissance "empiricism" was hardly more than magic by another name; (2) with few exceptions, Renaissance anti-Aristotelianism was not an introduction to the modern world but a longing for a far older and very mysterious one; (3) the Copernican "revolution" (1543), to the extent that it affected the sixteenth-century mind at all, drove thinking more in the direction of the *Pimander* than it did toward the *Novum Organum;* (4) the achievements in art, architecture, technology, science, and commerce, which are often cited to set the Renaissance off from its Medieval forebears, were firmly entrenched in a religious outlook, and this outlook, in its most defining aspects, was spiritual. In the light of these facts, we are to recognize that empiricism as we know it could not begin until its Renaissance roots were pulled up and withered; that rationalism as we know it could not begin until Aristotle was restored to Aristotelianism; that experimentalism, as a branch of *science*, could not begin until naturalism replaced spiritualism. The thesis advanced here, therefore, is that the modern era began not as a rejection of ancient wisdom, not as a political response to the authority of the Church, not as a dismissal of Scholasticism, and not as the triumph of perception over logic. The modern era began as a rejection of the Renaissance, which is to say, as the triumph of naturalism over spiritualism. To the extent that it may be called modern it is to be seen as an era in which small projects replaced grand ones, an era in which scientific humility replaced the limitless reach of magic. The Renaissance was philosophically conservative and scientifically radical. The seventeenth century reversed this, or at least rejected both the conservative and the radical molds. Leonardo announced the modern era and Francis Bacon attempted to define it. As can be discerned in his remarks quoted at the beginning of this chapter, Bacon was no admirer of empiricism—as empiricism was practiced in the Renaissance. He rebuked those who would attempt to construct theories from the limited material, or, as he said, "the narrowness and darkness of a few experiments."[1]

While scorning the Aristotelian form of empiricism, according to which experiments are performed in keeping with an initial metaphysical bias and one that must be satisfied by the "experiment," Bacon was recommending an empiricism of his own: the direct, theoretically neutral observation of nature for the purpose of learning the physical facts of the real world.

This form of empiricism, which Bacon construed to be as much at odds with Aristotle as it was with mysticism, is precisely the form that Gianfrancesco Pico construed as Aristotelianism's fatal flaw! Gianfrancesco's contention was that Aristotle based his epistemology on the faulty data of sense; Bacon's, that he did not limit his science to the facts of sense. What we learn from these contradictory complaints is, of course, that each age reads Aristotle in the way that pleases it most. Gianfrancesco's skepticism was heavily coated with Hermetism, Bacon's with naturalism.

The empirical movement launched by Bacon is the scientific movement itself. Empiricism, understood within this movement, is the epistemology that asserts that *the evidence of sense constitutes the primary data of all knowledge; that knowledge cannot exist unless this evidence has first been gathered; and that all subsequent intellectual processes must use this evidence and only this evidence in framing valid propositions about the real world.*

Rationalism, as received by our own time, is the product of the philosophical systems created by Descartes, Spinoza, and Leibniz. It is no coincidence that two of them, Descartes and Leibniz, were distinguished mathematicians. Descartes founded analytical geometry, and Leibniz invented the calculus independently of Newton. The modern rationalist, from the seventeenth century on, has shared with the ancient Pythagoreans and with the Plato of the "number theory," a vision of the real world as a system of mathematical, harmonic relationships. Persuaded by the proofs of mathematics that *certain* knowledge exists, he has been indifferent or hostile to the imprecise and ephemeral "truths" of sense. He has insisted that when reason explores the universe, a small set of fundamental and irrefutable principles are clear and that, from these, the more detailed facts and fabric of nature can be deduced rationally. It is ironic that what we now accept as empiricism is founded on that feature of Aristotle's so-called rationalism which was invented to challenge Plato's idealism. In fact, most post-Renaissance attacks on Aristotelian "rationalism" are cut from the same cloth as Aristotle's attack on Platonism.

What modern rationalism does retain of its Aristotelian origins is the contention that the very act of perception must assume a categorical framework if experience is to be anything other than a great blooming buzz of confusion. The mind must be so constituted as to segregate and organize sense data. It must be so equipped as to direct the senses, separate their illusory from their real content. One way or another, the rationalist position incorporates the concept of an *a priori* cognitive capacity. Without it, meaningful experience is not possible.

Rationalism, then, is the epistemological system that asserts that *all knowledge is the result of a rational analysis of the evidence of sense and that this very evidence cannot be gathered except by a rationally directing principle*. Accordingly, the primary "datum" of which our knowledge is comprised is that innate disposition called *the laws of thought*.

It is important to note that neither empiricism nor rationalism, so understood, is committed to idealism. Empiricism has led to idealistic epistemologies, as we shall see in our review of George Berkeley's philosophy. Rationalism, especially of the neo-Kantian variety, has also courted forms of idealism. But neither empiricism nor rationalism entails idealism, and some of the more illustrious spokesmen of both have occasionally rejected it. The rationalist is under no constraint to accept reality as but the perceivable manifestation of an idea, nor must the empiricist conclude, in believing what he sees, that reality vanishes when human sense is withdrawn. We must accentuate this fact because there is sometimes a tendency to identify empiricism and (particularly) rationalism with versions of solipsism. This tendency will not find support in the writings of either the major empiricists or the major rationalists.

We should also recognize a point of agreement between rationalists and empiricists which survived unimpaired until the advent of *empirical behaviorism* in the twentieth century. This common feature may best be labeled *mentalism*. The leading architects of empiricism—Berkeley, Locke, and Hume—all based their epistemologies upon what seemed to them to be the fixed dispositions of the mind. In other words, their philosophies were explicitly designed to account for the facts of *mental* life. While all agreed that the mind is furnished by the senses, they agreed as well that philosophy's task was to determine how this occurred and what can possibly be known given that it occurs. The empirical tradition, therefore, is in no sense *anti*mental, notwithstanding its emphasis on perception. Rationalism, of course, is unabashedly mentalistic. We must appreciate this common ground held by empiricists and rationalists if we are to comprehend the very substantial departure from tradition taken by the twentieth-century behaviorists. We will take up the rationalist tradition in the next chapter.

The Empiricists

1. FRANCIS BACON

Bacon was born to a ranking family, but his own star rose higher than all of theirs combined. Successively, he was a leading and prosperous attorney, a member of the Privy Council, the Lord Keeper of the Great Seal, the Chancellor of the Realm, and in 1618 he was named Baron Verulam by his admiring king, James I. It is a sign of his time that he was forced to resign from office in 1621, charged with accepting bribes. That the charge was valid is not to be questioned, only that there could have been no Bench in all of England had simon-pure been a condition of service. We will have a better comprehension of his *Novum Organum* after briefly examining the conditions leading up to and surrounding its authorship.

Luther's Reformation movement which, on the Continent, was a popular cause and one fired by the poverty consuming the German states, was to be absorbed by England on a different basis. There, a terrible rift had been infecting the affairs of Church and Throne for centuries. As early as the twelfth century English kings had sought to gain independence from Rome by contending that in temporal matters the Sovereign's will was the law of the land. The famous showdown between Henry II and Thomas à Becket, Bishop of Canterbury, which ended with the latter's murder (1170), was followed by a wave of Roman Catholic zeal threatening to reduce the throne to a form of vassalage. Throughout the later Middle Ages and the sixteenth century all varieties of intrigue were fashioned to maintain a delicate balance of power among English, European, and papal forces. It was in the reign of Henry VIII that the European reform movement had so threatened papal authority in Europe that an English king might take an extreme action. In 1533 Henry declared his marriage to Anne Boleyn legal, despite the pope's refusal to annul his current and fruitless marriage to Catherine. Anne lost her head within three years of their wedding day, charged with adultery, although her crime seems to have been the failure to produce a male heir. The marriage had lasted long enough, however, to yield a daughter, Elizabeth, later Elizabeth I, the most kingly queen in the long history of that office.

If the reign of Elizabeth (1558–1603) had embraced no more than the works of Shakespeare, it would still demand the attention of scholars. But the Elizabethan era amounted to more than even these. Its cultural achievements aside, it was the period in which Calvinism got its grip on the English mind, when Puritans began their holy vigil against pleasure, and when a throne that had long been cudgeled by papal Bulls found its moment of revenge. Catholics were no longer permitted to celebrate the Mass. Altars and icons were removed from the churches. Houses of suspected Catholics were entered and searched. The response from Rome was a decree from Pius V that announced Elizabeth an excommunicate and instructed English Catholics to ignore her laws. Recalling the circumstances of her birth, the oppressed Catholic majority now judged the Queen to be no more entitled to the crown than any other of Henry's bastards. Not unpredictably an Irish revolt was precipitated and was put down at a cost in lives and money almost unprecedented in England's history to that date. War with Spain followed and the defeat of the Spanish Armada began a period of oceanic rule which England enjoyed until our own century. But neither military success nor artistic accomplishments were able to mute the hostile cries of the religiously persecuted. The Catholic majority was outraged, and the small Puritan faction even more so. Elizabeth's niece, Mary, had been the exiled "Queen of Scots" for years and posed a constant threat to Elizabeth's publicly perceived legitimacy, for Mary Stuart was the great-granddaughter of Henry VII, and her pedigree was without corruption. Elizabeth had her beheaded in 1587, but by then Mary Stuart's son, James VI, was already twenty-one, was king of Scotland, and was on record as a defender of Protestantism. At the age of thirty-seven, he succeeded to the throne of England as James I. Within two years appeared "*The Proficience and Advancement of Learning*," (1605), Bacon's first major work. Elizabeth was dead and a time for renewal and rededication had arrived. Blood was to be spilled again in that most horrible of civil wars (1642–1649), but in the reign of James I (1603–1625) there was to be an interval of peace and ground-laying that would start English scholarship on a voyage from which it has never turned back. Bacon was its first captain and the *Novum Organum* its chart.

Many ideas developed in the *Novum Organum* were first set forth in the *Advancement of Learning*, a far earlier work and one serving rather as an outline for the *Novum Organum*. We will use the *Advancement of Learning*, therefore, to introduce the larger work.

Bacon's mission was fivefold: to delineate the principal causes of ignorance and disagreement; to specify the nature of true authority in matters intellectual; to indicate those areas of inquiry about which too little is known; to present methods able to accommodate the foregoing; to articulate the basis upon which any undertaking is worth the effort. On the question of method, the *Advancement* proves to be a skimpy text, but its deficiencies were ably overcome in the *Novum Organum*. On the last point, Bacon's position can be summarized very quickly: the value of an undertaking is assessed in terms of the potential benefit to the human race. If the project can do man little or no good in the daily affairs of life, there is the strongest presumption that it is worthless. This position, we see, is but the bold version of the pragmatic spirit that first blossomed in the Renaissance. It is also a specific disavowal of the aspect of Reformation theology that underestimated the value of human *works*. In Bacon's system, usefulness and worthiness are synonymous. This is made clear in a passage not yet devoid of the Hermetic tradition:

> "But the greatest error of all the rest is the mistaking or misplacing of the last or furthest end of knowledge. For men have entered into a desire of learning and knowledge . . . seldom sincerely to give a true account of their gift of reason, to the benefit and use of men . . . for the glory of the Creator and the relief of man's estate. But this is that which will indeed dignify and exalt knowledge, if contemplation and action may be more nearly and straitly conjoined and united together than they have been; a conjunction like unto that of the two highest planets, Saturn the planet of rest and contemplation, and Jupiter the planet of civil society and action."[2]

In regard to the issue of legitimate authority, the *Advancement* shows that Bacon was not the zealous and radical antitraditionalist so often conveyed by caricatures of his writing. He praises Aristotle often as well as other leading philosophers. However, he condemns those (and especially the Scholastics) who consult antiquity with such diffidence as to be unwilling to add a line or a reservation to Greek or Roman teaching:

> "For as water will not ascend higher than the level of the first springhead . . . so knowledge derived from Aristotle, and exempted from the liberty of examination, will not rise again higher than the knowledge of Aristotle."[3]

The complaint, then, is not with the ancients but with their disciples. Similarly those following in the steps of Luther—Luther, who had revived many ancient works to defend his charges against the Church— have become more interested in the words and the grammatical style of the older writers than they have in the very matters to which Luther was addressed:

> "Words are but the images of matter . . . to fall in love with them is all one as to fall in love with a picture."[4]

In addition to stultifying reverence for antiquity, there are human inventions that stand in the way of the advancement of learning—inventions of the mind and based on the gullibility of the mind. Bacon isolates three of these: *astrology*, *natural magic*, and *alchemy*.[5] As Aristotle was the "dictator" of the Scholastics, miracles, spirits, illusions, and magicians have come to master the common mind. A part of the source of these superstitions he attributes to too much concern for "final causes" and particularly to the inclusion of discussions of these final causes in the area of *physics* rather than *metaphysics*. Perhaps the most modern notion submitted in the *Advancement* is that which insists on the division of Natural Science into these two branches and the requirement that the issues in physics be treated with methods different from those purely logical devices normally employed in metaphysical analysis.[6] In addition to this division, Bacon argues that mathematics be reserved to metaphysical matters and, in this way, he stands foursquare against that rationalist (neo-Platonist) tradition which seeks to comprehend nature in terms of number theories, harmonies, and the like.*[7]

The portion of the *Advancement of Learning* that is of the greatest importance to the history of psychology are the sections dealing with subjects that have not received their due in the deliberations of natural philosophers. It is in these sections that Bacon invents the disciplines of theoretical and experimental psychology without naming them. Bacon's own words could not be clearer:

"We come therefore now to that knowledge whereunto the ancient oracle directeth us, which is *the knowledge of ourselves;* which deserveth the more accurate handling, by how much it toucheth us more nearly. This knowledge, as it is the end and term of natural philosophy in the intention of man, so notwithstanding it is but a portion of natural philosophy in the continent of nature. . . . (W)e proceed to Human Philosophy or Humanity, which hath two parts: the one considereth man segregate, or distributively; the other congregate, or in society. So as Human Philosophy is either Simple and Particular, or Conjugate and Civil. Humanity Particular consisteth of the same parts whereof man consisteth; that is, of knowledges which respect the Body, and of knowledges that respect the Mind . . . *how the one discloseth the other* and *how the one worketh upon the other* . . . the one is honored with the inquiry of Aristotle, and the other of Hippocrates."[8]

And then a little later in the essay:

"For Human Knowledge which concerns the Mind, it hath two parts; the one that enquireth of *the substance or nature of the soul or mind,*

---

* It is here also that Bacon recommends the study of mathematics as a means of promoting the mind's agility.

the other that enquireth of the faculties or functions thereof. Unto the
first of these, the considerations of *the original of the soul*, whether it
be *native or inventive*, and *how far it is exempted from the laws of
matter*."[9]

We cannot read these passages without being reminded of Aristotle's
De Anima, but we must recognize a telling difference: Bacon is presenting this subject matter as a branch of natural science and is reducing it to
a set of questions of an *experimental* nature. This is not reheated Aristotelianism!

In the concluding pages of the *Advancement*, Bacon presents his own
theories of Humanity and these turn out to be surprisingly nativistic. He
is persuaded that everyone can be identified in terms of several innate
characters or "tempers," that some minds *"are proportioned to great
matters, and others to small,"*[10] and that while some of these characteristics
"are inherent and not extern," others are caused by fortune.[11] Of the
inherent determinants he includes sex, age, nationality, disease, constitutional deformity, and beauty. The environmental determinants number
sovereignty, nobility or obscurity of birth, poverty and wealth, and
such ambiguous agencies as magistracy, privateness, prosperity, adversity,
constant fortune (luck?), variable fortune, rising *per saltum* (in a leap),
and rising *per gradus* (in humbler steps).

At no point in the essay does Bacon abandon or even question the
Hippocratic and Galenic theory of humours, but he is less rigidly
nativistic on this score than either the Hippocratics or Aristotle. Choosing
(out of context) the line of the *Metaphysics* that argues that what is *by
nature* cannot be changed by custom, he insists that even human nature
is alterable through practice, reward, and punishment.[12] He agrees with
the Philosopher that a stone hurled in the air a thousand times *"will not
learn to ascend,"* but he distinguishes between the fixed laws of mere
matter and those covering human conduct. The latter are not "peremp-
tory" but provide a certain "latitude." Since virtue and vice are, accordingly, only or largely habits, it is possible to create virtuous citizens
by a proper regimen. It is in this context that he praises Machiavelli for
having described what men do rather than what they *ought* to do. Bacon
is concerned with human nature in both its inherent and its acquired
respects. He recommends a psychology able to distinguish between the
two and able to manipulate the manipulable respect toward the better-
ment of the human condition. He is, in a word, demanding an "operative"
science to complement the purely speculative one bequeathed by Aristotle
and left unimproved by the Schoolmen.

What the *Advancement of Learning* establishes unambiguously is that
Bacon's empiricism was of a limited sort. He was committed without

reservation to the view that human psychology bears the indelible stamp of hereditary influence. Given this commitment he was forced to conclude that in regard to human conduct and human achievement, external variables could produce changes of a limited variety and degree. His was decidedly not a behavioristic empiricism or even an empirical psychology. Rather, it was a methodological empiricism and an epistemological empiricism—positions amplified in the *Novum Organum*.

If the *Advancement of Learning* is the work of a young man testing the waters of a new monarchy, the *Novum Organum* is the churlish scolding of a seasoned and respected scholar writing from the lofty position of a Baron of Verulam. Thus, while the effort of an older man, the *Novum* is less careful, less temperate, and less balanced and incomparably more influential than its predecessor. It was written as two books of Aphorisms, 130 in the first and 52 in the second. It is in Book II that the heralded method is disclosed but, after the brilliant, often witty and always challenging Book I, Book II proves to be a resoundingly pretentious and half-baked collection of veiled theories, Hermetic innuendos, Scholastic distinctions, and generally useless labels. Had only Book II survived, more than one Ph.D. dissertation would have been needed to establish precisely what the "Baconian" method was. Fortunately, in Book I Bacon offers it out of the crypt:

"Now for grounds of experience—since to experience we must come —we have as yet had either none or very weak ones. . . . Nothing duly investigated, nothing verified, nothing counted, weighed or measured, is to be found in natural history: and what in observation is loose and vague, is in information deceptive and treacherous. And if any one thinks that this is a strange thing to say, and something like an unjust complaint, seeing that Aristotle, himself so great a man, and supported by the wreath of so great a king, has composed so accurate a historia of animals . . . it seems that he does not rightly apprehend what it is that we are now about. For a natural history which is composed for its own sake is not like one . . . for the building up of philosophy. They differ in many ways, but especially this: that the former contains the variety of natural species only, and not experiments."[13]

Bacon's criticism of Aristotle is that the latter busied himself merely with noting and naming rather than searching for causes. So overwhelmed by the importance of his "final causes," Aristotle the naturalist mixed metaphysics with physics or, worse, failed to develop natural physics by treating its subject matter in a metaphysical way. Had Aristotle discovered the experimental approach, he would not have spent his time

on a merely historical assessment of the animal kingdom—that is, identifying the types of animals found in different places at different times—
but would have inquired into the physical (efficient and material) causes
of the variety.

The experiments envisaged by Bacon are of two sorts. He labels one
Experimenta lucifera (those that shed light) and the other *Experimenta
fructifera* (those that bear fruit). Science requires both. The first, which
are utterly devoid of a theoretical bias on the experimenter's part, are
simple inquiries into elementary cause-effect sequences:

> "Now experiments of this kind have one admirable property and con-
> dition; they never miss or fail. For since they are applied, not for the
> purpose of producing any particular effect, but only of discovering the
> natural cause of some effect, they answer the end equally well which-
> ever way they turn out; for they settle the question."[14]

The *experimenta lucifera*, modest in aim and useless by themselves, produce findings to be stored in the *Table of Discovery* to which other
scientists can refer. In time, the great Table is filled in and the searching
questions become obvious. Then, the *experimenta fructifera* are possible,
and the results of these are not only of great benefit to mankind but
also yield the basic and inviolable laws of nature. And if one wishes to
know to how broad a range of nature Bacon is willing to extend his
model, the answer is unequivocal:

> "I form a history and tables of discovery for anger, fear, shame, and
> the like; for matters political; and again for the mental operations of
> memory, composition, and division, judgment and the rest; not less than
> for heat, and cold, or light, or vegetation, or the like."[15]

We find throughout the *Novum* exhortations to the reader that he not
despair, that he recognize how long and arduous the path to useful truth
is but how great the success will be once it is navigated. The message is
movingly conveyed in the ninety-second aphorism of Book I:

> "But by far the greatest obstacle to the progress of science and to the
> undertaking of new tasks and provinences therein, is found in this—
> that men despair and think things impossible."[16]

What is the circumstance calling for these repeated encouragements? We
can answer this by recalling the social climate with which Bacon and,
later, Hobbes, Descartes and Locke were contending. Once again the
voices of doom were announcing from many pulpits that the end was

near, that man's corruption and moral fall were but pale copies of the gigantic destruction just over the earth's horizon. Once again, and with the well-worn tools of astrology, Hermetic frenzy, and biblical interpretation, the common people were convinced that the time had come, that the six thousand years had elapsed. Mankind has once more become *"the dregs of Adam's race,"* and the metaphysical poet, John Donne (1573–1631), can only lament:

"The world did in her cradle take a fall,
And turn'd her braines, and tooke a generall maime,
Wronging each joynt of th'universall frame.
The noblest part, man, felt it first; and than
Both beasts and plants, curst in the curse of man.
So did the world from the first houre decay,
That evening was beginning of the day,
And now the Springs and Sommers which we see,
Like sonnes of women after fiftie bee."[17]

The mood had been set by the fatigue of the Reformation, by the cooling of Renaissance achievement, by the collapse of governments, by poverty, hunger, and the sorry assortments of plague and civil wars. The fall of Rome had been an invitation to this sort of thing before, and the incomplete fall of the papacy served as a similar signal. The *Novum Organum* was as much a rejoinder to this mood as it was a detached exercise in scientific scholarship. Bacon was the first of a series of philosophers, principally English, to attempt to call a halt to all this. His essays, when reduced to their elemental, rhetorical injunction, all say something like: Stop the nonsense, get a hold on yourself, open your eyes and look at the world as it is. Put aside the pretensions of antique wisdom, the seductions of superstition, and easy conscience of surrender. Get busy with the affairs of life; let the dead bury their dead.

2. JOHN LOCKE (1632–1704)

There were two conflicting intellectual movements opposing the empiricism that Locke was to advance and while each of these—Skepticism and Rationalism—was at odds with the other, each was even more at odds with empiricism. Since Rationalism was (and has remained) an essentially Continental movement and since its principal architect, Descartes, was hardly a leading figure in British circles, we must assume that Locke's *Essay Concerning Human Understanding* was written as much in response to his skeptical countrymen as it was to Descartes' *Medita-*

tions. The habit in historical writing, and in histories of psychology especially, is to comprehend Locke's empiricism as a narrow debate between two small, superintellectual camps: one at Oxford, and the other at any house Descartes happened to be living in at the time. However, England in the second half of the seventeenth century provided a more immediate and at least as great an impetus as the untranslated Latin essays of a French geometer living in Amsterdam. Locke was intimately aware of Descartes' work, of Gassendi's *sensationist* attack on this work, of Pascal's suspicion of rationalism, and so forth. Thus, Locke's famous *Essay* must be read as an alternative to rationalism but not as a reply to it alone.

In the seventy years between the appearance of the *Novum Organum* and the publication of Locke's *Essay* (1690), the political face of England had been transformed. Three historic events occurred when Locke was ten: the beheading of Charles I, the beginning of the Civil War, and the birth of Isaac Newton. By the time the essay appeared, England had recovered reasonably well from the consequences of the first two but not the third.

Bacon's untutored countrymen, and many who were quite educated, were overcome by the prospect of the world's decay and by portents of imminent destruction. This is a feeling hard to sustain for long periods, and it soon gave place to a peculiar form of skepticism. Copernicanism had finally begun to sink in. The furious bickering between Reformationists and counter-Reformationists, between Lutherans and Calvinists, and between antipapist Catholics and papists led not merely to a war— which at least exhausted itself—but to a battle of opinions that seemed to show no sign of abating. Kepler's first two laws were published in 1609 and, when the *literati* digested and disseminated them, even the "perfect, celestial circles" that had survived Copernicus were now traduced to ellipses. This, of course, claimed the time and attention of countless theologians called upon to explain how Scripture had failed to note *this* feature of God's craft.

The combination of Luther, Copernicus, Calvin, young Newton, Elizabeth I, Bacon, and civil war was too much for any age to assimilate without raising some serious questions about whether *anything* can be known. Thus, Locke's contemporaries included a number of persuasive skeptics such as Joseph Glanvill (1636–1680), whose *Scepsis Scientifica* and *Lux Orientalis* revived an almost ancient form of cynical contempt for what presented itself as human understanding. *Pyrrhonism*, named after the Greek skeptic Pyrrho, was on the verge of becoming the new Scholasticism. The Doomsday perspective of Bacon's age was evolving into No-Nothingism, and Locke set out to stop it and replace it. In the Introduction to the *Essay*, he sounds Bacon's theme:

"If we can find out those measures whereby a rational creature, put in that state which man is in in this world, may and ought to govern his opinions and actions depending thereon, we need not be troubled that some other things escape our knowledge."[18]

He also leaves no doubt about the sort of analysis he is attempting. Unlike Hobbes and Descartes, whose psychological systems will be discussed later, Locke is completely neutral on the question of the biological or physical factors that may be responsible for the character of mental states and activities. He is specifically avoiding all questions regarding the physiological basis of thought:

"I shall not at present meddle with the physical consideration of the mind, or trouble myself to examine wherein its essence consists or by what motions of our spirits, or alterations of our bodies, we come to have any sensation by our organs, or any *ideas* in our understanding; and whether those ideas do, in their formation, any or all of them, depend on matter or not."[19]

The *Essay*, then, is not to be about brains, motions, or theological disputes. It is to be about the human understanding which, for Locke, is no more than the *ideas* possessed by the mind and reflected on by the mind. Locke's psychology is addressed to the origin, validity, and utility of ideas and these are only *"whatsoever is the* object *of the understanding when a man thinks."*[20]

In regard to the sources of our ideas (i.e., understanding), there are only two: *sensation* and *reflection*. The former is no more than the sensory apprehension of the particular objects of the physical world. We do not sense "universals," "species," "truths," "principles": we sense things and only things. As the organs of sense engage the material stuff of the world, the mind also has a perceptive faculty according to which it is able to examine its own contents. This faculty is *reflection* and, since the mind is furnished only through experience, reflection is comprised of that which the senses have provided. However, it is not comprised only of these. In addition, reflection includes the mind's ability to examine its operations (i.e., not only its contents) and these operations include the effects of the passions on our ideas.

What Locke proposes is a theory of knowledge based on two interacting processes. One of these is sensation, pure and simple, which leads to factual knowledge of the material world. The second is reflection, which is an internal sense able to examine the deposited sensations in the larger context of our general, emotional state. Reflection is that which removes understanding from the purely photographic process of recording items in space. Instead, through reflection, the human understanding is a *psychological* entity. This is not to say, however, that it is a spiritual one, since the feelings themselves are to be understood in empirical terms.

Locke's empirical psychology is associationistic, even in the mechanical sense, but it never denies those mentalistic attributes of human psychology which every person senses himself to be in possession of. He does not advance, that is, the associationistic form of psychology that Pavlov was to come to recommend, nor the materialistic form so prominently displayed by the early Epicurean philosophers or the Renaissance Averroists. In fact, he specifically rejects the suggestion that perception is merely the activation of the organs of sense. He speaks of the inattentive man in II.IX.4 of the *Essay* who, while inspecting an object of interest, is oblivious to a variety of sounds, despite the fact that there is no defect in the sense of hearing. For perception to occur, the mind must be directed at the object. It is not a passive process but, rather, an active transaction between the observer and the knowable world.

On the question of innate ideas, the *Essay* is uncompromisingly opposed. Locke insists, from the opening bell as it were, that man enters the world a *tabula rasa* and that all he will come to know will be the result of experience. He leaves room for the possibility that the fetus, once its sensory apparatus has taken form, will experience rudimentary sensations and, therefore, may enter the world with certain primitive ideas, but on no account can such ideas, if they exist, be considered innate.[21] Since knowledge is of particular, material things and since the infant could not possibly have had experience with such things prior to birth, there can be no sense in which the infant has "ideas." Nor, for that matter, can an adult have ideas about that with which his senses have had no commerce. In one of the most famous passages from the *Essay*, Locke applauds a proposition passed on to him by the French scholar Molineux, who has unconsciously anticipated an experimental issue that the twentieth century has found irresistible:

> "I shall here insert a problem of that very ingenious and studious promoter of real knowledge, the learned and worthy Mr. Molineux, which he was pleased to send me in a letter some months since: 'Suppose a man born blind, and now adult, and taught by his touch to distinguish between a cube and a sphere of the same metal and nighly of the same bigness, so as to tell, when he felt one and the other, which is the cube, which the sphere. Suppose the cube and sphere placed on a table and the blind man to be made to see: *quaere*, whether by his sight, before he touched them, he could now distinguish and tell which is the globe, which the cube?' To which the acute and judicious proposer answers: 'Not. For though he has obtained the experience of

how a globe, how a cube, affects his touch; yet he has not yet obtained the experience, that what affects his touch so or so, must affect his sight so or so. . . .' I agree with this thinking gentleman. . . . The blind man, at first sight, would not be able with certainty to say which was the globe, which the cube."[22]

Locke argues that thinking and perceiving are but different words for the same process. The ideas resulting from perception are initially simple but, through associated experiences and memory, the simple ideas are combined to form complex ones. However, no matter how complex our ideas become, they remain rooted to the soil of experience and nurtured by the reflective faculty. To say that we know is no more than to say that we have ideas. Knowledge itself is *"nothing but the perception of the connection of and agreement, or disagreement and repugnancy of any of our ideas."*[23] This agreement (and its converse) may be treated as a fourfold affair. First, there is the recognition that what is, is; that a thing cannot be and, at the same time, not be. After this "first act of the mind" comes our knowledge of *relations*, which is no more than the mind's awareness that certain ideas are related (e.g., mass and weight) and others not at all or less so (e.g., telephone number and annual rainfall). The third form of our knowledge of agreement is what Locke calls *coexistence* or what, in modern parlance, we would call a correlation. The word "gold" for example merely signifies color, malleability, weight, and so forth, such that when the word is uttered we know these properties by habitual association. Finally, we have the knowledge of *real existence*, such as "That is an apple." To summarize, we say that we know things in four ways: by *identity* (e.g., black is not white), by *relation* (e.g., the whole is equal to the sum of its parts), by *coexistence* (e.g., iron is attracted by a magnet), and by *real existence* (e.g., Big Ben is in London).

While the foregoing exhaust the foundations of our knowledge, they do not explain the degrees of knowledge. There are some things we are more confident about than others. Locke orders the certainty attaching to human knowledge as *intuitive*, *demonstrative*, and *sensitive*. By intuitive he means the sudden, undeliberated awareness of a truth; for example, a circle is not a triangle, or black is not white. No other idea is necessary for the mind to perceive such truths, and anyone who seeks to discredit the certainty of this form of knowledge *"has a mind to be a skeptic."*[24] Without intuitive knowledge, demonstrative certainty would not be possible. Thus, for us to recognize that two things equal to a third must be equal to each other—a recognition ensured by the incontrovertability of deductive proofs—we must have the capacity for *intuitive* knowledge of the kind just described. As intuitive knowledge forms the basis of sagacity or wisdom, demonstrative knowledge is the product of reasoning by which items that cannot be juxtaposed for purposes of comparison are reasonably juxtaposed by a juxtaposition of ideas. The major distinction between intuitive and demonstrative knowledge is that although both are completely resistant to doubt finally, only the former is absolutely undoubted initially. For example, no one doubts, from the moment the sentence is uttered, that "Black is not white." Initially, however, one might doubt that "two triangles with equal bases and constructed between parallel lines are equal." The latter can be proved and, once proved, is known to be *certainly* true. This certainty, however, may only come after the proof.

Between this pole of certainty occupied by intuition and demonstration and the opposite pole of the merely probable or possible—that is, the pole of mere faith or opinion—there is the *sensitive* knowledge of particulars. Sensitive knowledge is of two types: that which apprehends the *primary* qualities of substances, and that which involves *secondary* qualities. The distinction between these is fundamental. The *primary* qualities

"are discovered by our senses, and are in [things] even when we perceive them not; such as the bulk, figure, number, situation, and motion of the parts of bodies, which are really in them, whether we take notice of them or no. Secondly, the sensible secondary qualities which, depending on these, are nothing but the powers those substances have to produce several ideas in us by our senses; which ideas are not in the things themselves otherwise than as anything is in its cause. . . . Had we senses acute enough to discern the minute particles of bodies, and the real constitution on which their sensible qualities depend, I doubt not but that they would produce quite different ideas in us, and that which is now the yellow color of gold would then disappear, and instead of it we should see an admirable texture of parts of a certain size and figure."[25]

Sensitive knowledge, then, is part objective and part invented. Physical objects have specific primary qualities that the senses are equipped to perceive. These include size, shape, number, and motion. However, matter is particular and atomic, and the senses are not able to deal with matter at its own elemental level. Instead, the elementary particles stimulate the senses, and the latter report perceived matter whose secondary qualities are products of the act of perception itself. Were there no perceiver, these qualities would not exist. As a result of this, there will always be an "incurable ignorance," for "there is no discoverable connection between any secondary quality and those primary qualities that it depends on."[26]

While not raising this limitation specifically in the context of the mind-body problem, Locke has taken the position that it is simply not possible to establish a necessary connection between the actual physical attributes of matter and the psychological (perceptual) effects produced by them. The problem is not merely technical. That is, the problem would not disappear were we to possess instruments by which to discern the elementary composition of matter. Even if we knew, for example, the subatomic composition of gold, we would not be able to establish the connection between these particles and the experience of "yellow" produced by them. Our senses, just as our intuition and our reason, are of such a nature as to allow us to survive and prosper in the world as we find it but are not able to yield certain knowledge of all things. Our knowledge can go so far and no further.

Locke does not conclude, however, that just because secondary qualities are, in a sense, invented and just because there is a limit on what we can know that nothing can be known for certain. Nor does he accept the skeptical position that all knowledge is illusory. To those who contend that we cannot tell the difference between dreams and reality, who argue that all may be illusion, Locke replies with contemptuous indifference. Locke is concerned with contributing to the practical affairs of life and has no patience with sophistry. We have an immediate and intuitive comprehension of our existence—of the reality of our existence —and anyone denying it is not worth debating.[27]

Having established the sources of our knowledge and the limited degrees of our knowledge, Locke then defines what actually can be known. These fall into three categories. We know ourselves by intuition. We know God by reason (demonstration). Everything else that can be said to be known and that, in fact, exists is known by sensation.[28] In the dispute between nominalist and realist, Locke's position is undeviatingly nominalistic. The truth of so-called universal propositions is either merely tautologically true or it is a proposition about actual, physical entities whose essences are known. Thus, "gold is malleable" is true only to the extent that the word "gold" includes malleability in the sense of co-existence. Hence its malleability is not established by the proposition but by its actual, sensible properties:

"No existence of anything without us, but only of God, can certainly be known farther than our senses inform us."[29]

It is by virtue of *memory* that we do no need an endless repetition of events in order to be satisfied that we have knowledge of them. Our knowledge of causes and their effects is produced in us by repeated experiences. The durability and vividness of this knowledge are enhanced when our experiences are augmented by *pleasure* and *pain*.[30] The certain knowledge allowed by these processes is not perfect but it is *"as great as our condition needs."*[31] Memory fails not only because it weakens with time (i.e., because its "trace" decays) but also because we are not all gifted enough to retrieve what we want from the store of our memories.[32] However, within the limits of our sensory acuity, of our ability to focus our attention, and of our memory's ability to retain that with which the senses have furnished it, our knowledge of the real world can become so highly probably correct as to be, for all practical purposes, *certain*.

Since what we do depends upon what we know, at least according to the Lockean empiricist, the solution of the epistemological problems is tantamount to solving the problem of conduct. Locke's *Essay* thus addresses itself to the question of morality only briefly. His fuller development of the principles of governance and social conduct appears in his *Two Treatises on Government,* also published in 1690. Because of Locke's historic position in the cause of civil liberty, because of his insistence that the legitimacy of governments is rooted in the idea of a "social contract" between the governed and their appointed leaders, it is sometimes assumed that Locke's position on moral matters was one of mere situationism. Not only this, but it also is occasionally suggested that empiricism, as an epistemological system, is inescapably context-oriented on moral questions. This is not the place to examine Locke's theory of government, but we may pause to note his approach to moral questions in order to recognize that the empiricist position on such questions need not reduce moral proposition to public opinion.

Locke introduces his discussion of moral knowledge by first exploring the certainty of mathematical propositions. This requires a distinction between simple and complex ideas:

". . . simple ideas are not fictions of our fancies, but the natural and regular productions of things without us really operating upon us. . . . Thus, the idea of whiteness or bitterness, as it is in the mind, exactly answering that power which is in any body to produce it there, has all the real conformity it can or ought to have with things without us. . . . [However], all our complex ideas except those of substances being archetypes of the mind's own making, not intended to be the copies of anything, not referred to the existence of anything, as to their originals, cannot want any conformity necessary to real knowledge. For that which is not designed to represent anything but itself, can never be capable of a wrong representation, nor mislead us from the true apprehension of anything by its dislikeness to it; and such, excepting those of substances, are all our complex ideas: which . . . are combinations of ideas which the mind by its free choice puts together without considering any connection they have in nature."[33]

Now, is this to say that our complex ideas have nothing to do with reality? Not at all. Our complex ideas, except for those we have of substances, are not ideas about physical entities; but they are ideas, nonetheless. And, just as mathematical ideas are

"not the bare, empty vision or vain, insignificant chimeras of the brain,"[34]

so, also, moral ideas derive from the intuitive and demonstrative faculties of the ordered mind. Thus,

"our moral ideas as well as mathematical, being archetypes themselves, and so adequate and complete ideas, all the agreement or disagreement which we shall find in them will produce real knowledge, as well as in mathematical figures."[35]

Locke's argument is not that moral propositions have the sort of validity that attaches to our perception of motion or shape or that the canons of justice can be known the way we know, for example, that it is raining. Rather, he is arguing that most of what we know is *not* of the type, "It is raining" or, "The tram is moving." Our knowledge, from first to last, is *idea*. The idea results either from direct, sensory reactions or from logical demonstration or from intuition. None of these modes of knowing is perfect or all-inclusive. The geometer who reasons that a circle is a form containing 360° all of whose points are the same distance from its center may never be able to find such a figure in nature. That is, he may never *see* a perfect circle. This is not to say that such a figure is "unreal" or merely a creation of the mind. It is to say that, were nature to yield such a figure, that figure would be a circle and, furthermore, that given this definition of a circle, certain other properties necessarily follow. Moreover, given the nature of a circle, it matters not how we name it. The truths pertaining to it will be established by the demonstrative faculty of the mind and will be as certain as human knowledge can be.

"For the attaining of knowledge and certainty, it is requisite that we have determined ideas: and to make our knowledge real, it is requisite that the ideas answer their archetypes. . . . Nor will it be less true or certain because moral ideas are of our own making and naming."[36]

Where the "archetypes" of physical objects reside outside the mind, the archetypes of moral ideas reside within the mind, and these moral ideas are real and certain to the extent that our arguments and our observations of the human condition are made conformable to them. It is here, of course, that Locke's "archetypes" come uncomfortably close to the rationalist's notion of innate, moral sensibility. Indeed, the leap from these Lockian archetypes to Kant's *Categorical Imperative* is at its narrowest point in this discussion of the truth of moral propositions, and it is here also that Locke's credentials as a rationalist are above reproach.

3. GEORGE BERKELEY (1685–1783)

It is often suggested that Berkeley's major psychological work is his *New Theory of Vision*,[37] which lays down the experiential and geometric determinants of depth perception and takes Hobbes and Descartes to task for not recognizing the empirical foundation of such perceptual phenomena as the "moon illusion."[38] Were we concerned with the history of research in visual perception, it would be necessary to dissect Berkeley's theories which, for our present purposes, are ably summarized by the philosopher himself:

> "As we see distance, so we see magnitude. And we see both in the same way that we see shame or anger in the looks of a man. Those passions are themselves invisible; they are nevertheless let in by the eye along with colors and alterations of countenance which are the immediate object of vision, and which signify them for no other reason than barely because they have been observed to accompany them. Without which experience we should no more have taken blushing for a sign of shame than of gladness."[39]

We are not, in the present context, especially interested in his theories of depth perception, nor does the character of modern psychology derive from them. And on no account is the *New Theory of Vision* Berkeley's major psychological work nor the one referred to by those successors who had much to do with the creation of modern psychology. By far his most influential essay is *A Treatise Concerning the Principles of Human Knowledge*, published in 1710 and, in revised form, in 1734.[40] It is this *Treatise* that earned Berkeley such titles as "subjective idealist," "immaterialist," "spiritualist," and it is these titles which, in turn, have helped to make his small book one of the more misunderstood essays in philosophy. We will not review the long history of confusion and nearly libelous interpretations of the *Treatise*. Prof. A. A. Luce has set the record straight, and the interested reader may consult his informing clarification.[41] We are advised to examine the *Treatise* itself which, even more than Locke's *Essay*, is a *psychological* philosophy.

At the time of the writing of the *Treatise*, all the leading European rationalists had contributed their major works. In fact, of the three most influential rationalists—Descartes, Spinoza, and Leibniz—only Leibniz was still alive. Locke's most famous philosophical essay was already a classic, and Newton's celebrated *Principia* and *Mechanics* were joined by Galileo's achievements, together making the seventeenth century the most illustrious period of scientific creativity in history to date. We will not address ourselves to the rationalist tradition until the next chapter but we may note here that, by 1700, a tradition of European rationalism conspired with both Locke's empiricism and with the science of Newton and Galileo to create a decidedly materialistic perspective on the part of the intelligentsia. The downfall of Aristotle's ageless authority and the resulting disavowal of Scholasticism were already responsible for a form of religious skepticism bordering on atheism. Materialism, while still more than a century from becoming a religion in its own right, was fueling the skeptical fires. Even Descartes' dualism, which we shall study in the next chapter, was a grudging dualism according to which many, if not most, of the day-to-day affairs of the human community could be understood in essentially mechanical terms. It was this mechanical feature of social organization that Hobbes had presented as a full-blown political theory. What Berkeley set out to achieve, then, was nothing short of removing every trace of validity from materialism and to do this by refuting the latent or explicitly materialistic content both in Locke's *Essay* and in Descartes' and Hobbes' "geometric" theories of man and society. Berkeley's *Treatise* attempts the first of these, and his *New Theory of Vision*, the second. It will be easier to follow the more complicated reasoning of the former by remaining for a moment with his approach to the more limited objectives of the latter.

The rationalist account of visual perception and, particularly depth perception, was based on the geometric theory of optics. According to this theory, fully developed by Descartes but having very ancient roots, we see objects at a distance or near at hand on the basis of the angle formed by these objects when the interocular distance is treated as the base of a hypothetical triangle. The further the object is moved away, the smaller the apex angle becomes, such that, by Euclid's theorems, all visual, perceptual data can be deduced from the geometric principles that govern the science of optics. Perception, by this reasoning, is the way it is *necessarily*. A convergence of the eyes is necessary to maintain a clear view of an approaching object; a divergence of the eyes for a receding object. The muscles of the eyes therefore report the distance between the object and the observer. By calculating the degree of convergence or divergence, the observer is able to estimate the distance.

Berkeley's reply to this analysis is simply that no one sees things this way! When we examine an approaching or a receding object we do not, in fact, either compute the convergence of our eyes or the angle formed at the (invisible) apex of (invisible) triangles. Indeed, the untutored are as accurate in judging distances as are masters of optics and so it is not likely that a knowledge of optical rays, lines, and angles ever participates in our perceptual judgments. Quite simply, *distance is not visible* itself and it makes no sense at all to refer to "the perception of distance." While Berkeley does believe that interocular distance is the effective cue to distance, it is an *experience*, not a geometric calculation. In other words, we can only sense events and objects, not "empty" distance. Thus, the idea of distance must be rooted not in geometry or optics—neither of which the average man uses in judging distance—but in that which is available to all who might ever be able to experience distance. And this is *sensation*. We *learn* to judge distance and we learn it by being exposed not to the axioms of geometry but to the affairs of sense:

> "Not that there is any natural or necessary connection between the sensation we perceive by the turn of the eyes and greater or lesser distance. But—because the mind has, by constant experience, found the different sensations corresponding to the different dispositions of the eyes to be attended each with a different degree of distance in the object—there has grown a habitual or customary connection between those two sorts of ideas so that the mind no sooner perceives the sensation arising from the different turn it gives the eyes . . . but it withal perceives the different idea of distance which was wont to be connected with that sensation."[42]

We note in this passage, which is suggestive of the reasoning underlying the entire essay, that Berkeley is committed to an account of experience that is based on *other experiences only*. He specifically rejects the necessitarian argument of rationalists and mathematicians alike. He insists upon a "common sense" account which takes advantage of what all of us know to be true of the manner in which we make our judgments of distance and depth. He applies the same "common sense" standard to all experience: touch, hearing, smell, taste. An object, he argues, does not "look" round in the same way it "feels" round when the fingers explore its shape. We use the same words by an accident of learning, not by an identity of experience, less by the similarity of *species*.

In the light of this approach to perception, we are advised to expect that Berkeley will address the larger question of the principles of human knowledge in a novel way. He certainly does. He begins by specifying the real world as *immaterial* on the same basis as he rejects distance as something seen. We do not see "distance" and we not not see "matter." Rather, *we see*. Now, what is it that we see when we do? Berkeley answers:

> "It is indeed an opinion strangely prevailing amongst men, that houses, mountains, rivers, and, in a word, all sensible objects, have an existence, natural or real, distinct from their being perceived by the understanding. But, with how great an assurance and acquiescence soever this principle may be entertained in the world, yet whoever shall find in his heart to call it into question may, if I mistake not, perceive it to involve a manifest contradiction. For, what are the forementioned objects but things we perceive by sense? and what do we perceive besides our own ideas or sensations? and is it not plainly repugnant that any one of these, or any combination of them, should exist unperceived?"[43]

More than a century later, J. S. Mill would define matter as *"the permanent possibility of sensation"* and, in so defining it, reveal himself to be a Berkelian. Is this to say that Mill is a "subjective idealist"? No, and for the same reason that we are not to call Berkeley one if that term means that the one given it believes that matter is *created* by the ideas we have of it. It surely was not Berkeley who argued that the trees in a wood disappear if he is not there to see them. For Berkeley to argue that matter is invented by the mind would require that he consider the separate reality of both and the demonstrable proof of the existence of matter independent of mind. This is not a dualism Berkeley is likely to embrace:

> ". . . human knowledge may naturally be reduced to two heads— that of *ideas* and that of *spirits*. . . . And *first* as to ideas of unthinking things. Our knowledge of these hath been very much obscured and confounded, and we have been led into very dangerous errors, by supposing a twofold existence of the objects of sense—the one *intelligible* or in the mind, the other *real* and without the mind; whereby unthinking things are thought to have a natural subsistence of their own distinct from being perceived by spirits. This . . . is the very root of Scepticism."[44]

This passage illustrates Berkeley's conviction that materialism leads inescapably to skepticism and the latter is Berkeley's *nemesis*. We must recognize this because the label "subjective idealist" often is painted with the colors of skepticism. He insists that the dead-end of skepticism must be averted and that the only successful means of doing this is by erecting a system of "sound and real knowledge" which requires, first, an understanding of what is implied by the terms *thing, reality*, and *existence*.[45] With respect to the first, *thing* is *being* and the latter is of two radically different sorts, each having nothing in common with the other. One is being through *idea;* the other, being through *spirit*. The former impress themselves on the mind through the senses and *"are real things, or really do exist; this we do not deny, but we deny they can subsist without the minds which perceive them or that they are resemblances of any archetypes existing without the mind; since the very being of a sensation or idea consists in being perceived, and an idea can be like nothing but an idea."*[46]

Berkeley thus rejects Locke's "archetypes." What he is saying, in effect, is that Locke's primary and secondary qualities must reduce to secondary qualities only. Motion can be nothing if not *perceived* motion; number, only *perceived* number; form, but *perceived* form. Accordingly, there can be no difference between these so-called primary qualities and the secondary ones of color, heat, cold, and so forth. The "ideas," in Berkeley's unique use of the term, are *things* in the mind with a permanence and validity that cannot continue in the absence of mind. It is because of this that the materialists must fail to comprehend reality. It is also why the scientific theorist who abandons the facts of his own sensations and wanders forth into the purely verbal realm of physical laws of nature must contribute no more than nonsense in the garb of tautology. Thus, when Mr. Newton, the author of that *"great mechanical principle now in vogue,"* postulates the mutual attraction of matter, *"I do not perceive that anything is signified besides the effect itself,"*[47] and this effect can be nothing more than a *perceived* effect. It is the same Mr. Newton whose treatise on *Mechanics* grants an existence to time, space, and place outside the mind, and it is the same Bishop Berkeley who, in reply, must confess that he can conceive of none of these except as relative. Thus, *"to conceive motion there must be at least conceived two bodies . . . if there was one only body in being it could not possibly be moved."*[48] It is hardly necessary to note that Berkeley here anticipates the most important contribution to theoretical physics of the twentieth century. We are concerned, however, with the contribution these ideas made to psychology, and we will summarize them now.

Locke's theory of ideas was confused on several counts. It was dualistic without redemption in requiring a world of matter (primary qualities) able to appeal directly to mental "archetypes" and an additional, private, experiential world of perception dealing with and creating secondary qualities. Worse, there is no way of deriving the latter world from the former. We may list Berkeley's major epistemological contribution as the ridding of this dualism, or at least a very commendable attempt to do so. Where Locke still contended with the Nature-Spirit tensions and contradictions that so occupied the Renaissance mind, Berkeley broke away decisively. The court of last recourse for Berkeley was the court of Spirit wherein all reality finally resided. Ultimately the world, the universe, and all that lives are but perceptions held eternally in God's eye. So-called material objects exist in relation to our minds in the way that all exists in God's. This is Berkeley's simultaneous rebuttal of skepticism, materialism, and atheism. It was a revival of the historic Christian position before Aristotle had been elevated to the post of theologian.

Berkeley did not succeed in halting the progress of materialism, nor will the convinced atheist, if such there be, find his soul in Berkeley's *Treatise*. However, later empiricists, and especially David Hume, did find in the *Treatise* an able attack on nonsensory approaches to the problem of knowledge. Berkeley, in asserting that perception was the first and last criterion by which reality may be known and judged, succeeded in directing the attention of philosophers to the psychological dimension of all philosophical problems. In a word, he rendered epistemology a branch of psychology, and the two have never been divorced since. His empiricism was of the extreme sort and, as such, served as a justification for later forms of idealism which Berkeley himself would have considered nonsensical. His theories of perception were couched in the language of experimental science and constituted a model for subsequent investigators. Carrying on in the steps of Bacon and Locke, he further clarified the distinction between *words* and the things signified by them; between propositions that are (as Kant would call them) *analytical* and those that are *synthetic*, the former being logical and the latter empirical. In making these distinctions, he insisted that necessity does not inhere in nature but in the logical propositions we invent in our attempt to understand nature. In this, he anticipated Hume but, of course, did not equal him. To the extent that psychologists are interested in perception, in the contextual determinants of perception, in the relation between things and their (verbal) significations, Berkeley's *Treatise* has been seminal in the scientific development of the discipline. He did not write as much as Locke or Hume did, nor did his scholarship reach, as theirs did, to the farthest corners of political, civic, and moral concerns. But, on the specific epistemological issue to which all empiricists have been addressed, and on the specific points of contact between theories of knowledge and theories of psychological man, many empiricist contributions following his have been footnotes and epilogues. That he did more to frame the question than to answer it is only to acknowledge that Berkeley was a philosopher.

4. David Hume (1711–1776)

Twentieth-century philosophy in the English-speaking world is very nearly a creation of Hume's. It is always precarious to attempt to locate so important a figure within any context because his influence has persevered throughout such a variety of contexts. Still, as much as Hume was the founder and father of a new philosophy and one that continues to show his influence, he was also the product of eighteenth-century thought in England. Not only had Newton revolutionized science but such luminaries as John Milton, John Locke, Shaftesbury, Hutchinson, and Samuel Butler had provided the moral and intellectual foundations for a political liberalism that had not been witnessed since antiquity. Hume's most important work, *A Treatise of Human Nature*, was published in 1739–1740—nearly a century after the civil war, a half-century after Locke's *Essay*. Milton's *Areopagitica* (1644) had assaulted censorship of the press so effectively that J. S. Mill's *On Liberty*, two centuries later, could do little more than paraphrase it. Intellectual freedom was still a long way off but by the date of Hume's *Treatise*, the historic sources of authority—the military, the royalty, and the churches—were quite simply outnumbered. Hume died in the year of the American Revolution, thirteen years before the French Revolution. The former is as inconceivable without Milton, Locke, and Hume as the latter is without Voltaire, Diderot, Rousseau, and Montesquieu. Nor were the scholars on either side of the Channel unaware of each other. Voltaire celebrated the English empiricists in more than one essay, and Rousseau actually lived with Hume and was left a small pension in Hume's will. Thus it does not detract from the *Treatise* to place it on a continuum of liberal arguments presented in proud defiance against all who would defend the neglect, exploitation, or undignified position of the common man. Locke's *Essay* was intended to establish knowledge as something inseparable from those perceptual processes common to the great run of citizens. Berkeley's *Principles* went even further and included the material and scientific facts and laws of nature in the embrace of the human mind. Both the *Essay* and the *Principles* were reaffirmations of the ancient maxim of Protagoras, "Man—the measure of all things." Against this were counterpoised the leading rationalists whom we approach in the next chapter—those insisting on the validity of eternal propositions, natively imbedded in the human spirit, provable by the geometrically faultless methods of logic, safely beyond the frail apparatus of the individual. There were those like Hobbes, whose *Leviathan* (1651) was to demonstrate logically the necessity of political institutions. There were the Puritans demanding a return to simplicity and humility at a time when England was becoming the economic colossus of the world. And there were the joyous satirists —Pope, Addison, and Swift were great admirers of Berkeley, for example—who took advantage of the intensity and finality of the contests and thereby added measurably to the world's wealth of humor.

In the introduction to his *Treatise*, Hume singles out several of the new "natural philosophers" who, by his lights, have advanced the cause of truth. They include "*Mr. Locke, my Lord Shaftesbury, Dr. Mandeville, Mr. Hutchinson, Dr. Butler, &c.*"[49] We have already treated of Locke. To satisfy our purposes we must dismiss Mandeville as a satirical essayist and ignore Hutchinson completely. But Hume's inclusion of Shaftesbury and Butler demands comment, for both of them were leaders of the naturalistic (i.e., empiricistic) approach to moral philosophy. They were two of perhaps a dozen writers in the England of the early eighteenth century who labored to place ethics in that realm which, today, we would call psychology. Shaftesbury and Locke were very close, and Butler and Hume were contemporaries. Both of them, Shaftesbury and Butler, contended with persuasive eloquence that the moral and ethical dimensions of human life are to be understood in *human* terms. Both argued that the common man's self-interest, his need to live in society, his ability to perceive and learn from the consequences of his actions, his capacity to articulate his objectives and behave in a manner compatible with their attainment constituted the ultimate theory of values.[50] According to this view, moral "absolutes" can be so only to the extent that we are endowed with a *natural* faculty for perceiving wherein our interests lay—only to the extent that we can benefit from social instruction and will work to secure the praises of other human beings. Butler's emphasis on action as the standard of moral worth and on reward and punishment as the tools that forge our character would be repeated by Hume's good friend, Adam Smith, and would be installed as a systematic philosophy by Jeremy Bentham and the disciples of *Utilitarianism* in the nineteenth century. In acknowledging the contributions of Shaftesbury and Butler, Hume was not necessarily subscribing to the latter's instinct theory of virtue or Shaftesbury's empathy theory, about which we will say a few words, but was applauding their unwaveringly psychological approach to the issue of values. In short, he was applauding their rejection of rationalism and spiritualism as systems that could ever disclose the nature of morality in a way that would correspond to what the common man knew to be true.

In *An Inquiry Concerning Virtue or Merit* (1699), Shaftesbury had located all morality in the domain of intended actions and had argued that these actions, on the part of a reflective animal such as man, were to be understood as the product of a natural appetite or disposition or affection. With Darwin's vision (but not his data), he circumscribed all living things within a great system in which survival was the common motive. For man to survive and to know happiness, he balances his self-serving affections against those directed at the public good:

> "TO HAVE THE NATURAL AFFECTIONS . . . IS TO HAVE THE CHIEF MEANS AND POWER OF SELF ENJOYMENT: *And* THAT TO WANT THEM IS CERTAIN MISERY AND ILL. . . ."[51]

The goal for man is this self-enjoyment, and he proceeds to regulate the moral dimensions of his conduct in such a way as to secure it. While loyal to the teachings of Christ's church, Shaftesbury concludes that "religious Conscience *supposes* moral *or* natural *Conscience*"[52] and the latter is based upon a sentiment or affection according to which "*no Creature can maliciously and intentionally do ill, without being sensible at the same time that he deserves ill.*"[53] In this we have the basis of Kant's Categorical Imperative.

Butler carried forth the naturalistic school of virtue and made still clearer and wider the break with necessitarian doctrines:

> "That which renders beings capable of moral government, is their having a moral nature, and moral faculties of perception and action . . . we naturally and unavoidably approve of some actions, under the peculiar view of their being virtuous . . . and disapprove others as vicious. . . . That we have this moral approving and disapproving faculty, is certain from our experiencing it in ourselves, and recognizing it in each other."[54]

The sentimentalist theories of Shaftesbury and Butler were soon to undergo revolutionary transformations at the hands of Adam Smith and Jeremy Bentham, neither of whom was satisfied that we are endowed with an abiding longing for the *summum bonum*. Smith's *Theory of the Moral Sentiments* appeared about twenty years after Hume's *Treatise* and about twenty years before Bentham's *Principles of Morals and Legislation*. The steady progression from the innate moral sentiments propounded by Shaftesbury and Butler to the bold, Benthamist assertion of *morality-as-utility* provides one of the most uncluttered chapters in the history of political theory. We shall have more to say on these theories in later chapters. Now we may proceed to Hume's *Treatise*, a work firmly rooted in the naturalism and empiricism of his time.

Right at the outset, in his introduction to the 600-page work, Hume leaves no doubt as to his goal, his basic assumptions, and his opinion of earlier and contrary perspectives. His mission is to found a science of man which ultimately must include or set the boundaries on all other sciences. Human beings are not simply those who reason but are, as well, the worthy *objects* of reason and must be studied by the emerging instruments of "experimental philosophy," so recently forged by Bacon, Locke, and others. All truly important questions finally await an understanding of the human mind whose powers can be disclosed only through careful and exact experiments and observations.

> "And tho' we must endeavour to render all our principles as universal as possible, by tracing up our experiments to the utmost, and explaining all effects from the simplest and fewest causes, 'tis still certain we cannot go beyond experience; and any hypothesis, that pretends to discover the ultimate original qualities of human nature, ought at first to be rejected as presumptuous and chimerical."[55]

His ultimate objective is to establish the limit of human knowledge which, alas, falls short of being able to prove *"our most general and most refined principles beside our experience of their reality."*[56] In other words, notice is served on all who would promise extrasensory truths or irrefutable moral maxims.

The body of the *Treatise* is comprised of three broad topics: the Understanding (Book I), the Passions (Book II), and Morals (Book III). Hume's organization is not to be improved upon and we will discuss his psychological philosophy in the order in which he presents it.

Since the contents of the mind can come into being only through experience, it follows that the human understanding, most generally, must be based on perceptions. According to Hume, these are of two sorts: impressions and ideas. The former include sensations, passions, and emotions that are but the reports of stimulation of one sort or another. Ideas are only the persistence, in a weaker form, of prior impressions. In Hume's words, *"every simple idea has a simple impression which resembles it and every simple impression, a correspondent idea."*[57] Moreover, since the simple impressions always precede the corresponding idea in experience, we can be certain that the latter are the result of the former, and not vice versa. In other words, common experience belies the idealist assertion that the mind (idea) creates the sensation. And as for the notion of innate ideas, Hume simply dismisses it as unconfirmed in experience.[58]

Our impressions are of two varieties: sensation and reflection. The origin of sensations as psychological entities is something Hume cannot explain. He notes that a sensation—the vivid, conscious awareness of a thing—is of unknown cause and, in so noting, he joins a large army of philosophers unable to discern precisely how so many atoms, angles, or grams can come to be *sensed* in that very mental respect in which we use the term.[59] Once we have an impression and its corresponding idea, the mind reviews and combines different impressions by the process of reflection. Reflections are impressions also, but they are further removed from the initial impressions that give rise to sensation. By memory we are able to repeat or revive impressions and by imagination we are able to reconstruct impressions in the form of pure ideas.[59] We can make the distinction between memory and imagination clearer with an illustration. When we picture the face of a relative, we are employing memory; that is, we are simply reviving an actual sensation. When, however, we consider government to be necessary for the social good, we are not "picturing" any longer. Instead, we are abstracting from an assortment of specific impressions and ideas a general principle, and the faculty that allows this is the imagination.[60]

Simple ideas become associated to form complex ideas, and the bases upon which such associations are formed are "RESEMBLANCE, CONTIGUITY and CAUSE and EFFECT."[61] Experience teaches that we tend to associate those events that resemble each other, those that take place together in time and space, and those that provide instances of unerring succession. The way in which resemblance, contiguity, and causation produced associations of varying durability is to be explained in terms of the physiology of the brain.[62] (It is worth noting that Hume's physiological explanation is lifted out of whole cloth from Descartes and is rife with references to "spirits," "traces," etc.) On the question of actual material existence, Hume cannot refute Berkeley on a logical ground and therefore is content to recognize that " *'tis vain to ask, Whether there be a body or not? That is a point which we must take for granted in all our reasonings.*"[63] It is not reason that establishes the separate reality of things and distinguishes between them and perception. Rather, our *imaginations* (as heretofore defined) are responsible, and it is only on the basis of this imaginative faculty that we are given and driven to believe that our perceptions are *of* something. Thus, Hume is not attempting to prove that there is a separate, material world and an equally separate mental one. He is concerned instead with establishing the principles that force that opinion on us. As to these principles, he reduces them to *constancy* and *coherence*. The mountains we looked at yesterday are found to be in the same place when we come back and look again today. These experiences convince us that objects enjoy a constant existence separately from our immediate awareness of them. Similarly, even though objects do undergo some change over time, they continue to reflect a certain coherence in their relation to other objects.

That is, it is only by *assuming* a continuity of existence on the part of objects (even when we are not there to witness them) that we are able to establish a relation between objects instead of one between perceptions alone. In summary, we *believe* there are objects, distinct from our perception of them, because we *assume* they continue to exist in our absence, and we *assume* this because the same objects are perceived in roughly the same form when we return to where they were first perceived. The new impressions are compared with those earlier ones now stored in our memory, and when the resemblance is close, we suppose that the present object is the continuing one.[64]

This brings us to the question of how individual impressions and their correspondent ideas can give rise to the rich notions with which every mind is concerned. How, we ask, are *complex* ideas produced by the rather trivial consequences of perception? Hume's answer is that complex ideas result from the association of simple ones, as we have already noted, and that all our ideas, if they are more than utter fancy, can only derive from a complication of more elemental ones. The latter are inextricably tied to sensations and impressions. Our "understanding," properly called, can refer to nothing but these. Given this position, we can predict how Hume will approach the remaining problems of *Passions* and *Morals*.

As the arch psychological philosopher, Hume accords the passions a central place in epistemology. The passions of pride, love, humility, and hatred are connected to the ideas and sensations evinced by those objects toward which these passions are felt.[65] Thus, "agreeable" images give rise to agreeable passions. Hume assembles an admirable list of passions including benevolence, anger, malice, envy, contempt, amorousness, and respect. He presents his passions as opposing pairs and explains their appearance in terms of the individual's life-long experiences and in terms of the internal sense called *sympathy*:

"I have endeavored to prove that power and riches, or poverty and meanness, which give rise to love or hatred, without producing any original pleasure or uneasiness, operate upon us by means of a secondary sensation deriv'd from a sympathy with that pain or satisfaction which they produce in the person who possesses them."[66]

We see, then, that Hume is very much in the sentimentalist (empathist) tradition of Shaftesbury and Butler. Our emotions are natural, are elicited by sensations and impressions, are directed by the interior sense of sympathy. Thus, our loftiest sentiments and our most ennobling qualities—those of love, respect, and altruism—are, at base, effectively independent of rational considerations. We do not love because logic compels it; we are not benevolent because we have intellectual grounds for rejected selfishness; we are not malicious *with reason*. These sentiments or passions are produced in us by a history of associations, by the rewarding and punishing consequences of our conduct, and by those laws of thought summarized under the headings of resemblance, contiguity, and cause and effect.

The passions enter Hume's epistemology as a means of accounting for that which is central to this epistemology: *belief*. In quietly accepting Berkeley's "solution" to the paradox of matter, in accepting, that is, that what we know we know through our impressions and reflection, Hume is forced to the conclusion that our knowledge is *conviction*. Philosophy's task is to account for this conviction. Experience alone is not enough to explain the belief we have in our knowledge. While empiricism can account for knowledge—that is, can explain what we know of rain, dogs, and the moon—there is nothing in the experiences per se that will convey the belief we have in this knowledge. Belief, then, must be understood in terms different from sensation and impression. It is, alas, a *feeling* we have *about* our knowledge:

> "The imagination has the command over all its ideas, and can join and mix and vary them. . . . It may conceive fictitious objects. . . . It may set them, in a manner, before our eyes in their true colours. . . . But as it is impossible, that this faculty of imagination can ever, of itself, reach belief, it is evident that belief consists not in the peculiar nature or order of ideas, but in the *manner* of their conception, and in their *feeling* to the mind . . . (B)*elief* is something felt by the mind, which distinguishes the ideas of the judgment from the fictions of the imagination."[67]

He develops this argument to the point of concluding that reason is ever in the service of the passions. What passes for a rationally derived system of morals is, on closer inspection, no more than a commitment to what is pleasurable. We are moral to the extent that certain experiences and actions produce a satisfying state of affairs. Moral conduct arises from *"the natural sentiments of humanity,"*[68] which affect our reason but do not depend upon reason for their existence. The so-called moral virtues are no more voluntary than are other *natural abilities*. That is, we are no more voluntarily virtuous than we are voluntarily beautiful or deformed. It makes no more sense to reward or punish a person for his virtues than it does to reward or punish him for his height.[69] All we end up doing is praising or blaming people for doing that which pleases or displeases us and, while this is understandable, it cannot be said to be rational or defended by the canons of logic. In a word,

"all arguments concerning existence are founded on the relation of
cause and effect; . . . our knowledge of that relation is derived entirely from experience; . . . all our experimental conclusions proceed
upon the supposition that the future will be conformable to the past."[70]

If there is existence, it is *perceived* existence. That the existing object or
event is caused is a supposition—an invention of the mind—as is the
induction by which we assume the future will conform to the past. What
we judge to be moral are perceived acts that create agreeable or dis-
agreeable experiences within us. The "right" and "wrong" of a situation
are inextricably tied to beliefs, sentiments, dispositions, and native tendencies of the mind. "Right" and "wrong" are not *in* the events or *in* the
actors, except in the sense that a feeling is *in* percipient man.

We will return to Hume's position on causation in the next chapter
and will discuss the effect this position has had on the philosophy of
science in general and on psychology in particular.

Hume's psychological philosophy combines in a peculiar way a number
of conceptions which, in modern psychology, are normally in an antago-
nistic relationship. Epistemologically, he was an empiricist without reservation. Only two realms of knowledge exist: the demonstrative, which
is logical and purely verbal, and the factual, which is purely experiential.
Since ideas can be about things only, they cannot be innate. However,
while ideas are not innate, feelings are. We are, according to Hume, so
constituted as to respond passionately to certain classes of action. Our
appetites and the pleasures and pains attached to them give vividness to
our ideas and impressions, convictions to our knowledge. Precisely *how*
our constitution does this is only hinted at. Just as sensation itself is
treated as a "natural" quality of the mind to be understood by "anatomists," so also the moral sentiments are somehow part of our frame and,
presumably, amenable to (ultimate) biological explanation. We see, then,
that materialism is an implicit feature of Hume's psychology. The theory
of knowledge is empirical and associationistic; the theory of emotion,
nativistic; the final and unexpressed psychological theory, materialistic.
Hume was no exception to the general rule that an empirical philosophy,
soon or late, becomes either solipsism or psychological materialism.

5. Thomas Reid (1710–1796) and the "Common-Sense" Movement

Thomas Reid is a much underrated figure in histories of psychology
and philosophy, although his insights have been rediscovered several
times in both disciplines. That twentieth-century school of philosophy
fathered by G. E. Moore and dubbed the "common-sense" school is, in
outline, Reid's system in modern dress. Even Kant's famous if tortuous
"answer" to Hume, which we will review in the next chapter, was ably

anticipated by Reid as was the theoretically neutral and practical bent of modern behavioral science. It is especially surprising that modern commentators have been perfunctory in their attention, since Reid was widely read and admired by his own contemporaries in England, Scotland, and on the Continent. Perhaps he was too clear. We identify Reid with the "common-sense" movement and we are advised to pause in order to appreciate how congenial his time was to a movement of this sort.

The great figures in the line of British empiricists from Bacon to Hume were all influential outside England. Locke was adopted by the principal reformers of France, where he paid two extended visits. His *Treatise of Civil Government*, with its emphasis upon the human need for freedom and equality and its insistence on government's obligations to its citizens, perfectly complemented the spirit of the French *Enlightenment* that would culminate in the Revolution of 1789. The French *philosophes* may be said to derive from Montaigne (1533–1592), as the British empiricists did from Bacon, and it should be seen as more than coincidental that the French publisher who presented Locke's essay to the world of the *Enlightenment* was also responsible for the 1724 edition of Montaigne's collected works.[71] And it is far from coincidental that D'Alembert should write, in his introduction to Diderot's *Encyclopaedia* (1751):

> "Nothing is more indisputable than the existence of our sensations. Thus, in order to prove that they are the principle of all our knowledge, it suffices to show that they can be. . . . Why suppose that we have purely intellectual notions at the outset if all we need do in order to form them is to reflect upon our sensations?"[72]

The philosophers of England and France were at war with rationalism not merely on epistemological grounds but on political and social ones as well. Descartes' philosophy was, in the hands of Malebranche, a defense of religion and the perquisites of clerical office. Hobbes's *Leviathan* served others as that form of *Hobbism* that wields deductive logic in such a way that the divine rights of monarchs, the suffering of the poor, and the abuse of power, all have the legitimacy of Euclid's theorems. It is no accident, then, that the empirical epistemologists were also the empirical moralists and political theorists—no accident because their epistemologies were, in all significant respects, preliminary discourses on a *moral* treatise. That moral treatise would take many forms in several languages and nations: the Bill of Rights, the Rights of Man, Common Sense. Thomas Reid was central to this movement. He was not opposing Hume's skepticism merely to save God but, rather, to retain a philosophical foundation for a movement that extended even beyond the issue of faith.

When we recall Locke's willingness to accept the certitude of moral propositions with the same confidence displayed toward mathematical propositions, we are more willing to include Reid in the line of empiricists *despite* his assertion that the principles of common sense are innate. Locke and Reid are just two of many philosophers who can be fit into neat categories only if we are willing to look the other way. And in both cases, the willingness to take recourse to some sort of rationalist or nativist principle was prompted by the desire to avoid skepticism. For Locke, reducing the canons of morality to empirically observable factors could lead only to a form of moral relativism which, if pressed, would remove the validity of his political propositions. For Reid, Hume's philosophy leads not only to atheism but to absurdity. It was Hume who asserted that *"the errors in religion are dangerous; those in philosophy only ridiculous,"*[73] and it is Reid who sets out to ensure that the latter not be allowed to thrive just so the former might be averted.

In describing Reid as the founder of "common-sense" philosophy we mean to say not that he rested his case on the superstitions or shifting opinions of the man in the street but that he required philosophy to conform to that which every human being knows to be true—what philosophers themselves know to be true when freed from the pretensions of their trade. And, of the numerous pretentions endemic to the philosophical way of thinking, none is more absurd than the notion that our ideas are conditioned by the properties of things. *"We are commonly told by philosophers,"* says Reid, *"that we get the idea of extension by feeling along the extremities of a body, as if there was no manner of difficulty in the matter. I have sought with great pains, I confess, to find out how this idea can be got by feeling, but I have sought in vain."*[74] In reply to Berkeley's brand of idealism, Reid agrees to try on this point of view and to see what it produces:

"I resolve not to believe my senses. I break my nose against a post. . . . I step into a dirty kennel; and after twenty such wise and rational actions, I am taken up and clapped into a madhouse."[75]

To the Cartesian who shuns the senses in favor of reason, Reid can only observe that, since *"they came both out of the same shop,"* he is on as firm a ground accepting his senses as he is his reason.[76] According to Reid, Locke, Berkeley, and Hume all failed to distinguish between sensation and perception and as a result their use of the concept of "idea" was hopelessly muddled. A *sensation* is the direct experience of that which is in the mind, whereas a perception is of that which lies outside the mind. Note the following two sentences:

(a) "I feel a pain in my leg."
(b) "I see a rose in the garden."

In (a), while there is a verb (feel) and a grammatical object (pain), the difference is *only* grammatical in that "feel" and "pain" are one and the same. However, in (b), there is not only a grammatical distinction between the verb (see) and the object (rose) but an actual one.[77] Our perceptions, which come from "the mint of nature," are triggered by the actual objects in nature. It is these objects that constitute the language nature uses to speak to us. We do not *reason* that there must be an object when we perceive one. We know immediately and *instinctively* that such is the case. Hardness, coldness, and color, not less than motion, number, and form, are perceived by us through the peculiarities of our constitution. Sensation is a *natural sign* of hardness, no more provable than is the assertion that a thing cannot be and not be at the same time:

> ". . . (S)upposing we have got the conception of hardness, how come we by the *belief* of it? Is it self-evident, from comparing the ideas, that such a sensation could not be felt unless such a quality of bodies existed? No. Can it be proved by probable or certain arguments? No. Have we got this belief then by tradition, by education, or by experience? No. . . . Shall we then throw off this belief, as having no foundation in reason? Alas! it is not in our power; it triumphs over reason, and laughs at all the arguments of a philosopher. Even the author of the 'Treatise of Human Nature', though he saw no reason for this belief . . . could hardly conquer it in his speculative and solitary moments; at other times he fairly yielded to it, and confesses that he found himself under a necessity to do so."[78]

Reid was whimsically perplexed by Hume's willingness to doubt the validity of everything except those sensations and impressions from which his ideas were supposed to emerge. Why, asks Reid, did Hume find it necessary to stop at sensations? If causation is in the mind only, if virtue is but a certain "vivacity" our ideas have received, why accept even that there are sensations or impressions or ideas or belief or *anything*? The answer, of course, is that sensations, including Hume's sensations, cannot even be denied without the consequence of self-contradiction. Our sensations are not chimerical: we do avoid pain; we do believe certain impressions and not others despite the fact that there is nothing in an object that can command belief other than its reality.

To understand our sensations and our perceptions and the origins of our beliefs requires, on Reid's analysis, recourse to the notion of *natural faculties* that are intrinsic to our constitution. This is not to say that the mind has innate ideas; rather, it is naturally equipped to recognize that class of natural signs which are the "primary" and "secondary qualities" of Locke, the impressions and reflections of Hume, and Berkeley's *ideas*. It makes no more sense to ask about the rational justifications for accepting the natural faculties than to ask for a logical proof that the stomach digests food or, better, *why* the stomach digests food. In anticipation of Darwin, Reid notes that our survival in the real world requires that we be psychologically conversant with nature's objects. We are, accordingly *constitutionally* endowed in such a way as to reconstruct the world in psychologically meaningful and useful ways. The man in the street has neither the time nor the inclination to escape his idea of rain by thinking of entering his idea of a house. He does not keep himself alive—that is, he does not retain the idea of being alive—through the idea of eating his idea of food. Neither for that matter, does the philosopher, including the skeptical philosopher. That no argument of logic can distinguish among rain, life, food, and houses on the one hand, and our ideas of these on the other, is simply to note that man and his world are not composed of logic; that logic did not create the world; that when logic collides with those facts universally possessed by the human mind, it is logic that will be bent.

No one had better credentials as an atheist than David Hume's. Still, there is a respect in which his skeptical philosophy was a return to the Renaissance's inability to separate Nature and Spirit. More than Berkeley, because he was more influential than Berkeley, Hume seemed to "psychologize" the world while at the same time praising Newton and even trying to Newtonianize the mind. It was certainly not Hume's aim to foster a dualism of any sort, but the effect of his writings was to convey to some that we live in two radically different worlds: one, the *apparently* material world of causes, effects, moral truisms, and so forth; the other, the only knowable world that is, finally, subjective and ever conjectural. In terms of their respective influence or potential influence on psychology, Hume may be said to have psychologized philosophy to the point of making science a matter of conviction, whereas Reid, in basing psychology on the firm ground of natural causes, made conviction itself a possible subject of science. Among Reid's contemporaries was David Hartley, whose work will be considered in Chapter 9. He was one of the early theorists of the "reflex-conditioning" tradition, and his *Observations on Man* (1749) was the first important expression of psychological materialism to come out of the British empiricist school. Reid attacked this essay on the grounds of its excessive hypothesizing— its departure from Newton's maxims regarding the practice of science. It was not the materialism Reid objected to but the speculation. It is in his ringing denunciation of Hartley's theories that Reid's devotion to Baconian and Newtonian methodology is revealed:

"The effluvia of bodies make an impression upon the olfactory nerves; but make none upon the optic or auditory. No man has been able to give a shadow of reason for this. While this is the case, is it not better to confess our ignorance of the nature of those impressions made upon the nerves and brain in perception, than to flatter our pride with the conceit of knowledge which we have not, and to adulterate philosophy with the spurious brood of hypotheses?"[79]

In this also is Reid's influence on modern psychology felt. He demands that philosophical explanations conform to the facts and truths possessed by every human being. He requires that all hypothetical statements be avoided unless the overwhelming weight of indirect evidence is behind them. He insists that the world is real, that the senses are affected by this world, that perception is a report of this world. He justifies his position —which is called *representational realism*—in terms of what everyone, including the skeptic, learns from life in the world. Implicitly, he goes on to defend his brand of realism with the canons of survivalism; the skeptic's course leads us to step into a dirty kennel!

As Reid's influence spread to Europe, so too did it reach America, where a "common sense" movement culminated in the American *Pragmatism* and *Functionalism* of Dewey, James, and Peirce. This influence is the subject of a later chapter. In addition to laying the ground for pragmatism and functionalism, he fathered what has come to be called "*faculty psychology*," a form of psychological inquiry devoted to uncovering the natural faculties of man (and other animals) deemed essential to knowledge and conduct. In rooting these faculties in instincts or native dispositions, Reid began a branch of British empiricism that finally yielded Galton's theories of hereditary genius and McDougall's instinct-theory of emotion. On the way, "faculty psychology" would be assimilated by Gall and Spurzheim and would appear in ultramaterialist garb as *phrenology*. These, also, are subjects to be deferred. We note them here only to acknowledge how diffuse an influence Reid has had on psychology. Even the modern behaviorist, when he defends himself against those who demand theories, when he attempts to describe the sense in which "the law of effect" is a law, when he accounts for his indifference to neurological research and mechanisms, and when he articulates the principles of his program, ends up borrowing the commonsense arguments of Thomas Reid. A philosopher who has been successful in shaping the thought and practice of hereditarian and environmentalist alike, humanist and mechanist alike, is worthy of far more attention than Reid has received.

As Reid's epistemological position was of the commonsense sort, so also was his position on the question of the passions, emotion, free will, and moral conduct in general. Quite simply, these characteristics, most of which can be found throughout the animal kingdom, are so essential to society and to peace among the children of nature that their origins can be in none other than nature itself. On the natural appetites, for example, which even the lowly caterpillar displays in rejecting hundreds of different leaves until reaching the one that is "natural" to its diet, Reid comments:

> "The ends for which our natural appetites are given, are too evident to escape the observation of any man of the least reflection. Two of those I named are intended for the preservation of the individual, and the third for the continuance of the species."[80]

The same nature (God) responsible for these natural endowments has equipped us with the faculty of deliberation so that we may keep our appetites under control, so that we may recognize our duty to others and to God. This deliberative faculty is as self-evident as Euclid's theorems, and even the skeptic must employ it in order to doubt it. It is this very same faculty that allows our actions to be voluntary. Those who would point to exceptions, such as the madman, the delerious or intoxicated, are more aware of the exceptions than of the fact that they *are* exceptions.[81] The rules governing those in possession of their faculties are not over-thrown by instances of disease, deformity, or constitutional (native) deficiency.[82]

We will conclude our coverage of Reid with a review of his approach to the problem of universals, for it is in dealing with it, and especially with Hume's "solution," that he presents the early form of a *cognitive* psychology as contrasted with a perceptual or sensationist psychology.

Berkeley had accounted for general ideas, for example, the idea of "cat," in terms of an associationistic principle. Berkeley's theory, shared by Locke and Hume, was that all such general ideas are merely *particular* ideas melded together by words. Thus, once we have had repeated exposure to different, particular cats and have learned the word "cat," we use the word as a representation of *any* individual cat; that is, all cats, any one at a time. Hume not only agreed with this explanation but judged it to be one of the major advances in the recent history of philosophy. As Hume put it:

> "A particular idea becomes general by being annexed to a general term . . . [through] . . . customary conjunction. . . . Abstract ideas are therefore in themselves individual although they may become general in their representation. The image in the mind is only that of a particular object."[83]

Reid, the commonsense realist, offers the following observations on this theory which, as Reid notes, is the cornerstone of the Humean theory of ideas:

First, in asserting that every idea must finally reduce to an impression of quantity and quality, Hume makes it impossible for us to mean different things when we say, "This is a line" and "This is a line of three inches." It is not the case that when someone has the idea of "line," he has it only by picturing a particular line. He pictures no such thing.

Second, Reid agrees with Hume (and the Nominalists) that there can be no "abstract" triangle in the real world. However, attributes may be common to many individual objects, and to know this does not require that we make a mental picture of each individual object in order to weigh the similarities.

Third, when we have the idea of "lion" it does not come into being by having a particular lion eat a particular sheep; less by having the idea of lion eat the idea of sheep:

"If ideas differ from the object of sense only in strength and vivacity, it will follow, that the idea of a lion is a lion of less strength and vivacity."[84]

Fourth, in accounting for our assigning a term to a collection of particulars in terms of the *resemblance* among them, Hume either admits that we are capable of holding general ideas or, worse, he supports one hypothesis by taking recourse to the very principle he set out to reject.

Fifth, in proposing that when we use the general word it creates the idea of the individual in our minds, Hume flies in the face of the common experiences of mankind:

"I think a farmer can talk of his sheep, and his black cattle, without conceiving in his imagination one individual, with all its circumstances and proportions. If this be true, the whole of his [Hume's] theory of general ideas falls to the ground."[85]

Finally, Hume had offered as an illustration of his theory the suggestion that, for example, in a sphere of white marble, the form and the color are indistinguishable. Hume's point is that we mean no more by "form" than a particular distribution of light of a certain perceived hue. To this Reid replies:

"How foolish have mankind been to give different names, in all ages and in all languages, to things undistinguishable, and in effect the same?

Henceforth, in all books of science and of entertainment, we may substitute figure for colour, and colour for figure."[86]

In these arguments Reid was not defending the reality of Universals as conceived by the Medieval Realists. He was only pointing to the logical and practical limitations of the associationistic account endorsed by Berkeley, Locke, and Hume. He insisted that Hume's very employment of *resemblance* required an *a priori* faculty, or else there would be no way a general term could be applied to particulars. Further, he was reminding the sensationists that real people do not picture individual things when they think of the general words. Instead, the mind possesses the general concept which is now *mentally* independent of the things so represented. As the world of objects is a language nature has in order to communicate with us, our human language is a means by which the mind can free itself of particulars and of matter in general. We sense, we perceive, and we cognize. None is more "natural" than the other two; none requires logic as a proof.

Utilitarianism and Empiricism

There is a nearly irresistible urge, in attempting to account for the rise of utilitarianism, to point out that Thomas Reid's best student was Dugald Stewart (1753–1828), and Stewart's most able pupil was James Mill, and that James Mill was the principal disciple and a major expositor of Jeremy Bentham's political philosophy. The impression conveyed by such an intellectual pedigree is that the great political reform movement in England in the 1830s was born in the quiet studies of the University of Edinburgh and that its essential character was philosophical.

It is true that Dugald Stewart was mightily impressed with Reid, so much so that his *Elements of the Philosophy of the Human Mind* was devoted largely to qualifying and correcting those features of Reid's system that Stewart considered to be in error.[87] Through it all, however, he retained Reid's insistence on Baconian science, Reid's belief in the constitutional determinants of perception and thought, and Reid's "faculty" psychology as the proper starting point for a science of morals. He did not have much confidence, though, in appeals to common sense, nor did he share Reid's often haughty disregard for the role of reason in settling disputes. By and large, Stewart was concerned with the differences between natural science, moral science, and mathematics. (His father was professor of that subject at Edinburgh.) His effect on James Mill, we may guess, had more to do with the force of his personality, the liberality of his political convictions, his great personal charm. Of his specific intellectual contributions to Mill's development, we may cite two: he undermined confidence in that peculiar sort of mentalism with which Reid's psychology was rife and, in the process, he salvaged Hume's mechanical associationism. Reid's "innate mental dispositions" were of a sufficiently mysterious nature to keep theology in mental science and to keep physics out of it. Stewart, like Hume, traced many of these native qualities to language and to conventional figures of speech. Another of his students, Thomas Brown (1778–1820), may have summarized Stewart's criticism of Reid's psychology most aptly when he wrote:

> "To suppose the mind to exist in two different states, in the same moment, is a manifest absurdity. To the whole series of states of the mind, then, whatever the individual, momentary successive states may be, I give the name of our *consciousness*. . . . There are not sensations, thoughts, passions, *and also consciousness*, any more than there is *quadruped* or *animal*, as a separate being to be added to the wolves, tygers, elephants, and other living creatures. . . . The fallacy of conceiving consciousness to be something different from the feeling, which is said to be its *object*, has arisen, in a great measure, from the use of the personal pronoun *I*."*[88]

Brown followed Stewart in restoring a stricter associationism to psychology, and Mill followed both. Still, lest the impression of intellectual continuity become firm again, we must note that Mill did not even begin his university studies until the year after the publication of Bentham's *Principles of Morals and Legislation* (1789), and Bentham was hardly concerned with the philosophical hair-splitting that so occupied Thomas Reid's progeny at Edinburgh. Thus, to discover the connection—and an intimate one it is—between Utilitarianism and Empiricism, we must look

---

* Note the similarity between Thomas Brown's objection and what Prof. Ryle has called the *category error* in *The Concept of Mind* (1949, Hutchinson & Co., London). Ryle describes the foreign visitor to Oxford or Cambridge who asks, after seeing the classes, playing fields, offices, etc., "But where is the University?" Recall from Chapter 1, however, H. L. A. Hart's disavowal of behavioristic criteria for definitions. Oxford University did not come into being as a result of teachers and students simply finding themselves together on what was once a large and empty lot. First there was the *idea* of a university and then there was the choice of location, the construction of buildings, the admission of qualified students, etc. Thus, the foreigner's "category-mistake" may not be an error at all. It is quite conceivable that, after examining all the buildings and interviewing all the residents of Oxford, one still may plausibly ask, "But where is the University?" That is, he may be familiar with the original Charter, may perceive the original intentions and commitments of the University, and may decide that what is now going on *is not* Oxford University. In terms of Brown's version of the category-mistake, it would seem to make a little difference whether one uses the word "consciousness" or the word "feeling." Even if one agrees that "I am conscious of my toothache" means no more than "I have a toothache," one still must explain the feeling.

past that superficial and almost accidental chronology linking Reid, Stewart, Brown, Mill, and Bentham.

The distinction between politics and a political movement is that the latter seeks its defense in philosophy. When people are to be encouraged to give up certain traditions, when they are to be prodded into new political spheres, when they are incited to riot and rebel, they must, simultaneously, be convinced either that those principles to which they have subscribed have been violated or that the principles are invalid. Life in a society of law, no matter how mean and confining, generally is perceived as better than life amid anarchy. Improving one's condition is, at least in principle, always possible as long as one is alive and not imprisoned, and this fact is usually sufficient to discourage the masses from taking arms against their leaders.

Neither empiricism nor rationalism, as purely philosophical doctrines, entails any given form of government. Aristotle could argue against tyranny from the perspective of a rationalist, and Hobbes could argue for it from the same perspective. To the extent that a society of laws cannot prove, either experimentally or even empirically, the validity of those first principles upon which any system of law must be based, the legal and ethical tone of a society will necessarily be set by that form of discourse and invention normally associated with philosophical rationalism. Accordingly, when government fails and reform is in the air, philosophical rationalism becomes the innocent casualty in the war on law.

It cannot be mere chance that is responsible for the frequency with which periods of social turmoil and political reform are empirical in their philosophical complexion and the frequency with which periods of national birth and regrouping are rationalistic in their philosophical complexion. Recall the ultrarationalistic philosophies following Athens' defeat by Sparta, Rome's rise to power, the creation of the European community, and the post-Reformation period in France and Germany. Contrast this with the empirical Stoicism and materialism of late Rome, the empirical pragmatism of Europe in the Reformation, the political empiricism of England from the eighteenth century on. In these massive cultural and political movements, the empirically inclined luminaries have not so much denied that there are first principles or "self-evident" truths as they have asserted *different* first principles and "self-evident" truths. It is no more "self-evident" that *all men are created equal* than it is that kings have *divine rights*. John Locke, whose status as an empiricist requires no defense, begins his famous *Essay on Civil Government* with a very large number of assertions, none based on the evidence of sense, and few even possibly observable. He tries to imagine man in his original "state of nature" and concludes that, in such a state, nothing is more evident.

"than that creatures of the same species and rank, promiscuously born to all the same advantages of nature, and the use of the same faculties, should also be equal one amongst another without subordination or subjection, unless the lord and master of them all should, by any manifest declaration of his will, set one above another."[89]

But, *empirically*, what is this state of nature? And what observation or record of observations leads to the conclusion, than which none is more evident, that all men are similarly endowed at birth and have the same faculties in the same degree? And what of the notable exception, unless the lord and master of all (God) sets one above another? Is it not this very exception upon which all monarchies, all religious authority, all institutions of control have been based since the first pharaoh? And when Locke goes on to say that the state of nature "has a law of nature to govern it," is it not this presumed "law of nature" that dictates Caesar will rule and not follow?

Let us be sure to note, then, that the connection between empiricism and utilitarianism is historic, not logical. Locke, Berkeley, and Hume in England and the *philosophes* of the French *Enlightenment* had asserted the authority of experience in the affairs of state. At the grossest level, which is the only level from which political movements can draw inspiration from philosophy, the empiricists had identified truth with sense, validity with feeling, morality with sentiment. The influence of Thomas Reid, again at the grossest level, was one of making these empiricistic claims seem to rest on the natural constitution of the human frame. Jeremy Bentham's *Principles* was the coalescence of empiricism, sentimentalism, and commonsense philosophy, despite his rejection of "common-sense" schools which he described as *ipsedixitism*. While stubbornly regaling the intuitionists (e.g., Reid), he could still stand behind such aphorisms as

"pleasure is in *itself* a good . . . the only good: pain is in itself an evil; and, indeed, without exception, the only evil."[90]

This form of *ipsedixitism* can, of course, derive from nothing but intuition as this term was employed by those Bentham dismissed as intuitionists. Even in the superficially empirical language of the following passage, the strains of rationalism break through:

"Nature has placed mankind under the governance of two sovereign masters, *pain* and *pleasure*. It is for them alone to point out what we ought to do as well as to determine what we shall do. . . . They govern us in all we do, in all we say, in all we think. . . . The *principle of utility* recognises this subjection, and assumes it for the foundation of that system, the object of which is to rear the fabric of felicity by the hands of reason and law. Systems which attempt to question it, deal in sounds instead of sense, in caprice instead of reason, in darkness instead of light."[91]

Here was the English version of Rousseau's "Man is born free and is everywhere in chains"—the late eighteenth-century expansion of Locke's theory of the social contract. Bentham and James Mill had their historic meeting in 1808, and the *Benthamites* were founded. Utilitarianism in England would soon produce the Reform Bill of 1832. In France, its Continental version had already produced Napoleon.

Bentham's contribution to psychology can hardly be ignored. While the utilitarian emphasis upon pleasure and pain was, philosophically, far from original—arising as it did from more than a century of sentimentalist thinking—Bentham's attempt to quantify the doctrine created a bridge to science. His "pleasure principle" would find new expression in the psychoanalytic theories of Freud and in the research and theory of Thorndike. Indeed, behavioral science's tangled *law of effect* is but a restatement of Bentham's "two sovereigns." Less obviously, Bentham's legal prescriptions created a need for psychological inquiry. In Chapter XVI of his *Principles,* he is at some pain to establish the legal responsibility of citizens and the conditions that might confine either their claim to happiness or their ability to make such a claim. It is here that he addresses himself to the problems posed by insanity and mental deficiency and all but pleads for an Alfred Binet:

"For exhibiting the quantity of sensible heat in a human body we have a very tolerable sort of instrument, the thermometer; but for exhibiting the quantity of intelligence, we have no such instrument."[92]

In addition to these indirect effects upon psychology, effects that are very small relative to the contributions of Freud, Thorndike, and Binet themselves, Bentham directly set the tone of American psychology, and especially educational psychology, through his writings and through his major spokesman, James Mill. The bridge from utilitarianism to pragmatism is a short one. The distance from pragmatism to behaviorism is even shorter. As we shall see in later chapters one builder of these bridges was Charles Darwin.

Many, even most, of the ideas discussed in this chapter were written in response to an alternative perspective—rationalism. A good portion of Locke's *Essay* was devoted to issues raised by Descartes, just as Hume's *Treatise* was a reply to those who would challenge Locke's empiricism.

The *Treatise* went much further than a mere defense, however, and created a rationalistic streak among British and Scottish philosophers who, otherwise, were empiricists. We now will turn to this other system, which so boldly prefers mind to sense, logic to experiment, and certain truth to the inescapable probabilities of perception.

References

1. Francis Bacon, *Novum Organum*, LXIV. In *The Works of Francis Bacon*, Vol. I, Hurd & Houghton, Cambridge, 1878.

2. Francis Bacon, *Of the Proficience and Advancement of Learning Divine and Human*, op. cit., pp. 134–35.

3. Ibid., p. 128.

4. Ibid., p. 120.

5. Ibid., p. 127.

6. Ibid., p. 224.

7. Ibid., pp. 225–226.

8. Ibid., pp. 236–237.

9. Ibid., p. 254.

10. Ibid., p. 332.

11. Ibid., p. 334.

12. Ibid., p. 338.

13. Francis Bacon, *Novum Organum*, op. cit., XCVIII.

14. Ibid., XCIX.

15. Ibid., CXXVII.

16. Ibid., XCII.

17. John Donne, *Complete Poetry and Selected Prose*, edited by John Hayward, Random House, New York, 1936, p. 237. For an excellent analysis of this aspect of the Zeitgeist, consult *All Coherence Gone* by Victor Harris, University of Chicago Press, Chicago, 1949.

18. John Locke, *An Essay Concerning Human Understanding*, Henry Regnery Co., Chicago, 1956. An especially penetrating study of the skeptical forces operating in this period is Margaret Wiley's *The Subtle Knot: Creative Scepticism in Seventeenth-Century England*, Allen & Unwin, London, 1952.

19. Locke, op. cit., *Introduction*.

20. Ibid.

21. Locke, op. cit., Book II, Chap. IX, Sec. 7.

22. Ibid., II, IX, 8.

23. Ibid., IV, I, 2.

24. Ibid., IV, II, 1.

25. Ibid., II, XXIII, 9 and 11.

26. Ibid., IV, III, 12.

27. Ibid., IV, II, 14 and IV, IX, 3.

28. Ibid., IV, XI, 1.

29. Ibid., IV, XI, 13.

30. Ibid., IV, XI, 6.

31. Ibid., IV, XI, 8.

32. Ibid., II, X, 8.

33. Ibid., IV, IV, 5.

34. Ibid., IV, IV, 6.

35. Ibid., IV, IV, 7.

36. Ibid., IV, IV, 8.

37. George Berkeley, *An Essay Towards a New Theory of Vision* (1709). In Berkeley's *Works On Vision*, edited by Colin M. Turbayne, Library of Arts, Bobbs-Merrill, Indianapolis, 1963.

38. Ibid., Sec. 75.

39. Ibid., Sec. 65.

40. George Berkeley, *A Treatise Concerning the Principles of Human Knowledge* (1710), Open Court Edition, La Salle, Ill., 1963.

41. A. A. Luce, *Berkeley's Immaterialism*, Russell & Russell, New York, 1968.

42. George Berkeley, *An Essay Towards a New Theory of Vision*, op. cit., Sec. 17.

43. George Berkeley, *A Treatise Concerning the Principles of Human Knowledge*, op. cit., #4.

44. Ibid., #86.

45. Ibid., #89.

46. Ibid., #90.

47. Ibid., #103.

48. Ibid., #112.

49. David Hume, *A Treatise of Human Nature, Introduction*, edited by L. A. Selby-Bigge, Clarendon Press, Oxford, 1973.

50. The most readily available collection of essays by Shaftesbury, Butler, and other prominent sentamentalists is the Dover edition of *British Moralists*, 2 vols., edited by L. A. Selby-Bigge, Dover Books, New York, 1965.

51. Shaftesbury, *Inquiry Concerning Virtue or Merit*. In *British Moralists*, edited by L. A. Selby-Bigge, op. cit.

52. Ibid., p. 46.

53. Ibid.

54. Joseph Butler, *Of the Nature of Virtue*. In *British Moralists*, op. cit., p. 245.

55. Hume, *Treatise*, op. cit., p. XVII.

56. Ibid., p. XVIII.

57. Ibid., Book I, Pt. I, Sec. I.

58. Ibid., I, I, II.

59. Ibid., I, I, III.

60. Ibid., I, I, III.

61. Ibid., I, I, IV.

62. Ibid., I, IV, V; I, IV, I.

63. Ibid., I, IV, II and also I, IV, IV (quotation from p. 228).

64. Ibid., I, IV, II.

65. Ibid., II, II, IV and II, II, V.

66. Ibid., II, II, IX.

67. Hume, *An Enquiry Concerning Human Understanding*, Sec. V, Pt. II. In *Essential Works of David Hume*, edited by Ralph Cohen. Bantam Books, New York, 1965.

68. Hume, *Treatise*, op. cit., III, II, V.

69. Ibid., III, III, IV.

70. Hume, *Enquiry*, op. cit., Sec. IV, Pt. II.

71. Ira Wade, *The Intellectual Origins of the French Enlightenment*. Princeton University Press, New Jersey, 1971 (p. 89).

72. Jean Le Rond D'Alembert, *Preliminary Discourse to the Encyclopedia of Diderot*, translated by Richard N. Schwab. Quotation taken from p. 7 of the Introduction. Bobbs-Merrill, Indianapolis, 1963.

73. Hume, *Treatise*, op. cit., I, IV, VII.

74. Thomas Reid, *An Inquiry into the Human Mind on the Principles of Common Sense*. In *Between Hume and Mill: An Anthology of British Philosophy—1749–1843*, edited by Robert Brown. Random House, Modern Library, New York, 1970, p. 161.

75. Thomas Reid, op. cit., p. 175.

76. Ibid., p. 174.

77. Ibid., p. 173.

78. Ibid., p. 157.

79. Ibid., p. 187.

80. Thomas Reid, *Essays on the Active Powers of the Human Mind*, Essay III, Pt. II, Ch. I. Reprinted by MIT Press, Cambridge, Mass., 1969.

81. Ibid., Essay II, Ch. III.

82. Thomas Reid, *Essays on the Intellectual Powers of Man*, Essay II, Ch. 5 (*Of Perception*), reprinted by MIT Press, Cambridge, Mass., 1969.

83. Hume, *Treatise*, op. cit., I, I, VIII.

84. Reid, *Essays on the Intellectual Powers of Man*, op. cit., Essay V.

85. Ibid.

86. Ibid.

87. Dugald Stewart, *Elements of the Philosophy of the Human Mind*. Selections in *Between Hume and Mill*, op. cit.

88. Thomas Brown, *Lectures on the Philosophy of the Human Mind*, in *Between Hume and Mill, op. cit.*, p. 336.

89. John Locke: *An Essay Concerning the True Original, Extent and End of Civil Government: II: The State of Nature*. Reprinted in, *Social Contract*, edited by Sir Ernest Barker, Oxford University Press, New York, 1947.

90. Jeremy Bentham, *An Introduction to the Principles of Morals and Legislation*, Ch. X., Sec. XI. In *The Utilitarians*, Dolphin Books, New York, 1961.

91. Ibid., Ch. I, Sec. I.

92. Ibid., Ch. XV, Sec. XLIV.

8

□□□□□□□□□□□□□□□□□□□□□□□□□□□□□□

Rationalism

THE GEOMETRY OF THE MIND

The apology for rigid classification was first offered in Chapter 1 and has been repeated several times since. It is again in order, for *rationalism* is a term that has come to suggest so many meanings that nearly any objection to its application will stand on sure ground. More than one historian, for example, has referred to the French Enlightenment as "the Age of Reason" and its chief architects were all dedicated to reason. Yet, each of them—Voltaire, Diderot, D'Alembert, Condorcet—was an empiricist, at least according to the broad definition given in the previous chapter. Even Rousseau, so passionately romantic and, in the common sense of the term, idealistic, was durably empiricistic in addressing the major political questions of his time. And we have already observed that Locke's empiricism was still able to embrace intuition and the possibility of moral axioms whose certainty was as great as those of mathematics.

Apologies notwithstanding, however, there are fundamental differences between, on the one hand, Locke, Berkeley, Hume, James Mill, and J. S. Mill and, on the other, Descartes, Spinoza, Leibniz and Kant. To date, the differences have proved to be irreconcilable. More important for our present purposes, a distinguishable goup of "psychologies" has grown as a result of these differences. In this chapter, we will focus on two of these fundamental differences—the two that seem to be especially at odds and that played the greatest part by far in setting the infant science of psychology off on two separate paths. One difference is epistemological and centers on the issue of innate ideas. The other is methodological and concerns the relative roles to be played by (rational) deduction and (empirical-experimental) induction in the search for truth. Naturally enough, the epistemological bias virtually determines the

245

methodological prescriptions. Because these two issues, that of innate ideas and that of the deducibility of truth, are central to what concerns us most, we might best begin by examining the meaning of each.

Innate Ideas

Recall that Plato's theory of knowledge was, at the root, nativistic. In the *Meno*, the *Protagoras*, and elsewhere he insists that the eternal truths are locked within our souls, even before birth, and that learning, properly conceived, is *reminiscence*. In the *Theaetetus*, Socrates makes short shrift of that marvelously Humean maxim, "Man is the measure of all things," and notes that, were the senses enough, dog-faced baboons could qualify as philosophers.

The major portion of the Platonic legacy received by Aristotle, who was otherwise aloof to the theory of *ideas*, involved this skepticism toward the evidence of perception. Recognizing that the senses were responsive to changes in the material world, he concluded that they were of little service in the search for the unchanging. Accordingly, it was *metaphysics* that was to be the "first philosophy," and it was this ranking that Francis Bacon challenged.

In the medieval period, as we have noted, this same issue reappeared, this time in the form of the problem of *universals*. The eye can see one cat at a time but the mind "knows" of the "universal cat." Such knowledge assumes a knowing faculty that is not sensory and it is therefore a form of knowledge that cannot be *given* in experience. It is knowledge the mind must have *prior* to experience in order for experience to teach us anything.

The words "given" and "prior" are at the heart of the problem of innate ideas. In Chapter 2, we reviewed Aristotle's objections to the strict (Platonic) nativistic account which seemed to require that the infant enter the world knowing a number of things which, later in life, he would have so much trouble learning. Aristotle's jibe in this connection was the prototypic one and has been repeated in every generation by those seeking to disarm the nativist. The stock reply, of course, is that the child does not have difficulty with the truth but with the language he must learn in order to articulate it in the culturally approved form. And the rebuttal elicited by this defense is that the so-called knowledge is *only* linguistic in the first place. This then prompts the reply that were such truths merely verbal, there would have been no reason for every literate society in human history to have invented terms to express them!

Everyone tutored in arithmetic knows that there is no number so large that one cannot be added to it. No one knows this by experience in that no one has actually conducted the experiment and determined that the prediction succeeded. To say that we know this by inference or generalization is to impute to the fact the less-than-certain status that attaches to all other inferences. It is not merely likely that there is no number so large that one cannot be added to it. It is absolutely and irrefutably certain. If it is an inference, it is not the sort of inference generated by sensory knowledge or by experience. Since the fact is not established by experience in the first place and since it cannot be confirmed by experience and, finally, since, it *is* a fact, it must be one not *given* in experience. Thus, it is known *a priori*. The patient reader will discover in Chapter 11 how the empiricist deals with this problem—which he conceives to be linguistic—but for now we will train our attention on this sense of innate: that which could not possibly be given in experience. Employed this way, the term "innate idea," does not require that the infant be consciously aware of the fact or facts; only that, in maturity, he will know certain things for certain and that this knowledge will be the result of maturation alone, not instruction or experience. What is argued for is the existence of certain innate *principles* or *archetypes* of thought that assimilate experience and determine its *psychological* character. It is this meaning of *a priori* that continues to enliven psychological research and theory. It is a notion of innateness not wed to any particular period of maturation and surely not infancy. We do not have to grant the infant the ability to add in order to know that it is not experience that proves that no number is so great that it cannot be greater. The rationalists to be studied in this chapter all subscribed to the doctrine of innate ideas so defined.

Methodological Rationalism

The rationalist is distinguishable further from the empiricist by the method he adopts to discover nature's laws. As the term implies, rationalism is a commitment to thought, reflection, deductive rigor, an argumentative chain in which successive links are joined by the dictates of reason.

The empiricist traditionally has been content to discover what *is;* the rationalist, what must *must* be. The empiricist's evidence has always been the *data* of experience; the rationalist's, the necessary proofs following from his axioms and propositions. Integral to the rationalist tradition has been mathematics and particularly geometry. Euclid's theorems have served more than one leading rationalist as the model for epistemology. Logic, a kind of linguistic geometry, has been the method, standing in its own defense.

The rationalist's skeptical attitude toward the senses is based on the conviction that there are eternal truths, immutable and deducible. His nativistic bias derives readily from this position for, as Plato argued, a truth that cannot be *seen* must be present in the mind independently of experience. Thus, the rationalist does not reject the purely local and ephemeral facts of perception. Instead, he requires that they be incorporated within a logical system of the world, the truth of which is beyond sense but ever available to reason.

Psychology, in its prescientific period, was largely a debate between rationalists and empiricists. The great intellectual achievement, from Copernicus to Newton, was the marriage of these two perspectives and the fruit of this marriage was that hypothetico-deductive epistemology we know as science. We will return to this in Chapter 10. Our current examination of rationalism is intended to introduce the other partner. Science could not have been produced by radical empiricism and was not produced in those tens of centuries during which rationalism was the accepted system of inquiry. Broadly conceived, science seeks the laws of nature. These laws are rationalist inventions, as is the belief that such laws exist. Nature itself, however, is for the scientist a perceptual affair. The laws of science must describe nature as it is *experienced*, not the way it "ought" to be. To the extent that Aristotle had preconceived notions about how nature "ought" to be and to the extent that succeeding generations of rationalists were guided by his preconceptions, then, to these extents, the modern era begins with the rejection of the authority of Aristotle. Bacon, the empiricist, led the British movement away from Aristotle and his Scholastic following. On the Continent, the leading spokesman for the new era was René Descartes—no empiricist.

René Descartes (1596–1650)

Descartes stands in the same relation to the Continental tradition of rationalism as Bacon does in relation to British empiricism. Like Bacon, whom he mentions only rarely in his works and whose *Novum* was probably unknown to Descartes as he began his own *Discourse*, the French philosopher saw unbridled skepticism as his most powerful adversary. In this sense, and notwithstanding the considerable differences between the Baconian and the Cartesian solutions, both philosophers are to be understood in terms of a common intellectual source: Renaissance skepticism and its mystical alternatives.

We have already touched upon the skeptical strains of English scholarship in Bacon's time and we need not add much to the comments of the previous chapter in order to describe the nearly contemporary climate in

France early in the seventeenth century. Copernicus' *De Revolutionibus Oribus* (1543) made the case for the motion of the earth against Scholastic arguments to the contrary. Recall that Aristotle was quite willing to entertain the possibility and that, in finally coming out against it, he accepted the geocentric alternative only weakly. Still, in the politically charged climate of the late Renaissance, distinctions between Aristotle and his Scholastic disciples were crudely blurred such that any successful attack on the latter was taken as a telling refutation of the Philosopher as well.

In 1609 Johannes Kepler published the first two of his laws of planetary motion which required that planetary orbits be elliptical and, further, that the sun be the immobile center of the revolutions. In the same year Galileo had observed the moons of Jupiter with the aid of a telescope fashioned by his own hands. Astrology, theology, and much of the Hermetic *corpus* had an abiding commitment to a "sacred numerology" according to which "7" enjoyed a privileged place; for example, the seven days for creation, the seven days of the week, the seven sisters of the Pleiades, and the seven heavenly bodies. Galileo's observations demanded a recount. These developments, attending and following the Reformation, hardened the Church's stand against heresy. In Europe the consequences were greater and bloodier than in England. Bruno had been burned as a heretic in Descartes' lifetime (1600), and Galileo would be called before the Inquisitors in 1633, the year Descartes' *De Mundo*, which subscribed to the Copernican theory, could have been published had the author not held it back. Not long before Descartes' birth, wars between the Protestant Huguenots and French Catholics had ravaged the country. Indeed, *St. Bartholomew's Massacre* (1572) had ushered in a year of butchery grim even by the macabre standards of religious persecution. Ramus, the sedulous anti-Aristotelian at the University of Paris, was one of the first casualties of the *Massacre*, and this tells us that, at least in France, the line separating philosophical and Roman Catholic orthodoxy was vanishingly thin.

Here, then, was the climate of Descartes' early development: growing achievements in science, the residue of Hermetic mysticism, the sullen skepticism and cheery materialism of the followers of Montaigne, the harsh, retaliatory measures of traditional authority, the numbing conformity of unthinking "Aristotelians"—whom Aristotle himself would have despised. Descartes' rearing in this climate was traditional and upperclass, with his first instruction received at the hands of the Jesuits and emphasizing mathematics. From them he learned to respect learning itself, to devote himself to the ultimate purposes of Christianity, and to see in science, as it was known in his time, but another version of God's eternal wisdom and power. But from his own native genius, he learned to doubt, as well, and the great literary accomplishments of his life must be viewed as the triumphant reply to his own doubts. Even his lasting contributions to science and mathematics, his researches in optics and, especially, the optics of refraction, his application of algebra to geometry and consequent founding of analytic geometry, even these are supplementary to and intended as proofs of his larger, philosophical system, his *rationalism*.

Descartes' psychological theses are to be found in the *Discourse on Method*,[1] the Second and the Sixth of his *Meditations*,[2] and *The Passions of the Mind*.[3] His own summary of his broad and complex system was published in 1644 as the *Principles of Philosophy*.[4] His controversial and most influential *psychobiological* work, the *Treatise on Man and the Formation of the Fetus*, was published posthumously in 1664.[5] We will draw on several of these works in presenting the first rationalistic psychology of the modern era.

Descartes' "method," which is summarized in Part II of his *Discourse*,[6] is really only a four-part maxim about the way the unprejudiced mind should go about its business: first, to accept nothing as true except that whose truth presents itself to the mind with such clarity and vividness as to remove the merest element of doubt; second, to divide a problem into as many discriminable elements as possible; third, to work from the solution of the smallest problem gradually up to the solution of the grandest; finally, to guarantee that the solution thus arrived at is sufficiently general as to allow no exception. Having achieved success in uniting geometry and algebra through this method, Descartes was persuaded that it might profitably be extended to all sciences. To aid him in this grander enterprise, he adopts several "moral" maxims: he will obey the laws of his country and adhere firmly to the Faith; he will adopt his provisional skepticism as if it were a proven certitude until the weight of reason requires that it be rejected; he will adopt a kind of stoic resignation toward those matters beyond the control of any individual while recognizing that his thoughts at least were within the perimeter of his powers.[7]

Applying the method to epistemology, Descartes recognizes the limitations of the senses and adopts the skeptic's position that all is illusion and self-deception. Is there, then, *anything* that might justify our belief in it? Is it not just as plausible to assume that the entire fabric of apparent life is a fiction, an invention by nature assuring us of eternal ignorance?

"Whilst I thus wished to think that all was false, it was absolutely necessary that I, who thus thought, should be somewhat; and as I observed that this truth, I THINK, HENCE I AM, was so certain and of such evidence, that no ground of doubt, however extravagant, could be alleged by the Skeptics capable of shaking it, I concluded that I might, without scruple, accept it as the first principle of the Philosophy of which I was in search."[8]

The skeptic whose doubts extend as far as his very existence finally is caught in a contradiction: that which doubts must be; that which thinks must be. *Je pense donc je suis.* Even if the body is an illusion, even if all our actions and experiences are unreal, the ideas of the mind must exist, or doubt itself is impossible. It is reason, therefore, that gives indubitability to existence, not matter. The perfected existence of *triangle* is rationally provided even if there is no triangle to be found and even if a perfect one can never be formed materially. That the human mind can possess such perfected notions in an imperfect material world entails an immaterial author of perfection and this, of course, is God.

It is in the two concluding parts (V and VI) of the *Discourse* that Descartes reviews the many findings he has made in the biological and physical sciences using his method. He discusses the circulation of the blood and refers to the brilliant research "of a physician of England"[9] (William Harvey) for those who require experimental confirmation of that which reason can demonstrate. He also makes reference to unpublished treatises of his own which, because of their controversial elements, he has decided not to have published during his life. These include his essays in support of the Copernican system and, perhaps, his *Treatise on Man.* He also advises future workers to begin with reason and the immediate facts at hand before plunging forth into elaborate experiments, since the latter do not become necessary until knowledge is already well advanced and, in this recommendation, Descartes conveys the essential flavor of the hypothetico-deductive method.[10]

While disputes between the Greek Atomists and Idealists reflected an implicit disagreement over the status of mental as opposed to purely material realities, Descartes was the first to put the Mind-Body problem in a form requiring the attention of scientists and philosophers alike. It may even be proper to say that the differences between modern materialism and ancient atomism—and these differences are very great—are the result of Descartes' analysis of the Mind-Body problem and the solution he offered to it. Psychological materialism which, in the nineteenth century became *physiological psychology*, is founded on the explicit rejection of both his analysis and his solution. Both, however, have proved to be quite durable.

It is useful to begin with Descartes' solution: mind and matter are of a qualitatively different sort, are independent of each other and, on no account, is mind conceivably reducible to matter. Thus, Descartes is a *dualist*. He arrives at dualism, however, through the very skepticism to which his method commits him. He reviews his *cogito ergo sum* in the second *Meditation* and goes on to ask what sort of thing he is. He quickly dismisses Aristotle's definition of man as a rational animal because it fails to tell us what is "rational" and what is "animal." He then reviews the various attributes he *believes* he has: body, hands, feet, hunger and thirst, and so forth, and a number of things he does; for example, walking, hearing, sleeping. All these, however, can be illusory. That is, the only *necessary* attribute, made necessary by the *cogito*, is thinking. Thus he must be a *thinking thing:*

> "I suppose there exists an extremely powerful and . . . malignant being . . . directed toward deceiving me. Can I affirm that I possess any one of all those attributes of which I have lately spoken as belonging to the nature of body? . . . The first mentioned were the powers of nutrition and walking; but if it be true that I have no body it is true likewise that I am capable neither of walking nor of being nourished. Perception is another attribute of the soul; but perception too is impossible without the body. . . . Thinking is another attribute of the soul; and here I discover what properly belongs to myself. This alone is inseparable from me. I am, therefore, precisely speaking, only a thinking thing, that is, mind . . . or reason."[11]

Matter is extended and is, therefore, in a place. Mind is unextended. That the soul's intellection comes to affect the body indicates that it must be in some sort of intimate contact with the body. This conclusion, introduced in the sixth *Meditation*, is the entire topic of the *Passions of the Mind*. Before turning to it, we should note an especially subtle point raised in the sixth *Meditation* and representing that aspect of Cartesian philosophy that declares the existence of innate ideas. He accepts the empirical (Aristotelian) assertion that we possess a passive faculty of perception by which the external world impresses the senses. He does not doubt but that our knowledge of sensible things is created this way.

> "But this would be useless to me, if there did not also exist in me, or in some other thing, another active faculty capable of forming and producing those ideas."[12]

The truths of speculative geometry are, we may concede, truths *about* actual figures but not truths that can impress the passive faculty of perception. Only reason can analyze the figures of geometry in such a way as to discern the general truths. He is even more explicitly Platonic in the *Principles of Philosophy* when he explains the failure of some to know these general truths in terms of their being taken in by the sensations of the body.[13]

Descartes' major psychological problem and the one that has vexed dualists ever since is that of accounting for the manner in which an immaterial, unextended agent (the soul) can influence an extended, material substance (the body). How can an idea move a muscle if the idea has no mass? The seeming impossibility of this has led some to adopt either a materialistic monism, insisting that all finally reduces to matter, or a mentalistic monism, insisting that all finally reduces to mind, or a neutral monism, taking no side in the issue except to insist that, ultimately, all must reduce to one or the other or some third, presently unconceived alternative. Descartes did not resolve the dilemma in *The Passions of the Mind* but he subscribed to a position that veritably founded the dualist tradition. His analysis is as follows.

He reserves to the body all that can be imagined as pertaining to body: sensitivity, motion, extension, growth, decay. To the mind, however, he imputes that which is inconceivable in bodies: *thought*. He divides thought into that which impels voluntary action and that which is responsible for feeling.[14] Most of our perceptions are the result of the action of external objects on the sensory nerves, and many of our feelings such as heat, cold, pain, and hunger are also referable to similar neural mechanisms.[15] Our emotional feelings, however, which can occur in the absence of any external stimulus, and our reflections on these cannot exist in mere bodies and cannot, therefore, be attributed merely to our own bodies. These are in the province of the soul which, while not itself a body, is united as a principle to every part of the body.[16] When the body dies, the soul withdraws, but while the body lives, the will of the soul is influenced on the body and most especially through its ability to regulate the flow of animal spirits from the brain to all the nerves associated with experience, action, and feeling. Descartes' best guess is that the site of this control is the pineal gland which, unlike the other structures of the brain, is not duplicated on each side and is located propitiously in the center of the brain.[17] Men differ in part because their brains differ,[18] but in all cases the passions result from the flow of the animal spirits contained in the cavities of the brain.[19] The soul's ability to direct the spirits is made possible merely by its *willing* to do so and, through God, this will is free.[20] He offers an illustration:

> "If we see some animal approach us, the light reflected from its body depicts two images of it, one in each of our eyes. The two images, by way of the optic nerves, form two others in the interior surface of the brain. . . . The images then radiate toward the small gland which the

spirits encircle. . . . The two brain images form but one image on the gland which, acting immediately on the soul, causes it to see the shape of the animal. . . . The impressions which . . . a terrifying object makes on the gland causes fear in certain men, and yet in other men can excite courage and confidence . . . all brains are not constituted in the same manner."[21]

In this passage we have Descartes' introduction of the concept of the *reflex* which would engage the mind of eighteenth-century scientists throughout Europe. His own reluctance to include the soul in this purely materialist account of sensation and behavior would not be preserved by many of his outstanding successors in a more liberal period. Still, it is Descartes who first attempted to found biology on the same mathematical foundation that Kepler had given to astronomy. It was Descartes who insisted on placing the behavior of all animals and much of the behavior of man in the context of natural science. Moreover, it was Descartes who advised that we turn away from the search for Aristotle's final causes,[22] that we exercise reason instead of blind faith, that we place our trust in that which about us is beyond doubt: our own thoughts.

His direct contributions to psychology were impressive. That portion of his dualism that was materialistic is the cornerstone of modern neuro-psychology. His influential writings on the reflex-connections between sensation and action began a line of inquiry that culminated in the research and theory of Ivan Pavlov. His *Method*, a version of which was shared by Galileo, saved science from that vain ritual of fact-gathering that Bacon's *Novum* seemed to demand. In presenting thought and certain kinds of feeling as the distinguishing features of human beings, he prepared the way for an experimental psychology of consciousness that would be inaugurated by Wundt in the nineteenth century.

Indirectly, Descartes' influence is felt in psychology through the effect his writings had on Locke and, largely through Locke, on Berkeley and Hume. It was Descartes' position on innate ideas that marks the point of departure between the (British) empirical and the (Continental) rationalist schools. But even Locke, in his discussion of intuition, imagination, the axiomatic nature of moral precepts, and the reality of ideas, even Locke the empiricist in his battle with the skeptics, borrows more from Descartes than he rejects. Descartes' place in the ranks of speculative science and psychology is at the front and durably so. He was not an antiempiricist; he was just not only an empiricist. He was not an anti-materialist; he was merely not only a materialist. This is why it has been far easier to challenge one or another of his assertions than it has been to escape his presence even now, three centuries since his death. We will return to his physiological psychology in the next chapter.

Benedict de Spinoza (1632–1677)

Spain's wars with England and the defeat of the Spanish Armada in 1588 not only loosened the hold of the Roman Church throughout Europe but also made it difficult for Spain to continue to impose orthodoxy at home. Many of the Jews who had been forced by the Spanish Inquisition to adopt Catholicism now either began to rebel openly or to find their way out of Spain and into States eager to accept non-Catholic citizens. Holland was especially tolerant and it was to there that the Spinoza family migrated toward the end of the sixteenth century. Spinoza was thus reared as a Jew in the Christian city of Amsterdam at a time when the "new philosophy" (i.e., Descartes') was all the rage in intellectual quarters. What he borrowed from this new philosophy was sufficiently unorthodox to result in his excommunication from the Jewish community. What he assimilated from his training at home and in the Synagogue was enough to exclude him from the circle of important Christians. And, in finally granting to intuition a status even higher than that accorded to reason, he was unable to maintain a position among the intellectuals of the *Enlightenment*. He was something of a Maimonides among scholastics, a "naturalist" among mystics, a situationist among absolutists, an absolutist among skeptics. Spinoza lived a very difficult life.

Perhaps the best approach to Spinoza's psychology is through one of Blaise Pascal's *Pensées*:

> "I cannot forgive Descartes. In all his philosophy he would have been quite willing to dispense with God. But he could not help granting Him a flick of the forefinger to start the world in motion; beyond this, he has no further need of God."[23]

Descartes' system of philosophy took for granted the separate and independent categories of God, matter, and mind. While it was not suggested that the last two could exist without the first, it was implicit in Descartes' rational psychology that, once God's forefinger flicked, the balance of nature and natural events could be studied rationally. We have already described his impatience with the search for final causes and his resulting concern with efficient and material causes. These attitudes translate into one kind of Cartesianism, the kind that grants divine authorship in accounting for the world but restricts scientific and philosophical inquiry to methods and events with, we might say, theology held constant.

Unlike Pascal, Spinoza was not influential in his own time although Leibniz, despite his politically motivated protestations to the contrary, seems to have been impressed by a number of arguments appearing in

Spinoza's *Ethics*. We do not pause here to review Spinoza's psychology, therefore, because of its importance to seventeenth-century thought or even because of any direct impact it had on later scientific psychologists. It had little. Instead, we review it because it exposes the sensed tension between reason and passion, between free will and determinism, which has been so much a part of modern psychological thought. It also reflects an awareness that science will either incorporate God completely into its deliberations or must exclude him just as completely. Spinoza is important, then, as one who saw most clearly how new the new philosophy was.

Like Descartes, Leibniz, and Pascal, Spinoza was versed and active in science. He worked as a lens maker and had the fullest grasp of the principles of optics which were, of course, geometric. Like Descartes and Leibniz, he was convinced of *certain* truths in a world of apparent change. Unlike Descartes, he could find no reason in logic or experience to assume that mind, matter, and God were to be relegated to distinct categories. It followed that if God is the author of all, His presence must be in all since *"things which have nothing in common cannot be one the cause of the other."*[24] Thus, if God is the cause of all things, it makes no sense at all to talk about human freedom. Our very knowledge of good and evil is sufficient to prove that we were not born free for, if we were, this constraining knowledge would not exist.[25] Our "freedom" is of a different sort. Since God is a "thinking thing," our thoughts will either share in His or be imperfect. If imperfect, our actions will be compelled by passion rather than emotion. The distinction between the two is important. For Spinoza, a passion is a feeling toward that about which we have no clear idea, whereas an emotion is a feeling shaped by a distinct idea. So-called "blind rage" is an instance of passion, while love for our fellows is an emotion. But what does it mean to have a clear idea? The clear idea is none other than a rational awareness of the fact that what is *necessarily* is. *"The mind,"* says Spinoza, *"has greater power over the emotions and is less subject thereto, in so far as it understands all things as necessary."*[26] Thus, where Descartes' conception of body and soul (mind) required each to have some vague kind of interaction upon the other, Spinoza radically divides the psychological and the spiritual: learning, perception, memory, and emotion require a body and end with the end of the body.[27] There is an afterlife only in the sense that God, as a thinking thing, retains the idea of the essence of the given individual eternally.[28] Since this essence is *mind*, mind is eternal.[29]

So far, we are reading what, with no slight intended, may be called garden-variety Augustinianism, bordering on Berkeley's idealism. But when Spinoza turns to matters of direct, psychological consequence, his philosophy becomes radical. Rationalism becomes emotionalism in anticipation of Benthamism. What we call "good" and "evil," he says, is *"nothing else but the emotions of pleasure and pain."*[30] But pleasure and pain are, respectively, the mind's awareness of its strengths and its weaknesses.[31] It is the mind, not the body, that seeks to endure eternally and it is the mind that knows that this is possible only through its own activity, which is to say through its clear ideas. Passion, as a passive state, perception as a fleeting affair, and mere imagination as the repository of purely contingent events will not permit the mind to endure. The mind possessed by these is aware of its weakness, fearful of its transitoriness, and thus pained. Reason, however, and, more important, *intuition*, bring to the mind the clear idea of necessity whose possession is pleasure for the mind. The emotion so created is the most intense, since *"an emotion toward that which we conceive as necessary is, when other conditions are equal, more intense than an emotion towards that which is possible, or contingent, or non-necessary."*[32]

Spinoza's deterministic psychology is unreserved: *"The mind is determined to wish this or that by a cause, which has also been determined by another cause . . . and so on to infinity."*[33] The ultimate or first cause is God. To the extent that the mind is fixed on "adequate ideas," which are the ideas of necessity, it is active; otherwise, it is passive. When active, it endeavors to persist in its being, which is to say it strives for pleasure. Since this pleasure *is* the possession of adequate ideas and since the body is no such *necessary* entity and, finally, since things that have nothing in common cannot be the cause of one another, *"body cannot determine mind to think."*[34] However, it is in our nature to include the idea of our bodily existence in all of our ideas and, therefore, the mind is threatened by that which threatens the survival of the body. Intuitively we labor to preserve the activities of our bodies because of this sensed connection between bodily and mental survival. Since we believe that a threat to the body entails a threat to the activity of the mind, we strive to repress those ideas of the body's injury or demise.[35]

The categories of Spinoza's psychology are passion, emotion, reason, and intuition. All are determined and, to that extent, the will is not to be described as free. What makes us unique, when we are unique, is the presence of clear ideas or adequate ideas about the necessary causes of things, and these ideas lead back inevitably and inexorably to God. All else involves passive states of mind which, in the limiting case, would be eternal death. We are so constituted that our lives are devoted to perpetuating the existence of mental activity. The motive, at a superficial level, appears in the form of an egoistic quest for pleasure and aversion to pain. The unenlightened are moved in these respects by opinion rather than reason, and as a result of opinion and the laws of association they come to identify bodily death as the ultimate pain. Benignly, God has planted in man a higher sense, an intuitive awareness that *is* the active and impassable mind. But even when this mind grasps the essential nature of what is good, the emotions cannot be restrained by the truth of the knowledge, only by another and contrary emotion produced by such knowledge.[36] In this, Spinoza stands in agreement with the British sentimentalists, with Hume, and with Kant: reason alone will not produce moral conduct except to the extent that the rational exercise leads to or is correlated with the proper feeling. Our will is not the *free* cause of our actions but the *necessary* cause.[37] Given the will, action follows necessarily. Given the adequate idea, the will follows necessarily. Given God, the adequate idea, which is the idea that refers to Him, follows necessarily.

In his uncompleted essay, *On the Improvement of the Understanding*, Spinoza embellished his theory and offered a number of remarkably modern notions of learning and memory; for example, that memory is enhanced or degraded by the contextual features of the material to be memorized, that memory suffers when materials similar to those memorized are subsequently committed to memory, that memory is a brain process, that every idea must have a correlate in the real world.[38] It is here also that he makes the traditional rationalist distinction between mere sensations or perceptions and the active assimilation of experience by the intellect. Of the various modes of knowing, only opinion is inferior to mere experience. The highest mode is that by which the *essence* of a thing is known. We know the essence of a circle, for example, when we know that it is the line resulting when a stylus is fixed at one end. To know the essence of a thing is to know what *must* follow from the fact of its existence. To know an eternal truth is to know that, if it is true at all, its contrary *could not* be true. Thus, the Pythagorean theorem is an eternal truth in that there could not be a right-angle triangle the square of whose hypothenuse does not equal the sum of the squared sides. To know such truths and, indeed, to know even simple facts, is simultaneously to affirm and to negate. That is, every determination entails a negation. Once we have determined that Smith is an old man, we have, in this act of determination, denied that he is young, that he is female, that he is aluminum. To affirm is to limit. To define is to confine. The infinite, then, is either undefined (which Spinoza rejects) or is *self-defined*. To know an eternal truth is, therefore, to know the sense in which it is self-defining, self-causing. It is to know God.

We remarked that Spinoza did not speak to his age even if, in a peculiar way, he spoke for it. His recourse to associationistic principles of learning and memory was hardly original, and his egoistic theory of motivation, while infuriating, had been in the wind since Hobbes and since Montaigne before him. In striving for a unique form of *monism*, he offered a *pantheism* that is cut from the cloth of Pythagoreanism. God, as a thinking thing, inspires certain substances in a way that makes them thinking things. Such a pantheistic idealism had to be judged either as heresy or lunacy, and Spinoza's contemporaries were willing to offer both judgments. Not until the nineteenth century would his philosophy be taken seriously by a major philosopher and, in taking it seriously, Hegel would reject a good part of it and force the rest to conform to the Hegelian vision. If only to this extent, however, Spinoza must be included in a treatment of the rationalist tradition and that part of it subscribing to idealism. Hegel's own impact was so diffuse that anyone taken seriously by him came to figure in the heady debates between empiricists and rationalists in the nineteenth century. Therefore, when we examine Hegel's philosophy and record its influence on Husserl and the entire phenomenological movement, psychology's indirect debt to Spinoza will be clearer.

To Spinoza, also, we owe the insistence that philosophy and theology are different enterprises, that the former must be concerned with truth, no matter where it leads, while the latter must require reverence and a degree of compliance. Further, philosophy is a search for truths pertaining to *nature*, and God is known in nature through the laws of nature which, consequently, are necessary. Man, as a thinking thing driven to create pleasure in the mind, is constrained by nature to strive toward his essence and to be pained by its denial. The goal of psychological man, then, is self-actualization. In this, Spinoza serves as a model for a number of twentieth-century humanistic psychologists of whom the most notable is Abraham Maslow.

Spinoza was not a disciple of Descartes', and on a number of fundamental points he openly disagreed with him, for example, free will, dualism, the division of nature into compartments. He shared with Descartes a realization that Greek wisdom was not enough, that Christianity had to be more than Aristotelianism, that a rational creature, stripped of all superstition and unbiased in the face of nature, could know the truth. His rationalism was a naturalism without becoming a materialism. Spinoza did not doubt matter as did Berkeley, nor did he doubt mind as radical materialists did. He began with God and from that starting point he examined *thinking matter*. Implicitly, he defended materialism as applied to matter, since *only* materialism applies to that which is *only* matter—just as *only* idealism applies to a thinking thing when it is the thinking we wish to understand.

Gottfried Wilhelm von Leibniz (1646–1716)

Leibniz was only four years old when Descartes died. He lived in an intellectual climate dominated by Descartes and the "Cartesians," a climate rapidly becoming as uniform in its reverence for Descartes as the world of letters once had been toward Aristotle. Leibniz's father was Professor of Philosophy at Leipzig and, while both the father and mother were dead before he completed his university studies, Leibniz may be said to have been blessed with a stimulating early environment. He was exposed not only to the Greek and Latin classics but to the modern works of Bacon, Descartes, and Galileo.

Visits to London (brief) and Paris (four years) further exposed him to the most important ideas of the time. He met with Malebranche, the great Cartesian; he studied Pascal's treatises in mathematics and invented a calculating machine even better than Pascal's; through Huygens, his interest in optics was aroused; Hobbes' works enhanced his abiding concern with law, as the recently ended Thirty Years' War reminded him of the need for peace and tolerance. By way of introduction, we should also point out his discovery of differential calculus independently of Newton, and the bitter claims of priority that sounded across the English Channel for the better part of a decade.

Louis XIV had become king of France three years before Leibniz was born and died a year earlier than Leibniz. Thus, in addition to his own genius, his good head start, and the stimulating intellectual giants of his time, Leibniz passed his years in what were, perhaps, the most self-consciously cultivated and achievement-oriented six decades in the history of the modern world. We might underscore this by listing some of the authors whose works were published during the reign of Louis XIV or who were still alive at the time: Hobbes, Locke, Descartes, Newton, Pascal, Spinoza, Gassendi, Leibniz, Malebranche, Huygens Molière. Galileo had been dead only one year before Louis XIV acquired the throne. When the king died Voltaire was already nineteen and Hume's *Treatise* was only twenty years off. Of those on this list who were Leibniz's contemporaries or who just preceded him, Leibniz agreed with none. His role in the history of ideas is secure, his influence diffuse and recurrent. His specific contributions to psychology, while not as great, are revealing and are presented most clearly in his disagreements with Locke and with Descartes. In rejecting Locke's empirical psychology, he reasserted the cognitive, highly mentalistic and genetic character of human knowledge and feeling. And, in opposing Descartes' dualism, he rephrased the mind-body problem in a way that would render it more interesting to the modern era. We will begin with his antiempirical arguments.

Locke's *Essay on the Understanding*, published in 1690, came to Leibniz's attention in 1688 and he began to draft a rebuttal straightaway, although this rebuttal, *New Essays on the Understanding*,[39] did not appear until 1765. The reason is that Locke died the year Leibniz completed the work (1704), and Leibniz was not willing to argue with the dead. Accordingly, the *New Essays* became just one of many Leibnizian contributions not made generally available until after the author's death. Like the rest, the *New Essays* continues to influence the reflective mind.

Locke had begun Book II of his *Essay* with the central claim of all empiricists before and since:

> "Suppose the mind to be, as we say, white paper, void of all characters, without any ideas; how comes it to be furnished? Whence comes it by that vast store, which the busy and boundless fancy of man has painted on it with an almost endless variety? Whence has it all the materials of reason and knowledge? To this I answer, in one word, from experience."[40]

Leibniz's reply, a reply offered by all rationalists before and since, is that only some *thing* can be said to *have* an experience and such a thing must be a mind somehow prepared to have experiences of a given sort. He identifies Locke's position (incorrectly) with Aristotle's and attributes to the latter a statement also attributed to Aristotle by Duns Scotus, although we search in vain for this statement in any of Aristotle's works: "*Nothing is in the intellect which was not first in the senses.*" Leibniz replies, "*Nothing except the intellect itself.*"[41] He follows the introduction to his *New Essays* with a dialogue between Philalethes (friend of sleep) and Theophilus (friend of God),[42] who are, respectively, the empiricist and the rationalist. After giving Philalethes the lines from Locke's *Essay* (quoted above), he has Theophilus offer the Leibnizian position on the problem of knowledge and the solution:

> "This *tabula rasa*, of which so much is said, is in my opinion only a fiction which nature does not admit. . . . Uniform things and those which contain no variety are never anything but abstractions, like time, space, and other entities of pure mathematics. There is no body whatever whose parts are at rest, and there is no substance whatever that has nothing by which to distinguish it from every other . . . those who speak so frequently of this *tabula rasa*, after having taken away the ideas, cannot say what remain. . . . Experience is necessary, I admit, in order that the soul be determined to such or such thoughts, and in order that it take notice of the ideas which are in us; but by what means can experience and the senses give ideas? Has the soul windows, does it resemble tablets, is it like wax?"[43]

Experience is necessary, on Leibniz's account, in order that the soul *take notice* of the ideas that are *in us*. What experience provides is a context for our thoughts, a direction for our ideas, a means of aiming our attention, disposing ourselves to action of a certain kind. It is impossible that an experience will produce an idea for the simple reason that an experience involves the physical confrontation of matter and the organs of sense, and an idea has nothing to do with these mechanical transactions. Perception, however, which is not a mere experience and which assumes a rational, attentive mind, can lead to ideas; but perception is not mechanical and cannot be reduced to the mechanical.[44] It is precisely on this basis that Descartes' dualism is to be rejected. Leibniz is clearest on this in his *Monadology*, written two years before he died and presented as a condensation of his metaphysics:

> "Moreover, it must be confessed that *perception* and that which depends upon it are *inexplicable on mechanical grounds*. . . . And supposing there were a machine, so constructed as to think, feel, and have perception; it might be conceived as increased in size, while keeping the same proportions, so that one might go into it as into a mill. That being so, we should, on examining its interior, find only parts which work one upon another, and never anything by which to explain a perception."[45]

Perception is a uniquely *psychological* event. It is that of which we are *conscious*. It is qualitative in a way that no purely quantitative (i.e., material) phenomenon can imitate. As we walk through the great mill of the mind, observing the spinning wheels and crashing hammers, we find nothing by which the mill could have a perception; not that the mill does *not* have such perceptions or is not aware of itself but that nothing in its moving parts could convey as much. We will return to Leibniz's mill in the last chapter.

The mind-body interactionism advanced by Descartes thus seemed at once confused and meaningless to Leibniz. Mind, on the Leibnizian account, is a simple substance, a *monad*, not reducible to anything, not deriving its character from any source beyond itself, not extended. As with all simple substances, it is to be understood as a quality and not a quantity. In Leibniz's terms, its essence is *intensive* rather than extensive. The example of a point in mathematics is illustrative. A point is not a very small line or a very small fraction of a line. It is the idealized limit as extension approaches zero. Similarly, as quantity is stripped of its extensive features, there is a limit beyond which further reduction is not possible. This limit constitutes a quality of being, not a magnitude or extension. The limit of the body is also a simple substance; that is, a *monad*. Body as it is perceived is a composite whose extension derives from the assembly of simple substances. No two simple substances are alike. Each monad not only has a distinguishing quality but is the very "unit" of quality. Being dimensionless, it is not subject to modification from without. It has no window through which an external agency might enter and change it. In this respect, it makes no sense to speculate on the kind of interaction taking place between "mind" and "body" since each, properly conceived, is unique, independent, and ultimately unextended. Body and mind coexist and the relation between them is not causal but *harmonic*. If a note is loudly sounded in the presence of two resonators, we do not ask which of the resonators has established the sympathetic vibrations in the other. The two resonate in parallel as a result of being so constituted that, in the presence of the proper stimulus, each satisfies the conditions of its nature. So too with mind and body. Each, according to a *preestablished harmony*, exists compatibly with the other. The action of one is not caused by the other, as the mechanistic account requires; nor is the action of each reconciled to that of the other by some external "timekeeper" who occasionally steps in to make sure that all the clocks are on time—the view advanced by the philosophic *occasionalists*.

The universe is a collection of simple substances for which harmonic associations were established prior to their coming into being. Harmony is God's modality. If the monad is to change, it can do so only through an inner principle.[46] It is this internal principle, involving as it does a system of relations within the monad, that constitutes perception. This, however, differs from apperception or consciousness by which we not only perceive but know that we perceive. To the extent that every monad has an internal organization, it is perceptive. The monad whose internal principle allows both memory and perception may be called a soul.[47] It is clear from this that animals have souls. However, they do not have *rational* souls (i.e., minds) because, while they are able to perceive and even to retain the trace of former, consecutive perceptions, they are un-aware of *necessary* truths. Human beings too, insofar as their perceptions are simply united by memory, "*act like the lower animals, resembling the empirical physicians whose methods are those of mere practice without theory. Indeed, in three-fourths of our actions we are nothing but em-pirics.*"[48] It is only in our knowledge of a rule, of a necessary relationship, that we display the uniquely human quality of human life.

More than any previous philosopher, Leibniz was concerned with and wrote about an issue that would be at the core of modern psychology's problems: the *unconscious*. This is not to say that, in any complete sense, he anticipated Freud. Leibniz's use of the concept had little to do with the causes of motivation and nothing to do with psychopathology. He employs the concept, instead, in support of his position on the indestructi-bility of monads, on the distinction between perception and consciousness, and on the difference between the bare monad and the rational mind

Even in a dreamless sleep, the monad does not perish (for it can't) and, therefore, since it cannot exist without being affected in some way, perception, by definition, takes place. However, we are not aware of this perception because it is not accompanied by memory.[49] A number of unconscious (*insensible*) perceptions, stored in the mind, can add up in such a way as to break into consciousness. Indeed, there is a gradual scale separating the sleep of death from heightened awareness. We pass from one to the other in the smallest steps, one of which constitutes a *threshold*. Moreover, we retain all that has happened to us even though we might not be actively aware of much of it. The representations of the past remain in the mind creating "*an influence greater than people think. . . . The present is big with the future and laden with the past.*"[50]

As with Spinoza, it is not easy to carve out a niche for Leibniz in the history of psychology. As the dual enemy of empiricism and materialism, he cannot be located in that philosophical tradition that led to the installation of psychology as an experimental science. His writings make it clear that he believed one could deduce most of what our contemporary experimentalists are searching for, and what is not easily deduced is either trivial or readily available through common experience. We have already acknowledged his attention to the unconscious and his formal introduction of the concept of *subliminal* perception. That division of experimental psychology devoted to sensory thresholds has a debt to Leibniz here, but the debt is several times removed. Even his challenges to Locke were hardly more than what one can find in the *Protagoras* or the *Meno*, and Leibniz is the first to recognize that he has taken the Platonist position in the dispute.[51] His discussions of the unity of consciousness, of the role of memory in consciousness, and of the differences between consciousness on the one hand and both perception and memory on the other would surface again and again in both the theoretical and the experimental psychology of the late nineteenth century. Perhaps his most substantial direct effect on psychology—and, we might suspect, an unforeseen one—resulted from his telling criticism of Cartesian dualism. In illustrating its defects and contradictions, he did much to overturn Descartes' authority and to liberate thinking to the point of allowing an uncomplicated physiological psychology. Leibniz would not have applauded the reduction of mentalism to materialism—he specifically opposed it—but others would dismiss his caveats and focus instead on his successful refutations of Cartesianism.

Unlike Spinoza, Leibniz did little to restore idealism to a position of philosophic significance and, therefore, we are not even able to relate him to that tradition leading up to Hegelianism. But his emphasis upon activity and unity, the two abiding features of all and every simple substance (including *mind*), would reappear in the psychologies of

Brentano, James, the Gestalt school, and even early behaviorism. His monism would, as we have noted, inspire confidence in those who might examine brain in order to unearth mind. His attribution of soul to animals and his insistence on the continuous evolution of various levels of organization and relation would surely not retard the development of an experimental psychology of animal intelligence. His unswerving commitment to the presence of innate characteristics, his logical arguments in the behalf of the necessity of *a priori* dispositions of the mind, would constitute a starting point for one of the most influential philosophers of all time, Immanuel Kant.

Immanuel Kant (1724–1804)

The position in which philosophy, metaphysics, and science were left by Hume's *Treatise* was anything but reassuring. Rationalism was rendered deluded in its singular goal, the search for eternal truths. Epistemology was reduced to psychology, and an associationistic psychology, at that. What the *Treatise* denied was that necessity could be proved to exist in nature. It denied that logic confirms such necessity and that the senses ever perceive it. It affirmed the existence of *subjective* necessity as a habit of the mind. We judge B to be the effect of A when the two occur together in space and time, when A always precedes B and these perceived unions are constant. Since experience alone is responsible for our belief in causation and since, in principle, it is *"possible for all objects to become causes or effects to each other,"* we are forced to acknowledge that *"anything may produce anything."*[52]

Hume did not deny that events were caused. Rather, he insisted that our commitment to this view cannot rest upon any basis other than experience and, as such, the view can never sustain the added baggage of *necessity*. It may happen that A is always followed by B, that no one has ever recorded an exception, that the interval between the two is perfectly constant. Still, all we *know* is A and B. *"We are never sensible of any connection betwixt (them)."*[53] We have knowledge of the events and knowledge of the temporal connection between them. We have no knowledge of necessity. That is, experience will confirm only A . . . B; not A . . . necessarily . . . B. On the same basis, moral distinctions are not derived from reason but from experience (and the feelings resulting from it).[54] And, again on the same basis, there can be no logically compelling argument against those who assert that the rational faculties themselves are but the outcome of natural, material forces. For even though thought and matter seem to be different, experience suggests that *"they are constantly united; which being all the circumstances, that enter into the idea of cause and effect, when apply'd to the operations of matter, we may certainly conclude, that motion may be, and actually is, the cause of thought and perception.*"[55]

In a word, the *Treatise* removed moral precepts from the domain of the rationally deducible, removed necessity from the domain of cause and effect, and removed reason itself from the domain in which we locate the determinants of knowledge, feeling, and conduct. A rational philosophy designed to unearth necessary moral prescriptions must fail. A rational philosophy seeking to penetrate what *must* occur in nature must fail as well. The *Treatise* stripped natural science of "must" and moral science of "ought." Empirical psychology was all that survived.

If we are to appreciate the lasting contribution Kant made to psychology, we begin by examining a question that has tired philosophers for nearly two centuries: What was Kant's answer to Hume?[56] The answer is to be found in his towering achievement, *Critique of Pure Reason,*[57] in his summary and clarification of this work, *Prolegomena to Any Future Metaphysics,*[58] and in his *Groundwork of the Metaphysic of Morals.*[59] An implicit theory of psychology runs through every chapter of each of these and often the theory is explicit as well. In the following discussion, there is little chance that all of Kantian philosophy will be penetrated, but the psychology in this philosophy will be evident.

All the major philosophers of the eighteenth century were quick to note the distinction, a distinction made by Plato and by a good number of scholastics, between propositions that seek to add to our knowledge about a thing and those that only assert a semantic identity. When we say, for example, that a *body is an extended substance*, the predicate-term (extended substance) is, in fact, included in our concept of the subject (body) such that the proposition does not add anything to what the subject already contains. Locke, Berkeley, and Hume all devoted sections of their epistemological works to the relationship between words and things and to the fact that, very often, the only differences between things turn out to be a difference in the words we employ in describing them. The convention appearing in the eighteenth century was to label all such propositions in which the predicate is contained in the concept of the subject, *analytical.* Kant retained this term and employed another to represent those propositions whose predicates are not logically implied by their subjects, that is, those propositions that expand our factual knowledge. These he called *synthetic.*[60] When we say that *all bodies are heavy* we are making an assertion about bodies different from what is contained in the mere concept we have of a body. The same is true of statements of the sort, *The French are a people of average height; Protein is conducive to health;* and so forth. Being French does not logically entail being average in height; being protein does not logically entail good health on the part of the recipient. In noting the general position of philosophers on the matter of analytic and synthetic propositions, Kant formalized the distinction further by observing that the principle common to all analytic propositions is *the law of contradiction*.[61] We cannot say, "The man at the table is not the man at the table." In an affirmative analytic judgment, a contrary predicate will produce a contradiction. This is not the case with synthetic judgments, for no such contradiction results from, "The French are a people of above-average height." This distinction is what led all empirical philosophers, and Hume particularly, to subscribe to the view that analytical propositions are (a) logically necessary, meaning that if they are true, they *must* be true, (b) certain as opposed to probable, (c) *a priori* as opposed to given in experience. Since $a = a$ is necessarily true by the law of contradiction and since, on the empiricist account, nothing in experience is necessarily true, $a = a$ is said to be known *a priori*. By the same token, the same philosophers insisted that synthetic propositions (a) can only be contingently and never necessarily true, (b) can only be assigned a certain probability of truth and never certainty, and (c) can only be advanced or assessed *a posteriori*. No rational, *a priori* deduction will establish beyond doubt that "The French people are of average height." In the light of these terms and distinctions, we can summarize Hume's position on morals, on epistemology, and on ethics by noting that he placed all these issues in the domain of synthetical judgments. Whatever we say about knowledge or values can be true only contingently, only some of the time, and only *a posteriori*. Kant's task, then, is to prove that some synthetic judgments are true *a priori*, and Kant's answer to Hume is, in essence, that there are *a priori* synthetic truths. Put another way, Kant's mission is to return necessity to morals and to epistemology and thereby rescue metaphysics from mere opinion.

Before turning to Kant's analysis, we must recognize that he stands in agreement with Hume on many counts. On one of the cardinal empiricist points, he too insists that all judgments of experience are synthetical,[62] that objects are given to us by means of the senses and that thought itself, directly or indirectly, finally relates back to sensibility.[63] Kant, therefore, is not to be understood as one seeking to overturn empiricism but as one striving to determine its limits. It is in this regard that one might judge the empiricist movement as *culminating* in the *Critique of Pure Reason* rather than being swept aside by it.

Kant's critical analysis of Hume's claims predictably focuses on the Humean account of the concept of causation. The account is empirical, and Kant must determine the principles according to which experience yields the concept of cause. Alas, experience cannot yield the concept; experience *assumes* the concept. The proofs of this are contained in his famous *Analogies of Experience.* "*The principle of the analogies is: Experience is possible only through the representation of a necessary connection of perceptions.*"[64] He presents three such analogies. The first is addressed to the concept of object-permanence. For an object or event to have any real existence, it must exist in *time.* Time, however, is not *given* to experience by the object or event. Only through our "inner intuition," in which permanence is cognized *a priori,* can appearances take place *in time.*[65] There can be no relation in time unless that relation is grounded in permanence. We discover the weight of smoke, for example, by weighing the wood, burning the wood, and weighing the ashes. Matter is not conserved in the senses; that is, the wood is now gone and no smoke can any longer be seen. Still, because of the *a priori* category of the understanding, the category of thought we call *permanence,* we know that the weight of the smoke is just this difference between the weight of the wood and the weight of the ashes.[66] We can only call an appearance a "substance" because we are able to presuppose the existence of substance throughout time. This brings Kant to the Second Analogy: *Everything that happens, that is, begins to be, presupposes something upon which it follows according to a rule.*[67] It is this cryptic principle that is the kernel of Kant's answer to Hume, and it must be studied carefully.

Hume had argued that our concept of cause was to be explained in terms of contiguity (spatial), constant conjunction, and succession. Briefly, A and B take place in the same location, always together, and in an invariant order with A always preceding B. When these conditions are met, we say that "A is the cause of B." It is in the Second Analogy that Kant raises the question of the source of succession itself. We do not "see" time. We do not "perceive" intervals. We might *imagine* that a boat floating downstream *could* float upstream, but we do not apprehend the event in any but a fixed order: the boat now is here, *next* is there, *next* is there, and so forth. But what is the empirical basis of "next"? Quite simply, unless the understanding already possessed (*a priori*) the category, *time,* there could be no succession or constant conjunction. Conjunctions occur *in time,* but time is not *given* by the object. For us to be affected by the constant conjunction of events A and B, we must be able to experience A and B as events. What makes them events is that they stand out against a background of enduring states of affairs. Against an enduring background of silence, for example, chimes are heard. Chimes can only be events if they are separable from the enduring background. And the chimes can only be caused by the striking of the hammer if our perceptions are unfailingly ordered *in time.* Without the *a priori* category of understanding—in contrast to sensation alone—we would have no basis for judging the hammer to cause the chimes any better than the basis for judging the chimes to cause the hammer. Yet, we *never* make the latter mistake. The ordering is not contingent, it cannot be *a posteriori*, and it is hardly merely probable.

Prof. L. W. Beck has summarized the argument of the Second Analogy with an elegance and simplicity seldom displayed in the many treatments of "Kant's answer to Hume":

> "K. 'Everything that happens, that is, begins to be, presupposes something upon which it follows by rule.' (Kant's Second Analogy).
>
> P. Events can be distinguished from objective enduring states of affairs, even though our apprehension of each is serial (the accomplishment of Hume's task (a).
>
> H. Among events, we find empirically some pairs of similar ones which tend to be repeated, and we then make the inductive judgment: events like the first members of the pairs are causes of events like the second (the accomplishment of Hume's task (b).
>
> P implies K . . . H implies P, since if events cannot be distinguished, pairs of events cannot be found, and thus P is a necessary condition of H. Hence: H implies P and P implies K, therefore H implies K. That is Kant's answer to Hume."[68]

What Beck has shown is that Hume's account of causation requires, and logically requires in the sense of *necessarily* requiring, Kant's Second Analogy. Thus, Hume is not wrong, but he can be right only if the Second Analogy is granted and the Second Analogy confers on the understanding an *a priori* synthetic judgment.

The argument given in H (Hume's "succession" and "constant conjunction") can reduce the concept of causation to an inference from experience only by granting the percipient a basis for "first" and "next," and this basis is not, itself, grounded in experience but is assumed for experience to occur in the first place; that is, the Second Analogy. This is what Beck means by "H implies K." The Humean argument implies the Kantian argument.

Kant's analysis goes well beyond this question of the basis of causal inferences. The *Critique of Pure Reason* seeks to discover the foundations and principles of all knowledge, accepting at the outset that one foundation is, of course, the empirical. But, as the Humean account is insufficient to explain causation, Kant argues that the empirical account is insufficient to explain *anything* about human understanding except the conditions by which it becomes furnished with objects. What the understanding achieves is judgment. Judgment is based on *logical* functions. The latter are imposed upon the evidence of sense and are necessary prior to experience if experience is to have any meaning at all. These logical functions, which we possess intuitively, are the *pure concepts of the understanding* of which the following *Table of Categories* is exhaustive:[69]

I. Concept of Quantity	II. Concept of Quality
Unity	Reality
Plurality	Negation
Totality	Limitation
III. Concept of Relation:	IV. Concept of Modality:
Inherence & Subsistence	Possibility-Impossibility
Cause and Effect	Existence-Nonexistence
Community	Necessity-Contingency

These are the pure concepts of synthesis[70] which the understanding possesses *a priori* and without which experience would be impossible. These *categories* contain the possibility of all experience in general.[71] We confront the world of sensibility with an understanding already possessed of such pure concepts as: either a thing exists, or it does not exist, or it exists in a limited way; either A is possible or it is impossible; either it happens to follow B or it must. We can frame universal propositions (All men are mortal) only if we possess intuitively the category of *totality*, and there is nothing in experience that can give this. That we arrive at the proposition by induction or generalization from a large number of cases is not to deny the category but merely to cite the conditions under which it is invoked. Obviously, to think of "all men" requires that we know of "men," and we can only come to know them through experience. But we can never know "all" of anything through experience. The very process of inference assumes the concept of *quantity*, and the very process of generalization within a class assumes the concept of *relation*.

The foregoing is Kant's epistemological argument against empiricism and, more important for Kant, it is the introduction to the moral argument against the empiricist's *pleasure principle*. There is no doubt but that if one subscribes to an empiricist epistemology, he will have little patience with a moral science based on the "truths" of reason. Locke was willing to grant an axiomatic status to moral propositions, likening them to the propositions of geometry, but this truce with the rationalists was neither convincing nor long-lived. The Hume who cannot find necessity in the conjunction of natural events is hardly going to search for it in that conjunction of behavioral events we call moral conduct. Kant agrees that if epistemology were reducible to experience morality would be likewise. But having proved to his own satisfaction that epistemology cannot be reduced to the sensual domain and having established that this very world of sense is *contained* in the world of understanding, it must follow that the laws of experience are authored by those of reason.[72] Kant's metaphysics of morals thus is the crowning achievement of that rationalist morality to which Descartes, Spinoza, and Leibniz had devoted themselves. Moral precepts have the authority of reason not because they refer to something that does not occur in the real world but because our understanding of the real world is based on a rule without which understanding would be impossible. As the pure concepts of the understanding (i.e., the *categories*) form the logical foundations upon which all our knowledge of the natural world is based, so too there is an *a priori* rational principle which makes moral judgments inescapable, universal in form, and absolutely necessary to any explanation of the moral dimensions of life. It is not enough to argue that we judge "good" and "evil" on the basis of feeling unless one is able to explain why and how the given feeling attaches to the given act. The very attachment assumes a rule, and this rule is what Kant dubbed the Categorical Imperative: act in such a way that the maxim of your action could serve as a universal law of nature.[73]

In its varied forms, the Categorical Imperative includes a reverence for law, the insistence that man is an end and never a means to some other end. The very concept of law *assumes* a rational animal who *intends* good effects.[74] The mere (empirical) listing of the observed consequences of his actions will never disclose this intention, but the act itself could not have taken place had there not been the intention prior to it. To acknowledge this intention, the *fact* of intention, is to acknowledge simultaneously a *freedom of the will*. Its freedom is constrained in this sense: the very freedom requires that the will *make law*.[75] Reverence of the law is not acquired. The Categorical Imperative could not be acquired. The factual world of events could not be judged on a moral basis if there were not, *a priori*, pure moral concepts in the understanding. We are not "usually" or "contingently" ends in ourselves and not means toward some other end we have. We are necessarily ends in ourselves. We do not await the consequences of our actions in order to determine whether or not we *should* do unto others as we would have them do unto us. We understand that this is so or else we could never know guilt as long as we "got away" with what we did. There may be those who preach a situation-ethics, but they still draw the line at anarchy. And even those who might argue in favor of anarchy, if they are to argue at all, will begin with a principle and if that principle is ever to enjoy logical force, it will finally reduce to the Categorical Imperative—at which point, of course, it will contradict the claims of the anarchist.

Kant's influence in psychology has been far greater than is generally recognized. It is a commonplace in historical summaries to acknowledge his fame as a philosopher, to point to his nativistic emphasis and suggest its effect on some later psychologists. There are even those who have decided that Kant was really authoring a kind of anthropology and was anticipating subsequent instinct-theorists. He was decidedly not. It is, in fact, to his credit that he has influenced as many psychologists who have misunderstood him as he has those who have followed his reasoning. In subsequent chapters, we will have occasion to discuss theories of cognitive development, Gestalt psychology, genetic psychology, moral development. We will review the ideas of Wundt, Freud, Köhler, and their disciples. In these subsequent chapters, it will become clear that, with the exceptions of behavioral and physiological psychology, there is no area of contemporary psychological concern that does not rely on the major elements of Kant's philosophy. Such topics as the innate, logical structure of thought and language, the *a priori* principles of perceptual organization, the stages of cognitive and moral understanding, the concept of culture-neutral or culture-free methods of psychological assessment— these and many issues of lesser importance are hardly imaginable had the empiricistic persuasion prevailed to the exclusion of rationalism. Kant did not set out to save rationalism. Indeed, he had more admiration for Hume than for many of his detractors. He set out to establish the limits of knowledge and the conditions by which it takes place. In the process, he saved consciousness.

The Rationalist Legacy

It does not detract from Descartes, Leibniz, Spinoza, and Kant to recall the extent to which seventeenth- and eighteenth-century rationalism echoed many of the major lessons of Plato, St. Augustine, and St. Thomas. The *Theaetetus* was a reply to Protagoras' empiricist contentions, and its argument is not too different from that offered by Leibniz in the *New Essays*. The agreement on substantial psychological issues between Spinoza and St. Augustine is too marked to require further comment. Kant was unique, but in several respects his uniqueness is to be traced to an antirationalist way of treating the problems. He was, for example, uncompromising in his opposition to Berkeley's brand of idealism, he argued that mathematical judgments were synthetic, he denied the existence of innate ideas, at least as these had been described in the rationalist tradition. His *transcendental aesthetic* located psychological principles above the plane of experience. The new experimental psychology of the nineteenth century would thus have difficulty finding a place for Kant and ultimately succeeded in doing this only by ignoring the rest of his philosophical system. Those who came to play the major part in the creation of psychology as an independent discipline strived to impart to the enterprise the same rigor and objectivity enjoyed by physics or mathematics. Where the model was physics, the rationalist tradition was an encumbrance, and where the model was mathematics the enterprise failed, or seemed to fail. Even those who adopted a Kantian perspective on the mind still found it necessary to employ the methods of the empiricist. The exception, of course, was Wundt, whose works will be reviewed later. Wundt sought the best of two worlds in attempting to build an empirical science on the foundation of (rational) introspection. We may judge his success by observing that there are not many Wundtians around any longer.

Had there been no other movement in philosophy and philosophical psychology, the twentieth-century psychologist would still be actively engaged in assessing Leibniz's answer to Locke, and Kant's answer to Hume. Argument and analysis would continue to be the methods of choice. However, even as the seventeenth- and eighteenth-century philosophers carried on their disputes, there was a mammoth enterprise unfolding and at a rate that beggared the imagination of philosopher and layman alike: the enterprise of *science*, or what Bacon and, later, Newton, called "experimental philosophy." In its stubbornly and innocently pragmatic way, it drew upon both empiricism and rationalism for support and inspiration but wed itself to neither. In time, the empiricists would claim it, although no empirical philosopher of consequence ever made a contribution to it. Its real engines were skepticism and materialism: Descartes' method of doubt seeking assurance in technology. Its materialist foundations are the subject of the next chapter and, of its skeptical component, enough has been said in this and in the previous chapter.

What was the rationalist bequest? As we review the problems and methods of contemporary psychology, we find little direct evidence of a conscious commitment to the rationalist's vision. Research is addressed to behavioral engineering, brain physiology, social attitudes and influence, human learning and memory, individual differences. Only the light writing addressed to a popular audience continues to concern itself with the "mind," seldom with the soul, and never with the monads. But when we move from research to theory, the picture changes. Many would agree that by 1970 the three most influential theoretical attempts or, shall we say, the three theoretical issues commanding the greatest attention involve (a) the stage-specific cognitive capacities of man during development from infancy, (b) the *a priori* faculties, which must be granted if human language is to be understood, and (c) the species-specific processes, which must be assumed if we are to account for the range of emotional, intuitive, and "moral" dispositions observed throughout the animal kingdom. While (c) received its direct impetus from Darwin, (a) and (b) stem unadorned from the rationalist tradition. It is only in the methods employed to investigate these issues that these contemporary concerns can be described as "empirical." They are *rationalist* issues at the core and they are the visible signs of the rationalist legacy.

References

1. René Descartes, *Discourse on Method*. In *The Method, Meditations, and Philosophy of Descartes*, translated by John Veitch, Tudor, New York.
2. Descartes, *Meditations*. In John Veitch, translator, op. cit.
3. Descartes, *Les Passions de l'Ame*, translated as *The Passions of the Soul* by E. Haldane and G. R. T. Moss. In *The Philosophical Works of Descartes*, Dover Publications, New York, 1955.
4. Descartes, *Principles of Philosophy*. In John Veitch, op. cit.
5. Descartes, *Treatise on Man*. In *Descartes—Selections*, edited by R. M. Eaton, Scribner, New York, 1927.
6. Descartes, *Discourse on Method*, op. cit., Part II.
7. Ibid., Part III.
8. Ibid., Part IV (p. 171).
9. Ibid., Part V (p. 184).
10. Ibid., Part VI (p. 193).
11. Descartes, *Meditations*, op. cit., II.
12. Ibid., VI.
13. Descartes, *Principles of Philosophy*, op. cit., Part I, Sections XII and XLVII.
14. Descartes, *Les Passions*, op. cit., Article 17.
15. Ibid., Articles 23, 24.
16. Ibid., Article 30.
17. Ibid., Articles 31, 32.
18. Ibid., Article 39.
19. Ibid., Article 37.
20. Ibid., Article 41.
21. Ibid., Articles 35, 39.
22. Descartes, *Principles of Philosophy*, op. cit., Part I, Section XXVIII.
23. Blaise Pascal, *Pensées: Thoughts on Religion and Other Subjects*, translated by William Finlayson Trotter, Washington Square Press, New York, 1965. (*Pensée* #77).
24. Benedict de Spinoza, *Ethics*, Pt. I, Prop. III. In *The Chief Works of Benedict de Spinoza*, translated by R. H. M. Elwes, Dover Publications, New York, 1955.
25. Spinoza. *Ethics*, op. cit., Pt. IV, Prop. LXVIII.
26. Ibid., Pt. V, Prop. VI.
27. Ibid., Prop. XXI.
28. Ibid., Prop. XXII.
29. Ibid., Prop. XLI.
30. Ibid., Pt. IV, Prop. VIII.
31. Ibid., Pt. III, Props. LIII, LV.
32. Ibid., Pt. VI, Prop. XI.
33. Ibid., Pt. II, Prop. XLVIII.
34. Ibid., Pt. III, Prop. II.
35. Ibid., Prop. VIII.
36. Ibid., Pt. IV, Prop. XIV.
37. Ibid., Pt. I, Prop. XXXII.
38. Benedict de Spinoza. *On the Improvement of the Understanding*. In R. H. M. Elwes, op. cit., especially pp. 15–31.

39. Gottfried Wilhelm von Leibniz. *New Essays*. In *Leibniz—The Monadology and Other Philosophical Writings*, translated by Robert Latta, Oxford University Press, New York, 1898.

40. John Locke, *Essay on the Human Understanding*, II, I, 2.

41. Leibniz, *New Essays*, op. cit., Book II.

42. Ibid.

43. Ibid.

44. Ibid.

45. Leibniz, *Monadology*, op. cit., #17, in Robert Latta.

46. Ibid., #11.

47. Ibid., #19.

48. Ibid., #28.

49. Ibid., #20, 21.

50. Leibniz, *New Essays, Introduction*, op. cit., pp. 322–323.

51. Ibid., p. 358.

52. David Hume, *A Treatise of Human Nature*, I, III, XV, edited by L. A. Selby-Bigge, Clarendon, Oxford, 1973.

53. Ibid., I, IV, V.

54. Ibid., III, I, I.

55. Ibid., I, IV, IV.

56. A remarkably brief and extraordinarily lucid summary of the Hume-Kant dispute has been provided by Prof. L. W. Beck in his, *Once More Unto the Breach: Kant's Answer to Hume, Again. Ratio*, Vol. 9, No. *1*, pp. 33–37. I thank Prof. Tom Beauchamp for bringing this article to my attention.

57. Kant, *Critique of Pure Reason*, translated by Norman Kemp Smith, St. Martin's Press, New York, 1965.

58. Kant, *Prolegomena to Any Future Metaphysics*, Indianapolis, Bobbs-Merrill edition, Introduction by L. W. Beck, 1950.

59. Kant, *Groundwork of the Metaphysic of Morals*, translated by H. J. Paton, Harper & Row, Harper Torchbooks, New York, 1964.

60. Kant, *Critique of Pure Reason*, op. cit., Introduction to Section 4.

61. Kant, *Prolegomena*, op. cit., Section 2.

62. Ibid.

63. Kant, *Critique of Pure Reason*, op. cit., A19.

64. Ibid., A176; B218.

65. Ibid., A182; B225.

66. Ibid., A185.

67. Ibid., A189.

68. L. W. Beck, *Once More Unto the Breach: Kant's Answer to Hume, Again*, op. cit.

69. Kant, *Critique of Pure Reason*, op. cit., B106.

70. Ibid.

71. Ibid., B167.

72. Kant, *Fundamental Principles of the Metaphysic of Morals*, translated by Thomas K. Abbott, Library of Liberal Arts, Liberal Arts Press, New York, 1949, pp. 70–71.

73. Ibid., p. 19.

74. Kant, *Groundwork of the Metaphysic of Morals*, op. cit., pp. 68–69.

75. Ibid., p. 98.

9

□□□□□□□□□□□□□□□□□□□□□□□□□□□□□□

Materialism

THE ENLIGHTENED MACHINE

The Vexing Alternative

In the preceding two chapters, we have reviewed the philosophical psychologies of the English and Continental empiricists and rationalists. We restricted our sampling of thought to the seventeenth and eighteenth centuries, the period when these two perspectives became sufficiently definite and uncompromising to serve as alternatives. In Chapter 3, the very considerable similarities between Platonist and Aristotelian systems were noted. In subsequent chapters, equivalent similarities were observed to obtain between philosophers identified with one or another school. In the Renaissance, and really not until the Renaissance, did we find signs of a clear break, the break between Spiritualism and Naturalism. But in the Renaissance, there were only signs, not dramatic ruptures. The great separation took place in the irresolvable differences between the positions represented in Hume's *Treatise* and in Kant's *Critique*. Henceforth, empiricism and rationalism would hold out possibilities for radical departures and divisions. Unlike the differences that divided Greek Atomists and Platonists, the modern antagonisms would surface as completed systems of thought, rich in implications and recommendations for social organization, law, morality, economics, religion. By comparison, the disputes between orthodox Christians and Ockhamists in the thirteenth century and between the Florentine Aristotelians and Platonists in the fifteenth would be nearly negligible.

As great as the break between rationalism and empiricism was, however, there remained ground common enough for a Kant even to attempt to answer a Hume. The philosophical disputes of the seventeenth and

276

eighteenth centuries, to the extent that they were betwen rationalists and empiricists, were disputes about the same problems and disputes that began from identical starting points. Hume and Kant were both moved to explain the source of human knowledge, the nature of morality, the character of society. Broadly, they were both engaged in the "science of *mental* life." Neither of them subscribed to the vexing third alternative: law, morality, reason, and feeling were, in the last analysis, mere expressions of matter in motion. In Chapter 7, we noted that Locke declined to address the question of man's material nature. Berkeley openly rejected materialism and defiantly so. Hume, while tilting with the possibility, finally turned the matter over to the "anatomists."[1] Kant, too, recognized that a biological interpretation of his philosophy might be advanced, that his *categories* might be reduced to a neurological process, and he spurned the suggestion, noting that such a skeptical materialism would remove the element of *necessity* from the pure concepts of the understanding.[2] In short, neither Kant nor Hume nor any of the earlier figures in the two philosophical movements conceived of psychology as no more than or as something no different from physics. For all of them, it was and must remain a science of mental life and not merely science. However, in the same two centuries, a third movement was born and flourished: a movement toward physics and away from logic, a movement that grew to ignore the very terms of the rationalist-empiricist controversy, a movement that had more to do with the founding of psychology as a scientific discipline than did all the rationalists and empiricists combined. This was *Materialism*, whose seventeenth- and eighteenth-century character is the subject of the present chapter.

The Metaphor of the Machine

Every age of philosophical energy is animated by notions and events of a nonphilosophical complexion. Philosophers seek to understand and explain the truths of the world and they must take these truths as they find them. They are to be found, of course, outside philosophy: in the cosmos, in the world of matter, in the human mind, in the affairs of state.

Scholarship is a human enterprise and, no matter how narrow and technical it may become, no matter how ponderous or cultist its problems and methods may be, it never escapes the habits of the human mind. One of the most persistent of these habits is that which forces the mind to metaphor and simile when it seeks to comprehend an elusive phenomenon. And, among the many elusive phenomena, none is endowed with greater craft and agility than the mind itself. Thus, in their tireless attempt to comprehend the mind, philosophy and, later, psychology have constantly taken recourse to explanations of the sort, "it is like . . . " or "it is as if . . ." or "it is no more than . . . " Over the centuries, different metaphors and similes have gained and lost popularity. The pre-Socratics, with their special interest in hydraulics and hydrostatics and with their simplified four-element physics, were given to believe that psychological phenomena were to be understood in terms of the unique combination of earth, air, fire, and water. Platonism, which never extricated itself from its roots in the mystery religion of the Pythagoreans, focused on spiritual metaphors in an attempt to define that ineffable quality of mental life. Aristotle, surveying the unchallengeable truths of the syllogism, and noting the contingent nature of all nonlogical realities, advanced a dualistic psychology according to which some functions of the mind were "like" biological processes and others "like" eternal, logical verities. Accordingly, while the nutritive, sensitive, and locomotor faculties perish with the flesh, being of the flesh, the intellect survives "like" the truth of logic.

From the pre-Socratic period until the Age of Faith, the metaphor was Nature. All the divisions and antagonisms of competing philosophies are to be understood as different views of the nature of Nature and as differences of opinion regarding the ultimate nature of Nature: Is it material only or spiritual as well? Is it eternal or was there a beginning? Is it particulate and statistical or an essential and invariant form? Is it as perception records it or is experience mere illusion? The failure of philosophy to answer these questions and the failure of the very civilizations that raised such questions to survive were two of the chief causes of the rapid success of the Christian alternative. In the Western world, from the Patristic period until the seventeenth century, revelation was the ultimate authority. God was the reality and Nature was the metaphor. This is not to say that everyone shared this outlook. Indeed, Chapters 5 and 6 were devoted principally to those who sensed that the question was hardly settled. But the world is peopled by more than philosophers, many more. For all but the handful of seekers after truth, the Truth was revealed in the gospels and in the life of Christ. Those eager to understand either at another level could study the great Thomistic synthesis—the synthesis of Aristotle and Christian belief, or reason and faith.

We have pointed out, perhaps too often, that the Renaissance did not alter the essential temper of the Western mind as it grappled with the abiding questions. The major debates from 1350 to 1600 were between those who found God in "natural magic" and those who found Him in "spirit." Ficino's *Academy* sought to restore Platonism to Christianity, not to challenge scripture. Pomponazzi's Aristotelian school had no quibble with the Bible, nor were the heresies of Gianfrancesco Pico of a religious sort. And this speaks only to the affairs of academics. In the world at large, there were more important matters: war, pestilence, Reformation, starvation. Nature, as the metaphor, and God, as the reality, remained in their historic places.

The most significant scientific event of the Renaissance, Copernicus' theory of the earth's revolution, was judged by its author as no more than a footnote to God's great design. The same may be said of Kepler's assessment of his theory and Newton's of his. It is equally true of Galileo and of Locke and Descartes, of Leibniz and Spinoza. The greatest scholars in philosophy and science, even through much of the nineteenth century, labored under the light of Christian faith. Hume, of course, is the tantalizing exception, an exception even among seventeenth-century skeptics, of which there were many. The skeptics trained their doubts on man, not on God; on Aristotle, not on the Nazarene. In fact, several of the noteworthy skeptics were priests.

In the light of the foregoing, it is instructive to pause and to note a remarkable feature of contemporary psychology: no major spokesman for the discipline, no figure identified as one responsible for its methods and concerns, none who has provided a theory of consequence to contemporary endeavors, has argued that the religious message is necessary for an understanding of human psychology. Stated another way, we recognize that in the fifteen centuries beginning in A.D. 200, there is no record of a serious psychological work devoid of religious allusion and that, since 1930, there has not been a major psychological work expressing a need for spiritual terms in an attempt to comprehend the psychological dimensions of man. This striking shift in perspective cannot be explained as a product of rationalist-empiricist tensions—witness Locke and Leibniz. Nor is it to be understood in terms of some factual discovery in the natural sciences. Science, after all, has not discovered that there is no God. Moreover, it cannot even be understood as a gradual shift in perspective for, in the historical measure of time, it has been sudden. We are not able to establish all the causes, of course, but it is fair to say that we can discern its origin. The origin of this dramatic transformation in perspective, this historically unprecedented abandonment of an older and pervasive vision, is the seduction of a different metaphor: in this case, the metaphor of the *machine*.

The cautious reader will be ready to complain that the mechanistic outlook is hardly recent; that Zeno and Epicurus were beholden to it; that Ptolemy rendered it cosmic in scope; that the Scholastics were as wed to the machinelike precision of celestial motion as were the pre-Socratics. While this is a correct reading of history, it fails to distinguish between the mere metaphor and the seductive metaphor; between the metaphor that confirms and conforms to the balance of one's beliefs and the metaphor that creates a new belief; between the metaphor invented to represent reality and that which is so compelling as to be accepted as reality. We must ask, then, what there was in the mechanistic philosophy of seventeenth- and eighteenth-century thought that set the stage for the radical divorce now existing between psychology and its intellectual ancestry. What new feature was added or recognized? Who fashioned the wedge? We can only begin to answer this by discussing, all too briefly, a set of sociopolitical conditions and, coincident with those conditions, the extraordinary impact of Galileo on his contemporaries and immediate successors.

The political climates of England and France in the seventeenth and eighteenth centuries were touched upon in the preceding two chapters. The issues raised by the Reformation and the responses to these during the counter-Reformation remained hopelessly and perilously unsettled. Religious persecutions would continue in both countries until the nineteenth century, and religious toleration—always difficult to gauge—would become a political maxim only at the end of that century. Added to the death struggle of Protestant and Catholic, Protestant and Protestant, and Catholic and Catholic were the endless conflicts within the fraternity of European nations. The Roman Church, which had tied its fortunes to Aristotelianism, as understood by the Scholastics, found it necessary to take hardened stands on philosophical matters at a time when intellectual freedom was coming to rank as high as life itself in Paris. Descartes' *Method*, based on doubt and skepticism as points of departure, came close to heresy. The writings of Montaigne, filled with Erasmian charm and insolent wit, were proscribed, making them even more popular than would otherwise have been the case. The murder of Ramus, the famous anti-Aristotelian at the University of Paris, gave the liberal-leaning philosophers of the early seventeenth century still one more reason to resist the authority of Aristotelianism. But unlike all their predecessors, they had an irrefutable, scientific illustration of the failure of the Philosopher's *Metaphysics:* Galileo's laws of accelerated motion and Newton's general laws of motion.

Among the Thomistic proofs for the existence of God, the phenomenon of *motion* was central. Relying on the Aristotelian argument for a prime cause, the scholastic proof began with the contention that that which is in motion will seek a resting state unless impelled by a force external to itself; that is, eternal motion is impossible and, therefore, heavenly dynamics can be understood only in terms of a Prime Mover who constantly supplies the needed power. The planets move by the will of God, a proof providing a ready metaphor for human action as the result of human will. If the action of the planets required no recourse to the will of God, the actions of men might not either. More will be said on this later. What Newton demonstrated was that bodies set in motion would con-

tinue to move, linearly and eternally, unless acted upon by a force opposed
to their motion. Quite simply, once the bodies were set in motion, God's
will had no further work to do for the motion to continue forever. God
aside—for it was not God to whom Newton addressed his remarks—
Aristotle was wrong. He was also wrong, and Galileo proved it, in contending that the speed with which an object fell to the ground was proportional to its mass (weight). He was also wrong about the immobility
of the earth and about the motion of the sun. (Recall, however, that
Aristotle was far from dogmatic on this point.)

Had Galileo's contribution been limited to the unearthing of mere
factual errors in the corpus of Aristotelian science, his influence on his
own age and ours would have been negligible. The health of Christian belief never depended on the notions of a wise but pagan Greek about the
speed with which rocks and feathers fall to the earth. It depended even
less on the number of moons orbiting Saturn since, no matter how many
there are, they all came from the same shop. However, orthodox belief did
depend on the manner in which we go about *discovering* the truth, and
it was this that Galileo threatened.

In his *Discourse on the Two New Sciences*[3] Galileo virtually invented
the science of mechanics, passed it on in a form that has hardly been
changed, and tied each of its theorems and propositions to an *experimental* demonstration. Throughout this work, Aristotle falls on hard
times, even when credited with a truth. For example: Aristotle had some
idea of the principle of the lever—force bears to resistance a relationship
determined by the reciprocal of the distances separating the fulcrum from
the force and the resistance—derived and demonstrated by Archimedes.
Galileo acknowledged Aristotle's observation on the law of the lever,
but with a qualification, as usual:

> "Yes, I am willing to concede him priority in point of time; but as re-
> gards rigor of demonstration the first place must be given to Archi-
> medes."[4]

The most open attack on Aristotelianism appeared in Galileo's *Dialogue
on the Two Great Systems of the World*[5] (1632). The year following its
appearance found its author before the Inquisitors and called upon to renounce the heresy of Copernicanism. Copernicus was dead now for ninety
years, and Galileo was not the only philosopher-scientist to subscribe to
his theory. We may take it, then, that it was not merely the Copernicanism of the *Two Great Systems of the World* that troubled the Inquisitors but the ridicule heaped on the Aristotelian participating in the
dialogue.

Kepler (1571–1630) had advanced three laws of planetary motion, remarkable in their simplicity and predictive power, and these laws assumed the earth's elliptical movement around the sun. Galileo (1564–1642) accepted the Copernican-Keplerian theory and added to it a completed body of terrestrial Mechanics. William Harvey (1578–1657), who had studied with Galileo and the other great Paduans from 1598 to 1602, published his famous essay on the circulation of blood in 1628. It is to be noted that Harvey was Francis Bacon's physician—noted as a curio of history—but Harvey is to be seen as a disciple of Galileo's scientific method: one begins with a careful measurement of nature as it is found; one advances the simplest possible hypothesis sufficient to account for the measures obtained; one derives from the confirmed hypothesis those corollaries logically implied by the hypothesis; one proceeds to test the corollaries experimentally. The opinions of others, no matter how grand their genius may be, count for nothing. Truth is to be found after a test, not at the end of a dispute. The inscription adopted by the Royal Society, formed in 1662, is a testimony to Galileo's influence: *Nullius in verba.**

By far, the greatest contribution to science in the seventeenth century, if not in any century, was Isaac Newton's *Principia*. Newton (1642–1727) was the saint of seventeenth-century British intellectuals, a man whose influence spread far beyond the boundaries of science. He combined the theories of Kepler and Galileo in a triumphant synthesis, the universal law of gravitation. No longer was it necessary to require, as the Aristotelians did, that a different *physics* be applied to the heavens and the earth. Galileo had concluded the dialogue of the Second Day portentously:

"We do not encounter . . . difficulty, however, if we suppose the earth to move, a body so small, so inconsiderable in comparison with the whole universe that it could have no effect at all upon this."[6]

Newton, framing no hypotheses except those demanded by direct observation, placed this inconsiderable ball within the realm of many other balls and kept them all suspended by a law indifferent to human vanity, belief, or hope. In Book III of his *Principia*, he offers the *rules of reasoning* in philosophy:

"Rule I:
We are to admit no more causes of natural things than such as are both true and sufficient to explain their appearances.

Rule II:
Therefore to the same natural effects we must, as far as possible, assign the same causes . . .

* *On the words of no man.*

Rule IV:
In experimental philosophy we are to look upon propositions inferred
by general induction from phenomena as accurately or very nearly
true, notwithstanding any contrary hypotheses that may be imagined,
till such a time as other phenomena occur by which they may either be
made more accurate or liable to exceptions."[7]

Between 1609 and 1686—that is, in a span of a lifetime—Kepler had
published his laws of planetary motion (1609), Galileo had described sun
spots, the moon's rough surface, the "stars" of Jupiter (1609), and had invented *Mechanics* (1632), Harvey had published his *Excertatio* (1628),
Descartes, his *Discourse on Method* (1637), and Robert Hooke's *Micro-
graphia* (1665) laid the ground for microscopic anatomy. If we wonder
what the implications of this creative storm seemed to be to the enlightened bystander, we need only recall Voltaire's remark in *The
Ignorant Philosopher:*

". . . it would be very singular that all nature, all the planets, should
obey eternal laws, and that there should be a little animal, five feet high,
who, in contempt of these laws, could act as he pleased, solely according
to his caprice."[8]

The metaphor was becoming reality.

From Dualism to Monism

Descartes' enormous contribution to the scholarship of his day produced results he could not have anticipated. Three years before he died,
he received a pamphlet published anonymously in Belgium by a former
disciple, Regius. The pamphlet was in a form suitable for nailing on the
door of a church and it was written in a way that mimicked Descartes'
style. It was a polemic on the nature of the mind and it recommended a
radical materialism to those who might inquire into the nature of mind.
It offered twenty-one propositions and closed with one of Descartes' own
aphorisms, "No men more easily attain a great reputation for piety than
the superstitious and the hypocrites."[9] The propositions themselves were
uncompromising. The mind is no more than that which permits thought
to human beings; logic does not require any distinction between mind and
matter; all notions enter the mind through observation and tradition; no
idea can be said to be innate; perception is a process of the brain.[10]
Regius arrived at this view of the mind through his own inclinations
and probably from a hasty reading of *Les Passions de l'Âme*, which was

completed in 1646. It was not published until 1649 and Descartes regretted its publication. Regius either read the work in an early draft or decided, from conversations with Descartes about the work, that it supported the materialist-monist position. Several of the Articles in the book can be so construed. The origins of the animal spirits are traced to the brain such that the turbulence produced by stimulation of the senses becomes reflected in the actions of the muscles. In Article XVI, Descartes notes specifically that stimulation can produce orderly action without any intervention by the soul and in animals that lack souls.[11] Only thought and passion are in need of a soul for their existence. Perception, appetites, and even dreams and daydreams, are quite possible as a result of bodily actions.

Descartes quickly recorded his disagreement with Regius' manifesto, rejecting its propositions point by point. It was the twelfth Article that had challenged Descartes on the question of innate ideas, and Descartes' reply is instructive:

> "I never wrote or concluded that the mind required innate ideas which were in some sort different from its faculty of thinking; but when I observed the existence in me of certain thoughts which proceeded, not from extraneous objects nor from the determination of my will, but solely from the faculty of thinking which is within me, then . . . I termed (these) 'innate.' "[12]

Descartes goes on in his rebuttal to observe, yet another time, that there is nothing in an object that can be said to *contain* the idea we have of it. Thus, *all* ideas are innate if only in the sense that they have a quality not derivable from mere extension which, after all, is the very substance of object:

> ". . . no ideas of things, in the shape in which we envisage them by thought, are presented to us by the senses. So much so that in our ideas there is nothing which was not innate in the mind. . . . Nothing reaches our mind from external objects through the organs of sense beyond certain corporeal movements."[13]

Unlike his arguments in *Les Passions de l'Âme* which were often of a theological complexion, Descartes, in his rejoinder to Regius, presents the argument of the philosophical dualist: there is nothing in the physical stimulus resembling the mental image, nothing we can say in describing the stimulus that will permit us to deduce its psychological consequences. This argument, as we shall see in subsequent chapters, has lost none of its persuasiveness in contemporary philosophical discourse on the mind-body problem.

The pamphlet printed in Utrecht was a relatively minor irritation. In comparison, the challenges to Cartesianism presented by Pierre Gassendi (1592–1655) were titanic and were the very foundations of that anti-Cartesianism that flowered into eighteenth-century materialism. In his own time, Gassendi was ranked among the greatest philosophers of his age. His following was large and enthusiastic; his writings, influential; his command of science and mathematics, expert, or at least seemingly so. He established his libertine credentials early, authoring a text of *Paradoxes Against the Aristotelians* in 1624. More significantly, he became the center of a revival of interest in Epicurus and the other major Roman Stoics. The thrust of this revived Epicureanism was to install observational science in the place of (Cartesian) deductive, "axiomatic" science; to accept nature (including human nature) as matter; to oppose the authority of Aristotle at each instance of its assertion. While not a skeptic, Gassendi found it easier to adopt the skeptical posture when the only alternative was dogma devoid of empirical support. These orientations were marshaled for a critical attack on Cartesianism, one lasting six years and taking the form of published rebuttals answered, in print, by Descartes. We will not examine any part of the dispute other than that addressed to Descartes' dualism. It is worth noting, however, that Gassendi's critique was all-embracing and that, as Prof. Craig Brush has written, "Modern philosophy can add little or nothing significant to the objections made by Gassendi."[14]

It is in the Second and Sixth Meditations that Descartes presents his *psychophysical* dualism and it is in the rebuttals to these Meditations that Gassendi offers the monist alternative. Against the principal arguments for dualism, Gassendi registers the Epicurean complaints: (1) Why deny bodies the power to move themselves without the aid of a soul? Does not water flow and do not animals (judged to be without souls) walk?[15] (2) Since it is obvious that whatever *acts* is, why all the "beating around the bush" to establish that you (Descartes) are?[16] (3) What does it mean to say that you are "only a thinking thing"? Why exclude all other possibilities, such as you are a wind or a gas or a body? Even if it be granted that you only *know* you are a thinking thing, it does not necessarily follow that you are not other things as well.[17] (4) How can the mind reason without a brain, since even you (Descartes) have required that the brain organize and unite perceptions and actions?[18] (5) Even though the senses sometimes deceive, they often do not and we usually have the means of determining whether a given perception is valid or of questionable validity.[19] (6) If the mind is without extension, it can have no idea of extended things. The mind can be furnished by experience only if equipped, by its material nature, to respond to that which is physical. It may be said that you are composed of two bodies, one coarse and one subtle, and that only the former is immediately apparent. But it makes no sense to say that *you* or your mind is unextended.[20]

Even more than the specific objections to Descartes' dualism, Gassendi's writings reflect the impatient tone that every modernist displays toward a departing age. Gassendi was the most illustrious of the circle of visionaries that was brought and held together by Father Marsenne in Paris. They were all imbued with the spirit of Galileo, their Paduan saint, whose experimental and theoretical science constituted the final and invincible challenge to authority. Gassendi's works were known to and admired by Locke, whose empirical philosophy borrowed the spirit, if not the letter, of Gassendi's scholarship. Newton too acknowledged Gassendi's priority in advancing the law of inertia. While contemporary thought is not directly influenced by any of Gassendi's essays or discoveries, his position among his own contemporaries was one of considerable influence. Descartes' ambition to rest biology on a Keplerian foundation, to establish a mathematics of the life sciences while sparing the soul from materialism, was the ambition of the Gassendists but without the spiritual restrictions. Descartes' desire to combine physics and mathematics into an irrefutable body of knowledge was also an integral feature of the Gassendist program but with the rationalist element replaced by the experimentalism of Galileo. The Gassendists were the first *natural monists* of the modern era. When we refer to the origins of this perspective as "French Materialism," we are simultaneously acknowledging the role of Pierre Gassendi in the history of scientific psychology. He did less research than he inspired, but his inspiration was nearly without parallel.

Thomas Hobbes (1588–1679) and the Social Machine

The discussion of Hobbes could have been placed in either of the preceding two chapters as easily as in the present one. Texts devoted to the history of philosophy routinely list him as an early empiricist principally on the basis of such positions as that appearing in Part I of *Leviathan:* With the exception of *prudence*, which is *grounded* in experience,

> "there is no other act of man's mind, that I can remember, naturally planted in him, so, as to need no other thing, to the exercise of it, but to be born a man, and live with the use of his five Senses."[21]

But, two chapters later, Hobbes goes on to distinguish between sense and reason, noting that the latter is not "gotten by Experience only" and that Science, which is a knowledge of consequences, is something more than the mere facts of sense and memory.[22] Thus, while an epistemological empiricist, Hobbes is comfortable with methodological rationalism. In fact, one of the important sources of his scientific thinking was Galileo, whose hypothetico-deductive method provided possibilities utterly lacking in the methodological empiricism of Francis Bacon.

Leviathan appeared in 1651, when its author was already past sixty. Hobbes' earliest writings and training were in classics. His translations of Thucydides were authoritative. For five years (1621–1626) he served as a student-secretary to Francis Bacon and, later, for a time, as a tutor to Charles II. He was involved occasionally in the intellectual affairs of Fr. Marsenne's *libertines*, and it was through them that his visit to Florence and with Galileo was arranged (1634–1637). Although late appearing Hobbes' influence on his contemporaries was far from negligible notwithstanding the fact that the list of luminaries formed during his long life included Descartes, Locke, Newton, Gassendi, Milton, and Galileo.

Leviathan is a long and uneven work, consuming seven hundred pages of modern print and ranging topically from nutrition to demonology. Our present concerns warrant attention only to those parts of it which advance and defend the materialist perspective on man and society. The work, as a whole, is suffused with this perspective, but it is in Part One (*Of Man*) that our present interests are most repaid. Before turning to specific elements of Hobbes' philosophical psychology, we are advised to note the general view and aim of *Leviathan*.

The work appeared two years after the conclusion of the Civil War. One king had already been executed and the restored monarch, Charles II, faced a divided country, sapped of material and moral resources, and living in the growing shadow of a young and ambitious French regime. English letters were still laced with the gloomy predictions of the apocalypse and, like Bacon before and Locke just after, Hobbes must oppose despair:

> "The *Present* onely has a being in Nature; things *Past* have a being in the Memory onely, but things *to come* have no being at all."[23]

His goal is to establish the principles by which, in a word, civil strife might be averted. His method requires a determination of those aspects of human nature that conduce to war and peace and those instruments of governance that will work on and with this nature in such a way as to ensure national tranquillity. The metaphor of the machine is adopted (although it is to be doubted that Hobbes considered it a metaphor), and the laws of society are to be fathomed in the same way that Kepler and Galileo discovered laws in physics.

It was Hobbes' belief that a science of society could be established with the same rigor and sureness enjoyed by Mechanics. Since man possesses reason and thereby can come to know of cause-effect relations, there is no excuse for his continuing to live in the perilous and uncertain way endured by his ancestors. That he does so is simply to demonstrate that even a rational creature is given to absurdities. Hobbes considered the cardinal absurdities to include the following: (1) a lack of *method* such that we attempt to reason before we have agreed on the meaning of the terms we are reasoning about; (2) confusing the immaterial with the material such that we speak of "infusing Faith," not recognizing that "nothing can be *powred* or *breathed* into any thing but body; and that *extension* is *body*";[24] (3) a continuing belief in the reality of universals; (4) the use of metaphor instead of reality; (5) a devotion to scholastic terms such as *hypostatical, eternal-Now*, etc., which have no basis in experience at all. He will have none of these. "Words may be called metaphoricall; Bodies and Motions cannot."[25] Hobbes will speak of bodies and motions only. In other words, if man is to be understood scientifically, he is to be understood as matter in motion; if society is to be understood scientifically, it is to be understood as men in motion. Hobbes' plan is to establish first a kind of *biophysical behaviorism* and, from this, to deduce *sociology*.

The scientific analysis of man, that is, the biophysical behaviorism, begins in Chapter VI of *Leviathan*. The major variable—what might properly be called the seventeenth-century variable—is *motion*. Hobbes examines animal motion and notes that it takes two forms: *involuntary* ("vitall") and *intentional* ("animal"). The latter, which is the cause of all our grief and joy or very nearly so, is the motion "first fancied in our minds" before being executed by our limbs. While we cannot observe directly the source of this motion, it is none other than motion within the interior parts of the body, motion seeking to satisfy needs of the body. Thus, the motion is caused by appetites that can be subsumed under the label, *Desire*. Some appetites are native, such as those for food and drink and the avoiding of pain. But the vast majority of our desires "proceed from Experience."[26] The most basic desire, of course, is for the preservation of life. We judge ultimate good and ultimate evil in terms of our own desires and, since the chief of these is the desire for life itself, we will judge as good or as evil that which promises to preserve or that which threatens our lives. To live, we must have access to the necessities of life: nourishment and protection. Since resources are limited, we are, in the absence of government, in a state of war with our neighbors. We seek power in order to avert our own destruction. We value that which possesses power or confers power upon us, and this is true of the value we place on our fellow men. "The *Value*, or WORTH of a man, is as of all other things, his Price, that is to say, so much as would be given for the use of his Power."[27] What we call *dignity* is no more than this. The commonwealth prizes a man for what he can do for them. His status, then, is neither absolute nor permanent. It lasts as long as his power does.[28]

What is *honourable* is victory; dishonourable, defeat. Worthiness is fitness.[29] Our desire for power motivates us to search for causes, that is, to acquire science. When we lack this, we must content ourselves with the advice of others. It is in our search for ultimate causes that we discover God and, although we can never know the nature of God, we can and do infer His existence as a blind man infers that there *is* fire when told that fire warms us and when he then feels the warmth.[30] To the extent that religion grants power, it is judged as good and is desired. It will vary across cultures and be affected by the particular circumstances being faced by a given people.[31]

It is often surprising to the modern, Western reader who learns of Hobbes' devotion to monarchy and to the absolute powers of the state to discover that Hobbes arrives at this position from the assumption of the natural equality of all mankind. In fact, *Leviathan* is an object lesson to those who assume that a given philosophical or ethical bias logically entails a given political or social program. The argument for natural equality is presented at the beginning of Chapter XIII, and a lengthy quotation here is warranted:

"Nature hath made me so equall, in the faculties of body, and mind; as that though there bee found one man sometimes manifestly stronger in body, or of quicker mind than another; yet when all is reckoned together, the difference between man and man is not so considerable, as that one man can thereupon claim to himselfe any benefit, to which another may not pretend, as well as he. For as to the strength of body, the weakest has strength enough to kill the strongest, either by secret machination, or by confederacy with others, that are in the same danger with himselfe.

"And as to the faculties of the mind . . . I find yet a greater equality amongst men, than that of strength. For Prudence is but Experience; which equall time, equally bestowes on all men, in those things they equally apply themselves unto. That which may perhaps make such equality incredible, is but a vain conceit of ones owne wisdome, which amongst all men think they have in greater degree, than the Vulgar. . . . For they see their own wit at hand, and other mens at a distance. But this proveth rather that men are in that point equall, than unequall. For there is not ordinarily a greater signe of the equall distribution of any thing, than that every man is contented with his share."[32]

Because of this essential equality among men, there is no sufficient barrier to the assaults of one on another. That is, were there glaring inequalities in ability, the stronger would act with impunity; the weaker would submit without opposition. It is only because each has approximately the same chances of success as the other, each individual against each other and each group against another group, that the seeds of war are planted everywhere and for all time. Natural equality creates confidence and enmity. These, however, create the possibility of a violent death, dreaded by all. Thus, the desire for security calls upon each citizen to invest his personal power in the authority of a monarch. The duty to the sovereign last as long and no longer than "the power lasteth, by which he is able to protect them."[33]

Leviathan, in a truly remarkable way, integrated the major developments in seventeenth-century philosophy on both sides of the English Channel. With Descartes, Hobbes identified matter with extension. Siding with the Gassendists, he insisted that only body can affect body and that only *matter in motion* can serve as the subject of scientific inquiry. While applauding Bacon's *Novum Organum,* he saw in the works of Galileo what true science was to become: a rational approach to nature in which theory serves always as the handmaiden of fact.

Hobbes, for reasons that must be clear, was greatly respected by the nineteenth-century utilitarians. His program was pragmatic, mechanistic, objective, and, in a subtle way, egalitarian. He could find no source of human conduct other than the desire to survive and prosper. We cannot be sure that the Epicurean revival launched by Pierre Gassendi was seminal in this respect, but the presumptive evidence is substantial. His psychology was materialistic, hedonistic, behavioristic. The mind, while not doubted, is subject to the laws of physics just as is the *rest* of the body! To know the causes of a man's actions is to know his desires, to know his *needs*. Prime among these are the basic, biological requirements for survival. All other needs, acquired by experience and tradition, finally derive their force from these. In the introduction to *Leviathan* he wrote, "*Reward* and *Punishment* (by which fastned to the seate of the Soveraignty, every joynt and member is moved to performe his duty) are the *Nerves,* that do the same in the Body Naturall . . . *Concord, Health; Sedition, Sicknesse;* and *Civill war, Death.*"[34] Plato had examined the *Republic* in order to enlarge the canvas enough so that the nature of man could be discerned. Hobbes too saw the State as but an "artificial man." The difference, of course, is that Plato judged the ends of the State in terms of virtue; Hobbes, in terms of utility. Plato's metaphor was spirit; Hobbes', the machine.

Hobbes may be said not only to have initiated one of the first and most influential systems of materialistic philosophy in modern times but also one of the least compromised versions of *egoistic* ethics. His emphasis upon the motive for personal survival reappears continually as he addresses questions of morality. Hobbes is persuaded that what passes for benevolence, altruism, and other expressions of a principled regard for others must finally be analyzable in the terms of private gain and self-regard.

In Chapter 2, we paused to examine a classical defense of *egoism;* the one presented by Thrasymachus as an alternative to Socrates' ultra-rational theory of benevolence. Thrasymachus can find no reason to believe that the holder of *Gyges' Ring* will decline to avail himself of that which invisibility allows. Why would anyone defer the gratification of each and every desire except out of fear of reprisal? What reason has Smith to come to the rescue of Jones other than the possibility of reward or because he seeks to establish grounds for reciprocation?

The Socratic relaxation of the apparent tension between self-regard and altruism is based upon the theory than an enlightened individual can find happiness only in those actions that are good in themselves. Therefore, actions devoid of benevolence or indifferent to the needs of the State cannot produce happiness in the enlightened. Note, however, that this attempted solution plays readily into Hobbesian hands. Hobbes, even if he accepted the Socratic theory, is still able to insist that the happiness of the individual survives as the root-motive. Smith may, indeed, perform an act in the interest of the State but he does so *because it brings him pleasure.*

As with Hobbes' materialistic philosophy, his *egoistic* ethics would also undergo revision. Forms of it persist in all utilitarian theories and in those theories of value usually classified as "situation ethics." The eighteenth century sentimentalist or "empathy" theorists—Bernard Mandeville and Francis Hutcheson have already been cited—could not eschew the appeal or the challenge of *egoism.* Man might well be so framed as to possess an inborn concern for others but what is this concern other than the pleasure produced by actions of a certain kind? And from the proposition that value-laden thought and conduct are inescapably selfish, it is a small step to the proposition that each person must tailor for himself that set of tastes, opinions, and dispositions conformable with his own character, his *ego.* Here, of course, are the seeds of individualism and liberalism. From these would grow the overarching aims of personal growth and personal success that define the commercial tone of Victorian England. It was these elements of Hobbes' ethics that would reappear in Tom Paine's leaflets, in the antiroyalist literature of revolutionary France, in the British Reform Act (1832), and nearly every day in our own time as the liberated citizen celebrates the multiplication of his rights and the lessening of his duties. If one were to judge from the persisting and even growing signs of disillusionment displayed by those who have received the greatest share of egoistic benefits, one might conclude that Socrates had sensed something of a deep and durable nature, something missed or misunderstood even by Hobbes. Can a human being find pleasure in acts which themselves are not good?

The Reflex

Ours is a time of scientific specialization and, as the term suggests, "professionalism." When we read a history of psychology, we expect to find the names of Freud and Wundt and the usual philosophers. We are ready to admire a Descartes who, with all his concern for philosophy, still had time to contribute to optics and geometry; a Locke whose interests in government did not prevent him from providing a theory of the mind; a Galileo whose imagination was able to embrace astronomy, mechanics, and the philosophy of science. Our admiration takes the form of orphaning these figures as "universal geniuses," exceptions to the specialist's rule. While this attitude is understandable, it is not correct historically. If Locke has been an influential figure in the history of psychology, and he certainly has, then so also was Newton. The scholars of the seventeenth century were not "professionals." In the important respects, they assumed the *unity of science* to an extent the modern epoch hardly approximates. Newton, for example, was driven to a theory of vision and, particularly, to a theory of color vision, because he believed that the universal law of gravitation was *universal* and that its effects should be as apparent in a biological system as in planetary motion. Borelli, a colleague of Galileo's, studied the physiology of muscles in order to apply Galileo's principles of mechanics to systems that just happened to be alive. Descartes and Hobbes both sought to base their epistemologies upon the new science that was Mechanics. Descartes invented the physiological theory of reflexes with this in mind. To him and to his scientific contemporaries, it would have been inconceivable that there could be a "behavioral science" that was not, by the very fact, *physics*. Even Locke and Hume, disinclined to speculate on the biological basis of mind (disinclined, we may assume, because of the heavy weather suffered by Descartes at the hands of the Gassendists), both agreed that the issue was to be settled by "the anatomists." That is, while not addressing the question of materialism directly, Locke and Hume recognized it to be a *scientific* question. Hume was explicit:

> ". . . when the circulation of the blood . . . is clearly proved to have place in one creature . . . it forms a strong presumption, that the same principle has place in all . . . any theory . . . of the understanding, or the origin and connection of the passions in man will acquire additional authority, if we find, that the same theory is required to explain the same phenomena in all other animals."[35]

Descartes had said very much the same but had excluded animals from the domain of reason. Gassendi, however, had challenged this restriction, arguing that animals display memory, desire, and even a certain inductive capacity. Given the scientific climate of the second half of the seventeenth century, Descartes' dualistic path seemed to many to be too winding. When Newton's physics triumphed over Descartes', the latter's authority in all subjects fell into question, if not disrepute. His theory of the reflex had made action the consequence of stimulation and was designed to embrace a great part of all our conduct. Newton's laws, able to describe the motion of everything else, were judged by some to be immediately applicable to animal motion. (Recall Voltaire's remark, and it was Voltaire who brought Newton's work to the attention of the French.)

Descartes had envisaged the mechanism of the reflex to operate in the manner illustrated in the following figure. The arrow's image is conveyed by the optic nerves to the brain. The inverted image is set aright within the optic chiasm whence it passes to the pineal gland. Motor nerves receive "spirits" from the pineal gland in amounts determined by the force of the visual impression. Descartes considered the mechanism by which the nerves are actually energized by the spirits to be unfathomable.

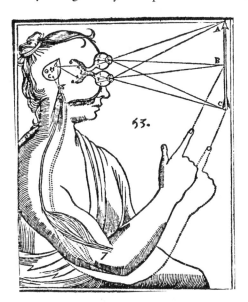

The *Treatise of Man* was a work that Descartes would not allow to be published in his lifetime. The work first appeared in 1662, twelve years after his death and seven years after Gassendi's. It is his most biological work, and it is in this treatise that the lurking monist in Descartes comes close to surfacing. The *Treatise* invokes the idea of a model or "machine-man" with a body like a statue. To this statue, anticipating Condillac, Descartes adds powers and functions by equipping it with sensory, motor, and reflex mechanisms. The essay includes the operation of feedback, emphasizes the muscular foundations of attention, and relates the quality of our experiences (or, the machine's experiences) to the action of the spirits flowing in and out of the pores of the brain. The spirits are rendered particulate, varying in mass and other qualities. As a result of these material differences, the spirits are able to mediate different emotions and the actions deriving from these emotions. Except for the faculty of reason, this machine simulates nearly perfectly a real man:

> "I desire you to consider, I say, that these functions imitiate those of a real man as perfectly as possible and that they follow naturally in this machine entirely from the disposition of the organs—no more nor less than do the movements of a clock. . . . Wherefor it is not necessary, on their account, to conceive of any vegitative or sensitive soul or any other principle of movement and life than its blood and its spirits, agitated by . . . those fires that occur in inanimate bodies."[36]

Newton's laws of motion were ideally suited to account for such a system:

> I. Every body continues in its state of rest or of uniform motion in a right line unless it is compelled to change that state by forces impressed upon it.
> II. The change of motion is proportional to the motive force impressed and is made in the direction of the right line in which that force is impressed.
> III. To every action there is always opposed an equal reaction; or, the mutual actions of two bodies upon each other are always equal and directed to contrary parts.

Today we accept these laws as determining the manner in which objects will react to imposed forces. In the seventeenth century, these were laws of "science," potentially as applicable to the mechanics of mental life as to billiard balls. Descartes' notion of "animal spirits" was transformed into the *vis nervosa* (nervous *force*), and the laws of the reflex were relegated to the science of physics. Increasingly, English empiricism and French materialism looked alike. The Gassendists and other anti-Cartesians could assert the failures of Cartesian physics (while subscribing to his theory of reflexes), and the empirical "experimental philosophers" in England could begin the grand program of reducing philosophy to science. In both quarters, the concept of the reflex was central. British empiricism had been, since Locke's *Essay*, associationistic. By the eighteenth century it was more compelling to some to speak not of the association of ideas but of a more mechanical association in a more mechanical entity. Here and there, experiments began to address the physiology of this reflex and, hand in hand, these experiments and entire mechanistic theories of psychology marched toward the century of materialism, the nineteenth.

Perhaps the most significant discovery of the eighteenth century in regard to the evolution of psychological materialism was made by Luigi Galvani, who in 1786 reported the results of experiments on the stimulation of the muscles of frogs by the application of an electrical pulse. Until the essentially *electrical* nature of nerve-muscle interactions was discovered, the mystery in Descartes' system was preserved. David Hartley (1705–1757) had already published his *Observations on Man*,[37] which had presented psychology as the science concerned with the mechanics of associationism. Hartley's thesis was self-consciously Newtonian, and prematurely so. Thomas Reid was only one of several philosophers to dismiss Hartley's "science" as having no basis whatever in observable fact. Thus, only with Galvani's discovery was it possible to advance a mechanistic psychology equipped with an actual mechanism. Such a psychology needed the biological equivalent of the colliding billiard balls, something tangible and measurable. Galvani did not discover the neural impulse itself, but he did establish that muscles could be caused to contract by the application of an electrical charge. The effect was dismissed by a number of scientists—including the great Alessandro Volta—who insisted that the human body was not even able to conduct a charge. This complaint was ingeniously set aside by one of the more elegant demonstrations in the history of the neural sciences. A small boy was suspended from a hook by a long rope. Hung from a separate beam were leaves of gold, placed just in front of the boy's nose. Then, a glass rod was rubbed briskly with cat's fur and placed against the boy's bare toes. The gold leaves were immediately drawn to the boy's nose, and the theory of electrical conduction by the human body entered the realm of indisputable fact. Experiment again had triumphed over dogma.

At about the same time that David Hartley was insisting without evidence that

> "each action results from the previous circumstances of the body and mind, in the same manner and with the same certainty as other effects do from their mechanical causes,"[38]

Robert Whytt (1714–1766) was repeating an experiment that had been performed years earlier by the physiologist Stephen Hales. Hales had observed that the decapitated frog could be induced to move its limbs by pinching them. Even without a brain, the frog would avoid a painful stimulus delivered to the extremities. A surgical severing of the spinal cord, however, eliminated the response. In his essay *"On the Vital and Other Involuntary Motions of Animals"* (1751), Whytt argued that the spinal cord was able to mediate stimuli and responses in the absence of activity of the brain.[39] What Hartley was speculating, Whytt was demonstrating and in so compelling a way that a Newtonian biology seemed to be merely a matter of time.

The concept of "association," and its mechanical equivalent, the "reflex arc," had the same status in eighteenth- and nineteenth-century physiology as "attraction" had in the physics of the seventeenth and eighteenth. Hartley illustrates the inextricable tie joining the emerging psychology to the established physics in the opening chapter of *Observations on Man:*

> "My chief design . . . is briefly to explain, establish, and apply the doctrines of *vibrations* and *association.* The first of these doctrines is taken from the hints concerning the performance of sensation and motion, which Sir Isaac Newton has given at the end of his Principia . . . the last from what Mr. Locke and other ingenious persons since his time have delivered concerning the influence of *association* over our opinions and affections."[40]

The essay then goes on to present ninety-one propositions regarding mental life, propositions embracing the simplest sensations and others designed to explain language, emotion, and dreams. All are based on the notion of a mechanical interaction between the organs of sense and the motor systems. Integrating these two systems is the brain. When we are stimulated, vibrations are established in the nerves and conveyed to the brain. After the stimulus has been removed, the vibrations persist, diminishing as a function of time. Memory, by this view, is the fading vibration induced by a bygone event. Learning is the establishment of a connection of what Newton had called "subtle forces" and Hume had described as the "gentle force," that is, a connection between *physical* events in the brain. The following theorem very nearly says it all:

> "If any sensation A, idea B, or muscular motion C, be associated for a sufficient number of times with any other sensation D, idea E, or muscular motion F, it will, at last, excite d, the simple idea belonging to the sensation D, the very idea E, or the very muscular motion F."[41]

Hume had said as much. Events occurring together, in unaltered sequence, often will come to be treated as causally related. Descartes, in describing the mechanism of nonspiritual action, had already specified the anatomical arrangements by which such sensory-motor events take place. Newton's "vibratiuncles" were but the earliest form of a *vis nervosa*. Hartley even finds support in Leibniz's "pre-established harmonies" which free the philosopher from having to explain how an immaterial soul directly activates a material body. Hartley's essay is, then, one of the great syntheses of the eighteenth century. He combines the physics (and method) of Newton with the physiology of Descartes; he avoids theological dilemmas by invoking the parallelism of Leibniz; he takes for granted the empirical associationism of Locke and Hume; he assumes, as Hume and every cobbler in England did, that pleasure and pain are the glue that binds our associations. Perhaps more than any single work previously published, Hartley's *Observations on Man* is a treatise in *modern* psychology. Its influence in the nineteenth century, as we shall see in the next chapter, was considerable.

"L'Homme Machine"

The luminaries of the French *Enlightenment*, whether atheists or theists, whether monarchists or anarchists, all shared in their contempt for dogma. Voltaire was the center and the engine of the movement. He admired England, wrote glowingly of the English people, praised them for their egalitarianism, their opposition to the Roman Church, and their tolerance. While history reveals that Voltaire's plaudits were overly generous, there is no doubt but that the Catholic influence in eighteenth-century France was oppressive. The *Enlightenment*, which cannot be said to have produced philosophic perspectives of lasting significance, was essentially a *political* movement posing as an intellectual enterprise. It is not surprising that the most original philosophical thinker in the group was Rousseau and that his only important contribution to philosophical thought is to be found in his additions to the "social contract" theory.

As political figures, the men and women of the *Enlightenment* saw in the new science and philosophy of their age a weapon that could protect them against the excesses of orthodoxy and, more, could drive a wedge between the received truths of religion and the complacent mass of believers. Politicized philosophy, like "political art," may have sudden effects, but not enduring ones. It may move people, but it does not advance the discipline in which it pretends membership. Voltaire himself introduced Newton to the French intellectuals but never fully comprehended Newtonian physics. Most of his competence in this subject was the gift of Mme. du Chatelet. This is not to say that Voltaire merely translated the *Principia* and chanted its laws. Rather, it is only to note that Voltaire's real interests in Newton's physics were extrascientific. He found in Newton another reason to oppose Cartesianism. The same may be said of Condillac (1715–1780), who translated Locke's *Essay* into French and whose *Essay on the Origin of Human Knowledge* remains one of the best analyses of Locke's empirical philosophy. It was Condillac who proposed the "sentient statue," standing in the path of a universe of stimuli, taking on psychological characteristics as a result of experience. It was Condillac's "statue" that served as the template for much of the materialistic philosophy of late eighteenth- and early nineteenth-century France. But Condillac was not particularly interested in the material basis of mind, and less in physiology. Nor was he simply a disciple of Locke's.[42] Rather, he was captivated by the antimetaphysical alternative of the English school, by the *philosophy of experience* celebrated by Voltaire, and no less so by Condillac's own cousin, d'Alembert. Again, the pull was not simply toward England but away from Descartes. Condillac was a priest. His enemy was clearly not the Church. His enemy was dogma, and especially philosophical dogma disguised as religion.

We have seen that Aristotelianism was an early casualty of the French religious wars. Galileo's "new sciences" were judged by the men and women of the *Enlightenment* as the definitive refutations of Peripatetic philosophy, although it is to be noted that their understanding of Galileo's physics was fuller than their understanding of Aristotle's *Metaphysics*. Cartesianism soon loomed as authoritarian as the *ism* so recently rejected. French intellectuals were now unanimous in their opposition to any assertion that flew in the face of fact and to any proposition not supported by the data of experience except those propositions set forth softly and humbly in the language of simple faith. No longer would they accept Thomism or Cartesianism as scientific. More significantly, no longer would they base government, social discourse, or the everyday affairs of life on foundations whose only claim to attention was custom or authority.

It is frivolous to date an idea and reckless to date large social movements. The eighteenth century was a century of revolution, but so was the sixteenth and, indeed, the seventeenth. The social, political, and economic changes that began most visibly in that period we so easily isolate as the Reformation are changes still taking place in our own time and often with revolutionary zeal and revolutionary consequences. Thus, it can only be apologetically that one advances the thesis that Gassendi, Newton, Voltaire, Rousseau, and their lesser contemporaries created a revolution in perspective that culminated in a revolution of classes. It is better and more accurate to put the thesis this way: The Reformation was an attack on institutions and this attack came to embrace the very idea of authority. With Hobbes, there was introduced the summoning utilitarian notion that the justification of governments is to be found in the safety they confer on human life. Galileo and Descartes, as scientists, contributed to the demise of that Aristotelian bastion which, for so long, had protected the claims of institutional authority. Descartes' additional contribution was that of publishing his major works in vulgar French, a policy embraced by every major French philosopher to follow. Locke, Hume, and their Continental counterparts, Gassendi and Condillac, translated the social reality into enduring philosophical systems. This is not to say that they were apologists for a movement. It is, however, to avoid the suggestion that they were the causes of the movement. They were, we prefer to say, participants and very influential ones at that.

We noted at the beginning of Chapter 7 that empirical philosophy does not *entail*, in the logical sense, materialism. (Berkeley was an ungrudging empiricist and a devout immaterialist.) But for the person who believes that the mind is furnished by experience alone, for the philosopher who can find no source of knowledge beyond the senses, the step to psychological materialism is short, logic to the contrary notwithstanding. Condillac's metaphor of the statue is a *material* metaphor. Hartley's vibrations —never witnessed by Hartley or anyone else—were not even presented as metaphor but as unseen reality. Recall that Locke and Hume specifically eschewed the temptation to theorize on the material causes of sensation and association. Hartley, a contemporary of Hume's, already displayed the attraction materialism always holds for the empiricist. Hobbes succumbed to it on the authority of Galileo; Hartley, on the authority of Newton's physics. In fact, there is a sense in which Descartes' dualistic psychology is understandable in terms of its not being an extension of an empirical philosophy.

In 1748 a book appeared bearing the title *L'Homme Machine*.[43] Its author, Julien Offroy de La Mettrie (1709–1751), was a physician, a self-exiled member of the court of Frederick the Great, and the boldest psychological materialist France had produced. The book caused a commotion even greater than that produced by his *Histoire Naturelle de l'Âme* (1745), whose sudden infamy had caused La Mettrie to move to Bavaria. Both books were relatively short, highly polemical, and hardly either philosophical or scientific as these adjectives are properly assigned. It is in *L'Homme Machine* that the soul is reduced to "an enlightened machine" and all the psychological faculties of man reduced to mere brain physiology. La Mettrie's "proofs" for these assertions are drawn from such otherwise irrelevant observations as the ability of a chicken to continue to run after its head has been removed, and the fact that the freshly removed heart of an animal will "jump" out of boiling water. His authorities include military officers who have told him tales of battle casualties but also include several of his own clinical observations. There is nothing in either book that the modern neurophysiologist or physiological psychologist would take very seriously, and less what a modern philosopher with his wits about him would pause to reread. The importance of *L'Homme Machine* is historical but not because it was especially influential, beyond the influence enjoyed by any book officially condemned. It is important in its style: porous, haughty, devoid of self-critical strains. It is the sort of book one writes on a dare or as a challenge. It is defiant but seldom clear on the issue or opinion to be defied. If the enemy were those who insisted that man is endowed with an immortal and incorporeal soul, the fact that chickens run after decapitation is utterly irrelevant. If the antagonist was the Cartesian who believed that the will is directed by the soul and that the soul directs its influence from a region of the brain, the behavior of hearts dropped into water is beside the point. La Mettrie, in summarizing the respects in which man is matter, went on to insist that he is only matter but this, as we know, cannot be established by materialist methods without committing the fallacy of *petitio principii*.

If La Mettrie had a direct influence on his successors it was on Pierre Cabanis (1757–1808), one of Napoleon's senators and a leading light in the French materialist movement. Both La Mettrie and Cabanis, however, have received more attention in histories of psychology than history warrants. It was Gassendi and the Gassendists who *founded* psychological materialism. Even Hobbes cannot compare to them in immediate influence. La Mettrie and Cabanis, both physicians and both lacking in that subtlety of mind that philosophy demands, contributed little to the historic debate between materialists and dualists, and nothing to the science spawned by the former. Both were products of the Gassendist tradition and both displayed the neo-Epicurean attitude of Gassendist philosophy. For both, happiness and morality, no less than sensation and action, were to be comprehended in material terms and were subjects of scientific analysis. Neither authored a bona fide materialist system. Indeed, neither had Gassendi. The system, of course, was there all along. It was the system of Galileo and Newton. But unlike Galileo and Newton, the French materialists were not physicists, were not incisive philosophers and, by and large, were not even scientists. Uncritically, they assumed psychophysical isomorphism and were thereby convinced that the laws of physics, the laws of society, and the laws of psychology were but three versions of the same material principles. Ironically these writers —d'Alembert, La Mettrie, Cabanis—are closer to a dominant contemporary perspective than were any of their more illustrious brothers. What they sensed, and what either eluded or embarrassed or failed to intrigue Locke, Hume, Leibniz, and Kant, was the growing possibility of wedding philosophy to anatomy. They were an eager group, forcing compatibilities where there was no ground other than enthusiasm for even speculating on the compatibilities. They saw into the next century.

The Scientific Context

Psychological materialism did not appear in a vacuum, nor is it to be understood simply as a consequence of the Gassendist rebuke of Cartesianism. We have devoted most of our attention to Galileo and Newton, by far the most important scientists of the seventeenth century and the men who gave the greatest impetus to eighteenth-century science. But there were many other, though smaller, contributions to the scientific spirit. La Mettrie, for example, studied with the great Dutch physician Hermann Boerhaave (1668–1738), whose treatises in chemistry had rejected *vitalism* and had insisted that all life processes were reducible to chemical processes. Antoine Lavoisier (1743–1794) convincingly demonstrated the conservation of matter in an experiment in which the steam from boiled water was condensed and collected. The notion of matter as being "neither created nor destroyed" is a late eighteenth-century one (discounting, as usual, the ancient Greek writers) and one with obvious religious implications. The same Lavoisier advanced the theory of chemical *elements* and, in a philosophical climate, this theory held out the promise of reducing the mysterious diversity of nature to its building blocks. We might underscore the growing materialism and *scientism* of La Mettrie's era by noting, without discussing, the scientists who were active and prominent at the time: Joseph Black (1728–1799), Charles Coulomb (1736–1806), Benjamin Franklin (1706–1790), Luigi Galvani (already cited), Stephen Hales (1677–1761), Albrecht von Haller (1708–1777), Karl Linnaeus (1707–1778), Joseph Priestly (1733–1804). It is the scientific achievement of this group that convinced some of the finest minds of the nineteenth century that the abiding questions could be answered at last and answered positively.

References

1. David Hume, *A Treatise of Human Nature*, Book I, Pt. I, Sec. II, edited by L. A. Selby-Bigge, Clarendon, Oxford, 1973.
2. Immanuel Kant, *Critique of Pure Reason*, translated by Norman Kemp Smith, St. Martin's Press, New York, 1965.
3. Galileo Galilei, *Dialogues Concerning Two New Sciences*, translated by Henry Crew and Alfonso de Salvio, Macmillan, Inc., New York, 1914.
4. Ibid., p. 110.
5. Galileo Galilei, *Dialogue Concerning the Two Great Systems of the World*. In *Classics of Modern Science*, edited by William S. Knickerbocker, Appleton-Century-Crofts, New York, 1927.
6. Ibid., *The Second Day*.
7. Isaac Newton, *Philosophiae Naturalis Principia: I. The Method of Natural*

Philosophy. In *Newton's Philosophy of Nature*, edited by H. S. Thayer, Hafner Publishing Co., New York, 1953.

8. Voltaire, *The Ignorant Philosopher*. Cited in *A History of Modern Science*, W. C. Dampier (p. 197), Cambridge University Press, Cambridge, 1966.

9. Descartes' response to the pamphlet includes the arguments of the pamphlet itself. It appears in Vol. I of *The Philosophical Works of Descartes*, translated by Elizabeth S. Haldane and G. R. T. Ross, first published in 1911 by Cambridge University Press and republished by Dover Publications, New York, 1955.

10. Ibid., pp. 433–434.

11. Ibid., p. 339.

12. Ibid., p. 442.

13. Ibid., p. 443.

14. *The Selected Works of Pierre Gassendi*, edited and translated by Craig R. Brush, Johnson Reprint Corp., New York, 1970. The introductory remarks by Prof. Brush are especially useful in establishing the context in which Gassendi's works were written.

15. Ibid., p. 174.

16. Ibid., p. 173.

17. Ibid., pp. 189–190.

18. Ibid., pp. 194–195.

19. Ibid., pp. 266–268.

20. Ibid., pp. 269–275.

21. Thomas Hobbes, *Leviathan*, Pt. I, Ch. 3, Pelican Classics, Penguin Books, England, 1974. This is the edition edited and discussed by C. B. Macpherson.

22. Ibid., Pt. I, Ch. 5.

23. Ibid.

24. Ibid.

25. Ibid., Pt. I, Ch. 6.

26. Ibid.

27. Ibid., Pt. I, Ch. 10.

28. Ibid.

29. Ibid.

30. Ibid., Pt. I., Ch. 11.

31. Ibid., Pt. I., Ch. 12.

32. Ibid., Pt. I., Ch. 13.

33. Ibid., Pt. II, Ch. 21.

34. Ibid., *Introduction* (p. 81).

35. David Hume, *An Enquiry Concerning Human Understanding*. Section IX. In *Essential Works of David Hume*, edited by Ralph Cohen, Bantam, New York, 1965.

36. René Descartes, *Treatise of Man*. French text with translation and commentary by Thomas Steele Hall. Harvard University Press, Cambridge, 1972. This excellent and much needed edition includes important notes by Prof. Hall that establish the pre-Cartesian authorities upon whom Descartes relied in constructing his psychobiological theory.

37. David Hartley, *Observations on Man*. In *Between Hume and Mill: An Anthology of British Philosophy 1749–1843*, edited by Robert Brown, Random House, Modern Library, New York, 1970.

38. Hartley, *Observations on Man*, op. cit., p. 84.

39. Robert Whytt, *An Essay on the Vital and Other Involuntary Motions of Animals*, Hamilton, Balfour, and Neill, Edinburgh, 1751.

40. Hartley, op. cit., pp. 5–16.

41. Ibid., p. 29.

42. Etienne Bonnot de Condillac, *An Essay on the Origin of Human Knowledge, Being a Supplement to Mr. Locke's Essay on the Human Understanding.* The most available edition is the facsimile reproduction of Thomas Nugent's translation of 1756. This facsimile, with an introduction by Robert Weyant, is published by Scholars' Facsimiles & Reprints, Gainesville, Florida, 1971. Note especially Prof. Weyant's discussion on pp. 17–18.

43. Julien Offray de La Mettrie, *L'Homme Machine*, 1748, Leiden. An English translation by M. W. Calkins is available.

THREE

Scientific Psychology

10

□□□□□□□□□□□□□□□□□□□□□□□□□□□□□□

The Nineteenth Century

THE AUTHORITY OF SCIENCE

A Note on the Debt to the Nineteenth Century

Contemporary psychology, in its broadest features, remains a nine-teenth-century enterprise. This is by no means to say that modern psy-chology is "old-fashioned" or behind the times. Still, it must be noted that the problems that consume the energy of the contemporary psychologist were either set forth explicitly in the nineteenth century or were intro-duced by those whose educational and cultural backgrounds were pro-vided by the unique perspective of the nineteenth century. Of those who can lay claim to a significant contribution to the manner in which the contemporary psychologist advances the discipline, only B. F. Skinner (1904–   ) was born in this century. All the rest—Lashley, Piaget, Freud, Adler, Hull, Pavlov, Tolman, Köhler, Watson, Dewey, James— are products of the century now under consideration. This fact is not a mere fact, but a suggestive and a revealing one. Modern psychology is not "modern" in the sense that modern physics and modern biology are. Re-cent discoveries of the molecular biology of the gene have transformed genetics into a discipline that Mendel scarcely would recognize, and the general theory of relativity has required the contemporary physicist to view the Newtonian universe through Einsteinian lenses.

In psychology, the situation is really quite different. The full range of its theoretical problems—from the study of personality and child develop-ment to inquiries into the neurophysiological basis of emotion or language to attempts to comprehend the determinants of social and national move-ments—can be traced directly to the thoughts and experiments of the psychologists and "natural philosophers" of the nineteenth century. Physicists no longer test the validity of Ohm's law or seek to discover whether, in fact, Maxwell's displacement current exists. They do not commit their lives to repeating those experiments that confirm the law of the conservation of energy or of angular momentum. Nor do they seek the "aether," or insist that light *must* be particulate *or* wave-mechanical. Physics still has problems, very substantial problems, and some are rooted in the nineteenth century. But it is not nineteenth-century physics that is brought to bear upon these problems now. The same may be said of chemistry and the more developed branches of biology. But in contemporary psychology, not only have the problems of the nineteenth century survived, but so have many of the methods developed in that century. More important than even this fact is that the contemporary perspective is largely the one bequeathed by the scholars of that time. This will be made clearer in the next chapter. For now, we need only remain mindful, as we explore the psychological endeavors of nineteenth-century philosophers and psychologists, that our subject is only partly historical.

The Legacy of the "Philosophes"

The great British philosophers who followed in Locke's path had a decidedly scientific orientation. They were all admirers of Newton and they all either recommended the new "experimental philosophy" or actually engaged in it. Some went the route of biological psychology; for example, Hartley; others, such as J. S. Mill, pursued the philosophy of science. In France too the disciples of Locke and Gassendi included philosophers of a seriously scientific nature, addressing their energies to specific, experimental questions. In the abiding tension between Nature and Spirit, they stood foursquare behind naturalism. But France, in the second half of the eighteenth century, hosted more than a group of industrious scientists and thoughtful philosophers. It hosted the *philosophes* of the *Enlightenment*, who had a greater effect upon the manner in which the average citizen of Paris viewed himself and his world than did the writings of any "respectable" philosopher. The intellectual groundwork for the French Revolution was not accomplished by Descartes, less by Locke or Newton. Rather, the groundwork was done by men and women who were literary people, not philosophers or scientists. It was done by dramatists, lawyers, and, as they called themselves, *dilettantes*. The most famous members of the group were, of course, Voltaire, Diderot, Rousseau, Condorcet, and D'Alembert.* Helvetius and Baron D'Holbach, though not members of

---

* No complete list can ignore Pierre Bayle (1647–1706) whose *Dictionnaire historique et critique* animated the scholarship of the Enlightenment with skeptical wit and an irreverent commitment to expose the pronouncements of authority to

the inner circle, derived inspiration from and voiced many of the central elements of the program of the *philosophes*. If we are to judge J. S. Mill as the nineteenth-century culmination of the empirical tradition created by Bacon, Hobbes, Locke, Newton, and Hume, then we must locate the source of Auguste Comte's *Positive Philosophy* in the French *Enlightenment*. Mill and Comte will occupy our attention shortly. But before turning to the specific and formalized contributions the nineteenth century made to psychology, we should have the major themes of the *Enlightenment* before us.

In the previous chapter, we noted that the French Materialists were engaged less in science than in politics or ideology. Accordingly, the works of La Mettrie, D'Holbach, and others had little influence on science in their own time or thereafter. The same must be said of the *Encyclopedists*. Neither D'Alembert nor Diderot contributed a method or a set of findings that served as a starting point for any major effort in science or in psychology. But, collectively, the *philosophes* did provide the starting point for all subsequent departures from orthodoxy. They established a liberated way of thinking and did this with such wit, craft, imagination, and penetration that defenders of the status quo inescapably invited ridicule. No single work summarizes their program nor can one be said to have launched the movement, but Voltaire's *Letters Concerning the English Nation*[1] came close to accomplishing both. As with a good many books of the *Enlightenment*, this one too was ordered burned by the *Parlement* (1734). The *Letters* are written in an offhand way, perfectly suited to the tastes and the time of busy and influential Frenchmen. They include praise for the pioneering efforts of Descartes but an utter dismissal of his metaphysics. Newton is offered as the master, and Bacon as his harbinger. The edition of the *Letters* condemned by the *Parlement* concluded with a waspish assault on Pascal's *Pensées*. Pascal's superstitions, his historical errors, his reliance on chance, his gloominess, are all pricked by the sharpest tongue in Europe.

Voltaire died in 1778. For nearly fifty years, his writings and very personality were the hub from which the scholarship of the *Enlightenment* radiated. He was enormously wealthy, and his influence was further increased by a close friendship with Frederick the Great of Prussia, the

---

the twin lights of reason and evidence. Bayle's ten-volume *Dictionary* and related writings made him a figure of great consequence to such illustrious contemporaries as Locke and Leibniz. Later, he would be hailed by Voltaire and would, as well, influence the thinking of scholars as different in outlook as Berkeley and Hume. Except for his summary dismissal of distinctions between "primary" and "secondary" (Lockean) qualities, however, Bayle provides little material for psychological analyses. His immediate followers in philosophy were inspired by his courageous and telling assaults on the chained mind, but the bulk of his writings remain only peripheral to matters of central concern to psychology.

poet-tyrant and most liberal king in Europe. Voltaire's example gave confidence to Diderot (1713–1784), whose *Encyclopédie* suffered a painful on-again, off-again experience at the hands of the *Parlement*. Indeed, many of the important works banned in France saw their way to Prussian publishers through the intercession of Voltaire. In his assertion of the superiority of the Lockean-Newtonian philosophy to that of Cartesianism, Voltaire set in motion a spirit of sensualism that led to Condillac and to Helvetius. The latter (1715–1771) published *A Treatise on Man, His Intellectual Faculties and His Education,*[2] which comes as close to twentieth-century environmentalism as any work written before 1900. It is in the *Treatise* that hereditary differences are dismissed as negligible and that the effects of training, reward, punishment, and experience are accorded first place in determining the character and accomplishments of the individual.

Voltaire also played a part, through Diderot, in the formation of Baron D'Holbach's materialistic philosophy, a materialism that soon took the form of polemical atheism. It was Holbach (1723–1789), as much as La Mettrie, who found the mechanistic portions of Descartes' psychology sufficient to account for morality, emotion, intellect, and language. It was Holbach who railed so vituperatively against established religion that the entire circle of *Encyclopedists* were soon treated as atheists, *en masse*.

Voltaire is credited with writing some twenty thousand letters to more than a thousand different correspondents. His plays moved the masses, his ideas, the *philosophes*. He, more than any other single voice in the eighteenth century, spoke the cause of freedom, reason, law, humanist ethics. He believed in God but was not religious. He believed in science but made no contribution to the literature of science. As with Diderot and Helvetius, he had received a Jesuit education and respected, all his days, the authority of reason. Many feared that he learned his lessons too well! He was no revolutionary, nor was he a "democrat" as that term is now employed. He insisted, however, that the ultimate validity of any government is rooted in its contributions to the welfare of its citizens, an idea that would become immortalized in Rousseau's *Contrat Social*. He, the *Encylopedists*, the growing power of the middle class, the conflicts between King and *Parlement*, between *Parlement* and Church, between Jesuit and Jansenist—these were the seeds of revolution and reform. All the leading figures of nineteenth-century science and natural philosophy looked back to the scholars of the *Enlightenment* for support and inspiration. We may summarize what they found when they looked back:

First, *the idea of progress*. In the works of Voltaire and, most particularly, in the rational materialism of Diderot and Condorcet, we discover repeatedly the notion of personal and cultural evolution. It is in *D'Alembert's Dream*[3] that Diderot presents the view of the whole as a collection of material parts, of the statue gaining its life from material reduction and subsequent evolution. And Condorcet (1743–1794), in his *Sketch for a Historical Picture of the Progress of the Human Mind*,[4] written as its author hid from the vengeful zealots of the Revolution—that is, from those whose new freedoms Condorcet had labored to secure—set to paper the idea that powered the entirety of the nineteenth century: the idea of progress.

Second, *the idea of nature*. If Voltaire, Diderot, D'Alembert, Condorcet, D'Holbach, Rousseau, and the rest can be said to have agreed on any single point—and the disagreements among the group were considerable—that point is philosophical *naturalism*. The world and everything in it are matter. The world is to be comprehended as matter in motion. Human reason, by which this comprehension becomes possible, must aim itself at nature and unearth nature's laws. To the Pascals who insist that we can never know everything, Voltaire's reply rings down the decades to our own day:

> "Let us console ourselves for not knowing the possible connections between a spider and the rings of Saturn, and continue to examine what is within our reach."[5]

Included in the idea of nature was the idea of natural law as applying to all spheres of reality. It was in this same period that Turgot and the *physiocrats* (*physis* = nature; *krateo* = power, sovereignty) argued for a "free market" economic policy whereby the "law" of supply and demand would set the "natural" value on goods and labor.

Third, *the idea of personal freedom*. Rousseau's greatest essay begins with the haunting picture of man, *born free and everywhere in chains*. Here is the spirit of the *Enlightenment*, transported by an Englishman to America and translated as *The Rights of Man*. Tom Paine would even become an elected member of the post-Revolution Assembly, notwithstanding the fact that he scarcely knew a word of French. He spoke the language without the words.

It is a scholar's bias to describe an epoch in such a way as to neglect all but the philosophy of the period—as if the titanic political and social upheavals of the time were trivially reducible to the ideas of an elite few, passing their manuscripts among themselves while sipping cognac in the *Salon* of Mme. du Duffand. It is an equivalent bias on the part of journalists to interpret the French Revolution in terms of the price of bread. The scholar and the journalist (or Marxist historian) are both right and both wrong. The price of bread in 1789 was quite high. It was also high in 1788, 1787, 1687, 1587, etc. Bread is seldom as cheap as the masses would wish. It is also true that by 1789 people were tired of war, outraged by the excesses of the courts of French kings, the lavish indulgences of their mistresses, the persecutions by the Church. But no king was more indulgent than Louis XIV, no church more persecutory than Spain's in 1480 (or England's a century later). Revolutions require more than high prices and fascism. Often, in fact, revolutions create higher prices and greater fascism. Revolutions require an idea, a compelling and essentially philosophical alternative, an altered perspective on nature and on self. Revolutions occur when people consider their present condition *unnatural* and when they are convinced that change will lead to progress. The era of the *Enlightenment* embraced the Seven Years' War (1756–1763) in which England, through the eloquence and nationalist lust of Pitt the elder, sided with Frederick against the combined forces of France and the Austria of Maria Theresa. The conclusion of that war, that useless and contrived war, found France and Prussia in bankruptcy, the once-fragmented German states on the verge of nationhood, and England a veritable empire. As Pitt had foreseen, the war made it impossible for France to protect her interests in the New World, had left England unchallenged on the seas, and Prussia bereft of any possibility of threatening English interests in Europe. Not only did France sink to insignificance as a colonial power in America but she lost her hold on India as well. Thus, when the price of bread reached new heights in the 1780s, it merely added to the Frenchman's conviction that his government could not do the sorts of things that are to be expected. The same England whose philosophers had triumphed over Descartes now triumphed over political France as well. Neither geometry nor the Church had prevented it.

The Legacy of Kant

Kant died at the beginning of the nineteenth century, but he is far more a member of the Age of Reason than he is the Age of Materialism. He set the tone of German philosophy for the entirety of the nineteenth century and, as a result, German "naturalism" would be ever barren of the strong empiricist elements of the naturalistic philosophies of France and England. German philosophy, that is, would come to accentuate the transcendentalism of Kant. The combination of naturalism and transcendentalism yielded that uniquely German creation, *Romantic Idealism*, whose principal architect was Johann Wolfgang von Goethe (1749–1832).

It was the poetry of Goethe that animated the German-speaking world with the spirit of *Sturm und Drang*. His *Sorrows of Young Werther* (1774) resulted in an epidemic of suicides. Naturalism, in the hands of Goethe, was the panpsychism of Leibniz, Spinoza's creative forces. Man stands hopelessly alone in an immense universe, torn by the stresses of life, and finding himself only through his own activity, through his *life*. The goal of life is the living of it, the activity and personal evolution, the reaching upward and outward. Life is love and passion. Kant's rejection of teleology was all Goethe needed to convince himself that the only end of human life is the activity that defines it. Nature is but a system of opposing forces: life and death, light and dark, love and hate.

Fitted to the demands of the new naturalism, Kant's *a priori* categories would become translated into a kind of *genetic* psychology that we have labeled *nativism*. The "pure understanding" would find representation in the experimentalist age in studies of consciousness, "imageless thought," and related nonempiricistic psychologies. In a tortuous way, the Kantian legacy would culminate in Gestalt psychology and phenomenology.

Empiricism in the Nineteenth Century

We concluded Chapter 7 with a discussion of the Utilitarian philosophy of Jeremy Bentham and observed that this system would be modified and promulgated by many, particularly J. S. Mill (1806–1873). We pick up the evolution of empiricism—this time as empirical *psychology*—with Mill.

There is no need to go into Mill's "conversion" to Benthamism and philosophical radicalism at age fifteen. His *Autobiography*[6] is widely quoted, and the missionary labors of his father, James Mill, in behalf of Benthamism have already been extolled. Mill never abandoned the broadest features of *Utilitarianism*, but he did recognize that Bentham's founding version of it was insufficient to meet the demands of the time. Unlike Bentham, who came to philosophy by way of law and economics, Mill's background was in classics, logic, and science. Where Bentham wrote in the grand style of the eighteenth-century universalists, Mill was more systematic and far less intuitive. His era was far more complex than Bentham's and he appreciated the complexities. Thus, we do not find the Mill of *On Liberty* attempting to "prove" the validity of freedom in terms of physics, or mathematics, or logic. Nor do we find the Mill of the *System of Logic* defending the inductive method in terms of economic or social considerations. Mill is a distinctively nineteenth-century gentleman, sophisticated, educated, liberal, and urbane. He is, in short, a modern as we would apply the term.

J. S. Mill's most important work in psychology was his *System of Logic* (1843), which was immediately successful and, through eight editions in his own lifetime, served as the handbook of the scientific community. The bulk of the work was devoted to a description of the principles of induction, the failure of purely rational approaches to matters of fact, the methods to be employed in establishing valid inferences, and the role of deductive processes in science. Contemporary science continues to rely on Mill's "methods," and our own easy commitment to the hypothetico-deductive method can be attributed to the immediate hold the *System of Logic* took on the scientific mind. Not many scientists in the late nineteenth century read Galileo; all of them read Mill.

The portion of the *System of Logic* most important to the appearance of experimental psychology is Book VI and especially Chapters III–VII.[7] Having laid the foundation for all science, Mill now addresses his attention to human nature as a subject of science:

> "It is a common notion, or at least it is implied in many common modes of speech, that the thoughts, feelings, and actions of sentient beings are not a subject of science. . . . This notion seems to involve some confusion of ideas, which it is necessary to begin by clearing up. Any facts are fitted, in themselves, to be a subject of science, which follow one another according to constant laws; although those laws may not have been discovered, nor even be discoverable by our existing resources."[8]

Mill offers an illustration from meteorology. We are not able, he says, to specify all the antecedent variables sufficient to produce rain, but we all agree that rainfall is the result of laws of nature. Thus, forecasting the weather is a probabilistic endeavor and may always be. That is, it may never be an *exact* science, but it is a science nonetheless.

> "The science of human nature is of this description. It falls far short of the standard of exactness now realized in Astronomy; but there is no reason that it should not be as much a science as . . . Astronomy."[9]

He notes that the subject matter of psychology embraces the thoughts, feelings, and actions of human beings and that these cannot be predicted with anywhere near the accuracy as that obtaining in astronomy. This limitation, however, does not indicate that psychology cannot be a science or even that it is not a science. We cannot foresee every circumstance in which an individual might be found, and the factors that conspire to form the individual character are so diverse that even if we knew these future circumstances, we might still not be able to predict how the individual will act. Nevertheless we must still accept that his actions, feelings, and thoughts *are caused*, that the causes are natural and, to that extent, knowable *in principle*. Some of the laws are, in fact, known already, according to Mill, and central among these are the laws of association, which Mill summarizes as follows:[10]

First, there is Hume's law according to which every mental impression has a corresponding idea. Once we have experienced X, we are able to recall X without its actual presentation. We are so constituted that we are able to form an idea or mental image of that which we have perceived.

Second, there is the law of connection such that the repeated, simultaneous (or immediately successive) presentation of two stimuli leads us to think of either when the other is later presented. This law, cited by all the empiricists, is most ably described, Mill tells us, by one James Mill, whose *Analysis of the Phenomena of the Human Mind* presents the law "with a masterly hand." The third law is one that renders the intensity of a stimulus relatively interchangeable with the frequency of its presentation. According to this law, a very intense X has the same effect upon the mind as a weaker Y that has been presented more frequently.

"These simple or elementary Laws of Mind have been ascertained by the ordinary methods of experimental inquiry; nor could they have been ascertained in any other manner. But a certain number of elementary laws having thus been obtained, it is a fair subject of scientific inquiry how far those laws can be made to go in explaining the actual phenomena. It is obvious that complex laws of thought and feeling not only may, but must be generated from these simple laws."[11]

Mill's empirical psychology was not of the radical sort. He certainly looked to education and the general cultural environment for the causes of individual differences, but he was equally persuaded that organic factors might be and probably are responsible for some of the more dramatic differences. He noted the advances being made in neurophysiology and neurology and believed that in time we would have a much better understanding of the relationship between brain physiology and the laws of the mind. However, as with Locke and Hume, he refused to take a position on the material basis of thought and noted that Hartley and his own father had displayed more confidence in the materialist account than was justified by available data.[12]

There is a second respect in which Mill's empirical psychology was conservative. He tended to doubt, notwithstanding the fact that psychology could and would develop empirical laws, that the science of psychology would ever be able to go beyond the given context in its attempts to predict human conduct, thought, and feeling. By an *empirical law*, Mill meant a law of regularities; Y follows X or is coincident with it in this setting, and we may infer that Y will follow X or be coincident with it in any setting greatly resembling this one. However, in a very different context, we are unable to specify precisely what the relationship, if any, will be between them. Since the human condition is ever changing, since history ordains ever different contexts, the laws of psychology will be empirical and of restricted generality.[13] Through the empirical laws, which allow us to predict the actual facts of conduct or thought or feeling in a given and restricted context, it is possible to deduce more general laws. These will not be merely empirical but will be exact. However, the price we pay for these exact laws is that they will not apply to facts but to tendencies. That is, from the empirical laws of association, we may inexactly predict that Henry Jones will form a stronger association between intense stimuli than he will between weak ones. There may be a race of men about whom this is not true. Yet, from this "situational law," we can deduce that, if there is thought at all, associations will be formed. Note that the law of associations does not predict or even attempt to predict the *exact* result of an experiment. Rather, it refers to the *tendency* of something to occur, other things being equal. That other things are never equal in the affairs of man is only to say that our exact laws will not be testable, not that they are not laws. Mill gave (invented) the name *ethology* to cover this science which is deduced from the empirical laws of psychology. As conceived by him, ethology was to be the science of *character* or that discipline concerned with the effects of environmental conditions on the laws of thought, feeling, and conduct. It was to be "the Exact Science of Human Nature" whose propositions are "hypothetical only, and affirm tendencies, not facts."[14] Modern ethology, of course, bears only a slight resemblance to Mill's expectations. This is not the occasion to examine the subtleties of Mill's plan for ethology, but we must, before leaving the point, draw attention to the ambiguous distinction between that which affirms a tendency and that which affirms a fact. It is worthwhile to draw attention to Mill's choice of words here because the *philosophical* behaviorism of several twentieth-century writers (e.g., Ryle) has come to rely heavily on the notion of dispositions and tendencies as opposed to observable facts.

The very mention of behaviorism, perhaps by one of those laws of association, brings one to Mill's version of *utilitarianism*. Over and against Kant's Categorical Imperative, which Mill sees as potentially admitting "the most outrageously immoral rules of conduct,"[15] Mill adopts the "happiness theory":

> "Questions of ultimate ends are not amenable to direct proof. Whatever can be proved to be good, must be so by being shown to be a means to something admitted to be good without proof."[16]

We judge medical science to be "good" because it conduces to health, but we have no way of showing that health itself is good. We accept this without proof, its ultimate sanction coming from the fact that all or very nearly all mankind will attempt to possess it. To those who reject utility as being no more than the measure of goodness employed by the beasts, Mill counters that there is nothing in utilitarianism that declares that human happiness is limited to pleasures of the flesh or bestial wants. Utilitarianism accepts the facts and the needs of the human intellect and recognizes that, for man, the greatest happiness is not confined to mere biological gratification. Pleasures differ in *quality* as well as in quantity and no utilitarian denies it:

> "If I am asked what I mean by difference of quality in pleasures, or what makes one pleasure more valuable than another merely as a pleasure, except its being greater in amount, there is but one possible answer. Of two pleasures, if there be one to which all or almost all who have experience of both give a decided preference, irrespective of any feeling of moral obligation to prefer it, that is the more desirable pleasure."[17]

Students of modern behaviorism will recognize in this passage the forerunner of that notion according to which it is the organism, not the psychologist, who defines the reinforcer. Pleasure and the quality of pleasure are to be judged in terms of what is sought by the individual when he has access to a variety of possibilities. Pain is that which is avoided by the individual when he is able to reveal his judgments in his conduct. And, lest the imaginative reader attempt to reconcile this view with some version of Kantian morality, Mill makes his own position utterly transparent:

> "There is, I am aware, a disposition to believe that a person who sees in moral obligation a transcendental fact, an objective reality belonging to the province of 'things in themselves', is likely to be more obedient to it than one who believes it to be entirely subjective, having its seat in human consciousness only. But whatever a person's opinion may be on this point of ontology, the force he is really urged by is his own subjective feeling, and is exactly measured by its strength. . . . It is not necessary, for the present purpose, to decide whether the feeling of duty is innate or implanted. Assuming it to be innate, it is an open question to what objects it naturally attaches itself. . . . If there be anything innate in the matter, I see no reason why the feeling which is innate should not be that of regard to the pleasures and pains of others. If there is any principle of morals which is intuitively obligatory, I should say it must be that. If so, the intuitive ethics *would* coincide with the utilitarian."[18]

Thus, Mill not only doubts that the intuitivist (i.e., Kantian) can ever prove his moral system but argues that even if, somehow, he is right, the utilitarian system can easily assimilate the "native" pleasures and pains. The important point, from Mill's perspective, is to understand the source of power that moral injunctions have. That source is none other than the pleasure or pain caused by our actions or anticipated as consequences of our actions. If there is such a thing as an ultimate morality, its sanctions derive from this consideration and only from this consideration.

The connection between utilitarianism and empiricism is direct. If morality is to be a knowable subject, then it must have a factual foundation. The latter requires that the elements of any moral philosophy be observable and that its propositions be, in principle, testable. On this account, utilitarianism, according to its adherents, is the *only* scientific moral system. Human acts can be assessed in terms of their consequences. When these are judged by those affected by them to have produced happiness, the acts may be judged as moral. When the consequences, as judged by the actual or potential recipients, are painful, the act is immoral. All other appeals must reduce to the utilitarian. All other standards must reduce to the subjective consequences on actual people.

We have observed the conservative elements of Mill's empirical psychology and now we must offset these with the radical character of his empirical philosophy. Unlike his forebears, Locke and Hume, who were willing to exclude at least the necessary truths of mathematics from the overall realm of empirical science, Mill argued that even these truths are finally to be understood as inferences from experience. In defining matter as the *"permanent possibility of sensation,"* he asserted *phenomenalism* as the fundamental epistemology. This is not to be confused with idealism, in any of its variants, since Mill was a confirmed believer in matter. Rather, he took the tenets of epistemological empiricism to their logical limit, which indeed requires that all statements about the material world must ultimately have perceptual counterparts or referents. Thus, to the extent that mathematical propositions are propositions about the real world, they too must have their source in the data of sense. This is a philosophical and not a psychological issue and is beyond our present purpose. It is enough to indicate, however, that this feature of Mill's empiricism rendered the entire enterprise suspect as, in many quarters, it now remains.*

Mill was influenced not only by the British tradition but by older con-

---

* J. S. Mill spoke not only with the most eloquent voice of his age but, in major respects, with one most accurately reflecting the tone of that age. His contemporary, the essayist John Morley, observed in his eulogy for Mill, "Much will one day have to be said as to the precise value of Mr. Mill's philosophical principles . . . However this trial may go, we shall at any rate be sure that with his reputation will stand or fall the intellectual repute of a whole generation of his countrymen." (*On the Death of Mr. Mill*, in: *John Morley, Nineteenth Century Essays,* University of Chicago Press, 1970.)

temporaries in France as well. Chief among these, and one of the most important figures in the experimentalism of the nineteenth century, was Auguste Comte (1798–1857), whose six-volume *Cours de philosophie positive* established *positivism* as a system of philosophy. By his own admission, Comte was led to his thinking principally by Condorcet's *Sketch* (cited above) with its emphasis on cultural evolution and intellectual progress. And in the best French tradition, Comte labored to convert the idea into a movement that can only be called political. In outline, Comte's position is that cultures pass through three distinct stages: the theological, which is superstitious the metaphysical, in which hidden physical forces or causes replace deities; finally, the scientific, in which *positive* knowledge replaces superstition and "metaphysics." The three stages must occur and in the order specified. At the transition point between one and the next, the culture finds itself in a *critical period*. An old perspective, which has been satisfying to the masses for an extended time, is now to be replaced by one whose virtues are only slightly sensed and only by the best minds of the period. Once the transition is complete, the culture enters an *organic* period: one of synthesis and discovery, growth and intellectual evolution.

Much along the same lines as those provided by Condorcet in his *Sketch* of intellectual progress, Comte's positivist doctrine required each new science to emerge from the principles of an older and more established one. Each science develops methods appropriate to its problems. Illustrative is the science of Sociology which Comte himself named. Its method was to be that of a comparison of cultures in various stages of evolution. And, through the discovered laws of sociology, all other sciences would be better comprehended, since all other sciences are the product of social evolution. Agreeing with Kant that the mind itself is not directly observable and recognizing that much of what presented itself as "psychology" was no more than philosophers attempting to discover the laws of the mind introspectively, Comte dismissed psychology as "an idle fancy, and a dream, when it is not an absurdity."[19] If the mind is to be studied, only two methods are available. The first, which Comte called *phrenological psychology* and which we shall discuss later in this chapter, involves research on the relation between brain processes and mental states and functions. The other is the direct observation of the *products* of mental life, and this, to Comte, was sociology. Of course, had the philosophical psychologists not attempted the impossible and conceited task of looking into their own minds and had, instead, appreciated the importance of *feeling* and *emotion*, they would have looked throughout the animal kingdom and discovered bona fide psychological principles. Convinced, however, that only man was rational and intelligent, they ignored this most promising investigative terrain.[20]

Comte's *positivism* was extended to embrace religion, ethics, and economics. He and his disciples advanced a view of science that placed it on a footing no different from the world's historic religions. Science would solve all problems, answer all questions, remove all doubts. To deny its power was to sink into metaphysical or, worse, theological torpor. To avail one's self of its methods was to set the world aright. Once more, the promises of Bacon, Hobbes, Descartes, and the *philosophes* returned to haunt the orthodox believers. Now they were told that there are two kinds of statements a man can make. One refers to the objects of sense, and it is a scientific statement. The other is nonsense!

Mill too was a positivist, although he disagreed on several counts with Comte's version. He (wisely) rejected phrenology, he accepted associationistic laws of the mind (even though the method of their proof might be "introspective"), and he refused to depart from strict empiricism even to the point of dogmatizing on what science *must* be. Still, his ethology was intended to complement Comte's sociology; his rules of inference were designed to yield positive knowledge; his appeal to the senses as the ultimate arbiters of truth was unashamedly Comtean. The ideas of Mill and Comte, paced through the revisions that all formulations undergo, culminated in the *logical positivism* of the Vienna circle: Wittgenstein, Schlick, Carnap, Reichenbach, and their followers. It was this group that introduced the twentieth century to the most coherent and critical attack on rationalism that had been witnessed since William of Ockham. According to the logical positivists—and they might just as well be called radical empiricists—the facts of the world are *sensations*, and all the laws of science are ultimately reducible to empirical propositions. Once we have exhausted the data of sense, there is nothing else that can be said either of the world or ourselves. These developments will be explored further in the next chapter.

Darwin and the Idea of Progress

Evolution, as a fact of perception and as a literary metaphor, is a dateless concept in the mind of man. Aristotle and Empedocles argued about its ontogenetic character, and Goethe extended it to the very processes of history. Condorcet, in his *Sketch*, analyzed the human experience as a series of stages, beginning with tribal communities and proceeding, in orderly succession, through nine more levels, the last being scientific in language and orientation.[21] Comte's *positivism* asserted the same, more formally and in far greater detail.

If evolution has been an abiding concept, so too has nature-as-enemy.

Every age and every person confront the challenges posed by the elements: plague, starvation, drought, illness, enfeeblement. Not only are these the ever-present features of life, but they have been perceived, since recorded history, as producing "heartier stocks," "fit specimens," and the like. The Spartan regimen recommended for Athenian youth in the *Republic* is defended on grounds such as these. The strongest metal is that tempered in the hottest flame. Even tribal initiation rites seem to respect the theory that asperity breeds future success. Darwin, then, is not to be accorded the honor of "discovering" either evolution or natural selection if by discovery we mean the same sort of process as that involved in Maxwell's discovery of the laws describing electromagnetic phenomena.

What Darwin (and, independently, Alfred Russell Wallace) discovered was that evolution, or "progress," is not only possible but inevitable and even, in a very ruthless fashion, mechanical. He and Wallace both read and acknowledged the ideas imparted by Thomas Malthus' *Essay on the Principle of Population.*[22] Malthus demonstrated, with mathematical rigor, that the breeding potential of the human race was staggering—but never realized. That is, it is possible for human beings to increase in number *geometrically*, but such increases do not occur. Clearly there must be an opposing force tending to limit populations. In describing what he called "the struggle for existence," Malthus presented war, pestilence, and starvation as the forces tending to prevent geometric increases in population. According to his analysis, whenever the rate of increase in population exceeds the rate of increase in the production of food, people *necessarily* will die.

In the *Origin of Species*, Darwin applied Malthusian concepts to all living systems. He presented the forces of nature as blind agents of selection, *natural selection*, which either favored or reduced the probability that a species would survive. Within any species, wide (natural) variations are apparent. The press of the environment favors certain variants and these, as a result, become more numerous. Darwin (1809–1882) published his works before Mendel's findings in genetics had become generally known and, as a result, the *Origin of Species* did not contain any modern notions about the mode of transmission of the various traits involved in survival. In fact, where Darwin was specific on this count, he was wrong. But he did recognize that mutations occur, that some of these were better suited to the conditions they faced, and that, as a result, they would come to prosper, often at the expense of the parent-type. The cheerful idea of progress entertained by the *philosophes* of the *Enlightenment* now took on a gloomier complexion. Progress is but the consequence of annihilation. New life appears and succeeds, while older forms perish. Supporting his theory with archaeological findings, Darwin relentlessly withstood the attacks of churchmen and skeptical scientists alike. If the Bible suggests that all living forms were created at the same time, the Bible is wrong. If Christian teaching insists that God made so many forms of life and no more, Christian teaching is wrong. If philosophers believe that man, through his will and accomplishments, has removed himself from the natural contexts in which survival never exceeds probability, the philosophers are wrong. Find a species of bird now in abundance and you will have the descendant of an avian form, different from the present one, which was unable to accommodate the demands of a changing environment. Man came into being as a successful variant of a primate-type no longer with us. Quite simply, he *evolved*.

Darwin's most important psychological work is *The Expression of the Emotions in Man and Animals*,[23] a book that may be said to have launched comparative psychology. Since the major strains of Darwinian theory are now widely known, we need only say a few words about his impact on psychological thought in the nineteenth century. By far, the greatest effect produced by Darwinism was that which located psychological man on a continuum of biological organization. In *The Expression of the Emotions*, Darwin examines the facial musculature of many species, *Homo sapiens* included, and notes not only the anatomical similarities (already well established) but the similarities in facial expression produced by conditions giving rise to similar emotions. The angry dog and the actor feigning anger both retract their lips back over their teeth, bare their teeth, and clench them. Signs of submission, of sexual attraction, and of melancholy are of a similar nature throughout phylogeny wherever we find the anatomical equipment necessary for the expression of affect. Natural selection has favored those species able to form "serviceable habits." It has led to the evolution of nervous systems so constructed as to produce behaviors leading to mating, to the avoidance of tissue-damaging stimuli, to the ingestion of nutritious foods. Not only is the present species the survivor of a long process of natural selection, but in the behavior and the emotions of this species, we will discover elaborated forms of those behaviors and feelings that characterize simpler types. In quasi-teleological terms, Darwinian ethology explained variations in the living world in terms of the ultimate goal of all life: the continuation of life. Attainment of this goal requires adaptation to the exigencies of the environment. The species that cannot adapt will vanish. In evolving into a new and different form, it, itself, must cease to be. The required evolution includes not only the anatomy of the species but its *functional* physiology as well—its habits, reflexes, and sensitivities. Psychological evolution is, therefore, concomitant with structural, anatomical evolution. Just as we are able to discern, in the structural nuances of more advanced species, the archetypical features of earlier forms, so also can we see, in the developed psychological equipment of the advanced species, traces of more primitive dispositions and abilities.*

It was not long after Darwin's *Origin of Species* that his cousin, Francis Galton (1822–1911), published his studies of *"hereditary genius"* (1869).[24] Galton had accepted the evolutionary theory without reservation and had accepted as well the epistemological empiricism that constituted England's national philosophy. Putting the two together could produce only one outcome: a theory of mental superiority based on the capacity of the senses! Galton's studies of the children of successful students indicated that mathematical ability "ran in families," although the environmentalist interpretation of the data received only a modest hearing. Galton needed only the Darwinian theory in order to explain why there is such great variability in human intelligence. He needed only an age of experimentalism and a burgeoning commercial empire to support his belief that the measurement of this variability was important. In selecting such tasks as those involving visual acuity and depth perception, Galton merely reflected one of the more innocent features of radical empiricism. In any case, a "mental measurement" tradition was begun which, lacking Malthusian restraints, has since grown geometrically.

Darwinian biology meant different things to different people, and it still does. It was illegal to teach the subject in a number of American states until relatively recently. To religionists of a fundamentalist stripe, the whole idea was out-and-out heresy. The theory required that the earth be much older than Scripture had indicated. It argued for the continuous creation of new forms; fundamentalism insisted on a "big-bang" origin of all forms. It demanded more of man than mere virtue in the

---

* It was Ernst Haeckel (1834–1919) who formalized this Darwinian proposition into the "biogenetic law" according to which ontogeny recapitulates phylogeny. But Henri Bergson (1859–1941), almost single-handedly, began to lead an intellectual movement against Darwin's materialistic theory of evolution. His *L'Évolution créatrice* (*Creative Evolution*), which was published in 1907, challenged evolutionary biology in terms very much like those used by the Gestalt psychologists in their arguments with associationists. Bergson found little plausibility in the notion that random processes could produce, in piecemeal fashion, such enormously complicated and functionally interdependent systems as those underlying vision, for example. Only a *creative* evolution, on Bergson's account, could lead to the degree of biological organization of which the higher species are evidence. This creative evolution is powered by an *élan original*, a divine agency that has authored free will as well. That Bergson's influence on contemporary psychology and especially contemporary American psychology has been less than commanding is to be understood in terms of the failure of such notions to be reduced to experimental modes of verification. Thus, we find Bergsonian ideas most prominently and perhaps uncomfortably located in that wide-ranging literature described as "existential psychology," "humanistic psychology," and "Gestalt" psychotherapy. Perhaps their most cogent integration is to be found in the hypotheses advanced by Prof. Jean Piaget whose discussions of "cognitive development" are richly shaded by notions akin to *creative evolution*.

struggle for survival and it allowed the *gradual* elimination of man himself. At best, it traduced the Day of Judgment into a painfully drawn-out affair.

To the middle-class commercialists of Victoria's empire, Darwinism was soon interpreted as a justifying ethic. The poor were poor "by nature." Since we are all engaged in an eternal struggle against the elements, since only certain "types" are properly adapted to the demand, it is inevitable that there will be the "haves" and the "have-nots." Given Galton's findings, it is even likely that the two classes will perpetuate their respective stations *hereditarily*.

To the Continental scholars, so much under the influence of Comtean *positivism* and the "three-stage" theory of cultural evolution, the Darwinian model pulled many diverse strands of thought together. The nervous system has evolved, consciousness has evolved, structure entails function. In Freud's words, "anatomy is destiny." Simultaneously there began to appear studies of comparative culture, comparative anatomy, and, alas, comparative psychology. Everything now made so much sense: the idea of progress, the enlightened machine, utilitarianism, the positive philosophy, young Werther besieged by the *Sturm und Drang* of his own feelings. A revolution was taking place, aptly titled by one historian, *heroic materialism*.

Nineteenth-Century Materialism

Alexander Bain (1818–1903), a close and admired associate of J. S. Mill, wrote the following to Mill in 1851, describing the progress he was making in his text in Psychology:

> "I have just finished rough drafting the first division . . . which includes the Sensations, Appetites, and Instincts. All through this portion I keep up a constant reference to the material structure of the parts concerned, it being my purpose to exhaust in this division the physiological basis of mental phenomena. . . . And although I neither can, nor at the present, desire to carry Anatomical explanation into the Intellect, I think that the state of the previous part of the subject will enable Intellect and Emotion to be treated to great advantage and in a manner altogether different from anything that has hitherto appeared. There is nothing I wish more than so to unite psychology and physiology that physiologists may be made to appreciate the true ends and drift of their researches into the nervous system."[25]

It was Bain who founded the essentially psychological journal, *Mind*. It was Bain who wrote the two most influential psychology texts to appear before the twentieth century.[26] What is it that prompted so physiological a bias in this empiricist? Why, unlike Locke, Hume, and even Mill, did Bain anchor empirical associationism to the science of physiology? To answer these questions we must review three extraordinary developments in neurophysiology that occurred in the decades immediately preceding Bain's own contributions. These were (1) the Bell-Magendie law, (2) the law of specific nerve energies, and (3) the "science" of phrenology.

The Bell-Magendie law is named after Sir Charles Bell (1774–1842) and François Magendie (1783–1855), who independently discovered the anatomical separation of sensory and motor functions of the spinal cord. Bell, reporting the finding to associates at a dinner party (1811), almost lost recognition to Magendie, who presented his work in the more durable form of a published scientific article (1822). Both demonstrated the ability to render an animal insensitive by compressing or transecting the dorsal member of a spinal nerve. The animal so treated was still able to *move* the surgically anaesthetized part of the body but did not respond to intense stimulation delivered to that region. Similarly, by ventral-root transection it was possible to elicit cries of pain from an animal who, nevertheless, could not withdraw its limb from the pain-producing stimulus. The Bell-Magendi law was important to psychological thinking on several counts. First, it provided clear, anatomical evidence of the sort of arrangement required by the Cartesian theory of sensory-motor functioning. Perhaps most significantly, it reinforced confidence in the experimental approach to the study of sensation and behavior. While the law did not disclose the actual mechanism of reflex-formation, it provided the structural foundation on which reflex mechanisms had to be based. The contribution thus extended a line of inquiry initiated by Descartes, receiving important experimental corroboration from the work of Stephen Hales and Robert Whytt, and theoretically rich amplification by David Hartley. Bain, the most psychological of the nineteenth-century associationists, readily perceived the importance of this law to his plan for a physiological psychology.

Bell himself had anticipated a form of the law of specific nerve energies, but most of the credit for this law is owed to one of the most prominent physiologists of the century, Johannes Müller (1801–1858), whose *Handbüch des Physiologie des Menschen* (1834–1840) was the most authoritative work of the period. The law, which has become a commonplace, asserts that the quality of experience is determined not by the features of the objective stimulus but by the particular nerves responding to it. An orthodox Kantian, Müller judged the law to be only plausible; that is, we do not sense the objective world as it is but come to know about it only in the translated form delivered by the organs of sense. The "thing in itself" remains a mystery. Our knowledge is the *subjectified* knowledge abstracted from the objects of sense and transformed by the organs of sense. Philosophical idealism aside, however, the law of specific nerve energies placed the qualitative and quantitative aspects of experience in the nerves, that is, in *nature*. It contributed a biological feature to epistemology in that the nature of knowledge now was inextricably tied to the characteristics of the "organs of knowledge."

Where the Bell-Magendie law and the law of specific nerve energies were important additions to an emerging physiological psychology, the concept of *localization of function*, as propounded and forged into a movement by Franz Joseph Gall (1758–1828), may be said to have created the discipline. We must quickly add, however, that Gall and his *phrenology* accelerated the appearance of physiological psychology in the sense of presenting notions that only a physiological psychology could successfully refute. Alexander Bain was much taken by phrenology, which reached the English-speaking world through J. G. Spurzheim's *The Physiognomical System of Drs. Gall and Spurzheim,*[27] and the translation of Gall's, *On the Functions of the Brain and Each of Its Parts: With Observations on the Possibility of Determining the Instincts, Propensities, and Talents, or the Moral and Intellectual Dispositions of Men and Animals, by the Configuration of the Brain and Head* (1835).[28] The title is presented here because it very nearly exhausts the theory contained in the work itself. It is in this work that Gall presented the four "incontestable truths" of phrenology:

". . . the brain alone has the great prerogative of being the organ of the mind. . . . The moral and intellectual dispositions are innate; their manifestation depends on organization; the brain is exclusively the organ of the mind; the brain is composed of as many particular and independent organs as there are fundamental powers of the mind."[29]

It is fortunate for the history of the neural sciences that the phrenology of Gall and Spurzheim was quickly challenged by a more sober group of thinkers. Yet for the better part of thirty years it was all the rage. Numerous journals devoted to the "science" sprouted in Europe, England, and the United States. It is only in our own century that the last of these disappeared. A good part of the success of the venture may be traced to Gall's deserved reputation as a neuroanatomist and to the salesmanship of Spurzheim. Moreover, the fundamental idea behind phrenolgy received some support from the neurological clinic, from common sense, and from the materialistic bent of nineteenth-century psychology. Even the caveman must have recognized that the head-end of his prey was uniquely effective in rendering the animal quiescent and, if the same caveman received nonlethal blows to his own skull, this recognition was further established. Greek and Egyptian medicine and its survival through the Renaissance had catalogued a number of functions mediated by the brain. Descartes, more than any previous writer, had popularized the role of the brain in experience and action. Following Descartes and the Gassendists, numberless investigators, here and there, began to disseminate their findings from neurosurgical patients, from clumsy studies of decapitated animals, from observations of the traumatically head-injured victims of war and civil strife. La Mettrie, of course, put the whole matter on the polemical foundation needed by any movement, and several of the more medically minded *philosophes*, trailing in La Mettrie's winding path, carried both the soul and the mind confidently into the brain. D'Holbach and Helvetius were most prominent in this respect.

Unlike La Mettrie, Gall actually had stature as a scientist and, coming almost a century after La Mettrie, had considerably more data with which to make his case. Even more important to the development of his theory than the growing number of experimental findings, however, was the firmly entrenched "faculty psychology" begun by Locke and developed by the later empirical philosophers of England and Scotland. As we discussed in Chapter 7, the idea of "faculties," as old as Aristotle's *De Anima*, received new life in the sentimentalist theories of seventeenth- and eighteenth-century England. By the time of Gall, it was common to accord to man not only the "internal light" (of reason) but also the faculties of empathy, justice, love, morality, etc., etc. Occasionally the list would become very long. Gall accepted these faculties, which is no more than to say that he acknowledged that people possessed such characteristics. Since they did, and since "the brain is exclusively the organ of the mind," it took only a slightly breathless exercise in deduction to conclude that each faculty enjoyed specific representation within the cerebral cortex.

Among those who took phrenology seriously, Bain was not the only scholar of substance. No less a figure than Herbert Spencer (1820–1903) more than toyed with the idea, and recall that Spencer was one of the earliest, most eloquent, and most successful defenders of Darwin's theories. Spencer, like Bain and Mill, was concerned that psychology take its place among the natural sciences and that it extricate itself from the purely speculative discipline of philosophy. Gall, understandably, held out the prospect of just such a liberation. In contending that morality, every bit as much as sensation and movement, was to be understood in terms of the organization and functional physiology of the nervous system, Gall gave psychologists precisely the foundation required for the development of an independent science. In addition, the broad features of phrenology did no violence to Darwinism. The latter, which emphasized instinctual drives, inherited habits, reflex mechanisms of survival, and naturally selected nervous processes, was actually an *ethological* or *comparative phrenology*, when understood a certain way. And, of course, this was the way the followers of Gall and Spurzheim understood it.

The polemical style of Spurzheim and the cultist flavor of this new science of phrenology invited immediate opposition from many quarters. The most telling criticisms were advanced by Pierre Flourens (1794–1867), who actually tested certain phrenological hypotheses experimentally. Flourens performed surgery on animals, including removal of the cerebral hemispheres, and also carefully noted pathologic changes in the brains of recently deceased patients who, prior to death, displayed a variety of neurological symptoms. It was Flourens who insisted that the cerebral mantle functions *as a whole*, that the magnitude of a deficit is not simply reducible to the amount of brain involved, and that similar deficits can result from lesions in any of several brain regions. While Flourens was struggling to defend the vitalistic and dualistic elements of Cartesianism, he was successful, nonetheless, in drawing attention to the purely scientific deficiencies of the phrenological theory.

Gall died before Darwin's great works were written. Spurzheim carried on, defending the master's system till his own death four years later in 1832. Both lived long enough to attract the attention and the admiration of Bain and Spencer and it was they who were able to see the connection between the concept of *localization of function* and evolutionism. Spencer, in his very widely read *Principles of Psychology*, divorced himself from the orthodox phrenology of his own day, but then added this:

> "Nevertheless, it seems to me that most physiologists have not sufficiently recognized the general truth of which Phrenology is an adumbration. Whoever calmly considers the question, cannot long resist the conviction that different parts of the cerebrum must, *in some way or other*, subserve different kinds of mental action. Localization of function is the law of all organization whatever; and it would be marvellous were there here an exception. . . . Any other hypothesis seems to me, on the face of it, untenable."[30]

Spencer, attempting to tie this to the theory of evolution, unfortunately accepted the Lamarckian notion of the inheritance of acquired characteristics and so was forced to argue that the learning, memory, and habits of a species appear in the next generation. Darwin, of course, was given to the same idea. But eliminating this error from the Spencerian system, we are left with a not-so-dated theory of mental function: the sensory fibers project to specific regions of the brain; repeated stimulation *somehow* results in a greater facility of neural transmission; chemically, prior experiences are stored within the cerebral hemispheres; the "subjective psychology" of association is but the other side of the "objective" or neurophysiological psychology within which the associations are physical. Added to this is the Darwinian contribution according to which the complexities of human neuroanatomical organization are to be understood as the evolved forms of a more primitive organization. Thus:

> "The claims of Psychology to rank as a distinct science are . . . not smaller but greater than those of any other science. If its phenomena are contemplated objectively, merely as nervo-muscular adjustments by which the higher organisms from moment to moment adapt their actions to environing co-existences and sequences, its degree of specialty, even then, entitles it to a separate place. The moment the element of feeling, or consciousness, is used to interpret nervo-muscular adjustments as thus exhibited in the living beings around, objective Psychology acquires an additional, and quite exceptional, distinction."[31]

This position was adopted and echoed by Alexander Bain. Never again, from the middle of the eighteenth century until the present day, would an associationistic psychology be devoid of evolutionary notions. Seldom would it be devoid of physiological hypotheses or references. Bain and Spencer, with the resounding support of Darwin's works, did all but found experimental psychology. They fought successfully for the independent status of the science. They presented the associationistic laws in a form never fully appreciated by their predecessors in empirical philosophy, proper. They cemented the new science to the new biology and the two have never been completely divided since. Revealingly, the first chapter of Spencer's *Principles* was titled *The Nervous System*, and this established a policy followed by textbook writers for nearly a century. They failed to found experimental psychology only in that they failed actually to engage in psychological research or to create the facilities with which such research could be conducted. Thus, it is to Wilhelm Wundt (1832–1920), who conducted research and who took the pains to construct and name a laboratory devoted exclusively to psychology, that the honor of "founder" is traditionally given.

Wundt opened psychology's first laboratory at the University at Leipzig in 1879. By that date Darwin's revolution was beginning to be generally appreciated throughout the scientific community. Bell, Magendie, Flourens, Gall, and Spurzheim had all made their varied contributions to the neural sciences. The great Hermann von Helmholtz (1821–1894) had not only written the classic works in the physiology of vision and hearing but had also measured the velocity of the neural impulse and had advanced the most compelling version of the law of the con-servation of energy. The latter two contributions are worth citing in apposition since each, in its own way, challenged the remnants of eighteenth-century vitalism. In discovering that the velocity of nervous conduction was not only measurable but even rather sluggish (maximum = 120 meters/sec), Helmholtz simultaneously put to rest the Cartesian view of the soul's ubiquitous influences on the body and the historic belief that mind is beyond the reach of observation. If the mind in-fluences the body, it does so through the brain, and the conducting path-ways and the brain perform their mission in measurably physical ways. Helmholtz was the most illustrious and independent of Müller's students and the most vocal opponent of the vitalistic elements in Müller's *Hand-buch*. Wundt, after receiving his degree, was Helmholtz's assistant for several years and may be said to have been intimately familiar with the major neurophysiological facts and theories of his time. It is clear that no German scientist of the period escaped the physicalistic (i.e., anti-vitalistic) climate created by Helmholtz, but it is equally clear that Wundt, in the history of psychology, was *sui generis*. Even today, one cannot read his *Principles of Physiological Psychology*[32] without being overwhelmed by his sensitivity to the experimental, philosophical, and biophysical problems uniquely affecting the new science. Of his many works, this one was the most important. It was not only one of the first (and one of the few) of his books to be translated into English but it was the most self-consciously programmatic.

With Bain and Spencer, Wundt saw the need to join the sciences of psychology and physiology. Unlike either Bain or Spencer, Wundt was a scientist—that is, a working scientist—and, as a result, he was far more concerned with the development of proper methods and measures. For these he looked to the recent discoveries of Gustav Fechner (1801–1876), also a Leipzig scientist. Fechner had published the landmark *Elemente der Psychophysik*[33] in 1860, the book that sought to express mathemati-cally the relationship between mental and physical events. It was in this work that Fechner's law was set forth according to which the strength of sensation is proportional to the logarithmic value of the intensity of stimulation. In the same work Fechner had demonstrated how the properly instructed laboratory subject, paced through a series of repeated measurements, would yield reliable data reducible to lawful description. No longer was it necessary to apologize for "introspective" techniques. Comte's critique of psychology seemed to vanish under the weight of Fechner's law. The *psychophysical* methods were simple to apply and were not unlike the methods used in any quantitative science called upon to deal with variable phenomena. Wundt, seldom lavish in his praise, notes only this:

"It is Fechner's service to have found and followed the true way; to have shown us how a 'mathematical psychology' may, within certain limits, be realized in practice. . . . He was the first to show how Herbart's idea of an 'exact psychology' might be turned to practical account."[34]

But for Wundt, neither the rational-mathematical deductive psychology of Herbart* [35] nor the dualism of Fechner could serve as the foundation of psychological science. Indeed, for Wundt, none of the earlier formulations was adequate. Of the British empiricistic psychology, he had this to say:

"In the psychological portion of their works, these writers usually adopt the theory of the 'association of ideas' elaborated in the English psychology of the eighteenth century. They adopt it for the good and sufficient reason that the doctrine of association, from David Hartley 1705–1757) down to Herbert Spencer (1820–1904), has itself for the most part attempted merely a physiological interpretation of the associative process."[36]

Psychology, from Wundt's perspective, must concern itself with the "*manifold of consciousness*" and arrive at an understanding of far more than the laws of association. The manifold of consciousness includes the mind's commerce with more than the objects of sense, with more than external stimuli. It embraces feelings, images, dreams, memories, attention, movement. And the psychology charged with the study of these processes is *experimental psychology*, the name given by Wundt himself. The science is to be the study of "mind" but by *mind*, Wundt is careful to dissociate himself from that long history of metaphysical speculation:

" 'Mind', 'intellect', 'reason', 'understanding', etc., are concepts . . . that existed before the advent of any scientific psychology. The fact that the naive consciousness always and everywhere points to internal

---

* Herbart's scientific psychology provided no room for innate ideas nor for *a priori* concepts. Rather, the elements of unconsciousness, including feelings, are to be understood in terms of the dynamical, mechanical laws of physics and are, therefore, mathematically expressible and deducible. He thus anticipated Fechner's psychophysical science and, in the Preface to the *Elemente*, Fechner acknowledges the debt: "To Herbart will always belong the credit not only of having been the first to point out the possibility of a mathematical treatment . . . but also of having made the first ingenious attempt to carry out such an enterprise; and everyone since Herbart will in this respect have to be second." (Gustav Fechner, *Elements of Psychophysics*, translated by Helmut Adler, edited by Davis H. Howes and Edwin G. Boring, Holt, Rinehart and Winston, New York, 1966. Originally published in 1860.)

experience as a special source of knowledge, may, therefore, be accepted for the moment as sufficient testimony to the rights of psychology as science. . . . 'Mind', will accordingly be the subject, to which we attribute all the separate facts of internal observation as predicates. The subject itself is determined wholly and exclusively by its predicates."[37]

Here, in a conservative and rather woolly fashion, Wundt hands down a manifesto of Humean proportion. By *mind* the psychologist will mean no more than and only that which is directly reportable as an observation of an internal event. If the mind thinks, feels, remembers, attends, and forgets, then a science of mind can be no more than experimental inquiries into the determinants of thinking, feeling, remembering, etc. When its predicates are exhausted, there is no metaphysical residue.

For Wundt, "psychology," "experimental psychology," and "physiological psychology" were three terms for the same subject. He rejected out of hand that form of materialism that insisted that mind was no more than matter or the mentalist assertion that mind was irreducible to matter. He rejected, that is, the grounding of his science in metaphysical disputes. Psychology henceforth was not to be a branch of philosophy, less of biology. It was to be the experimental science devoted to an analysis of the contents of consciousness or, as he put it, the manifold of conscious experience. Ultimately this analysis would converge upon equivalent analyses of the structure-function relationships of the nervous system. Wundt took a disinterested position in the Flourens-Gall controversy, well aware that Gall spoke without having the necessary facts and that Flourens, in opposing phrenology, dismissed more of the localization theory than the facts urged. He reviewed in his *Principles* the recently discovered technique of direct, electrical stimulation of the living animal's cerebral cortex,* the more established techniques of ablative surgery, and the various methods of clinical assay. He recognized early the severe limitations of each of these methods and also foresaw that none of them was a substitute for the introspective data easily secured from a conscious, healthy human being. He had a sophisticated awareness of the fact that the mind-body problem was not to evaporate

---

* Beginning in 1870, Fritsch and Hitzig published the results of their studies of the effects of direct electrical stimulation of the cerebral cortex of dogs. They demonstrated the topographic organization of sensation and movement on the cortical surface and further demonstrated the relatively separate cortical "strips" associated with sensory and motor capacities. Referring to their work, Wundt remarks on the "*simplicity of the structural plan*" [my italics], but the simplicity of 1875 has undergone some changes in the intervening century. (Wilhelm Wundt, *Principles of Physiological Psychology: Vol. I,* translated by E. B. Tichener from the (fifth) German edition of 1902, Macmillan, Inc., New York, 1904, p. 193.)

as a result of improved technology. He had, as well, a nearly modern disdain for the suggestion that it was psychology's responsibility to settle the matter. The topics, methods, and theories that define contemporary psychology have changed considerably since Wundt's time, but the essential attitude of the experimental psychologist today may be said to have originated in the Leipzig laboratory.

The "Idealist" Alternative

The Kantian legacy was briefly touched on earlier in this chapter, but the most important influences were neglected. These were the interpretations of Kantian philosophy by his immediate successors, Fichte (1762), Schelling (1775–1854), and Hegel (1770–1831). Together, they forged a unique form of *idealistic* psychology, which still affects the manner in which Continental psychology proceeds. We neglected this facet of the Kantian legacy in part because Kant himself may not have been eager to claim it and also because the movement was fueled by those empiricistic and materialistic perspectives we have just explored—fueled in the sense that this new idealism was a conscientious antagonist of empirical and physiological psychologies. Predictably, Wundt dismissed the system as no more than a "rational psychology" emerging from Kantian "nature philosophy" and having only negative effects on scientific psychology specifically and on natural science in general.[38]

Kant's role in the appearance of German *Idealism* is central, if miscast. While rejecting the subjective idealism of Berkeley, he described his own metaphysical position as *transcendental idealism* by which he meant to distinguish between the actual physical world of material objects and the sorts of knowledge we can ever have of those objects. The objects, for Kant, were "things in themselves" that could never be known empirically as "things in themselves." Rather, our empirical knowledge constitutes a translation of the real world, a translation performed by the pure categories of the understanding operating in conjunction with imperfect senses. To "know" is to interpret, not merely to sense, but in the very act of interpretation we suffuse objective nature with the categories. The mind that does this is not an "object" and, therefore, can never be known in the sense in which we know the natural world. This leads to the insistence, of course, that a *science* of psychology is scarcely imaginable. Wundt summarized the Kantian position this way:

"Kant once declared that psychology was incapable of ever raising itself to the rank of an exact natural science. The reasons that he gives . . . have often been repeated in later times. In the first place, Kant says, psychology cannot become an exact science because mathematics is inapplicable to the phenomena of the internal sense; the pure internal perception, in which mental phenomena must be constructed,—time, —has but one dimension. In the second place, however, it cannot even become an experimental science, because in it the manifold of internal observation cannot be arbitrarily varied,—still less, another thinking subject be submitted to one's experiments, conformably to the end in view; moreover, the very fact of observation means alteration of the observed object."[39]

We have seen that these objections did not prevent Wundt from committing his life to experimental psychology. Fechner had shown, to Wundt's satisfaction, that mathematics could, indeed, be applied to the phenomena of the "internal sense." Moreover, every branch of natural science must alter its objects in the process of observing them.

If Wundt did not perceive the Kantian objections to be telling, Fichte, Schelling, and Hegel accepted them as axiomatic. For Fichte, again in the Kantian tradition, the very freedom of the human will, in contrast to the deterministic character of purely physical processes, settled once and for all the question of a scientific psychology: there could be none. If there is to be a psychology, it must be a deductive, philosophical discipline that accepts as its subject the will and intentions of the self (*Ego*). The *ego* affirms itself through itself and not through recourse to external objects. In affirming itself, it forces nature to conform to its will and, indeed, may even be said to animate nature through its will. While the will is free, the spiritual ideals of human life impose upon it the constraint of *duty*, the neglect of which is the essence of evil. In these various elements—the self imposing its own character on nature, the transcendental nature of duty, the freedom of the will—Kant's metaphysics appears in the form of a psychology of personality.[40] Schelling's departures from Fichte's philosophical psychology require no mention here. In the significant respects, he and Fichte agreed; freedom of the will in an otherwise determined world of matter entails an inescapable dualism that no scientific psychology can eliminate. If we are to comprehend the nature of mind, our only method is that of the mind reflecting on itself and deducing the terms of its unity. Wundt, while rejecting the prescriptions of these idealists in the matter of method, could not extricate his psychology from their prescriptions regarding topic: the manifold of conscious experience.

The capstone of nineteenth-century German idealism is to be found in the philosophical and logical works of George Friedrich Hegel, whose influence on European thought is equaled, if at all, only by Descartes and Kant. Even if our present subject were the history of philosophy, it would hardly be possible to summarize "Hegelianism" in less than a very substantial chapter. Indeed, unless one is a professional philosopher, it is hazardous to attempt a summary of any sort. As with most productive scholars, Hegel underwent a change of mind from time to time. His writing suffers from the fatal combination of genius and literary awkwardness. The subjects of greatest interest to him—the Absolute, the Ineffable, Soul, Art, and Religion—tend to frustrate authors of the greatest literary skill, and Hegel is not one of these. Perhaps the clearest exposition of his system in the English language is the old but not dated study provided by Prof. W. T. Stace,[41] but even this work is so punctuated with Hegelian locutions as to leave the uninitiated . . . uninitiated. Russell surely has many advocates of his contention that Hegel is "the hardest to understand of all the great philosophers,"[42] and this from a man who believes that "almost all of Hegel's doctrines are false."[43] Be that as it may, Hegel invented *phenomenology*, was acclaimed by some otherwise moderate Englishmen as the new Aristotle, and caused Karl Marx to describe himself as "the pupil of that mighty thinker."* Hegel is not to be ignored.

Hegelian "doctrines," as Russell called them, are all derived from rational first principles. Completely rejecting Kant's *caveat* about the subjective nature of reason, Hegel declares that the truths of reason are necessary, nonarbitrary, and final. Through reason, the mind can dissect the apparent world such as to lay bare *its* reason. At this point, we must insert the distinction, the Hegelian distinction, between *reason* and *cause*. Hegel, while totally opposed to the thrust of empirical philosophy, readily appreciated Hume's arguments against *necessary* causal sequences. He agreed that no logical bridge could ever be constructed whereby one could proceed from an effect back to physical causes of a necessary nature. However, while *causes* do not logically entail effects, *reasons* do. Prof. Stace explains the emphasis this way:

> ". . . explanation involves the idea of logical necessity. It is just the apparent absence of necessity in the world which makes us complain that it is incomprehensible. Cold produces ice. This is a fact which simply *is*. We cannot see why it *must* be. . . . If, instead of being a mere fact, we could see that it is logical necessity; if we could see the *reason* of it, and that it follows from the reason as necessarily as a logical consequent from its antecedent, then we should understand it. . . . Thus, a philosophy which would genuinely explain the world will take as its first principle, not a cause but a reason. . . . This is the

* This remark appears in Karl Marx's Preface to the second edition of *Capital*. Marx moved away from orthodox Hegelianism in later years, but for a time he was as much a product of the Hegelian view of history and philosophy as anyone in the history of the movement.

fundamental Hegelian idea of explanation . . . it was for this that the Greeks, especially Aristotle, were groping, when they said that the first principle of the world is not prior to the world in time, i.e., as a cause is prior to its effect, but is *logically* prior to the world, i.e., as a logical antecedent is prior to its consequent."[44]

Reason, then, is the first principle and it explains itself. It determines itself and the world in that, unlike causal sequences, the sequence from reason to statements about the world is directed by logical necessity. To say that John Smith is dead "because a trigger was pulled" is not to explain *why* he is dead—only to note one of the antecedent causes of his demise. We explain *why* Smith is dead when we say that "Jones wanted him dead and it was Jones who pulled the trigger." The reason is prior to the cause. Where the effect is only contingently related to the cause, it is necessarily related to the reason. Harkening back to Kant's *Categories*, we can say that the characteristic of temporal succession is *logically* tied to the *a priori* concept of time.

Hegel's theory of psychology is presented most clearly in his *Encyclopaedia*[45] and his *Phenomenology of Mind*.[46] There has been something of a contest among historians to come up with as many people as possible who may be said to have anticipated the theories of Sigmund Freud. We do not seek this elusive prize in recognizing Hegel's part in the development of Freud's thinking. Hegel's philosophy of mind is rife with the concepts of stages of development, ego and antiego conflicts, intimations of a death wish. One could not be educated in the Austria of the 1860s and 1870s and not be influenced by the thoughts of Hegel.

The Hegelian philosophy of mind begins with the theory that the mind is a stage in the evolution of soul. Initially (and Platonically) the soul shares the realities of nature; as Stace describes this "natural soul," it is *the beginning of spirit*[47] and exists as mere being. It cannot reflect upon itself nor can it assimilate to itself the objective elements of the physical world. From this state of pure egoism, the soul, presumably through maturation, gains *sensibility* by which it is able to distinguish between itself and its contents. While the soul still cannot comprehend *external* objects, it has nonetheless an awareness of the difference between the feelings within it and itself. The "natural soul" is now the "feeling soul." This stage is followed by one in which the soul actually can receive external objects, can distinguish itself from the perceptual contents resulting from sensory experience, and can catalogue the elements of the physical world according to universal categories. The soul, now the "actual soul," recognizes itself *as its contents;* it is at one with its sensations, ideas, and feelings. Once the soul has expressed the ability to distinguish between itself and the objects of the external world, it may be said to have *consciousness* and to be *mind*. It is the study of this consciousness—as Wundt would later call it, the manifold of consciousness—that is *phenomenology*. Consciousness too passes through stages: *sensuous consciousness, sense perception,* and *intellect.* The first of these stages allows the mind to receive the "raw data" of experience, impressions devoid of cognitive features. The sensation is of an *event*—immediate and psychologically neutral. Perception, however, is another matter. Here, the observer adds to or brings to bear upon the merely sensuous the concept of the universal. Where the sensuous produces a "this" or a "that," the sense perception is of the form "What is *this?*":

> "Whatever we say in answer to this question invests the 'this' with a universal character. . . . To say that it is 'here' or 'now' is at once to apply concepts, or universals, to it; for 'here' and 'now' are both universals. . . . Everything belongs to the class of objects which are called 'this'. Hence, 'this' is a *class*-name and imports a universal."[48]

Sense perception, in applying the universal concept to each particular, establishes a contradiction—the contradiction between a particular object and a *class.* Perception, alone, cannot resolve the contradiction. This is the task of the intellect which, through its inventions of scientific laws and principles, recognizes the ultimate reality to be universals and particular objects to be mere appearances or instances. Once this developed form of consciousness has succeeded in abstracting the universal principle from each of the particular sense perceptions, it recognizes that its knowledge is *idea,* for universals are, by their nature, ideas. At this point, consciousness is led to self-consciousness or the awareness of the idea of self.*

It is hardly necessary to remind the modern reader of the "Hegelian" tone of much contemporary discourse not only within the community of professional psychologists but within the relatively nontechnical spheres of daily life. "Self-awareness," "self-actualization," "consciousness-raising," and related expressions of self-concern are directly attributable to Hegel and the neo-Hegelian idealists. The dialectical triad of *thesis, antithesis,* and *synthesis,* which Hegel advanced as laws of thought ex-

---

* The contemporary system of psychology bearing the closest resemblance to Hegelianism is, of course, the cognitive psychology of Prof. Jean Piaget. The Piagetian stages of cognitive development begin with *egocentrism* and culminate with the ability to identify the connection between particular instances and universal propositions. Indeed, the six-stage evolution of cognition described by Piaget fits neatly into the Hegelian three stages of sensuous consciousness, sense-perception, and intellect. Piaget's psychology, often defined as an *evolutionary epistemology,* has strived to document by experimental demonstration that logical structure of thought which Hegel deduced. It is not surprising, then, that contemporary challenges directed against Piagetian psychology are of a form almost indistinguishable from the British empiricists' attacks on Hegelianism.

pressed in logic, has now become a permanent fixture in the lexicon of undergraduate students and news commentators alike. In a subtler way, the triad found its way into Freudian theory: the *Id* asserting that most fundamental of all theses; the *Superego* standing in antithetical regard to it; the *Ego* emerging, synthetically, from the reconciliation of these counterpoised forces. Hegelianism, in its triumphant form, emerged in the middle years of the nineteenth century as Romanticism. In his *Reason in History*, he proclaimed that *nothing great in the world has been accomplished without passion*[49] and argued that the essential nature of man —not one at a time but as a collective of consciousnesses—is freedom, the irrepressible freedom of spirit. Renewing the ageless dichotomy, he dismissed matter as the passive victim of natural laws and asserted spirit as the only free force in the universe. He and Beethoven were born in the same year. One set Goethe to music, the other to philosophy. In all, we find the romantic expression of Condorcet's idea of progress. Escalated to the level of social action, we find a revolutionary spirit that has hardly begun to exhaust itself.

Karl Marx (1818–1883)

The historian of ideas is sorely tempted to discuss the roots of Marxist philosophy in a way that tends to trivialize the content of the philosophy. The temptation does not betoken or at least need not betoken enmity toward the philosophy or its author. Rather, from a purely philosophical perspective, so much of Marx's thought is derivative that a mere enumeration of Marxist principles obscures the brilliant originality of his work taken as a whole.

Offsetting this tendency toward underestimation is an error in the opposite direction. Marx has proved to be such a powerful figure in the social and political affairs of our own century that it becomes tempting to read too much depth and genius into the exclusively philosophical aspects of his writings.

For our present purposes, we seek to do no violence to the stature of the man in social and political history by observing the very marginal influence of his speculations on the evolution of modern psychology. Marx did not have a great effect either on contemporaries who figured centrally in psychology or on later psychologists who, in fact, shared his materialistic orientation. It is true that in the highly politicized decades of Soviet science there would be eager attempts to establish the connection between Marxist theory and Pavlovian psychology but these attempts seldom rose higher than the level of mere propaganda and were never taken seriously by scientists of enduring consequence.

Marx's failure to influence the course of psychological scholarship can be understood in a variety of ways. The nineteenth-century developments in psychology were of a largely experimental nature. Marx's approach was historiographical and, in the loose sense, logical and this was the very approach that the founders of experimental psychology were rejecting. Moreover, while Marx accorded "consciousness" a central role in his theory, it was a role that, on first inspection, was indistinguishable from Hegelianism and therefore not likely to be serviceable. But even more than these dissonances was the unbreachable separation between psychology's commitment to the study of the individual and Marx's undivided attention to broad social processes. In short, Marx was a sociologist at a time when psychology was being founded along biological lines. He discovered the psychology of alienation a century before social psychology would be prepared to study it. The same may be said of his recognition of those problems we now locate in such fields as "urban psychology," "industrial relations," and "community psychology." He saw the effects of industrialization on the family, on the worker, on the relations among states. In these effects he perceived economic forces as the engine of all social and cultural and intellectual evolution.

We have noted Marx's acknowledged debt to Hegel. It is also noteworthy that his doctoral dissertation analyzed the systems of Democritus and Epicurus, a dissertation that could only have steeped him in the *Enlightenment* scholarship of Diderot and Condorcet. Indeed, in *The German Ideology* (1845–46), where he discusses the successive stages of economic evolution in terms of tribal, state, feudal, and private ownership, we find almost a paraphrasing of Condorcet's *Sketch*. But unlike Condorcet or, for that matter, Epicurus, Marx was unwilling to place rational forces at the core of such evolution. For Marx, the materialism of consequence was *historic* materialism. He had no doubts but that man is so constituted biologically as to require and conform to historic materialism but Marx was not to digress into anatomical or physiological reflections about *Man* while a world of *men* were suffering under the yolk of industrialism. Nevertheless, he was aware of the direct connection between the psychological materialism of the *Enlightenment* and the philosophical justifications of communism. This awareness is almost glibly rendered in *The Holy Family*:

"As *Cartesian* materialism merges into *natural science proper*, the other branch of French materialism leads direct to *socialism* and *communism*. There is no need of any great penetration to see from the teaching of materialism on the original goodness and equal intellectual endowment of men, the omnipotence of experience, habit and education, and the influence of environment on man, the great significance of industry, the justification of enjoyment, etc., how necessarily materialism is connected with communism and socialism." (1845)

It is in the same work that Marx carries the analysis to its logical terminus. Since man is formed completely by his environment, by the social forces imposed upon him throughout his development, he cannot reasonably be held responsible for his crimes. These are the result of social evils and it is society that is to blame.

Perhaps it is too trite to observe that a fair fraction of the common-sense psychologies of history can be partitioned in terms of attention to similarities among men vs. attention to differences. With a broad brush, we can color with the same hues egalitarianism, behaviorism, Marxism, socialism; with another hue, elitism, idealism, capitalism. Marx, like the empiricists he so admired, was persuaded that the similarities among men were far greater than their diverse stations would suggest. Noting how the steam engine alone had transformed the very character of the English nation, he was convinced that economic systems of production had imposed artificial class-differences upon the human community and that these differences must be eradicated. In retrospect, we tend to dismiss much of this as a kind of "folk" psychology, realizing that individual differences among people are not trivial and judging also that the psychological character of our race appears to survive a remarkable range of social and economic systems. Although we have hardly exhausted the set of important cross-cultural studies of cognitive and perceptual processes, there would seem to be enough data now to cast doubt upon such cornerstones of Marxist psychology as, "The nature of individuals thus depends on the material conditions determining their production" (*The German Ideology*). But the issue here is not whether Marx was "right" or "wrong" any more than it is whether his century was "right" or "wrong." Instead, we are to discover in Marx*ism* that peculiar and fascinating theme uniting all the *isms* of the nineteenth century: positivism, materialism, utilitarianism, Hegelianism, pragmatism, experimentalism. And what unites these otherwise immiscible movements is the confident belief that the world or the human enterprise or the heavens or everything can finally be encompassed by a grand vision validated by a faultless method. Scholarship, neither before nor since, is displayed with such certainty and finality. In the major works of physics, political theory, psychology, biology, sociology, and even moral philosophy we discover an intellectual stridency and sureness that only amazes the twentieth century witness. In yet another way, this legacy of confidence also frustrates the modern citizen who is unable to locate the year when things started to go wrong; the time when certain physics became uncertain, when the knowable mind sunk once more to its historically unreachable depths, when the ping-pong rhythm of social organization gave way to cacophony.

There is yet another element in Marxist writing that warrants comment although it, too, has no direct bearing on the evolution of modern psychology, proper. The element is that of enmity and contempt, an element last present during the late-Renaissance and Reformation. The wit and charm of the *Enlightenment* are absent. The canons of civility are ignored. Logic and compassion lose their struggle with impatience.

Little is served by attempts to analyze the "psychology" of intellectual leaders. Their importance derives from the ideas they set forth, not from their motives or their personal idiosyncracies. However, it is not unremarkable that we find in Marx's works a temperament—even a hatefulness—that a Spencer or Bain or Mill never displayed. And it will not do to propose that British philosophers, uniformly, were of even disposition. Instead, what is at work in Marx's delivery is the passionate romanticism of Hegel; the Continental acceptance of emotion as a proper corollary of analysis. With the exception of La Mettrie and a few of the lesser lights of the *Enlightenment*, French scholarship avoided this almost completely. In England, the editors would perform the necessary surgery long before the work reached the typesetter.

In observing this feature of Marxist writing, we call attention to more than style. We call attention to the essential conservatism of nineteenth-century scholarship in Britain and France and the *radicalism* of Marx and his followers. Now, it could only be a cliché to let the matter rest here. *Of course*, Marx and his disciples were radicals, but the *utilitarians* were also radicals in their ambitions. The difference is a subtler one. Marx and his sympathizers, unlike their English contemporaries and unlike most of the leading intellectuals since the seventeenth century, were speaking directly to the people. They were applying the ideas and the recognized forms of philosophical discourse for ends that were clearly political. In their success, they introduced to scholarship a relevance that would have made even the *philosophes* uncomfortable. They brought into the debate those elements of society that the proper Victorian scholar had neutrally described as the "vulgar." Not depending on the mere force of rational discourse, the Marxists added the insurance of popular support. Philosophical adversaries now could not content themselves with reasoned rebuttals but would have to reckon with the collective wisdom of converted ideologues who, as the expression goes, knew which side their bread was buttered on. It would be unfair to hold Marx or Marxism responsible for the anti-intellectualism with which pragmatism is so bloated. But that self-defeating form of anti-intellectualism now commonly displayed by intellectuals themselves has its recent origins in Marxism. At its worst, it is intellectual thuggery. In its benign form, it is the captious skepticism of the Patristics, the fear that too much reason can weaken the faith.

The Freudian Synthesis[50]

We present Freud in a chapter dealing with psychology in the nineteenth century not merely because he was born in that century and not even because his first theoretical paper on hysteria appeared in the nineteenth century. We present Freud here because the entire complexion of his psychology is colored by the themes and disputes of intellectual and scientific discourse in the nineteenth century. This fact, however, has nothing to do with the peripheral fact, and one that is repeated with wearying regularity, that Freud "grew up," as they say, in something called "Victorian Vienna." In order to make the proper distinction between a description of the Freudian synthesis as a peculiarly nineteenth-century synthesis and that quasi-sociological "explanation" of Freud, we must refer back to the discussion of science presented in the first chapter.

While Prof. Kuhn's thesis might aptly be called a thesis regarding the "sociology of knowledge," we are not to saddle him with the liabilities and burdens courted by the "psychohistorian." To understand any phenomenon we must be able to step back from it; why else historical inquiry at all? And in stepping back from an essentially intellectual phenomenon, we must be careful not to confuse what *we* would have thought were we there but what we would have thought were we *there*. The difference between accentuating the subject and accentuating the adverb is one of the differences between fiction and history. Thus, to speak of the "sexually repressed" character of Victorian life is to impute to the era a feature it could only convey to those already under the influence of that very psychological system whose determinants we seek to discern. The silliness of "Freudian" interpretations of the origins of Freudian psychology is rooted in the fact that such interpretations require Freud to have been a Freudian prior to his being a Freudian!

What, in fact, he was prior to his major theoretical contributions to psychology was the product of that marvelously contradictory climate of German thought in which science was defined in the positivistic, deterministic, and physicalistic language of Helmholtz and in which philosophy was Hegelian. Let us review the prevailing forces. Freud was born in 1856. He completed his doctorate (in neurology) in 1881. Wundt's laboratory had already been in existence and in highly productive existence for two years. Helmholtz, now sixty years old, was the senior statesman of German science. Evolutionary theory, which most of the leading antivitalist biologists adopted as fact, had already been in print for more than twenty years. Darwin, himself, was dead only six years. His most ardent and able disciples, Thomas Huxley (1825–1894) and Herbert Spencer, were both alive, and Spencer especially was promoting the psychology of "instincts." If we wonder how much of the new science was part of young Freud's education, we need only recall that his mentor in neurophysiology and neurology was Prof. Ernst Brücke, himself a student of Müller's and one of Helmholtz's closest associates.

Philosophically the climate was overwhelmingly conditioned by Hegelianism. Psychology and phenomenology were two terms expressing the same subject: the subject of *consciousness*. The driving force in the universe was the free mind, a mind that had evolved from more primitive, nonreflecting, irrational substrates. Even Wundt, far from an Hegelian, had at least agreed that the subject matter of psychology was exhausted by the contents of consciousness. Wundt and Hegel also agreed on the central position of *feeling* in psychological life. If it is agreed that Freud had one of the great synthesizing minds of all time, we now have the list of major perspectives available for synthesis. We are in a position to review the synthesis that resulted.

His energies as a senior graduate student were devoted chiefly to neurophysiological research under Brücke's direction. We know he hoped for a professorial chair at the University of Vienna and that, as a Jew, his chances were negligible. The demands of marriage and family forced him into private practice in neurology, although, from the first, he never interrupted his research endeavors. Interestingly he is cited in Wundt's *Principles* for a published article on aphasia that appeared in 1891.[51] A number of his patients suffered from *hysteria* which, at the time, was the diagnostic category invented to account for sensory and motor deficits occurring in the absence of detectable neuropathology. The French pathologist Jean Charcot (1825–1893) had revived and given respectability to the practice of hypnosis and was employing it in the treatment of certain hysterical cases as well as for anaesthetic purposes. Freud attended Charcot's lectures (1885–1886) at the University of Paris. He returned to Vienna, eager to apply the new technique, which had already caught the attention of Joseph Breuer, another of Brücke's former pupils. Freud would later write:

> "Granted that it is a merit to have created psychoanalysis, it is not my merit. I was a student, busy with the passing of my last examinations, when another physician of Vienna, Dr. Joseph Breuer, made the first application of . . . [hypnosis] . . . to the case of an hysterical girl (1880–1882)."[52]

It was Breuer too who discovered, as one of his patients called it, the "talking cure" that later would receive the more impressive if less direct label, *catharsis*. While their medical relationship was not to last (though their friendship did), Freud and Breuer introduced the bare outlines of psychoanalytic theory in a series of jointly published papers beginning in 1895 and summarized in their *Studien über Hysterie*. Prof E. G. Boring gives a brief but searching insight into the theoretical bond between the two, Breuer being fourteen years the senior:

> "Breuer held that a certain amount of the organism's energy goes into intracerebral excitation and that there is a tendency in the organism to hold this excitation at a constant level. Psychic activity increases the excitation, discharging the energy. . . . What Breuer and Freud had from it, however, was the conception of psychic events' depending upon energy which is provided by the organism and which requires discharge when the level is too high. Because Brücke had trained them into being uncompromising physicalists, they slipped easily over from the brain to the mind."[53]

Under hypnosis, the patient's hysterical symptoms could be transferred from one part of his body to another. The hysterically paralyzed hand could be made to move, but with the consequence of immobilizing the intentional use of the leg. Sight could be restored, but with deafness following in its wake. Since the patient showed no understanding of the causes of his problem and since hypnotic induction could relieve the symptoms, Freud and Breuer concluded that the mechanism of symptom-formation was *unconscious*. Contrary to two widely held views, the symptoms were not feigned in an attempt to receive pity, nor were they limited to women. (*Hysteria*, itself, derives from the Greek for *uterus*.)

The unpopularity of Freud's notions, differences of opinion between him and Breuer, Breuer's desire to quit science for practice, all worked to drive the two apart. By 1900 their relationship was almost exclusively social. It was in 1900 that Freud's *Interpretation of Dreams* was published. In the following year, *The Psychopathology of Everyday Life* appeared. Thus, as the twentieth century began, he had a following. By 1920 there was a movement. By 1930 he was, and has since remained, the preeminent figure in modern theoretical psychology.

Central to Freud's system is the concept of *unconscious motivation*. Herbart and Fechner had both speculated about unconscious processes, and the idea is, of course, an abiding one in literature. But Freud's use of the concept was the first to be scientific. That is, in the sense in which the term was introduced in the first chapter, a *scientific explanation* was generated by Freud's treatment of the idea. It became a "covering law" from which one could deduce certain consequences. His recourse to the concept was based on the need to discover a force or agency by which behavior might be controlled independently of the patient's will. When

Breuer's patient was relieved by the cathartic method, it was clear to Freud that the power of particular memories to control behavior was reduced once the actual memories were revived. Accordingly (and here the metaphor of the *machine* becomes reality), he reasoned that painful thoughts are *repressed*, that they come to reside in the unconscious, and that the symptoms are the work done by the repressed elements—that is, psychic energy is conserved through symptom-formation. Only through a conscious reliving of the former trauma, an exhumation of it from the unconscious recesses, can the symptoms finally be removed. Short of this, they can only be moved about the body, disguised, accepted. Freud's own words could not be more descriptive:

> "*Hysterical patients suffer from reminiscences.* Their symptoms are the remnants and the memory symbols of certain (traumatic) experiences."[54]

Freud's quick renunciation of hypnosis is to be understood not only in terms of his Helmholtzian bias—he described hypnosis as "fanciful" and "mystical"—but also as the result of his inability to bring a number of patients "under." He abandoned it completely in favor of the cathartic method and its complement, *free association*. Reasoning that neurotic symptoms are the result of incomplete or unsuccessful repression, Freud sought to discover the traumatic episode in the patient's life by a sort of subterfuge. This involved an analysis of so-called slips-of-the-tongue (*parapraxes*), automatic or free associations, and, most salient of all, dreams.

For Freud the determinist, there was no more reason to consider dreams and parapraxes as uncaused than there is to consider normal speech or wakefulness uncaused. Thus, the "Freudian slip," no less than the disguised plots and fantasies of the dream world, under the penetrating lights of psychoanalysis, can be shown to have a direct bearing on the remnants of childhood traumas. These result from the very evolutionary progression that the human psyche undergoes on its way to an adult stage. Utterly consonant with Darwinism, Freudian theory rests on the notion of instinctual biological drives that impel the individual to act in such a way as to survive. The principle governing or defining all these drives is that of *pleasure*. The exercise of this principle is sexual gratification which, in its most advanced expression, involves heterosexual relations for the express purpose of procreation. However, the individual arrives at this level only after successfully passing through more primitive stages of gratification at any one of which he might be arrested by trauma. The stages are identified in terms of the particular source of pleasure: oral, anal, genital, phallic. The sexual "energy" devoted to this endless search for pleasure is the *libido*, which operates in the service of that most primitive and survivalistic element of psychological beings, the *Id*. Since the instincts of the Id are such as to lead to incestuous, murderous, and purely egoistic actions, no human society could survive its unrestrained expression. Every society, then, must "socialize" its young; develop in them a conscience, or *Superego*, which will direct the individual not away from gratification but toward socially acceptable means of gratification. The compromise between the impulses of the Id and the constraints of the Superego results in the self of whom we are aware, the *Ego*.

On the way to mature sexual motivation, this being the motive to procreate through heterosexual encounters, the child must select appropriate objects. The male child's natural proclivity is for his mother, who has been abidingly associated with gratification. However, to court one's mother is, simultaneously, to court a showdown with one's father, the effect of which is or may be castration. An Oedipal complex results in which the boy can only succeed in removing the threat of castration by becoming his father's equal, or by shifting his quest to another object. Pathological conditions result from the failure to resolve the tensions implicit in the Oedipal stage.

Even from this mere sketch of the Freudian theory of personality, we are able to appreciate the synthetic features of the system. The human personality *evolves*. Its origins are animalistic, survivalistic. Bentham's *pleasure principle* has been raised to the level of a medical or neurological reality. The engine of psychological growth is energy, which behaves according to the same sorts of laws prevailing in the physical world. As with physical energy, psychic energy is conserved, directed, partitioned, but never destroyed. As with Fichte and Schelling, Freud saw the world as a set of polarities, with the forces at one pole opposing those at the other, an Id struggling for supremacy over a Superego, a "life force" (*eros*) in heedless conflict with a "death wish" (*thanatos*), natural instincts driving the organism toward the next stage in the face of societal taboos and rites that might otherwise frustrate instinctual expression— and with all of this, Freud constantly asserting that the ultimate topic of psychological concern is consciousness in that daringly Hegelian sense: the knowing, feeling, mind in search of an Absolute that might bring it peace and harmony.

The Nineteenth Century's Invention

It was Alfred North Whitehead who credited the nineteenth century with having "invented the method of invention." It was the first period in history in which very nearly every important philosophical figure recognized the essential function of experimentation in the search for truth. It was also the first century in which the majority, the vast majority, of serious works in science were completely devoid of theological colorations.

The record of the century is particularly commendable in regard to psychology. When we examine the topics now filling the literature in professional psychology, we are hard pressed to find one that was not put forth—often in a form still to be improved upon—by those whose efforts we have examined in this chapter. Physiological psychology, little more than the product of polemicism in the eighteenth century, became a science in the hands of Flourens, Gall, Bell, Magendie, Helmholtz, and Wundt. Comparative psychology was invented by Spencer and Darwin. The psychology of individual differences is the creation of Francis Galton, as are several of the statistical procedures needed for such studies. Cognitive and *Gestalt* psychologies are so intimately tied to phenomenology that only a purist could deny Hegel and the neo-Hegelians the title of *founders*. Freud and the unconscious are near-synonyms. Our sense of what an experimental science is and ought to be is taken over, with only the slightest modifications, from J. S. Mill, and the general attitude toward the status of science remains largely the one advocated by Auguste Comte and his positivist disciples. Our fascination with hedonistic ethics, with the possibility of shaping the world through the processes of reward and punishment, is linearly traceable to Jeremy Bentham and the Utilitarian movement. Even our vaunted "humanistic" psychologies, with their focus on "self-actualization," personal growth, and individual freedom, have never improved upon the original formulations by the German Romantics. There will be more than one irritated reader, but at least one author will stand behind the claim that contemporary psychology is a footnote to the nineteenth century.

References

1. Voltaire, *Philosophical Letters*, translated by Ernest Dilworth, Bobbs-Merrill, Indianapolis, 1961.

2. Claude-Adrien Helvetius, *A Treatise on Man; His Intellectual Faculties and His Education*, translated by William Hooper, London, 1777.

3. Denis Diderot, *D'Alembert's Dream*. In *Diderot's Selected Writings*, edited by Lester G. Crocker and translated by Derek Coltman, Macmillan, Inc., New York, 1966, pp. 179–222.

4. Antoine-Nicolas De Condorcet, *Sketch for a Historical Picture of the Progress of the Human Mind*, translated by June Barraclough, with an introduction by Stuart Hampshire, Noonday Press, New York, 1955. (First published in 1795 in French.)

5. Voltaire, *On the Pensées of M. Pascal*. In *Philosophical Letters*, op. cit., p. 144.

6. J. S. Mill, *Autobiography*. The edited volume by F. E. Mineka (Toronto, 1963) is especially useful.

7. J. S. Mill, *A System of Logic, Ratiocinative and Inductive: Being a Connected View of the Principles of Evidence and the Methods of Scientific Investigation*, Longmans, Green, London, 1900.

8. Ibid., Book VI, Ch. III, Sec. 1.

9. Ibid., Sec. 2.

10. Ibid., Ch. IV, Sec. 3.

11. Ibid.

12. Ibid., Sec. 4.

13. Ibid., Ch. 5.

14. Ibid., Ch. V, Sec. 4.

15. J. S. Mill, *Utilitarianism.* In *The Utilitarians*, Dolphin Books, Doubleday, Garden City, N.Y., 1961, p. 404.

16. Ibid.

17. Ibid., pp. 408–409.

18. Ibid., pp. 432–433.

19. L. Levy-Bruhl, *The Philosophy of Auguste Comte,* translated by Frederic Harrison and published in English by Swan Sonnenschein, London, 1903. This was a most important edition, bringing the ideas of Comte to the English-speaking world. In America, in the 1850s, Henry Edger did much to advance the cause of positivism, but it was not really until Levy-Bruhl's careful study of the positivist program that a large number of philosophers in England and America seriously approached the system. On the earliest American forms, see *Positivism in the United States—1853–1861*, by Richmond Laurin Hawkins, Harvard University Press, Cambridge, Mass., 1938.

20. Levy-Bruhl, op. cit., pp. 191–193.

21. Antoine-Nicolas De Condorcet, *Sketch*, op cit.

22. Thomas Malthus, *An Essay on the Principle of Population as It Affects the Future Improvement of Society, with Remarks on the Speculations of Mr. Godwin, M. Condorcet, and Other Writers.* The essay has been reproduced in a paperback edition by the University of Michigan Press, Ann Arbor, 1959, with an introduction by Kenneth Boulding. The original appeared in 1798, in London.

23. Charles Darwin, *The Expression of the Emotions in Man and Animals*, Appleton-Century-Crofts, New York, 1896.

24. Francis Galton, *Hereditary Genius*, Macmillan, London, 1869.

25. The letter by Alexander Bain appears in R. M. Young's recent and excellent study, *Mind, Brain, and Adaptation in the Nineteenth Century*, Oxford University Press, Clarendon, 1970, pp. 102–103.

26. As Prof. Young notes, Bain's *The Senses and Intellect* (1855) and *The Emotions and the Will* (1859) comprised the two-volume set that served as the standard British psychology for nearly fifty years. Both were published in London by the Parker Publishing Co.

27. Johann G. Spurzheim, *The Physiognomical System of Drs. Gall and Spurzheim*, Baldwin, Cradock, & Joy, London, 1815.

28. François Joseph Gall, *On the Functions of the Brain and of Each of Its Parts*, etc., translated by Winslow Lewis. Six volumes, published in America by Marsh, Capen, and Lyon, Boston, 1835.

29. Gall, op cit.

30. Herbert Spencer, *The Principles of Psychology*, Appleton-Century-Crofts, New York, 1896, p. 573.

31. Ibid., p. 141.

32. Wilhelm Wundt, *Principles of Physiological Psychology: Vol. I*, translated by E. B. Titchener from the (fifth) German edition of 1902, Macmillan, Inc., New York, 1904.

33. Gustav Fechner, *Elements of Psychophysics*, translated by Helmut Adler, edited by Davis H. Howes and Edwin G. Boring, Holt, Rinehart and Winston, New York, 1966. (Originally published in 1860.)

34. Wundt, op. cit. pp. 6–7.

35. Johann Friedrich Herbart (1776–1841) was a student of Fichte's. He held the chair once occupied by Kant at Königsberg. Unlike Fichte, he envisaged a scientific psychology based on mathematical analyses, a view he advanced in his *Psychologie als Wissenschaft* (1824–1825).

36. Wundt, op. cit., pp. 9–10.

37. Ibid., p. 17.

38. Wundt, op. cit., pp. 8–9.

39. Ibid., p. 6.

40. To appreciate, in an historical way, the approach of Fichte, it is useful to consult expositions of his works written at the time he began to enjoy wide attention outside Germany. Particularly penetrating, in this respect, is C. C. Everett's *Fichte's Science of Knowledge*, S. C. Griggs and Company, Chicago, 1892. In the same regard, consult E. B. Talbot's *The Fundamental Principles of Fichte's Philosophy*, New York, 1906.

41. W. T. Stace, *The Philosophy of Hegel: A Systematic Exposition*. Originally published by Macmillan, Inc. 1924, this authoritative analysis of Hegel's *Encyclopaedia* and his *Phenomenology of Mind* is now available, softbound, from Dover Publications, New York, 1955.

42. Bertrand Russell, *A History of Western Philosophy*, Simon & Schuster, Clarion paperback edition, p. 730.

43. Ibid.

44. Stace, op. cit., Sec. 75.

45. English editions of Hegel's *Encyclopaedie* are available. The William Wallace translation (Oxford University Press, 1873) is available in later editions.

46. The authoritative translation of *Phenomenology of Mind* remains that by J. B. Baillie, London, 1910; 1931.

47. Stace, op. cit., p. 328.

48. Ibid., p. 343.

49. G. W. F. Hegel, *Reason in History: A General Introduction to the Philosophy of History*, translated by Robert S. Hartman. Bobbs-Merrill, Indianapolis, 1953, p. 29.

50. Some sentences in this brief review of Freud's theory have been borrowed from my *Psychology: A Study of Its Origins and Principles*, Dickenson Publishing Co., Encino, Calif., 1972.

51. Wundt, op. cit., p. 308. Here, in a footnote, Wundt refers to Freud's *Zur Auffassung der Aphasien* (1891).

52. S. Freud, *The Origins and Development of Psychoanalysis*, American Journal of Psychology, *21*, 1910.

53. E. G. Boring, *A History of Experimental Psychology*, Appleton-Century-Crofts, New York, 1951 edition, p. 709.

54. Freud, op. cit.

11

□□□□□□□□□□□□□□□□□□□□□□□□□□□□□□

Contemporary
Formulations

Method as Metaphysic

To describe contemporary psychology with the abrasive term "footnote" is to tilt with the error of *scholastica successionis civitatium*, which we pledged to avoid in the very first chapter. There is virtually no respect in which the contemporary psychologist diffidently searches the annals of nineteenth-century scholarship in order to discover the problems or methods appropriate to psychology. The most casual inspection of the courses and the texts in psychology, at both the undergraduate and the professional levels, will prove beyond doubt, if not beyond concern, that very little of the debt to the nineteenth century is consciously acknowledged. The aspiring psychologist might be expected to know something about "Mill's methods" and that Wundt founded the first laboratory devoted exclusively to psychological research. It is also the expectation of a faculty that its students will be conversant with the general features of Darwinian biology and the sensory-physiological theories of Helmholtz. But no one is asked any longer to pour over the works of Bain and Spencer, Fichte or Schelling, Kant or Hegel. Even William James is presented as a museum piece, and E. L. Thorndike as the author of a law and the prophet of a method that have both changed so much as to stun even Thorndike. No introductory course in psychology and certainly no concentration or "major" in psychological studies is considered complete or even respectable unless the great old names are periodically trotted out, dusted off, congratulated for having seen farther than most, and then gently returned to their crypts as psychology gets on with the serious business. Usually, as anyone willing to take the time

350

to glance through the more popular general and historical texts will see, the list of great old names is expeditiously contracted. "The Greeks" of course, are never neglected. Perhaps a few lines will be devoted to the fact—except it isn't a fact—that not very much of intellectual consequence took place from the fall of Rome until the Renaissance except, maybe, for St. Augustine and Thomas Aquinas. The "modern era" is then announced, homage is paid to Locke and Descartes and, with philosophy now out of the way, the study of *psychology* can begin.

It is this approach to the foundations of the discipline that virtually guarantees to each generation of psychologists the privilege of *rediscov*ering some of the most compelling ideas in the history of thought. It also confers on psychology that state of perpetual youth which is proclaimed by most of its spokesmen in all of its ages. Thus, Titchener could write in his very widely read *Primer*, "Psychology is a very old science; we have a complete treatise from the hand of Aristotle (384–322 B.C.). But the experimental method has only recently been adopted by psychologists."[1] From this, one might gather that science in ancient days had adopted the experimental method but that the science of psychology had not. The fact, of course, is that experiments in all fields of science did not really begin to take precedence over pure speculation until well into the eighteenth century and, at this time, experiments in perception began with the rest. By all relevant standards, the first psychology laboratory was installed late but not by more than fifty or seventy-five years. In fact, university laboratories, such as the one created by Wundt, were extremely rare until the nineteenth century, and appeared in Germany relatively late.[2] The government of the Revolution had executed Lavoisier in 1793 and only allowed the French *Académie des Sciences* to renew its activities in 1795 when everyone was convinced that libertarian rhetoric would not solve France's problems. It was, however, not until the educational reforms introduced by Napoleon that French universities became centers of excellence in experimental science. In Germany such endeavors began even later, but when Fechner looked for data to support his science of psychophysics, he had to look no further than E. H. Weber's *Der Tastsinn und das Gemeingefühl* (1846), which was already printed in a popular handbook.[3]

To repeat, psychology's adoption of an experimental outlook occurred at very nearly the same time as that outlook was shared generally by the community of sciences, and that time was the nineteenth century. It will not do, then, to insist upon the youth of psychology even as an experimental endeavor. Psychology is young in the sense of still conducting its affairs in the absence of a unifying theory of the kind advanced by Copernicus, Galileo, or Newton. To the extent that this is the case, we must be prepared to accept the possibility, though disturbing, not simply that psychology is young as a science but that *it is not a science at all*. We shall return to this in the final chapter when we examine the nature of psychological explanations and with Chapter 1 in mind.

The error of *scholastica successionis civitatium* is committed when, in the absence of clear evidence, it is assumed that the reappearance of an idea in a more recent culture must be the result of having borrowed it from an earlier one. We would fall into this trap were we to suggest, for example, that the modern behavioral scientist, studying the effects of shock or food-reward on the acquisition of behavior, was a disciple of Jeremy Bentham's. Even if it could be shown that the early twentieth-century architects of behaviorism were directly inspired by utilitarian writings, it would not follow that those currently engaged in such work are disciples in any useful sense of the term. Rather, a quite different claim is made here and at the end of the previous chapter. The claim is not that the nineteenth century provided contemporary psychology with an irresistible legacy but that contemporary psychology *is* nineteenth-century psychology in its most global respects and that its departures from nineteenth-century perspectives have not been the result of any factors that might be called "scientific." In short, to the extent that the contemporary psychologist rejects the methods and the terminology of the immediate past, he does so for reasons other than those that have produced analogous decisions on the part of physicists, biologists, and others. The contemporary physicist does not devote his energies to the search for phlogiston because he has established that there is no such thing. He does not labor to create perpetual motion machines because the conservation of energy legislates against them. The geneticist does not design experiments to test the inheritance of acquired characteristics because, within all but lethal ranges of environmental variation, the molecular biology of the gene is stable and, therefore, will not be altered as a result of learning or practice.

Shifting emphases in psychology are not based on the same considerations. In the first two decades of the present century, the most influential figures in American psychology were William James and E. B. Titchener. Titchener, in his *Primer*, offered a psychology not far removed from that of his mentor, Wundt. Psychology was to be experimental introspection:

"(W)hen we are trying to understand the mental processes of a child or a dog or an insect as shown by conduct and action, the outward signs of mental processes, . . . we must always fall back upon experimental introspection . . . we cannot imagine processes in another mind that we do not find in our own. Experimental introspection is thus our one reliable method of knowing ourselves; it is the sole gateway to psychology."[4]

William James, in much the same spirit, begins his *Text Book of Psychology* by defining the subject as the *description and explanation of states of consciousness.*[5]

Now, it is unmistakable to anyone surveying the contemporary psychological scene that there is hardly a vestige of the program envisaged by Titchener and James. The "rules of introspection" presented by the former are applied in no laboratory, appear in no advanced treatment of the discipline, form no part of the modern psychologist's training. The same may be said of James' division of the discipline into Sensation, Cerebration, and the Tendency to Action.[6] But observe the difference between this shift in emphasis or complete abandonment of interest and the changes that have occurred in physics and biology. We *do* have minds, we *are* conscious, and we *can* reflect upon our private experiences because we *have* them. Unlike phlogiston or the inheritance of acquired characteristics, these phenomena exist and are common in human experience. The absence of orthodox Wundtians or Titchenerians or Jamesians, therefore, cannot be attributed to the disappearance of their subjects. Rather, it is to be understood as the result of the inability of the accepted *method* of psychological inquiry to address these subjects. The contemporary psychologist, if only insensibly, has made a *metaphysical* commitment to a method and has, per force, eliminated from the domain of significant issues those that cannot be embraced by that method.

The method itself is not simply some variant of the experimental method. Titchener and James both subscribed to that. The method referred to here is broader than a set of actions or procedures. It includes a way of thinking about problems and a way of talking about them. The method needs a label and the one most commonly applied to it is *empirical*, but custom can be observed only with reservation. The historic empiricists, Locke, Berkeley, Hume, and Mill, would almost certainly be misled by the term as it is applied to this metaphysical commitment. A psychology striving to rid itself of mental predicates is one they could scarcely fathom. We may even suspect that their reaction to the notion of psychology as a "behavioral" science would vary from incredulity to whimsy. *Empirical*, if the contemporary usage is to be captured, must also suggest measurement, practicality, impersonality, ethical neutrality, (ironic) "antimetaphysical*ness.*" Contemporary journals, whether devoted to neuropsychology, clinical practice, animal learning, or family counseling, strive to reflect these "empirical" features.

To what extent is this pervasive aspect of contemporary psychology also a "footnote" to the nineteenth century? To answer this, we must once more pause to examine the impact of German *Idealism* and the response to it.

The philosophy of the *Enlightenment* had cut deeply into what were once held to be the rational justifications for faith. In England and France, scholarship turned decidedly in a secular direction whence it has never retreated. The failure of the French Revolution to change the general conditions of life endured by the French, and the excesses of that Revolution, promoted political conservatism on both sides of the English Channel. Napoleon's rise to power and the wars resulting from it led to a variety of unconnected religious, social, and political movements. In England there was a definite tightening up of traditional class distinctions and a growing enmity toward those liberal philosophies that many blamed for the problems in the world. The objective and ultrarational philosophies of the British empiricists were judged to have taken people away from religion and to have driven a wedge between daily life and the *transcendent* by which daily life becomes meaningful. To some, the only solution to this crisis in faith was to be found in the philosophies of idealism now overtaking Germany. Schelling's "nature philosophy" found a British audience as sympathetic as any to be found in his own country. The most eloquent and forceful leaders of this British idealist movement were the "Lake poets" and, especially, Coleridge (1772–1834) and Wordsworth (1770–1850). More keenly than any, they sensed the weakening of historic values, the creeping relativism in ethics and morality. Listen to Wordsworth calling up, from a time before Hume, the hero England lost:

"Milton! thou shouldst be living at this hour; England hath need of thee; she is a fen Of stagnant waters . . ." (*London*, 1802)

In his *Ode to Duty* and his *Character of the Happy Warrior*, there is the same assertion of traditional ideals—a call to higher purposes. Then he crowns his pleading with the fifth stanza of his *Intimations:*

"Our birth is but a sleep and a forgetting;
The Soul that rises with us, our life's Star,
 Hath had elsewhere its setting,
  And cometh from afar;
 Not in entire forgetfulness,
 And not in utter nakedness,
But trailing clouds of glory do we come
 From God, who is our home . . ."

Coleridge, with an even larger following, pressed the message against the breast of countless thousands with his *Ancient Mariner*, who found it *"sweeter than the marriage feast . . . to walk together to the kirk with a goodly company."* Here were the poets of nature, demanding a return to natural feelings including those of duty, morality, love of the unseen but well-known God who is accessible only to what Byron would describe as the *"Eternal Spirit of the chainless Mind."*

If one is to comprehend the spirit of Victorian England, it is necessary to try to unite the ostensibly contradictory forces of romance and industry, naturalism and experimentalism, freedom and duty, Puritan moral simplicity and imperial social opulence, sweatshops and philanthropy. Not only were these polarities constant but each occurred on a truly mammoth scale. While coal miners choked to death for pennies a day, John Constable painted landscapes one could nearly walk through. As Charles Bell teased out the spinal nerves and as Gall and Spurzheim sought to transform morality into neurology, Tennyson depicted the twisted fate of all materialists in his *Lucretius* who, convinced of his own insignificance, wracked by his *"poor little life that toddles half an hour,"* kills himself.

There is a sense, and an indefensible one at that, in which the Darwinian revolution was, itself, the melding of naturalist, romantic, and materialist tensions: man evolving from the slime of nature and rising, through instinctual duty to his own survival, to a position of temporary mastery over all that lives; man, *selected* by nature to play his present part. Not even Darwin, himself, whose works would come to serve as an authority against romantic idealism, was spared the influence of the Lake poets. He concludes *The Expression of the Emotions in Man and Animals* with the hypothesis that the very expression of an emotion (behaviorally) intensifies it and that this self-intensifying tendency has great adaptive value to the animal. Then, at the end of this long treatise, in which he has explored the *minutiae* of the facial muscles and bones of the jaw, Darwin finds support from a judge possessing *"wonderful knowledge of the human mind."*[7]

> "Is it not monstrous that this player here,
> But in a fiction, in a dream of passion,
> Could force his soul so to his own conceit,
> That, from her working, all his visage wann'd;
> Tears in his eyes, distraction in's aspect,
> A broken voice, and his whole function suiting
> With forms to his conceit? And all for nothing!"
>
> HAMLET, ii, 2

In the romantic poetry of Wordsworth and Coleridge, in the literary allusions of Darwin, we find the flavor of the internal conflicts raging in Victorian England. For the actual substance, we must turn to the essayists of the mid- and late nineteenth century—to Matthew Arnold whose essay *Culture and Anarchy* sought to commit an industrial and ruthlessly economic system to "sweetness and light," good manners, taste, reason, and a sense of place,[8] and to J. S. Mill whose *On Liberty* proclaimed the essential intellectual freedom of every individual and the right of that individual to be unconstrained by the state in all respects, short of the harm he might cause to others. And there was John Ruskin, whose style and penetration were briefly sampled in Chapter 6, who wrote of the history of art in such a way as to make architecture a lesson in morality —Ruskin, who reasserted the ideals of the Renaissance or, at least, what he perceived to be those ideals when he studied the buildings and paintings of the period. No single chapter, let alone several pages, can do justice to the restlessly agile and durable intelligence of the Victorians. Their period must be introduced, even this sparingly, in order for us to recognize the popular attitudes the scientific mind was fighting. In the most general respect, it was fighting *Hegelianism* but, at the same time, it was finding in that same *Hegelianism* the most ardent defense of freedom and progress. The romantic minds of this same period were fighting science and materialism but, in these very movements, the ideals of liberty, safety, dignified work, and freedom from want were preserved as objectives. The character of contemporary psychology is to be found in the failure of these two nineteenth-century forces to find a means of reconciliation. Only a divorce would end the dispute. It was Helmholtz who summarized matters most candidly:

> "It has been made of late a reproach against natural philosophy that it has struck out on a path of its own, and has separated itself more and more widely from the other sciences which are united by common philological and historical studies. The opposition has, in fact, been long apparent, and seems to me to have grown up mainly under the influence of the Hegelian philosophy, or, at any rate, to have been brought out into more distinct relief by that philosophy. . . . The sole object of Kant's 'Critical Philosophy' was to test the sources and the authority of our knowledge, and to fix a definite scope and standard for the researches of philosophy, as compared with other sciences. . . . [But Hegel's['Philosophy of Identity' was bolder. It started with the hypothesis that not only spiritual phenomena, but even the actual world —nature, that is, and man—were the result of an act of thought on the part of a creative mind, similar, it was supposed, in kind to the human mind. . . . The philosophers accused the scientific men of narrowness; the scientific men retorted that the philosophers were crazy. And so it came about that men of science began to lay some stress on the banishment of all philosophic influences from their work; while some of them, including men of the greatest acuteness, went so far as to condemn

philosophy altogether, not merely as useless, but as mischievous dreaming. Thus, it must be confessed, not only were the illegitimate pretensions of the Hegelian system to subordinate to itself all other studies rejected, but no regard was paid to the rightful claims of philosophy, that is, the criticism of the sources of cognition, and the definition of the functions of the intellect." (1862)*

All who entered psychology during the turmoil and all who have come since it was (temporarily) settled were to choose between some version of Hegelianism and the inductive science of Mill. Even the phenomenology of Brentano and Husserl,† so radically different from what Hegel had in mind, would be forged into a "descriptive psychology," more philosophy than psychology and never an "empirical" science. Thus, in Europe, where the idealist tradition was deepest, the psychologist could either become a Wundtian, a neo-Hegelian, or a physiologist in psychologist's clothing. In England and America the alternatives were quickly reduced. One was either a philosopher or an experimentalist. To fail to be the latter was to fail to be a psychologist. Note that this historical development was just that: historical and *not* scientific. No logical proof had been discovered by which it could be shown that a rationalistic psychology would fail. No experimental finding had made it clear that we lack a moral sense or a link with God or a love of beauty. No surgical

---

* This quotation is taken from W. C. Dampier, *A History of Science*, Cambridge University Press, pp. 291–292. Helmholtz rarely addressed himself to the philosophy of science. His closest associates (e.g., DuBois-Reymond, Brücke, Ludwig) knew him to be opposed to vitalism in all its forms. Even his paper on the conservation of energy was written from a self-consciously antivitalistic perspective. However, he was the least polemical of the nineteenth-century physicalists, letting his outstanding contributions in science speak for themselves.

† The phenomenological systems advanced by Brentano and by Husserl bear little relationship to what Hegel had called phenomenology. Recall that Hegel used the term to refer to that science concerned with the "manifold of consciousness." For Hegel, phenomenology was the science generated by an idealistic philosophy.

Franz Brentano (1838–1917) was a greater teacher than he was either a philosopher or a psychologist. His students included Husserl, Meinong, Carl Stumpf, and Christian Ehrenfels. Stumpf taught both Köhler and Koffka and was a very productive psychologist in his own right. Ehrenfels was the first to speak of *gestaltqualität*. It was Brentano's *Psychologie vom Empirischen Standpunkt* (1874) that promised a "descriptive psychology" able to discover universal laws of the perceiving mind. Edmund Husserl (1859–1938) studied with Brentano. His phenomenological theories underwent several revisions over the years but were never far removed from the insistence that a scientific or an experimental psychology could only arrive at the contingent (intentional) and fallible aspects of perception. He emphasized the role of reflection in experience—as opposed to the mere description of experience—as the means by which a mental science might be cultivated. Husserl's influence is found most in that aspect of phenomenological psychology that rejects experimental inquiry in favor of intuitive and logical analyses. For a discussion of Husserl's phenomenology, see Herbert Spiegelberg's *The Phenomenological Movement*, Vol. I, pp. 73–167, Mouton, The Hague, 1960.

procedure had established that the psychological dimensions of human life were readily reducible to neural mechanisms. Even "Mill's methods," now installed as the essential equipment of the new science, could claim neither the validity conferred by logic nor the reliability demanded by science, at least as these methods were applied in the psychology laboratory. Rather, what had taken place was the adoption of a metaphysical position not on the nature of *truth* but on the nature of *psychology*. The decision was made that psychology was no more than a certain kind of method, an "experimental" method, and that its subject matter would contain only those entries amenable to this method. Listen to another of the Leipzig graduates, Theodor Ziehen, introduce psychology in 1895:

> "The psychology which I shall present to you is not that old psychology which sought to investigate psychical phenomena in a more or less speculative way. That psychology has long been abandoned by those whose method of thought is that of the natural sciences, and empirical psychology has justly taken its place."[9]

E. W. Scripture, another Leipzig Ph. D., writing from Yale in 1897 put it this way:

> "The development of a science consists in the development of its means of extending and improving its method of observation. The great step that has lately been taken in psychology lies in the introduction of systematised observation, by means of experimental and clinical methods."[10]

Ziehen speaks of a "method of thought" endemic to the natural scientist and Scripture announces the introduction of an improved method of observation. But what is this "method of thought" and how had the method of observation been improved? We may turn to Titchener for an answer:

> "The rules for introspection are of two kinds: general and special. . . . Suppose, e.g., that you were trying to find out how small a difference you could distinguish in the smell of beeswax; that is how much greater the surface of the stimulus must be made if the sensation of smell is to become noticeably stronger. It would be a special rule that you should work only on dry days; for beeswax smells much stronger in wet than in fine weather. . . . The general rules of experimental introspection are as follows: (1) Be impartial . . . (2) Be attentive . . . (3) Be comfortable . . . (4) Be perfectly fresh."[11]

It is through these "methods" that Titchener hoped to discern the structure of consciousness; that is, to advance *Structuralism* as that division of psychological science having the same role as anatomy in the biological sciences. This "science" didn't last and, indeed, couldn't last. The most that *Structuralism* could ever have hoped to accomplish was the rediscovery of what every man, woman, and child know to be true during every waking hour of daily life. Having insisted upon a rupture with philosophical tradition and having affirmed the status of this new venture to be that of a "natural science," the founders of experimental psychology had to contract the domain of problems to . . . the smell of beeswax. Somehow, the laws of association would ultimately permit a coalescence of such findings into a complete description of the "elements of consciousness." The claim, for a while, was that the goal was reachable; that patient observation of "impartial, attentive, comfortable, and fresh" subjects would yield a natural science of the mind; that, indeed, the very observation *was* the natural science of the mind. But there was no "covering law," no theory worth the name, no independent set of measurements against which to validate the psychophysical methods. The data emerging from Wundtian studies—whether back at Leipzig or at Titchener's laboratory at Cornell—did not behave the way scientific data are supposed to. Even the most comfortable subject, try as he may, had trouble "introspecting" identically on separate occasions. Toward the end of his career, Titchener took up numismatics.

Notwithstanding the painfully apparent liabilities of the Wundtian-Titchenerian studies, the experimental method remained at the core of psychology, and still does. In a way, it is a method in search of a subject and, in the remainder of this chapter, we will review several of the possibilities unearthed along the way.

Behaviorism

We will call John B. Watson (1878–1958) the "father" of *Behaviorism* but only after acknowledging that fatherhood entails grandparents, at least one mate, and offspring. To this, we must add the fact that children are not to pay for the sins of the parents and that acquired characteristics are not inherited. And, since historical analysis involves a good deal more than genealogy, we leave the "paternalism" metaphor by remarking that the significant fact of "behaviorism" is not its authorship but its reception.

When Kurt Koffka (1886–1941, *vide infra*) presented his *Principles of Gestalt Psychology* (1935) as, among other things, a rebuttal of behaviorism, he observed that Americans possessed a very high regard for science, "accurate and earthbound" science, which produced in them, "an aversion, sometimes bordering on contempt, for metaphysics that tries to escape from the welter of mere facts into a loftier realm of ideas and ideals."[12]

He was, no doubt, reflecting on an American psychology that had begun to turn away from the problem of consciousness and toward the objective measurement of behavior. But in 1935 the trend was only a beginning. America, after all, was the country of William James and John Dewey, the country that Titchener had allowed to host structuralism. But it was not James or Dewey, and it was surely not Titchener, who called forth Koffka's stricture. Nor, we must observe, was it the mere fact that *behavior* was the subject of growing interest. And it certainly was not the very prominent place held by *animal* psychology in America, for Wundt never legislated against such an interest. In fact his *Lectures on Human and Animal Psychology* (1894) explicitly recommended it:

"The study of animal psychology may be approach from two different points of view. We may set out from the notion of a kind of comparative physiology of mind, a universal history of the development of mental life in the organic world. Or we may make human psychology the principal object of investigation. Then, the expressions of mental life in animals will be taken into account only so far as they throw light upon the evolution of consciousness in man. . . . Human psychology . . . may confine itself altogether to man, and generally has done so to far too great an extent. There are plenty of psychological text-books from which you would hardly gather that there was any other conscious life than the human."[13]

But American behaviorism was not just a commitment to study animal psychology, nor was it restricted to that aesthetic decision to examine behavior instead of something else. The behaviorism of John B. Watson was no less than the insistence that a scientific psychology must concern itself *only* with behavior and must abandon all interest in consciousness, mental states, introspection, unconscious processes, and other "ghosts." He announced the *ism* with unblemished lucidity in 1913:

"Psychology as the behaviorist views it is a purely experimental branch of natural science. Its theoretical goal is the prediction and control of behavior. Introspection forms no essential part of its methods, nor is the scientific value of its data dependent upon the readiness with which they lend themselves to interpretation in terms of consciousness. The behaviorist, in his efforts to get a unitary scheme of animal response, recognizes no dividing line between man and brute. The behavior of man, with all of its refinement and complexity, forms only a part of the behaviorist's total scheme of investigation."[14]

Structuralism, from Watson's point of view, is indefinite and self-serving in its methods, hopelessly out of control in its data, and committed to a mission that cannot succeed because it cannot ever end. There is no limit to the number of "experiences" one may have, especially since each may be attended by anywhere from *"three to nine states of clearness of attention."* Watson had, despite his search, never found a physician or lawyer or man of commerce who had even once found a use for the methods or findings of the structuralists. Clearly (to Watson) a venture so incapable of contributing to the practical affairs of life can have only a short future.

Having disposed of Titchener and the entire Wundtian tradition, Watson turned his attention—which was at least at the ninth state of clearness —to that *functionalist* school identified with James and Dewey. Watson frankly admits, and a good many psychologists have shared the admission, that he has never been able to understand just what functionalism is supposed to be, in contrast to Titchener's psychology. James, in his *Textbook of Psychology*, had complained of empirical associationism and of those who would describe a river in terms of *"pailsful, spoonsful, quartpotsful, barrelsful, and other moulded forms of water."*[15] He argued that the *stream of consciousness* cannot be arbitrarily fragmented to suit the needs of the experimental psychologist and that, therefore, any fractionation of consciousness into its structures could only lead to a distorted sense of what consciousness is. To discover the nature of consciouness, one must appreciate what it is *for*, in the Darwinian sense. One must, that is, discern its function; the part it plays in permitting man to adapt to the demands of the environment. This was James' position in 1882 before Titchener's structuralism even appeared, and when Titchener cites James in his *Primer*, it is invariably either in support of one of his own propositions or to borrow a mot from the master phrasemaker. John Dewey (1859–1952), also, attacked elementalism, arguing that the notion of reflex "units" fails to appreciate the coordinated nature of successful (i.e., *functional*) behavior.[16] But neither Titchener* nor Wundt† may

---

* Titchener here distinguishes between reflex movements, instincts, and more complex integrated movements. He argues that even the reflex movements are far from simple and are not the earliest phylogenetic units of action at all. (E. B. Titchener, *A Primer of Psychology*, Macmillan, Inc., New York, 1914, pp. 171–182.)

† In his chapter "Reflex Functions" (Ch. VI), in the *Principles of Physiological Psychology*, Wundt is careful to distinguish between reflex actions and intentional or willful action. He cautions (pp. 250–251) against extending the concept of the reflex so far that it fails to explain anything. The edition of the *Principles* referred to is that translated by Titchener and published by Macmillan, Inc., New York, 1904.

be said to have been naive on this point. What disturbed Watson was not that the functionalists found something lacking in structuralism but that they had yet to recommend a plausible method of correcting it.

Watson, in a steady stream of criticism and revolutionary rhetoric, struck no compromise with any of his immediate predecessors. Whether the subject was infant care[17] or the nature of comparative psychology[18] or the prescriptions for all psychological inquiry,[19] the message was the same: any branch of natural science must concern itself with the prediction of natural events; a science can study only that which can be observed; mental states and private experiences do not exist in the world of the publicly verifiable; behavior alone is the object of a truly scientific study. Wundt and Titchener, therefore, went wrong from the outset by assuming that the adoption of an experimental point of view was sufficient to install an enterprise as science. They made a proper methodological decision but selected for their study a subject that never could have achieved the status of scientific subjects. At each key point, according to Watson, the Wundtian and Titchenerian psychologies were given the wrong emphasis: the emphasis upon man instead of the animal kingdom in general; the emphasis upon experience instead of action; the emphasis upon existential rather than evolutionary considerations; the emphasis upon theoretical instead of practical considerations. Behaviorism, as defined by Watson and as understood ever since, is devoted to the shifting of each of these emphases.

It is difficult to assemble the various factors that led Watson to his manifesto. It is more difficult to isolate the factors responsible for the early success of behaviorism and for the mounting attention it has received over the past half-century.* He received his graduate education at Chicago during Dewey's tenure, but his subsequent attacks on the functionalism of the Chicago school suggest that Dewey's role was not a positive one. Dewey criticized the very "reflex arc" concept that Watson's later works would rely upon heavily. The philosophical *pragmatism* of James and C. S. Peirce† was, by now, nearly an "official" American

---

* The pragmatic bent of the Americans was keenly observed by Alexis de Tocqueville. In his classic, *Democracy in America*, he notes that, "in America the purely practical side of science is cultivated admirably, and trouble is taken about the theoretical side immediately necessary to application . . . But hardly anyone in the United States devotes himself to the essentially theoretical and abstract side of human knowledge." (From the edition of 1848, Volume II, Part I, Chapter 10).

† Charles Sanders Peirce (1839–1914) was the founder of pragmatism and exerted a great influence on William James. He was a logician and mathematician, not a psychologist and not especially pleased by the renditions of his system given by James. His principal epistemological concern was with meaning and over the years he evolved a theory of meaning that finally became the pragmatic theory of meaning. It may be summarized in a variety of ways, but the summaries tend to trivialize the concept. The meaning of a term, on the pragmatic account, cannot go beyond the

philosophy, and its insistence on the restriction of scientific terms to "observables" supported Watson's growing dissatisfaction with traditional formulations. A central tenet of Peirce's pragmatism is that the meaning of any concept, as applied to any *thing* in the natural world, can be no more than the *behavior* of that thing in a variety of clearly specified conditions. It was James who brought the ideas of Peirce, or at least the Jamesian reconstruction of these ideas, to the attention of large numbers of American philosophers and psychologists. Without belaboring the line of succession, we might simply observe the strong pragmatistic flavor of Watson's definitions and criteria of scientific discourse.

Far more important, however, than Dewey or James were the published works of E. L. Thorndike (1874–1949), who was a student of James' and whose *Animal Intelligence*[20] was a landmark in the history of so-called behavioral analysis. The work appeared in 1898 and described a series of experiments concerned with learning and memory in cats. Thorndike, with makeshift but serviceable equipment, plotted the speed with which animals escaped from a box in order to obtain food placed outside the box. He generated a series of "learning curves" which showed systematic improvement with increased practice. On the basis of these and related findings, Thorndike presented his famous *law of effect* according to which behavior is determined by its consequences. Behavior leading to "satisfying" states of affairs is more likely; behavior leading to unsatisfying states, less likely. Watson did not applaud Thorndike's choice of terms, finding the law of effect too mentalistic, but he did applaud the objective methods of measurement and the general demystification of the discipline.

Thorndike's "provisional" laws of learning, which he put forth as standing out *"clearly in every series of experiments on animal learning and in the entire history of the management of human affairs,"*[21] were of the sort we do not see any more in psychology:

> *"The Law of Effect is that:* Of several responses made to the same situation, those which are accompanied or closely followed by satisfaction to the animal will, other things being equal, be more firmly connected with the situation, so that, when it recurs, they will be more likely to recur; those which are accompanied or closely followed by discomfort to the animal will, other things being equal, have their connections with that situation weakened, so that, when it recurs, they will be less likely to recur. The greater the satisfaction or discomfort, the greater the strengthening or weakening of the bond.

---

actual objective features of that which the term is used to denote. Any distinction, therefore, between the actual behavior of an object or event and the definition given for the term used to represent that object or event is, literally, nonsense.

"The Law of Exercise is that: Any response to a situation will, other things being equal, be more strongly connected with the situation in proportion to the number of times it has been connected with that situation and to the average vigor and duration of the connections."[22]

There is little in either of these "laws" that could not be gleaned from Locke or Hume or Bentham or, for that matter, Aristotle. They are the classical laws of association with the addition of Darwinian and Benthamist principles. The difference, of course, is that the laws in Thorndike's case are supported by experimental findings. Still, it is not likely that anyone would have objected to either law even had experimental data not been presented. Practice makes perfect, as the aphorism goes, and we do tend to do the sorts of things we find satisfying. In their stated form, the laws are richly mentalistic and, as a result, pose no threat to those who believe that psychology is the science of the mind. This was not Thorndike's position, but his two laws allow such a construction. Under the law of effect, he employs terms such as "the same situation" and "satisfaction"; under the law of exercise, "a situation." These are psychological terms and fit easily into the introspective tradition whether Thorndike wanted them there or not. It is this fact that invited Watson's dissent:

"Most of the psychologists . . . believe habit formation is implanted by kind fairies. For example, Thorndike speaks of pleasure stamping in the successful movement and displeasure stamping out the unsuccessful movements."[23]

Instead of this, Watson elects to use the language of reflex physiology, recently developed by Ivan Pavlov (1849–1936). English translations of Pavlov's works began to appear after Watson's behavioristic lectures of 1912, but by the time of the 1930 edition of his *Behaviorism,* the complete Pavlovian system had been rendered into English.[24] We are not to make too much of Pavlov's effect upon Watson's thinking. The essentials of the latter's psychology were established before he learned of the Russian's theories and, even after mastering Pavlov's theories of conditioning, Watson could still observe:

"Most of the psychologists talk, too, quite volubly about the formation of new pathways in the brain, as though there were a group of tiny servants of Vulcan there who run through the nervous system with hammer and chisel digging new trenches and deepening old ones. . . . Since the advent of the conditioned reflex hypothesis in psychology with all of the simplifications (and I am often fearful that it may be an over-simplification!) I have had my own [views]."[25]

His own views involved the acceptance of the conditioned reflex as the "unit" of behavior and the notion that all more complex forms of behavior were compounded of these units. Prudently he resisted the temptation to set tiny servants to work in the brain. His explanation of psychological processes (i.e., the determinants of behavior) was to be of the descriptive variety, remaining relatively neutral on questions of physiological detail and relatively hostile on questions of mental referents. Psychology is to determine the manner in which elemental conditioned reflexes are built up to form complex habits. Our reactions to the world are to be understood in terms of these reflexes. Even our most vaunted capacity, that of language, is but the product of conditioned reflexes involving the laryngeal musculature.[26] Through conditioning (and in Humean fashion) *anything* can come to elicit a given response provided that it has been presented in conjunction with an unconditioned stimulus. By association, the previously neutral stimulus becomes the *substitute* for the unconditioned stimulus.[27]

> "The importance of stimulus substitution or stimulus conditioning cannot be overrated. . . . So far as we know now . . . we can take any stimulus calling out a standard reaction and substitute another stimulus for it."[28]

Since any desired behavior can be thus secured, Watson is prepared to reject even the concept of instincts, noting that man has been credited with a large number of them but that no recitation of the list tells us very much. He offers the example of the boomerang that returns to the place from which it was thrown. Its behavior is the result of its composition. Organisms also are composed of biological systems that are structured in such a way as to respond in stereotypical fashion to particular environmental features.[29] However, we need not invent a new instinct each time we observe a new pattern of behavior or a new stimulus-response connection. In fact, only when we study the infant, devoid of a conditioning history, are we in a position to say anything about innate dispositions. Watson, studying such infants, was persuaded that their only native, psychological apparatus are the primitive form of the emotions of rage, fear, and love.[30] He accepts these because, in the infant, he can find behavioral manifestations of them. He rejects out of hand the introspective method of James' for studying the emotions and he chortles at the long list of instincts that William McDougall (1871–1938) has made so popular.

Watson had begun his crusade as early as 1912 and had provided a seminal article by 1913 and a textual guide by 1924. In the *Introduction* to the 1930 edition of his *Behaviorism*, he reflected on the evolution of the behavioristic perspective thus:

". . . without behaviorism being overtly accepted, its influence has been profound during the eighteen years of its existence. To be convinced of this, one needs only to compare the contents of our journals title by title for 15 years before the advent of behaviorism and during the past 15 to 18 years. . . . Today, no university can escape the teaching of behaviorism . . . the younger generation of students demands at least some orientation in behaviorism."[31]

Watson, in this judgment, was correct. By 1930 the signs were unmistakable. Psychologists had divided into two camps—and *camps* is the apt description. In one were to be found the self-appointed scientists of the profession and, in the other, all the rest! The *scientists* were not yet "behavioral scientists," but they were students of animal behavior, of conditioned reflexes, of brain-behavior relations. Introspection was a fading method. Freud's influence was becoming international, but psychotherapy was still so mentalistic, so terminologically obtuse, that it was no threat to the new science of (real) psychology. There were, of course, still some problems. Watson's system was based on the notion that the full range of so-called purposive behavior could be accounted for in terms of the accretion of reflex connections. This seemed utterly implausible to anyone not ordained into the *ism*. Watsonian psychology also left out a topic that even the "scientists" were not willing to part with: *perception*. Watson's data, in the context of his ambitious system, were strikingly sparse and his proposed methods were daringly ambiguous. Promising to create "dentists" by Pavlovian conditioning, for example, left a good part of the psychological community incredulous, another part perplexed, and still another part in stitches. Quite simply, behaviorism could not have survived in the form bequeathed by Watson. Revisionism was in the air and it found its most articulate expression in B. F. Skinner's *The Behavior of Organisms* (1938).[32] Since its publication, the text has influenced American experimental psychology as much as any single work in the history of the discipline. Prof. Skinner (1904–) has revised the initial formulations of his behaviorism and has extended the system to embrace issues of a broad, social character.[33] Notwithstanding the alterations, behaviorism in Skinner's treatments has retained the following features:

Psychology is a natural science whose subject matter is restricted to the observable behavior of organisms. The aim of the science is the prediction and control of behavior. It does not strive to complement the biological sciences, nor does the validity of its principles depend upon findings in biology or neurophysiology. "Neurology cannot prove (behavioral) laws wrong if they are valid at the level of behavior. Not only are the laws of behavior independent of neurological support, they actually impose certain limiting conditions upon any science which undertakes to study the internal economy of the organism."[34] As a descriptive science concerned with (Humean) regularities between environmental antecedents and behavioral consequents, psychology need not strive toward theoretical systematicization. Its law is the law of effect with mentalism removed, that is, the law of effect expressed in purely operational terms. That which increases the probability of the behavior that precedes it is, by operational definition, a positive reinforcer. That which reduces the probability of the behavior that precedes it is a negative reinforcer. The behavior of interest to psychology is that which operates on the environment and thereby affects the survival of the organism. Pavlovian reflexes, while conditionable, tend to involve subsystems of the organism. They are, of course, intimately associated with the balance of the organism's adaptive capacities but do not directly and immediately result in those adjustments of the environment that *operant* behavior produces. Where the creation of a dentist by Pavlovian conditioning appears implausible, the very appearance of a dentist is *prima facie* evidence of the success of *operant conditioning*. Consciousness, free will, intention, and the like, for purposes of a scientific analysis of the determinants of behavior, need not be considered. The terms, themselves, are merely "verbal operants" invented by a society that finds mentalistic interpretations reinforcing.

The foregoing position does not occur in an intellectual vacuum. Nor does its reception, whether positive or hostile. The groundwork for "Skinnerian" psychology had been laid years, even centuries, earlier, perhaps as early as Ockham's rejection of *universals*. More proximately, it may be said to have begun with Hume and reached its first great plateau in the functional biology of Darwin, the utilitarianism of Mill, and the pragmatism of James. For James, *knowledge is utility*. At the time James was discovering C. S. Peirce, Ernst Mach (1838–1916) was promoting a similar movement in Vienna, a movement away from metaphysics (especially Kant's) and toward practicality. Peirce had already written his little classic, *How To Make Our Ideas Clear* (1900), offering such antimetaphysical notions as, "*To say a body is heavy means simply to say that it will fall.*" Einstein's challenge to complacent Newtonians even had physicists fearful of the metaphysical residue of "natural philosophy." Then too there was World War I, with its heightened nationalism and jingoism. Scholarly detachment could not survive that war which so intensified the long rift between Continental and English-speaking philosophy, psychology, and ethics. Recall Koffka's observations on the American devotion to "earthbound science" and aversion to "ideas and ideals." We are not to assess the scientific status of behaviorism either in terms of its origins or in terms of the social factors that may have led to its popularity. But to be assessed as a science, it had to come into being, and we would be remiss not to take note of that early twentieth-century atmosphere that was especially conducive to the behavioristic way of thinking. Watson's books and articles have the same anti-Hegelian ring (without ever mentioning Hegel) as the articles and books appearing at the same time in the philosophy literature of the English-speaking world.* Scientism had replaced religionism in intellectual circles, and psychology, forced again to choose between Nature and Spirit, now had the universal support of the sciences in choosing the former. We will examine the logical and scientific dimensions of this choice in the last chapter.

"Gestalt" Psychology (The Continental Reply)

The names associated with the founding of Gestalt psychology are those of Max Wertheimer (1880–1943), Kurt Koffka (1886–1941), and Wolfgang Köhler (1887–1967). The three worked together at the Psychological Institute of Frankfurt for several years, beginning in 1909. All psychologists are familiar with Wertheimer's "discovery" of the *phi phenomenon:* the apparent continuous movement produced by two different stimuli, spatially separated, and illuminated successively at brief intervals. Since stroboscopes were available as children's toys by 1910 and since the earliest motion pictures had been filmed some twenty-five years before, we must be careful about the sense in which we use the term *discovery.* It was not *apparent movement* that was discovered by the Frankfurt group but a new approach to psychology, an approach based on such perceptual phenomena as *phi.*

We can locate the spirit of Gestalt psychology as well as its philosophical orientation by reading Ivan Pavlov's *Criticism of Köhler's Idealistic Concepts* (1935).[35] It is not that there is anything especially "idealistic" in the Gestalt movement. None of the major treatises by the Gestalt psychologists contains an acknowledgment of Hegel's or Berkeley's influence. No Gestalt psychologist has ever denied the existence of matter or has suggested that the fundamental stuff of the universe is mental. But physiology by 1935, like psychology, had declared its opposition to metaphysical pronouncements. Pavlov is just one of the more famous spokesmen of that materialistic and associationistic school that judged any departure from the orthodox interpretation to be "idealism." If the Gestalt psychologists are to be united, in a loose way, with the German

---

* If the British philosophical reaction to Hegelianism is to be dated, we may cite G. E. Moore's *Principia Ethica* as the cogent starting point. In this work, Hegel's distinctions between "wholes" and the "sums of their parts" are rendered ambiguous and even meaningless (pp. 30 ff.). Darwinian notions are incorporated into ethics and, following Thomas Reid, "natural language" and "common sense" are restored to talk about principles of human conduct. (G. E. Moore, *Principia Ethica,* Cambridge University Press, 1903.)

idealist tradition of Kant, Hegel, and the neo-Hegelians, it must be through the notion of mental *categories* by which sense-data become organized percepts. At the risk of simplification, we might draw a parallel between Thorndike's experiments and those of Wertheimer, Koffka, and Köhler. It is this: Thorndike borrowed the philosophical principles of association, combined them with the utilitarian emphasis on the "pleasure principle," and created an experimental environment in which these principles could be demonstrated. The Gestaltists accepted the Kantian-Hegelian principle of the pure categories of the understanding brought them to bear on studies of visual perception, and thereby provided a laboratory demonstration of the role of the mind in organizing and transforming the raw facts of experience. The *phi* phenomenon, then, was just a means of displaying the essential premise of Gestalt psychology: perception is the result of an interaction between the physical characteristics of stimulation and the mental laws governing the experiences of the observer. The setting for demonstrating *phi* is a dark room in which one can present two illuminated stripes placed several inches apart. An interval can be found between the illumination of one stripe and that of its neighbor such that the observer reports, not two stripes, but the movement of one stripe from left to right, or right to left, depending on the order of illumination. The important point is this: nothing in the experimental arrangement, except the phenomenon itself, would lead to the prediction of apparent movement. That is, there is no physical feature of the environment that permits the prediction of the effect. A purely stimulus-bound description of the laboratory setting will be devoid of any allusion to motion. The motion is created by the observer. It is his perception of motion, not his response to motion that is the object of study. In short, it is the study of a mental as opposed to sensory or behavioral state.

Far from being an idealistic psychology, Gestalt psychology has always accentuated the role of brain dynamics in accounting for the large number and variety of Gestalt phenomena. Köhler insisted that the relationship between perception and neurophysiology was *isomorphic*, meaning that the structural features of the percept were matched by the structural features of the brain's functional organization:

". . . we are inclined to assume that when the self feels in one way or another referred to an object there actually is a field of force in the brain, which extends from the processes corresponding to the self to those corresponding to the object. The principle of isomorphism demands that in a given case the organization of experience and the underlying physiological facts have the same structure."[36]

The Gestalt critique of behaviorism is uncompromising.[37] The behavioristic reliance upon physiological reflexes is judged to be not only simplistic but at variance with even the physiological facts (*vide infra*). While presuming to model itself after physics, behaviorism fails to take from physics its most celebrated discoveries, those that allow a comprehension of dynamic processes. Even the very modern forms of behaviorism that labor so diligently to avoid commitment to any physiological theory or body of knowledge are still, by Köhler's lights, wed to the old associationistic principles of learning and their hedonistic corollaries. This is why behaviorism must always be embarrassed by the abilities of animals performing in settings that have not been trivialized by the demands of behaviorism. On this latter point, Köhler presents the results of his studies of chimpanzees that he conducted from 1913–1917 at the Anthropoid Station in Tenerife.[38] The experiments say more about the Gestalt view of psychology than many of the words written to describe the system. If the rat in a box is the image created by the term "behaviorism," then the chimp with two sticks in his hands is the symbol of the Gestalt laboratory.

It is axiomatic that all one will learn of the abilities of an animal is what the testing situation permits the animal to perform. Köhler's apes were called upon to solve problems. They would, for example, be confronted by a situation in which food was hung too high above them to be reached. Boxes were then strewn about the cage. The chimp soon solves the problem by stacking the boxes and climbing on them to reach the food. Then there is the most famous of the *insight* studies in which the animal is given two sticks, neither long enough to reach food placed beyond the cage. After some random activity and a good deal of looking at the sticks, the chimp suddenly joins them together, creating a single stick of twice the length, and proceeds to haul in his reward. The animal will also break off branches to achieve the same end. So, too, will they imitate the behavior of a human engaged in such tasks. And from such findings, Köhler concludes that the processes

> "*occur in chimpanzees, exactly as in man* . . . it is these 'impressions', which are not at all 'something that has been read into' the chimpanzees, but which belong to the elementary phenomenology of their behavior. . . . If *this* is an anthropomorphism, so then is the sentence: 'Chimpanzees have the same tooth formula as man.' "[39]

Later formulations of the Gestalt position, particularly those by E. C. Tolman (1886–1961), have retained the original emphasis upon *cognitive* as opposed to *performative* aspects of the psychology of learning. Tolman's *Cognitive Maps in Rats and Man* (1948)[40] is a summary and interpretation of a variety of Gestalt experiments on maze-learning and problem-solving in which the experimental animals seem to behave in terms of a "mental image" or "map" of the experimental situation rather than in terms of the purely associationistic demands of the situation. Here and elsewhere, the Gestaltist distinguishes between *performance*, which is under the control of rewards and punishments, and *learning*, which occurs whenever a complex organism has perceptual commerce with the immediate environment. Rats permitted to run freely in a maze come to solve the maze more quickly on subsequent occasions when food-reward is introduced than do animals without the original "irrelevant" experience. This so-called *latent learning* is assumed to violate the law of effect which requires reinforcement if learning is to occur. Similarly an animal receiving reward by responding to, say, a circle five inches in diameter and not rewarded for responses to one that is two and a half inches will subsequently choose one of ten inches over one of five inches. That is, after originally learning the choice of "5" vs. "2½," the animal, given the new choices, "10" vs. "5," does not choose the "5" (with which all previous rewards were associated) but, instead, chooses the *larger*. This, according to the Gestaltist, requires us to assume that what was originally learned was a *relationship* and not merely a physical value. This is taken as an instance of *transposition* in which the relational properties are abstracted from the stimulus elements. A more common instance of transposition occurs in music where the listener will recognize a melody played in different keys despite the fact that, from key to key, the actual notes are of completely different frequencies.

From the Gestalt point of view, latent learning and transpositional learning introduce fatal flaws into the traditional behavioristic perspective. The former is judged to be telling evidence against the law of effect and the latter against associationism. While as opposed to introspective psychology as any behaviorist, the Gestalt psychologist finds nothing in behaviorism that warrants its claims to superiority. It is one thing to assert that the Wundtian-Titchenerian psychology is "subjective" but quite another to deny the relevance of immediate experience to the study of man—and all other complex organisms. It is one thing to assert that the conditioned reflex comes about by virtue of the formation of reflex associations among cortical neurons but quite another to suggest that the brain is capable of *only* such "connections." It is one thing to demonstrate how practice and reward affect performance but a very different matter to submit that practice and reward are the *only* determinants of learning. In the light of these reservations, the Gestalt theorist offers his own findings and hypotheses:

1. Organisms do not merely respond to their environments; they have *transactions* with the environment.

2. The "environment" is not just the physical objects proximate to the animal but the outcome of an interaction between the perceptual predispositions of the organism and these physical objects. The effective stimulus, therefore, must always be specified from the organism's point of view.

3. The relationship between experience and action on the one hand and brain physiology on the other is *isomorphic*. Accordingly, to the extent that the experiences or the performances of the organism are not of a reflex nature, the underlying brain physiology also must not be of a reflex nature. Reflex organization within the brain is but one of the many forms of organization available to so complex a system.

4. Perception, as with all other fundamentally biological processes, is governed by laws or principles of organization. The laws of perception are such that the organism will impose upon the physical environment a certain *form* (*gestalt*) or organizational quality (*gestalt-qualität*). It is by virtue of this filtering and transforming of stimulus elements that the organism is able to deal with the demands of the environment in an economical and orderly way. In the following drawing we see two collections of six lines but, perceptually, we "see" something other than six lines on the right. We see three *groups* of two lines. *Grouping* is but one example of the imposition of *gestalt-qualität* upon the elements of sensation.

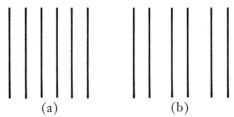

(a)   (b)

It is by virtue of the same principles of perceptual organization that we perceive a *constancy* of experience in the face of changing stimuli. Dinner plates are seen as round no matter what the angle of regard. Their circularity is apparent even though, in any plane other than the normal, they project ellipses on the retina. Shape-constancy violates the predictions of geometric optics because the latter does not take into account the *perceptual* principle of constancy. For the behaviorist or introspectionist to dismiss such effects as "illusory" is tantamount to their rejection of the bulk of human experience from the domain of psychological inquiry.

5. The naive *phenomenalism* of J. S. Mill, Titchener, and others must be abandoned. There is not a simple relationship between the world of

matter and the world of experience. We do not "see" objective stimuli, we transform them. If we can say, with Mill, that matter is the permanent possibility of sensation, then we must also say that sensation is the permanent possibility of perception:

> "(S)ensory organization constitutes a characteristic achievement of the nervous system. This emphasis has become necessary because some authors seem to think that, according to Gestalt Psychology, '*Gestalten*', i.e., segregated entities, exist outside the organism and simply extend or project themselves into the nervous system. This view, it must be realized, is entirely wrong."[41]

Like behaviorism, Gestalt psychology has splintered into a generous assortment of derivative enterprises. Not every contemporary "cognitive" psychologist expresses allegiance to Köhler's formulations, just as many "behavioral scientists" are quick to disavow kinship with Watson—and even with Skinner. Clark Hull (1884–1952), for example, has offered a behaviorism rich in mathematical notation and closely tied to physiology and evolutionary biology, but neither of these features characterizes the workaday activities of the current "operant" psychologist. In the Gestalt tradition, many investigators are carefully examining the nuances of perceptual organization, the rules of information-processing, and so forth, without worrying over *psychophysical isomorphism* or *Gestalt-qualität*. Around the world and with ever increasing comparability, laboratories are engaged in essentially descriptive work designed to establish the extent to which environmental modifications lead to alterations in the measurable features of behavior. Theoretical tensions have, at least for the moment, subsided and this must be appreciated as something of a victory for that modern behavioristic injunction against theorizing, physiologizing, and mathematizing.[42] The essentials of the Gestalt system still survive and flourish in the work of such European psychologists as Jean Piaget, whose theories of cognitive and moral development take recourse to neo-Hegelian concepts of evolutionary stages and to Gestalt concepts of innate perceptual dispositions and neuroperceptual isomorphism. Psycholinguistics too received its impetus from the nativistic and cognitive elements of the Gestalt psychologists but, like Piagetian psychology, it is considered by many behavioral psychologists to have little to do with psychology, proper. To these psychologists, the idea that language-structure is innate sounds very much like the instinct theories of the 1920s and 1930s and, even to those behaviorists who have abandoned the Watsonian version of behaviorism, Watson clearly held the day against McDougall!

Physiological Psychology

While it is true that behaviorism derived some inspiration from the writings of Ivan Pavlov, it is important to recognize that Pavlov hardly qualifies as a "behaviorist" in the sense in which that label has come to be applied. Pavlov was a physiologist by training and by commitment. His ambition was to articulate the laws of central nervous system function which accounted for the so-called psychological dimensions of life. His studies in Germany brought him in contact with the Helmholtzian school —principally with one of Helmholtz's colleagues, Carl Ludwig—but he was a declared physicalist before he ever left Russia.

In his speech accepting the Nobel Prize for pioneering research in gastric physiology, Pavlov (1909) introduced the concept of the conditioned reflex to the general scientific community. His important papers on reflex conditioning were not translated into English for several years, but the Nobel address then, as now, received wide attention. That the rest of his life would be devoted to the newly discovered phenomenon can be anticipated from his closing remarks on that occasion:

> "In point of fact, only one thing in life is of actual interest for us—our psychical experience. But its mechanism has been and still remains wrapped in mystery. All human resources—art, religion, literature, philosophy and historical science—have combined to throw light on this darkness. Man has at his disposal yet another powerful resource— natural science with its strictly objective methods. . . . The facts and considerations which I have placed before you are one of the numerous attempts to employ—in studying the mechanism of the highest vital manifestations in the dog, the representative of the animal kingdom which is man's best friend—a *consistent*, purely scientific method of thinking."[43]

Pavlovian psychology, some trivial aspects of which have recently been rediscovered and raised to the level of a "science" with the name "biofeedback," forms very little of contemporary *behavioral* psychology outside Russia. As a method of conditioning autonomic activity, it has had a great impact on the field of psychosomatic medicine. But the actual conditioning procedures themselves rarely appear in contemporary research except as part of some larger issue. It is generally agreed that autonomic conditioning takes place, that it does so in the manner first reported by Pavlov, and that it needs no more confirmation than do Galileo's findings. Even in his 1909 speech Pavlov was quick to note that "it has long been known that the sight of tasty food makes the mouth of a hungry man water."[44] Thus, even from the outset, the conditioning *effect* could hardly be called revolutionary. It is this fact that makes it difficult for the non-psychologist to understand, as he reads modern textbooks, how psychology was "revolutionized" by Pavlov. The point, of course, is that it was not his studies of the conditioned reflex that made Pavlov a figure to be contended with; it was the *theory* advanced on the basis of these studies. While Watson never had a sophisticated appreciation of the Pavlovian system, his behaviorism, as reviewed above, provides the essentials. We will not examine the details. In the broadest terms, the Pavlovian theory requires that all so-called psychic functions are reducible to reflex mechanisms within the brain. By the frequent association of a neutral stimulus with one having unconditional biological significance, the former comes to have the power of eliciting responses originally produced by the latter only. Stimuli thus associated are now conditional (or conditioned) stimuli. If they are presented repeatedly without the application of the unconditioned stimulus, they will lose their power of elicitation; that is, *extinction* will occur. Not only does the specific, conditioned stimulus acquire the power of the unconditioned stimulus, but those stimuli physically similar to the conditioned stimulus acquire this power by *generalization*. Thus, if a tone of 1000 Hz is paired with the delivery of powdered food to the mouth, the 1000 Hz tone will acquire the power to elicit salivation. So too will tones of 900 Hz, 1100 Hz, etc. The magnitude of the conditioned response will diminish in proportion to the difference between the initial conditioned stimulus and the test-stimulus. Stimulus generalization is explained in terms of the *irradiation* of cortical responses to stimuli. A given stimulus (e.g., the 1000 Hz tone) establishes a region of maximum activity within the cortex, and this activity radiates, decrementally, to adjacent regions of the cortex. Accordingly, a reflex-association is established which is strongest between "food" and 1000 Hz and weaker between "food" and a tone different from 1000 Hz. Combined with conditioned excitation of the cerebral cortex, there may be conditioned *inhibition*, such as that produced by the application of a second stimulus on all trials when no reward is to be administered. Responses to the pair "S+" and "S°" (where "+" refers to the application of reward and "°" to its absence) will be weaker than responses to "S+" alone.

These principles—conditioning, extinction, radiation, excitation, and inhibition—are the central elements of Pavlov's biological psychology. Conceptually, it is scarcely different from the reflex-associationism of Hartley or, for that matter, Descartes, with the dualism removed. Procedurally, however, it is radically different from any of its philosophical ancestors because of its reliance upon laboratory investigation and quantitative measurement. Since the case for this psychology is stated against the background of data, criticism was to take an experimental form and would come chiefly from Karl Lashley (1890–1958).

Lashley and Watson were colleagues for a time at Johns Hopkins and even coauthored a paper on the environmental determinants of homing behavior in birds (1915).[45] Lashley's training was in anatomy, but his life was devoted to physiological psychology. He was neither a "mentalist" nor an "idealist" but was quick to discern the deficiencies of that biological associationism fostered by Pavlov and, in less mature fashion, by his American disciples. If we were to summarize his role in twentieth-century developments in physiological psychology, we might say that he bore the same relationship to the Pavlovians that Flourens bore to the phrenologists. We are tempted to call him a Gestalt psychologist—a label that would not have offended him in the least—but his work possessed a rigor and systematic quality seldom found in the orthodox Gestalt tradition. Moreover, he did not merely speculate about the nervous system, he examined it directly. As with our treatments of other productive experimenters, we are not in a position to analyze the details of their research. Lashley's most important statements have been collected by his former students and may be consulted.[46] For historical purposes, a very brief review is sufficient.

Like Flourens, Lashley was sufficiently familiar with the clinical findings in neurology and neurosurgery to know that no simple relationship existed between a particular locus within the brain and complex psychological processes such as perception, learning, and memory. Like Köhler, he subscribed to a form of isomorphism regarding this relationship but not an elementarism. His own studies of the effects of surgical destruction of brain regions in animals trained to perform various discriminations proved that complex abilities survive the removal or maceration of even extensive amounts of cortical tissue. But other studies also revealed very substantial effects when restricted regions of the brain were disturbed or removed. Lashley framed two broad principles to account for as much of the data as any general statement was likely to embrace: the principle of *mass action* and that of *equipotentiality*. By *mass action* Lashley meant to convey the idea that when it comes to complex psychological processes, the brain functions *as a whole* and is to be understood as a whole. The principle of *equipotentiality* was invented to account for the otherwise perplexing fact that surgically produced deficits disappear in time. The deficits indicate that particular regions of the brain do serve specific functions, but postoperative recovery indicates that other regions of the brain are able to assume these functions when the primary area has been destroyed or removed.

If Pavlov's studies were careful, Lashley's were clever and even dramatic. A cat is equipped with an eye patch covering the right eye and is called upon to learn a visual discrimination, for example, to jump off a platform toward a circle but not toward a triangle. Once the animal has learned this to a criterion level of performance, the patch is removed from the right eye and placed over the left. On the very first test-trial, the cat performs as well as it did on the last training trial. Since the optic nerve involved in the original learning is not involved in the test of transfer, we must be cautious about the sorts of neural "associations" we are to posit in attempting to account for learning. Clearly it cannot be the impulses in the optic nerve that have become associated with specific motor discharges. With respect to the latter, Lashley had another finding to offer. If the motor roots of the spinal cord are compressed, the limb on the treated side becomes paralyzed, and impulses from the cord to the peripheral muscles are blocked. In time, the limb recovers. Animals so treated can be trained to emit appropriate responses with the normal limb during the period in which the treated limb is immobile. Now the trained animals undergo compression of the motor root on the normal side such that the limb that performed the task no longer can. Shortly after this, the initially treated limb has recovered. How does the animal perform? The answer is, *perfectly*. The limb that was not and could not have been involved in the actual learning is used as effectively as the now immobile limb that had been the "trained" limb. Again, if the associationist theory requires that specific sensory and specific motor elements be combined for learning to occur, the theory is wrong.

With respect to generalization and the "irradiation hypothesis" designed to account for it, Lashley presented data from transposition studies to show that the effective stimulus is not necessarily the one most closely represented cortically. Not only that, but in some sensory systems, the sensory outcome is not topographically represented at all. The experience of loudness, for example, is not based upon the anatomical juxtaposition of progressive "loudness" centers.

Perhaps Lashley's most significant findings were in the areas of learning and memory. He demonstrated in a variety of different experimental settings that the animal's ability to acquire a complex behavioral repertoire and to reproduce it after a long retention interval was not systematically related to specific loci within the cerebral cortex. He remarked whimsically that, after searching for the "engram" of memory for many years, he was forced to conclude that learning was simply not possible! Behind the wry comment was the *caveat* that the brain is not one of La Mettrie's clocks, nor is man Condillac's sentient statue. More recent findings in physiological psychology have shown that Lashley may have been too pessimistic in his position on localization of function and that he was certainly misled by his focus on the cerebral cortex to the exclusion of subcortical mechanisms. These findings have not, however, led to a revival of interest or hope in cortical reflexes as the *units of thought*. In his 1938 presentation of the new behaviorism, Skinner dwells at length on reflexes, reflex-reserves, reflex connections. By 1950, this language is replaced with a distinct aloofness toward neurological and physiological hypotheses. We must look to Lashley's works to find the source of this transition.

Satellites

We cannot leave this chapter on contemporary formulations without remarking on activities that enjoy substantial attention among modern psychologists but are not sufficiently original, explicit, or general to count as movements of intellectual consequence. This is not to dismiss such enterprises as unimportant, for they may come to affect the human condition more quickly and tellingly than will a fair fraction of the ideas we have explored thus far. It is to say, instead, that some of these undertakings are either so tied to a larger vision or so removed from any set of ideas that may fairly be said to comprise an intellectual tradition that a work devoted to the intellectual history of psychology cannot or need not find a place for them. Three such undertakings come to mind: *psychological testing, neo-Freudian theories of personality*, and what, for lack of a more descriptive label, will be called *genetic psychology*.

We mentioned Francis Galton in the previous chapter and observed that his interest in "intelligence" was tied to a larger commitment to Darwinian theory and epistemological empiricism. While Galton was one of the first to publish the results of attempts to measure intelligence, it was Alfred Binet (1857–1911) whose efforts along these lines were most influential. By 1916 American psychologists had already begun to modify Binet's tests for use in the United States, and since then the field of "mental testing" has grown almost uncontrollably, as any college student will readily agree. There are many controversies among those who construct these tests and even something of a "theory" behind each type of test. But when this large and varied enterprise is examined from a little distance, one is not able to discern divisions or perspectives of a compelling philosophical nature. Galton's influence is still felt in that the tests are designed to yield a normal distribution of scores reflecting, one is supposed to believe, the "natural variation" Darwin spoke of in describing the characteristics of plants and certain animals. But in the instance of psychological tests, the random variations are not found; they are imposed in that a test failing to yield scores that are thus distributed is considered to be a poor test. A homely analogy can be found in the difference between the size of feet and the size of shoes; that is, if shoe manufacturers

were to make shoes of all one length and if we were to judge the distribution of foot lengths in terms of shoe lengths, we would conclude that
feet do not vary! An analysis of this field does not have a place in the
present context but we must, by way of explaining our deletion of it
among the topics explored, propose that no analysis will succeed in
presenting the specialty as a fundamental force in the evolution of
psychology. It is a fruit bearing no seed.

Many interesting developments have taken place in clinical psychology
and in that branch of it devoted to theories of personality. Psychoanalytic
theory, by all contemporary lights, is far from the mechanical, physicalistic, system of Freud. None of the revisions, however, has either over-
thrown the Freudian view or presented a picture of man that intellectual
history had failed to perceive. There is much written these days about
"freedom," "self-actualization," "personal growth," and "humanism," but
this only looks new to those who have not yet gotten around to the
scholars of the Enlightenment, to Hegel, Mill, and their respective disciples. Where Freud's theory was instinctual in tone, the modified
perspectives tend to be more environmentalistic and hopeful. At best,
the differences between Freud and his revisionists are restatements of the
more careful and searching antagonisms between Locke and Leibniz,
Hume and Kant.

Genetic psychology has branched out prolifically to cover the spectrum
from insect tropisms to social institutions. The ethologists tend to require
genes to do far more than molecular biology will allow. While "genetic
engineering" has become another technological marvel of the twentieth
century, the underlying concepts were laid down by Plato in his *Republic*
and are as open to criticism as were Plato's. One hardly has an explanation
of aggression once told that "it" is "inherited." When the explanations
become more refined than this, they tend to fit into physiological psychology, proper, and are assessed, *ipso facto*, by any general assessment
of the parent discipline.

We close this chapter by recognizing that in the very long history of
speculation about the human mind, about the determinants of conduct,
experience, feeling, and motives, very similar themes have appeared, held
sway, and then retreated for a time. The nineteenth century was responsible for that scientific formulation of psychology that has served as
the model ever since. From that formulation the twentieth century
presents two broad possibilities that are compatible, notwithstanding
differences between them: behaviorism and physiological psychology,
the one deriving from empirical philosophy, the other from philosophical
materialism. Each of these now is offered with a certain tone of finality;
each is given to that historic locution, "man is nothing but . . ." Each,
in a different way, promises a more perfect world, one that is more

comprehensible and controllable. Each, in its way, proclaims to have removed the mysteries or, at least, to have provided the methods whereby any residual mysteries will be swept aside. In the next and final chapter, we will analyze these claims and the evidence upon which they are said to rest.

References

1. E. B. Titchener, *A Primer of Psychology*, Macmillan, Inc., New York, 1914, p. 32.

2. A brief but excellent discussion of this point is found in W. C. Dampier's *A History of Science*, Cambridge University Press, 1966 edition, pp. 288–290.

3. Fechner, in his *Elemente der Psychophysik*, cites R. Wagner's *Handwörterbuch der Physiologie*, III, ii, pp. 481–588, as the source containing Weber's findings and law. Gustav Fechner, *Elements of Psychophysics*, translated by Helmut Adler, Henry Holt Editions in Psychology, New York, 1966, p. 15.

4. Titchener, op. cit., p. 32.

5. William James, *A Text Book of Psychology*, Macmillan, New York, 1892, p. 1.

6. Ibid., pp. 6–8.

7. Charles Darwin, *The Expression of the Emotions in Man and Animals*, Appleton-Century-Crofts, New York, 1896, p. 366.

8. Matthew Arnold's *Culture and Anarchy* was first published in 1869 and can be found in any number of Arnold anthologies. Particularly good is the discussion by J. Dover Wilson, Cambridge University Press, Cambridge, 1932: Arnold's *Culture and Anarchy*.

9. Theodor Ziehen, *Introduction to Physiological Psychology*, Macmillan, Inc., New York, 1895, p. 1.

10. E. W. Scripture, *The New Psychology*, Scribner, New York, 1910, p. 2.

11. Titchener, op. cit., pp. 33–34.

12. Kurt Koffka, *Principles of Gestalt Psychology*, Harcourt Brace, Jovanovich, New York, 1935, p. 18.

13. Wilhelm Wundt, *Lectures on Human and Animal Psychology*, translated from the second German edition by J. E. Creighton and E. B. Titchener, Macmillan, Inc., New York, 1907, pp. 340–341.

14. John B. Watson, "*Psychology as the Behaviorist Views It*," *Psychological Review*, 20 (1913), 158–177.

15. James, *A Text Book of Psychology*, op. cit., p. 165.

16. John Dewey, *The Reflex Arc Concept in Psychology. Psychological Review*, 3 (1896), 357–370.

17. John B. Watson, *Psychological Care of Infant and Child*. Norton, New York, 1928.

18. John B. Watson, *Behavior: An Introduction to Comparative Psychology*, Holt, Rinehart and Winston, New York, 1914.

19. See also his *Psychology from the Standpoint of a Behaviorist*, Lippincott, Philadelphia, 1919; J. B. Watson and W. McDougall, *The Battle of Behaviorism*, Norton, New York, 1929.

20. In 1911, E. L. Thorndike published a collection of his experiments under the title *Animal Intelligence: Experimental Studies*. This seminal collection has been reprinted as a facsimile edition by the Hafner Publishing Co., Darien, Conn., 1970.

21. E. L. Thorndike, op. cit. p. 244.

22. Thorndike, op. cit., p. 244.

23. John B. Watson, *Behaviorism*, University of Chicago Press, 1924, p. 206.

24. Ivan Pavlov, *Conditioned Reflexes: An Investigation of the Physiological Activity of the Cerebral Cortex*, translated and edited by G. V. Anrep, Oxford University Press, London, 1927.

25. Watson, *Behaviorism*, op. cit., p. 206.

26. Ibid., p. 225.

27. Ibid., pp. 22–39.

28. Ibid., p. 24.

29. Ibid., p. 111–113.

30. Ibid., Ch. VII.

31. Ibid., Introduction, p. vii.

32. B. F. Skinner, *The Behavior of Organisms*, Appleton-Century-Crofts, New York, 1938.

33. Prof. Skinner has published widely as a social philosopher, a behavioral technologist, a philosopher of science, a novelist, and a laboratory investigator. These varied talents are loosely combined in *Science and Human Behavior*, Macmillan, New York, 1956. His prescriptions and proscriptions for a behavioral science appear in *Are Theories of Learning Necessary?* (*Psychological Review*, 57 (1950), 193–216) and in *The Science of Learning and the Art of Teaching* (*Harvard Educational Review* (Spring 1954), pp. 86–97). His utopian vision is shared in *Walden II* (Macmillan, Inc., New York, 1948) and defended in *Beyond Freedom and Dignity* (Knopf, New York, 1971).

34. Skinner, *The Behavior of Organisms*, op. cit., p. 432.

35. An extensive collection of Pavlov's lectures and papers has been translated and placed in a volume titled *Experimental Psychology and Other Essays*, Philosophical Library, New York, 1957. The quotation is taken from p. 599 of this work, translated from a lecture given in 1935.

36. Wolfgang Kohler, *Gestalt Psychology*, Liveright, New York, 1947, p. 177.

37. Ibid., pp. 7–41.

38. Wolfgang Kohler, *The Mentality of Apes*. Originally published in German. First English edition published by Routledge and Kegan Paul, London, 1925. Reprinted from the Ella Winter translation by Vintage Books, New York, 1959.

39. Ibid., p. 93, Vintage edition.

40. E. C. Tolman, *Cognitive Maps in Rats and Man*, Psychological Rev., 55 (1948), 189–208.

41. Kohler, *Gestalt Psychology*, op. cit., p. 94.

42. See Skinner's *The Science of Learning and the Art of Teaching*, op. cit.

43. Pavlov, *Experimental Psychology*, op. cit., p. 148.

44. Ibid., p. 141.

45. J. B. Watson and K. S. Lashley, *Homing and Related Activities of Birds*, Carnegie Institution, Department of Marine Biology, 1915, Vol. VII.

46. Karl S. Lashley, *The Neuropsychology of Lashley: Selected Papers of K. S. Lashley*, edited by F. A. Beach, McGraw-Hill, New York, 1960.

12

□□□□□□□□□□□□□□□□□□□□□□□□□□□□

Mind, Matter, and Utopias

Chivalric Ideals and Darwinian Necessity

It is Christian teaching that has promulgated the conception of a living God and the belief that we are children of God, made "in the image and likeness" of the Father. This pervasive conviction divides time into Ancient and Modern more thoroughly than even science does. Archimedes would have been in awe of Galileo, but he would have understood Galileo's mechanics completely. Galileo's religious faith would have been far more puzzling; the immortality of the soul, personal survival in a hereafter, the transubstantiation of the spirit, a day of judgment, original sin, the state of grace, the living saints, all would have boggled the Greek mind. That traces of these ideas may be found in the fragments of the pre-Socratics or in Orphism or in passages from Plato's *Dialogues* does not vitiate the central fact of the Greek outlook: that human life is a matter of little concern to the gods of Olympus who, as with man, must take their chances and accept their fate. No Greek god would sacrifice his only son in the name of human salvation, and no Greek peasant could do anything in this life that might earn him eternity among the Olympians. When Plato searched for a larger model whose properties might more readily disclose the essential nature of human life, he found the State. The model, from the Patristic age until the eighteenth century, was God himself. Man could know God by learning about man and could penetrate the psychological recesses of human life by knowing God. The two most vivid products of this altered perspective were Scholastic philosophy and Chivalry. One sought to discern God's plan through the marvels of human reason; the other to mimic the divine through strength, sacrifice, and swift justice.

The Medieval mind did not invent the idea of the hero. Greek and Roman lore offer all the examples one could ever ask for. But the heroic elements of the chivalric life were secondary to the idea of *duty*. The Greek hero, in his displays of fearless courage, exhibited his manhood; the knight-errant, his godliness. The Greek hero was called upon to fight against the odds (i.e., *Lachesis*), to do battle with fate (*Moira*), quietly resigned to the unalterable fact that, ultimately, chance and fate must triumph. The knight attacked the infidel whose sins were errors, whose soul would either perish or be won. No matter how many small skirmishes might be lost to the devil, God's ultimate victory was secure. The knight, then, could not be vanquished in any final sense. Only his body could be destroyed.

What have these Medieval institutions to do with modern psychology? What have they to do with the recent antecedents of modern psychology? An attempt to answer these questions can be found in Chapters 4 through 11. By way of summary, we may add this: psychology's interest in motivation, in moral perception, in human conduct, and in the laws of behavior has come into being principally in the wake of the ideas and practices dating from the Medieval epoch. Until the time of Galileo, the earth and its people were the subject of creation; soon after, they were the objects. The philosophical revolution introduced by Hume challenged the way scholars might talk about human nature, but even Hume could not alter the way they *felt* about it. Even this, however, was transformed by Darwinian biology. The latter converted the lion's pride, the mother robin's labors, and man's defiance to mere expressions of the immutable laws of nature. No special "interior light" guided human conduct along the paths of righteousness; no special ordinances had been legislated in man's behalf and to the disadvantage of his competitors; no abrupt beginning had set the varieties of living types in motion; no forces other than natural ones would determine their survival; no chivalrous act could suspend the justice of the jungle; no Scholastic analysis would bring charity to the struggle for existence. Where Plato would discover man's special nature in the attributes of the good State and where the Scholastics might find this nature in God's own, the modern psychologist henceforth would find this nature *in nature*. The soul was now an enlightened machine, and "enlightenment" was simply a synonym for adaptive potential. Henceforth, chivalry would be . . . ridiculous.

Historians, when their reading habits are proper, are not easily convinced that an idea or movement or *Zeitgeist* is brand-new. Given the two errors one may commit in reflecting on the character of his own time, the historian tends to commit the error of underestimation and to take for granted that very many previous periods were more interesting and portentous than his own. This is the error of conservatism and is the only error scholars are willing to excuse, even applaud. But the twentieth century has hosted events of a very special sort, a truly precedential sort, and modern psychology is not the least of them. Daring and troubling ideas are no longer confined to the inner circle of literate, sophisticated scholars equipped to take the time and the care to weigh them against the balance of thought. Now, the more daring the idea, the more likely it is to be broadly diffused by the most elaborate and rapid system of dissemination witnessed in history. Scarce resources conspire with a delicately balanced international economy to render every political decision one of staggering potential. And, of course, the mere *machinery* of the age allows some to transform their own and the lives of many, many others with alarming speed and irretrievability. We have, then, a federation of realities in our century never before seen—a federation of global and instant communication, able to homogenize perspectives, global needs able to instigate mammoth, popular responses, and a technology whose effects can be complete in a span of time that is short in comparison with the time it takes to reconsider. Under these circumstances, what man believes to be true about himself, what the human population recognizes to be its essential nature, are no longer merely academic matters. They are matters of historic proportion. They are historic in the same sense that the ideas that animated the Crusades were historic, in the sense that the chivalric ideal, the Roman *Dominate*, and the *Enlightenment* perspective were historic. They determine what people will do, what they will suffer, what they will demand, and what they will surrender. Great ideas have always had these consequences, but under the circumstances of modern life we must recognize that the consequences are amplified and by an unprecedented degree.

The ideas to be addressed in this chapter, while not invented by psychologists, have been refined and disseminated in large part by the psychologists of this century. They are ideas that have received the attention and support of influential sectors of the philosophical community and are quickly becoming the insensible convictions of the literate world at large. Described most tersely, the ideas are: *mind is brain* and *all behavior is conditioned, if it is not random*. We will refer to the former as the *identity* thesis and the latter as the *behavioristic* thesis. Each appears in a variety of ways, in radical or more conservative forms. Each permits a utopian vision according to which most of the regrettable features of the human condition can be eliminated by an existing or inchoate technology. Each denies the validity of all previous philosophical and psychological alternatives. Each rests its central claim on the authority of science, occasionally with indirect support from logical analysis. In the following sections, we will attempt to assess the evidence tending to favor or refute these theses.

Before beginning this analysis, it is profitable to draw the distinction between the speculative discourse of philosophers and the existence of a *Zeitgeist*. In the western world of our own century, the tensions prevailing a hundred years earlier have been largely relaxed owing to the supremacy gained by one of them: *positivism*. This supremacy is not intellectual or philosophical but social. That is, it is not the supremacy finally won by Copernicanism over Ptolemaicism but that won by, shall we say, *the Rights of Man* over *the Divine Right of Kings*. The Copernican theory succeeded finally because it conformed to the facts of science and the data of amplified observation. The march of egalitarianism and the retreat of elitism are not to be understood in these terms. Egalitarianism derives no support from science nor are the justifications for elitism disproved by perception or experimentation. Social movements seek philosophical and scientific sanctions but the movements themselves have a life of their own. They are historical movements tending to drag science and philosophy along with them and certainly not tarrying until the philosophers and scientists are convinced.

To the extent that positivism has triumphed in the struggle for man's allegiance, the victory has brought mixed results and few of the promised ones. Darwin's most forceful and effective disciple was Huxley who undertook to transform higher education into an essentially scientific education. He and his supporters, in essays and speeches, in symposia and light articles, drafted that division of mind that continues to occupy our attention: the division between science and humane letters. Today, when a leading spokesman for behavioral psychology, complains that students are still encouraged to read Plato if they wish to learn something about human behavior, we witness the survival of Huxley's attacks on those who would address the problems of the world with "a smattering of Greek."

While Huxley worked to replace *belles lettres* with science in English education, Ernest Renan was berating the "superficial humanism" extolled in the higher education of France.* It was Huxley, too, who would label the patrons of *belles lettres* the "Levites of Culture." What, after all, was gained from antique studies, from Latin grammar, or the rhetoric of Cicero? What does one know about himself or the natural world having read the idle speculations of Sallust or the pseudoscience of Lucretius? If our interest is in determining our origin and destiny, what more is

* Ernest Renan, "L'Instruction Superieur en France" (*Questions Contemporaines* [1868], Paris).

necessary than Darwin's scientific proposition, boldly offered in *The Descent of Man:*

"Our ancestor was a hairy quadruped with a tail and pointed ears, probably arboreal in his habits." (Part II, Ch. 21).

Huxley, Renan, and the less celebrated figures of Victorian naturalism did not go unchallenged. At Cambridge (1882) and later in America (1883–84) Matthew Arnold defended *belles lettres* and predicted that their temporary losses to the soldiers of science would be reversed; that there is something in the human frame that cannot avoid or ignore beauty and intellect. Arnold would argue that "the hairy quadruped with a tail and pointed ears"

"carried hidden in his nature, apparently, something destined to develop into a necessity for humane letters. Nay, more; we seem finally to be even led to the further conclusion that our hairy ancestor carried in his nature, also, a necessity for Greek."*

But the challenges were doomed from the outset. The industrial world had become entrenched, the metaphor of the machine a reality. Especially in America, the practical demands and the means of satisfying them consumed and quickened the popular mind. Emerson may well have been the herald of the age in declaring *work* to be the source of our majesty.

Positivism succeeded at the expense of romantic idealism but the success was not based upon any consideration that positivism, itself, demands. The history of social movements—itself a history of ideas in action—is animated by the desire of human beings to understand themselves, to control their short and long range fortunes, to place their loyalties in the care of worthy men and institutions, to discern meaning in daily life, to act upon the impulses of an awakened mind. It is true that the corpus of *belles lettres* has not answered the questions or settled the issues with which human life is sorely concerned. The fact is, of course, that science has not either. In its most defining respects, science is not even intended to address these matters.

The revolutionary climate sustained by the *Enlightenment* found neither support nor criticism in science. Rousseau's theory of the *social contract*, resting as it does on some putative need or sentiment of man "in the original state," is not a scientific theory and is not even a social theory capable of scientific assessment. We do not have access to men "in

---

* The collection, *Discourses in America*, written the year after Arnold's return from the States. His characterization of the American temperament of 1884 is not unlike that given by essayists in our own time.

the original state" nor would the "sentiments" of such a man be safely generalized to those living in less innocent environs. The status of the proposition that *"man is born free"* is no higher than that which insists that *"man is born in the image and service of God."* The same is true of the proposition, "science is the only route to positive knowledge." There is no experiment that will prove the claim; no observation that will render it beyond appeal; no historical record of prior proof; no experimental disconfirmation of alternative formulations. To accept that "science is the only route to positive knowledge" must be founded on the same considerations that lead to belief in ethical, moral, and religious propositions. The choice is largely aesthetic in tone and not evidential.

The two propositions that will occupy the balance of this chapter are of the same cloth. In declaring that "human behavior is completely determined" or that "the will is not free" or that "mind is matter only" or that "man is completely understandable by the methods of science," the theorist joins company with earlier sages who contended that "the will is so free that it can never be constrained" or that "man is just lower than the angels." These are not scientific propositions but philosophical speculations. What removes them from the domain of *belles lettres* is more the style than the content. Accordingly, their historical consequence does not result from their increased plausibility—they were no more or less plausible when advanced at any time in history—but from the increased allegiance they might command at a given time. In our own time, the materialistic (*identity*) thesis and the *behavioristic* thesis enjoy a large and growing following. The principle claims of these theses have appeared throughout the history of ideas. They can be found in the writings of the Greek *Atomists*, the Stoics and Epicureans, in Ockham and in Hobbes, in most of the works published by the *philosophes* and the British empiricists. It is often suggested that the prior failure of these ideas to dominate their times is to be understood as the failure of previous eras to develop a science able to deal with them. There is an alternative explanation: that the success or failure of such theses has little or nothing to do with science because the theses are not scientific propositions in the first place.

It is this alternative that is recommended here and defended in the balance of this chapter.

Minds and Bodies

One of the more persistent notions in philosophical speculation—and one that has animated psychological thought since the seventeenth century— is that the human mind is to be understood ultimately in material terms.

Such an idea is implicit in the atomistic theories of Democritus and Leucippus and has been explicit in the writings of countless philosophers from the Stoics and Epicureans on. It is the major premise of Gall's phrenological psychology as it was of La Mettrie's philosophical psychology. The essential contribution of Pavlovian psychology is also to be understood in these terms since, beyond the mere fact of the conditioned reflex, Pavlov's psychological system recommended an uncompromisingly materialistic perspective. Even the modern behaviorist, who for systematic and methodological reasons might prefer not to analyze biological processes himself, is generally (if conservatively) committed to a *materialist-monist* position. According to this position, the universe is not comprised of two mutually exclusive categories of "stuff," that is, "mental" and "material." It is comprised of only one and that is *material*. George Berkeley's *idealist-monist* alternative has not found a sympathetic audience in the scientific community since early in the nineteenth century and no significant figure in the brief history of experimental psychology has ever adopted it. It would be fair to say that no living experimental psychologist of exceptional repute has publicly declared that the issue remains open, although the neurobiologist Roger Sperry has at least tested the idea.[1]

Predictably, philosophers remain willing to debate the point and their journals, over the past half-century, have never been completely indifferent to the "mind-body" problem. But twentieth-century "scientific" psychology, which scarcely acknowledges a debt to the last two thousand years of philosophical scholarship, is in no direct way influenced by the arguments treated in contemporary philosophical journals.

Among so large and varied a group of professionals whose record of peaceful agreements is remarkably thin, it is surprising to find such a broad consensus. We cannot explain this consensus by simply observing that the metaphor of the machine has become the reality, since this observation does no more than restate the fact of theoretical agreement. "Why," the question remains, "has the metaphor become the reality?" One answer commonly forthcoming is that such great strides have been made in neurophysiology and neuropsychology that it seems to be only a matter of time before we are able to identify a specific brain process for each specific mental process. But this is hardly a justification for materialistic monism, since *dualism* does not require that there be no brain! Indeed, dualism does not even necessarily require that mental events not be the effects of neural causes. A modest dualism only asserts that there *are* mental events. To show, then, that such events are somehow caused by material events, far from establishing the validity of a monist position, virtually guarantees the validity of a dualist position. To say, that is, that "I have a mind that is an entity different from material entities" is to assert a proposition that cannot be falsified by *any* demonstration of the causes of the proposed mental entity. In other words, the putative strides that have been made in neurobiology, strides in the direction of discovering correlations between mental and neural events, do not bear directly on the monist-dualist issue and therefore do not provide logical support for complacent monism.

A second generic answer has to do with the metaphysical commitment to the so-called *unity of sciences*, proclaimed by Helmholtz and generally endorsed by those whose special training is in the natural sciences. The *unity of sciences* argument takes several forms and borrows liberally from Ockham's injunction against complicating the causes of an event when it can be explained by simpler ones. In most of its variants, the argument raises parsimony to the level of a universal principle and seeks support from such theoretical syntheses as those that unite chemistry and quantum physics. However, when the argument is used to defend the monist position in the mind-body dispute, it automatically becomes the fallacy of *petitio principii*. We hardly refute the dualist by telling him he is wrong! Since his proposition is that there is an entity in the real world that is *not* physical, our rebuttal must go beyond the assertion that all entities are physical. Put another way, it is the phenomenon of mind, itself, that serves as the most compelling and vexing challenge to the *unity of sciences* theses. The latter, therefore, cannot be used as an argument against that which denies it.

The third and more thoughtful generic answer is provided by a number of analytical philosophers who find in dualism not so much a metaphysical proposition as a set of logical and semantic deficiencies. They have argued that talk about minds and talk about brains are, when properly understood, talk about the same thing; that is, not that mental events are caused by physical ones but that there are *only* physical events, although we may use mentalistic terms to describe some of them. The promise offered by these philosophers is one that will eliminate dualism through a process of linguistic analysis. Two of the most frequently cited spokesmen for this position are Professors Gilbert Ryle and J. J. C. Smart. Ryle's *The Concept of Mind* (1949),[2] as a polemic against *"Descartes' Myth,"*[3] remains one of the seminal contributions to that field of inquiry that seeks to reformulate the mind-body issue into one that is principally linguistic.

Descartes' "myth," which Ryle recasts as *"the ghost in the machine,"* is, we are told, just one powerful instance of the common mistake of assuming that there are as many entities as we have words for them. It is to commit, again using Ryle's terms, a *category error*. Ryle speaks of the foreign visitor to Oxford who asks a question of this sort: "I've seen your buildings, and your student-body, your classes and administrative offices. I've been through the library and the residence halls and have listened to your debate teams. Now I would like to see *Oxford University*. Could you tell me where it is?" What the foreign visitor has failed to recognize is that there is not some *super*entity, *Oxford University*, above and beyond classes, students, libraries, and activities of the type mentioned. He has assumed, innocently and incorrectly, that a linguistic category necessarily implies existential status; that is, that something called *Oxford University* exists and is to be found *somewhere* beyond or different from the *places* where students, books, debates, and so forth, occur.

The mind-body thesis of the dualist, Ryle contends, is another version of the *category mistake*. Since the dualist talks of brains but also talks of dreams, ideas, experiences, and feelings, he assumes that the two categories of talk entail two categories of existence. What Ryle wants is for this talk to be translated into the *doings* and the *dispositions to do* of bodies, that is, of people. He does not argue that minds are merely brains or even that such an argument could make sense. What he does insist, however, is that dualism cannot succeed because it is riddled with category mistakes and insistent on the existence of ghosts. Instead of beating the dead horse of Cartesianism, Ryle would prefer to base psychology (and metaphysics) on an observational foundation. We thereby explain what is *mental* in terms of what people actually say and in terms of the observable factors that lead them to say it. Ryle's position is *behavioristic*, not in the sense of a commitment to theories of conditioning or laws of learning, but in the sense of demanding behavioral criteria in defining psychological terms. For Ryle, then, the mind-body problem is solved by being exposed as a pseudoproblem. It is not necessary to "prove" monism or dualism to be correct, even if one were to conceive of a way of doing so. Rather, it is necessary to recognize what we mean when we use mentalistic and physicalistic terms in discussing events of a psychological character. The events, themselves, are *behavioral*. Accordingly, a complete behavioral description exhausts the phenomenon under question. Terms of a nonbehavioral variety necessarily go beyond the phenomenon and invite category mistakes.

It would not be fair to Ryle to summarize his position as one of evasion; Ryle is one of the more forceful and lucid scholars of our time. Still, *The Concept of Mind* has not been and is not likely to become successful in converting all talk about human psychology to *performative* talk. When Ryle insists that we do not know what is in someone's mind until, by performance, that person tells us, he can only be reflecting on the limitations implicit in those so-called objective methods of knowing anything. That the mental states of Smith are *his* and only become available to us through some behavior on Smith's part is not to say that these states do not exist until we acknowledge them. Moreover, in creating dispositional categories in addition to purely descriptive behavioral ones, Ryle too courts the *category* error. To say that Smith is disposed to smoke cigarettes instead of saying that Smith has it in his mind to do so is to offer a distinction without a difference. In both cases we are imputing to Smith a quality of mind that is not observable and is only perilously inferrable. Smith may be disposed to smoke and not; he may unconsciously light a cigarette; he may be under hypnotic suggestion and be of the mind that cigarettes are pipes and matches, soap bubbles.

Ryle rebukes those ensnared by the "ghost in the machine":

"In unconscious reliance upon this dogma theorists and laymen alike constantly construe the adjectives by which we characterise performances as ingenious, wise, methodical, careful, witty, etc. as signalising the occurrence in someone's hidden stream of consciousness of special processes functioning as ghostly harbingers or, more specifically, as occult causes of the performances so characterised. . . . I am arguing that in describing the workings of a person's mind we are not describing a second set of shadowy operations . . . we are describing the ways in which parts of his conduct are managed."[4]

But what does it mean to refer to *part* of one's conduct? Ryle certainly is not proposing that what makes someone "ingenious" is a particular movement or reflex; that to be witty is to add or subtract a part of a behavioral whole.*[5] And what does it mean to say that someone's conduct is *managed* if not that some less than "shadowy" mental operation is engaged prior to the emission of behavior?

Ryle notes the error of assuming that mental activity is something that goes on in a *place* different from the *place* in which saying, feeling, and learning go on. He does not go so far as to say that all these go on in the brain, nor does he applaud that La Mettrian dogma. But if we are to accept that conduct is *managed*, that conduct is observable, that, to be observable, it must be material, then what are we to say of the *manager*? It is routinely noted that stimulation of the motor cortex results in the movement of limbs on the contralateral side. The anatomical paths associated with this effect are well known. Presumably, we are allowed, even on Ryle's account, to say that the animal's movement is produced *in* its muscles by activity *in* the nerves supplying these muscles and that the latter is initiated by events *in* the motor cortex. Why then are we, on Ryle's account, proscribed from saying that Smith's chess moves are *in*

---

* Ryle here notes the mechanistic and elementaristic bias of early behaviorism and dismisses it on this count.

Smith's brain? Ryle wants us to believe that the two statements, "Smith's chess move is in the motor cortex" and "Smith's chess move is one he had in his mind," are as different in their logical structure as are the statements, "Smith arrived in a flood of tears" and "Smith arrived in a taxi."[6] Once we recognize this, we are told, we will no longer seek to have matter absorb mind or mind absorb matter. Instead, the contrast between mind and matter will "be dissipated."[7] But no materialist-monist could possibly agree with Ryle on this point. If all talk about mental states and brain states must forever be as different as talk about Smith's tears and his means of transportation, then dualism—and not merely linguistic dualism—can look forward to a long life. While it is true that the same Smith is in tears and in a taxi, being in a taxi is not the *same* as being in tears, and there is no analysis that will make the two the same. However, if the contrast between mind and matter is to be "dissipated," it is precisely an identity that is needed. What we must show, if we are to witness this dissipation, is that brain-talk and mind-talk involve different languages only and that what is being spoken *about* is the same thing. Ryle has not shown this. In the most important respects, *The Concept of Mind* does not even attempt to do so. J. J. C. Smart, however, has tried to do precisely this, and we shall now proceed to his analysis of the issue.

Smart has been one of the most persuasive defenders of the identity thesis in modern times. He has attempted to raise the traditional dualistic objections to this thesis and to rebut them *seriatim*. It is instructive to review what Smart has chosen as the more compelling dualistic arguments and to assess his replies to them. In one of his most widely cited articles, *Sensations and Brain Processes*, he sets himself to the task of showing "that there are no philosophical arguments which compel us to be dualists"[8] and for the following reasons:

First, Ockham's razor and the *unity of sciences* doctrine both recommend a reduction of mind- and body-talk to a single set of terms if this is possible. Second, "That everything should be explicable in terms of physics . . . except the occurrence of sensations seems to [Smart] to be frankly unbelievable."[9] Next, the traditional claims of the dualist lack empirical and logical support. These claims, according to Smart, reduce to eight:

1. The language we use to describe sensations is not the same as that which we use to describe brain processes, and this suggests that the two are not identical.

2. Even if sensations are caused by brain processes, the relationship between the two—if there is one—is merely a *contingent* relationship, not the logically necessary relationship required of identities.

3. The very quality of sensations is of a different sort than the properties of brain processes; for example, we would hardly describe a brain

process as "yellow." (Smart finds this one of the most sophisticated objections.)

4. Sensations, such as afterimages, are not in a particular location, whereas brain processes are.

5. Brain processes can be described in topographic and intensive terms; for example, fast, slow, large, etc. The sensation of "yellow" cannot. (This is not very different from claim 3, but Smart includes it.)

6. Sensations are private and cannot be *wrong* in the sense that statements about brain processes can be wrong.

7. One can imagine himself turned into a rock or tree and still having sensations, even though there is no attending brain process.

8. If there were not sensations *in addition to* brain processes, a language of the former never would have evolved and become ingrained in the speech of man.

Smart's replies to each of these objections will be summarized but with no distortion, it is hoped, to his position:

1'. People knowing nothing about electrical discharges can still talk about lightning. This fact in no way repudiates the *identity* relationship between "lightning-talk" and "electrical discharge-talk."

2'. It may be that when we say we see "yellow" we do not *mean* that we are having a brain process of such and such a sort but that does not show that the two are not identical. We may not *mean* the same things when we report the Morning Star and the Evening Star, but the two are, in fact, the same star. (Note that this reply is not germane to its corresponding objection. The objection was based on the notion that the relationship between brain processes and sensations is *contingent;* that is, the rules of logic do not require that sensation-X follow brain process-X'. If X and X' are *causally* related, rather than logically related, they are not *identities*. The relationship between the Morning Star and the Evening Star is not a *contingent* relationship, nor is the relationship between lightning and the discharge of electricity.)

3'. Smart's reply to the third objection is involved and takes recourse to some hypothetical person he calls a "normal percipient." A person is said to be a more "normal percipient" than another person when, for example, he can make finer discriminations than that person. "Yellow," then, is the power a stimulus has to evoke a discriminating response from a normal percipient. The stimulus is a *physical* one and produces physical effects in the brain. The sensation, "yellow," *is* the brain process evoked by the stimulus.

4'. Smart insists that his thesis is *not* that a sensation (e.g., an afterimage) is a brain process but that the *experience* of the sensation (e.g., an afterimage) is a brain process.

5'. When we say we see "yellow," we leave open what is going on in the brain. I may say, for example, that "someone is using the phone." You may say, "Dr. Jones is using the phone." In this case, and unbeknownst to me, "someone" and "Dr. Jones" are identical.

6'. The language of introspection "has a different logic from the language of material processes." Smart believes that the brain process theory must be improved and widely accepted before we agree to use brain process-talk as comfortably as we now use sensation-talk.

7'. We can imagine that the Morning Star is not the Evening Star, but it is.

8'. The conventional language of society can be changed. If it is now dualistic, it is so because of misconceptions.

Smart's first reply is unimpeachable just as the objection to which it is a reply is somewhat jejune. His second reply, as we have noted, is not a reply to the corresponding objection. Moreover, if we are to distinguish between what we report as sensations and what we *mean* to report, we will, on Smart's account, have to find still another brain process to be the identity of *meaning*. Indeed, what could it mean to say that brain process-X *didn't mean* to report sensation-X?

In his third reply, Smart merely repeats his thesis; he does not validate it. His "normal percipient," in the limiting case, is able to make discriminations *no one* else can and, therefore, can be called "normal" only through a strange sort of synonymy. Equally perplexing is his fourth reply in which we are asked to distinguish between a sensation and the *experience of* a sensation, for example, between an afterimage and the *having* of an afterimage. What would it mean, however, to say, "I have had a sensation but not the experience of one"? In his fifth reply, he again (*vide supra* reply 2') inserts a bona fide logical identity as if his thesis had been proved and now requires only instructive illustrations. That "someone" is, indeed, "Dr. Jones," may be a fact of which we are unaware. However, once we learn that "he" *is* "Dr. Jones," we are no longer able to ask, "When is he Dr. Jones?" or "Under what conditions is he Dr. Jones?" We (or, better, he and his certifying institutions) have *stipulated* that that man over there using the telephone is to be called "Dr. Jones." There are, of course, many Dr. Joneses, but only one of them is he. It is the name we have given to an object, and we have established a *nominal* identity which, when asserted, can be no more than a tautology. Whatever the connection between events in the brain and our experiences, it surely is not of this kind.

Replies 6' and 8' are similar and before going to them we might just comment on reply 7' by observing that we can also imagine brain processes and sensations to be identical and be wrong! Now, in regard to replies 6' and 8', we have a different species of reply from the rest. It springs quite naturally from arguments based on Ockham's razor, the *unity of sciences*, and still another shibboleth, which we will call *learning the brain's language*. Each of these is rooted in an inductive process which, itself, is not amenable to logical validation; that is, Hume's achievement. Nature is under no compulsion to behave parsimoniously or, if so behaving, to continue to do so. Moreover, it is not at all clear "that everything should be explicable in terms of physics," nor is it clear that if everything else were explicable in terms of physics, sensations could not be exceptional in this respect. Prof. Smart finds this possibility "unbelievable," but he would be the last one to foist a religious conviction upon a reluctant audience. In urging us to be patient as significant advances in the brain process theory take shape, he is exercising a theorist's right and a prudent man's responsibility. But when he concludes his essay with the admission that "there is no conceivable experiment which could decide between materialism and epiphenomenalism,"[10] he leaves one in the lurch. If no *conceivable* experiment can settle the score between the identity thesis and a dualist alternative, what is it one is to wait for? More to the point, if the issue cannot *conceivably* be settled by experimentation, on what basis are we to agree that the issue is even related to the putative fact that "everything should be explicable in terms of physics"? Things are explicable in terms of physics to the extent that they are drawn from the universe of at least *conceivable* experiments and observations. There may be problems in physics that we cannot now solve experimentally and will be forever beyond our practical powers of experimentation. But none, in principle, is beyond our power to *conceive* of a relevant and even decisive experiment. Some physicists would even contend that once we have found a problem whose solution could not *conceivably* be of an experimental nature, we have found, *ipso facto*, a problem that is not scientific at all. If the mind-body problem is of such a sort, the kinds of findings generated by the neural sciences are not even relevant to the issue.

In the sixth objection and Smart's reply to it, we find an instance of the so-called *incorrigibility* hypothesis.[11] It is ambiguously illustrated by the contention that sensations and feelings are "private." They are not merely private—which can also be said of the material contents of Smith's desk—but they are peculiarly *irrefutable*. When Smith visits his dentist and announces that he has a toothache, his declaration is not the subject of confirmation. This is not to say that Smith cannot lie, nor is it to say that Smith may not have confused sensations that make it difficult for him to determine whether, in fact, his sensations are best described as an ache. It is to say, instead, that there is no assessment external to Smith's that has higher face-validity than his declaration. Even if we wished to corroborate his account by measuring the discharge patterns emitted by his dental nerves, our confidence in the data would, at some point, have to be based on the correlation between such neurographic recordings and the *reported sensations* of a sensible organism. That is, the validity of the extrapersonal assessment would be judged in terms of its agreement with the introspective or behavioral reports of pain. If we accept such introspective reports as data, then they are data of a unique sort in scientific inquiry for, while we may be mistaken about brain processes, the speed of light, and annual rainfall in London, we cannot be mistaken about our toothache; at least we cannot be provably mistaken about such sensations. The dentist could only be puzzled and amused by Smith if he came in to the clinic, clutching his swollen jaw, and announced, "I have a toothache, unless I am mistaken." Smith's brain processes do not enjoy this irrefutable status, nor do measures of these processes. Nor are these processes private *in principle* as are Smith's aches. Given this difference, it is difficult to believe that there is an argument in the offing that will show the two to be *identical*. And, if they are shown to be even invariably correlated such that process-X is always followed by sensation-X', we will have advanced the neural sciences enormously but simultaneously established that in addition to brain processes, there are sensations; that is, dualism succeeds, at least linguistically in that we will still need a term for the causally necessary (experiential) effects of (neural) antecedents. And more than *linguistic* dualism would follow from this (unlikely) experimental finding. What more is revealed in Smart's own example of "lightning" and "electrical discharges"? In a world devoid of visual organs, there is no "lightning," only electrical discharges. "Lightning," as a sensation, is not another word for discharges; it is a word for the effects of discharges on the "normal percipient." We do not continue to use "lightning" in 1975 because we are, as were our distant ancestors, ignorant of its causes. In fact, we do not use "lightning" to express a cause but an *effect upon us*. The hope that "lightning" will one day be replaced by statements about the effects of atmospheric discharges upon discharges in the brain is based on the shibboleth referred to as *learning the brain's language*. It has sudden appeal to an audience steeped in electronic inventions, tools for communication, and so forth. It suggests that the mind, properly understood as brain, is no more than a breakable code, soon to surrender to the same scientific methods that have rendered the balance of nature comprehensible. We set aside, for the moment, the question of *comprehensible to whom*, since this requires the reintroduction of the very mind we are now attempting to penetrate and expose as brain.

The metaphor of the *code* has become more frequently used because the molecular biologists succeeded in identifying the structural nuances of the DNA molecule. In La Mettrie's day the most impressive gadgets were clocks and, not surprisingly, his *l'Homme Machine* is rich in allusions to them. Similarly, discourse in neurology from the 1900s to the 1930s was punctuated by references to telephone switchboards and cables. Through the 1950s and 1960s, the preferred model was the computer which, now coupled with the metaphor of the *code*, calls on us to *learn the language of the brain*. But who are the US being called upon to engage in this inquiry? Is *brain* being asked to learn its own language? Put another way, if the language now used in writing this sentence is some kind of a reduced or translated version of "brain-language," and if mind and brain are identical, then this sentence is being written by brain. Moreover, the words and letters forming these passages and ideas are but symbols or coded forms of brain processes. But who can author a coded language without a knowledge of that original language on which the code is based? Indeed, on the account given by the strict materialist-monist, the statement "We must learn language of the brain" would have to be as unintelligible as the statement "I have to learn the language I am now speaking." Either that or we must assume Descartes' evil demon—this time the brain—committed to deceiving . . . what? Itself? Are we to assume that brain has generated an audible and visible language based on its intrinsic, neuroelectric, and chemical processes and, having generated this language, is now ignorant of the physical correlates of the symbols? Must we (i.e., *brains*) learn the language of brains because the brains have forgotten? The problem, of course, and Leibniz recognized it fully when he welcomed us to enter the mill, is that an ultimate description of brain processes can only be in terms of matter in motion. We will find no neuron in possession of a noun, no glial cell or combination of glial cells displaying a motive, no chunk of cortex having a memory. We may find a chunk of cortex which, when stimulated, leads to our recollection of a memory, but this no more gives the cortex the memory than our inscriptions in a diary gives the diary a memory.

What this discussion has attempted to disclose is not that dualism is established or that the identity thesis is beyond appeal. Rather, we are asked only to recognize that the materialist thesis is not confirmed by experimental findings, nor is it even confirmable by such findings; also, that it enjoys no privileged position in the hierarchy of logical plausibility. If this is accepted, we are then in a position to raise a question of historical consequence: Why has contemporary psychology invested so great a share of its resources and reputation in studies concerned with the relationship between brain physiology and behavior? If it is because the brain is intrinsically interesting, warranting the attention of science, then we must ask what the difference is between psychology and neurophysiology. No one seriously questions the desirability of learning as much as we can about brain dynamics and about the effects of brain activity and pathology upon the experiences and behavior of organisms. But psychology's commitment to an enterprise such as this can and properly should lead to the assimilation of the discipline by biology.

Inquisitiveness, within the laws of the land and the canons of ethics, needs no defense. The brain is as proper an object of study as is the liver or spleen, Neptune or Mars. But the contemporary psychologist has not been prone to present his neurological research as the product of such inquisitiveness alone. To it, he adds—or at least does not demur when others add—that studies of this type are essential to an understanding of the *mind*. This (hypothetical) psychologist is, he will insist, engaged in *science* and will quickly distinguish between what he does and what those nineteenth (or twentieth) century "introspectionists" were up to. Ironically, the introspectionists *were* studying the mind, and Wundt himself was well aware of the difference between that sort of study and neurophysiology.

Whether or not physiological psychology is *science* is less important historically than is the fact that many psychologists insist that it is. To the extent that it is indistinguishable from physiology—which is replete with the necessary covering laws and empirical methods of verification discussed in the first chapter—physiological psychology *is* a science, but is not psychology! That is, it achieves the desired status by abandoning its historic problems. Alchemy suffered the same fate, and the consequence was a very admirable one: modern chemistry. If the analogy is apt, the contemporary psychologist who has concluded that no amount of experimentation will succeed in converting brain into mind has three options. He can conclude, with the assailants of alchemy, that mind is not in brain and he can proceed to study mind in a nonphysiological way. This decision preserves the discipline of psychology. He can conclude that mind *is* brain, but this forces him into a maze of logical and methodological traps; for example, the use of nonhuman animals now becomes a practice of dubious consequence; the previously discussed problems with Smart's thesis suffuse his every effort; organisms lacking brains must be rejected from the arena of comparative psychology. In addition, this decision dissolves the discipline and prepares it for assimiliation. He can, finally, conclude (with Leibniz) that mind and brain are different and parallel entities, each conforming to its special essence and pacing off its harmonious journey in a way perfectly correlated with the other. In this case, he is metaphysically anachronistic. Few physiological psychologists will accept any but the second alternative, which is no more than to reacknowledge contemporary psychology's debt to the nineteenth century.

The Behavioristic Thesis

Many have been attracted to behaviorism in part because it is free of the difficulties suffered by various forms of psychological materialism. Behaviorism is under no compulsion to speak of brains or minds. As early as 1938, in his very first book, Prof. Skinner announced his psychology's independence in regard to neurology, and those who subscribe to the so-called *Skinnerian* version of behaviorism have remained neutral or indifferent on the question of the role of brain-talk in psychology. There is no contradicting the fact that the independent status of psychology as a historically unique discipline is better protected by the canons of behaviorism than by any alternative formulation. It has surrendered (without regrets) the mind to philosophy, the body to biology, and personality to the clinicians. In certain respects, behaviorism has liberated itself from the goals and methods of nineteenth-century science more successfully than has any other division of psychological inquiry. Its spokesmen, and Skinner must head this list, have declared themselves against attempts to invent grandiose theories, to provide satisfying explanations, to unite psychology with all other sciences, to unearth "mechanisms," to penetrate the "mind." In place of these historic and resoundingly failing missions, the behaviorists propose to provide a *descriptive science of behavior* permitting the prediction and control of the actions of organisms. The maxim that directs their inquiry is one or another form of the *law of effect,* and this law is as close as they come to out-and-out theorizing. With the unadorned ethic of the pragmatic utilitarian, they ask to be judged by what they can do, not by what they say or fail to say about "psychological man." They have introduced the methods of operant conditioning into classrooms, psychiatric clinics, vocational schools, industrial training programs, counseling chambers, and even playgrounds. The techniques of "behavior modification" are as at home in penal institutions as they are in the animal laboratory. Their application is recommended with the same confidence whether the "organism" is a white rat, a convicted felon, an autistic child, a performing seal, a schizophrenic patient, or a difficult student.

Critics of behaviorism have not been in short supply. Their attacks have been broad, often Delphic, sometimes ridiculous, and seldom dispassionate. Humanists (?) have condemned it as a "dehumanizing" psychology, theologians as a godless one, ethicists as amoral, nonbehavioristic psychologists as a reductionistic evasion. Philosophers in the tradition of the British empiricists have found it quite compelling; those in the Hegelian tradition, quite absurd. Political theorists in the line beginning with

Bentham have judged it to be nearly ideal; those in the Kantian succession, blatantly fascistic. Not even Freud attracted so diverse an assembly of friends and enemies. Far from chastening the advocates of behaviorism, all this attention and condemnation have called forth bold resolve, most recently evidenced in Skinner's *Beyond Freedom and Dignity*, which is intended to be the scientific justification of his utopian scheme.[12]

The most persistent complaint against behaviorism is that it fails to recognize the rational and intentional elements of human behavior. That is, in its devotion to unearthing the environmental *causes* of behavior, it ignores the private *reasons* of behavior. The accounts of behavior offered by it are therefore limited to the "whens" and "wheres" while stunningly silent on the matter of "why." In refusing to confront Smith's *reason* for doing X, the behaviorist neglects what some consider to be the most important psychological determinant of all; that is, *motivation*. The behaviorist's rejoinder is deceptively simple. What, he will ask, is added to a description of the publicly observable relations between responses and reinforcers when the concept of "motivation" is supplied? What can the term "motive" mean beyond the efficacy of a stimulus to control the behavior that obtains or avoids it? In regard to this demand for *reasons*, the behaviorist is interested only in determining what is responsible for the demand, itself. In summarizing the archetypical behavioristic account of what is responsible for this search for reasons, we will reach a fuller understanding of the totality of the behavioristic system. The following is a synthesis of many behavioristic works addressed to this question of *reasons*-explanations vs. *causes*-explanations.

Neither praise nor blame is entailed by a causal account of behavior. When we attribute Smith's walking, talking, and working to the effects of reinforcing stimuli, we remove his behavior from a judgmental domain and locate it in the domain of natural phenomena. However, when we impute *reasons* to Smith, we earn the right to judge Smith's intentions as something above and beyond his mere actions and above and beyond the mere consequences of these actions. We can say, for example, that Smith intended to kill Jones even though the bullet missed "its target." We can say, further, that Smith is a "bad sort," that he is wicked, worthy of our wrath, a candidate for punishment. Our own histories of reinforcement are such that we seek control over the behavior of others, and the right to judge is just this control. We are able to elevate ourselves to nobility of purpose as long as we can reduce Smith to an inferior station. Thus, one of the causes of our search for "reasons" is no more than the ability to control others.

Then too there is the component of social desirability in talk of "reasons." This is rooted in religiomystical traditions in which the priests and witch doctors are thought to possess unnatural powers and understandings. In modern society the residual of this tradition takes the form of applauding those able to "see more deeply" and "comprehend more richly" the "true" reasons of Smith's behavior. By retaining these religiomystical notions, we are in a position to reward ourselves with "perceptiveness" and "insight." Not content to deal with the Smith before us, we report that we have found the INNER MAN who is really responsible for what Smith does. Not everyone, of course, is blessed with such powers of intuition. Those of us who, unlike the common run of mankind, can see further, can unearth the quasi-private, brooding, and mysterious motives of the man-behind-the-man, now have a special status. It is in the nature of a special status that those who have it are in more complete control of the distribution of available resources, that is, *reinforcers*. Causal explanations, however, are, at least in principle, available to everyone. A society restricting the study of psychological man to the publicly observable and verifiable relationship between environmental events and behavioral outcomes is one in which each person has the same ability as does anyone else to judge and to decide.

Just as the search for and discovery of "reasons" place the observer in a position of privilege, belief in reasons as opposed to causes gives the actor a special power. Reasons, being private and, therefore, "his," put him in control, whereas *causes* put Nature in control. Industrial societies especially place a great premium on competition. Secondary reinforcers are distributed in such a way as to increase the behavior of the laboring community. Soon, titles and special distinctions are able to exert as great a control over behavior (including *verbal* behavior) as, in more primitive societies, food and shelter do. Accordingly, modern man is controlled in such a way as to emit those behaviors that seem to remove him from the direct control of others. It becomes increasingly important for him to refer to his "freedom" and his "dignity," since such imputations carry with them the possibility of special status. He is not merely an animal working for food but a self-motivated, self-actualizing *rational* creature and he can prove this by asserting *reasons* for his actions over and against their causes. But all he is doing is asserting; that is, he is merely engaged in the emission of *verbal operants* whose frequency of occurrence has been "shaped" by the same reinforcement contingencies as those associated with left-turns in a maze and bar-pressing in a "Skinner box." Those who criticize causal accounts by inserting "reasons" into Smith's "mind" are merely putting certain words into Smith's vocabulary, and these words get into his vocabulary in precisely the same way that bar-presses enter the behavioral vocabulary of the laboratory rat. The purely descriptive, causal account, on the other hand, allows a specification of the environmental sources of behavioral control. This specification is, in principle, complete, predictively powerful, pragmatically successful, and in no way improved by the inclusion of inner men, motives, reasons, spirits, wants, beliefs, or even neurons. Statements that begin,

Rats press bars . . .
Men pull levers . . .
Balls roll down inclined planes . . .
Planets revolve . . .

are to be followed by descriptions of *contingencies* in the observable world, not be references to unobservable, intangible, immeasurable, goals, dispositions, or intentions. *Goals*, if referred to at all, are understood as objects in the environment, not "in" the person, and can be specified only after the fact. They may be said to have been *reached*, not *sought*. Until society recognizes the essential truth of the foregoing, it will continue to praise and blame, to create heroes and villains, to be wracked by centuries of war, and to enjoy only accidental peace. Worse, it will look to geneticists and neurosurgeons to create "good stock" or "healthy brains," without realizing that all social problems are never more than *behavioral* problems and that most of these are soluble by methods we now possess.

> "An experimental analysis shifts the determination of behavior from autonomous man to the environment—an environment responsible both for the evolution of the species and for the repertoire acquired by each member. . . . Is man then 'abolished'? Certainly not as a species or as an individual achiever. It is autonomous inner man who is abolished, and that is a step forward."[13]

How does one begin to assess this thesis? The effect it has upon its audience is mixed. It sounds at once so reassuringly obvious and so patently ridiculous. It seems so very old and, at the same time, daringly original. It is philosophy, ethics, political theory, sociology, and psychotherapy wrapped up into one grand proclamation about issues that have engaged intellectual scrutiny for nearly thirty centuries. The careful reader, examining it for the first time, suspects that something has been left out but can find no fatal flaw. On reexamination, he begins to suspect, however, that the apparent invulnerability of the thesis may, just *may*, be the result of the failure of the thesis to say *anything!* We approach this possibility in a properly gingerly way, always wary of the critic's nemesis —the failure to understand the propositions he has set out to challenge.

We begin to appreciate the historical underpinnings of behaviorism by recognizing the system as Darwinian. It shares with all systematic psychologies since Wundt, and these include Freudian formulations, the conviction that the psychological dimensions of man have evolved, are present in lower forms of life, and are the outcome of transactions between the organism and its environment. In a nonmentalistic way, it subscribes to one or another form of "pleasure principle" that is judged to be responsible for the validity of the *law of effect*. What survives of the early Watsonian formulation is the emphasis upon practical application and objectivity, antimentalism, and indifference to philosophy. What survives of Pavlovian theory are the principles of generalization, reinforcement, and extinction. In a breathless attempt to label its essential and traditional character, then, we may describe the thesis and the *ism* as associationistic, hedonistic, utilitarian, and pragmatic. Unlike most earlier empiricistic psychologies, it has only the loosest ties to materialism, and these are of a conceptual rather than an operational or a programmatic nature. Each of these features of behaviorism exposes it to a particular set of objections, some of which are more telling than others.

When a psychological system or thesis is presented as one of Darwinian complexion, it is important to realize that this is not a demonstration of its validity but a call for clarification. We require clarification because that which is "Darwinian" is not reducible to a small set of descriptions or propositions. Evolutionary theory is, itself, in the process of evolving and is far from an adequate scientific theory. Indeed, as we get further away from the research and writings of molecular biologists, we find that evolutionary principles are thrown about in a way that can only be described as "loose talk." There is no "thing" in the world that is "selection," nor have we explained a phenotypic outcome by casually referring to "natural selection." The term *environment*, which psychologists tend to use as if it were a voltage or a weight, stands for a continuously changing and extraordinarily large and complex assortment of variables. For the organism capable of locomotion, the "environment" is never really permanent. For the organisms with memory, it is never really gone. Moreover, once the behaviorist commits himself to any version of evolutionary theory, he is required to accept the fact and the implications of genetic heterogeneity by virtue of which there can be no specification of selection pressures without a simultaneous specification of the hereditary nuances of the organisms under study. Ultraviolet radiation, which is a central feature of the environment of the honey bee, does not illuminate the world of man. Thus the *effective* environment is not what is loosely called the "environment," and the behaviorist who promises to bring behavior under the control of the "environment" by altering the latter may find that he has a new set of conditions to worry about each time the genotype of a behaving organism differs from the one he has just studied. What makes this fact important is the traditional indifference of behavioristic psychologists to genetic considerations. Indeed, it is frankly ironic that a system of psychology described as "evolutionary" should have such a spotless record of aloofness toward hereditary factors.

The common reply to those who question this neglect of genetics is that the *law of effect* applies to *all* organisms, regardless of hereditary nuances, since survival is impossible for organisms unable to secure rewards and avoid aversive stimulation. But, like "Darwinian," the "law of effect" does not refer unambiguously to a set of propositions or demonstrated facts. As formulated by Thorndike (Ch. XI), it is so rich in mentalistic terms and so tautologous in its logical structure that no modern behaviorist could possibly subscribe to it. That we and some other animals tend to do the things that give us pleasure is a fact that will embarrass no philosophical or psychological position on the nature of man that has ever been proposed. When the law of effect is recast to eliminate the mentalistic and motivational connotations—that is, when it is pared down to a simple, associationistic formulation—it courts still other difficulties. To say, for example, that the reinforcer is defined by the behavior of the organism rather than by the stipulations of the experimenter —to say, that is, that "X" is a reinforcer whenever it alters the probability of responses that precede it—is to run the risk of at least two pitfalls. One, and this has been overly exercised by those who reject behaviorism, is the proposal of *backward* causation; that is, the reinforcer works backwards in time to affect the behavior that precedes it. The second is to open up the domain of reinforcers so thoroughly that it would be impossible or at least impractical to locate the effective stimulus in an environmental space now filled with a veritable infinity of "reinforcers." The *backward causation* pitfall is averted by the behaviorist's insistence that the reinforcer does not work *back* upon the preceding behavior but *ahead* on the future behavior of the organism. This clarification, however, creates but another class of problems. If a rat presses a lever now and receives a pellet of food two days later, it is a verifiable fact that the bar-pressing behavior is no more probable than it was before the arrival of food. What is more probable is the behavior taking place *just before* the arrival of the pellet; that is, another instance of *backward* causation. It seems that the explanation based upon forward causation works only in the limited circumstance in which long chains of sequential behavior are involved, whereas *backward* causation must be invoked any time the delivery of "reward" is separated by long periods of time from the behavior preceding or following it. We are able to salvage the reduced form of the law of effect by arguing that a response sets up a pattern of neural activity that is still going on when food is delivered and that it is the neural "trace" that is reinforced by the reward. This hypothesis allows causation to work in the same way in the conditioning laboratory as it does in the balance of nature, but it requires the behavioristic thesis to tie itself to neurophysiological hypotheses, and this is a connection specifically disowned by Skinner and his disciples. Not only this, but in its neurophysiological form, the law of effect is no more confirmed than it is in purely behavioral contexts. We are no better informed in being told that "neural traces" are reinforced than in being told that behavior is. Conditioning has been observed at the level of single neurons, but for the behaviorist to invest his psychology in this sort of demonstration is, again, to surrender it to biology. This is not necessarily ill advised, but were the adoption to go forward, the once purely behavioral analysis would now be forced to endure all the logical and methodological problems that the mind-body issue has visited upon the physiological psychologist.

In addition to the ambiguity and the peculiar character of the law of effect, it has this negative bonus: it does not permit its defender to deduce from it the most significant findings to emerge from the experimental analysis of behavior. One of Skinner's many important findings is that pertaining to the effects of *schedules of reinforcement*. It has been found that behavior brought under the control of reinforcers that have been applied irregularly during the acquisition of a response is extremely resistant to extinction. The ability of random reinforcement to result in virtually unextinguishable responding is one of the most striking demonstrations in all of psychology. Yet there is no formulation of the law of effect that permits one to predict such an effect, nor is the effect logically deducible from the law that is asserted as covering it. Thus, even if we accept the modified, neurophysiological version of the law of effect, that is, the version that would allow scientific status, we are unable to use the law in framing explanations of behavioral events of interest. Referring back to the first chapter in which we reviewed the Hempelian model, we are forced to conclude that the behavioristic thesis either lacks a *covering law* or that the covering law does not *cover*. While this deficiency may have little bearing upon the practical utility of the behavioristic thesis, it ensures that that thesis will never be able to provide a scientific explanation of the phenomena it purports to embrace. Where physiological psychology earns the status of a science only by forfeiting its claim to being psychology, behavioristic psychology, it would seem, can only retain the status of psychology by surrendering its status as a science. Evidence of the recognition of this fact may be found in Skinner's most recent and very surprising flirtations with biology.[14] In these, he has attempted to present behavior as something akin to "digestion," but the net effect of the analogy is to move his psychological system back into the nineteenth century when the metaphor of the machine was the reigning theoretical device.

As with physiological psychology, the assets and liabilities of the behavioristic thesis concern us only to the extent that they tell us something about intellectual history, including the history now being written by our own age. The essentials of the behavioristic thesis can be found in the scholarship of all previous ages. Its mechanistic flavor is unadulterated Hobbism. Its only "law" is to be found in the writings of Epicurus, Marcus Aurelius, Ockham, Gassendi, La Mettrie, Locke, Hume, Bentham, Mill, and numerous less-distinguished commentators. Conditioning techniques have been developed to a level never attempted before, but this fact is one the historian must try to explain and not merely report. The techniques have been developed because many psychologists in the present century have labored to develop them and because modern society has supported their development. Endeavors which, in the seventeenth or eighteenth centuries, might have engaged only the animal trainer or those with domestic pets, now find expression in university laboratories the world over. Manufacturers have made available devices by which shocks can be transmitted over great distances in order to modify the behavior of children in playgrounds, pets in yards, and patients in psychiatric wards. These devices are new, but the idea is prehistoric. We must ask why the modern world is so eager to control behavior so thoroughly and so precisely. Yet to attempt to answer this is to go beyond the bounds of historical propriety. Others, less confined by the pressures of fact and more facile in the exercise of imagination, have already contributed many words in reply to this query. We may be satisfied here to observe that one principal difference between the modern world and its ancestry is not to be found in the sorts of utopias promised but in the eagerness to create them.

If behaviorism and materialism possess a common ground, it is that upon which rejections of *autonomous man* have always stood firm. Both have judged the very idea of autonomous man to be laden with mysticism, religiosity, and superstitious musing. The notion of "free will" in a determined universe violates every canon of parsimony, scientific unity, objectivity, and positivism. Kant's *categorical imperative* seems painfully whimsical to a world that has gone to war twice in less than a century; to a world in which vice, acquisitiveness, and selfish disregard are the abiding conditions and where moral vigor and individualism seem to be the fading relics of the Greek dream. The mind, itself, has come to be treated as a metaphysical fiction designed to obscure the essential fact of our determined, material, and temporary lives which, like the planet hosting them, are accidents of mindless creation. Modern man looks back upon the romantic visions of Wordsworth, the simple faith of the Medievalist, and the thrilling experiment begun in Athens the way he looks back upon his own childhood—the time before he learned the harsh realities of life. But every stage of personal development, just as every period in intellectual history, finds the participants believing that they have uncovered the "realities." Copernicus is the father of Ptolemy; Einstein, a more mature Newton. Our modern commitment to the methods and perspectives of science is no stronger than was the Medieval commitment to the syllogism or the Renaissance confidence in natural magic. Each age finds an idea that seems to reveal something that is common to the major events that occupy that age. Science both leads and follows the ages in which it finds a home. The psychologists of antiquity looked at their age and discovered law, illusion, cultural variety, courage, deception, and fate. Their psychologies made room for all of these. The Medievalist believed in a personal God of salvation and justice whose laws were immutable, rational, and inescapable. Medieval psychology quite naturally found the divine in the mind of man. And so on, down to our own time, the world we create comes, first, to serve as the metaphor of ourselves and, soon, as the reality of which we are but models or copies. Failing to find purpose and design in our world, we question the existence of purpose or design in ourselves. Looking everywhere and discovering only matter in motion, we begin to see the same in the mirror. It is one of the quiet triumphs of the human mind that it can exhaust itself in attempting to refute its existence.

Autonomous Man

It is not uncommon for the modern behaviorist or physiological psychologist to express disbelief when scholars entertaining other perspectives insist that a scientific account of human action and human experience is not any nearer than it was in pre-Socratic times. There is, mixed with this disbelief, a conviction often stated that those who do not subscribe to the behavioristic or physiological accounts are clutching at the straws of metaphysical dualism and religious mysticism. It seems that this reaction to the scholar's reservation is prompted by the view that such a reservation must be based on a denial of science's role in psychological studies.* That is, to reject the behavioristic or physiological accounts is somehow, *ipso facto*, tantamount to rejecting science itself. To believe, for example, that studies of the behavior of nonhuman organisms is not likely to illuminate the factors responsible for human conduct is, we are to understand, a rejection of Darwinian theory. To question whether neurophysiological findings bear directly on the question of psychic causation is to question determinism.

---

* For example, in *Beyond Freedom and Dignity*, Skinner complains that, ". . . no modern biologist or physicist would turn to Aristotle for help . . . but the dialogues of Plato are still assigned to students and cited as if they threw light on human behavior" (p. 3). Elsewhere he has proclaimed that "The methods of science no longer need verbal defense; one cannot throw a moon around the earth with dialectic" (*Harvard Educational Review*, 1954, *24*, p. 97.). Such passages are illustrative of that contemporary psychological attitude that animates the discipline with the insouciance of nineteenth century positivism.

There is a danger in this perspective, and the danger is greater to science than it is to those perspectives that are assumed to be hostile to the scientific vision. The danger is that of stagnation for, if there is a sure road to intellectual atrophy, it is paved with the complacent certainty that one's critics are deluded.

The twentieth-century behaviorists, especially Watson, Pavlov, and Skinner, have been faithfully given to concluding that objections to the behavioristic formulation are nothing short of a denial of determinism and Darwinism. Watson was fond of invoking the idea of "ghosts" whenever doubts about the behavioristic thesis were voiced. Skinner's preferred term is "autonomous man." Consistently the expositors of behaviorism have been ready to dismiss as "*idealism*" nearly the entire range of competing claims. Equally indiscriminately they have referred to physics as an ultimate arbiter, to evolutionary notions as unimpeachable defenses, and to practical success as the final criterion of validity.

We have already observed the ambiguous status of Darwinian concepts as introduced into discussions of behaviorism. The problem, however, is not limited to one of clarity, for even if Darwinian principles were employed with precision and consistency, they would not necessarily support the behavioristic thesis. The psychological features of human life are *data* that a Darwinian theory must be able to explain. Facts are not eliminated by invoking a theory unable to account for them. Rather, theories are rejected when they are unable to assimilate the facts. To the extent that Darwinian theory has *any* psychological implications, they can be discovered only when we have reason to believe that documented aspects of human psychology have direct analogues in the animal kingdom. These analogues, however, are not to be expected to vary only in quantitative respects. Indeed, it is one of the implicit deficiencies of the psychologist's employment of evolutionary theory that he requires interspecies comparisons to be made along a quantitative continuum. To do this is to be trapped by the appealing but incorrect assumption that structural analogies entail functional equivalence. No one denies that such homologous structures as fins, wings, and limbs function equivalently in allowing movement. However, the scientific principles that must be invoked in rendering a complete description of the determinants of swimming, flying, and walking are not identical. Locomotion is achieved at every level of biological organization in the animal world and in portions of the plant kingdom as well. To note that very substantial *qualitative* differences occur across species is not to deny Darwinian principles but to assert them. The Darwinian account can, for example, require all successful species to adapt their behaviors to the demands of their environments. It does not, however, require that this behavioral adaptation be achieved in exactly the same way or even in accordance with the same principles. Adaptation for one species may involve changes in the color of the coat or skin; for another, seasonal migration; for another, hibernation. All of these are *behavioral* adaptations and all can be comprehended by the Darwinian system. Nevertheless, except for the fact that these are adaptive behaviors, there is hardly a qualitative similarity to be found among coloration, migration, and hibernation. It is one thing to insist that behavior must conform to the demands of the environment but quite another to say that the conformity must be displayed in invariant fashion.

We realize, therefore, that to raise objections regarding the comparability of species in the matter of behavioral control is not the same as questioning the validity of evolutionary principles. This is not to say, however, that one is not allowed to raise such a question. If, for example, it could be shown that a particular aspect of human life is observed nowhere else in nature in any form even approximating its human expression, we would have to conclude either that selection pressures of an unknown variety were responsible or that the Darwinian model is simply not equipped to address the fact. Some have speculated that human language is just such a phenomenon; others, that consciousness is. This is not the place for an evaluation of such claims, although it is worth pointing out that the manner in which the child comes to display language has proved to be remarkably resistant to behavioristic analyses. "Consciousness," of course, has been legislated out of behaviorism since Watson, but this scarcely removes it from the real and knowable world. Indeed, it is that by which a real and knowable world becomes real and knowable in the first place. Even if language and consciousness were not present elsewhere in phylogeny, however, we would not have to reject Darwinism. Once we respect the fact that the species struggling for existence is under no compulsion to adopt the methods employed successfully by any other species, we will no longer fear that a challenge to behaviorism is a threat to Darwinism. The same is true, and for the same reasons, in our critiques of materialism. To acknowledge that current and historic formulations of the materialist-monist thesis do not succeed is not tantamount to denying the laws of physics, let alone lawfulness itself.

The very term *autonomous man* is not without its special problems. As used by Prof. Skinner, it is intended to stand for assertions of "free will," immaterialism, and the like. It is to suggest some fictional agent purported to live beyond the perimeter of scientific determinism. But if this usage is intended as a rebuke of any and every argument against the behavioristic thesis, it simply will not do. When we describe man as a rational, judging, discriminating, motivated, creative, and purposive creature, we are not necessarily proposing that he exists apart from the world or that these characteristics are independent of those natural regularities that ultimately are inscribed in the laws of science. We may only be saying that these are the sorts of characteristics the *behavioristic* thesis fails to explain; that is, what passes for behavioristic law is not a law. More subtly, we may be recognizing that, at least for the time being, the only relationship between the laws of physics and the principles of psychological life is a metaphorical one. *Of course* man obeys the laws of physics: when he jumps from a window, he falls; when he rows a boat, he works against damping forces; when he struts across the moon, he weighs less than he does on earth. No antagonist of behaviorism has based his dispute on the possibility of man's disobeying the laws of physics. Their validity, however, does not bear on the question of the validity of the behavioristic thesis which, in any of its forms, fails to resemble *any* physical law.

It is an undeniable law of physics that the mass and density of the human body are such, and that the viscosity of the earth's atmosphere is such, that no one will ever be able to escape the pull of gravity by beating his arms up and down. We accept this law and proceed to invent the airplane. Our reason is not recruited in attempts to violate the very laws of nature that this reason discovered. Rather, it embraces these laws in fashioning methods and instruments that permit us to adapt more successfully to the demands of the environment. These demands are none other than the laws of nature. We are, accordingly, not *autonomous* in the sense of being able to disregard natural laws, although we may be autonomous in disregarding what the behavioristic thesis has asserted to be a law of behavior. Obviously, if such a law were of the same sort as those of physics, there would be no reason to polemicize it into existence. It would apply whether we liked it or not.

The confusion between autonomy as *freedom to* and autonomy as *freedom from* has a history dating back to the Greek *Atomists*. We confronted it in Chapter 9 in the form of Voltaire's denial that a creature, five feet tall, could act according to his own caprice. The fact, however, is that he *can* act according to his own caprice. What he cannot do by caprice alone is *succeed*. Neither the laws of science nor the powers of logic can prevent a man from flapping his arms in a woeful attempt to join his avian friends. It is by the laws of science that we know he will fail. The laws ordaining his failure do not and never were intended to proscribe the attempt.

In its long and intriguing history, psychology has all too often been stalled or diverted by confusions of this kind. The philosophical psychologists, no less than the more recent generations of experimentalists, have been ready to translate discoveries in one realm of inquiry into psychological insights and usually without modification. By the same token, philosophical idealists and literary romantics have been far too grudging in their estimates of the relevance of science to the study of human nature. Darwin's theory, modern genetics, neurophysiology, biochemistry, and the experimental analysis of animal behavior are of obvious relevance to any discipline that has accepted human psychology as its subject. Along the way, students of this discipline may have good reason to adopt as working hypotheses any number of metaphors borrowed from science and from the arts. What history teaches, however, is that progress is retarded when scholars fail to distinguish between the metaphor and the fact the metaphor is intended to represent. Condillac's sentient statue, La Mettrie's clocks, and the telephone switchboards of the early part of this century have really had no part either in the evolution of neurophysiological science or in the refining of man's understanding of himself. Of course, the modern psychologist may very well ignore these lessons of history and proceed to deal with his subject in any way he sees fit. He is, after all, autonomous.

Horizons

In this last chapter, a disproportionate amount of space has been reserved for physiological and behavioristic psychologies because these are the only formulations sufficiently developed to allow historical and logical assessments of scientific status. There is no unified psychoanalytic theory, no formal social psychology. Even the brilliant efforts of Jean Piaget must be excluded since his theories of cognition and cognitive development have yet to be cast in such a way as to permit precise predictions of the effects of specific independent variables upon the psychological processes presumed to depend upon them. The rationalist and idealist elements in Piagetian psychology are too obvious to require further words here. The emphases it places upon evolution, universals, language, and logic derive almost directly from the European philosophical traditions established by Leibnitz, Kant, and Hegel. Piaget's system strives to embrace science and logic as the creations of human cognition. Accordingly, it is not clear that science and logic can, in turn, be brought to bear upon the system. As Aristotle might have observed, no method of demonstration can be used to prove itself!

Behaviorism and neuropsychology are not monolithic enterprises but evolving conceptualizations. It is nearly inconceivable that any future psychology will be devoid of their influence. While the behavior of organisms may not be *the* subject matter of a more developed psychology, it undoubtedly will be of special concern to that psychology. The question, then, is not whether behavior will survive as an issue but whether the contemporary form of behaviorism will dictate the manner in which the issue is addressed.

The same considerations apply to the neural sciences and physiological psychology. There is an undeniable relationship between the functional organization of the nervous system and those characteristics of animals and human beings which are described as "psychological." It would seem only likely that any more developed system of psychology will avail itself of the facts and methods generated by the neural sciences. However, there is now a two-thousand-year history of research and debate militating against any easy assurance that the mind-body problem will be solved in the laboratory. Simplifications die hard and the *logical behaviorism* of the 1930s is no exception. Increasingly, however, the number of serious philosophers willing to submit that all psychological predicates finally reduce to statements about performance or "dispositions to behave" shrinks.[15] *Dreaming* is "performative" only in a trivial way. What has one been told when Beethoven's Ninth Symphony is "explained" in terms of Beethoven's "performance" or "dispositions to behave"? The mind-body problem, which has refused to surrender to the techniques and devices of the laboratory, has been no more retiring in the face of philosophical positivism, *logical* or otherwise.

Much is to be said for the common-sense perspective of Thomas Reid and his contemporary disciples. In important ways, Reid's philosophy is the most durable protection against that virulent form of spiritualism that becomes popular when materialism fails. Recall the Pythagorean reaction to Anaxagoras' intellectualism, the Patristic reaction to Epicureanism, the Hermetic alternative to Scholasticism, and the Coleridgean reply to empiricism. In our own time, similar signs are in abundance. Science failed to create Utopia; it failed to "solve" the problem of mind; it failed to provide a new morality; it failed to prove or disprove the existence of God! Many, including scientists themselves, have responded to the disappointment by looking "East"; by abandoning once more the Apollonian vision in favor of the Dionysian. The mind that would not reduce to matter now creates it, moves it, defies it. On another account, matter has mind; plants listen to our songs as we and our surroundings merge into some ineffable "oneness" of peace and tranquility. What is old is, *ipso facto*, wiser and truer and more reliable. Progress in all its forms suffers the mark of vice. Simplicity, humility, and privation are called upon to settle issues beyond the range of analysis, courage, and grandeur. Competent investigators, having lost the struggle to comprehend consciousness in its most innocent form, consume hallucinogens in order to "expand" it. Recognizing that the creation of a science is difficult and often thankless work, some resign and proceed to traduce the entire effort into a form of *game* in which one plays a *role*.

There is a momentum to these developments. Historians cannot predict the future, let alone determine it. They can analyze the past whose effects are never completely neutralized by the mere passage of time. The past speaks to the modern world. It tells us not that science has failed but that it has limitations; not that psychology is pointless or immature but that, as with all intellectual ventures, is incomplete and evolving. Finally, it tells us that there is no more a single way of comprehending the psychological character of man than there is only one way to write a poem or build a church. The history of civilization displays confusion and evokes regrets but were it not for civilization there would be no standard of clarity and no basis for regret. The history of science, too, is rife with failure and banality but were it not for this very history, we would hardly be in a position to make the judgment. Psychology's history is no more than a profile of the larger history of civilization. As a creation of the human intelligence, it teaches by its errors as well as its success. The systems of psychology we create, even when steeped in blunders and contradiction, are *our* creations and allow us to discern characteristics of ours because they are our creations. Behaviorism and psychoanalytic theory, neuropsychology and phrenology, utilitarianism and pragmatism, may not have fared well as systems but they do reveal those qualities of mind, objects of hope, and collections of values and perceptions endemic to our species. The present work, which began as an attempt to locate psychology in the history of ideas, concludes with the obvious recognition that psychology *is* the history of ideas.

References

1. Roger Sperry, "A Modified Concept of Consciousness," *Psychological Review*, 1969, 76, 532–536. Prof. Sperry is a neurobiologist of international stature. His research on "split-brain" preparations was the pioneering foundation of contemporary theories of the cortical representation of cognitive functions. The paper referred to was sufficiently mentalistic to invite quick rebuttals, and Sperry has not, to this author's knowledge, attempted to expand the ideas introduced in this article. Later historians will be sure to note, however, that after several decades of relative silence in the technical journals, mind-talk and brain-talk appeared together, if uncomfortably, in 1969.

2. Gilbert Ryle, *The Concept of Mind*. Published originally in 1949 by Hutchinson & Co., Ltd, London. Barnes and Noble edition, 1959.

3. Ibid., Ch. I.

4. Ibid., p. 50.

5. Ibid., p. 328.

6. Ibid., p. 22.

7. Ibid.

8. Prof. Smart's thesis appears in a number of places. It can be found in *The Mind/Brain Identity Theory*, a collection of papers edited by C. V. Borst (St. Martin's Press, 1970). This is an excellent edition and is highly recommended for the reader interested in exploring the contemporary status of the issue. The Smart paper is titled, "Sensations and Brain Processes."

Critiques of this paper are provided by J. T. Stevenson and by Kurt Baier. It is Baier who discusses the "incorrigibility" hypothesis in his *Smart on Sensations*. In this same volume appear Prof. Smart's *Materialism* and an analysis of materialism by Prof. Norman Malcom. Further discussions of this issue and still another version of Smart's thesis can be found in *The Philosophy of Mind*, edited by V. G. Chappell, Prentice-Hall, Englewood, N.J., 1962.

9. Smart, *Sensations and Brain Processes, op. cit.*

10. Ibid.

11. Kurt Baier, *Smart on Sensations.* In C. V. Borst, op. cit., p. 95.

12. B. F. Skinner, *Beyond Freedom and Dignity*, Knopf, 1971; Bantam/Vintage paperback edition, 1972.

13. Ibid., Bantam/Vintage edition, p. 205.

14. B. F. Skinner, "The Steep and Thorny Way to a Science of Behavior," *American Psychologist*, 30 (1975), 42–49.

15. See Professor Hillary Putnam's *Brains and Behavior* for an excellent discussion of this. (*Analytical Philosophy*, R. J. Butler, Ed. New York, Barnes and Noble, 1965).

Bibliography

ABAILARD, P. *Glosses on Porphyry*, in *Selections from Medieval Philosophers*. Translated and edited by R. McKeon. New York: Scribner, 1929.

D'ALEMBERT, J. *Preliminary Discourse to the Encyclopedia of Diderot*. Translated by R. N. Schwab. Indianapolis: Bobbs-Merrill, 1963.

ANSELM, *Dialogus de Veritate*, translated by Richard McKeon, in *Selections from Medieval Philosophers*. New York: Scribner, 1929.

———. *Ontological Argument*, R. Taylor (ed.). New York: Doubleday, 1965.

AQUINAS, T. *Summa Contra Gentiles*, translated by Anton Pegis, in *Basic Writings of Thomas Aquinas*. New York: Random House, 1945.

———. *Summa Theologica*. Translated by Anton Pegis, in *Basic Writings of Thomas Aquinas*. New York: Random House, 1945.

ARISTOTLE. *Basic Works*. Translated by Richard McKeon. New York: Random House, 1941.

———. *History of the Animals*. Translated by A. L. Peck. Cambridge, Mass.: Harvard, 1970.

———. *On the Soul*. Greek text prepared by W. D. Ross. Oxford: Clarendon Press, 1961.

———. *The Protrepticus*. Translated by Anton-Hermann Chroust. South Bend, Ind.: Notre Dame, 1964.

ARNOLD, M. *Culture and Anarchy*. Cambridge, England: 1932.

AUGUSTINE. *Basic Writings of St. Augustine*. Whitney Oates (ed.). New York: Random House, 1948.

———. *The Confessions*. Translated by Rex Warner. New York: Mentor, 1963.

AURELIUS, M. *Meditations*, in *The Stoic and Epicurean Philosophers*. Whitney Oates (ed.). New York: Random House, 1940.

BACON, F. *Novum Organum*, in *The Works of Francis Bacon*. Vol. I, Cambridge, Mass.: Hurd & Houghton, 1878.

415

————. *Of the Proficience and Advancement of Learning Divine and Human*, in *The Works of Francis Bacon*. Vol. I, Cambridge, Mass.: Hurd & Houghton, 1878.

BACON, ROGER. *Opus Majus*. Vol. II, translated by R. B. Burke. Pennsylvania, 1928.

BAIN, A. *The Emotions and the Will*. London: Parker, 1859.

————. *The Senses and the Intellect*. London: Parker, 1855.

BECK, L. W. *Once More Unto the Breach: Kant's Answer to Hume, Again. Ratio*, Vol. 9, No. 1, pp. 33–37.

BENDER, F. L. *Karl Marx: The Essential Writings*. New York: Harper & Row, 1967.

BENGTSON, H. *The Greeks and the Persians from the Sixth to the Fourth Centuries*. New York: Delacorte, 1968.

BENTHAM, J. *An Introduction to the Principles of Morals and Legislation*, in *The Utilitarians*. New York: Dolphin, 1961.

BERGEN, T. G. and FISCH, M. H. (eds.). *The New Science of Giambattista Vico*. New York: Cornell, 1970.

BERGSON, H. *Creative Evolution*. Translated by Arthur Mitchell. London: Macmillan, 1911.

BERGSON, H. *Time and Free Will*. New York: Macmillan, 1950.

BERKELEY, G. *An Essay Towards a New Theory of Vision* (1709), in *Works on Vision*. Edited by C. M. Turbayne, Indianapolis: Bobbs-Merrill, 1963.

————. *A Treatise Concerning the Principles of Human Knowledge*. Open Court, La Salle, 1963.

BLOCH, M. *Feudal Society*. Chicago, 1961.

BOEHMER, H. *Martin Luther: Road to Reformation*. New York, 1957.

BOETHIUS. *Commentaries on the Isagogue of Porphyry, in Selections from Medieval Philosophers*. Translated and edited by R. McKeon. New York: Scribner, 1929.

————. *De Consolatione Philosophiae*. Translated by H. F. Stewart, New York: Putnam, 1926.

BORING, E. G. *A History of Experimental Psychology*. New York: Appleton-Century-Crofts, 1951.

BORST, C. V. (ed.) *The Mind/Brain Identity Theory*. New York: St. Martin's, 1970.

BROWN, T. *Lectures on the Philosophy of the Human Mind*, in *Between Hume and Mill: An Anthology of British Philosophy—1749–1843*. R. Brown (ed.), New York: Random House, 1970.

BRUSH, C. R. *The Selected Works of Pierre Gassendi*. New York: Johnson Reprint, 1970.

BURROUGHS, J. L. *Platonic Theology. Journal of the History of Ideas*, April, 1944.

BURY, J. S. et al. (eds.). *The Cambridge Ancient History*, Vol. IV. New York: Macmillan, 1926.

BUTLER, J. *Of the Nature of Virtue*, in *British Moralists*. L. A. Selby-Bigge, (ed.). New York: Dover, 1965.

CASSIRER, E., and KRISTELLER, P. O., and RANDALL, J. H. (eds.). *The Renaissance Philosophy of Man*. Chicago, 1948.

CICERO. *Letters of Marcus Tullius Cicero*. Translated by E. S. Shuckburgh in *The Harvard Classics*, Vol. 9. New York: Collier, 1909.

COLLINGWOOD, R. G. *The Idea of History*. New York: Oxford, 1972.

COMTE, A. *Introduction to Positive Philosophy*. Translated by F. Ferré, Indianapolis: Bobbs-Merrill, 1970.

CONDILLAC, E. B. de. *An Essay on the Origin of Human Knowledge, Being a Supplement to Mr. Locke's Essay on the Human Understanding*. Translated by T. Nugent (1756). Gainesville: Scholars Facsimiles & Reprints, 1971.

CONDORCET, A.-N. de. *Sketch for a Historical Picture of the Progress of the Human Mind*. Translated by J. Barraclough. New York: Noonday, 1955.

CORNFORD, F. M. *From Religion to Philosophy: A Study of the Origins of Western Speculation*. New York: Harper and Row, 1957.

COULTON, G. G. *Life in the Middle Ages*. Vol. *III*, New York: Macmillan, 1935.

CROMBIE, A. C. *Grosseteste and Experimental Science*, Oxford: Clarendon Press, 1953.

DAMPIER, W. C. *A History of Science*. Cambridge, England, 1966.

DARWIN, C. *The Expression of the Emotions in Man and Animals*. New York: Appleton-Century-Crofts, 1896.

———. *Origin of Species*. New York: Collier, 1909.

DESCARTES, R. *Discourse on Method*, in *The Method, Meditations, and Philosophy of Descartes*. Translated by J. Veitch. New York: Tudor, 1901.

———. *Meditations*. Translated by J. Veitch. New York: Tudor, 1901.

———. *Les Passions de L'Ame*. Translated by E. Haldane and G. R. T. Moss, in *The Philosophical Works of Descartes*. New York: Dover, 1955.

———. *Principles of Philosophy*. Translated by J. Veitch. New York: Tudor, 1901.

———. *Treatise on Man*, in *Descartes—Selections*. R. M. Eaton (ed.). New York: Scribner, 1927.

DEWEY, J. *The Reflex Arc Concept in Psychology, Psychological Review, 3*, (1896), 357–370.

DIDEROT, D. *D'Alembert's Dream*, in *Diderot's Selected Writings*. Translated by D. Coltman. New York: Macmillan, 1966.

DUNS SCOTUS, J. *Concerning Human Understanding*, in *Philosophical Writings*. Translated by A. Wolter. London: Nelson, 1962.

EPICTETUS. *Discourses*. Translated by P. E. Matheson, in *The Stoic and Epicurean Philosophers*. Whitney Oates (ed.). New York: Random House, 1940.

———. *Fragments*. Translated by P. E. Matheson, in *The Stoic and Epicurean Philosophers*. Whitney Oates (ed.), New York: Random House, 1940.

ERASMUS, D. *De Libero Arbitrio*. Translated by E. G. Rupp, in *Luther and Erasmus: Free Will and Salvation*. Library of Christian Classics, Vol. XVII. Philadelphia, 1969.

————. *Epistles.* Translated by F. M. Nichols, in *The Epistles of Erasmus,* Vol. I. London: Longmans, Green, 1901.

————. *The Praise of Folly.* Translated by H. H. Hudson. Princeton, 1941.

————. *Ten Colloquies.* Translated by C. R. Thompson, Indianapolis: Bobbs-Merrill, 1957.

ERICKSON, C. (ed.). *The Records of Medieval Europe.* New York: Doubleday, 1971.

EVERETT, C. C. *Fichte's Science of Knowledge.* Chicago: Griggs, 1892.

FECHNER, G. *Elements of Psychophysics.* Translated by H. Adler. New York: Holt, Rinehart, and Winston, 1966.

FICINO, M. *Five Questions Concerning the Mind.* Translated by J. L. Burroughs, in *The Renaissance Philosophy of Man.* Cassirer et al. (eds.). Chicago, 1948.

FREEMAN, K. *Ancilla to the Pre-Socratic Philosophers.* Oxford: Basil Blackwell, 1952.

FREUD, S. *The Origins and Development of Psychoanalysis, American Journal of Psychology, 21,* 1910.

————. *Psychopathology of Everyday Life,* in *The Basic Writings of Sigmund Freud.* A. A. Brill (ed.). New York: Random House, 1938.

————. *The Interpretation of Dreams.* Hogarth, London: 1953.

FUCHS, O. *The Psychology of Habit According to William of Ockham.* New York: Franciscan Institute, 1952.

GALEN. *On the Natural Faculties.* Translated by A. J. Brock. New York: Putnam, 1916.

GALILEI, GALILEO. *Dialogue Concerning the Two Great Systems of the World,* in *Classics of Modern Science.* W. S. Knickerbocker (ed.). New York: Appleton-Century-Crofts, 1927.

————. *Dialogues Concerning Two New Sciences.* Translated by H. Crew and A. de Salvio. New York: Macmillan, 1914.

GALL, F. J. *On the Functions of the Brain and of Each of Its Parts,* etc. Translated by W. Lewis, 6 vols. Boston: Marsh, Capen, and Lyon, 1835.

GALTON, F. *Hereditary Genius.* London: Macmillan, 1869.

GARIN, E. *Science and the Civic Life of the Italian Renaissance.* Translated by P. Munz, New York: Doubleday, 1969.

GLOTZ, G. *Ancient Greece at Work.* New York: Norton, 1967.

GUTHRIE, W. K. C. *The Greeks and Their Gods.* Boston: Beacon, 1950.

HARRIS, V. *All Coherence Gone.* Chicago, 1949.

HART, H. L. A. *The Concept of Law.* London: Oxford, 1961.

HARTLEY, D. *Observations on Man,* in *Between Hume and Mill: An Anthology of British Philosophy—1749–1843.* R. Brown (ed.). New York: Random House, 1970.

HASKINS, C. H. *Studies in the History of Medieval Science.* New York: Frederick Ungar, 1924.

————. *The Renaissance of the Twelfth Century.* Cambridge, Mass.: Harvard, 1927.

HAWKINS, R. L. *Positivism in the United States—1853–1861.* Cambridge, Mass.: Harvard, 1938.

HAYWARD, J. (ed.): *John Donne: Complete Poetry and Selected Prose.* New York: Random House, 1936.

HEGEL, G. W. F. *Encyclopaedie.* Translated by W. Wallace. Oxford, 1973.

———. *Phenomenology of Mind.* Translated by J. B. Baillie. London, 1910, 1931.

———. *Reason in History: A General Introduction to the Philosophy of History.* Translated by R. S. Hartman. Indianapolis: Bobbs-Merrill, 1953.

HELVETIUS, C. A. *A Treatise on Man; His Intellectual Faculties and His Education.* Translated by W. Hooper. London, 1777.

HEMPEL, C. *Aspects of Scientific Explanation and Other Essays in the Philosophy of Science.* New York: Free Press, 1965.

HERODOTUS. *The Persian Wars.* Translated by George Rawlinson, in *The Greek Historians.* F. R. B. Godolphin (ed.). New York: Random House, 1942.

HIPPOCRATES. *On Wounds in the Head,* in *Hippocrates.* Translated by W. H. S. Jones. New York: Putnam, 1923.

HOBBES, T. *Leviathan.* Baltimore, Penguin Classics, 1974.

HOLMES, G. *The Later Middle Ages 1272–1485.* New York: Norton, 1962.

HOLMES, O. W. *The Path of the Law.* Collected papers, 1920.

HOMER: *The Iliad.* Translated by Samuel Butler, M. M. Willcock (ed.). New York: Washington Square, 1966.

———. *The Odyssey.* Translated by Samuel Butler, M. M. Willcock (ed.). New York: Washington Square, 1966.

HUIZINGA, J. *The Waning of the Middle Ages.* New York: Doubleday, 1954.

HULL, C. L. *Principles of Behavior: An Introduction to Behavior Theory.* New York: Appleton-Century-Crofts, 1943.

HUME, D. *An Enquiry Concerning Human Understanding,* in *Essential Works of David Hume.* Ralph Cohen (ed.). New York: Bantam, 1965.

———. *A Treatise of Human Nature.* L. A. Selby-Bigge (ed.). New York: Dover, 1965.

HUSSERL, E. *Ideas: General Introduction to Pure Phenomenology.* Translated by W. R. B. Gibson. London: Collier-Macmillan, 1972.

JAEGER, W. *Aristotle: Fundamentals of the History of His Development.* Oxford: Clarendon, 1934.

JAMES, W. *A Text Book of Psychology.* New York: Macmillan, 1892.

JOHNSON, E. D. H. (ed.). *The World of the Victorians.* New York: Scribner, 1964.

JONES, W. H. S. *Hippocrates,* 3 vols. New York: Putnam, 1923.

KANT, I. *Critique of Pure Reason.* Translated by N. K. Smith. New York: St. Martin's, 1965.

———. *Fundamental Principles of the Metaphysic of Morals.* Translated by T. K. Abbott, New York: Liberal Arts, 1949.

———. *Groundwork of the Metaphysic of Morals.* Translated by H. J. Paton, New York: Harper & Row, 1964.

———. *Prolegomena to Any Future Metaphysics.* Translated by L. W. Beck, Indianapolis: Bobbs-Merrill, 1950.

KIRK, G. S. *Heraclitus: The Cosmic Fragments.* Cambridge (England), 1962.

KOFFKA, K. *Principles of Gestalt Psychology.* New York: Harcourt Brace, 1935.

KÖHLER, W. *Gestalt Psychology,* New York: Liveright, 1947.

————. *The Mentality of Apes.* London: Routledge and Kegan Paul, 1925.

KUHN, T. *The Structure of Scientific Revolutions.* Chicago, 1962.

LAKATOS, I. and MUSGRAVE, A. E. (eds.). *Criticism and the Growth of Knowledge.* Cambridge (England), 1970.

LA METTRIE, J. O. DE. *L'Homme Machine (Man, A Machine).* Translated by M. W. Calkins. New York: Open Court, 1912.

LASHLEY, K. S. *The Neuropsychology of Lashley: Selected Papers of K. S. Lashley.* Edited by F. A. Beach, et al. New York: McGraw-Hill, 1960.

LEIBNIZ, G. W. v. *Monadology,* in *Leibniz—The Monadology and Other Philosophical Writings.* Translated by R. Latta. Oxford, 1898.

————. v. *New Essays,* in *Leibniz—The Monadology and Other Philosophical Writings.* Translated by R. Latta. Oxford, 1898.

LEVY-BRUHL, L. *The Philosophy of Auguste Comte.* Translated by F. Harrison. London: Swan Sonnenschein, 1903.

LOCKE, J. *An Essay Concerning Human Understanding.* Chicago: Henry Regnery, 1956.

————. *An Essay Concerning the True Original, Extent and End of Civil Government: II: The State of Nature,* in *Social Contract.* E. Barker (ed.). Oxford, 1947.

LUCE, A. A. *Berkeley's Immaterialism.* New York: Russell & Russell, 1968.

LUCRETIUS. *De Rerum Natura.* Translated by Palmer Bovie. New York: Mentor, 1974.

LUTHER, M. *Twenty-seven Articles Respecting the Reformation of the Christian State.* In Vol. I., *Introduction to Contemporary Civilization in the West.* J. Buchler et al. (eds.). New York: Columbia, 1946.

MACAULAY, T. B. *History of England,* Vol. I. New York: Harper & Row, 1849.

MAGIE, D. (translator). *Scriptores Historiae Augustae,* 3 vols. New York: Putnam, 1922.

MALTHUS, T. *An Essay on the Principle of Population as It Affects the Future Improvement of Society, with Remarks on the Speculations of Mr. Godwin, M. Condorcet, and Other Writers.* Ann Arbor, Michigan, 1959.

MARX, K. and ENGELS, F. *The German Ideology.* S. Ryazanskaya (ed.). Moscow, 1964.

MILL, J. S. *A System of Logic, Ratiocinative and Inductive: Being a Connected View of the Principles of Evidence and the Methods of Scientific Investigation.* London: Longmans, Green, 1900.

————. *Utilitarianism,* in *The Utilitarians.* New York: Dolphin, 1961.

————. *Autobiography.* Toronto, 1963.

MILTON, J. *Areopagitica: A Speech for the Liberty of Unlicensed Printing to the Parliament of England.* New York: Collier (Harvard Classics), 1909.

MOLIÈRE: *Plays by Molière.* New York: Modern Library, 1924.

MORLEY, J. *Nineteenth Century Essays.* Selected and with an introduction by Peter Stansky. Chicago: Phoenix, 1970.

MUNZ, P. *Life in the Age of Charlemagne.* New York: Capricorn, 1971.

NEWTON, I. *Philosophiae Naturalis Principia: I. The Method of Natural Philosophy*, in *Newton's Philosophy of Nature*. H. S. Thayer (ed.). New York: Hafner, 1953.

NICHOLAS, B. *Roman Law.* Oxford: Clarendon, 1962.

PASCAL, B. *Pensées: Thoughts on Religion and Other Subjects.* Translated by W. F. Trotter. New York: Washington Square, 1965.

PAVLOV, I. *Conditioned Reflexes: An Investigation of the Physiological Activity of the Cerebral Cortex.* Translated by G. V. Anrep. London: Oxford, 1927.

————. *Experimental Psychology and Other Essays.* New York: Philosophical Library, 1957.

PETRARCH. *On His Own Ignorance.* Translated by H. Nachod, in *The Renaissance Philosophy of Man.* Cassirer et al. (eds.). Chicago, 1948.

PHILIP, J. A. *Pythagoras and Early Pythagoreanism.* Toronto, 1966.

PICO, GIOVANNI. *Oration on the Dignity of Man.* Translated by E. L. Forbes, in *The Renaissance Philosophy of Man.* Cassirer et al. (eds.). Chicago, 1948.

PIRENNE, H. *Medieval Cities: Their Origins and the Revival of Trade.* Translated by F. D. Halsey. Princeton, 1952.

PLATO. *The Dialogues.* Translated by Benjamin Jowett. New York: Random House, 1937. (in 2 volumes).

————. *Epistles.* Glenn R. Morrow (translator). Indianapolis: Bobbs-Merrill, 1962.

PLOTINUS. *The Enneads.* Translated by S. MacKenna, New York: Random House, 1957.

PLUTARCH. *The Lives of the Noble Grecians and Romans.* Translated by John Dryden and reprinted from the 1864 edition. New York: Random House.

POMPONAZZI, PIETRO. *On the Immortality of the Soul.* Translated by W. H. Hay, in *The Renaissance Philosophy of Man.* Cassirer et al. (eds.). Chicago, 1948.

POPPER, K. *The Logic of Scientific Discovery.* New York: Basic Books, 1959.

————. *Epistemology Without A Knowing Subject*, in *Proceedings of the Third International Congress for Logic, Methodology, and Philosophy of Science.* Rootselaar and Staal (eds.). Amsterdam, 1968.

————. *Normal Science and Its Dangers*, in *Proceedings of the Third International Congress for Logic, Methodology, and Philosophy of Science.* Rootselaar and Staal (eds.). Amsterdam, 1968.

POULET, G. *Studies in Human Time.* Baltimore: Johns Hopkins, 1956.

PUTNAM, H. *Brains and Behavior*, in *Analytical Philosophy.* R. J. Butler (ed.), New York: Barnes and Noble, 1965.

QUINE, W. V. O. *From a Logical Point of View.* Cambridge, Mass.: Harvard, 1953.

REID, T. *Essays on the Active Powers of the Human Mind.* Cambridge: M. I. T., 1969.

————. *Essays on the Intellectual Powers of Man.* Cambridge, M. I. T., 1969.

RICHTER, J. P. (ed.). *The Literary Works of Leonardo Da Vinci*, Vol. I. England: Phaidon, 1970.

ROBINSON, P. (translator). *The Writings of St. Francis of Assisi*. Philadelphia: Dolphin, 1906.

ROSS, J. B. and McLAUGHLIN, M. M. (eds.). *The Portable Renaissance Reader*. New York: Viking, 1973.

ROUSSEAU, JEAN-JACQUES. *The Social Contract* or, *Principles of Political Right* in *Social Contract*. Introduction by E. P. Barker, Oxford, 1947.

RUSKIN, J. *The Stones of Venice*, Vol. II. Philadelphia: Reuwee, Wattley & Walsh, 1851.

RUSSELL, B. *A History of Western Philosophy*, 14th ed., New York: Simon and Schuster (first printing, 1945).

————. *America: 1938–1944* in Volume 2, *The Autobiography of Bertrand Russell*. Boston: Little, Brown, 1968.

RYLE, G. *The Concept of Mind*. London: Hutchinson, 1949.

SCHMITT, C. B. *Gianfrancesco Pico della Mirandola and His Critique of Aristotle*. The Hague: Martinus Nijhoff, 1967.

SCOTUS, JOHN (ERIUGENA). *De Divisione Naturae*. Translated by Richard McKeon, in *Selections from Medieval Philosophers*. New York: Scribner, 1929.

SCRIPTURE, E. W. *The New Psychology*. New York: Scribner, 1910.

SHAFTESBURY. *Inquiry Concerning Virtue or Merit*, in *British Moralists*. L. A. Selby-Bigge (ed.). New York: Dover, 1965.

SKINNER, B. F. *The Behavior of Organisms*. New York: Appleton-Century-Crofts, 1938.

————. *Walden Two*. New York: Macmillan, 1948.

————. *Are Theories of Learning Necessary?*, *Psychological Review*, 57 (1950), 193–216.

————. *The Science of Learning and the Art of Teaching*. *Harvard Educational Review*, 1954 (Spring).

————. *Science and Human Behavior*. New York: Macmillan, 1956.

————. *Beyond Freedom and Dignity*. New York: Knopf, 1971.

————. *The Steep and Thorny Way to a Science of Behavior*, *American Psychologist*, 30 (1975), 42–49.

SMART, J. J. C. *Sensations and Brain Processes*, in *The Mind/Brain Identity Theory*. C. V. Borst (ed.). New York: St. Martin's, 1970.

SMITH, ADAM. *An Inquiry into the Nature and Causes of the Wealth of Nations*. New York: Collier (Harvard Classics), 1909.

SOUTHERN, R. W. *The Making of the Middle Ages*. New Haven: Yale, 1959.

SPENCER, H. *The Principles of Psychology*. New York: Appleton-Century-Crofts, 1896.

SPERRY, R. *A Modified Concept of Consciousness*, *Psychological Review*, 1969, 76, 532–536.

SPINOZA, B. DE. *Ethics*, in *The Chief Works of Benedict de Spinoza*. Translated by R. H. M. Elwes. New York: Dover, 1955.

————. *On the Improvement of the Understanding*, in *The Chief Works of Benedict de Spinoza*. Translated by R. H. M. Elwes. New York: Dover, 1955.

SPURZHEIM, J. G. *The Physiognomical System of Drs. Gall and Spurzheim.* London: Baldwin, Cradock, & Joy, 1815.

STACE, W. T. *The Philosophy of Hegel: A Systematic Exposition.* New York: Macmillan, 1924.

STEWART, D. *Elements of the Philosophy of the Human Mind,* in *Between Hume and Mill: Anthology of British Philosophy—1749-1843.* R. Brown (ed.). New York: Random House, 1970.

STRAUSS, L. *The Political Philosophy of Hobbes.* Translated by E. Sinclair. Chicago: Phoenix, 1952.

TALBOT, E. B. *The Fundamental Principles of Fichte's Philosophy.* New York, 1906.

TARÁN, L. *Parmenides.* Princeton, 1965.

TERTULLIAN. *Apologetical Works.* Translated by R. Arbesmann. Fathers of the Church, New York, 1950.

———. *De Spectaculis,* in *Corpus Scriptorum Ecclesiasticorum Latinorum.* Vienna: H. Hoppe, 1939.

THORNDIKE, E. L. *Animal Intelligence: Experimental Studies* (facsimiles). Connecticut: Hafner, 1970.

THUCYDIDES. *The Peloponnesian Wars.* Translated by Benjamin Jowett. New York: Washington Square, 1963.

TITCHENER, E. B. *A Primer of Psychology.* New York: Macmillan, 1914.

TOCQUEVILLE, A. *Democracy in America.* Translated by G. Lawrence. New York: Doubleday, 1969.

TOLMAN, E. C. *Cognitive Maps in Rats and Man. Psychological Review, 55* (1948). 189–208.

TRILLING, L. (ed.). *The Portable Matthew Arnold.* New York: Viking, 1972.

VALLA, L. *Dialogue on Free Will.* Translated by C. E. Trinkaus, in *The Renaissance Philosophy of Man,* Cassirer et al. (eds.). Chicago, 1948.

VOLTAIRE. *Philosophical Letters.* Translated by E. Dilworth. Indianapolis: Bobbs-Merrill, 1961.

WADE, I. *Intellectual Origins of the French Enlightenment.* Princeton, 1971.

WATSON, J. B. *Psychology as the Behaviorist Views It, Psychological Review,* 1913, 20. 158–177.

———. *Behavior: An Introduction to Comparative Psychology.* New York: Holt, Rinehart and Winston, 1914.

———. and LASHLEY, K. S. *Homing and Related Activities of Birds. Carnegie Institution.* 1915, Vol. VII.

———. *Psychology from the Standpoint of a Behaviorist.* Philadelphia: Lippincott, 1919.

———. *Behaviorism.* Chicago, 1924.

———. *Psychological Care of Infant and Child.* New York: Norton, 1928.

———. and McDOUGALL, W. *The Battle of Behaviorism.* New York: Norton, 1929.

WESTFALL, C. W. *In This Most Perfect Paradise: Alberti, Nicholas V, and the Invention of Conscious Urban Planning in Rome, 1447–55.* Pennsylvania, 1974.

WHYTT, R. *An Essay on the Vital and Other Involuntary Motions of Animals.* Edinburgh: Hamilton, Balfour, and Neill, 1751.

WIENER, P. P. (ed.). *Charles S. Peirce: Selected Writings.* New York: Dover, 1958.

WILEY, M. *The Subtle Knot: Creative Scepticism in Seventeenth-Century England.* London: Allen & Unwin, 1952.

WULF, M. DE. *An Introduction to Scholastic Philosophy.* New York: Dover, 1956.

WUNDT, W. *Principles of Physiological Psychology: Vol. I.* Translated by E. B. Titchener. New York: Macmillan, 1902.

————. *Lectures on Human and Animal Psychology.* Translated by J. E. Creighton and E. B. Titchener. New York: Macmillan, 1907.

XENOPHON. *Memorabilia.* Translated by E. C. Marchant. New York: Loeb Classical Library, 1923.

YATES, F. *Giordano Bruno and the Hermetic Tradition.* Chicago, 1964.

————. *The Art of Memory.* Chicago, 1966.

YOUNG, R. M. *Mind, Brain, and Adaptation in the Nineteenth Century.* Oxford, 1970.

ZIEHEN, T. *Introduction to Physiological Psychology.* New York: Macmillan, 1895.

ZIMMERN, A. E. *The Greek Commonwealth.* Oxford, 1924.

Index of Names

Index of Subjects

□■□■□■□■□■□■□■□■□■□■□■□■□■□■□■□■□■□

430